THE ENGLISH POETS

GENERAL EDITOR: CHRISTOPHER RICKS

Also available in this series

Robert Browning: The Poems, volume one
Robert Browning: The Poems, volume two
Robert Browning: The Ring and the Book
Edmund Spenser: The Faerie Queene
Henry Vaughan: The Complete Poems
William Wordsworth: The Poems, volume one
William Wordsworth: The Prelude
Sir Thomas Wyatt: The Complete Poems

William Wordsworth:
The Poems

VOLUME TWO

EDITED BY JOHN O. HAYDEN

NEW HAVEN AND LONDON
YALE UNIVERSITY PRESS

First published in 1977 in the United Kingdom in a paperback
edition by Penguin Books Limited in the series Penguin
English Poets. First published 1981 in the United States of
America by Yale University Press.

Printed in the United States of America.

Library of Congress Cataloging in Publication Data

Wordsworth, William, 1770–1850.
  The poems.

  (The English poets ; 7–8)
  Includes bibliographies and indexes.
  I. Hayden, John O. II. Title. III. Series:
English poets ; 7–8.
PR5850.F81   821'.7   81–2994
ISBN 0–300–02751–6 (v. 1)   AACR2
ISBN 0–300–02752–4 (v. 2)
ISBN 0–300–02754–0 (pbk. : v. 1)
ISBN 0–300–02755–9 (pbk. : v. 2)

10 9 8 7 6 5 4 3 2 1

Contents

[An asterisk preceding a title indicates either questionable
or partial authorship. Brackets around a title signifies the
unauthorized status of the title.]

Table of Dates

1770	*7 April* Born at Cockermouth, Cumberland to John Wordsworth, a lawyer.
1771	Dorothy Wordsworth, his only sister, born (three brothers: Richard b. 1768, John b. 1772, Christopher b. 1774).
1776–7	Attends nursery school in Penrith, along with Mary Hutchinson, his future wife.
1778	*c. 8 March* Ann Wordsworth, his mother, dies.
1779	Enters Hawkshead School.
1783	*30 December* His father dies.
1785	Earliest extant verse written (aetat. 15).
1787	Attends St John's College, Cambridge.
1789	Spends long vacation with his sister and Mary Hutchinson.
1790	Spends long vacation on a walking tour of France and Switzerland with Robert Jones, a college friend.
1791	*21 January* Receives B.A. degree. *26 November* Leaves for stay in France.
1792	Meets Michel Beaupuy and has an affair with Annette Vallon. *December* Returns to London. *15 December* A daughter, Anne-Caroline, by Annette Vallon, born at Orleans.
1793	*29 January* *An Evening Walk* and *Descriptive Sketches* published. *August–September* Walking tour over Salisbury Plain to Bristol, and thence through part of Wales.

1795   *January*   His friend Raisley Calvert dies, leaving Wordsworth a legacy.
August   Meets Samuel Taylor Coleridge.
September   Settles with Dorothy at Racedown, Dorset.

1797   *July*   Moves to Alfoxden, Somerset, to be near Coleridge at Nether Stowey.

1798   *10 July*   Visits Tintern Abbey.
September   *Lyrical Ballads* published (4 poems by Coleridge included).
16 September   Embarks for Germany with Coleridge and Dorothy.

1799   *May*   Returns to England (Sockburn-on-Tees).
20 December . Settles with Dorothy at Dove Cottage at Town-End, Grasmere.

1800   *January–September*   John Wordsworth visits.

1801   *January*   *Lyrical Ballads*, second edition (dated 1800), published in two volumes with the famous Preface.

1802   *Lyrical Ballads*, third edition, published with extended Preface and Appendix.
August   Visits Annette Vallon and Caroline at Calais.
4 October   Marries Mary Hutchinson.

1803   *18 June*   A son, John, born (other children: Dora b. 1804, Thomas b. 1806, Catharine b. 1808, William b. 1810).
August–September   Tours Scotland with Coleridge and Dorothy.

1804   Coleridge sails for Malta.

1805   *6 February*   John Wordsworth drowns.
May   *The Prelude* finished.
Lyrical Ballads, fourth edition, published.

1806   *August*   Coleridge returns from Malta.
November   Wordsworths move to Coleorton.

1807   *May*   *Poems in Two Volumes* published.

July Wordsworths return to Dove Cottage.

1808 *May* Wordsworths move to Allan Bank, Grasmere.

1809 *May* *The Convention of Cintra* tract published.

1810 *22 February* Essay on Epitaphs published in *The Friend*.

October Estrangement from Coleridge.

1811 *May* Wordsworths move to the Rectory, Grasmere.

1812 *May* Reconciliation with Coleridge.

Catharine and Thomas Wordsworth die.

1813 *March* Appointed Distributor of Stamps for Westmoreland.

May Wordsworths move to Rydal Mount, between Grasmere and Ambleside.

1814 Tours Scotland with his wife and Sara Hutchinson during the summer.

August *The Excursion* published.

1815 *March* *Poems* (first collected edition; in two volumes) published.

May *The White Doe of Rylstone* published.

1816 *May* *A Letter to a Friend of Burns* and *Thanksgiving Ode* published.

1817 *December* Meets John Keats in London.

1818 *Two Addresses to the Freeholders of Westmoreland* published.

1819 *April* *Peter Bell* published.

May *The Waggoner* published.

1820 *May* *The River Duddon* published.

July *The Miscellaneous Poems of William Wordsworth* (four volumes) published.

May–December Tours Continent with his wife and Dorothy.

1822 *March* *Ecclesiastical Sonnets* and *Memorials of a Tour on the Continent, 1820* published.

November *A Description of the Scenery of the Lakes* published.

1827 *February* Sir George Beaumont, patron, dies.

May Third collected edition of the *Poems* (five volumes) published.

1831 *September–October* Tours Scotland with his daughter and nephew, Charles; visits Sir Walter Scott.

1832 Fourth collected edition of the *Poems* (four volumes) published.

1834 *25 July* Coleridge dies.

1835 *January* *Yarrow Revisited and Other Poems* published.
Mental breakdown of Dorothy Wordsworth.

1836–7 Fifth collected edition of the *Poems* (in stereotype; six volumes) published.

1837 *March–August* Tours France and Italy with Henry Crabb Robinson.

1838 *June* One-volume edition of *The Sonnets* published.
21 July Receives D.C.L. from the University of Durham.

1839 *12 June* Receives D.C.L. from Oxford University.

1842 *April* *Poems, Chiefly of Early and Late Years* (with *The Borderers* and *Guilt and Sorrow*) published [volume VII of collected *Poems*].
July Resigns Distributorship of Stamps and receives pension.

1843 *April* Succeeds Southey as Poet Laureate.
Dictates notes on his poems to Isabella Fenwick.

1845 *November* Sixth collected edition of the *Poems* (one volume) published.

1847 *9 July* His daughter Dora dies.

1849–50 Seventh collected edition of the *Poems* (six volumes) published – the last edited by Wordsworth himself.

1850 *23 April* William Wordsworth dies.
July *The Prelude* published.

1855 *January* Dorothy Wordsworth dies.

1859 Mary Wordsworth dies.

Introduction

William Wordsworth has in many respects been fortunate in his editors. William Knight, Edward Dowden, Nowell C. Smith, and Ernest de Selincourt have assiduously uncovered and pieced together poems from manuscripts, have chased down allusions, quotations, and variants; and they have been assisted in a good part of this work by the myriad of minor editors of selected editions. Any editor of Wordsworth's poetry begins his task with a large debt to the past. Yet there is a good deal of work still to be done, even in a modest collected edition such as the present one.

The production of a clear and accurate text is the major consideration; for the standard text edited by Ernest de Selincourt in five volumes contains a number of errors. The substantive errors, such things as incorrect wording and collocation, number over eighty; and the accidental, such as unnecessary or mistaken changes in punctuation, paragraphing, and capitalization, occur on almost every page.

With these problems in mind I have returned to Wordsworth's own last edition of 1849–50, complying with his own words (in a letter to Alexander Dyce, 30 April 1830): 'You know what importance I attach to following strictly the last Copy of the text of an Author.' Of those poems not included in his last edition, I have given the latest version printed elsewhere during his lifetime where such exists; and where the poem is extant only in manuscript I have given the latest manuscript version. By a quirk of fate, a few poems first printed after Wordsworth's death now are available only in that printed form, which I have followed. A handful of manuscript poems (*The Three Graves* (Part I) *'There was a spot', Inscription for the Moss-Hut, The Cottager to Her Infant, In the First Page of an Album, The Lady*

Whom You Here Behold, Written in Mrs Field's Album, Upon the Sight of the Portrait of a Female Friend, and '*Prithee, gentle Lady*') I have not been able to examine in manuscript and for these have had to rely solely on later editions.

Once the text was determined, it was edited in a number of ways. The spelling has been modernized where it was merely archaic without a purpose. Hyphenated words, like *to-morrow*, and combinations of words, like *any one*, have been joined as one word, although an exception was made for *for ever*, which is often so spelled in Britain today. Where the sound of the word hasn't changed, obsolete spellings, such as *shew* (show) and *quire* (choir), have been modernized, but where the sound has changed, as in *sate* (sat), I have left the spelling as I found it.

The capitalization has also been respected, because Wordsworth apparently used capitals as a form of emphasis. The major exception is the consistent capitalization of pronouns referring to God, which in the original texts are capitalized only occasionally.

At the Dove Cottage Library there is a legend still told of a professor who had written a chapter on Wordsworth's punctuation and had come to check the original texts as an afterthought. The chapter had to be dropped (or the title changed to 'De Selincourt's Punctuation'), for Wordsworth's punctuation was fairly thoroughly modernized by his last editor.

Wordsworth has been said to overpunctuate, yet de Selincourt *adds* as much as he takes away. It might be better to say that Wordsworth's punctuation is merely different from modern accepted practice; sometimes, for example, he apparently uses commas for a pause. I have been chary of meddling with Wordsworth's rhythms and have left most of his punctuation intact. Only where a reader today might become confused have I made changes: where a comma occurs between the subject and its adjacent verb or where one has been omitted between several items in a series.

Unless bracketed the titles of the poems are those given them by Wordsworth in the last edition or in manuscript. I have changed the titles de Selincourt gave to other poems only when he overlooked a title provided by Wordsworth. The remaining titles originating with de Selincourt I have, however, placed in brackets to indicate their unauthorized status.

When poems have been printed from manuscript I have used brackets to show the state of the text. Where the brackets are empty a word or words were simply left blank by Wordsworth. A question-mark in brackets indicates that a word or words were written but are illegible. A word in brackets followed by a question-mark signifies illegibility and conjecture; with the question mark preceding, a bracketed word represents a blank in the manuscript and a conjecture. Bracketed letters also represent blanks and conjecture.

Rather than exclude or place poems of questionable authorship in a special section, I have included them in the text with the other poems. An asterisk preceding a title in the table of contents and in the text indicates either questionable or partial authorship. The reader should consult the notes for further information.

The arrangement of the poems undoubtedly represents my most important editorial decision. Even though William Knight, the most authoritative editor before de Selincourt, arranged his edition in chronological order of composition, such order is still considered by some to be untraditional, if not positively fraudulent because counter to the poet's own wishes.

The main contender is of course Wordsworth's own system of categories, which he used in all the collected editions during his lifetime. Supporters of his system, however, have always been few; Wordsworth himself was perhaps its only enthusiast. Even Ernest de Selincourt has admitted that the system 'will not stand logical examination', with Wordsworth shifting poems from one category to another in the various editions. De Selincourt nevertheless chose the system because of its 'supreme value': namely that it was Wordsworth's. Yet Wordsworth could be a great poet without being a great editor.

Some of the objections previously raised against the order of composition no longer hold. Problems of dating, for example, have largely yielded to the efforts of modern scholars, especially Mark Reed.

And the new dates to some extent eliminate another objection:

that the main reason for Wordsworth's categories in the first place has been ignored – 'that one poem should shade off happily into another' (letter to Henry Crabb Robinson, 6 April 1826). For, as James Scoggins has pointed out in his study of the two most important of Wordsworth's categories, the arrangement of 'Poems of Fancy' and 'Poems of Imagination' very nearly follow the order of composition (*Imagination and Fancy* [1966], p. 74). In any event, Wordsworth's argument based on the supposed offensiveness of abrupt transitions from one kind of poem to another rests on the premise that such transitions *should* offend the reader, not that they in fact *do* so. I doubt very much if most readers read through a volume from cover to cover, or even from the beginning of one section to the end.

The most forceful objection to order by composition is that datings, no matter how accurate, mislead. In the case of longer poems written over a period of years no real problem occurs, since only *The Excursion* is involved to any extent and consequently is easy enough to remember. Like Knight, I have placed the poem at the beginning of 1814, when it was completed. As for short poems in a series, I have left intact seven series that were written and published as a series. Of the poems in each series, most were written during a short period; and the few other poems, I believe, present no difficulty.

But even with Wordsworth's short poems there is a serious problem, inasmuch as he revised many of his poems, some of them extensively. If the poems are studied for evidence of the evolution of his poetic style, the reader should consult de Selincourt's edition for variants before drawing too specific conclusions. The problems of ordering poems whose composition dates are very tentative or span a number of years should bring the reader who is seriously interested in Wordsworth's stylistic development to the head-notes of the poems to determine how definite the order of the poems involved is.

Moreover, even with a poet who revised less than Wordsworth and the dating of whose poems is more certain than his, the study of poetic evolution would pose very complex problems and would require extreme caution. Still, it is a mistake to consider stylistic development as the only thing that can be examined from an arrangement by composition. Study of Wordsworth's developing interests in themes and forms, to the extent that they can be seen as separate from style, is another advantage of this arrangement.

Order of composition is in fact the standard method of ordering the works of most poets. Wordsworth himself considered it the proper method 'in the case of juvenile poems or those of advanced age' (letter to Henry Crabb Robinson, 27 April 1826). And chronology of composition is the method followed in selected editions and in anthologies, surely the most common forms in which Wordsworth's poems are read today.

By placing poems by date of composition, moreover, one of the disadvantages of Wordsworth's system is circumvented, namely the formation of the large clump of the poems that were not in the 1849–50 edition. They form a separate 'category' in de Selincourt's edition, a group of poems that have no literary reason whatsoever for combination.

Chronology of composition, therefore, seems to me the most reasonable of the methods for ordering Wordsworth's poems. Even in the absence of the above arguments, it would have won, I believe, by default: there is no other method that is as good. Information concerning Wordsworth's categories are, however, available in the head-notes to the poems.

The dates of composition of the poems written before 1815 are taken, often word for word, from Mark Reed's two studies of Wordsworth's chronology, although I have sometimes supplemented his lists with more specific terminal dates. After 1815 the dates of composition are derived from my own research.

The order of the poems in this edition, however, differs at times from Reed's lists. Although I do follow Reed's codes and their descending order of likelihood (probably, perhaps, possibly), unlike him I have usually given the probable dates precedence in the placement of the poems and have given priority to the composition of the bulk of a poem over the writing of a few lines. Within a particular year, moreover, the poems are given in the following order of dates of composition: (1) the exact date, (2) the month, (3) the season, (4) whether early or late within the year. Within a series of years, the poems are given by the earliest date of a substantial part of composition. For example, the dates of the poems of the year 1800 might read: 2 January 1800, 15 January 1800, January 1800, between January and April 1800, February 1800, early 1800, July 1800, summer 1800, 7 October 1800, probably 1800, possibly 1800, 1800–1801, probably 1800–1801. At times the ordering of the poems is thus only suggestive of the actual, unknown dates of composition.

Having ignored Wordsworth's wishes about the arrangement of the poems, I have been allowed by the format of this series of editions at least to follow his injunction that 'the poems should be left to speak for themselves' (letter to E. Moxon, 5 November 1845), with the notes placed at the end of the volumes. The scholarly sources for the information in the notes are usually not given unless the material is from an unfamiliar source (that is, not from a previous collected edition) or is merely speculative. Covering the same ground examined by so many editors does not allow for much that is original; consequently I take credit for little of the information in the notes beyond making numerous citations more definite.

Perhaps my principal contribution to Wordsworthian annotation is the limitation of the notes as strictly as possible to those that illuminate the text. The notes dictated by Wordsworth to Isabella Fenwick in 1843 have been especially trimmed to what is pertinent to the poems, either to their composition or to their meaning and form. The same is true of Wordsworth's own footnotes, except that I have been a bit more liberal in applying my rule. At the time of publication Wordsworth in these notes apparently thought he was aiding the reader in some way; the Fenwick notes, on the other hand, were originally intended only to satisfy the interest of Wordsworth's family and friends.

It is the nature of many of the annotations of Wordsworth's poems to point up the autobiographical nature of his poetry; this is especially true of the Fenwick notes. Such information, I believe, is useful in understanding the poems; but caution should be exerted not to treat the poems as if they are mere anecdotes from the life of the poet.

If a poem was printed in any collected edition before Wordsworth's death in 1850, the category to which he assigned it is given in the head-note to that poem at the rear of the volume. The first category date given is also the date of the first collected edition in which the poem appeared; if none is given and the date of first publication precedes 1850, the poem was not collected by Wordsworth. The poems first published in the *Lyrical Ballads* of 1798 and 1800 are cited as such in the head-notes, but often they were revised, and so care should be taken against reading them as if in their original forms. *The Prelude* has not been included in this edition, because it has already been published in an edition of its own by Penguin in 1971.

Few variants are given in the notes. Only those revisions of special interest are either noticed or quoted.

The Barberry-Tree is published with the consent of the Librarian on behalf of the Governing Body of Christ Church, Oxford; *Fragments on a Heroic Theme*, originally included in *The Early Wordsworthian Milieu*, ed. Z. S. Fink (1958) is published by permission of Oxford University Press; and *More may not be by Human Art Exprest* is reprinted from *Wordsworth's Pocket Notebook*, edited with commentary by George Harris Healey, copyright 1942, by Cornell University Press and used by permission of Cornell University Press.

I should like to acknowledge the generosity of the Dove Cottage Trustees in allowing me to publish new material from manuscripts under their care. Other libraries to which I am obliged for making available manuscripts in their possession are the British Museum; the Queen's Library, Windsor; Christ Church Library, Oxford; the Fitzwilliam Museum, Cambridge; the Pierpont Morgan Library, New York; the Huntington Library; and the Cornell University Library. The staffs of all these libraries were most helpful and generous with their time, as were also the staff of the Reading Room of the British Museum and the Interlibrary Loan Department of the Library of the University of California, Davis.

Perhaps my largest debt, in view of the immense work involved in producing an edition of this size, is to the typists who were so careful and concerned for the accuracy of text and notes. Elaine Bukhari was responsible for the text, Betty Kimura for the notes. Several work-study assistants also helped with this edition at various stages; I should like to thank them all for their diligent services. My work at the Dove Cottage Library was more productive than otherwise might have been the case because of the generous advice of two scholars present at the time, Paul Betz and Beth Darlington. Robert Kirkpatrick of the University of North Carolina gave me help on one poem, and my old friend, George Dekker, of Stanford University, read the introduction and offered advice on the edition as a whole. I should also like to thank my wife, who helped with the examination of manuscript material and put up with many inconveniences during the production of this edition.

These volumes are dedicated to Donald Davie.

Further Reading

[For further reading concerning *The Prelude* specifically, see J. C. Maxwell's edition of *The Prelude* in this series.]

EDITIONS

[For editions published during Wordsworth's lifetime, see the Table of Dates.]

The Poetical Works of William Wordsworth, 6 volumes, 1857 [the first edition to contain the Fenwick Notes].

Matthew Arnold, ed., *Poems of Wordsworth*, 1879 [a selected edition with the well-known introduction].

William Knight, ed., *The Poetical Works of William Wordsworth*, 11 volumes (the last three volumes contain the *Life*), 1882–9 [superseded by the 1896 edition].

Edward Dowden, ed., *The Poetical Works of William Wordsworth*, 7 volumes, 1892–3 [The Aldine Edition].

Thomas Hutchinson, ed., *The Poetical Works of William Wordsworth*, 5 volumes, 1895 [basis of the Oxford Standard Authors edition].

William Knight, ed., *The Poetical Works of William Wordsworth*, 8 volumes, 1896.

A. J. George, ed., *The Complete Poetical Works of Wordsworth*, Houghton Mifflin Co., Boston and New York, 1904 [Cambridge Edition].

Nowell C. Smith, ed., *The Poems of William Wordsworth*, 3 volumes, Methuen, 1908.

Ernest de Selincourt and Helen Darbishire, eds., *The Poetical Works of William Wordsworth*, 5 volumes,

Ernest de Selincourt and Helen Darbishire, eds., *The Poetical Works of William Wordsworth*, five volumes, Clarendon Press, 1940–49 [revised ed., volumes I–III, 1952–4; the standard edition].

Philip Wayne, ed., *Wordsworth's Poems*, three volumes, 1955 [Everyman edition].

W. J. B. Owen and J. W. Smyser, eds., *The Prose Works of William Wordsworth*, three volumes, Clarendon Press, 1974.

BIBLIOGRAPHIES AND REFERENCE WORKS

Bernbaum, Ernest, James V. Logan and Ford T. Swetnam, Jr., 'Wordsworth', in *The English Romantic Poets: A Review of Research and Criticism*, 3rd rev. ed., ed. Frank Jordan, New York, 1972.

Cooper, Lane, *A Concordance to the Poems of Wordsworth*, 1911.

Hayden, John O., *The Romantic Reviewers 1802–24*, Routledge & Kegan Paul, 1969 [chapter 3].

Healey, G. H., ed., *The Cornell Wordsworth Collection: A Catalogue*, Cornell University Press, 1957.

Henley, E. F. and D. H. Stam, eds., *Wordsworthian Criticism, 1945–1964; An Annotated Bibliography*, New York Public Library, 1965.

Logan, J. F., *Wordsworthian Criticism: A Guide and Bibliography*, Ohio State University Press, 1961.

Peacock, M. L., Jr., ed., *The Critical Opinions of William Wordsworth*, Johns Hopkins Press, 1950.

Reed, Mark, *Wordsworth: The Chronology of the Early Years 1770–1799*, Harvard University Press, 1967.

—, *Wordsworth: The Chronology of the Middle Years 1800–1815*, Harvard University Press, 1975.

Smith, Elsie, ed., *An Estimate of William Wordsworth by His Contemporaries 1793–1822*, Blackwell, 1932.

Stam, David H., *Wordsworthian Criticism, 1964–1973, an Annotated Bibliography*, New York Public Library, 1974.

Woodring, Carl, *Politics in English Romantic Poetry*, Harvard University Press, 1970 [chapter 4].

BIOGRAPHIES, LETTERS, AND JOURNALS

Broughton, L. N., ed., *Some Letters of the Wordsworth Family*, Cornell University Press, 1942.

—, ed., *Wordsworth and Reed: The Poet's Correspondence with His American Editor: 1836–1850*, Cornell University Press, 1933.

Burton, Mary E., ed., *The Letters of Mary Wordsworth*, Clarendon Press, 1958.

Coburn, Kathleen, ed., *The Letters of Sara Hutchinson*, Routledge and Kegan Paul, 1954.

De Selincourt, Ernest, ed., *Journals of Dorothy Wordsworth*, two volumes, New York, Macmillan, 1941.

—, ed., *The Letters of William and Dorothy Wordsworth: The Later Years*, three volumes, Clarendon Press, 1939.

Harper, G. M., *William Wordsworth: His Life, Works, and Influence*, 3rd ed., Scribners, 1929.

Margoliouth, H. M., *Wordsworth and Coleridge, 1795–1834*, Oxford University Press, 1953.

Moorman, Mary, ed., *Journals of Dorothy Wordsworth*, Oxford University Press, 1971 [The Alfoxden and Grasmere Journals].

—, ed., *The Letters of William and Dorothy Wordsworth*, arranged and edited by E. de Selincourt, 2nd ed., revised, Volume II. *The Middle Years, Part 1, 1806–1811*, Oxford University Press, 1969.

Moorman, Mary, and Alan G. Hill, eds., *Ibid.*, Volume III. *The Middle Years, Part 2, 1812–1820*, Oxford University Press, 1970.

Moorman, Mary, *William Wordsworth, A Biography: The Early Years, 1770–1803*, Clarendon Press, 1957.

—, *William Wordsworth, A Biography: The Later Years, 1803–1850*, Clarendon Press, 1965.

Morley, Edith J., ed., *Henry Crabb Robinson on Books and Their Writers*, three volumes, Longmans, Green, 1938.

Shaver, Chester L., ed., *The Letters of William and Dorothy*

Wordsworth, arranged and edited by E. de Selincourt, 2nd ed., revised, Volume I. *The Early Years, 1787–1805*, Oxford University Press, 1967.

Thompson, T. W., *Wordsworth's Hawkshead*, ed. Robert Woof, Oxford University Press, 1970.

Wordsworth, Christopher, *Memoirs of William Wordsworth, Poet-Laureate, D.C.L.*, two volumes, 1851.

SELECTED CRITICISM

Bateson, F. W., *Wordsworth: A Re-interpretation*, Longmans, Green, 1954.

Batho, Edith C., *The Later Wordsworth*, N.Y., Russell & Russell, 1963 [1933].

Beatty, Arthur, *William Wordsworth: His Doctrine and Art in Their Historical Relations*, 3rd ed., University of Wisconsin Press, 1960.

Bloom, Harold, *The Visionary Company: A Reading of English Romantic Literature*, 2nd ed., Cornell University Press, 1971 [Chapter 2].

Clarke, C. C., *Romantic Paradox: An Essay on the Poetry of Wordsworth*, Routledge & Kegan Paul, 1962.

Coleridge, Samuel Taylor, *Biographia Literaria*, ed. J. Shawcross, two volumes, Clarendon Press, 1907 [Chapters 4, 14, 17–20, 22].

Danby, J. F., *The Simple Wordsworth: Studies in the Poems 1797–1807*, Routledge & Kegan Paul, 1960.

Davie, Donald, *Selected Poems of William Wordsworth*, Hutchinson, 1962 [Introduction].

Davis, Jack, ed., *William Wordsworth*, Boston, Heath, 1963 [Collection of essays by various hands].

De Selincourt, Ernest, *Dorothy Wordsworth: A Biography*, Clarendon Press, 1933.

Dunklin, G. T., ed., *Wordsworth: Centenary Studies Presented at Cornell and Princeton Universities*, Princeton University Press, 1951 [Collection of essays by various hands].

Durrant, Geoffrey, *Wordsworth and the Great System: A Study of Wordsworth's Poetic Universe*, Cambridge University Press, 1970.

Ferry, David, *The Limits of Mortality: An Essay on Wordsworth's Major Poems*, Wesleyan University Press, 1959.

Garlitz, Barbara, 'The Baby's Debut: The Contemporary Reaction to Wordsworth's Poetry of Childhood', *Boston University Studies in English*, IV (1960), pp, 85–94.

Grob, Alan, *The Philosophic Mind: A Study of Wordsworth's Poetry and Thought 1797–1805*, Ohio State University Press, 1973.

Hartman, Geoffrey H., *Wordsworth's Poetry, 1787–1814*, Yale University Press, 1965.

Heffernan, James A. W., *Wordsworth's Theory of Poetry: The Transforming Imagination*, Cornell University Press, 1969.

Jones, John, *The Egotistical Sublime: A History of Wordsworth's Imagination*, Chatto & Windus, 1954.

Leavis, F. R., *Revaluation: Tradition and Development in English Poetry*, Chatto & Windus, 1936 [Chapter 5].

Marsh, Florence, *Wordsworth's Imagery: A Study in Poetic Vision*, Yale University Press, 1952.

Mayo, Robert, 'The Contemporaneity of the Lyrical Ballads', *Publications of the Modern Language Association*, LXIX (1954), pp. 486–522.

McMaster, Graham, ed., *William Wordsworth: Penguin Critical Anthology*, Penguin Books, 1972.

Miles, Josephine, *Wordsworth and the Vocabulary of Emotion*, University of California Press, 1942.

Owen, W. J. B., *Wordsworth as Critic*, University of Toronto Press, 1969.

Parrish, Stephen Maxfield, *The Art of the Lyrical Ballads*, Harvard University Press, 1973.

Perkins, David, *Wordsworth and the Poetry of Sincerity*, Harvard University Press, 1964.

Piper, H. W., *The Active Universe: Pantheism and the*

Concept of Imagination in the English Romantic Poets, Athlone Press, 1962.

Rader, Melvin, *Wordsworth: A Philosophical Approach*, Clarendon Press, 1967.

Read, Herbert, *Wordsworth*, Jonathan Cape, 1930.

Scoggins, James, *Imagination and Fancy: Complementary Modes in the Poetry of Wordsworth*, University of Nebraska Press, 1967.

Sheats, Paul D., *The Making of Wordsworth's Poetry 1785–88*, Harvard University Press, 1973.

Smith, James, 'Wordsworth: A Preliminary Survey', *Scrutiny*, VII (1938).

Sperry, W. L., *Wordsworth's Anti-Climax*, Harvard University Press, 1935.

Stallknecht, N. P., *Strange Seas of Thought: Studies in William Wordsworth's Philosophy of Man and Nature*, 2nd ed., Indiana University Press, 1958.

Thomson, A. W., ed., *Wordsworth's Mind and Art*, Oliver & Boyd, 1969 [Collection of essays by various hands].

Thorpe, C. D., 'The Imagination: Coleridge vs. Wordsworth', *Philological Quarterly*, XVIII (1939), pp. 1–18.

Trilling, Lionel, 'The Immortality Ode', in *The Liberal Imagination*, Secker & Warburg, 1951.

Willey, Basil, *The Eighteenth Century Background: Studies on the Idea of Nature in the Thought of the Period*, Chatto & Windus, 1941 [Chapter 12].

Woodring, Carl, *Wordsworth*, Boston, Houghton Mifflin, Co. 1965.

Wordsworth, Jonathan, *The Music of Humanity: A Critical Study of Wordsworth's 'Ruined Cottage'*, Nelson, 1969.

——, ed., *Bicentenary Wordsworth Studies in Memory of John Alban Finch*, Cornell University Press, 1970 [Collection of essays by various hands].

The Excursion

TO THE RIGHT HONOURABLE WILLIAM, EARL OF
LONSDALE, K.G.,
ETC., ETC.

Oft, through thy fair domains, illustrious Peer!
In youth I roamed, on youthful pleasures bent;
And mused in rocky cell or sylvan tent,
Beside swift-flowing Lowther's current clear.
– Now, by thy care befriended, I appear
Before thee, LONSDALE, and this Work present,
A token (may it prove a monument!)
Of high respect and gratitude sincere.
Gladly would I have waited till my task
10 Had reached its close; but Life is insecure,
And Hope full oft fallacious as a dream:
Therefore, for what is here produced, I ask
Thy favour; trusting that thou wilt not deem
The offering, though imperfect, premature.

WILLIAM WORDSWORTH.
Rydal Mount, Westmoreland,
July 29, 1814.

PREFACE TO THE EDITION OF 1814

The Title-page announces that this is only a portion of a
poem; and the Reader must be here apprised that it belongs to the second part of a long and laborious Work,
which is to consist of three parts. – The Author will can-
didly acknowledge that, if the first of these had been
completed, and in such a manner as to satisfy his own
mind, he should have preferred the natural order of publication, and have given that to the world first; but, as the
second division of the Work was designed to refer more to
passing events, and to an existing state of things, than the
others were meant to do, more continuous exertion was

naturally bestowed upon it, and greater progress made here than in the rest of the poem; and as this part does not depend upon the preceding, to a degree which will materially injure its own peculiar interest, the Author, complying with the earnest entreaties of some valued Friends, presents the following pages to the Public.

It may be proper to state whence the poem, of which The Excursion is a part, derives its Title of THE RECLUSE. – Several years ago, when the Author retired to his native mountains, with the hope of being enabled to construct a literary Work that might live, it was a reasonable thing that he should take a review of his own mind, and examine how far Nature and Education had qualified him for such employment. As subsidiary to this preparation, he undertook to record, in verse, the origin and progress of his own powers, as far as he was acquainted with them. That Work, addressed to a dear Friend, most distinguished for his knowledge and genius, and to whom the Author's Intellect is deeply indebted, has been long finished; and the result of the investigation which gave rise to it was a determination to compose a philosophical poem, containing views of Man, Nature, and Society; and to be entitled, The Recluse; as having for its principal subject the sensations and opinions of a poet living in retirement. – The preparatory poem is biographical, and conducts the history of the Author's mind to the point when he was emboldened to hope that his faculties were sufficiently matured for entering upon the arduous labour which he had proposed to himself; and the two Works have the same kind of relation to each other, if he may so express himself, as the ante-chapel has to the body of a gothic church. Continuing this allusion, he may be permitted to add, that his minor Pieces, which have been long before the Public, when they shall be properly arranged, will be found by the attentive Reader to have such connexion with the main Work as may give them claim to be likened to the little cells, oratories, and sepulchral recesses, ordinarily included in those edifices.

The Author would not have deemed himself justified in saying, upon this occasion, so much of performances either unfinished, or unpublished, if he had not thought that the labour bestowed by him upon what he has heretofore and now laid before the Public, entitled him to candid attention for such a statement as he thinks necessary to throw light upon his endeavours to please and, he would hope, to benefit his countrymen. – Nothing further need be added, than that the first and third parts of The Recluse will consist chiefly of meditations in the Author's own person; and that in the intermediate part (The Excursion) the intervention of characters speaking is employed, and something of a dramatic form adopted.

It is not the Author's intention formally to announce a system: it was more animating to him to proceed in a different course; and if he shall succeed in conveying to the mind clear thoughts, lively images, and strong feelings, the Reader will have no difficulty in extracting the system for himself. And in the meantime the following passage, taken from the conclusion of the first book of The Recluse, may be acceptable as a kind of *Prospectus* of the design and scope of the whole Poem.

'On Man, on Nature, and on Human Life,
Musing in solitude, I oft perceive
Fair trains of imagery before me rise,
Accompanied by feelings of delight
Pure, or with no unpleasing sadness mixed;
And I am conscious of affecting thoughts
And dear remembrances, whose presence soothes
Or elevates the Mind, intent to weigh
The good and evil of our mortal state.
10 – To these emotions, whencesoe'er they come,
Whether from breath of outward circumstance,
Or from the Soul – an impulse to herself –
I would give utterance in numerous verse.
Of Truth, of Grandeur, Beauty, Love, and Hope,
And melancholy Fear subdued by Faith;

Of blessèd consolations in distress;
Of moral strength, and intellectual Power;
Of joy in widest commonalty spread;
Of the individual Mind that keeps her own
20 Inviolate retirement, subject there
To Conscience only, and the law supreme
Of that Intelligence which governs all –
I sing: –"fit audience let m e find though few!"

      'So prayed, more gaining than he asked, the Bard –
In holiest mood. Urania, I shall need
Thy guidance, or a greater Muse, if such
Descend to earth or dwell in highest heaven!
For I must tread on shadowy ground, must sink
Deep – and, aloft ascending, breathe in worlds
30 To which the heaven of heavens is but a veil.
All strength – all terror, single or in bands,
That ever was put forth in personal form –
Jehovah – with his thunder, and the choir
Of shouting Angels, and the empyreal thrones –
I pass them unalarmed. Not Chaos, not
The darkest pit of lowest Erebus,
Nor aught of blinder vacancy, scooped out
By help of dreams – can breed such fear and awe
As fall upon us often when we look
40 Into our Minds, into the Mind of Man –
My haunt, and the main region of my song.
– Beauty – a living Presence of the earth,
Surpassing the most fair ideal Forms
Which craft of delicate Spirits hath composed
From earth's materials – waits upon my steps;
Pitches her tents before me as I move,
An hourly neighbour. Paradise, and groves
Elysian, Fortunate Fields – like those of old
Sought in the Atlantic Main – why should they be
50 A history only of departed things,
Or a mere fiction of what never was?
For the discerning intellect of Man,

When wedded to this goodly universe
In love and holy passion, shall find these
A simple produce of the common day.
– I, long before the blissful hour arrives,
Would chant, in lonely peace, the spousal verse
Of this great consummation: – and, by words
Which speak of nothing more than what we are,
60   Would I arouse the sensual from their sleep
Of Death, and win the vacant and the vain
To noble raptures; while my voice proclaims
How exquisitely the individual Mind
(And the progressive powers perhaps no less
Of the whole species) to the external World
Is fitted: – and how exquisitely, too –
Theme this but little heard of among men –
The external World is fitted to the Mind;
And the creation (by no lower name
70   Can it be called) which they with blended might
Accomplish: – this is our high argument.
– Such grateful haunts foregoing, if I oft
Must turn elsewhere – to travel near the tribes
And fellowships of men, and see ill sights
Of madding passions mutually inflamed;
Must hear Humanity in fields and groves
Pipe solitary anguish; or must hang
Brooding above the fierce confederate storm
Of sorrow, barricadoed evermore
80   Within the walls of cities – may these sounds
Have their authentic comment; that even these
Hearing, I be not downcast or forlorn! –
Descend, prophetic Spirit! that inspir'st
The human Soul of universal earth,
Dreaming on things to come; and dost possess
A metropolitan temple in the hearts
Of mighty Poets: upon me bestow
A gift of genuine insight; that my Song
With star-like virtue in its place may shine,
90   Shedding benignant influence, and secure,

Itself, from all malevolent effect
Of those mutations that extend their sway
Throughout the nether sphere! – and if with this
I mix more lowly matter; with the thing
Contemplated, describe the Mind and Man
Contemplating; and who, and what he was –
The transitory Being that beheld
This Vision; when and where, and how he lived; –
Be not this labour useless. If such theme
100 May sort with highest objects, then – dread Power!
Whose gracious favour is the primal source
Of all illumination – may my Life
Express the image of a better time,
More wise desires, and simpler manners; – nurse
My Heart in genuine freedom: – all pure thoughts
Be with me; – so shall thy unfailing love
Guide, and support, and cheer me to the end!'

BOOK FIRST
THE WANDERER

Argument

A summer forenoon. – The Author reaches a ruined Cottage
upon a Common, and there meets with a revered Friend, the
Wanderer, of whose education and course of life he gives an
account. – The Wanderer, while resting under the shade of the
Trees that surround the Cottage, relates the History of its last
Inhabitant.

'Twas summer, and the sun had mounted high:
Southward the landscape indistinctly glared
Through a pale steam; but all the northern downs,
In clearest air ascending, showed far off
A surface dappled o'er with shadows flung
From brooding clouds; shadows that lay in spots
Determined and unmoved, with steady beams
Of bright and pleasant sunshine interposed;
To him most pleasant who on soft cool moss
10 Extends his careless limbs along the front

Of some huge cave, whose rocky ceiling casts
A twilight of its own, an ample shade,
Where the wren warbles, while the dreaming man,
Half conscious of the soothing melody,
With side-long eye looks out upon the scene,
By power of that impending covert thrown
To finer distance. Mine was at that hour
Far other lot, yet with good hope that soon
Under a shade as grateful I should find
20 Rest, and be welcomed there to livelier joy.
Across a bare wide Common I was toiling
With languid steps that by the slippery turf
Were baffled; nor could my weak arm disperse
The host of insects gathering round my face,
And ever with me as I paced along.

   Upon that open moorland stood a grove,
The wished-for port to which my course was bound.
Thither I came, and there, amid the gloom
Spread by a brotherhood of lofty elms,
30 Appeared a roofless Hut; four naked walls
That stared upon each other! – I looked round,
And to my wish and to my hope espied
The Friend I sought; a Man of reverend age,
But stout and hale, for travel unimpaired.
There was he seen upon the cottage-bench,
Recumbent in the shade, as if asleep;
An iron-pointed staff lay at his side.

   Him had I marked the day before – alone
And stationed in the public way, with face
40 Turned toward the sun then setting, while that staff
Afforded, to the figure of the man
Detained for contemplation or repose,
Graceful support; his countenance as he stood
Was hidden from my view, and he remained
Unrecognized; but, stricken by the sight,
With slackened footsteps I advanced, and soon

A glad congratulation we exchanged
At such unthought-of meeting. – For the night
We parted, nothing willingly; and now
50 He by appointment waited for me here,
Under the covert of these clustering elms.

We were tried Friends: amid a pleasant vale,
In the antique market-village where was passed
My school-time, an apartment he had owned,
To which at intervals the Wanderer drew,
And found a kind of home or harbour there.
He loved me; from a swarm of rosy boys
Singled out me, as he in sport would say,
For my grave looks, too thoughtful for my years.
60 As I grew up, it was my best delight
To be his chosen comrade. Many a time,
On holidays, we rambled through the woods:
We sate – we walked; he pleased me with report
Of things which he had seen; and often touched
Abstrusest matter, reasonings of the mind
Turned inward; or at my request would sing
Old songs, the product of his native hills;
A skilful distribution of sweet sounds,
Feeding the soul, and eagerly imbibed
70 As cool refreshing water, by the care
Of the industrious husbandman, diffused
Through a parched meadow-ground, in time of drought.
Still deeper welcome found his pure discourse:
How precious when in riper days I learned
To weigh with care his words, and to rejoice
In the plain presence of his dignity!

Oh! many are the Poets that are sown
By Nature; men endowed with highest gifts,
The vision and the faculty divine;
80 Yet wanting the accomplishment of verse,
(Which, in the docile season of their youth,
It was denied them to acquire, through lack

Of culture and the inspiring aid of books,
Or haply by a temper too severe,
Or a nice backwardness afraid of shame)
Nor having e'er, as life advanced, been led
By circumstance to take unto the height
The measure of themselves, these favoured Beings,
All but a scattered few, live out their time,
90 Husbanding that which they possess within,
And go to the grave, unthought of. Strongest minds
Are often those of whom the noisy world
Hears least; else surely this Man had not left
His graces unrevealed and unproclaimed.
But, as the mind was filled with inward light,
So not without distinction had he lived,
Beloved and honoured – far as he was known.
And some small portion of his eloquent speech,
And something that may serve to set in view
100 The feeling pleasures of his loneliness,
His observations, and the thoughts his mind
Had dealt with – I will here record in verse;
Which, if with truth it correspond, and sink
Or rise as venerable Nature leads,
The high and tender Muses shall accept
With gracious smile, deliberately pleased,
And listening Time reward with sacred praise.

Among the hills of Athol he was born;
Where, on a small hereditary farm,
110 An unproductive slip of rugged ground,
His Parents, with their numerous offspring, dwelt;
A virtuous household, though exceeding poor!
Pure livers were they all, austere and grave,
And fearing God; the very children taught
Stern self-respect, a reverence for God's word,
And an habitual piety, maintained
With strictness scarcely known on English ground.

From his sixth year, the Boy of whom I speak,

In summer, tended cattle on the hills;
120 But, through the inclement and the perilous days
Of long-continuing winter, he repaired,
Equipped with satchel, to a school, that stood
Sole building on a mountain's dreary edge,
Remote from view of city spire, or sound
Of minster clock! From that bleak tenement
He, many an evening, to his distant home
In solitude returning, saw the hills
Grow larger in the darkness; all alone
Beheld the stars come out above his head,
130 And travelled through the wood, with no one near
To whom he might confess the things he saw.

So the foundations of his mind were laid.
In such communion, not from terror free,
While yet a child, and long before his time,
Had he perceived the presence and the power
Of greatness; and deep feelings had impressed
So vividly great objects that they lay
Upon his mind like substances, whose presence
Perplexed the bodily sense. He had received
140 A precious gift; for, as he grew in years,
With these impressions would he still compare
All his remembrances, thoughts, shapes, and forms;
And, being still unsatisfied with aught
Of dimmer character, he thence attained
An active power to fasten images
Upon his brain; and on their pictured lines
Intensely brooded, even till they acquired
The liveliness of dreams. Nor did he fail,
While yet a child, with a child's eagerness
150 Incessantly to turn his ear and eye
On all things which the moving seasons brought
To feed such appetite – nor this alone
Appeased his yearning: – in the after-day
Of boyhood, many an hour in caves forlorn,
And 'mid the hollow depths of naked crags

He sate, and even in their fixed lineaments,
Or from the power of a peculiar eye,
Or by creative feeling overborne,
Or by predominance of thought oppressed,
160 Even in their fixed and steady lineaments
He traced an ebbing and a flowing mind,
Expression ever varying!

              Thus informed,
He had small need of books; for many a tale
Traditionary, round the mountains hung,
And many a legend, peopling the dark woods,
Nourished Imagination in her growth,
And gave the Mind that apprehensive power
By which she is made quick to recognize
The moral properties and scope of things.
170 But eagerly he read, and read again,
Whate'er the minister's old shelf supplied;
The life and death of martyrs, who sustained,
With will inflexible, those fearful pangs
Triumphantly displayed in records left
Of persecution, and the Covenant – times
Whose echo rings through Scotland to this hour!
And there, by lucky hap, had been preserved
A straggling volume, torn and incomplete,
That left half-told the preternatural tale,
180 Romance of giants, chronicle of fiends,
Profuse in garniture of wooden cuts
Strange and uncouth; dire faces, figures dire,
Sharp-kneed, sharp-elbowed, and lean-ankled too,
With long and ghostly shanks – forms which once seen
Could never be forgotten!

              In his heart,
Where Fear sate thus, a cherished visitant,
Was wanting yet the pure delight of love
By sound diffused, or by the breathing air,
Or by the silent looks of happy things,

190 Or flowing from the universal face
Of earth and sky. But he had felt the power
Of Nature, and already was prepared,
By his intense conceptions, to receive
Deeply the lesson deep of love which he,
Whom Nature, by whatever means, has taught
To feel intensely, cannot but receive.

Such was the Boy – but for the growing Youth
What soul was his, when, from the naked top
Of some bold headland, he beheld the sun
200 Rise up, and bathe the world in light! He looked –
Ocean and earth, the solid frame of earth
And ocean's liquid mass, in gladness lay
Beneath him: – Far and wide the clouds were touched,
And in their silent faces could he read
Unutterable love. Sound needed none,
Nor any voice of joy; his spirit drank
The spectacle: sensation, soul, and form,
All melted into him; they swallowed up
His animal being; in them did he live,
210 And by them did he live; they were his life.
In such access of mind, in such high hour
Of visitation from the living God,
Thought was not; in enjoyment it expired.
No thanks he breathed, he proffered no request;
Rapt into still communion that transcends
The imperfect offices of prayer and praise,
His mind was a thanksgiving to the power
That made him; it was blessedness and love!

A Herdsman on the lonely mountain tops,
220 Such intercourse was his, and in this sort
Was his existence oftentimes *possessed*.
O then how beautiful, how bright, appeared
The written promise! Early had he learned
To reverence the volume that displays
The mystery, the life which cannot die;

But in the mountains did he *feel* his faith.
All things, responsive to the writing, there
Breathed immortality, revolving life,
And greatness still revolving; infinite:
230 There littleness was not; the least of things
Seemed infinite; and there his spirit shaped
Her prospects, nor did he believe, – he *saw*.
What wonder if his being thus became
Sublime and comprehensive! Low desires,
Low thoughts had there no place; yet was his heart
Lowly; for he was meek in gratitude,
Oft as he called those ecstasies to mind,
And whence they flowed; and from them he acquired
Wisdom, which works through patience; thence he
    learned
240 In oft-recurring hours of sober thought
To look on Nature with a humble heart,
Self-questioned where it did not understand,
And with a superstitious eye of love.

So passed the time; yet to the nearest town
He duly went with what small overplus
His earnings might supply, and brought away
The book that most had tempted his desires
While at the stall he read. Among the hills
He gazed upon that mighty orb of song,
250 The divine Milton. Lore of different kind,
The annual savings of a toilsome life,
His Schoolmaster supplied; books that explain
The purer elements of truth involved
In lines and numbers, and, by charm severe,
(Especially perceived where nature droops
And feeling is suppressed) preserve the mind
Busy in solitude and poverty.
These occupations oftentimes deceived
The listless hours, while in the hollow vale,
260 Hollow and green, he lay on the green turf
In pensive idleness. What could he do,

Thus daily thirsting, in that lonesome life,
With blind endeavours? Yet, still uppermost,
Nature was at his heart as if he felt,
Though yet he knew not how, a wasting power
In all things that from her sweet influence
Might tend to wean him. Therefore with her hues,
Her forms, and with the spirit of her forms,
He clothed the nakedness of austere truth.
270 While yet he lingered in the rudiments
Of science, and among her simplest laws,
His triangles – they were the stars of heaven,
The silent stars! Oft did he take delight
To measure the altitude of some tall crag
That is the eagle's birthplace, or some peak
Familiar with forgotten years, that shows
Inscribed upon its visionary sides,
The history of many a winter storm,
Or obscure records of the path of fire.

280   And thus before his eighteenth year was told,
Accumulated feelings pressed his heart
With still increasing weight; he was o'erpowered
By Nature; by the turbulence subdued
Of his own mind; by mystery and hope,
And the first virgin passion of a soul
Communing with the glorious universe.
Full often wished he that the winds might rage
When they were silent: far more fondly now
Than in his earlier season did he love
290 Tempestuous nights – the conflict and the sounds
That live in darkness. From his intellect
And from the stillness of abstracted thought
He asked repose; and, failing oft to win
The peace required, he scanned the laws of light
Amid the roar of torrents, where they send
From hollow clefts up to the clearer air
A cloud of mist, that smitten by the sun
Varies its rainbow hues. But vainly thus,

And vainly by all other means, he strove
300 To mitigate the fever of his heart.

In dreams, in study, and in ardent thought,
Thus was he reared; much wanting to assist
The growth of intellect, yet gaining more,
And every moral feeling of his soul
Strengthened and braced, by breathing in content
The keen, the wholesome, air of poverty,
And drinking from the well of homely life.
– But, from past liberty, and tried restraints,
He now was summoned to select the course
310 Of humble industry that promised best
To yield him no unworthy maintenance.
Urged by his Mother, he essayed to teach
A village-school – but wandering thoughts were then
A misery to him; and the Youth resigned
A task he was unable to perform.

That stern yet kindly Spirit, who constrains
The Savoyard to quit his naked rocks,
The freeborn Swiss to leave his narrow vales,
(Spirit attached to regions mountainous
320 Like their own stedfast clouds) did now impel
His restless mind to look abroad with hope.
– An irksome drudgery seems it to plod on,
Through hot and dusty ways, or pelting storm,
A vagrant Merchant under a heavy load
Bent as he moves, and needing frequent rest;
Yet do such travellers find their own delight;
And their hard service, deemed debasing now,
Gained merited respect in simpler times;
When squire, and priest, and they who round them dwelt
330 In rustic sequestration – all dependent
Upon the PEDLAR's toil – supplied their wants,
Or pleased their fancies, with the wares he brought.
Not ignorant was the Youth that still no few
Of his adventurous countrymen were led

By perseverance in this track of life
To competence and ease: – to him it offered
Attractions manifold; – and this he chose.
– His Parents on the enterprise bestowed
Their farewell benediction, but with hearts
340   Foreboding evil. From his native hills
He wandered far; much did he see of men,
Their manners, their enjoyments, and pursuits,
Their passions and their feelings; chiefly those
Essential and eternal in the heart,
That, 'mid the simpler forms of rural life,
Exist more simple in their elements,
And speak a plainer language. In the woods,
A lone Enthusiast, and among the fields,
Itinerant in this labour, he had passed
350   The better portion of his time; and there
Spontaneously had his affections thriven
Amid the bounties of the year, the peace
And liberty of nature; there he kept
In solitude and solitary thought
His mind in a just equipoise of love.
Serene it was, unclouded by the cares
Of ordinary life; unvexed, unwarped
By partial bondage. In his steady course,
No piteous revolutions had he felt,
360   No wild varieties of joy and grief.
Unoccupied by sorrow of its own,
His heart lay open; and, by nature tuned
And constant disposition of his thoughts
To sympathy with man, he was alive
To all that was enjoyed where'er he went,
And all that was endured; for, in himself
Happy, and quiet in his cheerfulness,
He had no painful pressure from within
That made him turn aside from wretchedness
370   With coward fears. He could *afford* to suffer
With those whom he saw suffer. Hence it came
That in our best experience he was rich,

And in the wisdom of our daily life.
For hence, minutely, in his various rounds,
He had observed the progress and decay
Of many minds, of minds and bodies too;
The history of many families;
How they had prospered; how they were o'erthrown
By passion or mischance, or such misrule
380   Among the unthinking masters of the earth
As makes the nations groan.

                              This active course
He followed till provision for his wants
Had been obtained; – the Wanderer then resolved
To pass the remnant of his days, untasked
With needless services, from hardship free.
His calling laid aside, he lived at ease:
But still he loved to pace the public roads
And the wild paths; and, by the summer's warmth
Invited, often would he leave his home
390   And journey far, revisiting the scenes
That to his memory were most endeared.
– Vigorous in health, of hopeful spirits, undamped
By worldly-mindedness or anxious care;
Observant, studious, thoughtful, and refreshed
By knowledge gathered up from day to day;
Thus had he lived a long and innocent life.

    The Scottish Church, both on himself and those
With whom from childhood he grew up, had held
The strong hand of her purity; and still
400   Had watched him with an unrelenting eye.
This he remembered in his riper age
With gratitude, and reverential thoughts.
But by the native vigour of his mind,
By his habitual wanderings out of doors,
By loneliness, and goodness, and kind works,
Whate'er, in docile childhood or in youth,

He had imbibed of fear or darker thought
Was melted all away; so true was this,
That sometimes his religion seemed to me
410 Self-taught, as of a dreamer in the woods;
Who to the model of his own pure heart
Shaped his belief, as grace divine inspired,
And human reason dictated with awe.
– And surely never did there live on earth
A man of kindlier nature. The rough sports
And teasing ways of children vexed not him;
Indulgent listener was he to the tongue
Of garrulous age; nor did the sick man's tale,
To his fraternal sympathy addressed,
Obtain reluctant hearing.

420   Plain his garb;
Such as might suit a rustic Sire, prepared
For sabbath duties; yet he was a man
Whom no one could have passed without remark.
Active and nervous was his gait; his limbs
And his whole figure breathed intelligence.
Time had compressed the freshness of his cheek
Into a narrower circle of deep red,
But had not tamed his eye; that, under brows
Shaggy and grey, had meanings which it brought
430 From years of youth; which, like a Being made
Of many Beings, he had wondrous skill
To blend with knowledge of the years to come,
Human, or such as lie beyond the grave.

So was He framed; and such his course of life
Who now, with no appendage but a staff,
The prized memorial of relinquished toils,
Upon that cottage-bench reposed his limbs,
Screened from the sun. Supine the Wanderer lay,
His eyes as if in drowsiness half shut,
440 The shadows of the breezy elms above

Dappling his face. He had not heard the sound
Of my approaching steps, and in the shade
Unnoticed did I stand some minutes' space.
At length I hailed him, seeing that his hat
Was moist with water-drops, as if the brim
Had newly scooped a running stream. He rose,
And ere our lively greeting into peace
Had settled, ' 'Tis,' said I, 'a burning day:
My lips are parched with thirst, but you, it seems,
450 Have somewhere found relief.' He, at the word,
Pointing towards a sweet-briar, bade me climb
The fence where that aspiring shrub looked out
Upon the public way. It was a plot
Of garden ground run wild, its matted weeds
Marked with the steps of those, whom, as they passed,
The gooseberry trees that shot in long lank slips,
Or currants, hanging from their leafless stems,
In scanty strings, had tempted to o'erleap
The broken wall. I looked around, and there,
460 Where two tall hedge-rows of thick alder boughs
Joined in a cold damp nook, espied a well
Shrouded with willow-flowers and plumy fern.
My thirst I slaked, and, from the cheerless spot
Withdrawing, straightway to the shade returned
Where sate the old Man on the cottage-bench;
And, while, beside him, with uncovered head,
I yet was standing, freely to respire,
And cool my temples in the fanning air,
Thus did he speak. 'I see around me here
470 Things which you cannot see: we die, my Friend,
Nor we alone, but that which each man loved
And prized in his peculiar nook of earth
Dies with him, or is changed; and very soon
Even of the good is no memorial left.
– The Poets, in their elegies and songs
Lamenting the departed, call the groves,
They call upon the hills and streams to mourn,
And senseless rocks; nor idly; for they speak,

In these their invocations, with a voice
480 Obedient to the strong creative power
Of human passion. Sympathies there are
More tranquil, yet perhaps of kindred birth,
That steal upon the meditative mind,
And grow with thought. Beside yon spring I stood,
And eyed its waters till we seemed to feel
One sadness, they and I. For them a bond
Of brotherhood is broken: time has been
When, every day, the touch of human hand
Dislodged the natural sleep that binds them up
490 In mortal stillness; and they ministered
To human comfort. Stooping down to drink,
Upon the slimy foot-stone I espied
The useless fragment of a wooden bowl,
Green with the moss of years, and subject only
To the soft handling of the elements:
There let it lie – how foolish are such thoughts!
Forgive them; – never – never did my steps
Approach this door but she who dwelt within
A daughter's welcome gave me, and I loved her
500 As my own child. Oh, Sir! the good die first,
And they whose hearts are dry as summer dust
Burn to the socket. Many a passenger
Hath blessed poor Margaret for her gentle looks,
When she upheld the cool refreshment drawn
From that forsaken spring; and no one came
But he was welcome; no one went away
But that it seemed she loved him. She is dead,
The light extinguished of her lonely hut,
The hut itself abandoned to decay,
510 And she forgotten in the quiet grave.

'I speak,' continued he, 'of One whose stock
Of virtues bloomed beneath this lowly roof.
She was a Woman of a steady mind,
Tender and deep in her excess of love;
Not speaking much, pleased rather with the joy

Of her own thoughts: by some especial care
Her temper had been framed, as if to make
A Being, who by adding love to peace
Might live on earth a life of happiness.
520 Her wedded Partner lacked not on his side
The humble worth that satisfied her heart:
Frugal, affectionate, sober, and withal
Keenly industrious. She with pride would tell
That he was often seated at his loom,
In summer, ere the mower was abroad
Among the dewy grass, – in early spring,
Ere the last star had vanished. – They who passed
At evening, from behind the garden fence
Might hear his busy spade, which he would ply,
530 After his daily work, until the light
Had failed, and every leaf and flower were lost
In the dark hedges. So their days were spent
In peace and comfort; and a pretty boy
Was their best hope, next to the God in heaven.

      'Not twenty years ago, but you I think
Can scarcely bear it now in mind, there came
Two blighting seasons, when the fields were left
With half a harvest. It pleased Heaven to add
A worse affliction in the plague of war:
540 This happy Land was stricken to the heart!
A Wanderer then among the cottages,
I, with my freight of winter raiment, saw
The hardships of that season: many rich
Sank down, as in a dream, among the poor;
And of the poor did many cease to be,
And their place knew them not. Meanwhile, abridged
Of daily comforts, gladly reconciled
To numerous self-denials, Margaret
Went struggling on through those calamitous years
550 With cheerful hope, until the second autumn,
When her life's Helpmate on a sick-bed lay,
Smitten with perilous fever. In disease

He lingered long; and, when his strength returned,
He found the little he had stored, to meet
The hour of accident or crippling age,
Was all consumed. A second infant now
Was added to the troubles of a time
Laden, for them and all of their degree,
With care and sorrow: shoals of artisans
560 From ill-requited labour turned adrift
Sought daily bread from public charity,
They, and their wives and children – happier far
Could they have lived as do the little birds
That peck along the hedge-rows, or the kite
That makes her dwelling on the mountain rocks!

'A sad reverse it was for him who long
Had filled with plenty, and possessed in peace,
This lonely Cottage. At the door he stood,
And whistled many a snatch of merry tunes
570 That had no mirth in them; or with his knife
Carved uncouth figures on the heads of sticks –
Then, not less idly, sought, through every nook
In house or garden, any casual work
Of use or ornament; and with a strange,
Amusing, yet uneasy, novelty,
He mingled, where he might, the various tasks
Of summer, autumn, winter, and of spring.
But this endured not; his good humour soon
Became a weight in which no pleasure was:
580 And poverty brought on a petted mood
And a sore temper: day by day he drooped,
And he would leave his work – and to the town
Would turn without an errand his slack steps;
Or wander here and there among the fields.
One while he would speak lightly of his babes,
And with a cruel tongue: at other times
He tossed them with a false unnatural joy:'
And 'twas a rueful thing to see the looks
Of the poor innocent children. "Every smile,"

590 Said Margaret to me, here beneath these trees,
"Made my heart bleed." '

                        At this the Wanderer paused;
And, looking up to those enormous elms,
He said, ' 'Tis now the hour of deepest noon.
At this still season of repose and peace,
This hour when all things which are not at rest
Are cheerful; while this multitude of flies
With tuneful hum is filling all the air;
Why should a tear be on an old Man's cheek?
Why should we thus, with an untoward mind,
600 And in the weakness of humanity,
From natural wisdom turn our hearts away;
To natural comfort shut our eyes and ears;
And, feeding on disquiet, thus disturb
The calm of nature with our restless thoughts?'

———————————

He spake with somewhat of a solemn tone:
But, when he ended, there was in his face
Such easy cheerfulness, a look so mild,
That for a little time it stole away
All recollection; and that simple tale
610 Passed from my mind like a forgotten sound.
A while on trivial things we held discourse,
To me soon tasteless. In my own despite,
I thought of that poor Woman as of one
Whom I had known and loved. He had rehearsed
Her homely tale with such familiar power,
With such an active countenance, an eye
So busy, that the things of which he spake
Seemed present; and, attention now relaxed,
A heart-felt chillness crept along my veins.
620 I rose; and, having left the breezy shade,
Stood drinking comfort from the warmer sun,
That had not cheered me long – ere, looking round
Upon that tranquil Ruin, I returned,

And begged of the old Man that, for my sake,
He would resume his story.

        He replied,
'It were a wantonness, and would demand
Severe reproof, if we were men whose hearts
Could hold vain dalliance with the misery
Even of the dead; contented thence to draw
630 A momentary pleasure, never marked
By reason, barren of all future good.
But we have known that there is often found
In mournful thoughts, and always might be found,
A power to virtue friendly; were't not so,
I am a dreamer among men, indeed
An idle dreamer! 'Tis a common tale,
An ordinary sorrow of man's life,
A tale of silent suffering, hardly clothed
In bodily form. – But without further bidding
I will proceed.

640   While thus it fared with them,
To whom this cottage, till those hapless years,
Had been a blessèd home, it was my chance
To travel in a country far remote;
And when these lofty elms once more appeared
What pleasant expectations lured me on
O'er the flat Common! – With quick step I reached
The threshold, lifted with light hand the latch;
But, when I entered, Margaret looked at me
A little while; then turned her head away
650 Speechless, – and, sitting down upon a chair,
Wept bitterly. I wist not what to do,
Nor how to speak to her. Poor Wretch! at last
She rose from off her seat, and then, – O Sir!
I cannot *tell* how she pronounced my name: –
With fervent love, and with a face of grief
Unutterably helpless, and a look
That seemed to cling upon me, she enquired

If I had seen her husband. As she spake
A strange surprise and fear came to my heart,
660   Nor had I power to answer ere she told
That he had disappeared – not two months gone.
He left his house: two wretched days had past,
And on the third, as wistfully she raised
Her head from off her pillow, to look forth,
Like one in trouble, for returning light,
Within her chamber-casement she espied
A folded paper, lying as if placed
To meet her waking eyes. This tremblingly
She opened – found no writing, but beheld
670   Pieces of money carefully enclosed,
Silver and gold. "I shuddered at the sight,"
Said Margaret, "for I knew it was his hand
That must have placed it there; and ere that day
Was ended, that long anxious day, I learned,
From one who by my husband had been sent
With the sad news, that he had joined a troop
Of soldiers, going to a distant land.
– He left me thus – he could not gather heart
To take a farewell of me; for he feared
680   That I should follow with my babes, and sink
Beneath the misery of that wandering life."

'This tale did Margaret tell with many tears:
And, when she ended, I had little power
To give her comfort, and was glad to take
Such words of hope from her own mouth as served
To cheer us both. But long we had not talked
Ere we built up a pile of better thoughts,
And with a brighter eye she looked around
As if she had been shedding tears of joy.
690   We parted. – 'Twas the time of early spring;
I left her busy with her garden tools;
And well remember, o'er that fence she looked,
And, while I paced along the foot-way path,
Called out, and sent a blessing after me,

With tender cheerfulness, and with a voice
That seemed the very sound of happy thoughts.

'I roved o'er many a hill and many a dale,
With my accustomed load; in heat and cold,
Through many a wood and many an open ground,
700 In sunshine and in shade, in wet and fair,
Drooping or blithe of heart, as might befall;
My best companions now the driving winds,
And now the "trotting brooks" and whispering trees,
And now the music of my own sad steps,
With many a short-lived thought that passed between,
And disappeared.

       I journeyed back this way,
When, in the warmth of midsummer, the wheat
Was yellow; and the soft and bladed grass,
Springing afresh, had o'er the hay-field spread
710 Its tender verdure. At the door arrived,
I found that she was absent. In the shade,
Where now we sit, I waited her return.
Her cottage, then a cheerful object, wore
Its customary look, – only, it seemed,
The honeysuckle, crowding round the porch,
Hung down in heavier tufts; and that bright weed,
The yellow stone-crop, suffered to take root
Along the window's edge, profusely grew
Blinding the lower panes. I turned aside,
720 And strolled into her garden. It appeared
To lag behind the season, and had lost
Its pride of neatness. Daisy-flowers and thrift
Had broken their trim border-lines, and straggled
O'er paths they used to deck: carnations, once
Prized for surpassing beauty, and no less
For the peculiar pains they had required,
Declined their languid heads, wanting support.
The cumbrous bind-weed, with its wreaths and bells,

Had twined about her two small rows of peas,
And dragged them to the earth.

730   Ere this an hour
Was wasted. – Back I turned my restless steps;
A stranger passed; and, guessing whom I sought,
He said that she was used to ramble far. –
The sun was sinking in the west; and now
I sate with sad impatience. From within
Her solitary infant cried aloud;
Then, like a blast that dies away self-stilled,
The voice was silent. From the bench I rose;
But neither could divert nor soothe my thoughts.
740 The spot, though fair, was very desolate –
The longer I remained, more desolate:
And, looking round me, now I first observed
The corner stones, on either side the porch,
With dull red stains discoloured, and stuck o'er
With tufts and hairs of wool, as if the sheep,
That fed upon the Common, thither came
Familiarly, and found a couching-place
Even at her threshold. Deeper shadows fell
From these tall elms; the cottage-clock struck eight; –
750 I turned, and saw her distant a few steps.
Her face was pale and thin – her figure, too,
Was changed. As she unlocked the door, she said,
"It grieves me you have waited here so long,
But, in good truth, I've wandered much of late;
And, sometimes – to my shame I speak – have need
Of my best prayers to bring me back again."
While on the board she spread our evening meal,
She told me – interrupting not the work
Which gave employment to her listless hands –
760 That she had parted with her elder child;
To a kind master on a distant farm
Now happily apprenticed. – "I perceive
You look at me, and you have cause; today
I have been travelling far; and many days

About the fields I wander, knowing this
Only, that what I seek I cannot find;
And so I waste my time: for I am changed;
And to myself," said she, "have done much wrong
And to this helpless infant. I have slept
770 Weeping, and weeping have I waked; my tears
Have flowed as if my body were not such
As others are; and I could never die.
But I am now in mind and in my heart
More easy; and I hope," said she, "that God
Will give me patience to endure the things
Which I behold at home."

It would have grieved
Your very soul to see her. Sir, I feel
The story linger in my heart; I fear
'Tis long and tedious; but my spirit clings
780 To that poor Woman: – so familiarly
Do I perceive her manner, and her look,
And presence; and so deeply do I feel
Her goodness, that, not seldom, in my walks
A momentary trance comes over me;
And to myself I seem to muse on One
By sorrow laid asleep; or borne away,
A human being destined to awake
To human life, or something very near
To human life, when he shall come again
790 For whom she suffered. Yes, it would have grieved
Your very soul to see her: evermore
Her eyelids drooped, her eyes downward were cast;
And, when she at her table gave me food,
She did not look at me. Her voice was low,
Her body was subdued. In every act
Pertaining to her house-affairs, appeared
The careless stillness of a thinking mind
Self-occupied; to which all outward things
Are like an idle matter. Still she sighed,
800 But yet no motion of the breast was seen,
No heaving of the heart. While by the fire

We sate together, sighs came on my ear,
I knew not how, and hardly whence they came.

'Ere my departure, to her care I gave,
For her son's use, some tokens of regard,
Which with a look of welcome she received;
And I exhorted her to place her trust
In God's good love, and seek his help by prayer.
I took my staff, and, when I kissed her babe,
810 The tears stood in her eyes. I left her then
With the best hope and comfort I could give:
She thanked me for my wish; – but for my hope
It seemed she did not thank me.
                    I returned,
And took my rounds along this road again
When on its sunny bank the primrose flower
Peeped forth, to give an earnest of the Spring.
I found her sad and drooping: she had learned
No tidings of her husband; if he lived,
She knew not that he lived; if he were dead,
820 She knew not he was dead. She seemed the same
In person and appearance; but her house
Bespake a sleepy hand of negligence;
The floor was neither dry nor neat, the hearth
Was comfortless, and her small lot of books,
Which, in the cottage-window, heretofore
Had been piled up against the corner panes
In seemly order, now, with straggling leaves
Lay scattered here and there, open or shut,
As they had chanced to fall. Her infant Babe
830 Had from its mother caught the trick of grief,
And sighed among its playthings. I withdrew,
And once again entering the garden saw,
More plainly still, that poverty and grief
Were now come nearer to her: weeds defaced
The hardened soil, and knots of withered grass:
No ridges there appeared of clear black mould,
No winter greenness; of her herbs and flowers,

It seemed the better part were gnawed away
Or trampled into earth; a chain of straw,
840 Which had been twined about the slender stem
Of a young apple-tree, lay at its root;
The bark was nibbled round by truant sheep.
– Margaret stood near, her infant in her arms,
And, noting that my eye was on the tree,
She said, "I fear it will be dead and gone
Ere Robert come again." When to the House
We had returned together, she enquired
If I had any hope: – but for her babe
And for her little orphan boy, she said,
850 She had no wish to live, that she must die
Of sorrow. Yet I saw the idle loom
Still in its place; his Sunday garments hung
Upon the self-same nail; his very staff
Stood undisturbed behind the door.

                       And when,
In bleak December, I retraced this way,
She told me that her little babe was dead,
And she was left alone. She now, released
From her maternal cares, had taken up
The employment common through these wilds, and gained,
860 By spinning hemp, a pittance for herself;
And for this end had hired a neighbour's boy
To give her needful help. That very time
Most willingly she put her work aside,
And walked with me along the miry road,
Heedless how far; and, in such piteous sort
That any heart had ached to hear her, begged
That, wheresoe'er I went, I still would ask
For him whom she had lost. We parted then –
Our final parting; for from that time forth
870 Did many seasons pass ere I returned
Into this tract again.

                      Nine tedious years;
From their first separation, nine long years,

She lingered in unquiet widowhood;
A Wife and Widow. Needs must it have been
A sore heart-wasting! I have heard, my Friend,
That in yon arbour oftentimes she sate
Alone, through half the vacant sabbath day;
And, if a dog passed by, she still would quit
The shade, and look abroad. On this old bench
880　For hours she sate; and evermore her eye
Was busy in the distance, shaping things
That made her heart beat quick. You see that path,
Now faint, – the grass has crept o'er its grey line;
There, to and fro, she paced through many a day
Of the warm summer, from a belt of hemp
That girt her waist, spinning the long-drawn thread
With backward steps. Yet ever as there passed
A man whose garments showed the soldier's red,
Or crippled mendicant in sailor's garb,
890　The little child who sate to turn the wheel
Ceased from his task; and she with faltering voice
Made many a fond enquiry; and when they,
Whose presence gave no comfort, were gone by,
Her heart was still more sad. And by yon gate,
That bars the traveller's road, she often stood,
And when a stranger horseman came, the latch
Would lift, and in his face look wistfully:
Most happy, if, from aught discovered there
Of tender feeling, she might dare repeat
900　The same sad question. Meanwhile her poor Hut
Sank to decay; for he was gone, whose hand,
At the first nipping of October frost,
Closed up each chink, and with fresh bands of straw
Chequered the green-grown thatch. And so she lived
Through the long winter, reckless and alone;
Until her house by frost, and thaw, and rain,
Was sapped; and while she slept, the nightly damps
Did chill her breast; and in the stormy day
Her tattered clothes were ruffled by the wind,
910　Even at the side of her own fire. Yet still

She loved this wretched spot, nor would for worlds
Have parted hence; and still that length of road,
And this rude bench, one torturing hope endeared,
Fast rooted at her heart: and here, my Friend, –
In sickness she remained; and here she died;
Last human tenant of these ruined walls!'

    The old Man ceased: he saw that I was moved;
From that low bench, rising instinctively
I turned aside in weakness, nor had power
920 To thank him for the tale which he had told.
I stood, and leaning o'er the garden wall
Reviewed that Woman's sufferings; and it seemed
To comfort me while with a brother's love
I blessed her in the impotence of grief.
Then towards the cottage I returned; and traced
Fondly, though with an interest more mild,
That secret spirit of humanity
Which, 'mid the calm oblivious tendencies
Of nature, 'mid her plants, and weeds, and flowers,
930 And silent overgrowings, still survived.
The old Man, noting this, resumed, and said,
'My Friend! enough to sorrow you have given,
The purposes of wisdom ask no more:
Nor more would she have craved as due to One
Who, in her worst distress, had ofttimes felt
The unbounded might of prayer; and learned, with soul
Fixed on the Cross, that consolation springs,
From sources deeper far than deepest pain,
For the meek Sufferer. Why then should we read
940 The forms of things with an unworthy eye?
She sleeps in the calm earth, and peace is here.
I well remember that those very plumes,
Those weeds, and the high spear-grass on that wall,
By mist and silent rain-drops silvered o'er,
As once I passed, into my heart conveyed
So still an image of tranquillity,
So calm and still, and looked so beautiful

Amid the uneasy thoughts which filled my mind,
That what we feel of sorrow and despair
950 From ruin and from change, and all the grief
That passing shows of Being leave behind,
Appeared an idle dream, that could maintain,
Nowhere, dominion o'er the enlightened spirit
Whose meditative sympathies repose
Upon the breast of Faith. I turned away,
And walked along my road in happiness.'

He ceased. Ere long the sun declining shot
A slant and mellow radiance, which began
To fall upon us, while, beneath the trees,
960 We sate on that low bench: and now we felt,
Admonished thus, the sweet hour coming on.
A linnet warbled from those lofty elms,
A thrush sang loud, and other melodies,
At distance heard, peopled the milder air.
The old Man rose, and, with a sprightly mien
Of hopeful preparation, grasped his staff;
Together casting then a farewell look
Upon those silent walls, we left the shade;
And, ere the stars were visible, had reached
970 A village-inn, – our evening resting-place.

BOOK SECOND
THE SOLITARY

Argument

The Author describes his travels with the Wanderer, whose
character is further illustrated. – Morning scene, and view of
a Village Wake. – Wanderer's account of a Friend whom he
purposes to visit. – View, from an eminence, of the Valley which
his Friend had chosen for his retreat. – Sound of singing from
below. – A funeral procession. – Descent into the Valley. –
Observations drawn from the Wanderer at sight of a book
accidentally discovered in a recess in the Valley. – Meeting
with the Wanderer's friend, the Solitary. – Wanderer's descrip–

tion of the mode of burial in this mountainous district. –
Solitary contrasts with this, that of the individual carried a few
minutes before from the cottage. – The cottage entered. – Description of the Solitary's apartment. – Repast there. – View,
from the window, of two mountain summits; and the Solitary's
description of the companionship they afford him. – Account
of the departed inmate of the cottage. – Description of a grand
spectacle upon the mountains, with its effect upon the Solitary's
mind. – Leave the house.

In days of yore how fortunately fared
The Minstrel! wandering on from hall to hall,
Baronial court or royal; cheered with gifts
Munificent, and love, and ladies' praise;
Now meeting on his road an armèd knight,
Now resting with a pilgrim by the side
Of a clear brook; – beneath an abbey's roof
One evening sumptuously lodged; the next,
Humbly in a religious hospital;
10 Or with some merry outlaws of the wood;
Or haply shrouded in a hermit's cell.
Him, sleeping or awake, the robber spared;
He walked – protected from the sword of war
By virtue of that sacred instrument
His harp, suspended at the traveller's side;
His dear companion wheresoe'er he went
Opening from land to land an easy way
By melody, and by the charm of verse.
Yet not the noblest of that honoured Race
20 Drew happier, loftier, more empassioned, thoughts
From his long journeyings and eventful life,
Than this obscure Itinerant had skill
To gather, ranging through the tamer ground
Of these our unimaginative days;
Both while he trod the earth in humblest guise
Accoutred with his burden and his staff;
And now, when free to move with lighter pace.

What wonder, then, if I, whose favourite school
Hath been the fields, the roads, and rural lanes,

30 Looked on this guide with reverential love?
Each with the other pleased, we now pursued
Our journey, under favourable skies.
Turn wheresoe'er we would, he was a light
Unfailing: not a hamlet could we pass,
Rarely a house, that did not yield to him
Remembrances; or from his tongue call forth
Some way-beguiling tale. Nor less regard
Accompanied those strains of apt discourse,
Which nature's various objects might inspire;
40 And in the silence of his face I read
His overflowing spirit. Birds and beasts,
And the mute fish that glances in the stream,
And harmless reptile coiling in the sun,
And gorgeous insect hovering in the air,
The fowl domestic, and the household dog –
In his capacious mind, he loved them all:
Their rights acknowledging he felt for all.
Oft was occasion given me to perceive
How the calm pleasures of the pasturing herd
50 To happy contemplation soothed his walk;
How the poor brute's condition, forced to run
Its course of suffering in the public road,
Sad contrast! all too often smote his heart
With unavailing pity. Rich in love
And sweet humanity, he was, himself,
To the degree that he desired, beloved.
Smiles of good-will from faces that he knew
Greeted us all day long; we took our seats
By many a cottage-hearth, where he received
60 The welcome of an Inmate from afar,
And I at once forgot, I was a Stranger.
– Nor was he loth to enter ragged huts,
Huts where his charity was blest; his voice
Heard as the voice of an experienced friend.
And, sometimes – where the poor man held dispute
With his own mind, unable to subdue
Impatience through inaptness to perceive

General distress in his particular lot;
Or cherishing resentment, or in vain
70 Struggling against it; with a soul perplexed,
And finding in herself no steady power
To draw the line of comfort that divides
Calamity, the chastisement of Heaven,
From the injustice of our brother men –
To him appeal was made as to a judge;
Who, with an understanding heart, allayed
The perturbation; listened to the plea;
Resolved the dubious point; and sentence gave
So grounded, so applied, that it was heard
80 With softened spirit, even when it condemned.

Such intercourse I witnessed, while we roved,
Now as his choice directed, now as mine;
Or both, with equal readiness of will,
Our course submitting to the changeful breeze
Of accident. But when the rising sun
Had three times called us to renew our walk,
My Fellow-traveller, with earnest voice,
As if the thought were but a moment old,
Claimed absolute dominion for the day.
90 We started – and he led me toward the hills,
Up through an ample vale, with higher hills
Before us, mountains stern and desolate;
But, in the majesty of distance, now
Set off, and to our ken appearing fair
Of aspect, with aërial softness clad,
And beautified with morning's purple beams.

The wealthy, the luxurious, by the stress
Of business roused, or pleasure, ere their time,
May roll in chariots, or provoke the hoofs
100 Of the fleet coursers they bestride, to raise
From earth the dust of morning, slow to rise;
And they, if blest with health and hearts at ease,
Shall lack not their enjoyment: – but how faint

Compared with ours! who, pacing side by side,
Could, with an eye of leisure, look on all
That we beheld; and lend the listening sense
To every grateful sound of earth and air;
Pausing at will – our spirits braced, our thoughts
Pleasant as roses in the thickets blown,
110 And pure as dew bathing their crimson leaves.

    Mount slowly, sun! that we may journey long,
By this dark hill protected from thy beams!
Such is the summer pilgrim's frequent wish;
But quickly from among our morning thoughts
'Twas chased away: for, toward the western side
Of the broad vale, casting a casual glance,
We saw a throng of people; – wherefore met?
Blithe notes of music, suddenly let loose
On the thrilled ear, and flags uprising, yield
120 Prompt answer; they proclaim the annual Wake,
Which the bright season favours. – Tabor and pipe
In purpose join to hasten or reprove
The laggard Rustic; and repay with boons
Of merriment a party-coloured knot,
Already formed upon the village-green.
– Beyond the limits of the shadow cast
By the broad hill, glistened upon our sight
That gay assemblage. Round them and above,
Glitter, with dark recesses interposed,
130 Casement, and cottage-roof, and stems of trees
Half-veiled in vapoury cloud, the silver steam
Of dews fast melting on their leafy boughs
By the strong sunbeams smitten. Like a mast
Of gold, the Maypole shines; as if the rays
Of morning, aided by exhaling dew,
With gladsome influence could re-animate
The faded garlands dangling from its sides.

    Said I, 'The music and the sprightly scene
Invite us; shall we quit our road, and join

140 These festive matins?' – He replied, 'Not loth
To linger I would here with you partake,
Not one hour merely, but till evening's close,
The simple pastimes of the day and place.
By the fleet Racers, ere the sun be set,
The turf of yon large pasture will be skimmed;
There, too, the lusty Wrestlers shall contend:
But know we not that he, who intermits
The appointed task and duties of the day,
Untunes full oft the pleasures of the day;
150 Checking the finer spirits that refuse
To flow, when purposes are lightly changed?
A length of journey yet remains untraced:
Let us proceed.' Then, pointing with his staff
Raised toward those craggy summits, his intent
He thus imparted: –
                              'In a spot that lies
Among yon mountain fastnesses concealed,
You will receive, before the hour of noon,
Good recompense, I hope, for this day's toil,
From sight of One who lives secluded there,
160 Lonesome and lost: of whom, and whose past life,
(Not to forestall such knowledge as may be
More faithfully collected from himself)
This brief communication shall suffice.

'Though now sojourning there, he, like myself,
Sprang from a stock of lowly parentage
Among the wilds of Scotland, in a tract
Where many a sheltered and well-tended plant
Bears, on the humblest ground of social life,
Blossoms of piety and innocence.
170 Such grateful promises his youth displayed:
And, having shown in study forward zeal,
He to the Ministry was duly called;
And straight, incited by a curious mind
Filled with vague hopes, he undertook the charge
Of Chaplain to a military troop

Cheered by the Highland bagpipe, as they marched
In plaided vest, – his fellow-countrymen.
This office filling, yet by native power
And force of native inclination made
180 An intellectual ruler in the haunts
Of social vanity, he walked the world,
Gay, and affecting graceful gaiety;
Lax, buoyant – less a pastor with his flock
Than a soldier among soldiers – lived and roamed
Where Fortune led: – and Fortune, who oft proves
The careless wanderer's friend, to him made known
A blooming Lady – a conspicuous flower,
Admired for beauty, for her sweetness praised;
Whom he had sensibility to love,
190 Ambition to attempt, and skill to win.

'For this fair Bride, most rich in gifts of mind,
Nor sparingly endowed with worldly wealth,
His office he relinquished; and retired
From the world's notice to a rural home.
Youth's season yet with him was scarcely past,
And she was in youth's prime. How free their love,
How full their joy! Till, pitiable doom!
In the short course of one undreaded year,
Death blasted all. Death suddenly o'erthrew
200 Two lovely Children – all that they possessed!
The Mother followed: – miserably bare
The one Survivor stood; he wept, he prayed
For his dismissal, day and night, compelled
To hold communion with the grave, and face
With pain the regions of eternity.
An uncomplaining apathy displaced
This anguish; and, indifferent to delight,
To aim and purpose, he consumed his days,
To private interest dead, and public care.
So lived he; so he might have died.
210   But now,
To the wide world's astonishment, appeared

A glorious opening, the unlooked-for dawn,
That promised everlasting joy to France!
Her voice of social transport reached even him!
He broke from his contracted bounds, repaired
To the great City, an emporium then
Of golden expectations, and receiving
Freights every day from a new world of hope.
Thither his popular talents he transferred;
220 And, from the pulpit, zealously maintained
The cause of Christ and civil liberty,
As one, and moving to one glorious end.
Intoxicating service! I might say
A happy service; for he was sincere
As vanity and fondness for applause,
And new and shapeless wishes, would allow.

    'That righteous cause (such power hath freedom)
      bound,
For one hostility, in friendly league,
Ethereal natures and the worst of slaves;
230 Was served by rival advocates that came
From regions opposite as heaven and hell.
One courage seemed to animate them all:
And, from the dazzling conquests daily gained
By their united efforts, there arose
A proud and most presumptuous confidence
In the transcendent wisdom of the age,
And her discernment; not alone in rights,
And in the origin and bounds of power
Social and temporal; but in laws divine,
240 Deduced by reason, or to faith revealed.
An overweening trust was raised; and fear
Cast out, alike of person and of thing.
Plague from this union spread, whose subtle bane
The strongest did not easily escape;
And He, what wonder! took a mortal taint.
How shall I trace the change, how bear to tell
That he broke faith with them whom he had laid

In earth's dark chambers, with a Christian's hope!
An infidel contempt of holy writ
250 Stole by degrees upon his mind; and hence
Life, like that Roman Janus, double-faced;
Vilest hypocrisy – the laughing, gay
Hypocrisy, not leagued with fear, but pride.
Smooth words he had to wheedle simple souls;
But, for disciples of the inner school,
Old freedom was old servitude, and they
The wisest whose opinions stooped the least
To known restraints; and who most boldly drew
Hopeful prognostications from a creed,
260 That, in the light of false philosophy,
Spread like a halo round a misty moon,
Widening its circle as the storms advance.

   'His sacred function was at length renounced;
And every day and every place enjoyed
The unshackled layman's natural liberty;
Speech, manners, morals, all without disguise.
I do not wish to wrong him; though the course
Of private life licentiously displayed
Unhallowed actions – planted like a crown
270 Upon the insolent aspiring brow
Of spurious notions – worn as open signs
Of prejudice subdued – still he retained,
'Mid much abasement, what he had received
From nature, an intense and glowing mind.
Wherefore, when humbled Liberty grew weak,
And mortal sickness on her face appeared,
He coloured objects to his own desire
As with a lover's passion. Yet his moods
Of pain were keen as those of better men,
280 Nay keener, as his fortitude was less:
And he continued, when worse days were come,
To deal about his sparkling eloquence,
Struggling against the strange reverse with zeal
That showed like happiness. But, in despite

Of all this outside bravery, within,
He neither felt encouragement nor hope:
For moral dignity, and strength of mind,
Were wanting; and simplicity of life;
And reverence for himself; and, last and best,
290 Confiding thoughts, through love and fear of Him
Before whose sight the troubles of this world
Are vain, as billows in a tossing sea.

'The glory of the times fading away –
The splendour, which had given a festal air
To self-importance, hallowed it, and veiled
From his own sight – this gone, he forfeited
All joy in human nature; was consumed,
And vexed, and chafed, by levity and scorn,
And fruitless indignation; galled by pride;
300 Made desperate by contempt of men who throve
Before his sight in power or fame, and won,
Without desert, what he desired; weak men,
Too weak even for his envy or his hate!
Tormented thus, after a wandering course
Of discontent, and inwardly opprest
With malady – in part, I fear, provoked
By weariness of life – he fixed his home,
Or, rather say, sate down by very chance,
Among these rugged hills; where now he dwells,
310 And wastes the sad remainder of his hours,
Steeped in a self-indulging spleen, that wants not
Its own voluptuousness; – on this resolved,
With this content, that he will live and die
Forgotten, – at safe distance from "a world
Not moving to his mind." '
                              These serious words
Closed the preparatory notices
That served my Fellow-traveller to beguile
The way, while we advanced up that wide vale.
Diverging now (as if his quest had been
320 Some secret of the mountains, cavern, fall

Of water, or some lofty eminence,
Renowned for splendid prospect far and wide)
We scaled, without a track to ease our steps,
A steep ascent; and reached a dreary plain,
With a tumultuous waste of huge hill tops
Before us; savage region! which I paced
Dispirited: when, all at once, behold!
Beneath our feet, a little lowly vale,
A lowly vale, and yet uplifted high
330   Among the mountains; even as if the spot
Had been from eldest time by wish of theirs
So placed, to be shut out from all the world!
Urn-like it was in shape, deep as an urn;
With rocks encompassed, save that to the south
Was one small opening, where a heath-clad ridge
Supplied a boundary less abrupt and close;
A quiet treeless nook, with two green fields,
A liquid pool that glittered in the sun,
And one bare dwelling; one abode, no more!
340   It seemed the home of poverty and toil,
Though not of want: the little fields, made green
By husbandry of many thrifty years,
Paid cheerful tribute to the moorland house.
– There crows the cock, single in his domain:
The small birds find in spring no thicket there
To shroud them; only from the neighbouring vales
The cuckoo, straggling up to the hill tops,
Shouteth faint tidings of some gladder place.

Ah! what a sweet Recess, thought I, is here!
350   Instantly throwing down my limbs at ease
Upon a bed of heath; – full many a spot
Of hidden beauty have I chanced to espy
Among the mountains; never one like this;
So lonesome, and so perfectly secure;
Not melancholy – no, for it is green,
And bright, and fertile, furnished in itself
With the few needful things that life requires.

– In rugged arms how softly does it lie,
How tenderly protected! Far and near
360 We have an image of the pristine earth,
The planet in its nakedness: were this
Man's only dwelling, sole appointed seat,
First, last, and single, in the breathing world,
It could not be more quiet: peace is here
Or nowhere; days unruffled by the gale
Of public news or private; years that pass
Forgetfully; uncalled upon to pay
The common penalties of mortal life,
Sickness, or accident, or grief, or pain.

370   On these and kindred thoughts intent I lay
In silence musing by my Comrade's side,
He also silent; when from out the heart
Of that profound abyss a solemn voice,
Or several voices in one solemn sound,
Was heard ascending; mournful, deep, and slow
The cadence, as of psalms – a funeral dirge!
We listened, looking down upon the hut,
But seeing no one: meanwhile from below
The strain continued, spiritual as before;
380 And now distinctly could I recognize
These words: – '*Shall in the grave thy love be known,
In death thy faithfulness?*' – 'God rest his soul!'
Said the old man, abruptly breaking silence, –
'He is departed, and finds peace at last!'

    This scarcely spoken, and those holy strains
Not ceasing, forth appeared in view a band
Of rustic persons, from behind the hut
Bearing a coffin in the midst, with which
They shaped their course along the sloping side
390 Of that small valley, singing as they moved;
A sober company and few, the men
Bare-headed, and all decently attired!
Some steps when they had thus advanced, the dirge

Ended; and, from the stillness that ensued
Recovering, to my Friend I said, 'You spake,
Methought, with apprehension that these rites
Are paid to Him upon whose shy retreat
This day we purposed to intrude.' – 'I did so,
But let us hence, that we may learn the truth:
400 Perhaps it is not he but someone else
For whom this pious service is performed;
Some other tenant of the solitude.'

    So, to a steep and difficult descent
Trusting ourselves, we wound from crag to crag,
Where passage could be won; and, as the last
Of the mute train, behind the heathy top
Of that off-sloping outlet, disappeared,
I, more impatient in my downward course,
Had landed upon easy ground; and there
410 Stood waiting for my Comrade. When behold
An object that enticed my steps aside!
A narrow, winding entry opened out
Into a platform – that lay, sheepfold-wise,
Enclosed between an upright mass of rock
And one old moss-grown wall; – a cool recess,
And fanciful! For where the rock and wall
Met in an angle, hung a penthouse, framed
By thrusting two rude staves into the wall
And overlaying them with mountain sods;
420 To weather-fend a little turf-built seat
Whereon a full-grown man might rest, nor dread
The burning sunshine, or a transient shower;
But the whole plainly wrought by children's hands!
Whose skill had thronged the floor with a proud show
Of baby-houses, curiously arranged;
Nor wanting ornament of walks between,
With mimic trees inserted in the turf,
And gardens interposed. Pleased with the sight,
I could not choose but beckon to my Guide,
430 Who, entering, round him threw a careless glance

Impatient to pass on, when I exclaimed,
'Lo! what is here?' and, stooping down, drew forth
A book, that, in the midst of stones and moss
And wreck of party-coloured earthenware,
Aptly disposed, had lent its help to raise
One of those petty structures. 'His it must be!'
Exclaimed the Wanderer, 'cannot but be his,
And he is gone!' The book, which in my hand
Had opened of itself (for it was swoln
440   With searching damp, and seemingly had lain
To the injurious elements exposed
From week to week,) I found to be a work
In the French tongue, a Novel of Voltaire,
His famous Optimist. 'Unhappy Man!'
Exclaimed my Friend: 'here then has been to him
Retreat within retreat, a sheltering-place
Within how deep a shelter! He had fits,
Even to the last, of genuine tenderness,
And loved the haunts of children: here, no doubt,
450   Pleasing and pleased, he shared their simple sports,
Or sate companionless; and here the book,
Left and forgotten in his careless way,
Must by the cottage-children have been found:
Heaven bless them, and their inconsiderate work!
To what odd purpose have the darlings turned
This sad memorial of their hapless friend!'

'Me,' said I, 'most doth it surprise, to find
Such book in such a place!' – 'A book it is,'
He answered, 'to the Person suited well,
460   Though little suited to surrounding things:
'Tis strange, I grant; and stranger still had been
To see the Man who owned it, dwelling here,
With one poor shepherd, far from all the world! –
Now, if our errand hath been thrown away,
As from these intimations I forebode,
Grieved shall I be – less for my sake than yours,
And least of all for him who is no more.'

By this, the book was in the old Man's hand;
And he continued, glancing on the leaves
470 An eye of scorn: – 'The lover,' said he, 'doomed
To love when hope hath failed him – whom no depth
Of privacy is deep enough to hide,
Hath yet his bracelet or his lock of hair,
And that is joy to him. When change of times
Hath summoned kings to scaffolds, do but give
The faithful servant, who must hide his head
Henceforth in whatsoever nook he may,
A kerchief sprinkled with his master's blood,
And he too hath his comforter. How poor,
480 Beyond all poverty how destitute,
Must that Man have been left, who, hither driven,
Flying or seeking, could yet bring with him
No dearer relique, and no better stay,
Than this dull product of a scoffer's pen,
Impure conceits discharging from a heart
Hardened by impious pride! – I did not fear
To tax you with this journey;' – mildly said
My venerable Friend, as forth we stepped
Into the presence of the cheerful light –
490 'For I have knowledge that you do not shrink
From moving spectacles; – but let us on.'

So speaking, on he went, and at the word
I followed, till he made a sudden stand:
For full in view, approaching through a gate
That opened from the enclosure of green fields
Into the rough uncultivated ground,
Behold the Man whom he had fancied dead!
I knew from his deportment, mien, and dress,
That it could be no other; a pale face,
500 A meagre person, tall, and in a garb
Not rustic – dull and faded like himself!
He saw us not, though distant but few steps;
For he was busy, dealing, from a store
Upon a broad leaf carried, choicest strings

Of red ripe currants; gift by which he strove,
With intermixture of endearing words,
To soothe a Child, who walked beside him, weeping
As if disconsolate. – 'They to the grave
Are bearing him, my Little-one,' he said,
510 'To the dark pit; but he will feel no pain;
His body is at rest, his soul in heaven.'

    More might have followed – but my honoured Friend
Broke in upon the Speaker with a frank
And cordial greeting. – Vivid was the light
That flashed and sparkled from the other's eyes;
He was all fire: no shadow on his brow
Remained, nor sign of sickness on his face.
Hands joined he with his Visitant, – a grasp,
An eager grasp; and many moments' space –
520 When the first glow of pleasure was no more,
And, of the sad appearance which at once
Had vanished, much was come and coming back –
An amicable smile retained the life
Which it had unexpectedly received,
Upon his hollow cheek. 'How kind,' he said,
'Nor could your coming have been better timed;
For this, you see, is in our narrow world
A day of sorrow. I have here a charge' –
And, speaking thus, he patted tenderly
530 The sun-burnt forehead of the weeping child –
'A little mourner, whom it is my task
To comfort; – but how came ye? – if yon track
(Which doth at once befriend us and betray)
Conducted hither your most welcome feet,
Ye could not miss the funeral train – they yet
Have scarcely disappeared.' 'This blooming Child,'
Said the old Man, 'is of an age to weep
At any grave or solemn spectacle,
Inly distressed or overpowered with awe,
540 He knows not wherefore; – but the boy today,
Perhaps is shedding orphan's tears; you also

Must have sustained a loss.' – 'The hand of Death,'
He answered, 'has been here; but could not well
Have fallen more lightly, if it had not fallen
Upon myself.' – The other left these words
Unnoticed, thus continuing. –
                  'From yon crag,
Down whose steep sides we dropped into the vale,
We heard the hymn they sang – a solemn sound
Heard anywhere, but in a place like this
550 'Tis more than human! Many precious rites
And customs of our rural ancestry
Are gone, or stealing from us; this, I hope,
Will last for ever. Oft on my way have I
Stood still, though but a casual passenger,
So much I felt the awfulness of life,
In that one moment when the corse is lifted
In silence, with a hush of decency;
Then from the threshold moves with song of peace,
And confidential yearnings, towards its home,
560 Its final home on earth. What traveller – who –
(How far soe'er a stranger) does not own
The bond of brotherhood, when he sees them go,
A mute procession on the houseless road;
Or passing by some single tenement
Or clustered dwellings, where again they raise
The monitory voice? But most of all
It touches, it confirms, and elevates,
Then, when the body, soon to be consigned
Ashes to ashes, dust bequeathed to dust,
570 Is raised from the church-aisle, and forward borne
Upon the shoulders of the next in love,
The nearest in affection or in blood;
Yea, by the very mourners who had knelt
Beside the coffin, resting on its lid
In silent grief their unuplifted heads,
And heard meanwhile the Psalmist's mournful plaint,
And that most awful scripture which declares
We shall not sleep, but we shall all be changed!

– Have I not seen – ye likewise may have seen –
580 Son, husband, brothers – brothers side by side,
And son and father also side by side,
Rise from that posture: – and in concert move,
On the green turf following the vested Priest,
Four dear supporters of one senseless weight,
From which they do not shrink, and under which
They faint not, but advance toward the open grave
Step after step – together, with their firm
Unhidden faces: he that suffers most,
He outwardly, and inwardly perhaps,
590 The most serene, with most undaunted eye! –
Oh! blest are they who live and die like these,
Loved with such love, and with such sorrow mourned!'

'That poor Man taken hence today,' replied
The Solitary, with a faint sarcastic smile
Which did not please me, 'must be deemed, I fear,
Of the unblest; for he will surely sink
Into his mother earth without such pomp
Of grief, depart without occasion given
By him for such array of fortitude.
600 Full seventy winters hath he lived, and mark!
This simple Child will mourn his one short hour,
And I shall miss him; scanty tribute! yet,
This wanting, he would leave the sight of men,
If love were his sole claim upon their care,
Like a ripe date which in the desert falls
Without a hand to gather it.'
                                        At this
I interposed, though loth to speak, and said,
'Can it be thus among so small a band
As ye must needs be here? in such a place
610 I would not willingly, methinks, lose sight
Of a departing cloud.' – ' 'Twas not for love' –
Answered the sick Man with a careless voice –
'That I came hither; neither have I found
Among associates who have power of speech,

Nor in such other converse as is here,
Temptation so prevailing as to change
That mood, or undermine my first resolve.'
Then, speaking in like careless sort, he said
To my benign Companion, – 'Pity 'tis
620   That fortune did not guide you to this house
A few days earlier; then would you have seen
What stuff the Dwellers in a solitude,
That seems by Nature hollowed out to be
The seat and bosom of pure innocence,
Are made of; an ungracious matter this!
Which, for truth's sake, yet in remembrance too
Of past discussions with this zealous friend
And advocate of humble life, I now
Will force upon his notice; undeterred
630   By the example of his own pure course,
And that respect and deference which a soul
May fairly claim, by niggard age enriched
In what she most doth value, love of God
And his frail creature Man; – but ye shall hear.
I talk – and ye are standing in the sun
Without refreshment!'
                      Quickly had he spoken,
And, with light steps still quicker than his words,
Led toward the Cottage. Homely was the spot;
And, to my feeling, ere we reached the door,
640   Had almost a forbidding nakedness;
Less fair, I grant, even painfully less fair,
Than it appeared when from the beetling rock
We had looked down upon it. All within,
As left by the departed company,
Was silent; save the solitary clock
That on mine ear ticked with a mournful sound. –
Following our Guide, we clomb the cottage-stairs
And reached a small apartment dark and low,
Which was no sooner entered than our Host
650   Said gaily, 'This is my domain, my cell,
My hermitage, my cabin, what you will –

I love it better than a snail his house.
But now ye shall be feasted with our best.'

So, with more ardour than an unripe girl
Left one day mistress of her mother's stores,
He went about his hospitable task.
My eyes were busy, and my thoughts no less,
And pleased I looked upon my grey-haired Friend,
As if to thank him; he returned that look,
660 Cheered, plainly, and yet serious. What a wreck
Had we about us! scattered was the floor,
And, in like sort, chair, window-seat, and shelf,
With books, maps, fossils, withered plants and flowers,
And tufts of mountain moss. Mechanic tools
Lay intermixed with scraps of paper, some
Scribbled with verse: a broken angling-rod
And shattered telescope, together linked
By cobwebs, stood within a dusty nook;
And instruments of music, some half-made,
670 Some in disgrace, hung dangling from the walls.
But speedily the promise was fulfilled;
A feast before us, and a courteous Host
Inviting us in glee to sit and eat.
A napkin, white as foam of that rough brook
By which it had been bleached, o'erspread the board;
And was itself half-covered with a store
Of dainties, – oaten bread, curd, cheese, and cream;
And cakes of butter curiously embossed,
Butter that had imbibed from meadow-flowers
680 A golden hue, delicate as their own
Faintly reflected in a lingering stream.
Nor lacked, for more delight on that warm day,
Our table, small parade of garden fruits,
And whortle-berries from the mountain side.
The Child, who long ere this had stilled his sobs,
Was now a help to his late comforter,
And moved, a willing Page, as he was bid,
Ministering to our need.

In genial mood,
While at our pastoral banquet thus we sate
690 Fronting the window of that little cell,
I could not, ever and anon, forbear
To glance an upward look on two huge Peaks,
That from some other vale peered into this.
'Those lusty twins,' exclaimed our host, 'if here
It were your lot to dwell, would soon become
Your prized companions. – Many are the notes
Which, in his tuneful course, the wind draws forth
From rocks, woods, caverns, heaths, and dashing shores;
And well those lofty brethren bear their part
700 In the wild concert – chiefly when the storm
Rides high; then all the upper air they fill
With roaring sound, that ceases not to flow,
Like smoke, along the level of the blast,
In mighty current; theirs, too, is the song
Of stream and headlong flood that seldom fails;
And, in the grim and breathless hour of noon,
Methinks that I have heard them echo back
The thunder's greeting. Nor have nature's laws
Left them ungifted with a power to yield
710 Music of finer tone; a harmony,
So do I call it, though it be the hand
Of silence, though there be no voice; – the clouds,
The mist, the shadows, light of golden suns,
Motions of moonlight, all come thither – touch,
And have an answer – thither come, and shape
A language not unwelcome to sick hearts
And idle spirits: – there the sun himself,
At the calm close of summer's longest day,
Rests his substantial orb; – between those heights
720 And on the top of either pinnacle,
More keenly than elsewhere in night's blue vault,
Sparkle the stars, as of their station proud.
Thoughts are not busier in the mind of man
Than the mute agents stirring there: – alone
Here do I sit and watch. –'

A fall of voice,
Regretted like the nightingale's last note,
Had scarcely closed this high-wrought strain of rapture
Ere with inviting smile the Wanderer said:
'Now for the tale with which you threatened us!'
730 'In truth the threat escaped me unawares:
Should the tale tire you, let this challenge stand
For my excuse. Dissevered from mankind,
As to your eyes and thoughts we must have seemed
When ye looked down upon us from the crag,
Islanders 'mid a stormy mountain sea,
We are not so; – perpetually we touch
Upon the vulgar ordinances of the world;
And he, whom this our cottage hath today
Relinquished, lived dependent for his bread
740 Upon the laws of public charity.
The Housewife, tempted by such slender gains
As might from that occasion be distilled,
Opened, as she before had done for me,
Her doors to admit this homeless Pensioner;
The portion gave of coarse but wholesome fare
Which appetite required – a blind dull nook,
Such as she had, the *kennel* of his rest!
This, in itself not ill, would yet have been
Ill borne in earlier life; but his was now
750 The still contentedness of seventy years.
Calm did he sit under the wide-spread tree
Of his old age; and yet less calm and meek,
Winningly meek or venerably calm,
Than slow and torpid; paying in this wise
A penalty, if penalty it were,
For spendthrift feats, excesses of his prime.
I loved the old Man, for I pitied him!
A task it was, I own, to hold discourse
With one so slow in gathering up his thoughts,
760 But he was a cheap pleasure to my eyes;
Mild, inoffensive, ready in *his* way,
And helpful to his utmost power: and there

Our housewife knew full well what she possessed!
He was her vassal of all labour, tilled
Her garden, from the pasture fetched her kine;
And, one among the orderly array
Of hay-makers, beneath the burning sun
Maintained his place; or heedfully pursued
His course, on errands bound, to other vales,
770 Leading sometimes an inexperienced child
Too young for any profitable task.
So moved he like a shadow that performed
Substantial service. Mark me now, and learn
For what reward! – The moon her monthly round
Hath not completed since our dame, the queen
Of this one cottage and this lonely dale,
Into my little sanctuary rushed –
Voice to a rueful treble humanized,
And features in deplorable dismay.
780 I treat the matter lightly, but, alas!
It is most serious: persevering rain
Had fallen in torrents; all the mountain-tops
Were hidden, and black vapours coursed their sides;
This had I seen, and saw; but, till she spake,
Was wholly ignorant that my ancient Friend –
Who at her bidding, early and alone,
Had clomb aloft to delve the moorland turf
For winter fuel – to his noontide meal
Returned not, and now, haply, on the heights
790 Lay at the mercy of this raging storm.
"Inhuman!" – said I, "was an old Man's life
Not worth the trouble of a thought? – alas!
This notice comes too late." With joy I saw
Her husband enter – from a distant vale.
We sallied forth together; found the tools
Which the neglected veteran had dropped,
But through all quarters looked for him in vain.
We shouted – but no answer! Darkness fell
Without remission of the blast or shower,
800 And fears for our own safety drove us home.

'I, who weep little, did, I will confess,
The moment I was seated here alone,
Honour my little cell with some few tears
Which anger and resentment could not dry.
All night the storm endured; and, soon as help
Had been collected from the neighbouring vale,
With morning we renewed our quest: the wind
Was fallen, the rain abated, but the hills
Lay shrouded in impenetrable mist;
810 And long and hopelessly we sought in vain:
Till, chancing on that lofty ridge to pass
A heap of ruin – almost without walls
And wholly without roof (the bleached remains
Of a small chapel, where, in ancient time,
The peasants of these lonely valleys used
To meet for worship on that central height) –
We there espied the object of our search,
Lying full three parts buried among tufts
Of heath-plant, under and above him strewn,
820 To baffle, as he might, the watery storm:
And there we found him breathing peaceably,
Snug as a child that hides itself in sport
'Mid a green hay-cock in a sunny field.
We spake – he made reply, but would not stir
At our entreaty; less from want of power
Than apprehension and bewildering thoughts.

'So was he lifted gently from the ground,
And with their freight homeward the shepherds moved
Through the dull mist, I following – when a step,
830 A single step, that freed me from the skirts
Of the blind vapour, opened to my view
Glory beyond all glory ever seen
By waking sense or by the dreaming soul!
The appearance, instantaneously disclosed,
Was of a mighty city – boldly say
A wilderness of building, sinking far
And self-withdrawn into a boundless depth,

Far sinking into splendour – without end!
Fabric it seemed of diamond and of gold,
840   With alabaster domes, and silver spires,
And blazing terrace upon terrace, high
Uplifted; here, serene pavilions bright,
In avenues disposed; there, towers begirt
With battlements that on their restless fronts
Bore stars – illumination of all gems!
By earthly nature had the effect been wrought
Upon the dark materials of the storm
Now pacified; on them, and on the coves
And mountain-steeps and summits, whereunto
850   The vapours had receded, taking there
Their station under a cerulean sky.
Oh, 'twas an unimaginable sight!
Clouds, mists, streams, watery rocks and emerald turf,
Clouds of all tincture, rocks and sapphire sky,
Confused, commingled, mutually inflamed,
Molten together, and composing thus,
Each lost in each, that marvellous array
Of temple, palace, citadel, and huge
Fantastic pomp of structure without name,
860   In fleecy folds voluminous, enwrapped.
Right in the midst, where interspace appeared
Of open court, an object like a throne
Under a shining canopy of state
Stood fixed; and fixed resemblances were seen
To implements of ordinary use,
But vast in size, in substance glorified;
Such as by Hebrew Prophets were beheld
In vision – forms uncouth of mightiest power
For admiration and mysterious awe.
870   This little Vale, a dwelling-place of Man,
Lay low beneath my feet; 'twas visible –
I saw not, but I felt that it was there.
That which I *saw* was the revealed abode
Of Spirits in beatitude: my heart
Swelled in my breast. – "I have been dead," I cried,

"And now I live! Oh! wherefore *do* I live?"
And with that pang I prayed to be no more! –
– But I forget our Charge, as utterly
I then forgot him: – there I stood and gazed:
880 The apparition faded not away,
And I descended.
      Having reached the house,
I found its rescued inmate safely lodged,
And in serene possession of himself,
Beside a fire whose genial warmth seemed met
By a faint shining from the heart, a gleam
Of comfort, spread over his pallid face.
Great show of joy the housewife made, and truly
Was glad to find her conscience set at ease;
And not less glad, for sake of her good name,
890 That the poor Sufferer had escaped with life.
But, though he seemed at first to have received
No harm, and uncomplaining as before
Went through his usual tasks, a silent change
Soon showed itself: he lingered three short weeks;
And from the cottage hath been borne today.

 'So ends my dolorous tale, and glad I am
That it is ended.' At these words he turned –
And, with blithe air of open fellowship,
Brought from the cupboard wine and stouter cheer,
900 Like one who would be merry. Seeing this,
My grey-haired Friend said courteously – 'Nay, nay,
You have regaled us as a hermit ought;
Now let us forth into the sun!' – Our Host
Rose, though reluctantly, and forth we went.

BOOK THIRD
DESPONDENCY

Argument

Images in the Valley. – Another Recess in it entered and described. – Wanderer's sensations. – Solitary's excited by the same
objects. – Contrast between these. – Despondency of the Solitary gently reproved. – Conversation exhibiting the Solitary's
past and present opinions and feelings, till he enters upon his
own History at length. – His domestic felicity. – Afflictions. –
Dejection. – Roused by the French Revolution. – Disappointment and disgust. – Voyage to America. – Disappointment and
disgust pursue him. – His return. – His languor and depression
of mind, from want of faith in the great truths of Religion, and
want of confidence in the virtue of Mankind.

A humming bee – a little tinkling rill –
A pair of falcons wheeling on the wing,
In clamorous agitation, round the crest
Of a tall rock, their airy citadel –
By each and all of these the pensive ear
Was greeted, in the silence that ensued,
When through the cottage-threshold we had passed,
And, deep within that lonesome valley, stood
Once more beneath the concave of a blue
10   And cloudless sky. – Anon exclaimed our Host,
Triumphantly dispersing with the taunt
The shade of discontent which on his brow
Had gathered, – 'Ye have left my cell, – but see
How Nature hems you in with friendly arms!
And by her help ye are my prisoners still.
But which way shall I lead you? – how contrive,
In spot so parsimoniously endowed,
That the brief hours, which yet remain, may reap
Some recompense of knowledge or delight?'
20   So saying, round he looked, as if perplexed;
And, to remove those doubts, my grey-haired Friend
Said – 'Shall we take this pathway for our guide? –

Upward it winds, as if, in summer heats,
Its line had first been fashioned by the flock
Seeking a place of refuge at the root
Of yon black Yew-tree, whose protruded boughs
Darken the silver bosom of the crag,
From which she draws her meagre sustenance.
There in commodious shelter may we rest.
30 Or let us trace this streamlet to its source;
Feebly it tinkles with an earthy sound,
And a few steps may bring us to the spot
Where, haply, crowned with flowerets and green herbs,
The mountain infant to the sun comes forth,
Like human life from darkness.' – A quick turn
Through a strait passage of encumbered ground,
Proved that such hope was vain: – for now we stood
Shut out from prospect of the open vale,
And saw the water, that composed this rill,
40 Descending, disembodied, and diffused
O'er the smooth surface of an ample crag,
Lofty, and steep, and naked as a tower.
All further progress here was barred; – And who,
Thought I, if master of a vacant hour,
Here would not linger, willingly detained?
Whether to such wild objects he were led
When copious rains have magnified the stream
Into a loud and white-robed waterfall,
Or introduced at this more quiet time.

50 Upon a semicirque of turf-clad ground,
The hidden nook discovered to our view
A mass of rock, resembling, as it lay
Right at the foot of that moist precipice,
A stranded ship, with keel upturned, that rests
Fearless of winds and waves. Three several stones
Stood near, of smaller size, and not unlike
To monumental pillars: and, from these
Some little space disjoined, a pair were seen,
That with united shoulders bore aloft

60 A fragment, like an altar, flat and smooth:
Barren the tablet, yet thereon appeared
A tall and shining holly, that had found
A hospitable chink, and stood upright,
As if inserted by some human hand
In mockery, to wither in the sun,
Or lay its beauty flat before a breeze,
The first that entered. But no breeze did now
Find entrance; – high or low appeared no trace
Of motion, save the water that descended,
70 Diffused adown that barrier of steep rock,
And softly creeping, like a breath of air,
Such as is sometimes seen, and hardly seen,
To brush the still breast of a crystal lake.

   'Behold a cabinet for sages built,
Which kings might envy!' – Praise to this effect
Broke from the happy old Man's reverend lip;
Who to the Solitary turned, and said,
'In sooth, with love's familiar privilege,
You have decried the wealth which is your own.
80 Among these rocks and stones, methinks, I see
More than the heedless impress that belongs
To lonely nature's casual work: they bear
A semblance strange of power intelligent,
And of design not wholly worn away.
Boldest of plants that ever faced the wind,
How gracefully that slender shrub looks forth
From its fantastic birthplace! And I own,
Some shadowy intimations haunt me here,
That in these shows a chronicle survives
90 Of purposes akin to those of Man,
But wrought with mightier arm than now prevails.
– Voiceless the stream descends into the gulf
With timid lapse; – and lo! while in this strait
I stand – the chasm of sky above my head
Is heaven's profoundest azure; no domain
For fickle, short-lived clouds to occupy,

Or to pass through; but rather an abyss
In which the everlasting stars abide;
And whose soft gloom, and boundless depth, might
    tempt
100 The curious eye to look for them by day.
   – Hail Contemplation! from the stately towers,
Reared by the industrious hand of human art
To lift thee high above the misty air
And turbulence of murmuring cities vast;
From academic groves, that have for thee
Been planted, hither come and find a lodge
To which thou mayst resort for holier peace, –
From whose calm centre thou, through height or depth,
Mayst penetrate, wherever truth shall lead;
110 Measuring through all degrees, until the scale
Of time and conscious nature disappear,
Lost in unsearchable eternity!'

   A pause ensued; and with minuter care
We scanned the various features of the scene:
And soon the Tenant of that lonely vale
With courteous voice thus spake –
                  'I should have grieved
Hereafter, not escaping self-reproach,
If from my poor retirement ye had gone
Leaving this nook unvisited: but, in sooth,
120 Your unexpected presence had so roused
My spirits, that they were bent on enterprise;
And, like an ardent hunter, I forgot,
Or, shall I say? – disdained, the game that lurks
At my own door. The shapes before our eyes
And their arrangement, doubtless must be deemed
The sport of Nature, aided by blind Chance
Rudely to mock the works of toiling Man.
And hence, this upright shaft of unhewn stone,
From Fancy, willing to set off her stores
130 By sounding titles, hath acquired the name
Of Pompey's pillar; that I gravely style

My Theban obelisk; and, there, behold
A Druid cromlech! – thus I entertain
The antiquarian humour, and am pleased
To skim along the surfaces of things,
Beguiling harmlessly the listless hours.
But if the spirit be oppressed by sense
Of instability, revolt, decay,
And change, and emptiness, these freaks of Nature
140   And her blind helper Chance, do *then* suffice
To quicken, and to aggravate – to feed
Pity and scorn, and melancholy pride,
Not less than that huge Pile (from some abyss
Of mortal power unquestionably sprung)
Whose hoary diadem of pendent rocks
Confines the shrill-voiced whirlwind, round and round
Eddying within its vast circumference,
On Sarum's naked plain – than pyramid
Of Egypt, unsubverted, undissolved –
150   Or Syria's marble ruins towering high
Above the sandy desert, in the light
Of sun or moon. – Forgive me, if I say
That an appearance which hath raised your minds
To an exalted pitch (the self-same cause
Different effect producing) is for me
Fraught rather with depression than delight,
Though shame it were, could I not look around,
By the reflection of your pleasure, pleased.
Yet happier in my judgement, even than you
160   With your bright transports fairly may be deemed,
The wandering Herbalist, – who, clear alike
From vain, and, that worse evil, vexing thoughts,
Casts, if he ever chance to enter here,
Upon these uncouth Forms a slight regard
Of transitory interest, and peeps round
For some rare floweret of the hills, or plant
Of craggy fountain; what he hopes for wins,
Or learns, at least, that 'tis not to be won:
Then, keen and eager, as a fine-nosed hound

170 By soul-engrossing instinct driven along
    Through wood or open field, the harmless Man
    Departs, intent upon his onward quest! –
    Nor is that Fellow-wanderer, so deem I,
    Less to be envied, (you may trace him oft
    By scars which his activity has left
    Beside our roads and pathways, though, thank Heaven!
    This covert nook reports not of his hand)
    He who with pocket-hammer smites the edge
    Of luckless rock or prominent stone, disguised
180 In weather-stains or crusted o'er by Nature
    With her first growths, detaching by the stroke
    A chip or splinter – to resolve his doubts;
    And, with that ready answer satisfied,
    The substance classes by some barbarous name,
    And hurries on; or from the fragments picks
    His specimen, if but haply interveined
    With sparkling mineral, or should crystal cube
    Lurk in its cells – and thinks himself enriched,
    Wealthier, and doubtless wiser, than before!
190 Intrusted safely each to his pursuit,
    Earnest alike, let both from hill to hill
    Range; if it please them, speed from clime to clime;
    The mind is full – and free from pain their pastime.'

    'Then,' said I, interposing, 'One is near,
    Who cannot but possess in your esteem
    Place worthier still of envy. May I name,
    Without offence, that fair-faced cottage-boy?
    Dame Nature's pupil of the lowest form,
    Youngest apprentice in the school of art!
200 Him, as we entered from the open glen,
    You might have noticed, busily engaged,
    Heart, soul, and hands, – in mending the defects
    Left in the fabric of a leaky dam
    Raised for enabling this penurious stream
    To turn a slender mill (that new-made plaything)
    For his delight – the happiest he of all!'

'Far happiest,' answered the desponding Man,
'If, such as now he is, he might remain!
Ah! what avails imagination high
210 Or question deep? what profits all that earth,
Or heaven's blue vault, is suffered to put forth
Of impulse or allurement, for the Soul
To quit the beaten track of life, and soar
Far as she finds a yielding element
In past or future; far as she can go
Through time or space – if neither in the one,
Nor in the other region, nor in aught
That Fancy, dreaming o'er the map of things,
Hath placed beyond these penetrable bounds,
220 Words of assurance can be heard; if nowhere
A habitation, for consummate good,
Or for progressive virtue, by the search
Can be attained, – a better sanctuary
From doubt and sorrow, than the senseless grave?'

'Is this,' the grey-haired Wanderer mildly said,
'The voice, which we so lately overheard,
To that same child, addressing tenderly
The consolations of a hopeful mind?
"*His body is at rest, his soul in heaven.*"
230 These were your words; and, verily, methinks
Wisdom is ofttimes nearer when we stoop
Than when we soar.' –
                        The Other, not displeased,
Promptly replied – 'My notion is the same.
And I, without reluctance, could decline
All act of inquisition whence we rise,
And what, when breath hath ceased, we may become.
Here are we, in a bright and breathing world.
Our origin, what matters it? In lack
Of worthier explanation, say at once
240 With the American (a thought which suits
The place where now we stand) that certain men
Leapt out together from a rocky cave;

And these were the first parents of mankind:
Or, if a different image be recalled
By the warm sunshine, and the jocund voice
Of insects chirping out their careless lives
On these soft beds of thyme-besprinkled turf,
Choose, with the gay Athenian, a conceit
As sound – blithe race! whose mantles were bedecked
250 With golden grasshoppers, in sign that they
Had sprung, like those bright creatures, from the soil
Whereon their endless generations dwelt.
But stop! – these theoretic fancies jar
On serious minds: then, as the Hindoos draw
Their holy Ganges from a skiey fount,
Even so deduce the stream of human life
From seats of power divine; and hope, or trust,
That our existence winds her stately course
Beneath the sun, like Ganges, to make part
260 Of a living ocean; or, to sink engulfed,
Like Niger, in impenetrable sands
And utter darkness: thought which may be faced,
Though comfortless! –
              Not of myself I speak;
Such acquiescence neither doth imply,
In me, a meekly-bending spirit soothed
By natural piety; nor a lofty mind,
By philosophic discipline prepared
For calm subjection to acknowledged law;
Pleased to have been, contented not to be.
270 Such palms I boast not; – no! to me, who find,
Reviewing my past way, much to condemn,
Little to praise, and nothing to regret,
(Save some remembrances of dream-like joys
That scarcely seem to have belonged to me)
If I must take my choice between the pair
That rule alternately the weary hours,
Night is than day more acceptable; sleep
Doth, in my estimate of good, appear
A better state than waking; death than sleep:

280 Feelingly sweet is stillness after storm,
     Though under covert of the wormy ground!

         'Yet be it said, in justice to myself,
     That in more genial times, when I was free
     To explore the destiny of human kind
     (Not as an intellectual game pursued
     With curious subtlety, from wish to cheat
     Irksome sensations; but by love of truth
     Urged on, or haply by intense delight
     In feeding thought, wherever thought could feed)
290 I did not rank with those (too dull or nice,
     For to my judgement such they then appeared,
     Or too aspiring, thankless at the best)
     Who, in this frame of human life, perceive
     An object whereunto their souls are tied
     In discontented wedlock; nor did e'er,
     From me, those dark impervious shades, that hang
     Upon the region whither we are bound,
     Exclude a power to enjoy the vital beams
     Of present sunshine. – Deities that float
300 On wings, angelic Spirits! I could muse
     O'er what from eldest time we have been told
     Of your bright forms and glorious faculties,
     And with the imagination rest content,
     Not wishing more; repining not to tread
     The little sinuous path of earthly care,
     By flowers embellished, and by springs refreshed.
     – "Blow winds of autumn! – let your chilling breath
     Take the live herbage from the mead, and strip
     The shady forest of its green attire, –
310 And let the bursting clouds to fury rouse
     The gentle brooks! – Your desolating sway,
     Sheds," I exclaimed, "no sadness upon me,
     And no disorder in your rage I find.
     What dignity, what beauty, in this change
     From mild to angry, and from sad to gay,
     Alternate and revolving! How benign,

How rich in animation and delight,
How bountiful these elements – compared
With aught, as more desirable and fair,
320 Devised by fancy for the golden age;
Or the perpetual warbling that prevails
In Arcady, beneath unaltered skies,
Through the long year in constant quiet bound,
Night hushed as night, and day serene as day!"
– But why this tedious record? – Age, we know,
Is garrulous; and solitude is apt
To anticipate the privilege of Age.
From far ye come; and surely with a hope
Of better entertainment: – let us hence!'

330   Loth to forsake the spot, and still more loth
To be diverted from our present theme,
I said, 'My thoughts, agreeing, Sir, with yours,
Would push this censure farther; – for, if smiles
Of scornful pity be the just reward
Of Poesy thus courteously employed
In framing models to improve the scheme
Of Man's existence, and recast the world,
Why should not grave Philosophy be styled,
Herself, a dreamer of a kindred stock,
340 A dreamer yet more spiritless and dull?
Yes, shall the fine immunities she boasts
Establish sounder titles of esteem
For her, who (all too timid and reserved
For onset, for resistance too inert,
Too weak for suffering, and for hope too tame)
Placed, among flowery gardens curtained round
With world-excluding groves, the brotherhood
Of soft Epicureans, taught – if they
The ends of being would secure, and win
350 The crown of wisdom – to yield up their souls
To a voluptuous unconcern, preferring
Tranquillity to all things. Or is she,'
I cried, 'more worthy of regard, the Power,

Who, for the sake of sterner quiet, closed
The Stoic's heart against the vain approach
Of admiration, and all sense of joy?'

His countenance gave notice that my zeal
Accorded little with his present mind;
I ceased, and he resumed. – 'Ah! gentle Sir,
360   Slight, if you will, the *means*; but spare to slight
The *end* of those, who did, by system, rank,
As the prime object of a wise man's aim,
Security from shock of accident,
Release from fear; and cherished peaceful days
For their own sakes, as mortal life's chief good,
And only reasonable felicity.
What motive drew, what impulse, I would ask,
Through a long course of later ages, drove,
The hermit to his cell in forest wide;
370   Or what detained him, till his closing eyes
Took their last farewell of the sun and stars,
Fast anchored in the desert? – Not alone
Dread of the persecuting sword, remorse,
Wrongs unredressed, or insults unavenged
And unavengeable, defeated pride,
Prosperity subverted, maddening want,
Friendship betrayed, affection unreturned,
Love with despair, or grief in agony; –
Not always from intolerable pangs
380   He fled; but, compassed round by pleasure, sighed
For independent happiness; craving peace,
The central feeling of all happiness,
Not as a refuge from distress or pain,
A breathing-time, vacation, or a truce,
But for its absolute self; a life of peace,
Stability without regret or fear;
That hath been, is, and shall be evermore! –
Such the reward he sought; and wore out life,
There, where on few external things his heart
390   Was set, and those his own; or, if not his,

Subsisting under nature's stedfast law.

    'What other yearning was the master tie
Of the monastic brotherhood, upon rock
Aërial, or in green secluded vale,
One after one, collected from afar,
An undissolving fellowship? – What but this,
The universal instinct of repose,
The longing for confirmed tranquillity,
Inward and outward; humble, yet sublime:
400   The life where hope and memory are as one;
Where earth is quiet and her face unchanged
Save by the simplest toil of human hands
Or seasons' difference; the immortal Soul
Consistent in self-rule; and heaven revealed
To meditation in that quietness! –
Such was their scheme: and though the wished-for end
By multitudes was missed, perhaps attained
By none, they for the attempt, and pains employed,
Do, in my present censure, stand redeemed
410   From the unqualified disdain, that once
Would have been cast upon them by my voice
Delivering her decisions from the seat
Of forward youth – that scruples not to solve
Doubts, and determine questions, by the rules
Of inexperienced judgement, ever prone
To overweening faith; and is inflamed,
By courage, to demand from real life
The test of act and suffering, to provoke
Hostility – how dreadful when it comes,
420   Whether affliction be the foe, or guilt!

    'A child of earth, I rested, in that stage
Of my past course to which these thoughts advert,
Upon earth's native energies; forgetting
That mine was a condition which required
Nor energy, nor fortitude – a calm
Without vicissitude; which, if the like

Had been presented to my view elsewhere,
I might have even been tempted to despise.
But no – for the serene was also bright;
430 Enlivened happiness with joy o'erflowing,
With joy, and – oh! that memory should survive
To speak the word – with rapture! Nature's boon,
Life's genuine inspiration, happiness
Above what rules can teach, or fancy feign;
Abused, as all possessions *are* abused
That are not prized according to their worth.
And yet, what worth? what good is given to men,
More solid than the gilded clouds of heaven?
What joy more lasting than a vernal flower? –
440 None! 'tis the general plaint of human kind
In solitude: and mutually addressed
From each to all, for wisdom's sake: – This truth
The priest announces from his holy seat:
And, crowned with garlands in the summer grove,
The poet fits it to his pensive lyre.
Yet, ere that final resting-place be gained,
Sharp contradictions may arise, by doom
Of this same life, compelling us to grieve
That the prosperities of love and joy
450 Should be permitted, oft-times, to endure
So long, and be at once cast down for ever.
Oh! tremble, ye, to whom hath been assigned
A course of days composing happy months,
And they as happy years; the present still
So like the past, and both so firm a pledge
Of a congenial future, that the wheels
Of pleasure move without the aid of hope:
For Mutability is Nature's bane;
And slighted Hope *will* be avenged; and, when
460 Ye need her favours, ye shall find her not;
But in her stead – fear – doubt – and agony!'

This was the bitter language of the heart:
But, while he spake, look, gesture, tone of voice,

Though discomposed and vehement, were such
As skill and graceful nature might suggest
To a proficient of the tragic scene
Standing before the multitude, beset
With dark events. Desirous to divert
Or stem the current of the speaker's thoughts,
470 We signified a wish to leave that place
Of stillness and close privacy, a nook
That seemed for self-examination made;
Or, for confession, in the sinner's need,
Hidden from all men's view. To our attempt
He yielded not; but, pointing to a slope
Of mossy turf defended from the sun,
And on that couch inviting us to rest,
Full on that tender-hearted Man he turned
A serious eye, and his speech thus renewed.

480   'You never saw, your eyes did never look
On the bright form of Her whom once I loved: –
Her silver voice was heard upon the earth,
A sound unknown to you; else, honoured Friend!
Your heart had borne a pitiable share
Of what I suffered, when I wept that loss,
And suffer now, not seldom, from the thought
That I remember, and can weep no more. –
Stripped as I am of all the golden fruit
Of self-esteem; and by the cutting blasts
490 Of self-reproach familiarly assailed;
Yet would I not be of such wintry bareness
But that some leaf of your regard should hang
Upon my naked branches: – lively thoughts
Give birth, full often, to unguarded words;
I grieve that, in your presence, from my tongue
Too much of frailty hath already dropped;
But that too much demands still more.
                                        You know,
Revered Compatriot – and to you, kind Sir,
(Not to be deemed a stranger, as you come

500 Following the guidance of these welcome feet
To our secluded vale) it may be told –
That my demerits did not sue in vain
To One on whose mild radiance many gazed
With hope, and all with pleasure. This fair Bride –
In the devotedness of youthful love,
Preferring me to parents, and the choir
Of gay companions, to the natal roof,
And all known places and familiar sights
(Resigned with sadness gently weighing down
510 Her trembling expectations, but no more
Than did to her due honour, and to me
Yielded, that day, a confidence sublime
In what I had to build upon) – this Bride,
Young, modest, meek, and beautiful, I led
To a low cottage in a sunny bay,
Where the salt sea innocuously breaks,
And the sea breeze as innocently breathes,
On Devon's leafy shores; – a sheltered hold,
In a soft clime encouraging the soil
520 To a luxuriant bounty! – As our steps
Approach the embowered abode – our chosen seat –
See, rooted in the earth, her kindly bed,
The unendangered myrtle, decked with flowers,
Before the threshold stands to welcome us!
While, in the flowering myrtle's neighbourhood,
Not overlooked but courting no regard,
Those native plants, the holly and the yew,
Gave modest intimation to the mind
How willingly their aid they would unite
530 With the green myrtle, to endear the hours
Of winter, and protect that pleasant place.
– Wild were the walks upon those lonely Downs,
Track leading into track; how marked, how worn
Into bright verdure, between fern and gorse,
Winding away its never-ending line
On their smooth surface, evidence was none:
But, there, lay open to our daily haunt,

A range of unappropriated earth,
Where youth's ambitious feet might move at large;
540   Whence, unmolested wanderers, we beheld
The shining giver of the day diffuse
His brightness o'er a tract of sea and land
Gay as our spirits, free as our desires;
As our enjoyments, boundless. – From those heights
We dropped, at pleasure, into sylvan combs;
Where arbours of impenetrable shade,
And mossy seats, detained us side by side,
With hearts at ease, and knowledge in our hearts
"That all the grove and all the day was ours."

550   'O happy time! still happier was at hand;
For Nature called my Partner to resign
Her share in the pure freedom of that life,
Enjoyed by us in common. – To my hope,
To my heart's wish, my tender Mate became
The thankful captive of maternal bonds;
And those wild paths were left to me alone.
There could I meditate on follies past;
And, like a weary voyager escaped
From risk and hardship, inwardly retrace
560   A course of vain delights and thoughtless guilt,
And self-indulgence – without shame pursued.
There, undisturbed, could think of and could thank
Her whose submissive spirit was to me
Rule and restraint – my guardian – shall I say
That earthly Providence, whose guiding love
Within a port of rest had lodged me safe;
Safe from temptation, and from danger far?
Strains followed of acknowledgement addressed
To an Authority enthroned above
570   The reach of sight; from whom, as from their source,
Proceed all visible ministers of good
That walk the earth – Father of heaven and earth,
Father, and king, and judge, adored and feared!
These acts of mind, and memory, and heart,

And spirit – interrupted and relieved
By observations transient as the glance
Of flying sunbeams, or to the outward form
Cleaving with power inherent and intense,
As the mute insect fixed upon the plant
580 On whose soft leaves it hangs, and from whose cup
It draws its nourishment imperceptibly –
Endeared my wanderings; and the mother's kiss
And infant's smile awaited my return.

    'In privacy we dwelt, a wedded pair,
Companions daily, often all day long;
Not placed by fortune within easy reach
Of various intercourse, nor wishing aught
Beyond the allowance of our own fireside,
The twain within our happy cottage born,
590 Inmates, and heirs of our united love;
Graced mutually by difference of sex,
And with no wider interval of time
Between their several births than served for one
To establish something of a leader's sway;
Yet left them joined by sympathy in age;
Equals in pleasure, fellows in pursuit.
On these two pillars rested as in air
Our solitude.
                    It soothes me to perceive,
Your courtesy withholds not from my words
600 Attentive audience. But, oh! gentle Friends,
As times of quiet and unbroken peace,
Though, for a nation, times of blessedness,
Give back faint echoes from the historian's page;
So, in the imperfect sounds of this discourse,
Depressed I hear, how faithless is the voice
Which those most blissful days reverberate.
What special record can, or need, be given
To rules and habits, whereby much was done,
But all within the sphere of little things;
610 Of humble, though, to us, important cares,

And precious interests? Smoothly did our life
Advance, swerving not from the path prescribed;
Her annual, her diurnal, round alike
Maintained with faithful care. And you divine
The worst effects that our condition saw
If you imagine changes slowly wrought,
And in their progress unperceivable;
Not wished for; sometimes noticed with a sigh,
(Whate'er of good or lovely they might bring)
620 Sighs of regret, for the familiar good
And loveliness endeared which they removed.

  'Seven years of occupation undisturbed
Established seemingly a right to hold
That happiness; and use and habit gave
To what an alien spirit had acquired
A patrimonial sanctity. And thus,
With thoughts and wishes bounded to this world,
I lived and breathed; most grateful – if to enjoy
Without repining or desire for more,
630 For different lot, or change to higher sphere,
(Only except some impulses of pride
With no determined object, though upheld
By theories with suitable support) –
Most grateful, if in such wise to enjoy
Be proof of gratitude for what we have;
Else, I allow, most thankless. – But, at once,
From some dark seat of fatal power was urged
A claim that shattered all. – Our blooming girl,
Caught in the gripe of death, with such brief time
640 To struggle in as scarcely would allow
Her cheek to change its colour, was conveyed
From us to inaccessible worlds, to regions
Where height, or depth, admits not the approach
Of living man, though longing to pursue.
– With even as brief a warning – and how soon,
With what short interval of time between,
I tremble yet to think of – our last prop,

Our happy life's only remaining stay –
The brother followed; and was seen no more!

650   'Calm as a frozen lake when ruthless winds
Blow fiercely, agitating earth and sky,
The Mother now remained; as if in her,
Who, to the lowest region of the soul,
Had been erewhile unsettled and disturbed,
This second visitation had no power
To shake; but only to bind up and seal;
And to establish thankfulness of heart
In Heaven's determinations, ever just.
The eminence whereon her spirit stood,
660 Mine was unable to attain. Immense
The space that severed us! But, as the sight
Communicates with heaven's ethereal orbs
Incalculably distant; so, I felt
That consolation may descend from far
(And that is intercourse, and union, too,)
While, overcome with speechless gratitude,
And, with a holier love inspired, I looked
On her – at once superior to my woes
And partner of my loss. – O heavy change!
670 Dimness o'er this clear luminary crept
Insensibly; – the immortal and divine
Yielded to mortal reflux; her pure glory,
As from the pinnacle of worldly state
Wretched ambition drops astounded, fell
Into a gulf obscure of silent grief,
And keen heart-anguish – of itself ashamed,
Yet obstinately cherishing itself:
And, so consumed, she melted from my arms;
And left me, on this earth, disconsolate!

680   'What followed cannot be reviewed in thought;
Much less, retraced in words. If she, of life
Blameless, so intimate with love and joy
And all the tender motions of the soul,

Had been supplanted, could I hope to stand –
Infirm, dependent, and now destitute?
I called on dreams and visions, to disclose
That which is veiled from waking thought; conjured
Eternity, as men constrain a ghost
To appear and answer; to the grave I spake
690 Imploringly; – looked up, and asked the Heavens
If Angels traversed their cerulean floors,
If fixed or wandering star could tidings yield
Of the departed spirit – what abode
It occupies – what consciousness retains
Of former loves and interests. Then my soul
Turned inward, – to examine of what stuff
Time's fetters are composed; and life was put
To inquisition, long and profitless!
By pain of heart – now checked – and now impelled –
700 The intellectual power, through words and things,
Went sounding on, a dim and perilous way!
And from those transports, and these toils abstruse,
Some trace am I enabled to retain
Of time, else lost; – existing unto me
Only by records in myself not found.

'From that abstraction I was roused, – and how?
Even as a thoughtful shepherd by a flash
Of lightning startled in a gloomy cave
Of these wild hills. For, lo! the dread Bastille,
710 With all the chambers in its horrid towers,
Fell to the ground: – by violence overthrown
Of indignation; and with shouts that drowned
The crash it made in falling! From the wreck
A golden palace rose, or seemed to rise,
The appointed seat of equitable law
And mild paternal sway. The potent shock
I felt: the transformation I perceived,
As marvellously seized as in that moment
When, from the blind mist issuing, I beheld
720 Glory – beyond all glory ever seen,

Confusion infinite of heaven and earth,
Dazzling the soul. Meanwhile, prophetic harps
In every grove were ringing, "War shall cease;
Did ye not hear that conquest is abjured?
Bring garlands, bring forth choicest flowers, to deck
The tree of Liberty." – My heart rebounded;
My melancholy voice the chorus joined;
– "Be joyful all ye nations; in all lands,
Ye that are capable of joy be glad!
730   Henceforth, whate'er is wanting to yourselves
In others ye shall promptly find; – and all,
Enriched by mutual and reflected wealth,
Shall with one heart honour their common kind."

'Thus was I reconverted to the world;
Society became my glittering bride,
And airy hopes my children. – From the depths
Of natural passion, seemingly escaped,
My soul diffused herself in wide embrace
Of institutions, and the forms of things;
740   As they exist, in mutable array,
Upon life's surface. What, though in my veins
There flowed no Gallic blood, nor had I breathed
The air of France, not less than Gallic zeal
Kindled and burned among the sapless twigs
Of my exhausted heart. If busy men
In sober conclave met, to weave a web
Of amity, whose living threads should stretch
Beyond the seas, and to the farthest pole,
There did I sit, assisting. If, with noise
750   And acclamation, crowds in open air
Expressed the tumult of their minds, my voice
There mingled, heard or not. The powers of song
I left not uninvoked; and, in still groves,
Where mild enthusiasts tuned a pensive lay
Of thanks and expectations, in accord
With their belief, I sang Saturnian rule
Returned, – a progeny of golden years

Permitted to descend, and bless mankind.
– With promises the Hebrew Scriptures teem:
760 I felt their invitation; and resumed
A long-suspended office in the House
Of public worship, where, the glowing phrase
Of ancient inspiration serving me,
I promised also, – with undaunted trust
Foretold, and added prayer to prophecy;
The admiration winning of the crowd;
The help desiring of the pure devout.

'Scorn and contempt forbid me to proceed!
But History, time's slavish scribe, will tell
770 How rapidly the zealots of the cause
Disbanded – or in hostile ranks appeared;
Some, tired of honest service; these, outdone,
Disgusted therefore, or appalled, by aims
Of fiercer zealots – so confusion reigned,
And the more faithful were compelled to exclaim,
As Brutus did to Virtue, "Liberty,
I worshipped thee, and find thee but a Shade!"

'Such recantation had for me no charm,
Nor would I bend to it; who should have grieved
780 At aught, however fair, that bore the mien
Of a conclusion, or catastrophe.
Why then conceal, that, when the simply good
In timid selfishness withdrew, I sought
Other support, not scrupulous whence it came;
And, by what compromise it stood, not nice?
Enough if notions seemed to be high-pitched,
And qualities determined. – Among men
So charactered did I maintain a strife
Hopeless, and still more hopeless every hour;
790 But, in the process, I began to feel
That, if the emancipation of the world
Were missed, I should at least secure my own,
And be in part compensated. For rights,

Widely – inveterately usurped upon,
I spake with vehemence; and promptly seized
All that Abstraction furnished for my needs
Or purposes; nor scrupled to proclaim,
And propagate, by liberty of life,
Those new persuasions. Not that I rejoiced,
800 Or even found pleasure, in such vagrant course,
For its own sake; but farthest from the walk
Which I had trod in happiness and peace,
Was most inviting to a troubled mind;
That, in a struggling and distempered world,
Saw a seductive image of herself.
Yet, mark the contradictions of which Man
Is still the sport! Here Nature was my guide,
The Nature of the dissolute; but thee,
O fostering Nature! I rejected – smiled
810 At others' tears in pity; and in scorn
At those, which thy soft influence sometimes drew
From my unguarded heart. – The tranquil shores
Of Britain circumscribed me; else, perhaps
I might have been entangled among deeds,
Which, now, as infamous, I should abhor –
Despise, as senseless: for my spirit relished
Strangely the exasperation of that Land,
Which turned an angry beak against the down
Of her own breast; confounded into hope
820 Of disencumbering thus her fretful wings.

    'But all was quieted by iron bonds
Of military sway. The shifting aims,
The moral interests, the creative might,
The varied functions and high attributes
Of civil action, yielded to a power
Formal, and odious, and contemptible.
– In Britain, ruled a panic dread of change;
The weak were praised, rewarded, and advanced;
And, from the impulse of a just disdain,
830 Once more did I retire into myself.

There feeling no contentment, I resolved
To fly, for safeguard, to some foreign shore,
Remote from Europe; from her blasted hopes;
Her fields of carnage, and polluted air.

   'Fresh blew the wind, when o'er the Atlantic Main
The ship went gliding with her thoughtless crew;
And who among them but an Exile, freed
From discontent, indifferent, pleased to sit
Among the busily-employed, not more
840 With obligation charged, with service taxed,
Than the loose pendant – to the idle wind
Upon the tall mast streaming. But, ye Powers
Of soul and sense mysteriously allied,
O, never let the Wretched, if a choice
Be left him, trust the freight of his distress
To a long voyage on the silent deep!
For, like a plague, will memory break out;
And, in the blank and solitude of things,
Upon his spirit, with a fever's strength,
850 Will conscience prey. – Feebly must they have felt
Who, in old time, attired with snakes and whips
The vengeful Furies. *Beautiful* regards
Were turned on me – the face of her I loved;
The Wife and Mother pitifully fixing
Tender reproaches, insupportable!
Where now that boasted liberty? No welcome
From unknown objects I received; and those,
Known and familiar, which the vaulted sky
Did, in the placid clearness of the night,
860 Disclose, had accusations to prefer
Against my peace. Within the cabin stood
That volume – as a compass for the soul –
Revered among the nations. I implored
Its guidance; but the infallible support
Of faith was wanting. Tell me, why refused
To One by storms annoyed and adverse winds;
Perplexed with currents; of his weakness sick;

Of vain endeavours tired; and by his own,
And by his nature's, ignorance, dismayed!

870   'Long wished-for sight, the Western World appeared;
And, when the ship was moored, I leaped ashore
Indignantly – resolved to be a man,
Who, having o'er the past no power, would live
No longer in subjection to the past,
With abject mind – from a tyrannic lord
Inviting penance, fruitlessly endured:
So, like a fugitive, whose feet have cleared
Some boundary, which his followers may not cross
In prosecution of their deadly chase,
880   Respiring I looked round. – How bright the sun,
The breeze how soft! Can anything produced
In the old World compare, thought I, for power
And majesty with this gigantic stream,
Sprung from the desert? And behold a city
Fresh, youthful, and aspiring! What are these
To me, or I to them? As much at least
As he desires that they should be, whom winds
And waves have wafted to this distant shore,
In the condition of a damaged seed,
890   Whose fibres cannot, if they would, take root.
Here may I roam at large; – my business is,
Roaming at large, to observe, and not to feel
And, therefore, not to act – convinced that all
Which bears the name of action, howsoe'er
Beginning, ends in servitude – still painful,
And mostly profitless. And, sooth to say,
On nearer view, a motley spectacle
Appeared, of high pretensions – unreproved
But by the obstreperous voice of higher still;
900   Big passions strutting on a petty stage;
Which a detached spectator may regard
Not unamused. – But ridicule demands
Quick change of objects; and, to laugh alone,
At a composing distance from the haunts

Of strife and folly, though it be a treat
As choice as musing Leisure can bestow;
Yet, in the very centre of the crowd,
To keep the secret of a poignant scorn,
Howe'er to airy Demons suitable,
910 Of all unsocial courses, is least fit
For the gross spirit of mankind, – the one
That soonest fails to please, and quickliest turns
Into vexation.
         Let us, then, I said,
Leave this unknit Republic to the scourge
Of her own passions; and to regions haste,
Whose shades have never felt the encroaching axe,
Or soil endured a transfer in the mart
Of dire rapacity. There, Man abides,
Primeval Nature's child. A creature weak
920 In combination, (wherefore else driven back
So far, and of his old inheritance
So easily deprived?) but, for that cause,
More dignified, and stronger in himself;
Whether to act, judge, suffer, or enjoy.
True, the intelligence of social art
Hath overpowered his forefathers, and soon
Will sweep the remnant of his line away;
But contemplations, worthier, nobler far
Than her destructive energies, attend
930 His independence, when along the side
Of Mississippi, or that northern stream
That spreads into successive seas, he walks;
Pleased to perceive his own unshackled life,
And his innate capacities of soul,
There imaged: or when, having gained the top
Of some commanding eminence, which yet
Intruder ne'er beheld, he thence surveys
Regions of wood and wide savannah, vast
Expanse of unappropriated earth,
940 With mind that sheds a light on what he sees;
Free as the sun, and lonely as the sun,

Pouring above his head its radiance down
Upon a living and rejoicing world!

'So, westward, toward the unviolated woods
I bent my way; and, roaming far and wide,
Failed not to greet the merry Mocking-bird;
And, while the melancholy Muccawiss
(The sportive bird's companion in the grove)
Repeated, o'er and o'er, his plaintive cry,
950 I sympathized at leisure with the sound;
But that pure archetype of human greatness,
I found him not. There, in his stead, appeared
A creature, squalid, vengeful, and impure;
Remorseless, and submissive to no law
But superstitious fear, and abject sloth.

'Enough is told! Here am I – ye have heard
What evidence I seek, and vainly seek;
What from my fellow-beings I require,
And either they have not to give, or I
960 Lack virtue to receive; what I myself,
Too oft by wilful forfeiture, have lost
Nor can regain. How languidly I look
Upon this visible fabric of the world,
May be divined – perhaps it hath been said: –
But spare your pity, if there be in me
Aught that deserves respect: for I exist,
Within myself, not comfortless. – The tenour
Which my life holds, he readily may conceive
Whoe'er hath stood to watch a mountain brook
970 In some still passage of its course, and seen,
Within the depths of its capacious breast,
Inverted trees, rocks, clouds, and azure sky;
And, on its glassy surface, specks of foam,
And conglobated bubbles undissolved,
Numerous as stars; that, by their onward lapse,
Betray to sight the motion of the stream,
Else imperceptible. Meanwhile, is heard

A softened roar, or murmur; and the sound
Though soothing, and the little floating isles
980 Though beautiful, are both by Nature charged
With the same pensive office; and make known
Through what perplexing labyrinths, abrupt
Precipitations, and untoward straits,
The earth-born wanderer hath passed; and quickly,
That respite o'er, like traverses and toils
Must he again encounter. – Such a stream
Is human Life; and so the Spirit fares
In the best quiet to her course allowed;
And such is mine, – save only for a hope
990 That my particular current soon will reach
The unfathomable gulf, where all is still!'

BOOK FOURTH
DESPONDENCY CORRECTED

Argument

State of feeling produced by the foregoing Narrative. – A belief
in a superintending Providence the only adequate support
under affliction. – Wanderer's ejaculation. – Acknowledges the
difficulty of a lively faith. – Hence immoderate sorrow. – Exhortations. – How received. – Wanderer applies his discourse
to that other cause of dejection in the Solitary's mind. – Disappointment from the French Revolution. – States grounds of
hope, and insists on the necessity of patience and fortitude with
respect to the course of great revolutions. – Knowledge the
source of tranquillity. – Rural Solitude favourable to knowledge
of the inferior Creatures; Study of their habits and ways recommended; exhortation to bodily exertion and communion with
Nature. – Morbid Solitude pitiable. – Superstition better than
apathy. – Apathy and destitution unknown in the infancy of
society. – The various modes of Religion prevented it. – Illustrated in the Jewish, Persian, Babylonian, Chaldean, and Grecian
modes of belief. – Solitary interposes. –Wanderer points out the
influence of religious and imaginative feeling in the humble
ranks of society, illustrated from present and past times. – These
principles tend to recall exploded superstitions and Popery. –

Wanderer rebuts this charge, and contrasts the dignities of the
Imagination with the presumptous littleness of certain modern
Philosophers. – Recommends other lights and guides. – Asserts
the power of the Soul to regenerate herself; Solitary asks how. –
Reply. – Personal appeal. – Exhortation to activity of body renewed. – How to commune with Nature. – Wanderer concludes
with a legitimate union of the imagination, affections, understanding, and reason. – Effect of his discourse. – Evening;
Return to the Cottage.

Here closed the Tenant of that lonely vale
His mournful narrative – commenced in pain,
In pain commenced, and ended without peace:
Yet tempered, not unfrequently, with strains
Of native feeling, grateful to our minds;
And yielding surely some relief to his,
While we sate listening with compassion due.
A pause of silence followed; then, with voice
That did not falter though the heart was moved,
The Wanderer said: –

10   'One adequate support
For the calamities of mortal life
Exists – one only; an assured belief
That the procession of our fate, howe'er
Sad or disturbed, is ordered by a Being
Of infinite benevolence and power;
Whose everlasting purposes embrace
All accidents, converting them to good.
– The darts of anguish *fix* not where the seat
Of suffering hath been thoroughly fortified
20 By acquiescence in the Will supreme
For time and for eternity; by faith,
Faith absolute in God, including hope,
And the defence that lies in boundless love
Of his perfections; with habitual dread
Of aught unworthily conceived, endured
Impatiently, ill-done, or left undone,
To the dishonour of His holy name.
Soul of our Souls, and safeguard of the world!

Sustain, Thou only canst, the sick of heart;
30 Restore their languid spirits, and recall
Their lost affections unto Thee and Thine!'

Then, as we issued from that covert nook,
He thus continued, lifting up his eyes
To heaven: – 'How beautiful this dome of sky;
And the vast hills, in fluctuation fixed
At Thy command, how awful! Shall the Soul,
Human and rational, report of Thee
Even less than these? – Be mute who will, who can,
Yet I will praise thee with impassioned voice:
40 My lips, that may forget thee in the crowd,
Cannot forget thee here; where Thou hast built,
For Thy own glory, in the wilderness!
Me didst Thou constitute a priest of Thine,
In such a temple as we now behold
Reared for Thy presence: therefore, am I bound
To worship, here, and everywhere – as one
Not doomed to ignorance, though forced to tread,
From childhood up, the ways of poverty;
From unreflecting ignorance preserved,
50 And from debasement rescued. – By Thy grace
The particle divine remained unquenched;
And, 'mid the wild weeds of a rugged soil,
Thy bounty caused to flourish deathless flowers,
From paradise transplanted: wintry age
Impends; the frost will gather round my heart;
If the flowers wither, I am worse than dead!
– Come, labour, when the worn-out frame requires
Perpetual sabbath; come, disease and want;
And sad exclusion through decay of sense;
60 But leave me unabated trust in Thee –
And let Thy favour, to the end of life,
Inspire me with ability to seek
Repose and hope among eternal things –
Father of heaven and earth! and I am rich,
And will possess my portion in content!

'And what are things eternal? – powers depart,'
The grey-haired Wanderer stedfastly replied,
Answering the question which himself had asked,
'Possessions vanish, and opinions change,
70 And passions hold a fluctuating seat:
But, by the storms of circumstance unshaken,
And subject neither to eclipse nor wane,
Duty exists; – immutably survive,
For our support, the measures and the forms,
Which an abstract intelligence supplies;
Whose kingdom is, where time and space are not.
Of other converse which mind, soul, and heart,
Do, with united urgency, require,
What more that may not perish? – Thou, dread source,
80 Prime, self-existing cause and end of all
That in the scale of being fill their place;
Above our human region, or below,
Set and sustained; – Thou, who didst wrap the cloud
Of infancy around us, that Thyself,
Therein, with our simplicity awhile
Mightst hold, on earth, communion undisturbed;
Who from the anarchy of dreaming sleep,
Or from its death-like void, with punctual care,
And touch as gentle as the morning light,
90 Restor'st us, daily, to the powers of sense
And reason's stedfast rule – Thou, Thou alone
Art everlasting, and the blessed Spirits,
Which Thou includest, as the sea her waves:
For adoration Thou endur'st; endure
For consciousness the motions of Thy will;
For apprehension those transcendent truths
Of the pure intellect, that stand as laws
(Submission constituting strength and power)
Even to Thy Being's infinite majesty!
100 This universe shall pass away – a work
Glorious! because the shadow of Thy might,
A step, or link, for intercourse with Thee.
Ah! if the time must come, in which my feet

No more shall stray where meditation leads,
By flowing stream, through wood, or craggy wild,
Loved haunts like these; the unimprisoned Mind
May yet have scope to range among her own,
Her thoughts, her images, her high desires.
If the dear faculty of sight should fail,
110 Still, it may be allowed me to remember
What visionary powers of eye and soul
In youth were mine; when, stationed on the top
Of some huge hill – expectant, I beheld
The sun rise up, from distant climes returned
Darkness to chase, and sleep; and bring the day
His bounteous gift! or saw him toward the deep
Sink, with a retinue of flaming clouds
Attended; then, my spirit was entranced
With joy exalted to beatitude;
120 The measure of my soul was filled with bliss,
And holiest love; as earth, sea, air, with light,
With pomp, with glory, with magnificence!

'Those fervent raptures are for ever flown;
And, since their date, my soul hath undergone
Change manifold, for better or for worse:
Yet cease I not to struggle, and aspire
Heavenward; and chide the part of me that flags,
Through sinful choice; or dread necessity
On human nature from above imposed.
130 'Tis, by comparison, an easy task
Earth to despise; but, to converse with heaven –
This is not easy: – to relinquish all
We have, or hope, of happiness and joy,
And stand in freedom loosened from this world,
I deem not arduous; but must needs confess
That 'tis a thing impossible to frame
Conceptions equal to the soul's desires;
And the most difficult of tasks to *keep*
Heights which the soul is competent to gain.
140 – Man is of dust: ethereal hopes are his,

Which, when they should sustain themselves aloft,
Want due consistence; like a pillar of smoke,
That with majestic energy from earth
Rises; but, having reached the thinner air,
Melts, and dissolves, and is no longer seen.
From this infirmity of mortal kind
Sorrow proceeds, which else were not; at least,
If grief be something hallowed and ordained,
If, in proportion, it be just and meet,
150 Yet, through this weakness of the general heart,
Is it enabled to maintain its hold
In that excess which conscience disapproves.
For who could sink and settle to that point
Of selfishness; so senseless who could be
As long and perseveringly to mourn
For any object of his love, removed
From this unstable world, if he could fix
A satisfying view upon that state
Of pure, imperishable, blessedness,
160 Which reason promises, and holy writ
Ensures to all believers? – Yet mistrust
Is of such incapacity, methinks,
No natural branch; despondency far less;
And, least of all, is absolute despair.
– And, if there be whose tender frames have drooped
Even to the dust; apparently, through weight
Of anguish unrelieved, and lack of power
An agonizing sorrow to transmute;
Deem not that proof is here of hope withheld
170 When wanted most; a confidence impaired
So pitiably, that, having ceased to see
With bodily eyes, they are borne down by love
Of what is lost, and perish through regret.
Oh! no, the innocent Sufferer often sees
Too clearly; feels too vividly; and longs
To realize the vision, with intense
And over–constant yearning; – there – there lies
The excess, by which the balance is destroyed.

Too, too contracted are these walls of flesh,
180 This vital warmth too cold, these visual orbs,
Though inconceivably endowed, too dim
For any passion of the soul that leads
To ecstasy; and, all the crooked paths
Of time and change disdaining, takes its course
Along the line of limitless desires.
I, speaking now from such disorder free,
Nor rapt, nor craving, but in settled peace,
I cannot doubt that they whom you deplore
Are glorified; or, if they sleep, shall wake
190 From sleep, and dwell with God in endless love.
Hope, below this, consists not with belief
In mercy, carried infinite degrees
Beyond the tenderness of human hearts:
Hope, below this, consists not with belief
In perfect wisdom, guiding mightiest power,
That finds no limits but her own pure will.

'Here then we rest; not fearing for our creed
The worst that human reasoning can achieve,
To unsettle or perplex it: yet with pain
200 Acknowledging, and grievous self-reproach,
That, though immovably convinced, we want
Zeal, and the virtue to exist by faith
As soldiers live by courage; as, by strength
Of heart, the sailor fights with roaring seas.
Alas! the endowment of immortal power
Is matched unequally with custom, time,
And domineering faculties of sense
In *all*; in most with superadded foes,
Idle temptations; open vanities,
210 Ephemeral offspring of the unblushing world;
And, in the private regions of the mind,
Ill-governed passions, ranklings of despite,
Immoderate wishes, pining discontent,
Distress and care. What then remains? – To seek
Those helps for his occasions ever near

Who lacks not will to use them; vows, renewed
On the first motion of a holy thought;
Vigils of contemplation; praise; and prayer –
A stream, which, from the fountain of the heart
220 Issuing, however feebly, nowhere flows
Without access of unexpected strength.
But, above all, the victory is most sure
For him, who, seeking faith by virtue, strives
To yield entire submission to the law
Of conscience – conscience reverenced and obeyed,
As God's most intimate presence in the soul,
And His most perfect image in the world.
– Endeavour thus to live; these rules regard;
These helps solicit; and a stedfast seat
230 Shall then be yours among the happy few
Who dwell on earth, yet breathe empyreal air,
Sons of the morning. For your nobler part,
Ere disencumbered of her mortal chains,
Doubt shall be quelled and trouble chased away;
With only such degree of sadness left
As may support longings of pure desire;
And strengthen love, rejoicing secretly
In the sublime attractions of the grave.'

        While, in this strain, the venerable Sage
240 Poured forth his aspirations, and announced
His judgements, near that lonely house we paced
A plot of green-sward, seemingly preserved
By nature's care from wreck of scattered stones,
And from encroachment of encircling heath:
Small space! but, for reiterated steps,
Smooth and commodious; as a stately deck
Which to and fro the mariner is used
To tread for pastime, talking with his mates,
Or haply thinking of far-distant friends,
250 While the ship glides before a steady breeze.
Stillness prevailed around us: and the voice
That spake was capable to lift the soul

Toward regions yet more tranquil. But, methought,
That he, whose fixed despondency had given
Impulse and motive to that strong discourse,
Was less upraised in spirit than abashed;
Shrinking from admonition, like a man
Who feels that to exhort is to reproach.
Yet not to be diverted from his aim,
The Sage continued: –

260   'For that other loss,
The loss of confidence in social man,
By the unexpected transports of our age
Carried so high, that every thought, which looked
Beyond the temporal destiny of the Kind,
To many seemed superfluous – as, no cause
Could e'er for such exalted confidence
Exist; so, none is now for fixed despair:
The two extremes are equally disowned
By reason: if, with sharp recoil, from one
270 You have been driven far as its opposite,
Between them seek the point whereon to build
Sound expectations. So doth he advise
Who shared at first the illusion; but was soon
Cast from the pedestal of pride by shocks
Which Nature gently gave, in woods and fields;
Nor unreproved by Providence, thus speaking
To the inattentive children of the world:
"Vain-glorious Generation! what new powers
On you have been conferred? what gifts, withheld
280 From your progenitors, have ye received,
Fit recompense of new desert? what claim
Are ye prepared to urge, that my decrees
For you should undergo a sudden change;
And the weak functions of one busy day,
Reclaiming and extirpating, perform
What all the slowly-moving years of time,
With their united force, have left undone?
By nature's gradual processes be taught;
By story be confounded! Ye aspire

290 Rashly, to fall once more; and that false fruit,
     Which, to your overweening spirits, yields
     Hope of a fight celestial, will produce
     Misery and shame. But Wisdom of her sons
     Shall not the less, though late, be justified."

       'Such timely warning,' said the Wanderer, 'gave
     That visionary voice; and, at this day,
     When a Tartarean darkness overspreads
     The groaning nations; when the impious rule,
     By will or by established ordinance,
300 Their own dire agents, and constrain the good
     To acts which they abhor; though I bewail
     This triumph, yet the pity of my heart
     Prevents me not from owning, that the law,
     By which mankind now suffers, is most just.
     For by superior energies; more strict
     Affiance in each other; faith more firm
     In their unhallowed principles; the bad
     Have fairly earned a victory o'er the weak,
     The vacillating, inconsistent good.
310 Therefore, not unconsoled, I wait – in hope
     To see the moment, when the righteous cause
     Shall gain defenders zealous and devout
     As they who have opposed her; in which Virtue
     Will, to her efforts, tolerate no bounds
     That are not lofty as her rights; aspiring
     By impulse of her own ethereal zeal.
     That spirit only can redeem mankind;
     And when that sacred spirit shall appear,
     Then shall *our* triumph be complete as theirs.
320 Yet, should this confidence prove vain, the wise
     Have still the keeping of their proper peace;
     Are guardians of their own tranquillity.
     They act, or they recede, observe, and feel;
     "Knowing the heart of man is set to be
     The centre of this world, about the which
     Those revolutions of disturbances

Still roll; where all the aspècts of misery
Predominate; whose strong effects are such
As he must bear, being powerless to redress;
330 *And that unless above himself he can*
Erect himself, how poor a thing is Man!"

'Happy is he who lives to understand,
Not human nature only, but explores
All natures, – to the end that he may find
The law that governs each; and where begins
The union, the partition where, that makes
Kind and degree, among all visible Beings;
The constitutions, powers, and faculties,
Which they inherit, – cannot step beyond, –
340 And cannot fall beneath; that do assign
To every class its station and its office,
Through all the mighty commonwealth of things;
Up from the creeping plant to sovereign Man.
Such converse, if directed by a meek,
Sincere, and humble spirit, teaches love:
For knowledge is delight; and such delight
Breeds love: yet, suited as it rather is
To thought and to the climbing intellect,
It teaches less to love, than to adore;
350 If that be not indeed the highest love!'

'Yet,' said I, tempted here to interpose,
'The dignity of life is not impaired
By aught that innocently satisfies
The humbler cravings of the heart; and he
Is still a happier man, who, for those heights
Of speculation not unfit, descends;
And such benign affections cultivates
Among the inferior kinds; not merely those
That he may call his own, and which depend,
360 As individual objects of regard,
Upon his care, from whom he also looks
For signs and tokens of a mutual bond;

But others, far beyond this narrow sphere,
Whom, for the very sake of love, he loves.
Nor is it a mean praise of rural life
And solitude, that they do favour most,
Most frequently call forth, and best sustain,
These pure sensations; that can penetrate
The obstreperous city; on the barren seas
370   Are not unfelt; and much might recommend,
How much they might inspirit and endear,
The loneliness of this sublime retreat!'

'Yes,' said the Sage, resuming the discourse
Again directed to his downcast Friend,
'If, with the froward will and grovelling soul
Of man, offended, liberty is here,
And invitation every hour renewed,
To mark *their* placid state, who never heard
Of a command which they have power to break,
380   Or rule which they are tempted to transgress:
These, with a soothed or elevated heart,
May we behold; their knowledge register;
Observe their ways; and, free from envy, find
Complacence there: – but wherefore this to you?
I guess that, welcome to your lonely hearth,
The redbreast, ruffled up by winter's cold
Into a "feathery bunch," feeds at your hand:
A box, perchance, is from your casement hung
For the small wren to build in; – not in vain,
390   The barriers disregarding that surround
This deep abiding place, before your sight
Mounts on the breeze the butterfly; and soars,
Small creature as she is, from earth's bright flowers,
Into the dewy clouds. Ambition reigns
In the waste wilderness: the Soul ascends
Drawn towards her native firmament of heaven,
When the fresh eagle, in the month of May,
Upborne, at evening, on replenished wing,
This shaded valley leaves; and leaves the dark

400 Empurpled hills, conspicuously renewing
A proud communication with the sun
Low sunk beneath the horizon! – List! – I heard,
From yon huge breast of rock, a voice sent forth
As if the visible mountain made the cry.
Again!' – The effect upon the soul was such
As he expressed: from out the mountain's heart
The solemn voice appeared to issue, startling
The blank air – for the region all around
Stood empty of all shape of life, and silent
410 Save for that single cry, the unanswered bleat
Of a poor lamb – left somewhere to itself,
The plaintive spirit of the solitude!
He paused, as if unwilling to proceed,
Through consciousness that silence in such place
Was best, the most affecting eloquence.
But soon his thoughts returned upon themselves,
And, in soft tone of speech, thus he resumed.

'Ah! if the heart, too confidently raised,
Perchance too lightly occupied, or lulled
420 Too easily, despise or overlook
The vassalage that binds her to the earth,
Her sad dependence upon time, and all
The trepidations of mortality,
What place so destitute and void – but there
The little flower her vanity shall check;
The trailing worm reprove her thoughtless pride?

'These craggy regions, these chaotic wilds,
Does that benignity pervade, that warms
The mole contented with her darksome walk
430 In the cold ground; and to the emmet gives
Her foresight, and intelligence that makes
The tiny creatures strong by social league;
Supports the generations, multiplies
Their tribes, till we behold a spacious plain
Or grassy bottom, all, with little hills –

Their labour, covered, as a lake with waves;
Thousands of cities, in the desert place
Built up of life, and food, and means of life!
Nor wanting here, to entertain the thought,
440 Creatures that in communities exist,
Less, as might seem, for general guardianship
Or through dependence upon mutual aid,
Than by participation of delight
And a strict love of fellowship, combined.
What other spirit can it be that prompts
The gilded summer flies to mix and weave
Their sports together in the solar beam,
Or in the gloom of twilight hum their joy?
More obviously the self-same influence rules
450 The feathered kinds; the fieldfare's pensive flock,
The cawing rooks, and sea-mews from afar,
Hovering above these inland solitudes,
By the rough wind unscattered, at whose call
Up through the trenches of the long-drawn vales
Their voyage was begun: nor is its power
Unfelt among the sedentary fowl
That seek yon pool, and there prolong their stay
In silent congress; or together roused
Take flight; while with their clang the air resounds.
460 And, over all, in that ethereal vault,
Is the mute company of changeful clouds;
Bright apparition, suddenly put forth,
The rainbow smiling on the faded storm;
The mild assemblage of the starry heavens;
And the great sun, earth's universal lord!

'How bountiful is Nature! he shall find
Who seeks not; and to him, who hath not asked,
Large measures shall be dealt. Three sabbath-days
Are scarcely told, since, on a service bent
470 Of mere humanity, you clomb those heights;
And what a marvellous and heavenly show
Was suddenly revealed! – the swains moved on,

And heeded not: you lingered, you perceived
And felt, deeply as living man could feel.
There is a luxury in self-dispraise;
And inward self-disparagement affords
To meditative spleen a grateful feast.
Trust me, pronouncing on your own desert,
You judge unthankfully: distempered nerves
480 Infect the thoughts: the languor of the frame
Depresses the soul's vigour. Quit your couch –
Cleave not so fondly to your moody cell;
Nor let the hallowed powers, that shed from heaven
Stillness and rest, with disapproving eye
Look down upon your taper, through a watch
Of midnight hours, unseasonably twinkling
In this deep Hollow, like a sullen star
Dimly reflected in a lonely pool.
Take courage, and withdraw yourself from ways
490 That run not parallel to nature's course.
Rise with the lark! your matins shall obtain
Grace, be their composition what it may,
If but with hers performed; climb once again,
Climb every day, those ramparts; meet the breeze
Upon their tops, adventurous as a bee
That from your garden thither soars, to feed
On new-blown heath; let yon commanding rock
Be your frequented watch-tower; roll the stone
In thunder down the mountains; with all your might
500 Chase the wild goat; and if the bold red deer
Fly to those harbours, driven by hound and horn
Loud echoing, add your speed to the pursuit;
So, wearied to your hut shall you return,
And sink at evening into sound repose.'

    The Solitary lifted toward the hills
A kindling eye: – accordant feelings rushed
Into my bosom, whence these words broke forth:
'Oh! what a joy it were, in vigorous health,
To have a body (this our vital frame

510 With shrinking sensibility endued,
    And all the nice regards of flesh and blood)
    And to the elements surrender it
    As if it were a spirit! – How divine,
    The liberty, for frail, for mortal, man
    To roam at large among unpeopled glens
    And mountainous retirements, only trod
    By devious footsteps; regions consecrate
    To oldest time! and, reckless of the storm
    That keeps the raven quiet in her nest,
520 Be as a presence or a motion – one
    Among the many there; and while the mists
    Flying, and rainy vapours, call out shapes
    And phantoms from the crags and solid earth
    As fast as a musician scatters sounds
    Out of an instrument; and while the streams
    (As at a first creation and in haste
    To exercise their untried faculties)
    Descending from the region of the clouds,
    And starting from the hollows of the earth
530 More multitudinous every moment, rend
    Their way before them – what a joy to roam
    An equal among mightiest energies;
    And haply sometimes with articulate voice,
    Amid the deafening tumult, scarcely heard
    By him that utters it, exclaim aloud,
    "Rage on, ye elements! let moon and stars
    Their aspects lend, and mingle in their turn
    With this commotion (ruinous though it be)
    From day to night, from night to day, prolonged!" '

540   'Yes,' said the Wanderer, taking from my lips
    The strain of transport, 'whosoe'er in youth
    Has, through ambition of his soul, given way
    To such desires, and grasped at such delight,
    Shall feel congenial stirrings late and long,
    In spite of all the weakness that life brings,
    Its cares and sorrows; he, though taught to own

The tranquillizing power of time, shall wake,
Wake sometimes to a noble restlessness –
Loving the sports which once he gloried in.

550   'Compatriot, Friend, remote are Garry's hills,
The streams far distant of your native glen;
Yet is their form and image here expressed
With brotherly resemblance. Turn your steps
Wherever fancy leads; by day, by night,
Are various engines working, not the same
As those with which your soul in youth was moved,
But by the great Artificer endowed
With no inferior power. You dwell alone;
You walk, you live, you speculate alone;
560   Yet doth remembrance, like a sovereign prince,
For you a stately gallery maintain
Of gay or tragic pictures. You have seen,
Have acted, suffered, travelled far, observed
With no incurious eye; and books are yours,
Within whose silent chambers treasure lies
Preserved from age to age; more precious far
Than that accumulated store of gold
And orient gems, which, for a day of need,
The Sultan hides deep in ancestral tombs.
570   These hoards of truth you can unlock at will:
And music waits upon your skilful touch,
Sounds which the wandering shepherd from these heights
Hears, and forgets his purpose; – furnished thus,
How can you droop, if willing to be upraised?

'A piteous lot it were to flee from Man –
Yet not rejoice in Nature. He, whose hours
Are by domestic pleasures uncaressed
And unenlivened; who exists whole years
Apart from benefits received or done
580   'Mid the transactions of the bustling crowd;
Who neither hears, nor feels a wish to hear,
Of the world's interests – such a one hath need

Of a quick fancy and an active heart,
That, for the day's consumption, books may yield
Food not unwholesome; earth and air correct
His morbid humour, with delight supplied
Or solace, varying as the seasons change.
– Truth has her pleasure-grounds, her haunts of ease
And easy contemplation; gay parterres,
590   And labyrinthine walks, her sunny glades
And shady groves in studied contrast – each,
For recreation, leading into each:
These may he range, if willing to partake
Their soft indulgences, and in due time
May issue thence, recruited for the tasks
And course of service Truth requires from those
Who tend her altars, wait upon her throne,
And guard her fortresses. Who thinks, and feels,
And recognizes ever and anon
600   The breeze of nature stirring in his soul,
Why need such man go desperately astray,
And nurse "the dreadful appetite of death?"
If tired with systems, each in its degree
Substantial, and all crumbling in their turn,
Let him build systems of his own, and smile
At the fond work, demolished with a touch;
If unreligious, let him be at once,
Among ten thousand innocents, enrolled
A pupil in the many-chambered school,
610   Where superstition weaves her airy dreams.

   'Life's autumn past, I stand on winter's verge;
And daily lose what I desire to keep:
Yet rather would I instantly decline
To the traditionary sympathies
Of a most rustic ignorance, and take
A fearful apprehension from the owl
Or death-watch: and as readily rejoice,
If two auspicious magpies crossed my way; –
To this would rather bend than see and hear

620   The repetitions wearisome of sense,
      Where soul is dead, and feeling hath no place;
      Where knowledge, ill begun in cold remark
      On outward things, with formal inference ends;
      Or, if the mind turn inward, she recoils
      At once – or, not recoiling, is perplexed –
      Lost in a gloom of uninspired research;
      Meanwhile, the heart within the heart, the seat
      Where peace and happy consciousness should dwell,
      On its own axis restlessly revolving,
630   Seeks, yet can nowhere find, the light of truth.

     'Upon the breast of new-created earth
      Man walked; and when and wheresoe'er he moved,
      Alone or mated, solitude was not.
      He heard, borne on the wind, the articulate voice
      Of God; and Angels to his sight appeared
      Crowning the glorious hills of paradise;
      Or through the groves gliding like morning mist
      Enkindled by the sun. He sate – and talked
      With wingèd Messengers; who daily brought
640   To his small island in the ethereal deep
      Tidings of joy and love. – From those pure heights
      (Whether of actual vision, sensible
      To sight and feeling, or that in this sort
      Have condescendingly been shadowed forth
      Communications spiritually maintained,
      And intuitions moral and divine)
      Fell Human-kind – to banishment condemned
      That flowing years repealed not: and distress
      And grief spread wide; but Man escaped the doom
650   Of destitution; – solitude was not.
      – Jehovah – shapeless Power above all Powers,
      Single and one, the omnipresent God,
      By vocal utterance, or blaze of light,
      Or cloud of darkness, localized in heaven;
      On earth, enshrined within the wandering ark;

Or, out of Sion, thundering from his throne
Between the Cherubim – on the chosen Race
Showered miracles, and ceased not to dispense
Judgements, that filled the land from age to age
660 With hope, and love, and gratitude, and fear;
And with amazement smote; – thereby to assert
His scorned, or unacknowledged, sovereignty.
And when the One, ineffable of name,
Of nature indivisible, withdrew
From mortal adoration or regard,
Not then was Deity engulfed; nor Man,
The rational creature, left, to feel the weight
Of his own reason, without sense or thought
Of higher reason and a purer will,
670 To benefit and bless, through mightier power: –
Whether the Persian – zealous to reject
Altar and image, and the inclusive walls
And roofs of temples built by human hands –
To loftiest heights ascending, from their tops,
With myrtle-wreathed tiara on his brow,
Presented sacrifice to moon and stars,
And to the winds and mother elements,
And the whole circle of the heavens, for him
A sensitive existence, and a God,
680 With lifted hands invoked, and songs of praise:
Or, less reluctantly to bonds of sense
Yielding his soul, the Babylonian framed
For influence undefined a personal shape;
And, from the plain, with toil immense, upreared
Tower eight times planted on the top of tower,
That Belus, nightly to his splendid couch
Descending, there might rest; upon that height
Pure and serene, diffused – to overlook
Winding Euphrates, and the city vast
690 Of his devoted worshippers, far-stretched,
With grove and field and garden interspersed;
Their town, and foodful region for support
Against the pressure of beleaguering war.

'Chaldean Shepherds, ranging trackless fields,
Beneath the concave of unclouded skies
Spread like a sea, in boundless solitude,
Looked on the polar star, as on a guide
And guardian of their course, that never closed
His stedfast eye. The planetary Five
700   With a submissive reverence they beheld;
Watched, from the centre of their sleeping flocks,
Those radiant Mercuries, that seemed to move
Carrying through ether, in perpetual round,
Decrees and resolutions of the Gods;
And, by their aspects, signifying works
Of dim futurity, to Man revealed.
– The imaginative faculty was lord
Of observations natural; and, thus
Led on, those shepherds made report of stars
710   In set rotation passing to and fro,
Between the orbs of our apparent sphere
And its invisible counterpart, adorned
With answering constellations, under earth,
Removed from all approach of living sight
But present to the dead; who, so they deemed,
Like those celestial messengers beheld
All accidents, and judges were of all.

'The lively Grecian, in a land of hills,
Rivers and fertile plains, and sounding shores, –
720   Under a cope of sky more variable,
Could find commodious place for every God,
Promptly received, as prodigally brought,
From the surrounding countries, at the choice
Of all adventurers. With unrivalled skill,
As nicest observation furnished hints
For studious fancy, his quick hand bestowed
On fluent operations a fixed shape;
Metal or stone, idolatrously served.
And yet – triumphant o'er this pompous show
730   Of art, this palpable array of sense,

On every side encountered; in despite
Of the gross fictions chanted in the streets
By wandering Rhapsodists; and in contempt
Of doubt and bold denial hourly urged
Amid the wrangling schools – a SPIRIT hung,
Beautiful region! o'er thy towns and farms,
Statues and temples, and memorial tombs;
And emanations were perceived; and acts
Of immortality, in Nature's course,
740 Exemplified by mysteries, that were felt
As bonds, on grave philosopher imposed
And armèd warrior; and in every grove
A gay or pensive tenderness prevailed,
When piety more awful had relaxed.
– "Take, running river, take these locks of mine" –
Thus would the Votary say – "this severed hair,
My vow fulfilling, do I here present,
Thankful for my belovèd child's return.
Thy banks, Cephisus, he again hath trod,
750 Thy murmurs heard; and drunk the crystal lymph
With which thou dost refresh the thirsty lip,
And, all day long, moisten these flowery fields!"
And doubtless, sometimes, when the hair was shed
Upon the flowing stream, a thought arose
Of Life continuous, Being unimpaired;
That hath been, is, and where it was and is
There shall endure, – existence unexposed
To the blind walk of mortal accident;
From diminution safe and weakening age;
760 While man grows old, and dwindles, and decays;
And countless generations of mankind
Depart; and leave no vestige where they trod.

'We live by Admiration, Hope, and Love;
And, even as these are well and wisely fixed,
In dignity of being we ascend.
But what is error?' – 'Answer he who can!'
The Sceptic somewhat haughtily exclaimed:

'Love, Hope, and Admiration – are they not
Mad Fancy's favourite vassals? Does not life
770 Use them, full oft, as pioneers to ruin,
Guides to destruction? Is it well to trust
Imagination's light when reason's fails,
The unguarded taper where the guarded faints?
– Stoop from those heights, and soberly declare
What error is; and, of our errors, which
Doth most debase the mind; the genuine seats
Of power, where are they? Who shall regulate,
With truth, the scale of intellectual rank?'

    'Methinks,' persuasively the Sage replied,
780 'That for this arduous office you possess
Some rare advantages. Your early days
A grateful recollection must supply
Of much exalted good by Heaven vouchsafed
To dignify the humblest state. – Your voice
Hath, in my hearing, often testified
That poor men's children, they, and they alone,
By their condition taught, can understand
The wisdom of the prayer that daily asks
For daily bread. A consciousness is yours
790 How feelingly religion may be learned
In smoky cabins, from a mother's tongue –
Heard while the dwelling vibrates to the din
Of the contiguous torrent, gathering strength
At every moment – and, with strength, increase
Of fury; or, while snow is at the door,
Assaulting and defending, and the wind,
A sightless labourer, whistles at his work –
Fearful; but resignation tempers fear,
And piety is sweet to infant minds.
800 – The Shepherd-lad, that in the sunshine carves,
On the green turf, a dial – to divide
The silent hours; and who to that report
Can portion out his pleasures, and adapt,
Throughout a long and lonely summer's day

His round of pastoral duties, is not left
With less intelligence for *moral* things
Of gravest import. Early he perceives,
Within himself, a measure and a rule,
Which to the sun of truth he can apply,
810   That shines for him, and shines for all mankind.
Experience daily fixing his regards
On nature's wants, he knows how few they are,
And where they lie, how answered and appeased.
This knowledge ample recompense affords
For manifold privations; he refers
His notions to this standard; on this rock
Rests his desires; and hence, in after-life,
Soul-strengthening patience, and sublime content.
Imagination – not permitted here
820   To waste her powers, as in the worldling's mind,
On fickle pleasures, and superfluous cares,
And trivial ostentation – is left free
And puissant to range the solemn walks
Of time and nature, girded by a zone
That, while it binds, invigorates and supports.
Acknowledge, then, that whether by the side
Of his poor hut, or on the mountain-top,
Or in the cultured field, a Man so bred
(Take from him what you will upon the score
830   Of ignorance or illusion) lives and breathes
For noble purposes of mind: his heart
Beats to the heroic song of ancient days;
His eye distinguishes, his soul creates.
And those illusions, which excite the scorn
Or move the pity of unthinking minds,
Are they not mainly outward ministers
Of inward conscience? with whose service charged
They came and go, appeared and disappear,
Diverting evil purposes, remorse
840   Awakening, chastening an intemperate grief,
Or pride of heart abating: and, whene'er
For less important ends those phantoms move,

Who would forbid them, if their presence serve,
On thinly-peopled mountains and wild heaths,
Filling a space, else vacant, to exalt
The forms of Nature, and enlarge her powers?

'Once more to distant ages of the world
Let us revert, and place before our thoughts
The face which rural solitude might wear
850   To the unenlightened swains of pagan Greece.
– In that fair clime, the lonely herdsman, stretched
On the soft grass through half a summer's day,
With music lulled his indolent repose:
And, in some fit of weariness, if he,
When his own breath was silent, chanced to hear
A distant strain, far sweeter than the sounds
Which his poor skill could make, his fancy fetched,
Even from the blazing chariot of the sun,
A beardless Youth, who touched a golden lute,
860   And filled the illumined groves with ravishment.
The nightly hunter, lifting a bright eye
Up towards the crescent moon, with grateful heart
Called on the lovely wanderer who bestowed
That timely light, to share his joyous sport:
And hence, a beaming Goddess with her Nymphs,
Across the lawn and through the darksome grove,
Not unaccompanied with tuneful notes
By echo multiplied from rock or cave,
Swept in the storm of chase; as moon and stars
870   Glance rapidly along the clouded heaven,
When winds are blowing strong. The traveller slaked
His thirst from rill or gushing fount, and thanked
The Naiad. Sunbeams, upon distant hills
Gliding apace, with shadows in their train,
Might, with small help from fancy, be transformed
Into fleet Oreads sporting visibly.
The Zephyrs fanning, as they passed, their wings,
Lacked not, for love, fair objects whom they wooed
With gentle whisper. Withered boughs grotesque,

880 Stripped of their leaves and twigs by hoary age,
From depth of shaggy covert peeping forth
In the low vale, or on steep mountain-side;
And, sometimes, intermixed with stirring horns
Of the live deer, or goat's depending beard, –
These were the lurking Satyrs, a wild brood
Of gamesome Deities; or Pan himself,
The simple shepherd's awe-inspiring God!'

    The strain was aptly chosen; and I could mark
Its kindly influence, o'er the yielding brow
890 Of our Companion, gradually diffused;
While, listening, he had paced the noiseless turf,
Like one whose untired ear a murmuring stream
Detains; but tempted now to interpose,
He with a smile exclaimed: –
                    ' 'Tis well you speak
At a safe distance from our native land,
And from the mansions where our youth was taught.
The true descendants of those godly men
Who swept from Scotland, in a flame of zeal,
Shrine, altar, image, and the massy piles
900 That harboured them, – the souls retaining yet
The churlish features of that after-race
Who fled to woods, caverns, and jutting rocks,
In deadly scorn of superstitious rites,
Or what their scruples construed to be such –
How, think you, would they tolerate this scheme
Of fine propensities, that tends, if urged
Far as it might be urged, to sow afresh
The weeds of Romish phantasy, in vain
Uprooted; would re-consecrate our wells
910 To good Saint Fillan and to fair Saint Anne;
And from long banishment recall Saint Giles,
To watch again with tutelary love
O'er stately Edinborough throned on crags?
A blessed restoration, to behold
The patron, on the shoulders of his priests,

Once more parading through her crowded streets
Now simply guarded by the sober powers
Of science, and philosophy, and sense!'

  This answer followed. – 'You have turned my thoughts
920 Upon our brave Progenitors, who rose
Against idolatry with warlike mind,
And shrunk from vain observances, to lurk
In woods, and dwell under impending rocks
Ill-sheltered, and oft wanting fire and food;
Why? – for this very reason that they felt,
And did acknowledge, wheresoe'er they moved,
A spiritual presence, ofttimes misconceived,
But still a high dependence, a divine
Bounty and government, that filled their hearts
930 With joy, and gratitude, and fear, and love;
And from their fervent lips drew hymns of praise,
That through the desert rang. Though favoured less,
Far less, than these, yet such, in their degree,
Were those bewildered Pagans of old time.
Beyond their own poor natures and above
They looked; were humbly thankful for the good
Which the warm sun solicited, and earth
Bestowed; were gladsome, – and their moral sense
They fortified with reverence for the Gods;
940 And they had hopes that overstepped the Grave.

  'Now, shall our great Discoverers,' he exclaimed,
Raising his voice triumphantly, 'obtain
From sense and reason less than these obtained,
Though far misled? Shall men for whom our age
Unbaffled powers of vision hath prepared,
To explore the world without and world within,
Be joyless as the blind? Ambitious spirits –
Whom earth, at this late season, hath produced
To regulate the moving spheres, and weigh
950 The planets in the hollow of their hand;
And they who rather dive than soar, whose pains

Have solved the elements, or analysed
The thinking principle – shall they in fact
Prove a degraded Race? and what avails
Renown, if their presumption make them such?
Oh! there is laughter at their work in heaven!
Enquire of ancient Wisdom; go, demand
Of mighty Nature, if 'twas ever meant
That we should pry far off yet be unraised;
960   That we should pore, and dwindle as we pore,
Viewing all objects unremittingly
In disconnexion dead and spiritless;
And still dividing, and dividing still,
Break down all grandeur, still unsatisfied
With the perverse attempt, while littleness
May yet become more little; waging thus
An impious warfare with the very life
Of our own souls!
                And if indeed there be
An all-pervading Spirit, upon whom
970   Our dark foundations rest, could he design
That this magnificent effect of power,
The earth we tread, the sky that we behold
By day, and all the pomp which night reveals;
That these – and that superior mystery
Our vital frame, so fearfully devised,
And the dread soul within it – should exist
Only to be examined, pondered, searched,
Probed, vexed, and criticized? – Accuse me not
Of arrogance, unknown Wanderer as I am,
980   If, having walked with Nature threescore years,
And offered, far as frailty would allow,
My heart a daily sacrifice to Truth,
I now affirm of Nature and of Truth,
Whom I have served, that their DIVINITY
Revolts, offended at the ways o men
Swayed by such motives, to such ends employed;
Philosophers, who, though the human soul
Be of a thousand faculties composed,

And twice ten thousand interests, do yet prize
990 This soul, and the transcendent universe,
No more than as a mirror that reflects
To proud Self-love her own intelligence;
That one, poor, finite object, in the abyss
Of infinite Being, twinkling restlessly!

'Nor higher place can be assigned to him
And his compeers – the laughing Sage of France. –
Crowned was he, if my memory do not err,
With laurel planted upon hoary hairs,
In sign of conquest by his wit achieved
1000 And benefits his wisdom had conferred;
His stooping body tottered with wreaths of flowers
Opprest, far less becoming ornaments
Than Spring oft twines about a mouldering tree;
Yet so it pleased a fond, a vain, old Man,
And a most frivolous people. Him I mean
Who penned, to ridicule confiding faith,
This sorry Legend; which by chance we found
Piled in a nook, through malice, as might seem,
Among more innocent rubbish.' – Speaking thus,
1010 With a brief notice when, and how, and where,
We had espied the book, he drew it forth;
And courteously, as if the act removed,
At once, all traces from the good Man's heart
Of unbenign aversion or contempt,
Restored it to its owner. 'Gentle Friend,'
Herewith he grasped the Solitary's hand,
'You have known lights and guides better than these.
Ah! let not aught amiss within dispose
A noble mind to practise on herself,
1020 And tempt opinion to support the wrongs
Of passion: whatsoe'er be felt or feared,
From higher judgement-seats make no appeal
To lower: can you question that the soul
Inherits an allegiance, not by choice
To be cast off, upon an oath proposed

By each new upstart notion? In the ports
Of levity no refuge can be found,
No shelter, for a spirit in distress.
He, who by wilful disesteem of life
1030 And proud insensibility to hope,
Affronts the eye of Solitude, shall learn
That her mild nature can be terrible;
That neither she nor Silence lack the power
To avenge their own insulted majesty.

'O blest seclusion! when the mind admits
The law of duty; and can therefore move
Through each vicissitude of loss and gain,
Linked in entire complacence with her choice;
When youth's presumptuousness is mellowed down,
1040 And manhood's vain anxiety dismissed;
When wisdom shows her seasonable fruit,
Upon the boughs of sheltering leisure hung
In sober plenty; when the spirit stoops
To drink with gratitude the crystal stream
Of unreproved enjoyment; and is pleased
To muse, and be saluted by the air
Of meek repentance, wafting wall-flower scents
From out the crumbling ruins of fallen pride
And chambers of transgression, now forlorn.
1050 O, calm contented days, and peaceful nights!
Who, when such good can be obtained, would strive
To reconcile his manhood to a couch
Soft, as may seem, but, under that disguise,
Stuffed with the thorny substance of the past
For fixed annoyance; and full oft beset
With floating dreams, black and disconsolate,
The vapoury phantoms of futurity?

'Within the soul a faculty abides,
That with interpositions, which would hide
1060 And darken, so can deal that they become

Contingencies of pomp; and serve to exalt
Her native brightness. As the ample moon,
In the deep stillness of a summer even
Rising behind a thick and lofty grove,
Burns, like an unconsuming fire of light,
In the green trees; and, kindling on all sides
Their leafy umbrage, turns the dusky veil
Into a substance glorious as her own,
Yea, with her own incorporated, by power
1070 Capacious and serene. Like power abides
In man's celestial spirit; virtue thus
Sets forth and magnifies herself; thus feeds
A calm, a beautiful, and silent fire,
From the encumbrances of mortal life,
From error, disappointment – nay, from guilt;
And sometimes, so relenting justice wills,
From palpable oppressions of despair.'

The Solitary by these words was touched
With manifest emotion, and exclaimed;
1080 'But how begin? and whence? – "The Mind is free –
Resolve," the haughty Moralist would say,
"This single act is all that we demand."
Alas! such wisdom bids a creature fly
Whose very sorrow is, that time hath shorn
His natural wings! – To friendship let him turn
For succour; but perhaps he sits alone
On stormy waters, tossed in a little boat
That holds but him, and can contain no more!
Religion tells of amity sublime
1090 Which no condition can preclude; of One
Who sees all suffering, comprehends all wants,
All weakness fathoms, can supply all needs:
But is that bounty absolute? – His gifts,
Are they not, still, in some degree, rewards
For acts of service? Can His love extend
To hearts that own not Him? Will showers of grace,
When in the sky no promise may be seen,

Fall to refresh a parched and withered land?
Or shall the groaning Spirit cast her load
At the Redeemer's feet?'

1100   In rueful tone,
With some impatience in his mien, he spake:
Back to my mind rushed all that had been urged
To calm the Sufferer when his story closed;
I looked for counsel as unbending now;
But a discriminating sympathy
Stooped to this apt reply: –
                         'As men from men
Do, in the constitution of their souls,
Differ, by mystery not to be explained;
And as we fall by various ways, and sink
1110 One deeper than another, self-condemned,
Through manifold degrees of guilt and shame;
So manifold and various are the ways
Of restoration, fashioned to the steps
Of all infirmity, and tending all
To the same point, attainable by all –
Peace in ourselves, and union with our God.
For you, assuredly, a hopeful road
Lies open: we have heard from you a voice
At every moment softened in its course
1120 By tenderness of heart; have seen your eye,
Even like an altar lit by fire from heaven,
Kindle before us. – Your discourse this day,
That, like the fabled Lethe, wished to flow
In creeping sadness, through oblivious shades
Of death and night, has caught at every turn
The colours of the sun. Access for you
Is yet preserved to principles of truth,
Which the imaginative Will upholds
In seats of wisdom, not to be approached
1130 By the inferior Faculty that moulds,
With her minute and speculative pains,
Opinion, ever changing!
                         I have seen

A curious child, who dwelt upon a tract
Of inland ground, applying to his ear
The convolutions of a smooth-lipped shell;
To which, in silence hushed, his very soul
Listened intensely; and his countenance soon
Brightened with joy; for from within were heard
Murmurings, whereby the monitor expressed
1140 Mysterious union with its native sea.
Even such a shell the universe itself
Is to the ear of Faith; and there are times,
I doubt not, when to you it doth impart
Authentic tidings of invisible things;
Of ebb and flow, and ever-during power;
And central peace, subsisting at the heart
Of endless agitation. Here you stand,
Adore, and worship, when you know it not;
Pious beyond the intention of your thought;
1150 Devout above the meaning of your will.
– Yes, you have felt, and may not cease to feel.
The estate of man would be indeed forlorn
If false conclusions of the reasoning power
Made the eye blind, and closed the passages
Through which the ear converses with the heart.
Has not the soul, the being of your life,
Received a shock of awful consciousness,
In some calm season, when these lofty rocks
At night's approach bring down the unclouded sky,
1160 To rest upon their circumambient walls;
A temple framing of dimensions vast,
And yet not too enormous for the sound
Of human anthems, – choral song, or burst
Sublime of instrumental harmony,
To glorify the Eternal! What if these
Did never break the stillness that prevails
Here, – if the solemn nightingale be mute,
And the soft woodlark here did never chant
Her vespers, – Nature fails not to provide
1170 Impulse and utterance. The whispering air

Sends inspiration from the shadowy heights,
And blind recesses of the caverned rocks;
The little rills, and waters numberless,
Inaudible by daylight, blend their notes
With the loud streams: and often, at the hour
When issue forth the first pale stars, is heard,
Within the circuit of this fabric huge,
One voice – the solitary raven, flying
Athwart the concave of the dark blue dome,
1180 Unseen, perchance above all power of sight –
An iron knell! with echoes from afar
Faint – and still fainter – as the cry, with which
The wanderer accompanies her flight
Through the calm region, fades upon the ear,
Diminishing by distance till it seemed
To expire; yet from the abyss is caught again,
And yet again recovered!
                    But descending
From these imaginative heights, that yield
Far-stretching views into eternity,
1190 Acknowledge that to Nature's humbler power
Your cherished sullenness is forced to bend
Even here, where her amenities are sown
With sparing hand. Then trust yourself abroad
To range her blooming bowers, and spacious fields,
Where on the labours of the happy throng
She smiles, including in her wide embrace
City, and town, and tower, – and sea with ships
Sprinkled; – be our Companion while we track
Her rivers populous with gliding life;
1200 While, free as air, o'er printless sands we march,
Or pierce the gloom of her majestic woods;
Roaming, or resting under grateful shade
In peace and meditative cheerfulness;
Where living things, and things inanimate,
Do speak, at Heaven's command, to eye and ear,
And speak to social reason's inner sense,
With inarticulate language.

                              For, the Man –
        Who, in this spirit, communes with the Forms
        Of nature, who with understanding heart
1210   Both knows and loves such objects as excite
        No morbid passions, no disquietude,
        No vengeance, and no hatred – needs must feel
        The joy of that pure principle of love
        So deeply, that, unsatisfied with aught
        Less pure and exquisite, he cannot choose
        But seek for objects of a kindred love
        In fellow-natures and a kindred joy.
        Accordingly he by degrees perceives
        His feelings of aversion softened down;
1220   A holy tenderness pervade his frame.
        His sanity of reason not impaired,
        Say rather, all his thoughts now flowing clear,
        From a clear fountain flowing, he looks round
        And seeks for good; and finds the good he seeks:
        Until abhorrence and contempt are things
        He only knows by name; and, if he hear,
        From other mouths, the language which they speak,
        He is compassionate; and has no thought,
        No feeling, which can overcome his love.

1230   'And further; by contemplating these Forms
        In the relations which they bear to man,
        He shall discern, how, through the various means
        Which silently they yield, are multiplied
        The spiritual presences of absent things.
        Trust me, that for the instructed, time will come
        When they shall meet no object but may teach
        Some acceptable lesson to their minds
        Of human suffering, or of human joy.
        So shall they learn, while all things speak of man,
1240   Their duties from all forms; and general laws,
        And local accidents, shall tend alike
        To rouse, to urge; and, with the will, confer
        The ability to spread the blessings wide

Of true philanthropy. The light of love
Not failing, perseverance from their steps
Departing not, for them shall be confirmed
The glorious habit by which sense is made
Subservient still to moral purposes,
Auxiliar to divine. That change shall clothe
1250 The naked spirit, ceasing to deplore
The burden of existence. Science then
Shall be a precious visitant; and then,
And only then, be worthy of her name:
For then her heart shall kindle; her dull eye,
Dull and inanimate, no more shall hang
Chained to its object in brute slavery;
But taught with patient interest to watch
The processes of things, and serve the cause
Of order and distinctness, not for this
1260 Shall it forget that its most noble use,
Its most illustrious province, must be found
In furnishing clear guidance, a support
Not treacherous, to the mind's *excursive* power.
– So build we up the Being that we are;
Thus deeply drinking-in the soul of things,
We shall be wise perforce; and, while inspired
By choice, and conscious that the Will is free,
Shall move unswerving, even as if impelled
By strict necessity, along the path
1270 Of order and of good. Whate'er we see,
Or feel, shall tend to quicken and refine
The humblest functions of corporeal sense;
Shall fix, in calmer seats of moral strength,
Earthly desires; and raise, to loftier heights
Of divine love, our intellectual soul.'

Here closed the Sage that eloquent harangue,
Poured forth with fervour in continuous stream,
Such as, remote, 'mid savage wilderness,
An Indian Chief discharges from his breast
1280 Into the hearing of assembled tribes,

In open circle seated round, and hushed
As the unbreathing air, when not a leaf
Stirs in the mighty woods. – So did he speak:
The words he uttered shall not pass away
Dispersed, like music that the wind takes up
By snatches, and lets fall, to be forgotten;
No – they sank into me, the bounteous gift
Of one whom time and nature had made wise,
Gracing his doctrine with authority
1290 Which hostile spirits silently allow;
Of one accustomed to desires that feed
On fruitage gathered from the tree of life;
To hopes on knowledge and experience built;
Of one in whom persuasion and belief
Had ripened into faith, and faith become
A passionate intuition; whence the Soul,
Though bound to earth by ties of pity and love,
From all injurious servitude was free.

The Sun, before his place of rest were reached,
1300 Had yet to travel far, but unto us,
To us who stood low in that hollow dell,
He had become invisible, – a pomp
Leaving behind of yellow radiance spread
Over the mountain-sides, in contrast bold
With ample shadows, seemingly, no less
Than those resplendent lights, his rich bequest;
A dispensation of his evening power.
– Adown the path that from the glen had led
The funeral train, the Shepherd and his Mate
1310 Were seen descending: – forth to greet them ran
Our little Page: the rustic pair approach;
And in the Matron's countenance may be read
Plain indication that the words, which told
How that neglected Pensioner was sent
Before his time into a quiet grave,
Had done to her humanity no wrong:
But we are kindly welcomed – promptly served

With ostentatious zeal. – Along the floor
Of the small Cottage in the lonely Dell
1320 A grateful couch was spread for our repose;
Where, in the guise of mountaineers, we lay,
Stretched upon fragrant heath, and lulled by sound
Of far-off torrents charming the still night,
And, to tired limbs and over-busy thoughts,
Inviting sleep and soft forgetfulness.

BOOK FIFTH
THE PASTOR

Argument

Farewell to the Valley. – Reflections. – A large and populous
Vale described. – The Pastor's Dwelling, and some account of
him. – Church and Monuments. – The Solitary musing, and
where. – Roused. – In the Churchyard the Solitary communicates
the thoughts which had recently passed through his mind. –
Lofty tone of the Wanderer's discourse of yesterday adverted
to. – Rite of Baptism, and the professions accompanying it,
contrasted with the real state of human life. – Apology for the
Rite. – Inconsistency of the best men. – Acknowledgement that
practise falls far below the injunctions of duty as existing in the
mind. – General complaint of a falling-off in the value of life
after the time of youth. – Outward appearances of content and
happiness in degree illusive. – Pastor approaches. – Appeal
made to him. – His answer. – Wanderer in sympathy with him.
– Suggestion that the least ambitious enquirers may be most
free from error. – The Pastor is desired to give some portraits
of the living or dead from his own observation of life among
these Mountains – and for what purpose. – Pastor consents. –
Mountain cottage. – Excellent qualities of its Inhabitants. –
Solitary expresses his pleasure; but denies the praise of virtue
to worth of this kind. – Feelings of the Priest before he enters
upon his account of persons interred in the Churchyard. –
Graves of unbaptized Infants. – Funeral and sepulchral observances, whence. – Ecclesiastical Establishments, whence
derived. – Profession of belief in the doctrine of Immortality.

'Farewell, deep Valley, with thy one rude House,
And its small lot of life-supporting fields,

And guardian rocks! – Farewell, attractive seat!
To the still influx of the morning light
Open, and day's pure cheerfulness, but veiled
From human observation, as if yet
Primeval forests wrapped thee round with dark
Impenetrable shade; once more farewell,
Majestic circuit, beautiful abyss,
10 By Nature destined from the birth of things
For quietness profound!'
                                    Upon the side
Of that brown ridge, sole outlet of the vale
Which foot of boldest stranger would attempt,
Lingering behind my comrades, thus I breathed
A parting tribute to a spot that seemed
Like the fixed centre of a troubled world.
Again I halted with reverted eyes;
The chain that would not slacken, was at length
Snapt, – and, pursuing leisurely my way,
20 How vain, thought I, is it by change of place
To seek that comfort which the mind denies;
Yet trial and temptation oft are shunned
Wisely; and by such tenure do we hold
Frail life's possessions, that even they whose fate
Yields no peculiar reason of complaint
Might, by the promise that is here, be won
To steal from active duties, and embrace
Obscurity, and undisturbed repose.
– Knowledge, methinks, in these disordered times,
30 Should be allowed a privilege to have
Her anchorites, like piety of old;
Men, who, from faction sacred, and unstained
By war, might, if so minded, turn aside
Uncensured, and subsist, a scattered few
Living to God and nature, and content
With that communion. Consecrated be
The spots where such abide! But happier still
The Man, whom, furthermore, a hope attends
That meditation and research may guide

40 His privacy to principles and powers
Discovered or invented; or set forth,
Through his acquaintance with the ways of truth,
In lucid order; so that, when his course
Is run, some faithful eulogist may say,
He sought not praise, and praise did overlook
His unobtrusive merit; but his life,
Sweet to himself, was exercised in good
That shall survive his name and memory.

Acknowledgements of gratitude sincere
50 Accompanied these musings; fervent thanks
For my own peaceful lot and happy choice;
A choice that from the passions of the world
Withdrew, and fixed me in a still retreat;
Sheltered, but not to social duties lost,
Secluded, but not buried; and with song
Cheering my days, and with industrious thought;
With the ever-welcome company of books;
With virtuous friendship's soul-sustaining aid,
And with the blessings of domestic love.

60 Thus occupied in mind I paced along,
Following the rugged road, by sledge or wheel
Worn in the moorland, till I overtook
My two Associates, in the morning sunshine
Halting together on a rocky knoll,
Whence the bare road descended rapidly
To the green meadows of another vale.

Here did our pensive Host put forth his hand
In sign of farewell. 'Nay,' the old Man said,
'The fragrant air its coolness still retains;
70 The herds and flocks are yet abroad to crop
The dewy grass; you cannot leave us now,
We must not part at this inviting hour.'
He yielded, though reluctant; for his mind
Instinctively disposed him to retire

To his own covert; as a billow, heaved
Upon the beach, rolls back into the sea.
– So we descend: and winding round a rock
Attain a point that showed the valley – stretched
In length before us; and, not distant far,
80   Upon a rising ground a grey church-tower,
Whose battlements were screened by tufted trees.
And toward a crystal Mere, that lay beyond
Among steep hills and woods embosomed, flowed
A copious stream with boldly-winding course;
Here traceable, there hidden – there again
To sight restored, and glittering in the sun.
On the stream's bank, and everywhere, appeared
Fair dwellings, single, or in social knots;
Some scattered o'er the level, others perched
90   On the hill-sides, a cheerful quiet scene,
Now in its morning purity arrayed.

'As 'mid some happy valley of the Alps,'
Said I, 'once happy, ere tyrannic power,
Wantonly breaking in upon the Swiss,
Destroyed their unoffending commonwealth,
A popular equality reigns here,
Save for yon stately House beneath whose roof
A rural lord might dwell.' – 'No feudal pomp,
Or power,' replied the Wanderer, 'to that House
100   Belongs, but there in his allotted Home
Abides, from year to year, a genuine Priest,
The shepherd of his flock; or, as a king
Is styled, when most affectionately praised,
The father of his people. Such is he;
And rich and poor, and young and old, rejoice
Under his spiritual sway. He hath vouchsafed
To me some portion of a kind regard;
And something also of his inner mind
Hath he imparted – but I speak of him
As he is known to all.
110   The calm delights

Of unambitious piety he chose,
And learning's solid dignity; though born
Of knightly race, nor wanting powerful friends.
Hither, in prime of manhood, he withdrew
From academic bowers. He loved the spot –
Who does not love his native soil? – he prized
The ancient rural character, composed
Of simple manners, feelings unsupprest
And undisguised, and strong and serious thought;
120 A character reflected in himself,
With such embellishment as well beseems
His rank and sacred function. This deep vale
Winds far in reaches hidden from our sight,
And one a turreted manorial hall
Adorns, in which the good Man's ancestors
Have dwelt through ages – Patrons of this Cure.
To them, and to his own judicious pains,
The Vicar's dwelling, and the whole domain,
Owes that presiding aspect which might well
130 Attract your notice; statelier than could else
Have been bestowed, through course of common chance,
On an unwealthy mountain Benefice.'

   This said, oft pausing, we pursued our way;
Nor reached the village-churchyard till the sun
Travelling at steadier pace than ours, had risen
Above the summits of the highest hills,
And round our path darted oppressive beams.

   As chanced, the portals of the sacred Pile
Stood open; and we entered. On my frame,
140 At such transition from the fervid air,
A grateful coolness fell, that seemed to strike
The heart, in concert with that temperate awe
And natural reverence which the place inspired.
Not raised in nice proportions was the pile,
But large and massy; for duration built;
With pillars crowded, and the roof upheld

By naked rafters intricately crossed,
Like leafless underboughs, in some thick wood,
All withered by the depth of shade above.
150 Admonitory texts inscribed the walls,
Each, in its ornamental scroll, enclosed;
Each also crowned with wingèd heads – a pair
Of rudely-painted Cherubim. The floor
Of nave and aisle, in unpretending guise,
Was occupied by oaken benches ranged
In seemly rows; the chancel only showed
Some vain distinctions, marks of earthly state
By immemorial privilege allowed;
Though with the Encincture's special sanctity
160 But ill according. An heraldic shield,
Varying its tincture with the changeful light,
Imbued the altar-window; fixed aloft
A faded hatchment hung, and one by time
Yet undiscoloured. A capacious pew
Of sculptured oak stood here, with drapery lined;
And marble monuments were here displayed
Thronging the walls; and on the floor beneath
Sepulchral stones appeared, with emblems graven
And foot-worn epitaphs, and some with small
170 And shining effigies of brass inlaid.

The tribute by these various records claimed,
Duly we paid, each after each, and read
The ordinary chronicle of birth,
Office, alliance, and promotion – all
Ending in dust; of upright magistrates,
Grave doctors strenuous for the mother-church,
And uncorrupted senators, alike
To king and people true. A brazen plate,
Not easily deciphered, told of one
180 Whose course of earthly honour was begun
In quality of page among the train
Of the eighth Henry, when he crossed the seas
His royal state to show, and prove his strength

In tournament, upon the fields of France.
Another tablet registered the death,
And praised the gallant bearing, of a Knight
Tried in the sea-fights of the second Charles.
Near this brave Knight his Father lay entombed;
And, to the silent language giving voice,
190 I read, – how in his manhood's earlier day
He, 'mid the afflictions of intestine war
And rightful government subverted, found
One only solace – that he had espoused
A virtuous Lady tenderly beloved
For her benign perfections; and yet more
Endeared to him, for this, that, in her state
Of wedlock richly crowned with Heaven's regard,
She with a numerous issue filled his house,
Who throve, like plants, uninjured by the storm
200 That laid their country waste. No need to speak
Of less particular notices assigned
To Youth or Maiden gone before their time,
And Matrons and unwedded Sisters old;
Whose charity and goodness were rehearsed
In modest panegyric.
                              'These dim lines,
What would they tell?' said I, – but, from the task
Of puzzling out that faded narrative,
With whisper soft my venerable Friend
Called me; and, looking down the darksome aisle,
210 I saw the Tenant of the lonely vale
Standing apart; with curvèd arm reclined
On the baptismal font; his pallid face
Upturned, as if his mind were rapt, or lost
In some abstraction; – gracefully he stood,
The semblance bearing of a sculptured form
That leans upon a monumental urn
In peace, from morn to night, from year to year.

   Him from that posture did the Sexton rouse;
Who entered, humming carelessly a tune,

220 Continuation haply of the notes
That had beguiled the work from which he came,
With spade and mattock o'er his shoulder hung;
To be deposited, for future need,
In their appointed place. The pale Recluse
Withdrew; and straight we followed, – to a spot
Where sun and shade were intermixed; for there
A broak oak, stretching forth its leafy arms
From an adjoining pasture, overhung
Small space of that green churchyard with a light
230 And pleasant awning. On the moss-grown wall
My ancient Friend and I together took
Our seats; and thus the Solitary spake,
Standing before us: –
                              'Did you note the mien
Of that self-solaced, easy-hearted churl,
Death's hireling, who scoops out his neighbour's grave,
Or wraps an old acquaintance up in clay,
All unconcerned as he would bind a sheaf,
Or plant a tree? And did you hear his voice?
I was abruptly summoned by the sound
240 From some affecting images and thoughts,
Which then were silent; but crave utterance now.

'Much,' he continued, with dejected look,
'Much, yesterday, was said in glowing phrase
Of our sublime dependencies, and hopes
For future states of being; and the wings
Of speculation, joyfully outspread,
Hovered above our destiny on earth:
But stoop, and place the prospect of the soul
In sober contrast with reality,
250 And man's substantial life. If this mute earth
Of what it holds could speak, and every grave
Were as a volume, shut, yet capable
Of yielding its contents to eye and ear,
We should recoil, stricken with sorrow and shame,
To see disclosed, by such dread proof, how ill

That which is done accords with what is known
To reason, and by conscience is enjoined;
How idly, how perversely, life's whole course,
To this conclusion, deviates from the line,
260 Or of the end stops short, proposed to all
At her aspiring outset.
                Mark the babe
Not long accustomed to this breathing world;
One that hath barely learned to shape a smile,
Though yet irrational of soul, to grasp
With tiny finger – to let fall a tear;
And, as the heavy cloud of sleep dissolves,
To stretch his limbs, bemocking, as might seem,
The outward functions of intelligent man;
A grave proficient in amusive feats
270 Of puppetry, that from the lap declare
His expectations, and announce his claims
To that inheritance which millions rue
That they were ever born to! In due time
A day of solemn ceremonial comes;
When they, who for this Minor hold in trust
Rights that transcend the loftiest heritage
Of mere humanity, present their Charge,
For this occasion daintily adorned,
At the baptismal font. And when the pure
280 And consecrating element hath cleansed
The original stain, the child is there received
Into the second ark, Christ's church, with trust
That he, from wrath redeemed, therein shall float
Over the billows of this troublesome world
To the fair land of everlasting life.
Corrupt affections, covetous desires,
Are all renounced; high as the thought of man
Can carry virtue, virtue is professed;
A dedication made, a promise given
290 For due provision to control and guide,
And unremitting progress to ensure
In holiness and truth.'

'You cannot blame,'
Here interposing fervently I said,
'Rites which attest that Man by nature lies
Bedded for good and evil in a gulf
Fearfully low; nor will your judgement scorn
Those services, whereby attempt is made
To lift the creature toward that eminence
On which, now fallen, erewhile in majesty
300 He stood; or if not so, whose top serene
At least he feels 'tis given him to descry;
Not without aspirations, evermore
Returning, and injunctions from within
Doubt to cast off and weariness; in trust
That what the Soul perceives, if glory lost,
May be, through pains and persevering hope,
Recovered; or, if hitherto unknown,
Lies within reach, and one day shall be gained.'

'I blame them not,' he calmly answered – 'no;
310 The outward ritual and established forms
With which communities of men invest
These inward feelings, and the aspiring vows
To which the lips give public utterance
Are both a natural process; and by me
Shall pass uncensured; though the issue prove,
Bringing from age to age its own reproach,
Incongruous, impotent, and blank. – But, oh!
If to be weak is to be wretched – miserable,
As the lost Angel by a human voice
320 Hath mournfully pronounced, then, in my mind,
Far better not to move at all than move
By impulse sent from such illusive power, –
That finds and cannot fasten down; that grasps
And is rejoiced, and loses while it grasps;
That tempts, emboldens – for a time sustains,
And then betrays; accuses and inflicts
Remorseless punishment; and so retreads
The inevitable circle: better far

Than this, to graze the herb in thoughtless peace,
330   By foresight or remembrance, undisturbed!

'Philosophy! and thou more vaunted name
Religion! with thy statelier retinue,
Faith, Hope, and Charity – from the visible world
Choose for your emblems whatsoe'er ye find
Of safest guidance or of firmest trust –
The torch, the star, the anchor; nor except
The cross itself, at whose unconscious feet
The generations of mankind have knelt
Ruefully seized, and shedding bitter tears,
340   And through that conflict seeking rest – of you,
High-titled Powers, am I constrained to ask,
Here standing, with the unvoyageable sky
In faint reflection of infinitude
Stretched overhead, and at my pensive feet
A subterraneous magazine of bones,
In whose dark vaults my own shall soon be laid,
Where are your triumphs? your dominion where?
And in what age admitted and confirmed?
– Not for a happy land do I enquire,
350   Island or grove, that hides a blessèd few
Who, with obedience willing and sincere,
To your serene authorities conform;
But whom, I ask, of individual Souls,
Have ye withdrawn from passion's crooked ways,
Inspired, and thoroughly fortified? – If the heart
Could be inspected to its inmost folds
By sight undazzled with the glare of praise,
Who shall be named – in the resplendent line
Of sages, martyrs, confessors – the man
360   Whom the best might of faith, wherever fixed,
For one day's little compass, has preserved
From painful and discreditable shocks
Of contradiction, from some vague desire
Culpably cherished, or corrupt relapse
To some unsanctioned fear?'

'If this be so,
And Man,' said I, 'be in his noblest shape
Thus pitiably infirm; then, He who made,
And who shall judge the creature, will forgive.
– Yet, in its general tenor, your complaint
370 Is all too true; and surely not misplaced:
For, from this pregnant spot of ground, such thoughts
Rise to the notice of a serious mind
By natural exhalation. With the dead
In their repose, the living in their mirth,
Who can reflect, unmoved, upon the round
Of smooth and solemnized complacencies,
By which, on Christian lands, from age to age
Profession mocks performance? Earth is sick,
And Heaven is weary, of the hollow words
380 Which States and Kingdoms utter when they talk
Of truth and justice. Turn to private life
And social neighbourhood; look we to ourselves;
A light of duty shines on every day
For all; and yet how few are warmed or cheered!
How few who mingle with their fellow-men
And still remain self-governed, and apart,
Like this our honoured Friend; and thence acquire
Right to expect his vigorous decline,
That promises to the end a blest old age!'

390   'Yet,' with a smile of triumph thus exclaimed
The Solitary, 'in the life of man,
If to the poetry of common speech
Faith may be given, we see as in a glass
A true reflection of the circling year,
With all its seasons. Grant that Spring is there,
In spite of many a rough untoward blast,
Hopeful and promising with buds and flowers;
Yet where is glowing Summer's long rich day,
That *ought* to follow faithfully expressed?
400 And mellow Autumn, charged with bounteous fruit,
Where is she imaged? in what favoured clime

Her lavish pomp, and ripe magnificence?
– Yet, while the better part is missed, the worse
In man's autumnal season is set forth
With a resemblance not to be denied,
And that contents him; bowers that hear no more
The voice of gladness, less and less supply
Of outward sunshine and internal warmth;
And, with this change, sharp air and falling leaves,
410 Foretelling aged Winter's desolate sway.

    'How gay the habitations that bedeck
This fertile valley! Not a house but seems
To give assurance of content within;
Embosomed happiness, and placid love;
As if the sunshine of the day were met
With answering brightness in the hearts of all
Who walk this favoured ground. But chance-regards,
And notice forced upon incurious ears;
These, if these only, acting in despite
420 Of the encomiums by my Friend pronounced
On humble life, forbid the judging mind
To trust the smiling aspect of this fair
And noiseless commonwealth. The simple race
Of mountaineers (by nature's self removed
From foul temptations, and by constant care
Of a good shepherd tended, as themselves
Do tend their flocks) partake man's general lot
With little mitigation. They escape,
Perchance, the heavier woes of guilt; feel not
430 The tedium of fantastic idleness:
Yet life, as with the multitude, with them
Is fashioned like an ill-constructed tale;
That on the outset wastes its gay desires,
Its fair adventures, its enlivening hopes,
And pleasant interests – for the sequel leaving
Old things repeated with diminished grace;
And all the laboured novelties at best
Imperfect substitutes, whose use and power

Evince the want and weakness whence they spring.'

440   While in this serious mood we held discourse,
The reverend Pastor toward the churchyard gate
Approached; and, with a mild respectful air
Of native cordiality, our Friend
Advanced to greet him. With a gracious mien
Was he received, and mutual joy prevailed.
Awhile they stood in conference, and I guess
That he, who now upon the mossy wall
Sate by my side, had vanished, if a wish
Could have transferred him to the flying clouds,
450   Or the least penetrable hiding-place
In his own valley's rocky guardianship.
– For me, I looked upon the pair, well pleased:
Nature had framed them both, and both were marked
By circumstance, with intermixture fine
Of contrast and resemblance. To an oak
Hardy and grand, a weather-beaten oak,
Fresh in the strength and majesty of age,
One might be likened: flourishing appeared,
Though somewhat past the fulness of his prime,
460   The other – like a stately sycamore,
That spreads, in gentle pomp, its honied shade.

A general greeting was exchanged; and soon
The Pastor learned that his approach had given
A welcome interruption to discourse
Grave, and in truth too often sad. – 'Is Man
A child of hope? Do generations press
On generations, without progress made?
Halts the individual, ere his hairs be grey,
Perforce? Are we a creature in whom good
470   Preponderates, or evil? Doth the will
Acknowledge reason's law? A living power
Is virtue, or no better than a name,
Fleeting as health or beauty, and unsound?
So that the only substance which remains,

(For thus the tenor of complaint hath run)
Among so many shadows, are the pains
And penalties of miserable life,
Doomed to decay, and then expire in dust!
– Our cogitations this way have been drawn,
480 These are the points,' the Wanderer said, 'on which
Our inquest turns. – Accord, good Sir! the light
Of your experience to dispel this gloom:
By your persuasive wisdom shall the heart
That frets, or languishes, be stilled and cheered.'

'Our nature,' said the Priest, in mild reply,
'Angels may weigh and fathom: they perceive,
With undistempered and unclouded spirit,
The object as it is; but, for ourselves,
That speculative height *we* may not reach.
490 The good and evil are our own; and we
Are that which we would contemplate from far.
Knowledge, for us, is difficult to gain –
Is difficult to gain, and hard to keep –
As virtue's self; like virtue is beset
With snares; tried, tempted, subject to decay.
Love, admiration, fear, desire, and hate,
Blind were we without these: through these alone
Are capable to notice or discern
Or to record; we judge, but cannot be
500 Indifferent judges. 'Spite of proudest boast,
Reason, best reason, is to imperfect man
An effort only, and a noble aim;
A crown, an attribute of sovereign power,
Still to be courted – never to be won.
– Look forth, or each man dive into himself;
What sees he but a creature too perturbed;
That is transported to excess; that yearns,
Regrets, or trembles, wrongly, or too much;
Hopes rashly, in disgust as rash recoils;
510 Battens on spleen, or moulders in despair?
Thus comprehension fails, and truth is missed;

Thus darkness and delusion round our path
Spread, from disease, whose subtle injury lurks
Within the very faculty of sight.

'Yet for the general purposes of faith
In Providence, for solace and support,
We may not doubt that who can best subject
The will to reason's law, can strictliest live
And act in that obedience, he shall gain
520   The clearest apprehension of those truths,
Which unassisted reason's utmost power
Is too infirm to reach. But, waiving this,
And our regards confining within bounds
Of less exalted consciousness, through which
The very multitude are free to range,
We safely may affirm that human life
Is either fair and tempting, a soft scene
Grateful to sight, refreshing to the soul,
Or a forbidding tract of cheerless view;
530   Even as the same is looked at, or approached.
Thus, when in changeful April fields are white
With new-fallen snow, if from the sullen north
Your walk conduct you hither, ere the sun
Hath gained his noontide height, this churchyard, filled
With mounds transversely lying side by side
From east to west, before you will appear
An unillumined, blank, and dreary plain,
With more than wintry cheerlessness and gloom
Saddening the heart. Go forward, and look back;
540   Look, from the quarter whence the lord of light,
Of life, of love, and gladness doth dispense
His beams; which, unexcluded in their fall,
Upon the southern side of every grave
Have gently exercised a melting power;
Then will a vernal prospect greet your eye,
All fresh and beautiful, and green and bright,
Hopeful and cheerful: – vanished is the pall
That overspread and chilled the sacred turf,

Vanished or hidden; and the whole domain,
550 To some, too lightly minded, might appear
A meadow carpet for the dancing hours.
– This contrast, not unsuitable to life,
Is to that other state more apposite,
Death and its two-fold aspect! wintry – one,
Cold, sullen, blank, from hope and joy shut out;
The other, which the ray divine hath touched,
Replete with vivid promise, bright as spring.'

'We see, then, as we feel,' the Wanderer thus
With a complacent animation spake,
560 'And in your judgement, Sir! the mind's repose
On evidence is not to be ensured
By act of naked reason. Moral truth
Is no mechanic structure, built by rule;
And which, once built, retains a stedfast shape
And undisturbed proportions; but a thing
Subject, you deem, to vital accidents;
And, like the water-lily, lives and thrives,
Whose root is fixed in stable earth, whose head
Floats on the tossing waves. With joy sincere
570 I re-salute these sentiments confirmed
By your authority. But how acquire
The inward principle that gives effect
To outward argument; the passive will
Meek to admit; the active energy,
Strong and unbounded to embrace, and firm
To keep and cherish? how shall man unite
With self-forgetting tenderness of heart
An earth-despising dignity of soul?
Wise in that union, and without it blind!'

580   'The way,' said I, 'to court, if not obtain
The ingenuous mind, apt to be set aright;
This, in the lonely dell discoursing, you
Declared at large; and by what exercise

From visible nature, or the inner self
Power may be trained, and renovation brought
To those who need the gift. But, after all,
Is aught so certain as that man is doomed
To breathe beneath a vault of ignorance?
The natural roof of that dark house in which
590   His soul is pent! How little can be known –
This is the wise man's sigh; how far we err –
This is the good man's not unfrequent pang!
And they perhaps err least, the lowly class
Whom a benign necessity compels
To follow reason's least ambitious course;
Such do I mean who, unperplexed by doubt,
And unincited by a wish to look
Into high objects farther than they may,
Pace to and fro, from morn till eventide,
600   The narrow avenue of daily toil
For daily bread.'
                    'Yes,' buoyantly exclaimed
The pale Recluse – 'praise to the sturdy plough,
And patient spade; praise to the simple crook,
And ponderous loom – resounding while it holds
Body and mind in one captivity;
And let the light mechanic tool be hailed
With honour; which, encasing by the power
Of long companionship, the artist's hand,
Cuts off that hand, with all its world of nerves,
610   From a too busy commerce with the heart!
– Inglorious implements of craft and toil,
Both ye that shape and build, and ye that force,
By slow solicitation, earth to yield
Her annual bounty, sparingly dealt forth
With wise reluctance; you would I extol,
Not for gross good alone which ye produce,
But for the impertinent and ceaseless strife
Of proofs and reasons ye preclude – in those
Who to your dull society are born,
620   And with their humble birthright rest content.

       – Would I had ne'er renounced it!'

                                A slight flush
Of moral anger previously had tinged
The old Man's cheek; but, at this closing turn
Of self-reproach, it passed away. Said he,
'That which we feel we utter; as we think
So have we argued; reaping for our pains
No visible recompense. For our relief
You,' to the Pastor turning thus he spake,
'Have kindly interposed. May I entreat
630   Your further help? The mine of real life
Dig for us; and present us, in the shape
Of virgin ore, that gold which we, by pains
Fruitless as those of aëry alchemists,
Seek from the torturing crucible. There lies
Around us a domain where you have long
Watched both the outward course and inner heart:
Give us, for our abstractions, solid facts;
For our disputes, plain pictures. Say what man
He is who cultivates yon hanging field;
640   What qualities of mind she bears, who comes,
For morn and evening service, with her pail,
To that green pasture; place before our sight
The family who dwell within yon house
Fenced round with glittering laurel; or in that
Below, from which the curling smoke ascends.
Or rather, as we stand on holy earth,
And have the dead around us, take from them
Your instances; for they are both best known,
And by frail man most equitably judged.
650   Epitomize the life; pronounce, you can,
Authentic epitaphs on some of these
Who, from their lowly mansions hither brought,
Beneath this turf lie mouldering at our feet:
So, by your records, may our doubts be solved;
And so, not searching higher, we may learn
To prize the breath we share with human kind;
And look upon the dust of man with awe.'

The Priest replied – 'An office you impose
For which peculiar requisites are mine;
660   Yet much, I feel, is wanting – else the task
Would be most grateful. True indeed it is
That they whom death has hidden from our sight
Are worthiest of the mind's regard; with these
The future cannot contradict the past:
Mortality's last exercise and proof
Is undergone; the transit made that shows
The very Soul, revealed as she departs.
Yet, on your first suggestion, will I give,
Ere we descend into these silent vaults,
One picture from the living.
670   You behold,
High on the breast of yon dark mountain, dark
With stony barrenness, a shining speck
Bright as a sunbeam sleeping till a shower
Brush it away, or cloud pass over it;
And such it might be deemed – a sleeping sunbeam;
But 'tis a plot of cultivated ground,
Cut off, an island in the dusky waste;
And that attractive brightness is its own.
The lofty site, by nature framed to tempt
680   Amid a wilderness of rocks and stones
The tiller's hand, a hermit might have chosen,
For opportunity presented, thence
Far forth to send his wandering eye o'er land
And ocean, and look down upon the works,
The habitations, and the ways of men,
Himself unseen! But no tradition tells
That ever hermit dipped his maple dish
In the sweet spring that lurks 'mid yon green fields;
And no such visionary views belong
690   To those who occupy and till the ground,
High on that mountain where they long have dwelt
A wedded pair in childless solitude.
A house of stones collected on the spot,
By rude hands built, with rocky knolls in front,

Backed also by a ledge of rock, whose crest
Of birch-trees waves over the chimney top;
A rough abode – in colour, shape, and size,
Such as in unsafe times of border-war
Might have been wished for and contrived, to elude
700 The eye of roving plunderer – for their need
Suffices; and unshaken bears the assault
Of their most dreaded foe, the strong South-west
In anger blowing from the distant sea.
– Alone within her solitary hut;
There, or within the compass of her fields,
At any moment may the Dame be found,
True as the stock-dove to her shallow nest
And to the grove that holds it. She beguiles
By intermingled work of house and field
710 The summer's day, and winter's; with success
Not equal, but sufficient to maintain,
Even at the worst, a smooth stream of content,
Until the expected hour at which her Mate
From the far-distant quarry's vault returns;
And by his converse crowns a silent day
With evening cheerfulness. In powers of mind,
In scale of culture, few among my flock
Hold lower rank than this sequestered pair:
But true humility descends from heaven;
720 And that best gift of heaven hath fallen on them;
Abundant recompense for every want.
– Stoop from your height, ye proud, and copy these!
Who, in their noiseless dwelling-place, can hear
The voice of wisdom whispering scripture texts
For the mind's government, or temper's peace;
And recommending for their mutual need,
Forgiveness, patience, hope, and charity!'

'Much was I pleased,' the grey-haired Wanderer said,
'When to those shining fields our notice first
730 You turned; and yet more pleased have from your lips
Gathered this fair report of them who dwell

In that retirement; whither, by such course
Of evil hap and good as oft awaits
A tired way-faring man, once *I* was brought
While traversing alone yon mountain-pass.
Dark on my road the autumnal evening fell,
And night succeeded with unusual gloom,
So hazardous that feet and hands became
Guides better than mine eyes – until a light
740 High in the gloom appeared, too high, methought,
For human habitation; but I longed
To reach it, destitute of other hope.
I looked with steadiness as sailors look
On the north star, or watch-tower's distant lamp,
And saw the light – now fixed – and shifting now –
Not like a dancing meteor, but in line
Of never-varying motion, to and fro.
It is no night-fire of the naked hills,
Thought I – some friendly covert must be near.
750 With this persuasion thitherward my steps
I turn, and reach at last the guiding light;
Joy to myself! but to the heart of her
Who there was standing on the open hill,
(The same kind Matron whom your tongue hath praised)
Alarm and disappointment! The alarm
Ceased, when she learned through what mishap I came,
And by what help had gained those distant fields.
Drawn from her cottage, on that aëry height,
Bearing a lantern in her hand she stood,
760 Or paced the ground – to guide her Husband home,
By that unwearied signal, kenned afar;
An anxious duty! which the lofty site,
Traversed but by a few irregular paths,
Imposes, whensoe'er untoward chance
Detains him after his accustomed hour
Till night lies black upon the ground. "But come,
Come," said the Matron, "to our poor abode;
Those dark rocks hide it!" Entering, I beheld
A blazing fire – beside a cleanly hearth

770 Sate down; and to her office, with leave asked,
The Dame returned.
            Or ere that glowing pile
Of mountain turf required the builder's hand
Its wasted splendour to repair, the door
Opened, and she re-entered with glad looks,
Her Helpmate following. Hospitable fare,
Frank conversation, made the evening's treat:
Need a bewildered traveller wish for more?
But more was given; I studied as we sate
By the bright fire, the good Man's form, and face
780 Not less than beautiful; an open brow
Of undisturbed humanity; a cheek
Suffused with something of a feminine hue;
Eyes beaming courtesy and mild regard;
But, in the quicker turns of the discourse,
Expression slowly varying, that evinced
A tardy apprehension. From a fount
Lost, thought I, in the obscurities of time,
But honoured once, those features and that mien
May have descended, though I see them here.
790 In such a man, so gentle and subdued,
Withal so graceful in his gentleness,
A race illustrious for heroic deeds,
Humbled, but not degraded, may expire.
This pleasing fancy (cherished and upheld
By sundry recollections of such fall
From high to low, ascent from low to high,
As books record, and even the careless mind
Cannot but notice among men and things)
Went with me to the place of my repose.

800   'Roused by the crowing cock at dawn of day,
I yet had risen too late to interchange
A morning salutation with my Host,
Gone forth already to the far-off seat
Of his day's work. "Three dark mid-winter months
Pass," said the Matron, "and I never see,

Save when the sabbath brings its kind release,
My helpmate's face by light of day. He quits
His door in darkness, nor till dusk returns.
And, through Heaven's blessing, thus we gain the bread
810 For which we pray; and for the wants provide
Of sickness, accident, and helpless age.
Companions have I many; many friends,
Dependants, comforters – my wheel, my fire,
All day the house-clock ticking in mine ear,
The cackling hen, the tender chicken brood,
And the wild birds that gather round my porch.
This honest sheep-dog's countenance I read;
With him can talk; nor blush to waste a word
On creatures less intelligent and shrewd.
820 And if the blustering wind that drives the clouds
Care not for me, he lingers round my door,
And makes me pastime when our tempers suit; –
But, above all, my thoughts are my support,
My comfort: – would that they were oftener fixed
On what, for guidance in the way that leads
To heaven, I know, by my Redeemer taught."
The Matron ended – nor could I forbear
To exclaim – "O happy! yielding to the law
Of these privations, richer in the main! –
830 While thankless thousands are opprest and clogged
By ease and leisure; by the very wealth
And pride of opportunity made poor;
While tens of thousands falter in their path,
And sink, through utter want of cheering light;
For you the hours of labour do not flag;
For you each evening hath its shining star,
And every sabbath-day its golden sun." '

'Yes!' said the Solitary with a smile
That seemed to break from an expanding heart,
840 'The untutored bird may found, and so construct,
And with such soft materials line, her nest
Fixed in the centre of a prickly brake,

That the thorns wound her not; they only guard.
Powers not unjustly likened to those gifts
Of happy instinct which the woodland bird
Shares with her species, nature's grace sometimes
Upon the individual doth confer,
Among her higher creatures born and trained
To use of reason. And, I own that, tired
850   Of the ostentatious world – a swelling stage
With empty actions and vain passions stuffed,
And from the private struggles of mankind
Hoping far less than I could wish to hope,
Far less than once I trusted and believed –
I love to hear of those, who, not contending
Nor summoned to contend for virtue's prize,
Miss not the humbler good at which they aim,
Blest with a kindly faculty to blunt
The edge of adverse circumstance, and turn
860   Into their contraries the petty plagues
And hindrances with which they stand beset.
In early youth, among my native hills,
I knew a Scottish Peasant who possessed
A few small crofts of stone-encumbered ground;
Masses of every shape and size, that lay
Scattered about under the mouldering walls
Of a rough precipice; and some, apart,
In quarters unobnoxious to such chance,
As if the moon had showered them down in spite.
870   But he repined not. Though the plough was scared
By these obstructions, "round the shady stones
A fertilizing moisture," said the Swain,
"Gathers, and is preserved; and feeding dews
And damps, through all the droughty summer day
From out their substance issuing, maintain
Herbage that never fails: no grass springs up
So green, so fresh, so plentiful, as mine!"
But thinly sown these natures; rare, at least,
The mutual aptitude of seed and soil
880   That yields such kindly product. He, whose bed

Perhaps yon loose sods cover, the poor Pensioner
Brought yesterday from our sequestered dell
Here to lie down in lasting quiet, he,
If living now, could otherwise report
Of rustic loneliness: that grey-haired Orphan –
So call him, for humanity to him
No parent was – feelingly could have told,
In life, in death, what solitude can breed
Of selfishness, and cruelty, and vice;
890 Or, if it breed not, hath not power to cure.
– But your compliance, Sir! with our request
My words too long have hindered.'
                    Undeterred,
Perhaps incited rather, by these shocks,
In no ungracious opposition, given
To the confiding spirit of his own
Experienced faith, the reverend Pastor said,
Around him looking; 'Where shall I begin?
Who shall be first selected from my flock
Gathered together in their peaceful fold?'
900 He paused – and having lifted up his eyes
To the pure heaven, he cast them down again
Upon the earth beneath his feet; and spake: –

  'To a mysteriously-united pair
This place is consecrate; to Death and Life,
And to the best affections that proceed
From their conjunction; consecrate to faith
In Him who bled for man upon the cross;
Hallowed to revelation; and no less
To reason's mandates; and the hopes divine
910 Of pure imagination; – above all,
To charity, and love, that have provided,
Within these precincts, a capacious bed
And receptacle, open to the good
And evil, to the just and the unjust;
In which they find an equal resting-place:
Even as the multitude of kindred brooks

And streams, whose murmur fills this hollow vale,
Whether their course be turbulent or smooth,
Their waters clear or sullied, all are lost
920 Within the bosom of yon crystal Lake,
And end their journey in the same repose!

'And blest are they who sleep; and we that know,
While in a spot like this we breathe and walk,
That all beneath us by the wings are covered
Of motherly humanity, outspread
And gathering all within their tender shade,
Though loth and slow to come! A battlefield,
In stillness left when slaughter is no more,
With this compared, makes a strange spectacle!
930 A dismal prospect yields the wild shore strewn
With wrecks, and trod by feet of young and old
Wandering about in miserable search
Of friends or kindred, whom the angry sea
Restores not to their prayer! Ah! who would think
That all the scattered subjects which compose
Earth's melancholy vision through the space
Of all her climes – these wretched, these depraved,
To virtue lost, insensible of peace,
From the delights of charity cut off,
940 To pity dead, the oppressor and the opprest;
Tyrants who utter the destroying word,
And slaves who will consent to be destroyed –
Were of one species with the sheltered few,
Who, with a dutiful and tender hand,
Lodged, in a dear appropriated spot,
This file of infants; some that never breathed
The vital air; others, which, though allowed
That privilege, did yet expire too soon,
Or with too brief a warning, to admit
950 Administration of the holy rite
That lovingly consigns the babe to the arms
Of Jesus, and his everlasting care.
These that in trembling hope are laid apart;

And the besprinkled nursling, unrequired
Till he begins to smile upon the breast
That feeds him; and the tottering little-one
Taken from air and sunshine when the rose
Of infancy first blooms upon his cheek;
The thinking, thoughtless, school-boy; the bold youth
960 Of soul impetuous, and the bashful maid
Smitten while all the promises of life
Are opening round her; those of middle age,
Cast down while confident in strength they stand,
Like pillars fixed more firmly, as might seem,
And more secure, by very weight of all
That, for support, rests on them; the decayed
And burdensome; and lastly, that poor few
Whose light of reason is with age extinct;
The hopeful and the hopeless, first and last,
970 The earliest summoned and the longest spared –
Are here deposited, with tribute paid
Various, but unto each some tribute paid;
As if, amid these peaceful hills and groves,
Society were touched with kind concern,
And gentle "Nature grieved, that one should die;"
Or, if the change demanded no regret,
Observed the liberating stroke – and blessed.

'And whence that tribute? wherefore these regards?
Not from the naked *Heart* alone of Man
980 (Though claiming high distinction upon earth
As the sole spring and fountain-head of tears,
His own peculiar utterance for distress
Or gladness) – No,' the philosophic Priest
Continued, ' 'tis not in the vital seat
Of feeling to produce them, without aid
From the pure soul, the soul sublime and pure;
With her two faculties of eye and ear,
The one by which a creature, whom his sins
Have rendered prone, can upward look to heaven;
990 The other that empowers him to perceive

The voice of Deity, on height and plain,
Whispering those truths in stillness, which the WORD,
To the four quarters of the winds, proclaims.
Not without such assistance could the use
Of these benign observances prevail:
Thus are they born, thus fostered, thus maintained;
And by the care prospective of our wise
Forefathers, who, to guard against the shocks,
The fluctuation and decay of things,
1000 Embodied and established these high truths
In solemn institutions: – men convinced
That life is love and immortality,
The being one, and one the element.
There lies the channel, and original bed,
From the beginning, hollowed out and scooped
For Man's affections – else betrayed and lost,
And swallowed up 'mid deserts infinite!
This is the genuine course, the aim, and end
Of prescient reason; all conclusions else
1010 Are abject, vain, presumptuous, and perverse.
The faith partaking of those holy times,
Life, I repeat, is energy of love
Divine or human; exercised in pain,
In strife, in tribulation; and ordained,
If so approved and sanctified, to pass,
Through shades and silent rest, to endless joy.'

BOOK SIXTH
THE CHURCHYARD AMONG THE MOUNTAINS

Argument

Poet's Address to the State and Church of England. – The
Pastor not inferior to the ancient Worthies of the Church. – He
begins his Narratives with an instance of unrequited Love. –
Anguish of mind subdued, and how. – The lonely Miner. – An
instance of perseverance. – Which leads by contrast to an
example of abused talents, irresolution, and weakness. – Solitary,
applying this covertly to his own case, asks for an instance of

some Stranger, whose dispositions may have led him to end his days here. – Pastor, in answer, gives an account of the harmonizing influence of Solitude upon two men of opposite principles, who had encountered agitations in public life. – The rule by which Peace may be obtained expressed, and where. – Solitary hints at an overpowering Fatality. – Answer of the Pastor. – What subjects he will exclude from his Narratives. – Conversation upon this. – Instance of an unamiable character, a Female, and why given. – Contrasted with this, a meek sufferer, from unguarded and betrayed love. – Instance of heavier guilt, and its consequences to the Offender. – With this instance of a Marriage Contract broken is contrasted one of a Widower, evidencing his faithful affection towards his deceased wife by his care of their female Children.

Hail to the crown by Freedom shaped – to gird
An English Sovereign's brow! and to the throne
Whereon he sits! Whose deep foundations lie
In veneration and the people's love;
Whose steps are equity, whose seat is law.
– Hail to the State of England! And conjoin
With this a salutation as devout,
Made to the spiritual fabric of her Church;
Founded in truth; by blood of Martyrdom
10 Cemented; by the hands of Wisdom reared
In beauty of holiness, with ordered pomp,
Decent and unreproved. The voice, that greets
The majesty of both, shall pray for both;
That, mutually protected and sustained,
They may endure long as the sea surrounds
This favoured Land, or sunshine warms her soil.

     And O, ye swelling hills, and spacious plains!
Besprent from shore to shore with steeple-towers,
And spires whose 'silent finger points to heaven;'
20 Nor wanting, at wide intervals, the bulk
Of ancient minster lifted above the cloud
Of the dense air, which town or city breeds
To intercept the sun's glad beams – may ne'er
That true succession fail of English hearts,

Who, with ancestral feeling, can perceive
What in those holy structures ye possess
Of ornamental interest, and the charm
Of pious sentiment diffused afar,
And human charity, and social love.
30 – Thus never shall the indignities of time
Approach their reverend graces, unopposed;
Nor shall the elements be free to hurt
Their fair proportions; nor the blinder rage
Of bigot zeal madly to overturn;
And, if the desolating hand of war
Spare them, they shall continue to bestow,
Upon the thronged abodes of busy men
(Depraved, and ever prone to fill the mind
Exclusively with transitory things)
40 An air and mien of dignified pursuit;
Of sweet civility, on rustic wilds.

The Poet, fostering for his native land
Such hope, entreats that servants may abound
Of those pure altars worthy; ministers
Detached from pleasure, to the love of gain
Superior, insusceptible of pride,
And by ambitious longings undisturbed;
Men, whose delight is where their duty leads
Or fixes them; whose least distinguished day
50 Shines with some portion of that heavenly lustre
Which makes the sabbath lovely in the sight
Of blessèd angels, pitying human cares.
– And, as on earth it is the doom of truth
To be perpetually attacked by foes
Open or covert, be that priesthood still,
For her defence, replenished with a band
Of strenuous champions, in scholastic arts
Thoroughly disciplined; nor (if in course
Of the revolving world's disturbances
60 Cause should recur, which righteous Heaven avert!
To meet such trial) from their spiritual sires

Degenerate; who, constrained to wield the sword
Of disputation, shrunk not, though assailed
With hostile din, and combating in sight
Of angry umpires, partial and unjust;
And did, thereafter, bathe their hands in fire,
So to declare the conscience satisfied:
Nor for their bodies would accept release;
But, blessing God and praising him, bequeathed
70 With their last breath, from out the smouldering flame,
The faith which they by diligence had earned,
Or, through illuminating grace, received,
For their dear countrymen, and all mankind.
O high example, constancy divine!

Even such a Man (inheriting the zeal
And from the sanctity of elder times
Not deviating, – a priest, the like of whom,
If multiplied, and in their stations set,
Would o'er the bosom of a joyful land
80 Spread true religion and her genuine fruits)
Before me stood that day; on holy ground
Fraught with the relics of mortality,
Exalting tender themes, by just degrees
To lofty raised; and to the highest, last;
The head and mighty paramount of truths, –
Immortal life, in never-fading worlds,
For mortal creatures, conquered and secured.

That basis laid, those principles of faith
Announced, as a preparatory act
90 Of reverence done to the spirit of the place,
The Pastor cast his eyes upon the ground;
Not, as before, like one oppressed with awe,
But with a mild and social cheerfulness;
Then to the Solitary turned, and spake.

'At morn or eve, in your retired domain,
Perchance you not unfrequently have marked

A Visitor – in quest of herbs and flowers;
Too delicate employ, as would appear,
For one, who, though of drooping mien, had yet
100 From nature's kindliness received a frame
Robust as ever rural labour bred.'

   The Solitary answered: 'Such a Form
Full well I recollect. We often crossed
Each other's path; but, as the Intruder seemed
Fondly to prize the silence which he kept,
And I as willingly did cherish mine,
We met, and passed, like shadows. I have heard,
From my good Host, that being crazed in brain
By unrequited love, he scaled the rocks,
110 Dived into caves, and pierced the matted woods,
In hope to find some virtuous herb of power
To cure his malady!'
               The Vicar smiled, –
'Alas! before tomorrow's sun goes down
His habitation will be here: for him
That open grave is destined.'
                   'Died he then
Of pain and grief?' the Solitary asked,
'Do not believe it; never could that be!'

   'He loved,' the Vicar answered, 'deeply loved,
Loved fondly, truly, fervently; and dared
120 At length to tell his love, but sued in vain;
Rejected, yea repelled; and, if with scorn
Upon the haughty maiden's brow, 'tis but
A high-prized plume which female Beauty wears
In wantonness of conquest, or puts on
To cheat the world, or from herself to hide
Humiliation, when no longer free.
That he could brook, and glory in; – but when
The tidings came that she whom he had wooed
Was wedded to another, and his heart
130 Was forced to rend away its only hope;

Then, Pity could have scarcely found on earth
An object worthier of regard than he,
In the transition of that bitter hour!
Lost was she, lost; nor could the Sufferer say
That in the act of preference he had been
Unjustly dealt with; but the Maid was gone!
Had vanished from his prospects and desires;
Not by translation to the heavenly choir
Who have put off their mortal spoils – ah no!
140 She lives another's wishes to complete, –
"Joy be their lot, and happiness," he cried,
"His lot and hers, as misery must be mine!"

'Such was that strong concussion; but the Man,
Who trembled, trunk and limbs, like some huge oak
By a fierce tempest shaken, soon resumed
The stedfast quiet natural to a mind
Of composition gentle and sedate,
And, in its movements, circumspect and slow.
To books, and to the long-forsaken desk,
150 O'er which enchained by science he had loved
To bend, he stoutly re-addressed himself,
Resolved to quell his pain, and search for truth
With keener appetite (if that might be)
And closer industry. Of what ensued
Within the heart no outward sign appeared
Till a betraying sickliness was seen
To tinge his cheek; and through his frame it crept
With slow mutation unconcealable;
Such universal change as autumn makes
160 In the fair body of a leafy grove
Discoloured, then divested.
                                        'Tis affirmed
By poets skilled in nature's secret ways
That Love will not submit to be controlled
By mastery: – and the good Man lacked not friends
Who strove to instil this truth into his mind,
A mind in all heart-mysteries unversed.

"Go to the hills," said one, "remit a while
This baneful diligence: – at early morn
Court the fresh air, explore the heaths and woods;
170　And, leaving it to others to foretell,
By calculations sage, the ebb and flow
Of tides, and when the moon will be eclipsed,
Do you, for your own benefit, construct
A calendar of flowers, plucked as they blow
Where health abides, and cheerfulness, and peace."
The attempt was made; – 'tis needless to report
How hopelessly; but innocence is strong,
And an entire simplicity of mind
A thing most sacred in the eye of Heaven;
180　That opens, for such sufferers, relief
Within the soul, fountains of grace divine;
And doth commend their weakness and disease
To Nature's care, assisted in her office
By all the elements that round her wait
To generate, to preserve, and to restore;
And by her beautiful array of forms
Shedding sweet influence from above; or pure
Delight exhaling from the ground they tread.'

'Impute it not to impatience, if,' exclaimed
190　The Wanderer, 'I infer that he was healed
By perserverance in the course prescribed.'

'You do not err: the powers, that had been lost
By slow degrees, were gradually regained;
The fluttering nerves composed; the beating heart
In rest established; and the jarring thoughts
To harmony restored. – But yon dark mould
Will cover him, in the fulness of his strength,
Hastily smitten by a fever's force;
Yet not with stroke so sudden as refused
200　Time to look back with tenderness on her
Whom he had loved in passion; and to send
Some farewell words – with one, but one, request;

That, from his dying hand, she would accept
Of his possessions that which most he prized;
A book, upon whose leaves some chosen plants,
By his own hand disposed with nicest care,
In undecaying beauty were preserved;
Mute register, to him, of time and place,
And various fluctuations in the breast;
210   To her, a monument of faithful love
Conquered, and in tranquillity retained!

    'Close to his destined habitation, lies
One who achieved a humbler victory,
Though marvellous in its kind. A place there is
High in these mountains, that allured a band
Of keen adventurers to unite their pains
In search of precious ore: they tried, were foiled –
And all desisted, all, save him alone.
He, taking counsel of his own clear thoughts,
220   And trusting only to his own weak hands,
Urged unremittingly the stubborn work,
Unseconded, uncountenanced; then, as time
Passed on, while still his lonely efforts found
No recompense, derided; and at length,
By many pitied, as insane of mind;
By others dreaded as the luckless thrall
Of subterranean Spirits feeding hope
By various mockery of sight and sound;
Hope after hope, encouraged and destroyed.
230   – But when the lord of seasons had matured
The fruits of earth through space of twice ten years,
The mountain's entrails offered to his view
And trembling grasp the long-deferred reward.
Not with more transport did Columbus greet
A world, his rich discovery! But our Swain,
A very hero till his point was gained,
Proved all unable to support the weight
Of prosperous fortune. On the fields he looked
With an unsettled liberty of thought,

240 Wishes and endless schemes; by daylight walked
Giddy and restless; ever and anon
Quaffed in his gratitude immoderate cups;
And truly might be said to die of joy!
He vanished; but conspicuous to this day
The path remains that linked his cottage-door
To the mine's mouth; a long and slanting track,
Upon the rugged mountain's stony side,
Worn by his daily visits to and from
The darksome centre of a constant hope.
250 This vestige, neither force of beating rain,
Nor the vicissitudes of frost and thaw
Shall cause to fade, till ages pass away;
And it is named, in memory of the event,
The PATH OF PERSEVERANCE.'
                              'Thou from whom
Man has his strength,' exclaimed the Wanderer, 'oh!
Do Thou direct it! To the virtuous grant
The penetrative eye which can perceive
In this blind world the guiding vein of hope;
That, like this Labourer, such may dig their way,
260 "Unshaken, unseduced, unterrified;"
Grant to the wise *his* firmness of resolve!'

'That prayer were not superfluous,' said the Priest,
'Amid the noblest relics, proudest dust,
That Westminster, for Britain's glory, holds
Within the bosom of her awful pile,
Ambitiously collected. Yet the sigh,
Which wafts that prayer to heaven, is due to all,
Wherever laid, who living fell below
Their virtue's humbler mark; a sigh of *pain*
270 If to the opposite extreme they sank.
How would you pity her who yonder rests;
Him, farther off; the pair, who here are laid;
But, above all, that mixture of earth's mould
Whom sight of this green hillock to my mind
Recalls!

He lived not till his locks were nipped
By seasonable frost of age; nor died
Before his temples, prematurely forced
To mix the manly brown with silver grey,
Gave obvious instance of the sad effect
280 Produced, when thoughtless Folly hath usurped
The natural crown that sage Experience wears.
Gay, volatile, ingenious, quick to learn,
And prompt to exhibit all that he possessed
Or could perform; a zealous actor, hired
Into the troop of mirth, a soldier, sworn
Into the lists of giddy enterprise –
Such was he; yet, as if within his frame
Two several souls alternately had lodged,
Two sets of manners could the Youth put on;
290 And, fraught with antics as the Indian bird
That writhes and chatters in her wiry cage,
Was graceful, when it pleased him, smooth and still
As the mute swan that floats adown the stream,
Or, on the waters of the unruffled lake,
Anchors her placid beauty. Not a leaf,
That flutters on the bough, lighter than he;
And not a flower, that droops in the green shade,
More winningly reserved! If ye enquire
How such consummate elegance was bred
300 Amid these wilds, this answer may suffice;
'Twas Nature's will; who sometimes undertakes,
For the reproof of human vanity,
Art to outstrip in her peculiar walk.
Hence, for this Favourite – lavishly endowed
With personal gifts, and bright instinctive wit,
While both, embellishing each other, stood
Yet farther recommended by the charm
Of fine demeanour, and by dance and song,
And skill in letters – every fancy shaped
310 Fair expectations; nor, when to the world's
Capacious field forth went the Adventurer, there
Were he and his attainments overlooked,

Or scantily rewarded; but all hopes,
Cherished for him, he suffered to depart,
Like blighted buds; or clouds that mimicked land
Before the sailor's eye; or diamond drops
That sparkling decked the morning grass; or aught
That *was* attractive, and hath ceased to be!

'Yet, when this Prodigal returned, the rites
320   Of joyful greeting were on him bestowed,
Who, by humiliation undeterred,
Sought for his weariness a place of rest
Within his Father's gates. – Whence came he? – clothed
In tattered garb, from hovels where abides
Necessity, the stationary host
Of vagrant poverty; from rifted barns
Where no one dwells but the wide-staring owl
And the owl's prey; from these bare haunts, to which
He had descended from the proud saloon,
330   He came, the ghost of beauty and of health,
The wreck of gaiety! But soon revived
In strength, in power refitted, he renewed
His suit to Fortune; and she smiled again
Upon a fickle Ingrate. Thrice he rose,
Thrice sank as willingly. For he – whose nerves
Were used to thrill with pleasure, while his voice
Softly accompanied the tuneful harp,
By the nice finger of fair ladies touched
In glittering halls – was able to derive
340   No less enjoyment from an abject choice.
Who happier for the moment – who more blithe
Than this fallen Spirit? in those dreary holds
His talents lending to exalt the freaks
Of merry-making beggars, – now, provoked
To laughter multiplied in louder peals
By his malicious wit; then, all enchained
With mute astonishment, themselves to see
In their own arts outdone, their fame eclipsed,
As by the very presence of the Fiend

350   Who dictates and inspires illusive feats,
      For knavish purposes! The city, too,
      (With shame I speak it) to her guilty bowers
      Allured him, sunk so low in self-respect
      As there to linger, there to eat his bread,
      Hired minstrel of voluptuous blandishment;
      Charming the air with skill of hand or voice,
      Listen who would, be wrought upon who might,
      Sincerely wretched hearts, or falsely gay.
      – Such the too frequent tenor of his boast
360   In ears that relished the report; – but all
      Was from his Parents happily concealed;
      Who saw enough for blame and pitying love.
      They also were permitted to receive
      His last, repentant breath; and closed his eyes,
      No more to open on that irksome world
      Where he had long existed in the state
      Of a young fowl beneath one mother hatched,
      Though from another sprung, different in kind:
      Where he had lived, and could not cease to live,
370   Distracted in propensity; content
      With neither element of good or ill;
      And yet in both rejoicing; man unblest;
      Of contradictions infinite the slave,
      Till his deliverance, when Mercy made him
      One with himself, and one with them that sleep.'

      ''Tis strange,' observed the Solitary, 'strange
      It seems, and scarcely less than pitiful,
      That in a land where charity provides
      For all that can no longer feed themselves,
380   A man like this should choose to bring his shame
      To the parental door; and with his sighs
      Infect the air which he had freely breathed
      In happy infancy. He could not pine
      Through lack of converse; no – he must have found
      Abundant exercise for thought and speech,
      In his dividual being, self-reviewed,

Self-catechized, self-punished. – Some there are
Who, drawing near their final home, and much
And daily longing that the same were reached,
390   Would rather shun than seek the fellowship
Of kindred mould. – Such haply here are laid?'

        'Yes,' said the Priest, 'the Genius of our hills –
Who seems, by these stupendous barriers cast
Round his domain, desirous not alone
To keep his own, but also to exclude
All other progeny – doth sometimes lure,
Even by his studied depth of privacy,
The unhappy alien hoping to obtain
Concealment, or seduced by wish to find,
400   In place from outward molestation free,
Helps to internal ease. Of many such
Could I discourse; but as their stay was brief,
So their departure only left behind
Fancies, and loose conjectures. Other trace
Survives, for worthy mention, of a pair
Who, from the pressure of their several fates,
Meeting as strangers, in a petty town
Whose blue roofs ornament a distant reach
Of this far-winding vale, remained as friends
410   True to their choice; and gave their bones in trust
To this loved cemetery, here to lodge
With unescutcheoned privacy interred
Far from the family vault. – A Chieftain one
By right of birth; within whose spotless breast
The fire of ancient Caledonia burned:
He, with the foremost whose impatience hailed
The Stuart, landing to resume, by force
Of arms, the crown which bigotry had lost,
Aroused his clan; and, fighting at their head,
420   With his brave sword endeavoured to prevent
Culloden's fatal overthrow. Escaped
From that disastrous rout, to foreign shores
He fled; and when the lenient hand of time

Those troubles had appeased, he sought and gained,
For his obscured condition, an obscure
Retreat, within this nook of English ground.

'The other, born in Britain's southern tract,
Had fixed his milder loyalty, and placed
His gentler sentiments of love and hate,
430   There, where *they* placed them who in conscience prized
The new succession, as a line of kings
Whose oath had virtue to protect the land
Against the dire assaults of papacy
And arbitrary rule. But launch thy bark
On the distempered flood of public life,
And cause for most rare triumph will be thine
If, spite of keenest eye and steadiest hand,
The stream, that bears thee forward, prove not, soon
Or late, a perilous master. He – who oft,
440   Beneath the battlements and stately trees
That round his mansion cast a sober gloom,
Had moralized on this, and other truths
Of kindred import, pleased and satisfied –
Was forced to vent his wisdom with a sigh
Heaved from the heart in fortune's bitterness,
When he had crushed a plentiful estate
By ruinous contest, to obtain a seat
In Britain's senate. Fruitless was the attempt:
And while the uproar of that desperate strife
450   Continued yet to vibrate on his ear,
The vanquished Whig, under a borrowed name,
(For the mere sound and echo of his own
Haunted him with sensations of disgust
That he was glad to lose) slunk from the world
To the deep shade of those untravelled Wilds;
In which the Scottish Laird had long possessed
An undisturbed abode. Here, then, they met,
Two doughty champions; flaming Jacobite
And sullen Hanoverian! You might think
460   That losses and vexations, less severe

Than those which they had severally sustained,
Would have inclined each to abate his zeal
For his ungrateful cause; no, – I have heard
My reverend Father tell that, 'mid the calm
Of that small town encountering thus, they filled,
Daily, its bowling-green with harmless strife;
Plagued with uncharitable thoughts the church;
And vexed the market-place. But in the breasts
Of these opponents gradually was wrought,
470   With little change of general sentiment,
Such leaning towards each other, that their days
By choice were spent in constant fellowship;
And if, at times, they fretted with the yoke,
Those very bickerings made them love it more.

'A favourite boundary to their lengthened walks
This Churchyard was. And, whether they had come
Treading their path in sympathy and linked
In social converse, or by some short space
Discreetly parted to preserve the peace,
480   One spirit seldom failed to extend its sway
Over both minds, when they awhile had marked
The visible quiet of this holy ground,
And breathed its soothing air; – the spirit of hope
And saintly magnanimity; that – spurning
The field of selfish difference and dispute,
And every care which transitory things,
Earth and the kingdoms of the earth, create –
Doth, by a rapture of forgetfulness,
Preclude forgiveness, from the praise debarred,
490   Which else the Christian virtue might have claimed.

'There live who yet remember here to have seen
Their courtly figures, seated on the stump
Of an old yew, their favourite resting-place.
But as the remnant of the long-lived tree
Was disappearing by a swift decay,
They, with joint care, determined to erect,

Upon its site, a dial, that might stand
For public use preserved, and thus survive
As their own private monument: for this
500 Was the particular spot, in which they wished
(And Heaven was pleased to accomplish the desire)
That, undivided, their remains should lie.
So, where the mouldered tree had stood, was raised
Yon structure, framing, with the ascent of steps
That to the decorated pillar lead,
A work of art more sumptuous than might seem
To suit this place; yet built in no proud scorn
Of rustic homeliness; they only aimed
To ensure for it respectful guardianship.
510 Around the margin of the plate, whereon
The shadow falls to note the stealthy hours,
Winds an inscriptive legend.' – At these words
Thither we turned; and gathered, as we read,
The appropriate sense, in Latin numbers couched:
'*Time flies; it is his melancholy task*
To bring, and bear away, delusive hopes,
And re-produce the troubles he destroys.
But, while his blindness thus is occupied,
Discerning Mortal! do thou serve the will
520 *Of Time's eternal Master, and that peace,*
Which the world wants, shall be for thee confirmed!'

'Smooth verse, inspired by no unlettered Muse,'
Exclaimed the Sceptic, 'and the strain of thought
Accords with nature's language; – the soft voice
Of yon white torrent falling down the rocks
Speaks, less distinctly, to the same effect.
If, then, their blended influence be not lost
Upon our hearts, not wholly lost, I grant,
Even upon mine, the more we are required
530 To feel for those among our fellow-men,
Who, offering no obeisance to the world,
Are yet made desperate by "too quick a sense
Of constant infelicity," cut off

From peace like exiles on some barren rock,
Their life's appointed prison; not more free
Than sentinels, between two armies, set,
With nothing better, in the chill night air,
Than their own thoughts to comfort them. Say why
That ancient story of Prometheus chained
540   To the bare rock, on frozen Caucasus;
The vulture, the inexhaustible repast
Drawn from his vitals? Say what meant the woes
By Tantalus entailed upon his race,
And the dark sorrows of the line of Thebes?
Fictions in form, but in their substance truths,
Tremendous truths! familiar to the men
Of long-past times, nor obsolete in ours.
Exchange the shepherd's frock of native grey
For robes with regal purple tinged; convert
550   The crook into a sceptre; give the pomp
Of circumstance; and here the tragic Muse
Shall find apt subjects for her highest art.
Amid the groves, under the shadowy hills,
The generations are prepared; the pangs,
The internal pangs, are ready; the dread strife
Of poor humanity's afflicted will
Struggling in vain with ruthless destiny.'

'Though,' said the Priest in answer, 'these be terms
Which a divine philosophy rejects,
560   We, whose established and unfailing trust
Is in controlling Providence, admit
That, through all stations, human life abounds
With mysteries; – for, if Faith were left untried,
How could the might, that lurks within her, then
Be shown? her glorious excellence – that ranks
Among the first of Powers and Virtues – proved?
Our system is not fashioned to preclude
That sympathy which you for others ask;
And I could tell, not travelling for my theme
570   Beyond these humble graves, of grievous crimes

And strange disasters; but I pass them by,
Loth to disturb what Heaven hath hushed in peace.
– Still less, far less, am I inclined to treat
Of Man degraded in his Maker's sight
By the deformities of brutish vice:
For, in such portraits, though a vulgar face
And a coarse outside of repulsive life
And unaffecting manners might at once
Be recognized by all –' 'Ah! do not think,'
580 The Wanderer somewhat eagerly exclaimed,
'Wish could be ours that you, for such poor gain,
(Gain shall I call it? – gain of what? – for whom?)
Should breathe a word tending to violate
Your own pure spirit. Not a step we look for
In slight of that forbearance and reserve
Which common human-heartedness inspires,
And mortal ignorance and frailty claim,
Upon this sacred ground, if nowhere else.'

'True,' said the Solitary, 'be it far
590 From us to infringe the laws of charity.
Let judgement here in mercy be pronounced;
This, self-respecting Nature prompts, and this
Wisdom enjoins; but if the thing we seek
Be genuine knowledge, bear we then in mind
How, from his lofty throne, the sun can fling
Colours as bright on exhalations bred
By weedy pool or pestilential swamp,
As by the rivulet sparkling where it runs,
Or the pellucid lake.'
                              'Small risk,' said I,
600 'Of such illusion do we here incur;
Temptation here is none to exceed the truth;
No evidence appears that they who rest
Within this ground, were covetous of praise,
Or of remembrance even, deserved or not.
Green is the Churchyard, beautiful and green,
Ridge rising gently by the side of ridge,

A heaving surface, almost wholly free
From interruption of sepulchral stones,
And mantled o'er with aboriginal turf
610 And everlasting flowers. These Dalesmen trust
The lingering gleam of their departed lives
To oral record, and the silent heart;
Depositories faithful and more kind
Than fondest epitaph: for, if those fail,
What boots the sculptured tomb? And who can blame,
Who rather would not envy, men that feel
This mutual confidence; if, from such source,
The practise flow, – if thence, or from a deep
And general humility in death?
620 Nor should I much condemn it, if it spring
From disregard of time's destructive power,
As only capable to prey on things
Of earth, and human nature's mortal part.

'Yet – in less simple districts, where we see
Stone lift its forehead emulous of stone
In courting notice; and the ground all paved
With commendations of departed worth;
Reading, where'er we turn, of innocent lives,
Of each domestic charity fulfilled,
630 And sufferings meekly borne – I, for my part,
Though with the silence pleased that here prevails,
Among those fair recitals also range,
Soothed by the natural spirit which they breathe.
And, in the centre of a world whose soil
Is rank with all unkindness, compassed round
With such memorials, I have sometimes felt,
It was no momentary happiness
To have *one* Enclosure where the voice that speaks
In envy or detraction is not heard;
640 Which malice may not enter; where the traces
Of evil inclinations are unknown;
Where love and pity tenderly unite
With resignation; and no jarring tone

Intrudes, the peaceful concert to disturb
Of amity and gratitude.'
                              'Thus sanctioned,'
The Pastor said, 'I willingly confine
My narratives to subjects that excite
Feelings with these accordant; love, esteem,
And admiration; lifting up a veil,
650　A sunbeam introducing among hearts
Retired and covert; so that ye shall have
Clear images before your gladdened eyes
Of nature's unambitious underwood,
And flowers that prosper in the shade. And when
I speak of such among my flock as swerved
Or fell, those only shall be singled out
Upon whose lapse, or error, something more
Than brotherly forgiveness may attend;
To such will we restrict our notice, else
Better my tongue were mute.
660　 And yet there are,
I feel, good reasons why we should not leave
Wholly untraced a more forbidding way.
For, strength to persevere and to support,
And energy to conquer and repel –
These elements of virtue, that declare
The native grandeur of the human soul –
Are oft-times not unprofitably shown
In the perverseness of a selfish course:
Truth every day exemplified, no less
670　In the grey cottage by the murmuring stream
Than in fantastic conqueror's roving camp,
Or 'mid the factious senate unappalled
Whoe'er may sink, or rise – to sink again,
As merciless proscription ebbs and flows.

　'There,' said the Vicar, pointing as he spake,
'A woman rests in peace; surpassed by few
In power of mind, and eloquent discourse.
Tall was her stature; her complexion dark

And saturnine; her head not raised to hold
680 Converse with heaven, nor yet deprest towards earth,
But in projection carried, as she walked
For ever musing. Sunken were her eyes;
Wrinkled and furrowed with habitual thought
Was her broad forehead; like the brow of one
Whose visual nerve shrinks from a painful glare
Of overpowering light. – While yet a child,
She, 'mid the humble flowerets of the vale,
Towered like the imperial thistle, not unfurnished
With its appropriate grace, yet rather seeking
690 To be admired, than coveted and loved.
Even at that age she ruled, a sovereign queen,
Over her comrades; else their simple sports,
Wanting all relish for her strenuous mind,
Had crossed her only to be shunned with scorn.
– Oh! pang of sorrowful regret for those
Whom, in their youth, sweet study has enthralled,
That they have lived for harsher servitude,
Whether in soul, in body, or estate!
Such doom was hers; yet nothing could subdue
700 Her keen desire of knowledge, nor efface
Those brighter images by books imprest
Upon her memory, faithfully as stars
That occupy their places, and, though oft
Hidden by clouds, and oft bedimmed by haze,
Are not to be extinguished, nor impaired.

'Two passions, both degenerate, for they both
Began in honour, gradually obtained
Rule over her, and vexed her daily life;
An unremitting, avaricious thrift;
710 And a strange thraldom of maternal love,
That held her spirit, in its own despite,
Bound – by vexation, and regret, and scorn,
Constrained forgiveness, and relenting vows,
And tears, in pride suppressed, in shame concealed –
To a poor dissolute Son, her only child.

– Her wedded days had opened with mishap,
Whence dire dependence. What could she perform
To shake the burden off? Ah! there was felt,
Indignantly, the weakness of her sex.
720 She mused, resolved, adhered to her resolve;
The hand grew slack in alms-giving, the heart
Closed by degrees to charity; heaven's blessing
Not seeking from that source, she placed her trust
In ceaseless pains – and strictest parsimony
Which sternly hoarded all that could be spared,
From each day's need, out of each day's least gain.

'Thus all was re-established, and a pile
Constructed, that sufficed for every end,
Save the contentment of the builder's mind;
730 A mind by nature indisposed to aught
So placid, so inactive, as content;
A mind intolerant of lasting peace,
And cherishing the pang her heart deplored.
Dread life of conflict! which I oft compared
To the agitation of a brook that runs
Down a rocky mountain, buried now and lost
In silent pools, now in strong eddies chained;
But never to be charmed to gentleness:
Its best attainment fits of such repose
740 As timid eyes might shrink from fathoming.

'A sudden illness seized her in the strength
Of life's autumnal season. – Shall I tell
How on her bed of death the Matron lay,
To Providence submissive, so she thought;
But fretted, vexed, and wrought upon, almost
To anger, by the malady that griped
Her prostrate frame with unrelaxing power,
As the fierce eagle fastens on the lamb?
She prayed, she moaned; – her husband's sister watched
750 Her dreary pillow, waited on her needs;
And yet the very sound of that kind foot
Was anguish to her ears! "And must she rule,"

This was the death-doomed Woman heard to say
In bitterness, "and must she rule and reign,
Sole Mistress of this house, when I am gone?
Tend what I tended, calling it her own!"
Enough; – I fear, too much. – One vernal evening,
While she was yet in prime of health and strength,
I well remember, while I passed her door
760 Alone, with loitering step, and upward eye
Turned towards the planet Jupiter that hung
Above the centre of the Vale, a voice
Roused me, her voice; it said, "That glorious star
In its untroubled element will shine
As now it shines, when we are laid in earth
And safe from all our sorrows." With a sigh
She spake, yet, I believe, not unsustained
By faith in glory that shall far transcend
Aught by these perishable heavens disclosed
770 To sight or mind. Nor less than care divine
Is divine mercy. She, who had rebelled,
Was into meekness softened and subdued;
Did, after trials not in vain prolonged,
With resignation sink into the grave;
And her uncharitable acts, I trust,
And harsh unkindnesses are all forgiven,
Though, in this Vale, remembered with deep awe.'

The Vicar paused; and toward a seat advanced,
A long stone-seat, fixed in the Churchyard wall;
780 Part shaded by cool sycamore, and part
Offering a sunny resting-place to them
Who seek the House of worship, while the bells
Yet ring with all their voices, or before
The last hath ceased its solitary knell.
Beneath the shade we all sate down; and there
His office, uninvited, he resumed.

'As on a sunny bank, a tender lamb

Lurks in safe shelter from the winds of March,
Screened by its parent, so that little mound
790 Lies guarded by its neighbour; the small heap
Speaks for itself; an Infant there doth rest;
The sheltering hillock is the Mother's grave.
If mild discourse, and manners that conferred
A natural dignity on humblest rank;
If gladsome spirits, and benignant looks,
That for a face not beautiful did more
Than beauty for the fairest face can do;
And if religious tenderness of heart,
Grieving for sin, and penitential tears
800 Shed when the clouds had gathered and distained
The spotless ether of a maiden life;
If these may make a hallowed spot of earth
More holy in the sight of God or Man;
Then, o'er that mould, a sanctity shall brood
Till the stars sicken at the day of doom.

'Ah! what a warning for a thoughtless man,
Could field or grove, could any spot of earth,
Show to his eye an image of the pangs
Which it hath witnessed; render back an echo
810 Of the sad steps by which it hath been trod!
There, by her innocent Baby's precious grave,
And on the very turf that roofs her own,
The Mother oft was seen to stand, or kneel
In the broad day, a weeping Magdalene.
Now she is not; the swelling turf reports
Of the fresh shower, but of poor Ellen's tears
Is silent; nor is any vestige left
Of the path worn by mournful tread of her
Who, at her heart's light bidding, once had moved
820 In virgin fearlessness, with step that seemed
Caught from the pressure of elastic turf
Upon the mountains gemmed with morning dew,
In the prime hour of sweetest scents and airs.
– Serious and thoughtful was her mind; and yet,

By reconcilement exquisite and rare,
The form, port, motions, of this Cottage-girl
Were such as might have quickened and inspired
A Titian's hand, addrest to picture forth
Oread or Dryad glancing through the shade
830   What time the hunter's earliest horn is heard
Startling the golden hills.
                   A wide-spread elm
Stands in our valley, named THE JOYFUL TREE;
From dateless usage which our peasants hold
Of giving welcome to the first of May
By dances round its trunk. – And if the sky
Permit, like honours, dance and song, are paid
To the Twelfth Night, beneath the frosty stars
Or the clear moon. The queen of these gay sports,
If not in beauty yet in sprightly air,
840   Was hapless Ellen. – No one touched the ground
So deftly, and the nicest maiden's locks
Less gracefully were braided; – but this praise,
Methinks, would better suit another place.

'She loved, and fondly deemed herself beloved.
– The road is dim, the current unperceived,
The weakness painful and most pitiful,
By which a virtuous woman, in pure youth,
May be delivered to distress and shame.
Such fate was hers. – The last time Ellen danced,
850   Among her equals, round THE JOYFUL TREE,
She bore a secret burden; and full soon
Was left to tremble for a breaking vow, –
Then, to bewail a sternly-broken vow,
Alone, within her widowed Mother's house.
It was the season of unfolding leaves,
Of days advancing toward their utmost length,
And small birds singing happily to mates
Happy as they. With spirit-saddening power
Winds pipe through fading woods; but those blithe notes
860   Strike the deserted to the heart; I speak

Of what I know, and what we feel within.
– Beside the cottage in which Ellen dwelt
Stands a tall ash-tree; to whose topmost twig
A thrush resorts and annually chants,
At morn and evening from that naked perch,
While all the undergrove is thick with leaves,
A time-beguiling ditty, for delight
Of his fond partner, silent in the nest.
– "Ah why," said Ellen, sighing to herself,
870 "Why do not words, and kiss, and solemn pledge,
And nature that is kind in woman's breast,
And reason that in man is wise and good,
And fear of Him who is a righteous judge;
Why do not these prevail for human life,
To keep two hearts together, that began
Their spring-time with one love, and that have need
Of mutual pity and forgiveness, sweet
To grant, or be received; while that poor bird –
O come and hear him! Thou who hast to me
880 Been faithless, hear him, though a lowly creature,
One of God's simple children that yet know not
The universal Parent, how he sings
As if he wished the firmament of heaven
Should listen, and give back to him the voice
Of his triumphant constancy and love;
The proclamation that he makes, how far
His darkness doth transcend our fickle light!"

'Such was the tender passage, not by me
Repeated without loss of simple phrase,
890 Which I perused, even as the words had been
Committed by forsaken Ellen's hand
To the blank margin of a Valentine,
Bedropped with tears. 'Twill please you to be told
That, studiously withdrawing from the eye
Of all companionship, the Sufferer yet
In lonely reading found a meek resource:
How thankful for the warmth of summer days,

When she could slip into the cottage-barn,
And find a secret oratory there;
900 Or, in the garden, under friendly veil
Of their long twilight, pore upon her book
By the last lingering help of the open sky
Until dark night dismissed her to her bed!
Thus did a waking fancy sometimes lose
The unconquerable pang of despised love.

'A kindlier passion opened on her soul
When that poor Child was born. Upon its face
She gazed as on a pure and spotless gift
Of unexpected promise, where a grief
910 Or dread was all that had been thought of, – joy
Far livelier than bewildered traveller feels,
Amid a perilous waste that all night long
Hath harassed him toiling through fearful storm,
When he beholds the first pale speck serene
Of day-spring, in the gloomy east, revealed,
And greets it with thanksgiving. "Till this hour,"
Thus, in her Mother's hearing Ellen spake,
"There was a stony region in my heart;
But He, at whose command the parchèd rock
920 Was smitten, and poured forth a quenching stream,
Hath softened that obduracy, and made
Unlooked-for gladness in the desert place,
To save the perishing; and, henceforth, I breathe
The air with cheerful spirit, for thy sake,
My Infant! and for that good Mother dear,
Who bore me; and hath prayed for me in vain; –
Yet not in vain; it shall not be in vain."
She spake, nor was the assurance unfulfilled;
And if heart-rending thoughts would oft return,
930 They stayed not long. – The blameless Infant grew;
The Child whom Ellen and her Mother loved
They soon were proud of; tended it and nursed;
A soothing comforter, although forlorn;
Like a poor singing-bird from distant lands;

Or a choice shrub, which he, who passes by
With vacant mind, not seldom may observe
Fair-flowering in a thinly-peopled house,
Whose window, somewhat sadly, it adorns.

'Through four months' space the Infant drew its food
940 From the maternal breast; then scruples rose;
Thoughts, which the rich are free from, came and crossed
The fond affection. She no more could bear
By her offence to lay a twofold weight
On a kind parent willing to forget
Their slender means: so, to that parent's care
Trusting her child, she left their common home,
And undertook with dutiful content
A Foster-mother's office.
                              'Tis, perchance,
Unknown to you that in these simple vales
950 The natural feeling of equality
Is by domestic service unimpaired;
Yet, though such service be, with us, removed
From sense of degradation, not the less
The ungentle mind can easily find means
To impose severe restraints and laws unjust,
Which hapless Ellen now was doomed to feel:
For (blinded by an over-anxious dread
Of such excitement and divided thought
As with her office would but ill accord)
960 The pair, whose infant she was bound to nurse,
Forbad her all communion with her own:
Week after week, the mandate they enforced.
– So near! yet not allowed, upon that sight
To fix her eyes – alas! 'twas hard to bear!
But worse affliction must be borne – far worse;
For 'tis Heaven's will – that, after a disease
Begun and ended within three days' space,
Her child should die; as Ellen now exclaimed,
Her own – deserted child! – Once, only once,
970 She saw it in that mortal malady;

And, on the burial-day, could scarcely gain
Permission to attend its obsequies.
She reached the house, last of the funeral train;
And someone, as she entered, having chanced
To urge unthinkingly their prompt departure,
"Nay," said she, with commanding look, a spirit
Of anger never seen in her before,
"Nay, ye must wait my time!" and down she sate,
And by the unclosed coffin kept her seat
980 Weeping and looking, looking on and weeping,
Upon the last sweet slumber of her Child,
Until at length her soul was satisfied.

'You see the Infant's Grave; and to this spot,
The Mother, oft as she was sent abroad,
On whatsoever errand, urged her steps:
Hither she came; here stood, and sometimes knelt
In the broad day, a rueful Magdalene!
So call her; for not only she bewailed
A mother's loss, but mourned in bitterness
990 Her own transgression; penitent sincere
As ever raised to heaven a streaming eye!
– At length the parents of the foster-child,
Noting that in despite of their commands
She still renewed and could not but renew
Those visitations, ceased to send her forth;
Or, to the garden's narrow bounds, confined.
I failed not to remind them that they erred;
For holy Nature might not thus be crossed,
Thus wronged in woman's breast: in vain I pleaded –
1000 But the green stalk of Ellen's life was snapped,
And the flower drooped; as every eye could see,
It hung its head in mortal languishment.
– Aided by this appearance, I at length
Prevailed; and, from those bonds released, she went
Home to her mother's house.
                                    The Youth was fled;
The rash betrayer could not face the shame

Or sorrow which his senseless guilt had caused;
And little would his presence, or proof given
Of a relenting soul, have now availed;
1010 For, like a shadow, he was passed away
From Ellen's thoughts; had perished to her mind
For all concerns of fear, or hope, or love,
Save only those which to their common shame,
And to his moral being appertained:
Hope from that quarter would, I know, have brought
A heavenly comfort; there she recognized
An unrelaxing bond, a mutual need;
There, and, as seemed, there only.
                                    She had built,
Her fond maternal heart had built, a nest
1020 In blindness all too near the river's edge;
That work a summer flood with hasty swell
Had swept away; and now her Spirit longed
For its last flight to heaven's security.
– The bodily frame wasted from day to day;
Meanwhile, relinquishing all other cares,
Her mind she strictly tutored to find peace
And pleasure in endurance. Much she thought,
And much she read; and brooded feelingly
Upon her own unworthiness. To me,
1030 As to a spiritual comforter and friend,
Her heart she opened; and no pains were spared
To mitigate, as gently as I could,
The sting of self-reproach, with healing words.
Meek Saint! through patience glorified on earth!
In whom, as by her lonely hearth she sate,
The ghastly face of cold decay put on
A sun-like beauty, and appeared divine!
May I not mention – that, within those walls,
In due observance of her pious wish,
1040 The congregation joined with me in prayer
For her soul's good? Nor was that office vain.
– Much did she suffer: but, if any friend,
Beholding her condition, at the sight

Gave way to words of pity or complaint,
She stilled them with a prompt reproof, and said,
"He who afflicts me knows what I can bear;
And, when I fail, and can endure no more,
Will mercifully take me to Himself."
So, through the cloud of death, her Spirit passed
1050 Into that pure and unknown world of love
Where injury cannot come: – and here is laid
The mortal Body by her Infant's side.'

   The Vicar ceased; and downcast looks made known
That each had listened with his inmost heart.
For me, the emotion scarcely was less strong
Or less benign than that which I had felt
When seated near my venerable Friend,
Under those shady elms, from him I heard
The story that retraced the slow decline
1060 Of Margaret, sinking on the lonely heath
With the neglected house to which she clung.
– I noted that the Solitary's cheek
Confessed the power of nature. – Pleased though sad,
More pleased than sad, the grey-haired Wanderer sate;
Thanks to his pure imaginative soul
Capacious and serene; his blameless life,
His knowledge, wisdom, love of truth, and love
Of human kind! He was it who first broke
The pensive silence, saying: –
                    'Blest are they
1070 Whose sorrow rather is to suffer wrong
Than to do wrong, albeit themselves have erred.
This tale gives proof that Heaven most gently deals
With such, in their affliction. – Ellen's fate,
Her tender spirit, and her contrite heart,
Call to my mind dark hints which I have heard
Of one who died within this vale, by doom
Heavier, as his offence was heavier far.
Where, Sir, I pray you, where are laid the bones
Of Wilfred Armathwaite?'

The Vicar answered,

1080 'In that green nook, close by the Churchyard wall,
Beneath yon hawthorn, planted by myself
In memory and for warning, and in sign
Of sweetness where dire anguish had been known,
Of reconcilement after deep offence –
There doth he rest. No theme his fate supplies
For the smooth glozings of the indulgent world;
Nor need the windings of his devious course
Be here retraced; – enough that, by mishap
And venial error, robbed of competence,

1090 And her obsequious shadow, peace of mind,
He craved a substitute in troubled joy;
Against his conscience rose in arms, and, braving
Divine displeasure, broke the marriage-vow.
That which he had been weak enough to do
Was misery in remembrance; he was stung,
Stung by his inward thoughts, and by the smiles
Of wife and children stung to agony.
Wretched at home, he gained no peace abroad;
Ranged through the mountains, slept upon the earth,

1100 Asked comfort of the open air, and found
No quiet in the darkness of the night,
No pleasure in the beauty of the day.
His flock he slighted: his paternal fields
Became a clog to him, whose spirit wished
To fly – but whither! And this gracious Church,
That wears a look so full of peace and hope
And love, benignant mother of the vale,
How fair amid her brood of cottages!
She was to him a sickness and reproach.

1110 Much to the last remained unknown: but this
Is sure, that through remorse and grief he died;
Though pitied among men, absolved by God,
He could not find forgiveness in himself;
Nor could endure the weight of his own shame.

'Here rests a Mother. But from her I turn

And from her grave. – Behold – upon that ridge,
That, stretching boldly from the mountain side,
Carries into the centre of the vale
Its rocks and woods – the Cottage where she dwelt;
1120 And where yet dwells her faithful Partner, left
(Full eight years past) the solitary prop
Of many helpless Children. I begin
With words that might be prelude to a tale
Of sorrow and dejection; but I feel
No sadness, when I think of what mine eyes
See daily in that happy family.
– Bright garland form they for the pensive brow
Of their undrooping Father's widowhood,
Those six fair Daughters, budding yet – not one,
1130 Not one of all the band, a full-blown flower.
Deprest, and desolate of soul, as once
That Father was, and filled with anxious fear,
Now, by experience taught, he stands assured,
That God, who takes away, yet takes not half
Of what he seems to take; or gives it back,
Not to our prayer, but far beyond our prayer;
He gives it – the boon produce of a soil
Which our endeavours have refused to till,
And hope hath never watered. The Abode,
1140 Whose grateful owner can attest these truths,
Even were the object nearer to our sight,
Would seem in no distinction to surpass
The rudest habitations. Ye might think
That it had sprung self-raised from earth, or grown
Out of the living rock, to be adorned
By nature only; but, if thither led,
Ye would discover, then, a studious work
Of many fancies, prompting many hands.

'Brought from the woods the honeysuckle twines
1150 Around the porch, and seems, in that trim place,
A plant no longer wild; the cultured rose

There blossoms, strong in health, and will be soon
Roof-high; the wild pink crowns the garden-wall,
And with the flowers are intermingled stones
Sparry and bright, rough scatterings of the hills.
These ornaments, that fade not with the year,
A hardy Girl continues to provide;
Who, mounting fearlessly the rocky heights,
Her Father's prompt attendant, does for him
1160 All that a boy could do, but with delight
More keen and prouder daring; yet hath she,
Within the garden, like the rest, a bed
For her own flowers and favourite herbs, a space,
By sacred charter, holden for her use.
– These, and whatever else the garden bears
Of fruit or flower, permission asked or not,
I freely gather; and my leisure draws
A not unfrequent pastime from the hum
Of bees around their range of sheltered hives
1170 Busy in that enclosure; while the rill,
That sparkling thrids the rocks, attunes his voice
To the pure course of human life which there
Flows on in solitude. But, when the gloom
Of night is falling round my steps, then most
This Dwelling charms me; often I stop short,
(Who could refrain?) and feed by stealth my sight
With prospect of the company within,
Laid open through the blazing window: – there
I see the eldest Daughter at her wheel
1180 Spinning amain, as if to overtake
The never-halting time; or, in her turn,
Teaching some Novice of the sisterhood
That skill in this or other household work,
Which, from her Father's honoured hand, herself,
While she was yet a little-one, had learned.
Mild Man! he is not gay, but they are gay;
And the whole house seems filled with gaiety.
– Thrice happy, then, the Mother may be deemed,
The Wife, from whose consolatory grave

1190 I turned, that ye in mind might witness where,
And how, her Spirit yet survives on earth!'

[The next three Ridges – those upon the left –
By close connexion with our present thoughts
Tempt me to add, in praise of humble worth,
Their brief and unobtrusive history.
– One Hillock, ye may note, is small and low,
Sunk almost to a level with the plain
By weight of time; the Others, undepressed,
Are bold and swelling. There a Husband sleeps,
1200 Deposited, in pious confidence
Of glorious resurrection with the just,
Near the loved Partner of his early days;
And, in the bosom of that family mould,
A second Wife is gathered to his side;
The approved Assistant of an arduous course
From his mid noon of manhood to old age!
He also of his Mate deprived, was left
Alone – 'mid many Children: One a Babe
Orphaned as soon as born. Alas! 'tis not
1210 In course of nature that a Father's wing
Should warm these Little-ones; and can he *feed*?
That was a thought of agony more keen.
For, hand in hand with Death, by strange mishap
And chance-encounter on their diverse road,
The ghastlier shape of Poverty had entered
Into that House, unfeared and unforeseen.
He had stepped forth, in time of urgent need,
The generous Surety of a Friend: and now
The widowed Father found that all his rights
1220 In his paternal fields were undermined.
Landless he was and pennyless. – The dews
Of night and morn that wet the mountain sides,
The bright stars twinkling on their dusky tops,
Were conscious of the pain that drove him forth
From his own door, he knew not when – to range
He knew not where; distracted was his brain,

His heart was cloven; and full oft he prayed,
In blind despair, that God would take them all.
– But suddenly, as if in one kind moment
1230 To encourage and reprove, a gleam of light
Broke from the very bosom of that cloud
Which darkened the whole prospect of his days.
For He who now possessed the joyless right
To force the Bondsman from his house and lands,
In pity, and by admiration urged
Of his unmurmuring and considerate mind
Meekly submissive to the law's decree,
Lightened the penalty with liberal hand.
– The desolate Father raised his head and looked
1240 On the wide world in hope. Within these walls,
In course of time was solemnized the vow
Whereby a virtuous Woman, of grave years
And of prudential habits, undertook
The sacred office of a wife to him,
Of Mother to his helpless family.
– Nor did she fail, in nothing did she fail,
Through various exercise of twice ten years,
Save in some partial fondness for that Child
Which at the birth she had received, the Babe
1250 Whose heart had known no Mother but herself.
– By mutual efforts; by united hopes;
By daily-growing help of boy and girl,
Trained early to participate that zeal
Of industry, which runs before the day
And lingers after it; by strong restraint
Of an economy which did not check
The heart's more generous motions towards themselves
Or to their neighbours; and by trust in God;
This Pair insensibly subdued the fears
1260 And troubles that beset their life: and thus
Did the good Father and his second Mate
Redeem at length their plot of smiling fields.
These, at this day, the eldest Son retains:
The younger Offspring, through the busy world,

Have all been scattered wide, by various fates;
But each departed from the native Vale,
In beauty flourishing, and moral worth.']

BOOK SEVENTH
THE CHURCHYARD AMONG THE MOUNTAINS
(*continued*)

Argument

Impression of these Narratives upon the Author's mind. –
Pastor invited to give account of certain Graves that lie apart. –
Clergyman and his Family. – Fortunate influence of change of
situation. – Activity in extreme old age. – Another Clergyman,
a character of resolute Virtue. – Lamentations over mis-directed
applause. – Instance of less exalted excellence in a deaf man. –
Elevated character of a blind man. – Reflection upon Blindness.
– Interrupted by a Peasant who passes – his animal cheerfulness
and careless vivacity. – He occasions a digression on the fall of
beautiful and interesting Trees. – A female Infant's Grave. –
Joy at her Birth. – Sorrow at her Departure. – A youthful
Peasant – his patriotic enthusiasm and distinguished qualities
– his untimely death. – Exultation of the Wanderer, as a
patriot, in this Picture. – Solitary how affected. – Monument of
a Knight. – Traditions concerning him. – Peroration of the
Wanderer on the transitoriness of things and the revolutions of
society. – Hints at his own past Calling. – Thanks the Pastor.

While thus from theme to theme the Historian passed,
The words he uttered, and the scene that lay
Before our eyes, awakened in my mind
Vivid remembrance of those long-past hours;
When, in the hollow of some shadowy vale,
(What time the splendour of the setting sun
Lay beautiful on Snowdon's sovereign brow,
On Cader Idris, or huge Penmanmaur)
A wandering Youth, I listened with delight
10   To pastoral melody or warlike air,
Drawn from the chords of the ancient British harp
By some accomplished Master, while he sate

Amid the quiet of the green recess,
And there did inexhaustibly dispense
An interchange of soft or solemn tunes,
Tender or blithe; now, as the varying mood
Of his own spirit urged, – now, as a voice
From youth or maiden, or some honoured chief
Of his compatriot villagers (that hung
20 Around him, drinking in the impassioned notes
Of the time-hallowed minstrelsy) required
For their heart's ease or pleasure. Strains of power
Were they, to seize and occupy the sense;
But to a higher mark than song can reach
Rose this pure eloquence. And, when the stream
Which overflowed the soul was passed away,
A consciousness remained that it had left,
Deposited upon the silent shore
Of memory, images and precious thoughts,
30 That shall not die, and cannot be destroyed.

'These grassy heaps lie amicably close,'
Said I, 'like surges heaving in the wind
Along the surface of a mountain pool:
Whence comes it, then, that yonder we behold
Five graves, and only five, that rise together
Unsociably sequestered, and encroaching
On the smooth play-ground of the village-school?'

The Vicar answered, – 'No disdainful pride
In them who rest beneath, nor any course
40 Of strange or tragic accident, hath helped
To place those hillocks in that lonely guise.
– Once more look forth, and follow with your sight
The length of road that from yon mountain's base
Through bare enclosures stretches, 'till its line
Is lost within a little tuft of trees;
Then, reappearing in a moment, quits
The cultured fields; and up the heathy waste,
Mounts, as you see, in mazes serpentine,

Led towards an easy outlet of the vale.
50 That little shady spot, that sylvan tuft,
By which the road is hidden, also hides
A cottage from our view; though I discern
(Ye scarcely can) amid its sheltering trees
The smokeless chimney-top. –
                                        All unembowered
And naked stood that lowly Parsonage
(For such in truth it is, and appertains
To a small Chapel in the vale beyond)
When hither came its last Inhabitant.
Rough and forbidding were the choicest roads
60 By which our northern wilds could then be crossed;
And into most of these secluded vales
Was no access for wain, heavy or light.
So, at his dwelling-place the Priest arrived
With store of household goods, in panniers slung
On sturdy horses graced with jingling bells,
And on the back of more ignoble beast;
That, with like burden of effects most prized
Or easiest carried, closed the motley train.
Young was I then, a schoolboy of eight years;
70 But still, methinks, I see them as they passed
In order, drawing toward their wished-for home.
– Rocked by the motion of a trusty ass
Two ruddy children hung, a well-poised freight,
Each in his basket nodding drowsily;
Their bonnets, I remember, wreathed with flowers,
Which told it was the pleasant month of June;
And, close behind, the comely Matron rode,
A woman of soft speech and gracious smile,
And with a lady's mien. – From far they came,
80 Even from Northumbrian hills; yet theirs had been
A merry journey, rich in pastime, cheered
By music, prank, and laughter-stirring jest;
And freak put on, and arch word dropped – to swell
The cloud of fancy and uncouth surmise
That gathered round the slowly-moving train.

– "Whence do they come? and with what errand charged?
Belong they to the fortune-telling tribe
Who pitch their tents under the green-wood tree?
Or Strollers are they, furnished to enact
90 Fair Rosamond, and the Children of the Wood,
And, by that whiskered tabby's aid, set forth
The lucky venture of sage Whittington,
When the next village hears the show announced
By blast of trumpet?" Plenteous was the growth
Of such conjectures, overheard, or seen
On many a staring countenance portrayed
Of boor or burgher, as they marched along.
And more than once their steadiness of face
Was put to proof, and exercise supplied
100 To their inventive humour, by stern looks,
And questions in authoritative tone,
From some staid guardian of the public peace,
Checking the sober steed on which he rode,
In his suspicious wisdom; oftener still,
By notice indirect, or blunt demand
From traveller halting in his own despite,
A simple curiosity to ease:
Of which adventures, that beguiled and cheered
Their grave migration, the good pair would tell,
110 With undiminished glee, in hoary age.

'A Priest he was by function; but his course
From his youth up, and high as manhood's noon,
(The hour of life to which he then was brought)
Had been irregular, I might say, wild;
By books unsteadied, by his pastoral care
Too little checked. An active, ardent mind;
A fancy pregnant with resource and scheme
To cheat the sadness of a rainy day;
Hands apt for all ingenious arts and games;
120 A generous spirit, and a body strong
To cope with stoutest champions of the bowl;
Had earned for him sure welcome, and the rights

Of a prized visitant, in the jolly hall
Of country 'squire; or at the statelier board
Of duke or earl, from scenes of courtly pomp
Withdrawn, – to while away the summer hours
In condescension among rural guests.

'With these high comrades he had revelled long,
Frolicked industriously, a simple Clerk
130 By hopes of coming patronage beguiled
Till the heart sickened. So, each loftier aim
Abandoning and all his showy friends,
For a life's stay (slender it was, but sure)
He turned to this secluded chapelry;
That had been offered to his doubtful choice
By an unthought-of patron. Bleak and bare
They found the cottage, their allotted home;
Naked without, and rude within; a spot
With which the Cure not long had been endowed:
140 And far remote the chapel stood, – remote,
And, from his Dwelling, unapproachable,
Save through a gap high in the hills, an opening
Shadeless and shelterless, by driving showers
Frequented, and beset with howling winds.
Yet cause was none, whate'er regret might hang
On his own mind, to quarrel with the choice
Or the necessity that fixed him here;
Apart from old temptations, and constrained
To punctual labour in his sacred charge.
150 See him a constant preacher to the poor!
And visiting, though not with saintly zeal,
Yet, when need was, with no reluctant will,
The sick in body, or distrest in mind;
And, by as salutary change, compelled
To rise from timely sleep, and meet the day
With no engagement, in his thoughts, more proud
Or splendid than his garden could afford,
His fields, or mountains by the heath-cock ranged,
Or the wild brooks; from which he now returned

160   Contented to partake the quiet meal
     Of his own board, where sat his gentle Mate
     And three fair Children, plentifully fed
     Though simply, from their little household farm;
     Nor wanted timely treat of fish or fowl
     By nature yielded to his practised hand; –
     To help the small but certain comings-in
     Of that spare benefice. Yet not the less
     Theirs was a hospitable board, and theirs
     A charitable door.
                So days and years
170   Passed on; – the inside of that rugged house
     Was trimmed and brightened by the Matron's care,
     And gradually enriched with things of price,
     Which might be lacked for use or ornament.
     What, though no soft and costly sofa there
     Insidiously stretched out its lazy length,
     And no vain mirror glittered upon the walls,
     Yet were the windows of the low abode
     By shutters weather-fended, which at once
     Repelled the storm and deadened its loud roar.
180   Their snow-white curtains hung in decent folds;
     Tough moss, and long-enduring mountain plants,
     That creep along the ground with sinuous trail,
     Were nicely braided; and composed a work
     Like Indian mats, that with appropriate grace
     Lay at the threshold and the inner doors;
     And a fair carpet, woven of homespun wool
     But tinctured daintily with florid hues,
     For seemliness and warmth, on festal days,
     Covered the smooth blue slabs of mountain-stone
190   With which the parlour-floor, in simplest guise
     Of pastoral homesteads, had been long inlaid.

     'Those pleasing works the Housewife's skill produced:
     Meanwhile the unsedentary Master's hand
     Was busier with his task – to rid, to plant,
     To rear for food, for shelter, and delight;

A thriving covert! And when wishes, formed
In youth, and sanctioned by the riper mind,
Restored me to my native valley, here
To end my days; well pleased was I to see
200 The once-bare cottage, on the mountain-side,
Screened from assault of every bitter blast;
While the dark shadows of the summer leaves
Danced in the breeze, chequering its mossy roof.
Time, which had thus afforded willing help
To beautify with nature's fairest growths
This rustic tenement, had gently shed,
Upon its Master's frame, a wintry grace;
The comeliness of unenfeebled age.

'But how could I say, gently? for he still
210 Retained a flashing eye, a burning palm,
A stirring foot, a head which beat at nights
Upon its pillow with a thousand schemes.
Few likings had he dropped, few pleasures lost;
Generous and charitable, prompt to serve;
And still his harsher passions kept their hold –
Anger and indignation. Still he loved
The sound of titled names, and talked in glee
Of long-past banquetings with high-born friends:
Then, from those lulling fits of vain delight
220 Uproused by recollected injury, railed
At their false ways disdainfully, – and oft
In bitterness, and with a threatening eye
Of fire, incensed beneath its hoary brow.
– Those transports, with staid looks of pure good-will,
And with soft smile, his consort would reprove.
She, far behind him in the race of years,
Yet keeping her first mildness, was advanced
Far nearer, in the habit of her soul,
To that still region whither all are bound.
230 Him might we liken to the setting sun
As seen not seldom on some gusty day,
Struggling and bold, and shining from the west

With an inconstant and unmellowed light;
She was a soft attendant cloud, that hung
As if with wish to veil the restless orb;
From which it did itself imbibe a ray
Of pleasing lustre. – But no more of this;
I better love to sprinkle on the sod
That now divides the pair, or rather say,
240   That still unites them, praises, like heaven's dew,
Without reserve descending upon both.

'Our very first in eminence of years
This old Man stood, the patriarch of the Vale!
And, to his unmolested mansion, death
Had never come, through space of forty years;
Sparing both old and young in that abode.
Suddenly then they disappeared: not twice
Had summer scorched the fields; not twice had fallen,
On those high peaks, the first autumnal snow,
250   Before the greedy visiting was closed,
And the long-privileged house left empty – swept
As by a plague. Yet no rapacious plague
Had been among them; all was gentle death,
One after one, with intervals of peace.
A happy consummation! an accord
Sweet, perfect, to be wished for! save that here
Was something which to mortal sense might sound
Like harshness, – that the old grey-headed Sire,
The oldest, he was taken last, survived
260   When the meek Partner of his age, his Son,
His Daughter, and that late and high-prized gift,
His little smiling Grandchild, were no more.

' "All gone, all vanished! he deprived and bare,
How will he face the remnant of his life?
What will become of him?" we said, and mused
In sad conjectures – "Shall we meet him now
Haunting with rod and line the craggy brooks?
Or shall we overhear him, as we pass,

Striving to entertain the lonely hours
270 With music?" (for he had not ceased to touch
The harp or viol which himself had framed,
For their sweet purposes, with perfect skill.)
"What titles will he keep? will he remain
Musician, gardener, builder, mechanist,
A planter, and a rearer from the seed?
A man of hope and forward-looking mind
Even to the last!" – Such was he, unsubdued.
But Heaven was gracious; yet a little while,
And this Survivor, with his cheerful throng
280 Of open projects, and his inward hoard
Of unsunned griefs, too many and too keen,
Was overcome by unexpected sleep,
In one blest moment. Like a shadow thrown
Softly and lightly from a passing cloud,
Death fell upon him, while reclined he lay
For noontide solace on the summer grass,
The warm lap of his mother earth: and so,
Their lenient term of separation past,
That family (whose graves you there behold)
290 By yet a higher privilege once more
Were gathered to each other.'
                    Calm of mind
And silence waited on these closing words;
Until the Wanderer (whether moved by fear
Lest in those passages of life were some
That might have touched the sick heart of his Friend
Too nearly, or intent to reinforce
His own firm spirit in degree deprest
By tender sorrow for our mortal state)
Thus silence broke: – 'Behold a thoughtless Man
300 From vice and premature decay preserved
By useful habits, to a fitter soil
Transplanted ere too late. – The hermit, lodged
Amid the untrodden desert, tells his beads,
With each repeating its allotted prayer,
And thus divides and thus relieves the time;

Smooth task, with *his* compared, whose mind could string,
Not scantily, bright minutes on the thread
Of keen domestic anguish; and beguile
A solitude, unchosen, unprofessed;
Till gentlest death released him.

310   Far from us
Be the desire – too curiously to ask
How much of this is but the blind result
Of cordial spirits and vital temperament,
And what to higher powers is justly due.
But you, Sir, know that in a neighbouring vale
A Priest abides before whose life such doubts
Fall to the ground; whose gifts of nature lie
Retired from notice, lost in attributes
Of reason, honourably effaced by debts

320 Which her poor treasure-house is content to owe,
And conquests over her dominion gained,
To which her frowardness must needs submit.
In this one Man is shown a temperance – proof
Against all trials; industry severe
And constant as the motion of the day;
Stern self-denial round him spread, with shade
That might be deemed forbidding, did not there
All generous feelings flourish and rejoice;
Forbearance, charity in deed and thought,

330 And resolution competent to take
Out of the bosom of simplicity
All that her holy customs recommend,
And the best ages of the world prescribe.
– Preaching, administering, in every work
Of his sublime vocation, in the walks
Of worldly intercourse between man and man,
And in his humble dwelling, he appears
A labourer, with moral virtue girt,
With spiritual graces, like a glory, crowned.'

340   'Doubt can be none,' the Pastor said, 'for whom
This portraiture is sketched. The great, the good,

The well-beloved, the fortunate, the wise, –
These titles emperors and chiefs have borne,
Honour assumed or given: and him, the WONDERFUL,
Our simple shepherds, speaking from the heart,
Deservedly have styled. – From his abode
In a dependent chapelry that lies
Behind yon hill, a poor and rugged wild,
Which in his soul he lovingly embraced,
350 And, having once espoused, would never quit;
Into its graveyard will ere long be borne
That lowly, great, good Man. A simple stone
May cover him; and by its help, perchance,
A century shall hear his name pronounced,
With images attendant on the sound;
Then, shall the slowly-gathering twilight close
In utter night; and of his course remain
No cognizable vestiges, no more
Than of this breath, which shapes itself in words
360 To speak of him, and instantly dissolves.'

     The Pastor pressed by thoughts which round his theme
Still lingered, after a brief pause, resumed;
'Noise is there not enough in doleful war,
But that the heaven-born poet must stand forth,
And lend the echoes of his sacred shell,
To multiply and aggravate the din?
Pangs are there not enough in hopeless love –
And, in requited passion, all too much
Of turbulence, anxiety, and fear –
370 But that the minstrel of the rural shade
Must tune his pipe, insidiously to nurse
The perturbation in the suffering breast,
And propagate its kind, far as he may?
– Ah who (and with such rapture as befits
The hallowed theme) will rise and celebrate
The good man's purposes and deeds; retrace
His struggles, his discomfitures deplore,
His triumphs hail, and glorify his end;

That virtue, like the fumes and vapoury clouds
380 Through fancy's heat redounding in the brain,
And like the soft infections of the heart,
By charm of measured words may spread o'er field,
Hamlet, and town; and piety survive
Upon the lips of men in hall or bower;
Not for reproof, but high and warm delight,
And grave encouragement, by song inspired?
– Vain thought! but wherefore murmur or repine?
The memory of the just survives in heaven:
And, without sorrow, will the ground receive
390 That venerable clay. Meanwhile the best
Of what lies here confines us to degrees
In excellence less difficult to reach,
And milder worth: nor need we travel far
From those to whom our last regards were paid,
For such example.
                        Almost at the root
Of that tall pine, the shadow of whose bare
And slender stem, while here I sit at eve,
Oft stretches toward me, like a long straight path
Traced faintly in the greensward; there, beneath
400 A plain blue stone, a gentle Dalesman lies,
From whom, in early childhood, was withdrawn
The precious gift of hearing. He grew up
From year to year in loneliness of soul;
And this deep mountain-valley was to him
Soundless, with all its streams. The bird of dawn
Did never rouse this Cottager from sleep
With startling summons; not for his delight
The vernal cuckoo shouted; not for him
Murmured the labouring bee. When stormy winds
410 Were working the broad bosom of the lake
Into a thousand thousand sparkling waves,
Rocking the trees, or driving cloud on cloud
Along the sharp edge of yon lofty crags,
The agitated scene before his eye
Was silent as a picture: evermore

Were all things silent, wheresoe'er he moved.
Yet, by the solace of his own pure thoughts
Upheld, he duteously pursued the round
Of rural labours; the steep mountain-side
420 Ascended, with his staff and faithful dog;
The plough he guided, and the scythe he swayed;
And the ripe corn before his sickle fell
Among the jocund reapers. For himself,
All watchful and industrious as he was,
He wrought not: neither field nor flock he owned:
No wish for wealth had place within his mind;
Nor husband's love, nor father's hope or care.

'Though born a younger brother, need was none
That from the floor of his paternal home
430 He should depart, to plant himself anew.
And when, mature in manhood, he beheld
His parents laid in earth, no loss ensued
Of rights to him; but he remained well pleased,
By the pure bond of independent love,
An inmate of a second family;
The fellow-labourer and friend of him
To whom the small inheritance had fallen.
– Nor deem that his mild presence was a weight
That pressed upon his brother's house; for books
440 Were ready comrades whom he could not tire;
Of whose society the blameless Man
Was never satiate. Their familiar voice,
Even to old age, with unabated charm
Beguiled his leisure hours; refreshed his thoughts;
Beyond its natural elevation raised
His introverted spirit; and bestowed
Upon his life an outward dignity
Which all acknowledged. The dark winter night,
The stormy day, each had its own resource;
450 Song of the muses, sage historic tale,
Science severe, or word of holy Writ
Announcing immortality and joy

To the assembled spirits of just men
Made perfect, and from injury secure.
– Thus soothed at home, thus busy in the field,
To no perverse suspicion he gave way,
No languor, peevishness, nor vain complaint:
And they, who were about him, did not fail
In reverence, or in courtesy; they prized
460 His gentle manners: and his peaceful smiles,
The gleams of his slow-varying countenance,
Were met with answering sympathy and love.

'At length, when sixty years and five were told,
A slow disease insensibly consumed
The powers of nature: and a few short steps
Of friends and kindred bore him from his home
(Yon cottage shaded by the woody crags)
To the profounder stillness of the grave.
– Nor was his funeral denied the grace
470 Of many tears, virtuous and thoughtful grief;
Heart-sorrow rendered sweet by gratitude.
And now that monumental stone preserves
His name, and unambitiously relates
How long, and by what kindly outward aids,
And in what pure contentedness of mind,
The sad privation was by him endured.
– And yon tall pine-tree, whose composing sound
Was wasted on the good Man's living ear,
Hath now its own peculiar sanctity;
480 And, at the touch of every wandering breeze,
Murmurs, not idly, o'er his peaceful grave.

'Soul-cheering Light, most bountiful of things!
Guide of our way, mysterious comforter!
Whose sacred influence, spread through earth and heaven,
We all too thanklessly participate,
Thy gifts were utterly withheld from him
Whose place of rest is near yon ivied porch.
Yet, of the wild brooks ask if he complained;

Ask of the channelled rivers if they held
490 A safer, easier, more determined, course.
What terror doth it strike into the mind
To think of one, blind and alone, advancing
Straight toward some precipice's airy brink!
But, timely warned, *He* would have stayed his steps,
Protected, say enlightened, by his ear;
And on the very edge of vacancy
Not more endangered than a man whose eye
Beholds the gulf beneath. – No floweret blooms
Throughout the lofty range of these rough hills,
500 Nor in the woods, that could from him conceal
Its birthplace; none whose figure did not live
Upon his touch. The bowels of the earth
Enriched with knowledge his industrious mind;
The ocean paid him tribute from the stores
Lodged in her bosom; and, by science led,
His genius mounted to the plains of heaven.
– Methinks I see him – how his eye-balls rolled,
Beneath his ample brow, in darkness paired, –
But each instinct with spirit; and the frame
510 Of the whole countenance alive with thought,
Fancy, and understanding; while the voice
Discoursed of natural or moral truth
With eloquence, and such authentic power,
That, in his presence, humbler knowledge stood
Abashed, and tender pity overawed.'

'A noble – and, to unreflecting minds,
A marvellous spectacle,' the Wanderer said,
'Beings like these present! But proof abounds
Upon the earth that faculties, which seem
520 Extinguished, do not, *therefore*, cease to be.
And to the mind among her powers of sense
This transfer is permitted, – not alone
That the bereft their recompense may win;
But for remoter purposes of love
And charity; nor last nor least for this,

That to the imagination may be given
A type and shadow of an awful truth;
How, likewise, under sufferance divine,
Darkness is banished from the realms of death,
530   By man's imperishable spirit, quelled.
Unto the men who see not as we see
Futurity was thought, in ancient times,
To be laid open, and they prophesied.
And know we not that from the blind have flowed
The highest, holiest, raptures of the lyre;
And wisdom married to immortal verse?'

    Among the humbler Worthies, at our feet
Lying insensible to human praise,
Love, or regret, – *whose* lineaments would next
540   Have been portrayed, I guess not; but it chanced
That, near the quiet churchyard where we sate,
A team of horses, with a ponderous freight
Pressing behind, adown a rugged slope,
Whose sharp descent confounded their array,
Came at that moment, ringing noisily.

    'Here,' said the Pastor, 'do we muse, and mourn
The waste of death; and lo! the giant oak
Stretched on his bier – that massy timber wain;
Nor fail to note the Man who guides the team.'

550   He was a peasant of the lowest class:
Grey locks profusely round his temples hung
In clustering curls, like ivy, which the bite
Of winter cannot thin; the fresh air lodged
Within his cheek, as light within a cloud;
And he returned our greeting with a smile.
When he had passed, the Solitary spake;
'A Man he seems of cheerful yesterdays
And confident tomorrows; with a face
Not worldly-minded, for it bears too much
560   Of Nature's impress, – gaiety and health,

Freedom and hope; but keen, withal, and shrewd.
His gestures note, – and hark! his tones of voice
Are all vivacious as his mien and looks.'

The Pastor answered, 'You have read him well.
Year after year is added to his store
With *silent* increase: summers, winters – past,
Past or to come; yea, boldly might I say,
Ten summers and ten winters of a space
That lies beyond life's ordinary bounds,
570 Upon his sprightly vigour cannot fix
The obligation of an anxious mind,
A pride in having, or a fear to lose;
Possessed like outskirts of some large domain,
By anyone more thought of than by him
Who holds the land in fee, its careless lord!
Yet is the creature rational, endowed
With foresight; hears, too, every sabbath day,
The Christian promise with attentive ear;
Nor will, I trust, the Majesty of Heaven
580 Reject the incense offered up by him,
Though of the kind which beasts and birds present
In grove or pasture; cheerfulness of soul,
From trepidation and repining free.
How many scrupulous worshippers fall down
Upon their knees, and daily homage pay
Less worthy, less religious even, than his!

'This qualified respect, the old Man's due,
Is paid without reluctance; but in truth,'
(Said the good Vicar with a fond half-smile)
590 'I feel at times a motion of despite
Towards one, whose bold contrivances and skill,
As you have seen, bear such conspicuous part
In works of havoc; taking from these vales,
One after one, their proudest ornaments.
Full oft his doings leave me to deplore
Tall ash-tree, sown by winds, by vapours nursed,

In the dry crannies of the pendent rocks;
Light birch, aloft upon the horizon's edge,
A veil of glory for the ascending moon;
600 And oak whose roots by noontide dew were damped,
And on whose forehead inaccessible
The raven lodged in safety. – Many a ship
Launched into Morecamb-bay, to *him* hath owed
Her strong knee-timbers, and the mast that bears
The loftiest of her pendants; He, from park
Or forest, fetched the enormous axle-tree
That whirls (how slow itself!) ten thousand spindles:
And the vast engine labouring in the mine,
Content with meaner prowess, must have lacked
610 The trunk and body of its marvellous strength,
If his undaunted enterprise had failed
Among the mountain coves.
                              Yon household fir,
A guardian planted to fence off the blast,
But towering high the roof above, as if
Its humble destination were forgot –
That sycamore, which annually holds
Within its shade, as in a stately tent
On all sides open to the fanning breeze,
A grave assemblage, seated while they shear
620 The fleece-encumbered flock – the JOYFUL ELM,
Around whose trunk the maidens dance in May –
And the LORD'S OAK – would plead their several rights
In vain, if he were master of their fate;
His sentence to the axe would doom them all.
But, green in age and lusty as he is,
And promising to keep his hold on earth
Less, as might seem, in rivalship with men
Than with the forest's more enduring growth,
His own appointed hour will come at last;
630 And, like the haughty Spoilers of the world,
This keen Destroyer, in his turn, must fall.

'Now from the living pass we once again:

From Age,' the Priest continued, 'turn your thoughts;
From Age, that often unlamented drops,
And mark that daisied hillock, three spans long!
– Seven lusty Sons sate daily round the board
Of Gold-rill side; and, when the hope had ceased
Of other progeny, a Daughter then
Was given, the crowning bounty of the whole;
640   And so acknowledged with a tremulous joy
Felt to the centre of that heavenly calm
With which by nature every mother's soul
Is stricken in the moment when her throes
Are ended, and her ears have heard the cry
Which tells her that a living child is born;
And she lies conscious, in a blissful rest,
That the dread storm is weathered by them both.

   'The Father – him at this unlooked-for gift
A bolder transport seizes. From the side
650   Of his bright hearth, and from his open door,
Day after day the gladness is diffused
To all that come, almost to all that pass;
Invited, summoned, to partake the cheer
Spread on the never-empty board, and drink
Health and good wishes to his new-born girl,
From cups replenished by his joyous hand.
– Those seven fair brothers variously were moved
Each by the thoughts best suited to his years:
But most of all and with most thankful mind
660   The hoary grandsire felt himself enriched;
A happiness that ebbed not, but remained
To fill the total measure of his soul!
– From the low tenement, his own abode,
Whither, as to a little private cell,
He had withdrawn from bustle, care, and noise,
To spend the sabbath of old age in peace,
Once every day he duteously repaired
To rock the cradle of the slumbering babe:
For in that female infant's name he heard

670   The silent name of his departed wife;
      Heart-stirring music! hourly heard that name;
      Full blest he was, "Another Margaret Green,"
      Oft did he say, "was come to Gold-rill side."

       'Oh! pang unthought of, as the precious boon
      Itself had been unlooked-for; oh! dire stroke
      Of desolating anguish for them all!
      – Just as the Child could totter on the floor,
      And, by some friendly finger's help upstayed,
      Ranged round the garden walk, while she perchance
680   Was catching at some novelty of spring,
      Ground-flower, or glossy insect from its cell
      Drawn by the sunshine – at that hopeful season
      The winds of March, smiting insidiously,
      Raised in the tender passage of the throat
      Viewless obstruction; whence, all unforewarned,
      The household lost their pride and soul's delight.
      – But time hath power to soften all regrets,
      And prayer and thought can bring to worst distress
      Due resignation. Therefore, though some tears
690   Fail not to spring from either Parent's eye
      Oft as they hear of sorrow like their own,
      Yet this departed Little-one, too long
      The innocent troubler of their quiet, sleeps
      In what may now be called a peaceful bed.

       'On a bright day – so calm and bright, it seemed
      To us, with our sad spirits, heavenly-fair –
      These mountains echoed to an unknown sound;
      A volley, thrice repeated o'er the Corse
      Let down into the hollow of that grave,
700   Whose shelving sides are red with naked mould.
      Ye rains of April, duly wet this earth!
      Spare, burning sun of midsummer, these sods,
      That they may knit together, and therewith
      Our thoughts unite in kindred quietness!
      Nor so the Valley shall forget her loss.

Dear Youth, by young and old alike beloved,
To me as precious as my own! – Green herbs
May creep (I wish that they would softly creep)
Over thy last abode, and we may pass
710   Reminded less imperiously of thee; –
The ridge itself may sink into the breast
Of earth, the great abyss, and be no more;
Yet shall not thy remembrance leave our hearts,
Thy image disappear!
                    The Mountain-ash
No eye can overlook, when 'mid a grove
Of yet unfaded trees she lifts her head
Decked with autumnal berries, that outshine
Spring's richest blossoms; and ye may have marked,
By a brook-side or solitary tarn,
720   How she her station doth adorn: the pool
Glows at her feet, and all the gloomy rocks
Are brightened round her. In his native vale
Such and so glorious did this Youth appear;
A sight that kindled pleasure in all hearts
By his ingenuous beauty, by the gleam
Of his fair eyes, by his capacious brow,
By all the graces with which nature's hand
Had lavishly arrayed him. As old bards
Tell in their idle songs of wandering gods,
730   Pan or Apollo, veiled in human form:
Yet, like the sweet-breathed violet of the shade,
Discovered in their own despite to sense
Of mortals (if such fables without blame
May find chance-mention on this sacred ground)
So, through a simple rustic garb's disguise,
And through the impediment of rural cares,
In him revealed a scholar's genius shone;
And so, not wholly hidden from men's sight,
In him the spirit of a hero walked
740   Our unpretending valley. – How the quoit
Whizzed from the Stripling's arm! If touched by him,
The inglorious football mounted to the pitch

Of the lark's flight, – or shaped a rainbow curve,
Aloft, in prospect of the shouting field!
The indefatigable fox had learned
To dread his perseverance in the chase.
With admiration would he lift his eyes
To the wide-ruling eagle, and his hand
Was loth to assault the majesty he loved:
750 Else had the strongest fastnesses proved weak
To guard the royal brood. The sailing glead,
The wheeling swallow, and the darting snipe,
The sportive sea-gull dancing with the waves,
And cautious water-fowl, from distant climes,
Fixed at their seat, the centre of the Mere,
Were subject to young Oswald's steady aim,
And lived by his forbearance.

From the coast
Of France a boastful Tyrant hurled his threats;
Our Country marked the preparation vast
760 Of hostile forces; and she called – with voice
That filled her plains, that reached her utmost shores,
And in remotest vales was heard – to arms!
– Then, for the first time, here you might have seen
The shepherd's grey to martial scarlet changed,
That flashed uncouthly through the woods and fields.
Ten hardy Striplings, all in bright attire,
And graced with shining weapons, weekly marched,
From this lone valley, to a central spot
Where, in assemblage with the flower and choice
770 Of the surrounding district, they might learn
The rudiments of war; ten – hardy, strong,
And valiant; but young Oswald, like a chief
And yet a modest comrade, led them forth
From their shy solitude, to face the world,
With a gay confidence and seemly pride;
Measuring the soil beneath their happy feet
Like Youths released from labour, and yet bound
To most laborious service, though to them
A festival of unencumbered ease;

780   The inner spirit keeping holiday,
     Like vernal ground to sabbath sunshine left.

     'Oft have I marked him, at some leisure hour,
     Stretched on the grass, or seated in the shade,
     Among his fellows, while an ample map
     Before their eyes lay carefully outspread,
     From which the gallant teacher would discourse,
     Now pointing this way, and now that. – "Here flows,"
     Thus would he say, "the Rhine, that famous stream!
     Eastward, the Danube toward this inland sea,
790   A mightier river, winds from realm to realm;
     And, like a serpent, shows his glittering back
     Bespotted – with innumerable isles:
     Here reigns the Russian, there the Turk; observe
     His capital city!" Thence, along a tract
     Of livelier interest to his hopes and fears,
     His finger moved, distinguishing the spots
     Where wide-spread conflict then most fiercely raged;
     Nor left unstigmatized those fatal fields
     On which the sons of mighty Germany
800   Were taught a base submission. – "Here behold
     A nobler race, the Switzers, and their land,
     Vales deeper far than these of ours, huge woods,
     And mountains white with everlasting snow!"
     – And, surely, he, that spake with kindling brow,
     Was a true patriot, hopeful as the best
     Of that young peasantry, who, in our days,
     Have fought and perished for Helvetia's rights –
     Ah, not in vain! – or those who, in old time,
     For work of happier issue, to the side
810   Of Tell came trooping from a thousand huts,
     When he had risen alone! No braver Youth
     Descended from Judean heights, to march
     With righteous Joshua; nor appeared in arms
     When grove was felled, and altar was cast down,
     And Gideon blew the trumpet, soul-inflamed,
     And strong in hatred of idolatry.'

The Pastor, even as if by these last words
Raised from his seat within the chosen shade,
Moved towards the grave; – instinctively his steps
820 We followed; and my voice with joy exclaimed:
'Power to the Oppressors of the world is given,
A might of which they dream not. Oh! the curse,
To be the awakener of divinest thoughts,
Father and founder of exalted deeds;
And, to whole nations bound in servile straits,
The liberal donor of capacities
More than heroic! this to be, nor yet
Have sense of one connatural wish, nor yet
Deserve the least return of human thanks;
830 Winning no recompense but deadly hate
With pity mixed, astonishment with scorn!'

When this involuntary strain had ceased,
The Pastor said: 'So Providence is served;
The forkèd weapon of the skies can send
Illumination into deep, dark holds,
Which the mild sunbeam hath not power to pierce.
Ye Thrones that have defied remorse, and cast
Pity away, soon shall ye quake with *fear!*
For, not unconscious of the mighty debt
840 Which to outrageous wrong the sufferer owes,
Europe, through all her habitable bounds,
Is thirsting for *their* overthrow, who yet
Survive, as pagan temples stood of yore,
By horror of their impious rites, preserved;
Are still permitted to extend their pride,
Like cedars on the top of Lebanon
Darkening the sun.
                          But less impatient thoughts,
And love "all hoping and expecting all,"
This hallowed grave demands, where rests in peace
850 A humble champion of the better cause;
A Peasant-youth, so call him, for he asked
No higher name; in whom our country showed,

As in a favourite son, most beautiful.
In spite of vice, and misery, and disease,
Spread with the spreading of her wealthy arts,
England, the ancient and the free, appeared
In him to stand before my swimming eyes,
Unconquerably virtuous and secure.
– No more of this, lest I offend his dust:
860 Short was his life, and a brief tale remains.

'One day – a summer's day of annual pomp
And solemn chase – from morn to sultry noon
His steps had followed, fleetest of the fleet,
The red-deer driven along its native heights
With cry of hound and horn; and, from that toil
Returned with sinews weakened and relaxed,
This generous Youth, too negligent of self,
Plunged – 'mid a gay and busy throng convened
To wash the fleeces of his Father's flock –
870 Into the chilling flood. Convulsions dire
Seized him, that self-same night; and through the space
Of twelve ensuing days his frame was wrenched,
Till nature rested from her work in death.
To him, thus snatched away, his comrades paid
A soldier's honours. At his funeral hour
Bright was the sun, the sky a cloudless blue –
A golden lustre slept upon the hills;
And if by chance a stranger, wandering there,
From some commanding eminence had looked
880 Down on this spot, well pleased would he have seen
A glittering spectacle; but every face
Was pallid: seldom hath that eye been moist
With tears, that wept not then; nor were the few,
Who from their dwellings came not forth to join
In this sad service, less disturbed than we.
They started at the tributary peal
Of instantaneous thunder, which announced,
Through the still air, the closing of the Grave;
And distant mountains echoed with a sound

890 Of lamentation, never heard before!'

The Pastor ceased. – My venerable Friend
Victoriously upraised his clear bright eye;
And, when that eulogy was ended, stood
Enrapt, as if his inward sense perceived
The prolongation of some still response,
Sent by the ancient Soul of this wide land,
The Spirit of its mountains and its seas,
Its cities, temples, fields, its awful power,
Its rights and virtues – by that Deity
900 Descending, and supporting his pure heart
With patriotic confidence and joy.
And, at the last of those memorial words,
The pining Solitary turned aside;
Whether through manly instinct to conceal
Tender emotions spreading from the heart
To his worn cheek; or with uneasy shame
For those cold humours of habitual spleen
That, fondly seeking in dispraise of man
Solace and self-excuse, had sometimes urged
910 To self-abuse a not ineloquent tongue.
– Right toward the sacred Edifice his steps
Had been directed; and we saw him now
Intent upon a monumental stone,
Whose uncouth form was grafted on the wall,
Or rather seemed to have grown into the side
Of the rude pile; as oft-times trunks of trees,
Where nature works in wild and craggy spots,
Are seen incorporate with the living rock –
To endure for aye. The Vicar, taking note
920 Of his employment, with a courteous smile
Exclaimed –
          'The sagest Antiquarian's eye
That task would foil;' then, letting fall his voice
While he advanced, thus spake: 'Tradition tells
That, in Eliza's golden days, a Knight
Came on a war-horse sumptuously attired,

And fixed his home in this sequestered vale.
'Tis left untold if here he first drew breath,
Or as a stranger reached this deep recess,
Unknowing and unknown. A pleasing thought
930 I sometimes entertain, that haply bound
To Scotland's court in service of his Queen,
Or sent on mission to some northern Chief
Of England's realm, this vale he might have seen
With transient observation; and thence caught
An image fair, which, brightening in his soul
When joy of war and pride of chivalry
Languished beneath accumulated years,
Had power to draw him from the world, resolved
To make that paradise his chosen home
940 To which his peaceful fancy oft had turned.

'Vague thoughts are these; but, if belief may rest
Upon unwritten story fondly traced
From sire to son, in this obscure retreat
The Knight arrived, with spear and shield, and borne
Upon a Charger gorgeously bedecked
With broidered housings. And the lofty Steed –
His sole companion, and his faithful friend,
Whom he, in gratitude, let loose to range
In fertile pastures – was beheld with eyes
950 Of admiration and delightful awe,
By those untravelled Dalesmen. With less pride,
Yet free from touch of envious discontent,
They saw a mansion at his bidding rise,
Like a bright star, amid the lowly band
Of their rude homesteads. Here the Warrior dwelt;
And, in that mansion, children of his own,
Or kindred, gathered round him. As a tree
That falls and disappears, the house is gone;
And, through improvidence or want of love
960 For ancient worth and honourable things,
The spear and shield are vanished, which the Knight
Hung in his rustic hall. One ivied arch

Myself have seen, a gateway, last remains
Of that foundation in domestic care
Raised by his hands. And now no trace is left
Of the mild-hearted Champion, save this stone,
Faithless memorial! and his family name
Borne by yon clustering cottages, that sprang
From out the ruins of his stately lodge:
970 These, and the name and title at full length, –
𝔖ir 𝔄lfred 𝔍rt�ing, with appropriate words
Accompanied, still extant, in a wreath
Or posy, girding round the several fronts
Of three clear-sounding and harmonious bells,
That in the steeple hang, his pious gift.'

'So fails, so languishes, grows dim, and dies,'
The grey-haired Wanderer pensively exclaimed,
'All that this world is proud of. From their spheres
The stars of human glory are cast down;
980 Perish the roses and the flowers of kings,
Princes, and emperors, and the crowns and palms
Of all the mighty, withered and consumed!
Nor is power given to lowliest innocence
Long to protect her own. The man himself
Departs; and soon is spent the line of those
Who, in the bodily image, in the mind,
In heart or soul, in station or pursuit,
Did most resemble him. Degrees and ranks,
Fraternities and orders – heaping high
990 New wealth upon the burden of the old,
And placing trust in privilege confirmed
And re-confirmed – are scoffed at with a smile
Of greedy foretaste, and from the secret stand
Of Desolation, aimed: to slow decline
These yield, and these to sudden overthrow:
Their virtue, service, happiness, and state
Expire; and nature's pleasant robe of green,
Humanity's appointed shroud, enwraps
Their monuments and their memory. The vast Frame

1000 Of social nature changes evermore
Her organs and her members, with decay
Restless, and restless generation, powers
And functions dying and produced at need, –
And by this law the mighty whole subsists:
With an ascent and progress in the main;
Yet, oh! how disproportioned to the hopes
And expectations of self-flattering minds!

'The courteous Knight, whose bones are here interred,
Lived in an age conspicuous as our own
1010 For strife and ferment in the minds of men;
Whence alteration in the forms of things,
Various and vast. A memorable age!
Which did to him assign a pensive lot –
To linger 'mid the last of those bright clouds
That, on the steady breeze of honour, sailed
In long procession calm and beautiful.
He who had seen his own bright order fade,
And its devotion gradually decline,
(While war, relinquishing the lance and shield,
1020 Her temper changed, and bowed to other laws)
Had also witnessed, in his morn of life,
That violent commotion, which o'erthrew,
In town and city and sequestered glen,
Altar, and cross, and church of solemn roof,
And old religious house – pile after pile;
And shook their tenants out into the fields,
Like wild beasts without home! Their hour was come;
But why no softening thought of gratitude,
No just remembrance, scruple, or wise doubt?
1030 Benevolence is mild; nor borrows help,
Save at worst need, from bold impetuous force,
Fitliest allied to anger and revenge.
But Human-kind rejoices in the might
Of mutability; and airy hopes,
Dancing around her, hinder and disturb
Those meditations of the soul that feed

The retrospective virtues. Festive songs
Break from the maddened nations at the sight
Of sudden overthrow; and cold neglect
1040 Is the sure consequence of slow decay.

'Even,' said the Wanderer, 'as that courteous Knight,
Bound by his vow to labour for redress
Of all who suffer wrong, and to enact
By sword and lance the law of gentleness,
(If I may venture of myself to speak,
Trusting that not incongruously I blend
Low things with lofty) I too shall be doomed
To outlive the kindly use and fair esteem
Of the poor calling which my youth embraced
1050 With no unworthy prospect. But enough;
— Thoughts crowd upon me — and 'twere seemlier now
To stop, and yield our gracious Teacher thanks
For the pathetic records which his voice
Hath here delivered; words of heartfelt truth,
Tending to patience when affliction strikes;
To hope and love; to confident repose
In God; and reverence for the dust of Man.'

BOOK EIGHTH
THE PARSONAGE

Argument

Pastor's apology and apprehensions that he might have detained
his Auditors too long, with the Pastor's invitation to his house.
— Solitary disinclined to comply — rallies the Wanderer — and
playfully draws a comparison between his itinerant profession
and that of the Knight-errant — which leads to Wanderer's
giving an account of changes in the Country from the manufacturing spirit. — Favourable effects. — The other side of the
picture, and chiefly as it has affected the humbler classes. —
Wanderer asserts the hollowness of all national grandeur if
unsupported by moral worth. — Physical science unable to
support itself. — Lamentations over an excess of manufacturing

industry among the humbler Classes of Society. – Picture of a
Child employed in a Cotton-mill. – Ignorance and degradation
of Children among the agricultural Population reviewed. –
Conversation broken off by a renewed Invitation from the
Pastor. – Path leading to his House. – Its appearance described.
– His Daughter. – His Wife. – His Son (a Boy) enters with his
Companion. – Their happy appearance. – The Wanderer how
affected by the sight of them.

The pensive Sceptic of the lonely vale
To those acknowledgements subscribed his own,
With a sedate compliance, which the Priest
Failed not to notice, inly pleased, and said: –
'If ye, by whom invited I began
These narratives of calm and humble life,
Be satisfied, 'tis well, – the end is gained;
And in return for sympathy bestowed
And patient listening, thanks accept from me.
10   – Life, death, eternity! momentous themes
Are they – and might demand a seraph's tongue,
Were they not equal to their own support;
And therefore no incompetence of mine
Could do them wrong. The universal forms
Of human nature, in a spot like this,
Present themselves at once to all men's view:
Ye wished for act and circumstance, that make
The individual known and understood;
And such as my best judgement could select
20   From what the place afforded, have been given;
Though apprehensions crossed me that my zeal
To his might well be likened, who unlocks
A cabinet stored with gems and pictures – draws
His treasures forth, soliciting regard
To this, and this, as worthier than the last,
Till the spectator, who awhile was pleased
More than the exhibitor himself, becomes
Weary and faint, and longs to be released.
– But let us hence! my dwelling is in sight,
And there –'

30   At this the Solitary shrunk
With backward will; but, wanting not address
That inward motion to disguise, he said
To his Compatriot, smiling as he spake:
– 'The peaceable remains of this good Knight
Would be disturbed, I fear, with wrathful scorn,
If consciousness could reach him where he lies
That one, albeit of these degenerate times,
Deploring changes past, or dreading change
Foreseen, had dared to couple, even in thought,
40 The fine vocation of the sword and lance
With the gross aims and body-bending toil
Of a poor brotherhood who walk the earth
Pitied, and, where they are not known, despised.

   'Yet, by the good Knight's leave, the two estates
Are graced with some resemblance. Errant those,
Exiles and wanderers – and the like are these;
Who, with their burden, traverse hill and dale,
Carrying relief for nature's simple wants.
– What though no higher recompense be sought
50 Than honest maintenance, by irksome toil
Full oft procured, yet may they claim respect,
Among the intelligent, for what this course
Enables them to be and to perform.
Their tardy steps give leisure to observe,
While solitude permits the mind to feel;
Instructs, and prompts her to supply defects
By the division of her inward self
For grateful converse: and to these poor men
Nature (I but repeat your favourite boast)
60 Is bountiful – go wheresoe'er they may;
Kind nature's various wealth is all their own.
Versed in the characters of men; and bound,
By ties of daily interest, to maintain
Conciliatory manners and smooth speech;
Such have been, and still are in their degree,
Examples efficacious to refine

Rude intercourse; apt agents to expel,
By importation of unlooked-for arts,
Barbarian torpor, and blind prejudice;
70 Raising, through just gradation, savage life
To rustic, and the rustic to urbane.
– Within their moving magazines is lodged
Power that comes forth to quicken and exalt
Affections seated in the mother's breast,
And in the lover's fancy; and to feed
The sober sympathies of long-tried friends.
– By these Itinerants, as experienced men,
Counsel is given; contention they appease
With gentle language; in remotest wilds,
80 Tears wipe away, and pleasant tidings bring;
Could the proud quest of chivalry do more?'

'Happy,' rejoined the Wanderer, 'they who gain
A panegyric from your generous tongue!
But, if to these Wayfarers once pertained
Aught of romantic interest, it is gone.
Their purer service, in this realm at least,
Is past for ever. – An inventive Age
Has wrought, if not with speed of magic, yet
To most strange issues. I have lived to mark
90 A new and unforeseen creation rise
From out the labours of a peaceful Land
Wielding her potent enginery to frame
And to produce, with appetite as keen
As that of war, which rests not night or day,
Industrious to destroy! With fruitless pains
Might one like me *now* visit many a tract
Which, in his youth, he trod, and trod again,
A lone pedestrian with a scanty freight,
Wished-for, or welcome, wheresoe'er he came –
100 Among the tenantry of thorpe and vill;
Or straggling burgh, of ancient charter proud,
And dignified by battlements and towers
Of some stern castle, mouldering on the brow

Of a green hill or bank of rugged stream.
The foot-path faintly marked, the horse-track wild,
And formidable length of plashy lane,
(Prized avenues ere others had been shaped
Or easier links connecting place with place)
Have vanished – swallowed up by stately roads
110 Easy and bold, that penetrate the gloom
Of Britain's farthest glens. The Earth has lent
Her waters, Air her breezes; and the sail
Of traffic glides with ceaseless intercourse,
Glistening along the low and woody dale;
Or, in its progress, on the lofty side
Of some bare hill, with wonder kenned from far.

'Meanwhile, at social Industry's command,
How quick, how vast an increase! From the germ
Of some poor hamlet, rapidly produced
120 Here a huge town, continuous and compact,
Hiding the face of earth for leagues – and there,
Where not a habitation stood before,
Abodes of men irregularly massed
Like trees in forests, – spread through spacious tracts,
O'er which the smoke of unremitting fires
Hangs permanent, and plentiful as wreaths
Of vapour glittering in the morning sun.
And, wheresoe'er the traveller turns his steps,
He sees the barren wilderness erased,
130 Or disappearing; triumph that proclaims
How much the mild Directress of the plough
Owes to alliance with these new-born arts!
– Hence is the wide sea peopled, – hence the shores
Of Britain are resorted to by ships
Freighted from every climate of the world
With the world's choicest produce. Hence that sum
Of keels that rest within her crowded ports,
Or ride at anchor in her sounds and bays;
That animating spectacle of sails
140 That, through her inland regions, to and fro

Pass with the respirations of the tide,
Perpetual, multitudinous! Finally,
Hence a dread arm of floating power, a voice
Of thunder daunting those who would approach
With hostile purposes the blessèd Isle,
Truth's consecrated residence, the seat
Impregnable of Liberty and Peace.

    'And yet, O happy Pastor of a flock
Faithfully watched, and, by that loving care
150 And Heaven's good providence, preserved from taint!
With you I grieve, when on the darker side
Of this great change I look; and there behold
Such outrage done to nature as compels
The indignant power to justify herself;
Yea, to avenge her violated rights,
For England's bane. – When soothing darkness spreads
O'er hill and vale,' the Wanderer thus expressed
His recollections, 'and the punctual stars,
While all things else are gathering to their homes,
160 Advance, and in the firmament of heaven
Glitter – but undisturbing, undisturbed;
As if their silent company were charged
With peaceful admonitions for the heart
Of all-beholding Man, earth's thoughtful lord;
Then, in full many a region, once like this
The assured domain of calm simplicity
And pensive quiet, an unnatural light
Prepared for never-resting Labour's eyes
Breaks from a many-windowed fabric huge;
170 And at the appointed hour a bell is heard,
Of harsher import than the curfew-knoll
That spake the Norman Conqueror's stern behest –
A local summons to unceasing toil!
Disgorged are now the ministers of day;
And, as they issue from the illumined pile,
A fresh band meets them, at the crowded door –
And in the courts – and where the rumbling stream,

That turns the multitude of dizzy wheels,
Glares, like a troubled spirit, in its bed
180   Among the rocks below. Men, maidens, youths,
Mother and little children, boys and girls,
Enter, and each the wonted task resumes
Within this temple, where is offered up
To Gain, the master idol of the realm,
Perpetual sacrifice. Even thus of old
Our ancestors, within the still domain
Of vast cathedral or conventual church,
Their vigils kept; where tapers day and night
On the dim altar burned continually,
190   In token that the House was evermore
Watching to God. Religious men were they;
Nor would their reason, tutored to aspire
Above this transitory world, allow
That there should pass a moment of the year,
When in their land the Almighty's service ceased.

'Triumph who will in these profaner rites
Which we, a generation self-extolled,
As zealously perform! I cannot share
His proud complacency: – yet do I exult,
200   Casting reserve away, exult to see
An intellectual mastery exercised
O'er the blind elements; a purpose given,
A perseverance fed; almost a soul
Imparted – to brute matter. I rejoice,
Measuring the force of those gigantic powers
That, by the thinking mind, have been compelled
To serve the will of feeble-bodied Man.
For with the sense of admiration blends
The animating hope that time may come
210   When, strengthened, yet not dazzled, by the might
Of this dominion over nature gained,
Men of all lands shall exercise the same
In due proportion to their country's need;
Learning, though late, that all true glory rests,

All praise, all safety, and all happiness,
Upon the moral law. Egyptian Thebes,
Tyre, by the margin of the sounding waves,
Palmyra, central in the desert, fell;
And the Arts died by which they had been raised.
220 – Call Archimedes from his buried tomb
Upon the grave of vanished Syracuse,
And feelingly the Sage shall make report
How insecure, how baseless in itself,
Is the Philosophy whose sway depends
On mere material instruments; – how weak
Those arts, and high inventions, if unpropped
By virtue. – He, sighing with pensive grief,
Amid his calm abstractions, would admit
That not the slender privilege is theirs
230 To save themselves from blank forgetfulness!'

When from the Wanderer's lips these words had fallen,
I said, 'And, did in truth those vaunted Arts
Possess such privilege, how could we escape
Sadness and keen regret, we who revere,
And would preserve as things above all price,
The old domestic morals of the land,
Her simple manners, and the stable worth
That dignified and cheered a low estate?
Oh! where is now the character of peace,
240 Sobriety, and order, and chaste love,
And honest dealing, and untainted speech,
And pure good-will, and hospitable cheer;
That made the very thought of country-life
A thought of refuge, for a mind detained
Reluctantly amid the bustling crowd?
Where now the beauty of the sabbath kept
With conscientious reverence, as a day
By the almighty Lawgiver pronounced
Holy and blest? and where the winning grace
250 Of all the lighter ornaments attached
To time and season, as the year rolled round?'

'Fled!' was the Wanderer's passionate response,
'Fled utterly! or only to be tràced
In a few fortunate retreats like this;
Which I behold with trembling, when I think
What lamentable change, a year – a month –
May bring; that brook converting as it runs
Into an instrument of deadly bane
For those, who, yet untempted to forsake
260   The simple occupations of their sires,
Drink the pure water of its innocent stream
With lip almost as pure. – Domestic bliss
(Or call it comfort, by a humbler name,)
How art thou blighted for the poor Man's heart!
Lo! in such neighbourhood, from morn to eve,
The habitations empty! or perchance
The Mother left alone, – no helping hand
To rock the cradle of her peevish babe;
No daughters round her, busy at the wheel,
270   Or in dispatch of each day's little growth
Of household occupation; no nice arts
Of needle-work; no bustle at the fire,
Where once the dinner was prepared with pride;
Nothing to speed the day, or cheer the mind;
Nothing to praise, to teach, or to command!

'The Father, if perchance he still retain
His old employments, goes to field or wood,
No longer led or followed by the Sons;
Idlers perchance they were, – but in *his* sight;
280   Breathing fresh air, and treading the green earth;
Till their short holiday of childhood ceased,
Ne'er to return! That birthright now is lost.
Economists will tell you that the State
Thrives by the forfeiture – unfeeling thought,
And false as monstrous! Can the mother thrive
By the destruction of her innocent sons
In whom a premature necessity
Blocks out the forms of nature, preconsumes

The reason, famishes the heart, shuts up
290   The infant Being in itself, and makes
Its very spring a season of decay!
The lot is wretched, the condition sad,
Whether a pining discontent survive,
And thirst for change; or habit hath subdued
The soul deprest, dejected – even to love
Of her close tasks, and long captivity.

'Oh, banish far such wisdom as condemns
A native Briton to these inward chains,
Fixed in his soul, so early and so deep;
300   Without his own consent, or knowledge, fixed!
He is a slave to whom release comes not,
And cannot come. The boy, where'er he turns,
Is still a prisoner; when the wind is up
Among the clouds, and roars through the ancient woods;
Or when the sun is shining in the east,
Quiet and calm. Behold him – in the school
Of his attainments? no; but with the air
Fanning his temples under heaven's blue arch.
His raiment, whitened o'er with cotton-flakes
310   Or locks of wool, announces whence he comes.
Creeping his gait and cowering, his lip pale,
His respiration quick and audible;
And scarcely could you fancy that a gleam
Could break from out those languid eyes, or a blush
Mantle upon his cheek. Is this the form,
Is that the countenance, and such the port,
Of no mean Being? One who should be clothed
With dignity befitting his proud hope;
Who, in his very childhood, should appear
320   Sublime from present purity and joy!
The limbs increase; but liberty of mind
Is gone for ever; and this organic frame,
So joyful in its motions, is become
Dull, to the joy of her own motions dead;
And even the touch, so exquisitely poured

Through the whole body, with a languid will
Performs its functions; rarely competent
To impress a vivid feeling on the mind
Of what there is delighful in the breeze,
330 The gentle visitations of the sun,
Or lapse of liquid element – by hand,
Or foot, or lip, in summer's warmth – perceived.
– Can hope look forward to a manhood raised
On such foundations?'
                              'Hope is none for him!'
The pale Recluse indignantly exclaimed,
'And tens of thousands suffer wrong as deep.
Yet be it asked, in justice to our age,
If there were not, before those arts appeared,
These structures rose, commingling old and young,
340 And unripe sex with sex, for mutual taint;
If there were not, *then*, in our far-famed Isle,
Multitudes, who from infancy had breathed
Air unimprisoned, and had lived at large;
Yet walked beneath the sun, in human shape,
As abject, as degraded? At this day,
Who shall enumerate the crazy huts
And tottering hovels, whence do issue forth
A ragged Offspring, with their upright hair
Crowned like the image of fantastic Fear;
350 Or wearing, (shall we say?) in that white growth
An ill-adjusted turban, for defence
Or fierceness, wreathed around their sunburnt brows,
By savage Nature? Shrivelled are their lips;
Naked, and coloured like the soil, the feet
On which they stand; as if thereby they drew
Some nourishment, as trees do by their roots,
From earth, the common mother of us all.
Figure and mien, complexion and attire,
Are leagued to strike dismay; but outstretched hand
360 And whining voice denote them suppliants
For the least boon that pity can bestow.
Such on the breast of darksome heaths are found;

And with their parents occupy the skirts
Or furze-clad commons; such are born and reared
At the mine's mouth under impending rocks;
Or dwell in chambers of some natural cave;
Or where their ancestors erected huts,
For the convenience of unlawful gain,
In forest purlieus; and the like are bred,
370 All England through, where nooks and slips of ground
Purloined, in times less jealous than our own,
From the green margin of the public way,
A residence afford them, 'mid the bloom
And gaiety of cultivated fields.
Such (we will hope the lowest in the scale)
Do I remember oft-times to have seen
'Mid Buxton's dreary heights. In earnest watch,
Till the swift vehicle approach, they stand;
Then, following closely with the cloud of dust,
380 An uncouth feat exhibit, and are gone
Heels over head, like tumblers on a stage.
– Up from the ground they snatch the copper coin,
And, on the freight of merry passengers
Fixing a steady eye, maintain their speed;
And spin – and pant – and overhead again,
Wild pursuivants! until their breath is lost,
Or bounty tires – and every face, that smiled
Encouragement, hath ceased to look that way.
– But, like the vagrants of the gypsy tribe,
390 These, bred to little pleasure in themselves,
Are profitless to others.
                  Turn we then
To Britons born and bred within the pale
Of civil polity, and early trained
To earn, by wholesome labour in the field,
The bread they eat. A sample should I give
Of what this stock hath long produced to enrich
The tender age of life, ye would exclaim,
"Is this the whistling plough-boy whose shrill notes
Impart new gladness to the morning air!"

400   Forgive me if I venture to suspect
That many, sweet to hear of in soft verse,
Are of no finer frame. Stiff are his joints;
Beneath a cumbrous frock, that to the knees
Invests the thriving churl, his legs appear,
Fellows to those that lustily upheld
The wooden stools for everlasting use,
Whereon our fathers sate. And mark his brow!
Under whose shaggy canopy are set
Two eyes – not dim, but of a healthy stare –
410   Wide, sluggish, blank, and ignorant, and strange –
Proclaiming boldly that they never drew
A look or motion of intelligence
From infant-conning of the Christ-cross-row,
Or puzzling through a primer, line by line,
Till perfect mastery crown the pains at last.
– What kindly warmth from touch of fostering hand,
What penetrating power of sun or breeze,
Shall e'er dissolve the crust wherein his soul
Sleeps, like a caterpillar sheathed in ice?
420   This torpor is no pitiable work
Of modern ingenuity; no town
Nor crowded city can be taxed with aught
Of sottish vice or desperate breach of law,
To which (and who can tell where or how soon?)
He may be roused. This Boy the fields produce:
His spade and hoe, mattock and glittering scythe,
The carter's whip that on his shoulder rests
In air high-towering with a boorish pomp,
The sceptre of his sway; his country's name,
430   Her equal rights, her churches and her schools –
What have they done for him? And, let me ask,
For tens of thousands uninformed as he?
In brief, what liberty of *mind* is here?'

    This ardent sally pleased the mild good Man,
To whom the appeal couched in its closing words
Was pointedly addressed; and to the thoughts

That, in assent or opposition, rose
Within his mind, he seemed prepared to give
Prompt utterance; but the Vicar interposed
440   With invitation urgently renewed.
    – We followed, taking as he led, a path
Along a hedge of hollies dark and tall,
Whose flexible boughs low bending with a weight
Of leafy spray, concealed the stems and roots
That gave them nourishment. When frosty winds
Howl from the north, what kindly warmth, methought,
Is here – how grateful this impervious screen!
    – Not shaped by simple wearing of the foot
On rural business passing to and fro
450   Was the commodious walk: a careful hand
Had marked the line, and strewn its surface o'er
With pure cerulean gravel, from the heights
Fetched by a neighbouring brook. – Across the vale
The stately fence accompanied our steps;
And thus the pathway, by perennial green
Guarded and graced, seemed fashioned to unite,
As by a beautiful yet solemn chain,
The Pastor's mansion with the house of prayer.

      Like image of solemnity, conjoined
460   With feminine allurement soft and fair,
The mansion's self displayed; – a reverend pile
With bold projections and recesses deep;
Shadowy, yet gay and lightsome as it stood
Fronting the noontide sun. We paused to admire
The pillared porch, elaborately embossed;
The low wide windows with their mullions old;
The cornice, richly fretted, of grey stone;
And that smooth slope from which the dwelling rose,
By beds and banks Arcadian of gay flowers
470   And flowering shrubs, protected and adorned:
Profusion bright! and every flower assuming
A more than natural vividness of hue
From unaffected contrast with the gloom

Of sober cypress, and the darker foil
Of yew, in which survived some traces, here
Not unbecoming, of grotesque device
And uncouth fancy. From behind the roof
Rose the slim ash and massy sycamore,
Blending their diverse foliage with the green
480 Of ivy, flourishing and thick, that clasped
The huge round chimneys, harbour of delight
For wren and redbreast, – where they sit and sing
Their slender ditties when the trees are bare.
Nor must I leave untouched (the picture else
Were incomplete) a relique of old times
Happily spared, a little Gothic niche
Of nicest workmanship; that once had held
The sculptured image of some patron-saint,
Or of the blessèd Virgin, looking down
490 On all who entered those religious doors.

But lo! where from the rocky garden-mount
Crowned by its antique summer-house – descends,
Light as the silver fawn, a radiant Girl;
For she hath recognized her honoured friend,
The Wanderer ever welcome! A prompt kiss
The gladsome child bestows at his request;
And, up the flowery lawn as we advance,
Hangs on the old Man with a happy look,
And with a pretty, restless hand of love.
500 – We enter – by the Lady of the place
Cordially greeted. Graceful was her port:
A lofty stature undepressed by time,
Whose visitation had not wholly spared
The finer lineaments of form and face;
To that complexion brought which prudence trusts in
And wisdom loves. – But when a stately ship
Sails in smooth weather by the placid coast
On homeward voyage, – what if wind and wave,
And hardship undergone in various climes,
510 Have caused her to abate the virgin pride,

And that full trim of inexperienced hope
With which she left her haven – not for this,
Should the sun strike her, and the impartial breeze
Play on her streamers, fails she to assume
Brightness and touching beauty of her own,
That charm all eyes. So bright, so fair, appeared
This goodly Matron, shining in the beams
Of unexpected pleasure. – Soon the board
Was spread, and we partook a plain repast.

520   Here, resting in cool shelter, we beguiled
The mid-day hours with desultory talk;
From trivial themes to general argument
Passing, as accident or fancy led,
Or courtesy prescribed. While question rose
And answer flowed, the fetters of reserve
Dropping from every mind, the Solitary
Resumed the manners of his happier days;
And in the various conversation bore
A willing, nay, at times, a forward part;
530 Yet with the grace of one who in the world
Had learned the art of pleasing, and had now
Occasion given him to display his skill,
Upon the stedfast 'vantage-ground of truth.
He gazed, with admiration unsuppressed,
Upon the landscape of the sun-bright vale,
Seen, from the shady room in which we sate,
In softened pérspective; and more than once
Praised the consummate harmony serene
Of gravity and elegance, diffused
540 Around the mansion and its whole domain;
Not, doubtless, without help of female taste
And female care. – 'A blessed lot is yours!'
The words escaped his lip, with a tender sigh
Breathed over them: but suddenly the door
Flew open, and a pair of lusty Boys
Appeared, confusion checking their delight.
– Not brothers they in feature or attire,

But fond companions, so I guessed, in field,
And by the river's margin – whence they come,
550 Keen anglers with unusual spoil elated.
One bears a willow-pannier on his back,
The boy of plainer garb, whose blush survives
More deeply tinged. Twin might the other be
To that fair girl who from the garden-mount
Bounded: – triumphant entry this for him!
Between his hands he holds a smooth blue stone,
On whose capacious surface see outspread
Large store of gleaming crimson-spotted trouts;
Ranged side by side, and lessening by degrees
560 Up to the dwarf that tops the pinnacle.
Upon the board he lays the sky-blue stone
With its rich freight; their number he proclaims;
Tells from what pool the noblest had been dragged;
And where the very monarch of the brook,
After long struggle, had escaped at last –
Stealing alternately at them and us
(As doth his comrade too) a look of pride:
And, verily, the silent creatures made
A splendid sight, together thus exposed;
570 Dead – but not sullied or deformed by death,
That seemed to pity what he could not spare.

But O, the animation in the mien
Of those two boys! yea in the very words
With which the young narrator was inspired,
When, as our questions led, he told at large
Of that day's prowess! Him might I compare,
His looks, tones, gestures, eager eloquence,
To a bold brook that splits for better speed,
And at the self-same moment, works its way
580 Through many channels, ever and anon
Parted and re-united: his compeer
To the still lake, whose stillness is to sight
As beautiful – as grateful to the mind.
– But to what object shall the lovely Girl

Be likened? She whose countenance and air
Unite the graceful qualities of both,
Even as she shares the pride and joy of both.

My grey-haired Friend was moved; his vivid eye
Glistened with tenderness; his mind, I knew,
590 Was full; and had, I doubted not, returned,
Upon this impulse, to the theme – erewhile
Abruptly broken off. The ruddy boys
Withdrew, on summons to their well-earned meal;
And He – to whom all tongues resigned their rights
With willingness, to whom the general ear
Listened with readier patience than to strain
Of music, lute or harp, a long delight
That ceased not when his voice had ceased – as One
Who from truth's central point serenely views
600 The compass of his argument – began
Mildly, and with a clear and steady tone.

BOOK NINTH
DISCOURSE OF THE WANDERER AND AN EVENING
VISIT TO THE LAKE

Argument

Wanderer asserts that an active principle pervades the Universe,
its noblest seat the human soul. – How lively this principle is in
Childhood. – Hence the delight in old Age of looking back upon
Childhood. – The dignity, powers, and privileges of Age
asserted. – These not to be looked for generally but under a just
government. – Right of a human Creature to be exempt from
being considered as a mere Instrument. – The condition of
multitudes deplored. – Former conversation recurred to, and
the Wanderer's opinions set in a clearer light. – Truth placed
within reach of the humblest. – Equality. – Happy state of
the two Boys again adverted to. – Earnest wish expressed for
a System of National Education established universally by
Government. – Glorious effects of this foretold. – Walk to the
Lake. – Grand spectacle from the side of a hill. – Address of
Priest to the Supreme Being – in the course of which he contrasts

with ancient Barbarism the present appearance of the scene
before him. – The change ascribed to Christianity. – Apos-
trophe to his flock, living and dead. – Gratitude to the Almighty.
– Return over the Lake. – Parting with the Solitary. – Under
what circumstances.

'To every Form of being is assigned,'
Thus calmly spake the venerable Sage,
'An *active* Principle: – howe'er removed
From sense and observation, it subsists
In all things, in all natures; in the stars
Of azure heaven, the unenduring clouds,
In flower and tree, in every pebbly stone
That paves the brooks, the stationary rocks,
The moving waters, and the invisible air.
10 Whate'er exists hath properties that spread
Beyond itself, communicating good,
A simple blessing, or with evil mixed;
Spirit that knows no insulated spot,
No chasm, no solitude; from link to link
It circulates, the Soul of all the worlds.
This is the freedom of the universe;
Unfolded still the more, more visible,
The more we know; and yet is reverenced least,
And least respected in the human Mind,
20 Its most apparent home. The food of hope
Is meditated action; robbed of this
Her sole support, she languishes and dies.
We perish also; for we live by hope
And by desire; we see by the glad light
And breathe the sweet air of futurity;
And so we live, or else we have no life.
Tomorrow – nay perchance this very hour
(For every moment hath its own tomorrow!)
Those blooming Boys, whose hearts are almost sick
30 With present triumph, will be sure to find
A field before them freshened with the dew
Of other expectations; – in which course
Their happy year spins round. The youth obeys

A like glad impulse; and so moves the man
'Mid all his apprehensions, cares, and fears, –
Or so he ought to move. Ah! why in age
Do we revert so fondly to the walks
Of childhood – but that there the Soul discerns
The dear memorial footsteps unimpaired
40 Of her own native vigour; thence can hear
Reverberations; and a choral song,
Commingling with the incense that ascends,
Undaunted, toward the imperishable heavens,
From her own lonely altar?
                         Do not think
That good and wise ever will be allowed,
Though strength decay, to breathe in such estate
As shall divide them wholly from the stir
Of hopeful nature. Rightly it is said
That Man descends into the VALE of years;
50 Yet have I thought that we might also speak,
And not presumptuously, I trust, of Age,
As of a final EMINENCE; though bare
In aspect and forbidding, yet a point
On which 'tis not impossible to sit
In awful sovereignty; a place of power,
A throne, that may be likened unto his,
Who, in some placid day of summer, looks
Down from a mountain-top, – say one of those
High peaks, that bound the vale where now we are.
60 Faint, and diminished to the gazing eye,
Forest and field, and hill and dale appear,
With all the shapes over their surface spread:
But, while the gross and visible frame of things
Relinquishes its hold upon the sense,
Yea almost on the Mind herself, and seems
All unsubstantialized, – how loud the voice
Of waters, with invigorated peal
From the full river in the vale below,
Ascending! For on that superior height
70 Who sits, is disencumbered from the press

Of near obstructions, and is privileged
To breathe in solitude, above the host
Of ever-humming insects, 'mid thin air
That suits not them. The murmur of the leaves
Many and idle, visits not his ear:
This he is freed from, and from thousand notes
(Not less unceasing, not less vain than these,)
By which the finer passages of sense
Are occupied; and the Soul, that would incline
80   To listen, is prevented or deterred.

'And may it not be hoped, that, placed by age
In like removal, tranquil though severe,
We are not so removed for utter loss;
But for some favour, suited to our need?
What more than that the severing should confer
Fresh power to commune with the invisible world,
And hear the mighty stream of tendency
Uttering, for elevation of our thought,
A clear sonorous voice, inaudible
90   To the vast multitude; whose doom it is
To run the giddy round of vain delight,
Or fret and labour on the Plain below.

'But, if to such sublime ascent the hopes
Of Man may rise, as to a welcome close
And termination of his mortal course;
Them only can such hope inspire whose minds
Have not been starved by absolute neglect;
Nor bodies crushed by unremitting toil;
To whom kind Nature, therefore, may afford
100   Proof of the sacred love she bears for all;
Whose birthright Reason, therefore, may ensure.
For me, consulting what I feel within
In times when most existence with herself
Is satisfied, I cannot but believe,
That, far as kindly Nature hath free scope

And Reason's sway predominates; even so far,
Country, society, and time itself,
That saps the individual's bodily frame,
And lays the generations low in dust,
110 Do, by the almighty Ruler's grace, partake
Of one maternal spirit, bringing forth
And cherishing with ever-constant love,
That tires not, nor betrays. Our life is turned
Out of her course, wherever man is made
An offering, or a sacrifice, a tool
Or implement, a passive thing employed
As a brute mean, without acknowledgement
Of common right or interest in the end;
Used or abused, as selfishness may prompt.
120 Say, what can follow for a rational soul
Perverted thus, but weakness in all good,
And strength in evil? Hence an after-call
For chastisement, and custody, and bonds,
And oft-times Death, avenger of the past,
And the sole guardian in whose hands we dare
Entrust the future. – Not for these sad issues
Was Man created; but to obey the law
Of life, and hope, and action. And 'tis known
That when we stand upon our native soil,
130 Unelbowed by such objects as oppress
Our active powers, those powers themselves become
Strong to subvert our noxious qualities:
They sweep distemper from the busy day,
And make the chalice of the big round year
Run o'er with gladness; whence the Being moves
In beauty through the world; and all who see
Bless him, rejoicing in his neighbourhood.'

'Then,' said the Solitary, 'by what force
Of language shall a feeling heart express
140 Her sorrow for that multitude in whom
We look for health from seeds that have been sown
In sickness, and for increase in a power

That works but by extinction? On themselves
They cannot lean, nor turn to their own hearts
To know what they must do; their wisdom is
To look into the eyes of others, thence
To be instructed what they must avoid:
Or rather, let us say, how least observed,
How with most quiet and most silent death,
150 With the least taint and injury to the air
The oppressor breathes, their human form divine,
And their immortal soul, may waste away.'

The Sage rejoined, 'I thank you – you have spared
My voice the utterance of a keen regret,
A wide compassion which with you I share.
When, heretofore, I placed before your sight
A Little-one, subjected to the arts
Of modern ingenuity, and made
The senseless member of a vast machine,
160 Serving as doth a spindle or a wheel;
Think not, that, pitying him, I could forget
The rustic Boy, who walks the fields, untaught;
The slave of ignorance, and oft of want,
And miserable hunger. Much, too much,
Of this unhappy lot, in early youth
We both have witnessed, lot which I myself
Shared, though in mild and merciful degree:
Yet was the mind to hinderances exposed,
Through which I struggled, not without distress
170 And sometimes injury, like a lamb enthralled
'Mid thorns and brambles; or a bird that breaks
Through a strong net, and mounts upon the wind,
Though with her plumes impaired. If they, whose souls
Should open while they range the richer fields
Of merry England, are obstructed less
By indigence, their ignorance is not less,
Nor less to be deplored. For who can doubt
That tens of thousands at this day exist
Such as the boy you painted, lineal heirs

180 Of those who once were vassals of her soil,
    Following its fortunes like the beasts or trees
    Which it sustained. But no one takes delight
    In this oppression; none are proud of it;
    It bears no sounding name, nor ever bore;
    A standing grievance, an indigenous vice
    Of every country under heaven. My thoughts
    Were turned to evils that are new and chosen,
    A bondage lurking under shape of good, –
    Arts, in themselves beneficent and kind,
190 But all too fondly followed and too far; –
    To victims, which the merciful can see
    Nor think that they are victims – turned to wrongs,
    By women, who have children of their own,
    Beheld without compassion; yea with praise!
    I spake of mischief by the wise diffused
    With gladness, thinking that the more it spreads
    The healthier, the securer, we become;
    Delusion which a moment may destroy!
    Lastly I mourned for those whom I had seen
200 Corrupted and cast down, on favoured ground,
    Where circumstance and nature had combined
    To shelter innocence, and cherish love;
    Who, but for this intrusion, would have lived,
    Possessed of health, and strength, and peace of mind;
    Thus would have lived, or never have been born.

    'Alas! what differs more than man from man!
    And whence that difference? Whence but from himself?
    For see the universal Race endowed
    With the same upright form! – The sun is fixed,
210 And the infinite magnificence of heaven
    Fixed, within reach of every human eye;
    The sleepless ocean murmurs for all ears;
    The vernal field infuses fresh delight
    Into all hearts. Throughout the world of sense,
    Even as an object is sublime or fair,
    That object is laid open to the view

Without reserve or veil; and as a power
Is salutary, or an influence sweet,
Are each and all enabled to perceive
220   That power, that influence, by impartial law.
Gifts nobler are vouchsafed alike to all;
Reason, and, with that reason, smiles and tears;
Imagination, freedom in the will;
Conscience to guide and check; and death to be
Foretasted, immortality conceived
By all, – a blissful immortality,
To them whose holiness on earth shall make
The Spirit capable of heaven, assured.
Strange, then, nor less than monstrous, might be deemed
230   The failure, if the Almighty, to this point
Liberal and undistinguishing, should hide
The excellence of moral qualities
From common understanding; leaving truth
And virtue, difficult, abstruse, and dark;
Hard to be won, and only by a few;
Strange, should He deal herein with nice respects,
And frustrate all the rest! Believe it not:
The primal duties shine aloft – like stars;
The charities that soothe, and heal, and bless,
240   Are scattered at the feet of Man – like flowers.
The generous inclination, the just rule,
Kind wishes, and good actions, and pure thoughts –
No mystery is here! Here is no boon
For high – yet not for low; for proudly graced –
Yet not for meek of heart. The smoke ascends
To heaven as lightly from the cottage-hearth
As from the haughtiest palace. He, whose soul
Ponders this true equality, may walk
The fields of earth with gratitude and hope;
250   Yet, in that meditation, will he find
Motive to sadder grief, as we have found;
Lamenting ancient virtues overthrown,
And for the injustice grieving, that hath made
So wide a difference between man and man.

'Then let us rather fix our gladdened thoughts
Upon the brighter scene. How blest that pair
Of blooming Boys (whom we beheld even now)
Blest in their several and their common lot!
A few short hours of each returning day
260 The thriving prisoners of their village-school:
And thence let loose, to seek their pleasant homes
Or range the grassy lawn in vacancy;
To breathe and to be happy, run and shout
Idle, – but no delay, no harm, no loss;
For every genial power of heaven and earth,
Through all the seasons of the changeful year,
Obsequiously doth take upon herself
To labour for them; bringing each in turn
The tribute of enjoyment, knowledge, health,
270 Beauty, or strength! Such privilege is theirs,
Granted alike in the outset of their course
To both; and, if that partnership must cease,
I grieve not,' to the Pastor here he turned,
'Much as I glory in that child of yours,
Repine not for his cottage-comrade, whom
Belike no higher destiny awaits
Than the old hereditary wish fulfilled;
The wish for liberty to live – content
With what Heaven grants, and die – in peace of mind,
280 Within the bosom of his native vale.
At least, whatever fate the noon of life
Reserves for either, sure it is that both
Have been permitted to enjoy the dawn;
Whether regarded as a jocund time,
That in itself may terminate, or lead
In course of nature to a sober eve.
Both have been fairly dealt with; looking back
They will allow that justice has in them
Been shown, alike to body and to mind.'

290   He paused, as if revolving in his soul
Some weighty matter; then, with fervent voice

And an impassioned majesty, exclaimed –

'O for the coming of that glorious time
When, prizing knowledge as her noblest wealth
And best protection, this imperial Realm,
While she exacts allegiance, shall admit
An obligation, on her part, to *teach*
Them who are born to serve her and obey;
Binding herself by statute to secure
300 For all the children whom her soil maintains
The rudiments of letters, and inform
The mind with moral and religious truth,
Both understood and practised, – so that none,
However destitute, be left to droop
By timely culture unsustained; or run
Into a wild disorder; or be forced
To drudge through a weary life without the help
Of intellectual implements and tools;
A savage horde among the civilized,
310 A servile band among the lordly free!
This sacred right, the lisping babe proclaims
To be inherent in him, by Heaven's will,
For the protection of his innocence;
And the rude boy – who, having overpast
The sinless age, by conscience is enrolled,
Yet mutinously knits his angry brow,
And lifts his wilful hand on mischief bent,
Or turns the godlike faculty of speech
To impious use – by process indirect
320 Declares his due, while he makes known his need.
– This sacred right is fruitlessly announced,
This universal plea in vain addressed,
To eyes and ears of parents who themselves
Did, in the time of their necessity,
Urge it in vain; and, therefore, like a prayer
That from the humblest floor ascends to heaven,
It mounts to reach the State's parental ear;
Who, if indeed she own a mother's heart,

And be not most unfeelingly devoid
330 Of gratitude to Providence, will grant
The unquestionable good – which, England, safe
From interference of external force,
May grant at leisure; without risk incurred
That what in wisdom for herself she doth,
Others shall e'er be able to undo.

'Look! and behold, from Calpe's sunburnt cliffs
To the flat margin of the Baltic sea,
Long-reverenced titles cast away as weeds;
Laws overturned; and territory split,
340 Like fields of ice rent by the polar wind,
And forced to join in less obnoxious shapes
Which, ere they gain consistence, by a gust
Of the same breath are shattered and destroyed.
Meantime the sovereignty of these fair Isles
Remains entire and indivisible:
And, if that ignorance were removed, which breeds
Within the compass of their several shores
Dark discontent, or loud commotion, each
Might still preserve the beautiful repose
350 Of heavenly bodies shining in their spheres.
– The discipline of slavery is unknown
Among us, – hence the more do we require
The discipline of virtue; order else
Cannot subsist, nor confidence, nor peace.
Thus, duties rising out of good possest
And prudent caution needful to avert
Impending evil, equally require
That the whole people should be taught and trained.
So shall licentiousness and black resolve
360 Be rooted out, and virtuous habits take
Their place; and genuine piety descend,
Like an inheritance, from age to age.

'With such foundations laid, avaunt the fear

Of numbers crowded on their native soil,
To the prevention of all healthful growth
Through mutual injury! Rather in the law
Of increase and the mandate from above
Rejoice! – and ye have special cause for joy.
– For, as the element of air affords
370 An easy passage to the industrious bees
Fraught with their burdens; and a way as smooth
For those ordained to take their sounding flight
From the thronged hive, and settle where they list
In fresh abodes – their labour to renew;
So the wide waters, open to the power,
The will, the instincts, and appointed needs
Of Britain, do invite her to cast off
Her swarms, and in succession send them forth;
Bound to establish new communities
380 On every shore whose aspect favours hope
Or bold adventure; promising to skill
And perseverance their deserved reward.

   'Yes,' he continued, kindling as he spake,
'Change wide, and deep, and silently performed,
This Land shall witness; and as days roll on,
Earth's universal frame shall feel the effect;
Even till the smallest habitable rock,
Beaten by lonely billows, hear the songs
Of humanized society; and bloom
390 With civil arts, that shall breathe forth their fragrance,
A grateful tribute to all-ruling Heaven.
From culture, unexclusively bestowed
On Albion's noble Race in freedom born,
Expect these mighty issues: from the pains
And faithful care of unambitious schools
Instructing simple childhood's ready ear:
Thence look for these magnificent results!
– Vast the circumference of hope – and ye
Are at its centre, British Lawgivers;
400 Ah! sleep not there in shame! Shall Wisdom's voice

From out the bosom of these troubled times
Repeat the dictates of her calmer mind,
And shall the venerable halls ye fill
Refuse to echo the sublime decree?
Trust not to partial care a general good;
Transfer not to futurity a work
Of urgent need. – Your Country must complete
Her glorious destiny. Begin even now,
Now, when oppression, like the Egyptian plague
410 Of darkness, stretched o'er guilty Europe, makes
The brightness more conspicuous that invests
The happy Island where ye think and act;
Now, when destruction is a prime pursuit,
Show to the wretched nations for what end
The powers of civil polity were given.'

    Abruptly here, but with a graceful air,
The Sage broke off. No sooner had he ceased
Than, looking forth, the gentle Lady said,
'Behold the shades of afternoon have fallen
420 Upon this flowery slope; and see – beyond –
The silvery lake is streaked with placid blue;
As if preparing for the peace of evening.
How temptingly the landscape shines! The air
Breathes invitation; easy is the walk
To the lake's margin, where a boat lies moored
Under a sheltering tree.' – Upon this hint
We rose together: all were pleased; but most
The beauteous girl, whose cheek was flushed with joy.
Light as a sunbeam glides along the hills
430 She vanished – eager to impart the scheme
To her loved brother and his shy compeer.
– Now was there bustle in the Vicar's house
And earnest preparation. – Forth we went,
And down the vale along the streamlet's edge
Pursued our way, a broken company,
Mute or conversing, single or in pairs.
Thus having reached a bridge, that overarched

The hasty rivulet where it lay becalmed
In a deep pool, by happy chance we saw
440 A twofold image; on a grassy bank
A snow-white ram, and in the crystal flood
Another and the same! Most beautiful,
On the green turf, with his imperial front
Shaggy and bold, and wreathèd horns superb,
The breathing creature stood; as beautiful,
Beneath him, showed his shadowy counterpart.
Each had his glowing mountains, each his sky,
And each seemed centre of his own fair world:
Antipodes unconscious of each other,
450 Yet, in partition, with their several spheres,
Blended in perfect stillness, to our sight!

'Ah! what a pity were it to disperse,
Or to disturb, so fair a spectacle,
And yet a breath can do it!'
                                    These few words
The Lady whispered, while we stood and gazed
Gathered together, all in still delight,
Not without awe. Thence passing on, she said
In like low voice to my particular ear,
'I love to hear that eloquent old Man
460 Pour forth his meditations, and descant
On human life from infancy to age.
How pure his spirit! in what vivid hues
His mind gives back the various forms of things,
Caught in their fairest, happiest, attitude!
While he is speaking, I have power to see
Even as he sees; but when his voice hath ceased,
Then, with a sigh, sometimes I feel, as now,
That combinations so serene and bright
Cannot be lasting in a world like ours,
470 Whose highest beauty, beautiful as it is,
Like that reflected in yon quiet pool,
Seems but a fleeting sunbeam's gift, whose peace
The sufferance only of a breath of air!'

More had she said – but sportive shouts were heard
Sent from the jocund hearts of those two Boys,
Who, bearing each a basket on his arm,
Down the green field came tripping after us.
With caution we embarked; and now the pair
For prouder service were addrest; but each,
480 Wishful to leave an opening for my choice,
Dropped the light oar his eager hand had seized.
Thanks given for that becoming courtesy,
Their place I took – and for a grateful office
Pregnant with recollections of the time
When, on thy bosom, spacious Windermere!
A Youth, I practised this delightful art;
Tossed on the waves alone, or 'mid a crew
Of joyous comrades. Soon as the reedy marge
Was cleared, I dipped, with arms accordant, oars
490 Free from obstruction; and the boat advanced
Through crystal water, smoothly as a hawk,
That, disentangled from the shady boughs
Of some thick wood, her place of covert, cleaves
With correspondent wings the abyss of air.
– 'Observe,' the Vicar said, 'yon rocky isle
With birch-trees fringed; my hand shall guide the helm,
While thitherward we shape our course; or while
We seek that other, on the western shore;
Where the bare columns of those lofty firs,
500 Supporting gracefully a massy dome
Of sombre foliage, seem to imitate
A Grecian temple rising from the Deep.'

'Turn where we may,' said I, 'we cannot err
In this delicious region.' – Cultured slopes,
Wild tracts of forest-ground, and scattered groves,
And mountains bare, or clothed with ancient woods,
Surrounded us; and, as we held our way
Along the level of the glassy flood,
They ceased not to surround us; change of place,
510 From kindred features diversely combined,

Producing change of beauty ever new.
– Ah! that such beauty, varying in the light
Of living nature, cannot be portrayed
By words, nor by the pencil's silent skill;
But is the property of him alone
Who hath beheld it, noted it with care,
And in his mind recorded it with love!
Suffice it, therefore, if the rural Muse
Vouchsafe sweet influence, while her Poet speaks
520 Of trivial occupations well devised,
And unsought pleasures springing up by chance;
As if some friendly Genius had ordained
That, as the day thus far had been enriched
By acquisition of sincere delight,
The same should be continued to its close.

One spirit animating old and young,
A gypsy-fire we kindled on the shore
Of the fair Isle with birch-trees fringed – and there,
Merrily seated in a ring, partook
530 A choice repast – served by our young companions
With rival earnestness and kindred glee.
Launched from our hands the smooth stone skimmed
    the lake;
With shouts we raised the echoes; – stiller sounds
The lovely Girl supplied – a simple song,
Whose low tones reached not to the distant rocks
To be repeated thence, but gently sank
Into our hearts; and charmed the peaceful flood.
Rapaciously we gathered flowery spoils
From land and water; lilies of each hue –
540 Golden and white, that float upon the waves,
And court the wind; and leaves of that shy plant,
(Her flowers were shed) the lily of the vale,
That loves the ground, and from the sun withholds
Her pensive beauty; from the breeze her sweets.

Such product, and such pastime, did the place

And season yield; but, as we re-embarked,
Leaving, in quest of other scenes, the shore
Of that wild spot, the Solitary said
In a low voice, yet careless who might hear,
550 'The fire, that burned so brightly to our wish,
Where is it now? – Deserted on the beach –
Dying, or dead! Nor shall the fanning breeze
Revive its ashes. What care we for this,
Whose ends are gained? Behold an emblem here
Of one day's pleasure, and all mortal joys!
And, in this unpremeditated slight
Of that which is no longer needed, see
The common course of human gratitude!'

    This plaintive note disturbed not the repose
560 Of the still evening. Right across the lake
Our pinnace moves; then, coasting creek and bay,
Glades we behold, and into thickets peep,
Where couch the spotted deer; or raise our eyes
To shaggy steeps on which the careless goat
Browsed by the side of dashing waterfalls;
And thus the bark, meandering with the shore,
Pursued her voyage, till a natural pier
Of jutting rock invited us to land.

    Alert to follow as the Pastor led,
570 We clomb a green hill's side; and, as we clomb,
The Valley, opening out her bosom, gave
Fair prospect, intercepted less and less,
O'er the flat meadows and indented coast
Of the smooth lake, in compass seen: – far off,
And yet conspicuous, stood the old Church-tower,
In majesty presiding over fields
And habitations seemingly preserved
From all intrusion of the restless world
By rocks impassable and mountains huge.

580   Soft heath this elevated spot supplied,

And choice of moss-clad stones, whereon we couched
Or sate reclined; admiring quietly
The general aspect of the scene; but each
Not seldom over anxious to make known
His own discoveries; or to favourite points
Directing notice, merely from a wish
To impart a joy, imperfect while unshared.
That rapturous moment never shall I forget
When these particular interests were effaced
590 From every mind! – Already had the sun,
Sinking with less than ordinary state,
Attained his western bound; but rays of light –
Now suddenly diverging from the orb
Retired behind the mountain-tops or veiled
By the dense air – shot upwards to the crown
Of the blue firmament – aloft, and wide:
And multitudes of little floating clouds,
Through their ethereal texture pierced – ere we,
Who saw, of change were conscious – had become
600 Vivid as fire; clouds separately poised, –
Innumerable multitude of forms
Scattered through half the circle of the sky;
And giving back, and shedding each on each,
With prodigal communion, the bright hues
Which from the unapparent fount of glory
They had imbibed, and ceased not to receive.
That which the heavens displayed, the liquid deep
Repeated; but with unity sublime!

  While from the grassy mountain's open side
610 We gazed, in silence hushed, with eyes intent
On the refulgent spectacle, diffused
Through earth, sky, water, and all visible space,
The Priest in holy transport thus exclaimed:

  'Eternal Spirit! universal God!
Power inaccessible to human thought,
Save by degrees and steps which thou hast deigned

To furnish; for this effluence of thyself,
To the infirmity of mortal sense
Vouchsafed; this local transitory type
620 Of thy paternal splendours, and the pomp
Of those who fill thy courts in highest heaven,
The radiant Cherubim; – accept the thanks
Which we, thy humble Creatures, here convened,
Presume to offer; we, who – from the breast
Of the frail earth, permitted to behold
The faint reflections only of thy face –
Are yet exalted, and in soul adore!
Such as they are who in thy presence stand
Unsullied, incorruptible, and drink
630 Imperishable majesty streamed forth
From thy empyreal throne, the elect of earth
Shall be – divested at the appointed hour
Of all dishonour, cleansed from mortal stain.
– Accomplish, then, their number; and conclude
Time's weary course! Or if, by thy decree,
The consummation that will come by stealth
Be yet far distant, let thy Word prevail,
Oh! let thy Word prevail, to take away
The sting of human nature. Spread the law,
640 As it is written in thy holy book,
Throughout all lands: let every nation hear
The high behest, and every heart obey;
Both for the love of purity, and hope
Which it affords, to such as do thy will
And persevere in good, that they shall rise,
To have a nearer view of Thee, in heaven.
– Father of good! this prayer in bounty grant,
In mercy grant it, to Thy wretched sons.
Then, nor till then, shall persecution cease,
650 And cruel wars expire. The way is marked,
The guide appointed, and the ransom paid.
Alas! the nations, who of yore received
These tidings, and in Christian temples meet
The sacred truth to acknowledge, linger still;

Preferring bonds and darkness to a state
Of holy freedom, by redeeming love
Proffered to all, while yet on earth detained.

  'So fare the many; and the thoughtful few,
Who in the anguish of their souls bewail
660 This dire perverseness, cannot choose but ask,
Shall it endure? – Shall enmity and strife,
Falsehood and guile, be left to sow their seed;
And the kind never perish? Is the hope
Fallacious, or shall righteousness obtain
A peaceable dominion, wide as earth,
And ne'er to fail? Shall that blest day arrive
When they, whose choice or lot it is to dwell
In crowded cities, without fear shall live
Studious of mutual benefit; and he,
670 Whom Morn awakens, among dews and flowers
Of every clime, to till the lonely field,
Be happy in himself? – The law of faith
Working through love, such conquest shall it gain,
Such triumph over sin and guilt achieve?
Almighty Lord, Thy further grace impart!
And with that help the wonder shall be seen
Fulfilled, the hope accomplished; and Thy praise
Be sung with transport and unceasing joy.

  'Once,' and with mild demeanour, as he spake,
680 On us the venerable Pastor turned
His beaming eye that had been raised to Heaven,
'Once, while the Name, Jehovah, was a sound
Within the circuit of this sea-girt isle
Unheard, the savage nations bowed the head
To Gods delighting in remorseless deeds;
Gods which themselves had fashioned, to promote
Ill purposes, and flatter foul desires.
Then, in the bosom of yon mountain-cove,
To those inventions of corrupted man
690 Mysterious rites were solemnized; and there –

Amid impending rocks and gloomy woods –
Of those terrific Idols some received
Such dismal service, that the loudest voice
Of the swoln cataracts (which now are heard
Soft murmuring) was too weak to overcome,
Though aided by wild winds, the groans and shrieks
Of human victims, offered up to appease
Or to propitiate. And, if living eyes
Had visionary faculties to see
700 The thing that hath been as the thing that is,
Aghast we might behold this crystal Mere
Bedimmed with smoke, in wreaths voluminous,
Flung from the body of devouring fires,
To Taranis erected on the heights
By priestly hands, for sacrifice performed
Exultingly, in view of open day
And full assemblage of a barbarous host;
Or to Andates, female Power! who gave
(For so they fancied) glorious victory.
710 – A few rude monuments of mountain-stone
Survive; all else is swept away. – How bright
The appearances of things! From such, how changed
The existing worship; and with those compared,
The worshippers how innocent and blest!
So wide the difference, a willing mind
Might almost think, at this affecting hour,
That paradise, the lost abode of man,
Was raised again: and to a happy few,
In its original beauty, here restored.

720   'Whence but from Thee, the true and only God,
And from the faith derived through Him who bled
Upon the cross, this marvellous advance
Of good from evil; as if one extreme
Were left, the other gained. – O ye, who come
To kneel devoutly in yon reverend Pile,
Called to such office by the peaceful sound
Of sabbath bells; and ye, who sleep in earth,

All cares forgotten, round its hallowed walls!
For you, in presence of this little band
730   Gathered together on the green hill-side,
Your Pastor is emboldened to prefer
Vocal thanksgivings to the eternal King;
Whose love, whose counsel, whose commands, have made
Your very poorest rich in peace of thought
And in good works; and him, who is endowed
With scantiest knowledge, master of all truth
Which the salvation of his soul requires.
Conscious of that abundant favour showered
On you, the children of my humble care,
740   And this dear land, our country, while on earth
We sojourn, have I lifted up my soul,
Joy giving voice to fervent gratitude.
These barren rocks, your stern inheritance;
These fertile fields, that recompense your pains;
The shadowy vale, the sunny mountain-top;
Woods waving in the wind their lofty heads,
Or hushed; the roaring waters, and the still –
They see the offering of my lifted hands,
They hear my lips present their sacrifice,
750   They know if I be silent, morn or even:
For, though in whispers speaking, the full heart
Will find a vent; and thought is praise to Him,
Audible praise, to Thee, omniscient Mind,
From whom all gifts descend, all blessings flow!'

This vesper-service closed, without delay,
From that exalted station to the plain
Descending, we pursued our homeward course,
In mute composure, o'er the shadowy lake,
Under a faded sky. No trace remained
760   Of those celestial splendours; grey the vault –
Pure, cloudless, ether; and the star of eve
Was wanting; but inferior lights appeared
Faintly, too faint almost for sight; and some
Above the darkened hills stood boldly forth

In twinkling lustre, ere the boat attained
Her mooring-place; where, to the sheltering tree,
Our youthful Voyagers bound fast her prow,
With prompt yet careful hands. This done, we paced
The dewy fields; but ere the Vicar's door
770 Was reached, the Solitary checked his steps;
Then, intermingling thanks, on each bestowed
A farewell salutation; and, the like
Receiving, took the slender path that leads
To the one cottage in the lonely dell:
But turned not without welcome promise made
That he would share the pleasures and pursuits
Of yet another summer's day, not loth
To wander with us through the fertile vales,
And o'er the mountain-wastes. 'Another sun,'
780 Said he, 'shall shine upon us, ere we part;
Another sun, and peradventure more;
If time, with free consent, be yours to give,
And season favours.'
                  To enfeebled Power,
From this communion with uninjured Minds,
What renovation had been brought; and what
Degree of healing to a wounded spirit,
Dejected, and habitually disposed
To seek, in degradation of the Kind,
Excuse and solace for her own defects;
790 How far those erring notions were reformed;
And whether aught, of tendency as good
And pure, from further intercourse ensued;
This – if delightful hopes, as heretofore,
Inspire the serious song, and gentle Hearts
Cherish, and lofty Minds approve the past –
My future labours may not leave untold.

Composed in One of the Valleys of Westmoreland, on Easter Sunday

With each recurrence of this glorious morn
That saw the Saviour in his human frame
Rise from the dead, erewhile the Cottage-dame
Put on fresh raiment – till that hour unworn:
Domestic hands the home-bred wool had shorn,
And she who span it culled the daintiest fleece,
In thoughtful reverence to the Prince of Peace,
Whose temples bled beneath the platted thorn.
A blest estate when piety sublime
10 These humble props disdained not! O green dales!
Sad may *I* be who heard your sabbath chime
When Art's abused inventions were unknown;
Kind Nature's various wealth was all your own;
And benefits were weighed in Reason's scales!

Composed at Cora Linn in Sight of Wallace's Tower

'– How Wallace fought for Scotland, left the name
Of Wallace to be found, like a wild flower,
All over his dear Country; left the deeds
Of Wallace, like a family of ghosts,
To people the steep rocks and river banks,
Her natural sanctuaries, with a local soul
Of independence and stern liberty.' MS.

Lord of the vale! astounding Flood;
The dullest leaf in this thick wood
Quakes – conscious of thy power;
The caves reply with hollow moan;
And vibrates, to its central stone,
Yon time-cemented Tower!

And yet how fair the rural scene!
For thou, O Clyde, hast ever been

Beneficent as strong;
10   Pleased in refreshing dews to steep
The little trembling flowers that peep
Thy shelving rocks among.

Hence all who love their country, love
To look on thee – delight to rove
Where they thy voice can hear;
And, to the patriot-warrior's Shade,
Lord of the vale! to Heroes laid
In dust, that voice is dear!

Along thy banks, at dead of night
20   Sweeps visibly the Wallace Wight;
Or stands, in warlike vest,
Aloft, beneath the moon's pale beam,
A Champion worthy of the stream,
Yon grey tower's living crest!

But clouds and envious darkness hide
A Form not doubtfully descried: –
Their transient mission o'er,
O say to what blind region flee
These Shapes of awful phantasy?
30   To what untrodden shore?

Less than divine command they spurn;
But this we from the mountains learn,
And this the valleys show;
That never will they deign to hold
Communion where the heart is cold
To human weal and woe.

The man of abject soul in vain
Shall walk the Marathonian plain;
Or thrid the shadowy gloom,
40   That still invests the guardian Pass,
Where stood, sublime, Leonidas
Devoted to the tomb.

And let no Slave his head incline,
Or kneel, before the votive shrine
By Uri's lake, where Tell
Leapt, from his storm-vext boat, to land,
Heaven's Instrument, for by his hand
That day the Tyrant fell.

*Suggested by a Beautiful Ruin upon One of the
Islands of Loch Lomond, a Place Chosen for the
Retreat of a Solitary Individual,
from Whom this Habitation Acquired the Name
of*

The Brownie's Cell

I

To barren heath, bleak moor, and quaking fen,
Or depth of labyrinthine glen;
Or into trackless forest set
With trees, whose lofty umbrage met;
World-wearied Men withdrew of yore;
(Penance their trust, and prayer their store;)
And in the wilderness were bound
To such apartments as they found;
Or with a new ambition raised;
10 That God might suitably be praised.

II

High lodged the *Warrior*, like a bird of prey,
Or where broad waters round him lay:
But this wild Ruin is no ghost
Of his devices – buried, lost!
Within this little lonely isle
There stood a consecrated Pile;
Where tapers burned, and mass was sung,
For them whose timid Spirits clung
To mortal succour, though the tomb
20 Had fixed, for ever fixed, their doom!

III

Upon those servants of another world
When madding Power her bolts had hurled,
Their habitation shook; – it fell,
And perished, save one narrow cell;
Whither, at length, a Wretch retired
Who neither grovelled nor aspired:
He, struggling in the net of pride,
The future scorned, the past defied;
Still tempering, from the unguilty forge
30 Of vain conceit, an iron scourge!

IV

Proud Remnant was he of a fearless Race,
Who stood and flourished face to face
With their perennial hills; – but Crime,
Hastening the stern decrees of Time,
Brought low a Power, which from its home
Burst, when repose grew wearisome;
And, taking impulse from the sword,
And, mocking its own plighted word,
Had found, in ravage widely dealt,
40 Its warfare's bourn, its travel's belt!

V

All, all were dispossessed, save him whose smile
Shot lightning through this lonely Isle!
No right had he but what he made
To this small spot, his leafy shade;
But the ground lay within that ring
To which he only dared to cling;
Renouncing here, as worse than dead,
The craven few who bowed the head
Beneath the change; who heard a claim
50 How loud! yet lived in peace with shame.

VI

From year to year this shaggy Mortal went
(So seemed it) down a strange descent:

Till they, who saw his outward frame,
Fixed on him an unhallowed name;
Him, free from all malicious taint,
And guiding, like the Patmos Saint,
A pen unwearied – to indite,
In his lone Isle, the dreams of night;
Impassioned dreams, that strove to span
60   The faded glories of his Clan!

VII
Suns that through blood their western harbour sought,
And stars that in their courses fought;
Towers rent, winds combating with woods,
Lands deluged by unbridled floods;
And beast and bird that from the spell
Of sleep took import terrible; –
These types mysterious (if the show
Of battle and the routed foe
Had failed) would furnish an array
70   Of matter for the dawning day!

VIII
How disappeared He? – ask the newt and toad,
Inheritors of his abode;
The otter crouching undisturbed,
In her dank cleft; – but be thou curbed,
O froward Fancy! 'mid a scene
Of aspect winning and serene;
For those offensive creatures shun
The inquisition of the sun!
And in this region flowers delight,
80   And all is lovely to the sight.

IX
Spring finds not here a melancholy breast,
When she applies her annual test
To dead and living; when her breath
Quickens, as now, the withered heath; –

Nor flaunting Summer – when he throws
His soul into the briar-rose;
Or calls the lily from her sleep
Prolonged beneath the bordering deep;
Nor Autumn, when the viewless wren
90 Is warbling near the BROWNIE'S Den.

X
Wild Relique! beautous as the chosen spot
In Nysa's isle, the embellished grot;
Whither, by care of Libyan Jove,
(High Servant of paternal Love)
Young Bacchus was conveyed – to lie
Safe from his step-dame Rhea's eye;
Where bud, and bloom, and fruitage, glowed,
Close-crowding round the infant-god;
All colours, – and the liveliest streak
100 A foil to his celestial cheek!

Effusion in the Pleasure-Ground on the Banks of the Bran, near Dunkeld

'The waterfall, by a loud roaring, warned us when we must expect it. We were first, however, conducted into a small apartment, where the Gardener desired us to look at a picture of Ossian, which, while he was telling the history of the young Artist who executed the work, disappeared, parting in the middle – flying asunder as by the touch of magic – and lo! we are at the entrance of a splendid apartment, which was almost dizzy and alive with waterfalls, that tumbled in all directions; the great cascade, opposite the window, which faced us, being reflected in innumerable mirrors upon the ceiling and against the walls.' – *Extract from the Journal of my Fellow-Traveller.*

What He – who, 'mid the kindred throng
Of Heroes that inspired his song,
Doth yet frequent the hill of storms,
The stars dim-twinkling through their forms!

What! Ossian here – a painted Thrall,
Mute fixture on a stuccoed wall;
To serve – an unsuspected screen
For show that must not yet be seen;
And, when the moment comes, to part
10 And vanish by mysterious art;
Head, harp, and body, split asunder,
For ingress to a world of wonder;
A gay saloon, with waters dancing
Upon the sight wherever glancing;
One loud cascade in front, and lo!
A thousand like it, white as snow –
Streams on the walls, and torrent-foam
As active round the hollow dome,
Illusive cataracts! of their terrors
20 Not stripped, nor voiceless in the mirrors,
That catch the pageant from the flood
Thundering adown a rocky wood.
What pains to dazzle and confound!
What strife of colour, shape and sound
In this quaint medley, that might seem
Devised out of a sick man's dream!
Strange scene, fantastic and uneasy
As ever made a maniac dizzy,
When disenchanted from the mood
30 That loves on sullen thoughts to brood!

    O Nature – in thy changeful visions,
Through all thy most abrupt transitions
Smooth, graceful, tender, or sublime –
Ever averse to pantomime,
Thee neither do they know nor us
Thy servants, who can trifle thus;
Else verily the sober powers
Of rock that frowns, and stream that roars,
Exalted by congenial sway
40 Of Spirits, and the undying Lay,
And Names that moulder not away,

Had wakened some redeeming thought
More worthy of this favoured Spot;
Recalled some feeling – to set free
The Bard from such indignity!

   The Effigies of a valiant Wight
I once beheld, a Templar Knight;
Not prostrate, not like those that rest
On tombs, with palms together prest,
50 But sculptured out of living stone,
And standing upright and alone,
Both hands with rival energy
Employed in setting his sword free
From its dull sheath – stern sentinel
Intent to guard St Robert's cell;
As if with memory of the affray
Far distant, when, as legends say,
The Monks of Fountain's thronged to force
From its dear home the Hermit's corse,
60 That in their keeping it might lie,
To crown their abbey's sanctity.
So had they rushed into the grot
Of sense despised, a world forgot,
And torn him from his loved retreat,
Where altar-stone and rock-hewn seat
Still hint that quiet best is found,
Even by the *Living*, under ground;
But a bold Knight, the selfish aim
Defeating, put the Monks to shame,
70 There where you see his Image stand
Bare to the sky, with threatening brand
Which lingering NID is proud to show
Reflected in the pool below.

   Thus, like the men of earliest days,
Our sires set forth their grateful praise:
Uncouth the workmanship, and rude!
But, nursed in mountain solitude,

Might some aspiring artist dare
To seize whate'er, through misty air,
80 A ghost, by glimpses, may present
Of imitable lineament,
And give the phantom an array
That less should scorn the abandoned clay;
Then let him hew with patient stroke
An Ossian out of mural rock,
And leave the figurative Man –
Upon thy margin, roaring Bran! –
Fixed, like the Templar of the steep,
An everlasting watch to keep;
90 With local sanctities in trust,
More precious than a hermit's dust;
And virtues through the mass infused,
Which old idolatry abused.

What though the Granite would deny
All fervour to the sightless eye;
And touch from rising suns in vain
Solicit a Memnonian strain;
Yet, in some fit of anger sharp,
The wind might force the deep-grooved harp
100 To utter melancholy moans
Not unconnected with the tones
Of soul-sick flesh and weary bones;
While grove and river notes would lend,
Less deeply sad, with these to blend!

Vain pleasures of luxurious life,
For ever with yourselves at strife;
Through town and country both deranged
By affectations interchanged,
And all the perishable gauds
110 That heaven-deserted man applauds;
When will your hapless patrons learn
To watch and ponder – to discern
The freshness, the everlasting youth,

Of admiration sprung from truth;
From beauty infinitely growing
Upon a mind with love o'erflowing –
To sound the depths of every Art
That seeks its wisdom through the heart?

    Thus (where the intrusive Pile, ill-graced
120 With baubles of theatric taste,
O'erlooks the torrent breathing showers
On motley bands of alien flowers
In stiff confusion set or sown,
Till Nature cannot find her own,
Or keep a remnant of the sod
Which Caledonian Heroes trod)
I mused; and, thirsting for redress,
Recoiled into the wilderness.

'From the dark chambers of dejection freed'

From the dark chambers of dejection freed,
Spurning the unprofitable yoke of care,
Rise, GILLIES, rise: the gales of youth shall bear
Thy genius forward like a wingèd steed.
Though bold Bellerophon (so Jove decreed
In wrath) fell headlong from the fields of air,
Yet a rich guerdon waits on minds that dare,
If aught be in them of immortal seed,
And reason govern that audacious flight
10 Which heaven-ward they direct. – Then droop not thou,
Erroneously renewing a sad vow
In the low dell 'mid Roslin's faded grove:
A cheerful life is what the Muses love,
A soaring spirit is their prime delight.

Yarrow Visited
September, 1814

And is this – Yarrow? – *This* the Stream
Of which my fancy cherished,
So faithfully, a waking dream?
An image that hath perished!
O that some Minstrel's harp were near,
To utter notes of gladness,
And chase this silence from the air,
That fills my heart with sadness!

Yet why? – a silvery current flows
10 With uncontrolled meanderings;
Nor have these eyes by greener hills
Been soothed, in all my wanderings.
And, through her depths, Saint Mary's Lake
Is visibly delighted;
For not a feature of those hills
Is in the mirror slighted.

A blue sky bends o'er Yarrow vale,
Save where that pearly whiteness
Is round the rising sun diffused,
20 A tender hazy brightness;
Mild dawn of promise! that excludes
All profitless dejection;
Though not unwilling here to admit
A pensive recollection.

Where was it that the famous Flower
Of Yarrow Vale lay bleeding?
His bed perchance was yon smooth mound
On which the herd is feeding:
And haply from this crystal pool,
30 Now peaceful as the morning,
The Water-wraith ascended thrice –
And gave his doleful warning.

Delicious is the Lay that sings
The haunts of happy Lovers,
The path that leads them to the grove,
The leafy grove that covers:
And Pity sanctifies the Verse
That paints, by strength of sorrow,
The unconquerable strength of love;
40   Bear witness, rueful Yarrow!

But thou, that didst appear so fair
To fond imagination,
Dost rival in the light of day
Her delicate creation:
Meek loveliness is round thee spread,
A softness still and holy;
The grace of forest charms decayed,
And pastoral melancholy.

That region left, the vale unfolds
50   Rich groves of lofty stature,
With Yarrow winding through the pomp
Of cultivated nature;
And, rising from those lofty groves,
Behold a Ruin hoary!
The shattered front of Newark's Towers,
Renowned in Border story.

Fair scenes for childhood's opening bloom,
For sportive youth to stray in;
For manhood to enjoy his strength;
60   And age to wear away in!
Yon cottage seems a bower of bliss,
A covert for protection
Of tender thoughts, that nestle there –
The brood of chaste affection.

How sweet, on this autumnal day,
The wild-wood fruits to gather,

And on my True-love's forehead plant
A crest of blooming heather!
And what if I enwreathed my own!
70 'Twere no offence to reason;
The sober Hills thus deck their brows
To meet the wintry season.

I see – but not by sight alone,
Loved Yarrow, have I won thee;
A ray of fancy still survives –
Her sunshine plays upon thee!
Thy ever-youthful waters keep
A course of lively pleasure;
And gladsome notes my lips can breathe,
80 Accordant to the measure.

The vapours linger round the Heights,
They melt, and soon must vanish;
One hour is theirs, nor more is mine –
Sad thought, which I would banish,
But that I know, where'er I go,
Thy genuine image, Yarrow!
Will dwell with me – to heighten joy,
And cheer my mind in sorrow.

Laodamia

'With sacrifice before the rising morn
Vows have I made by fruitless hope inspired;
And from the infernal Gods, 'mid shades forlorn
Of night, my slaughtered Lord have I required;
Celestial pity I again implore; –
Restore him to my sight – great Jove, restore!'

So speaking, and by fervent love endowed
With faith, the Suppliant heavenward lifts her hands;
While, like the sun emerging from a cloud,

10 Her countenance brightens – and her eye expands;
   Her bosom heaves and spreads, her stature grows;
   And she expects the issue in repose.

O terror! what hath she perceived? – O joy!
   What doth she look on? – whom doth she behold?
   Her Hero slain upon the beach of Troy?
His vital presence? his corporeal mould?
   It is – if sense deceive her not – 'tis He!
   And a God leads him, wingèd Mercury!

Mild Hermes spake – and touched her with his wand
20 That calms all fear; 'Such grace hath crowned thy
      prayer,
   Laodamía! that at Jove's command
Thy Husband walks the paths of upper air:
   He comes to tarry with thee three hours' space;
   Accept the gift, behold him face to face!'

Forth sprang the impassioned Queen her Lord to clasp;
   Again that consummation she essayed;
   But unsubstantial Form eludes her grasp
As often as that eager grasp was made.
   The Phantom parts – but parts to re-unite,
30 And re-assume his place before her sight.

'Protesiláus, lo! thy guide is gone!
   Confirm, I pray, the vision with thy voice:
   This is our palace, – yonder is thy throne;
Speak, and the floor thou tread'st on will rejoice.
   Not to appal me have the gods bestowed
   This precious boon; and blest a sad abode.'

'Great Jove, Laodamía! doth not leave
   His gifts imperfect: – Spectre though I be,
   I am not sent to scare thee or deceive;
40 But in reward of thy fidelity.
   And something also did my worth obtain;
   For fearless virtue bringeth boundless gain.

'Thou knowest, the Delphic oracle foretold
That the first Greek who touched the Trojan strand
Should die; but me the threat could not withhold:
A generous cause a victim did demand;
And forth I leapt upon the sandy plain;
A self-devoted chief – by Hector slain.'

'Supreme of Heroes – bravest, noblest, best!
50 Thy matchless courage I bewail no more,
Which then, when tens of thousands were deprest
By doubt, propelled thee to the fatal shore;
Thou found'st – and I forgive thee – here thou art –
A nobler counsellor than my poor heart.

'But thou, though capable of sternest deed,
Wert kind as resolute, and good as brave;
And he, whose power restores thee, hath decreed
Thou should'st elude the malice of the grave:
Redundant are thy locks, thy lips as fair
60 As when their breath enriched Thessalian air.

'No Spectre greets me, – no vain Shadow this;
Come, blooming Hero, place thee by my side!
Give, on this well-known couch, one nuptial kiss
To me, this day, a second time thy bride!'
Jove frowned in heaven: the conscious Parcae threw
Upon those roseate lips a Stygian hue.

'This visage tells thee that my doom is past:
Nor should the change be mourned, even if the joys
Of sense were able to return as fast
70 And surely as they vanish. Earth destroys
Those raptures duly – Erebus disdains:
Calm pleasures there abide – majestic pains.

'Be taught, O faithful Consort, to control
Rebellious passion: for the Gods approve
The depth, and not the tumult, of the soul;

A fervent, not ungovernable, love.
Thy transports moderate; and meekly mourn
When I depart, for brief is my sojourn –'

'Ah, wherefore? – Did not Hercules by force
80 Wrest from the guardian Monster of the tomb
Alcestis, a reanimated corse,
Given back to dwell on earth in vernal bloom?
Medea's spells dispersed the weight of years,
And Aeson stood a youth 'mid youthful peers.

'The Gods to us are merciful – and they
Yet further may relent: for mightier far
Than strength of nerve and sinew, or the sway
Of magic potent over sun and star,
Is love, though oft to agony distrest,
90 And though his favourite seat be feeble woman's breast.

'But if thou goest, I follow –' 'Peace!' he said, –
She looked upon him and was calmed and cheered;
The ghastly colour from his lips had fled;
In his deportment, shape, and mien, appeared
Elysian beauty, melancholy grace,
Brought from a pensive though a happy place.

He spake of love, such love as Spirits feel
In worlds whose course is equable and pure;
No fears to beat away – no strife to heal –
100 The past unsighed for, and the future sure;
Spake of heroic arts in graver mood
Revived, with finer harmony pursued;

Of all that is most beauteous – imaged there
In happier beauty; more pellucid streams,
An ampler ether, a diviner air,
And fields invested with purpureal gleams;
Climes which the sun, who sheds the brightest day
Earth knows, is all unworthy to survey.

Yet there the Soul shall enter which hath earned
110 That privilege by virtue. – 'Ill,' said he,
'The end of man's existence I discerned,
Who from ignoble games and revelry
Could draw, when we had parted, vain delight,
While tears were thy best pastime, day and night;

'And while my youthful peers before my eyes
(Each hero following his peculiar bent)
Prepared themselves for glorious enterprise
By martial sports, – or, seated in the tent,
Chieftains and kings in council were detained;
120 What time the fleet at Aulis lay enchained.

'The wished-for wind was given: – I then revolved
The oracle, upon the silent sea;
And, if no worthier led the way, resolved
That, of a thousand vessels, mine should be
The foremost prow in pressing to the strand, –
Mine the first blood that tinged the Trojan sand.

'Yet bitter, oft-times bitter, was the pang
When of thy loss I thought, belovèd Wife!
On thee too fondly did my memory hang,
130 And on the joys we shared in mortal life, –
The paths which we had trod – these fountains, flowers;
My new-planned cities, and unfinished towers.

'But should suspense permit the Foe to cry,
"Behold they tremble! – haughty their array,
Yet of their number no one dares to die?"
In soul I swept the indignity away:
Old frailties then recurred: – but lofty thought,
In act embodied, my deliverance wrought.

'And Thou, though strong in love, art all too weak
140 In reason, in self-government too slow;
I counsel thee by fortitude to seek

Our blest re-union in the shades below.
The invisible world with thee hath sympathized;
Be thy affections raised and solemnized.

'Learn, by a mortal yearning, to ascend –
Seeking a higher object. Love was given,
Encouraged, sanctioned, chiefly for that end;
For this the passion to excess was driven –
That self might be annulled: her bondage prove
150   The fetters of a dream, opposed to love.' –

Aloud she shrieked! for Hermes reappears!
Round the dear Shade she would have clung – 'tis vain:
The hours are past – too brief had they been years;
And him no mortal effort can detain:
Swift, toward the realms that know not earthly day,
He through the portal takes his silent way,
And on the palace-floor a lifeless corse She lay.

Thus, all in vain exhorted and reproved,
She perished; and, as for a wilful crime,
160   By the just Gods whom no weak pity moved,
Was doomed to wear out her appointed time,
Apart from happy Ghosts, that gather flowers
Of blissful quiet 'mid unfading bowers.

– Yet tears to human suffering are due;
And mortal hopes defeated and o'erthrown
Are mourned by man, and not by man alone,
As fondly he believes. – Upon the side
Of Hellespont (such faith was entertained)
A knot of spiry trees for ages grew
170   From out the tomb of him for whom she died;
And ever, when such stature they had gained
That Ilium's walls were subject to their view,
The trees' tall summits withered at the sight;
A constant interchange of growth and blight!

Lines Written on a Blank Leaf in a Copy of the Author's Poem 'The Excursion', upon Hearing of the Death of the Late Vicar of Kendal

To public notice, with reluctance strong,
Did I deliver this unfinished Song;
Yet for one happy issue; – and I look
With self-congratulation on the Book
Which pious, learned, MURFITT saw and read; –
Upon my thoughts his saintly Spirit fed;
He conned the new-born Lay with grateful heart –
Foreboding not how soon he must depart;
Unweeting that to him the joy was given
10 Which good men take with them from earth to heaven.

*[Passage from Mary Barker's Lines Addressed to a Noble Lord (His Lordship will know why)]

[Bracketed matter was written by Mary Barker.]

[If, of meaner happiness
Thou wouldst know, or thou wouldst guess,
Come and see us when we climb]
Old Helvellyn's brow sublime.
See us, when we spread the sail,
Fearless of the mountain-gale,
Or, disturb with dashing oars
The bright picture of the shores,
And the azure sky – imprest
10 On that water's glassy breast.

Come! our merry meal partake
While we float along the Lake;
Or beside some crystal rill,
Where we cool our wine at will,

See us feasting – Earth our board!
There, is spread the dainty hoard,
On her flower-embroidered cloth,
That cares not for the fretting moth:
And, belike, a stately broom
20 Self-adorned with golden bloom,
And, enwreathed with climbing fern,
Frames in the midst a rich epergne;
Or a bush with roses drest,
As if in honour of the feast.

Nothing (trust the Muse) want we
Of luxurious dignity.
What can sumptuous London boast
That is not ours at lighter cost?
Couch of heather – thymy seat
30 For a social circle meet;
And – apart for moody man,
Sofa on the Grecian plan;
Curtained round with leafy boughs,
Which the wild-goat loves to browse;
And some shapely rock or stone,
All with softest moss o'ergrown,
Open for the breeze to fan;
Listless Loiterer's Ottoman!

Thus we revel, free from care:
40 Happy Children – Ladies fair,
[Lords and Knights and Squires attending,
Wit and sense and music blending.]
Come! let no proud notions tease thee,
And our PONDS shall better please thee
Than those now dishonoured Seas,
With their shores and Cyclades,
Stocked with Pachas, Seraskiers,
Slaves, and turbaned Buccaneers;
Sensual Mussulmen atrocious,
50 Renegados, more ferocious!

Heroes suited to the trances
Of thy crude, distempered fancies.

[Ever in the obscure delighting,
All thy images affrighting,
Sad and fearful stories telling,
Or on vice and folly dwelling,
Break off thy ignoble fetters,
Learn to reverence thy Betters!]
Come, and listen to a measure
60   Framed by Hope for lasting pleasure;
Listen, till thy heart be sure
That nothing monstrous can endure.
To unlearn thyself, repair
Hither, or grow wise elsewhere;
Striving to become the creature
Of a genuine English nature!

Artegal and Elidure
(See the Chronicle of Geoffrey of Monmouth and Milton's History of England)

Where be the temples which in Britain's Isle,
For his paternal Gods, the Trojan raised?
Gone like a morning dream, or like a pile
Of clouds that in cerulean ether blazed!
Ere Julius landed on her white-cliffed shore,
    They sank, delivered o'er
To fatal dissolution; and, I ween,
No vestige then was left that such had ever been.

Nathless, a British record (long concealed
10   In old Armorica, whose secret springs
No Gothic conqueror ever drank) revealed
The marvellous current of forgotten things;
How Brutus came, by oracles impelled,
    And Albion's giants quelled,

A brood whom no civility could melt,
'Who never tasted grace, and goodness ne'er had felt.'

By brave Corineus aided, he subdued,
And rooted out the intolerable kind;
And this too-long-polluted land imbued
20   With goodly arts and usages refined;
Whence golden harvests, cities, warlike towers,
    And pleasure's sumptuous bowers;
Whence all the fixed delights of house and home,
Friendships that will not break, and love that cannot
    roam.

O, happy Britain! region all too fair
For self-delighting fancy to endure
That silence only should inhabit there,
Wild beasts, or uncouth savages impure!
But, intermingled with the generous seed,
30   Grew many a poisonous weed;
Thus fares it still with all that takes its birth
From human care, or grows upon the breast of earth.

Hence, and how soon! that war of vengeance waged
By Guendolen against her faithless lord;
Till she, in jealous fury unassuaged,
Had slain his paramour with ruthless sword:
Then, into Severn hideously defiled,
    She flung her blameless child,
Sabrina, – vowing that the stream should bear
40   That name through every age, her hatred to declare.

So speaks the Chronicle, and tells of Lear
By his ungrateful daughters turned adrift.
Ye lightnings, hear his voice! – they cannot hear,
Nor can the winds restore his simple gift.
But One there is, a Child of nature meek,
    Who comes her Sire to seek;
And he, recovering sense, upon her breast
Leans smilingly, and sinks into a perfect rest.

There too we read of Spenser's fairy themes,
50 And those that Milton loved in youthful years;
The sage enchanter Merlin's subtle schemes;
The feats of Arthur and his knightly peers;
Of Arthur, – who, to upper light restored,
   With that terrific sword
Which yet he brandishes for future war,
Shall lift his country's fame above the polar star!

What wonder, then, if in such ample field
Of old tradition, one particular flower
Doth seemingly in vain its fragrance yield,
60 And bloom unnoticed even to this late hour?
Now, gentle Muses, your assistance grant,
   While I this flower transplant
Into a garden stored with Poesy;
Where flowers and herbs unite, and haply some weeds be,
That, wanting not wild grace, are from all mischief free!

A KING more worthy of respect and love
Than wise Gorbonian ruled not in his day;
And grateful Britain prospered far above
All neighbouring countries through his righteous sway;
70 He poured rewards and honours on the good;
   The oppressor he withstood;
And while he served the Gods with reverence due,
Fields smiled, and temples rose, and towns and cities
   grew.

He died, whom Artegal succeeds – his son;
But how unworthy of that sire was he!
A hopeful reign, auspiciously begun,
Was darkened soon by foul iniquity.
From crime to crime he mounted, till at length
   The nobles leagued their strength
80 With a vexed people, and the tyrant chased;
And, on the vacant throne, his worthier Brother placed.

From realm to realm the humbled Exile went,
Suppliant for aid his kingdom to regain;
In many a court, and many a warrior's tent,
He urged his persevering suit in vain.
Him, in whose wretched heart ambition failed,
  Dire poverty assailed;
And, tired with slights his pride no more could brook,
He towards his native country cast a longing look.

90 Fair blew the wished-for wind – the voyage sped;
He landed; and, by many dangers scared,
'Poorly provided, poorly followèd,'
To Calaterium's forest he repaired.
How changed from him who, born to highest place,
  Had swayed the royal mace,
Flattered and feared, despised yet deified,
In Troynovant, his seat by silver Thames's side!

From that wild region where the crownless King
Lay in concealment with his scanty train,
100 Supporting life by water from the spring,
And such chance food as outlaws can obtain,
Unto the few whom he esteems his friends
  A messenger he sends;
And from their secret loyalty requires
Shelter and daily bread, – the sum of his desires.

While he the issue waits, at early morn
Wandering by stealth abroad, he chanced to hear
A startling outcry made by hound and horn,
From which the tusky wild boar flies in fear;
110 And, scouring towards him o'er the grassy plain,
  Behold the hunter train!
He bids his little company advance
With seeming unconcern and steady countenance.

The royal Elidure, who leads the chase,
Hath checked his foaming courser: — can it be!

Methinks that I should recognize that face,
Though much disguised by long adversity!
He gazed rejoicing, and again he gazed,
   Confounded and amazed –
120 'It is the king, my brother!' and, by sound
Of his own voice confirmed, he leaps upon the ground.

Long, strict, and tender was the embrace he gave,
Feebly returned by daunted Artegal;
Whose natural affection doubts enslave,
And apprehensions dark and criminal.
Loth to restrain the moving interview,
   The attendant lords withdrew;
And, while they stood upon the plain apart,
Thus Elidure, by words, relieved his struggling heart.

130 'By heavenly Powers conducted, we have met;
– O Brother! to my knowledge lost so long,
But neither lost to love, nor to regret,
Nor to my wishes lost; – forgive the wrong,
(Such it may seem) if I thy crown have borne,
   Thy royal mantle worn:
I was their natural guardian; and 'tis just
That now I should restore what hath been held in trust.'

A while the astonished Artegal stood mute,
Then thus exclaimed: 'To me, of titles shorn,
140 And stripped of power! me, feeble, destitute,
To me a kingdom! spare the bitter scorn:
If justice ruled the breast of foreign kings,
   Then, on the wide-spread wings
Of war, had I returned to claim my right;
This will I here avow, not dreading thy despite.'

'I do not blame thee,' Elidure replied;
'But, if my looks did with my words agree,
I should at once be trusted, not defied,
And thou from all disquietude be free.

150   May the unsullied Goddess of the chase,
     Who to this blessèd place
  At this blest moment led me, if I speak
  With insincere intent, on me her vengeance wreak!

  'Were this same spear, which in my hand I grasp,
  The British sceptre, here would I to thee
  The symbol yield; and would undo this clasp,
  If it confined the robe of sovereignty.
  Odious to me the pomp of regal court,
     And joyless sylvan sport,
160   While thou art roving, wretched and forlorn,
  Thy couch the dewy earth, thy roof the forest thorn!'

  Then Artegal thus spake: 'I only sought
  Within this realm a place of safe retreat;
  Beware of rousing an ambitious thought;
  Beware of kindling hopes, for me unmeet!
  Thou art reputed wise, but in my mind
     Art pitiably blind:
  Full soon this generous purpose thou mayst rue,
  When that which has been done no wishes can undo.

170   'Who, when a crown is fixed upon his head,
  Would balance claim with claim, and right with right?
  But thou – I know not how inspired, how led –
  Wouldst change the course of things in all men's sight!
  And this for one who cannot imitate
     Thy virtue, who may hate:
  For, if, by such strange sacrifice restored,
  He reign, thou still must be his king, and sovereign lord;

  'Lifted in magnanimity above
  Aught that my feeble nature could perform,
180   Or even conceive; surpassing me in love
  Far as in power the eagle doth the worm:
  I, Brother! only should be king in name,
     And govern to my shame;

A shadow in a hated land, while all
Of glad or willing service to thy share would fall.'

'Believe it not,' said Elidure; 'respect
Awaits on virtuous life, and ever most
Attends on goodness with dominion decked,
Which stands the universal empire's boast;
190   This can thy own experience testify:
     Nor shall thy foes deny
That, in the gracious opening of thy reign,
Our father's spirit seemed in thee to breathe again.

'And what if o'er that bright unbosoming
Clouds of disgrace and envious fortune passed!
Have we not seen the glories of the spring
By veil of noontide darkness overcast?
The frith that glittered like a warrior's shield,
    The sky, the gay green field,
200   Are vanished; gladness ceases in the groves,
And trepidation strikes the blackened mountain-coves.

'But is that gloom dissolved? how passing clear
Seems the wide world, far brighter than before!
Even so thy latent worth will re-appear,
Gladdening the people's heart from shore to shore;
For youthful faults ripe virtues shall atone;
    Re-seated on thy throne,
Proof shalt thou furnish that misfortune, pain,
And sorrow, have confirmed thy native right to reign.

210   'But, not to overlook what thou mayst know,
Thy enemies are neither weak nor few;
And circumspect must be our course, and slow,
Or from my purpose ruin may ensue.
Dismiss thy followers; – let them calmly wait
    Such change in thy estate
As I already have in thought devised;
And which, with caution due, may soon be realized.'

The Story tells what courses were pursued,
Until king Elidure, with full consent
220 Of all his peers, before the multitude,
Rose, – and, to consummate this just intent,
Did place upon his brother's head the crown,
   Relinquished by his own;
Then to his people cried, 'Receive your lord,
Gorbonian's first-born son, your rightful king restored!'

The people answered with a loud acclaim:
Yet more; – heart-smitten by the heroic deed,
The reinstated Artegal became
Earth's noblest penitent; from bondage freed
230 Of vice – thenceforth unable to subvert
   Or shake his high desert.
Long did he reign; and, when he died, the tear
Of universal grief bedewed his honoured bier.

Thus was a Brother by a Brother saved;
With whom a crown (temptation that hath set
Discord in hearts of men till they have braved
Their nearest kin with deadly purpose met)
'Gainst duty weighed, and faithful love, did seem
   A thing of no esteem;
240 And, from this triumph of affection pure,
He bore the lasting name of 'pious Elidure!'

To B. R. Haydon

High is our calling, Friend! – Creative Art
(Whether the instrument of words she use,
Or pencil pregnant with ethereal hues,)
Demands the service of a mind and heart,
Though sensitive, yet, in their weakest part,
Heroically fashioned – to infuse
Faith in the whispers of the lonely Muse,
While the whole world seems adverse to desert.

And, oh! when Nature sinks, as oft she may,
10   Through long-lived pressure of obscure distress,
Still to be strenuous for the bright reward,
And in the soul admit of no decay,
Brook no continuance of weak-mindedness –
Great is the glory, for the strife is hard!

November 1

How clear, how keen, how marvellously bright
The effluence from yon distant mountain's head,
Which, strewn with snow smooth as the sky can shed,
Shines like another sun – on mortal sight
Uprisen, as if to check approaching Night,
And all her twinkling stars. Who now would tread,
If so he might, yon mountain's glittering head –
Terrestrial, but a surface, by the flight
Of sad mortality's earth-sullying wing,
10   Unswept, unstained? Nor shall the aërial Powers
Dissolve that beauty, destined to endure,
White, radiant, spotless, exquisitely pure,
Through all vicissitudes, till genial Spring
Has filled the laughing vales with welcome flowers.

September, 1815

While not a leaf seems faded; while the fields,
With ripening harvest prodigally fair,
In brightest sunshine bask; this nipping air,
Sent from some distant clime where Winter wields
His icy scimitar, a foretaste yields
Of bitter change, and bids the flowers beware;
And whispers to the silent birds, 'Prepare
Against the threatening foe your trustiest shields.'
For me, who under kindlier laws belong
10   To Nature's tuneful choir, this rustling dry

Through leaves yet green, and yon crystalline sky,
Announce a season potent to renew,
'Mid frost and snow, the instinctive joys of song,
And nobler cares than listless summer knew.

Ode: The Morning of the Day Appointed for a General Thanksgiving. January 18, 1816

I

Hail, orient Conqueror of gloomy Night!
Thou that canst shed the bliss of gratitude
On hearts howe'er insensible or rude;
Whether thy punctual visitations smite
The haughty towers where monarchs dwell;
Or thou, impartial Sun, with presence bright
Cheer'st the low threshold of the peasant's cell!
Not unrejoiced I see thee climb the sky
In naked splendour, clear from mist or haze,
Or cloud approaching to divert the rays,
Which even in deepest winter testify
 Thy power and majesty,
Dazzling the vision that presumes to gaze.
– Well does thine aspect usher in this Day;
As aptly suits therewith that modest pace
 Submitted to the chains
That bind thee to the path which God ordains
 That thou shalt trace,
Till, with the heavens and earth, thou pass away!
20 Nor less, the stillness of these frosty plains,
Their utter stillness, and the silent grace
Of yon ethereal summits white with snow
(Whose tranquil pomp and spotless purity
 Report of storms gone by
 To us who tread below),
Do with the service of this Day accord.
– Divinest Object which the uplifted eye
Of mortal man is suffered to behold;

Thou, who upon those snow-clad Heights has poured
30 Meek lustre, nor forget'st the humble Vale;
Thou who dost warm Earth's universal mould,
And for thy bounty wert not unadored
    By pious men of old;
Once more, heart-cheering Sun, I bid thee hail!
Bright be thy course today, let not this promise fail!

II
    'Mid the deep quiet of this morning hour,
All nature seems to hear me while I speak,
By feelings urged that do not vainly seek
Apt language, ready as the tuneful notes
40 That stream in blithe succession from the throats
    Of birds, in leafy bower,
Warbling a farewell to a vernal shower.
– There is a radiant though a short-lived flame,
That burns for Poets in the dawning east;
And oft my soul hath kindled at the same,
When the captivity of sleep had ceased;
But He who fixed immoveably the frame
Of the round world, and built, by laws as strong,
    A solid refuge for distress –
50   The towers of righteousness;
He knows that from a holier altar came
The quickening spark of this day's sacrifice;
Knows that the source is nobler whence doth rise
    The current of this matin song;
      That deeper far it lies
Than aught dependent on the fickle skies.

III
    Have we not conquered? – by the vengeful sword?
Ah no, by dint of Magnanimity;
    That curbed the baser passions, and left free
60 A loyal band to follow their liege Lord
Clear-sighted Honour, and his staid Compeers,
Along a track of most unnatural years;

In execution of heroic deeds
Whose memory, spotless as the crystal beads
Of morning dew upon the untrodden meads,
Shall live enrolled above the starry spheres.
He, who in concert with an earthly string
  Of Britain's acts would sing,
  He with enraptured voice will tell
70 Of One whose spirit no reverse could quell;
Of One that 'mid the failing never failed –
Who paints how Britain struggled and prevailed
Shall represent her labouring with an eye
  Of circumspect humanity;
Shall show her clothed with strength and skill,
  All martial duties to fulfil;
Firm as a rock in stationary fight;
In motion rapid as the lightning's gleam;
Fierce as a flood-gate bursting at midnight
80 To rouse the wicked from their giddy dream –
Woe, woe to all that face her in the field!
Appalled she may not be, and cannot yield.

IV

  And thus is *missed* the sole true glory
  That can belong to human story!
  At which they only shall arrive
  Who through the abyss of weakness dive.
The very humblest are too proud of heart;
And one brief day is rightly set apart
For Him who lifteth up and layeth low;
90 For that Almighty God to whom we owe,
Say not that we have vanquished – but that we survive.

V

 How dreadful the dominion of the impure!
Why should the Song be tardy to proclaim
That less than power unbounded could not tame
That soul of Evil – which, from hell let loose,
Had filled the astonished world with such abuse

As boundless patience only could endure?
– Wide-wasted regions – cities wrapt in flame –
Who sees, may lift a streaming eye
100 To Heaven; – who never saw, may heave a sigh;
But the foundation of our nature shakes,
And with an infinite pain the spirit aches,
When desolated countries, towns on fire,
    Are but the avowed attire
Of warfare waged with desperate mind
Against the life of virtue in mankind
    Assaulting without ruth
    The citadels of truth;
While the fair gardens of civility,
110   By ignorance defaced,
    By violence laid waste,
Perish without reprieve for flower or tree.

VI

    A crouching purpose – a distracted will –
Opposed to hopes that battened upon scorn,
And to desires whose ever-waxing horn
Not all the light of earthly power could fill;
Opposed to dark, deep plots of patient skill,
And to celerities of lawless force;
Which, spurning God, had flung away remorse –
120 What could they gain but shadows of redress?
– So bad proceeded propagating worse;
And discipline was passion's dire excess.
Widens the fatal web, its lines extend,
And deadlier poisons in the chalice blend.
When will your trials teach you to be wise?
– O prostrate Lands, consult your agonies!

VII

    No more – the guilt is banished,
And, with the guilt, the shame is fled;
And, with the guilt and shame, the Woe hath vanished,
130 Shaking the dust and ashes from her head!

– No more – these lingerings of distress
Sully the limpid stream of thankfulness.
What robe can Gratitude employ
So seemly as the radiant vest of Joy?
What steps so suitable as those that move
In prompt obedience to spontaneous measures
Of glory, and felicity, and love,
Surrendering the whole heart to sacred pleasures?

VIII
  O Britain! dearer far than life is dear,
140   If one there be
    Of all thy progeny
Who can forget thy prowess, never more
Be that ungrateful Son allowed to hear
Thy green leaves rustle or thy torrents roar.
As springs the lion from his den,
   As from a forest-brake
   Upstarts a glistering snake,
The bold Arch-despot re-appeared; – again
Wide Europe heaves, impatient to be cast,
150   With all her armèd Powers,
   On that offensive soil, like waves upon a thousand
    shores.
The trumpet blew a universal blast!
But Thou art foremost in the field: – there stand:
Receive the triumph destined to thy hand!
All States have glorified themselves; – their claims
Are weighed by Providence, in balance even;
And now, in preference to the mightiest names,
To Thee the exterminating sword is given.
Dread mark of approbation, justly gained!
160 Exalted office, worthily sustained!

IX
   Preserve, O Lord! within our hearts
   The memory of Thy favour,

That else insensibly departs,
And loses its sweet savour!
Lodge it within us! – as the power of light
Lives inexhaustibly in precious gems,
Fixed on the front of Eastern diadems,
So shine our thankfulness for ever bright!
What offering, what transcendent monument
170   Shall our sincerity to Thee present?
– Not work of hands; but trophies that may reach
To highest Heaven – the labour of the Soul;
That builds, as thy unerring precepts teach,
Upon the internal conquests made by each,
Her hope of lasting glory for the whole.
Yet will not heaven disown nor earth gainsay
The outward service of this day;
Whether the worshippers entreat
Forgiveness from God's mercy-seat;
180   Or thanks and praises to His throne ascend
That He has brought our warfare to an end,
And that we need no second victory! –
Ha! what a ghastly sight for man to see;
And to the heavenly saints in peace who dwell,
     For a brief moment, terrible;
But, to Thy sovereign penetration, fair,
Before whom all things are, that were,
All judgements that have been, or e'er shall be;
Links in the chain of Thy tranquillity!
190   Along the bosom of this favoured Nation,
Breathe Thou, this day, a vital undulation!
     Let all who do this land inherit
     Be conscious of Thy moving spirit!
Oh, 'tis a goodly Ordinance, – the sight,
Though sprung from bleeding war, is one of pure delight;
Bless Thou the hour, or ere the hour arrive,
When a whole people shall kneel down in prayer,
And, at one moment, in one rapture, strive
With lip and heart to tell their gratitude
200   For Thy protecting care,

Their solemn joy – praising the Eternal Lord
    For tyranny subdued,
And for the sway of equity renewed,
For liberty confirmed, and peace restored!

X

    But hark – the summons! – down the placid lake
Floats the soft cadence of the church-tower bells;
Bright shines the Sun, as if his beams would wake
The tender insects sleeping in their cells;
Bright shines the Sun – and not a breeze to shake
210   The drops that tip the melting icicles.
      O, enter now his temple gate!
Inviting words – perchance already flung
(As the crowd press devoutly down the aisle
Of some old Minster's venerable pile)
From voices into zealous passion stung,
While the tubed engine feels the inspiring blast,
And has begun – its clouds of sound to cast
      Forth towards empyreal Heaven,
      As if the fretted roof were riven.
220 *Us,* humbler ceremonies now await;
But in the bosom, with devout respect
The banner of our joy we will erect,
And strength of love our souls shall elevate:
For to a few collected in His name,
Their heavenly Father will incline an ear
Gracious to service hallowed by its aim; –
Awake! the majesty of God revere!
    Go – and with foreheads meekly bowed
Present your prayers – go – and rejoice aloud –
230   The Holy One will hear!
And what, 'mid silence deep, with faith sincere,
Ye, in your low and undisturbed estate,
Shall simply feel and purely meditate –
Of warnings – from the unprecedented might,
Which, in our time, the impious have disclosed;
And of more arduous duties thence imposed

Upon the future advocates of right;
  Of mysteries revealed,
  And judgements unrepealed,
240 Of earthly revolution,
  And final retribution, –
 To His omniscience will appear
An offering not unworthy to find place,
On this high DAY OF THANKS, before the Throne of
 Grace!

Siege of Vienna Raised by John Sobieski
February, 1816

O, for a kindling touch from that pure flame
Which ministered, erewhile, to a sacrifice
Of gratitude, beneath Italian skies,
In words like these: 'Up, Voice of song! proclaim
Thy saintly rapture with celestial aim:
For lo! the Imperial City stands released
From bondage threatened by the embattled East,
And Christendom respires; from guilt and shame
Redeemed, from miserable fear set free
10 By one day's feat, one mighty victory.
 – Chant the Deliverer's praise in every tongue!
The cross shall spread, the crescent hath waxed dim;
He conquering, as in joyful Heaven is sung,
HE CONQUERING THROUGH GOD, AND GOD BY HIM.'

Ode: 1814

————Carmina possumus
Donare, et pretium dicere muneri.
Non incisa notis marmora publicis,
Per quae spiritus et vita redit bonis
Post mortem ducibus,
———— clarius indicant
Laudes, quam ———— Pierides; neque,

Si chartae sileant quod bene feceris,
Mercedem tuleris. – Hor. Car. 8. Lib. 4.

I

When the soft hand of sleep had closed the latch
On the tired household of corporeal sense,
And Fancy, keeping unreluctant watch,
Was free her choicest favours to dispense;
I saw, in wondrous pérspective displayed,
A landscape more august than happiest skill
Of pencil ever clothed with light and shade;
An intermingled pomp of vale and hill,
City, and naval stream, suburban grove,

10   And stately forest where the wild deer rove;
Nor wanted lurking hamlet, dusky towns,
And scattered rural farms of aspect bright;
And, here and there, between the pastoral downs,
The azure sea upswelled upon the sight.
Fair prospect, such as Britain only shows!
But not a living creature could be seen
Through its wide circuit, that, in deep repose,
And, even to sadness, lonely and serene,
Lay hushed; till – through a portal in the sky

20   Brighter than brightest loop-hole, in a storm,
Opening before the sun's triumphant eye –
Issued, to sudden view, a glorious Form!
Earthward it glided with a swift descent:
Saint George himself this Visitant must be;
And, ere a thought could ask on what intent ,
He sought the regions of humanity,
A thrilling voice was heard, that vivified
City and field and flood; – aloud it cried –
    'Though from my celestial home,

30   Like a Champion, armed I come;
On my helm the dragon crest,
And the red cross on my breast;
I, the Guardian of this Land,
Speak not now of toilsome duty;

Well obeyed was that command –
Whence bright days of festive beauty;
Haste, Virgins, haste! – the flowers which summer gave
    Have perished in the field;
But the green thickets plenteously shall yield
40   Fit garlands for the brave,
That will be welcome, if by you entwined;
Haste, Virgins, haste; and you, ye Matrons grave,
Go forth with rival youthfulness of mind,
    And gather what ye find
Of hardy laurel and wild holly boughs –
To deck your stern Defenders' modest brows!
    Such simple gifts prepare,
Though they have gained a worthier meed;
    And in due time shall share
50 Those palms and amaranthine wreaths
Unto their martyred Countrymen decreed,
In realms where everlasting freshness breathes!'

II
    And lo! with crimson banners proudly streaming,
And upright weapons innocently gleaming,
Along the surface of a spacious plain
Advance in order the redoubted Bands,
And there receive green chaplets from the hands
    Of a fair female train –
    Maids and Matrons, dight
    In robes of dazzling white;
While from the crowd bursts forth a rapturous noise
    By the cloud-capt hills retorted;
    And a throng of rosy boys
    In loose fashion tell their joys;
And grey-haired sires, on staffs supported,
Look round, and by their smiling seem to say,
'Thus strives a grateful Country to display
The mighty debt which nothing can repay!'

III
> Anon before my sight a palace rose
70 Built of all precious substances, – so pure
> And exquisite, that sleep alone bestows
> Ability like splendour to endure:
> Entered, with streaming thousands, through the gate,
> I saw the banquet spread beneath a Dome of state,
> A lofty Dome, that dared to emulate
> The heaven of sable night
> With starry lustre; yet had power to throw
> Solemn effulgence, clear as solar light,
> Upon a princely company below,
80 While the vault rang with choral harmony,
> Like some Nymph-haunted grot beneath the roaring sea.
> – No sooner ceased that peal, than on the verge
> Of exultation hung a dirge
> Breathed from a soft and lonely instrument,
>> That kindled recollections
>> Of agonized affections;
> And, though some tears the strain attended,
>> The mournful passion ended
> In peace of spirit, and sublime content!

IV
90 But garlands wither; festal shows depart,
> Like dreams themselves; and sweetest sound –
>> (Albeit of effect profound)
>> It was – and it is gone!
> Victorious England! bid the silent Art
> Reflect, in glowing hues that shall not fade,
> Those high achievements; even as she arrayed
> With second life the deed of Marathon
>> Upon Athenian walls;
> So may she labour for thy civic halls:
100 And be the guardian spaces
>> Of consecrated places,
> As nobly graced by Sculpture's patient toil;
> And let imperishable Columns rise

Fixed in the depths of this courageous soil;
Expressive signals of a glorious strife,
And competent to shed a spark divine
Into the torpid breast of daily life; –
Records on which, for pleasure of all eyes,
　　　The morning sun may shine
110　With gratulation thoroughly benign!

V

　　　And ye, Pierian Sisters, sprung from Jove
And sage Mnemosyne, – full long debarred
From your first mansions, exiled all too long
From many a hallowed stream and grove,
Dear native regions where ye wont to rove,
Chanting for patriot heroes the reward
　　　Of never-dying song!
Now (for, though Truth descending from above
The Olympian summit hath destroyed for aye
120　Your kindred Deities, *Ye* live and move,
Spared for obeisance from perpetual love
For privilege redeemed of godlike sway)
Now, on the margin of some spotless fountain,
Or top serene of unmolested mountain,
Strike audibly the noblest of your lyres,
And for a moment meet the soul's desires!
That I, or some more favoured Bard, may hear
What ye, celestial Maids! have often sung
Of Britain's acts, – may catch it with rapt ear,
130　And give the treasure to our British tongue!
So shall the characters of that proud page
Support their mighty theme from age to age;
And, in the desert places of the earth,
When they to future empires have given birth,
So shall the people gather and believe
The bold report, transferred to every clime;
And the whole world, not envious but admiring,
　　　And to the like aspiring,
Own – that the progeny of this fair Isle

140 Had power as lofty actions to achieve
As were performed in man's heroic prime;
Nor wanted, when their fortitude had held
Its even tenor, and the foe was quelled,
A corresponding virtue to beguile
The hostile purpose of wide-wasting Time –
That not in vain they laboured to secure,
For their great deeds, perpetual memory,
And fame as largely spread as land and sea,
By Works of spirit high and passion pure!

Ode

I

Who rises on the banks of Seine,
And binds her temples with the civic wreath?
What joy to read the promise of her mien!
How sweet to rest her wide-spread wings beneath!
But they are ever playing,
And twinkling in the light,
And, if a breeze be straying,
That breeze she will invite;
And stands on tiptoe, conscious she is fair,
10 And calls a look of love into her face,
And spreads her arms, as if the general air
Alone could satisfy her wide embrace.
– Melt, Principalities, before her melt!
Her love ye hailed – her wrath have felt!
But She through many a change of form hath gone,
And stands amidst you now an armèd creature,
Whose panoply is not a thing put on,
But the live scales of a portentous nature;
That, having forced its way from birth to birth,
20 Stalks round – abhorred by Heaven, a terror to the
Earth!

II

    I marked the breathings of her dragon crest;
My Soul, a sorrowful interpreter,
In many a midnight vision bowed
Before the ominous aspect of her spear;
Whether the mighty beam, in scorn upheld,
Threatened her fòes, – or, pompously at rest,
Seemed to bisect her orbèd shield,
As stretches a blue bar of solid cloud
Across the setting sun and all the fiery west.

III

30   So did she daunt the Earth, and God defy!
And, wheresoe'er she spread her sovereignty,
Pollution tainted all that was most pure.
– Have we not known – and live we not to tell –
That Justice seemed to hear her final knell?
Faith buried deeper in her own deep breast
Her stores, and sighed to find them insecure!
And Hope was maddened by the drops that fell
From shades, her chosen place of short-lived rest.
Shame followed shame, and woe supplanted woe –
40 Is this the only change that time can show?
How long shall vengeance sleep? Ye patient Heavens,
    how long?
– Infirm ejaculation! from the tongue
Of Nations wanting virtue to be strong
Up to the measure of accorded might,
And daring not to feel the majesty of right!

IV

    Weak Spirits are there – who would ask,
Upon the pressure of a painful thing,
The lion's sinews, or the eagle's wing;
Or let their wishes loose, in forest-glade,
50   Among the lurking powers
        Of herbs and lowly flowers,
Or seek, from saints above, miraculous aid –

That Man may be accomplished for a task
Which his own nature hath enjoined; – and why?
If, when that interference hath relieved him,
      He must sink down to languish
In worse than former helplessness – and lie
      Till the caves roar, – and, imbecility
      Again engendering anguish,
60 The same weak wish returns, that had before deceived
      him.

V

  But Thou, supreme Disposer! mayst not speed
The course of things, and change the creed
Which hath been held aloft before men's sight
Since the first framing of societies,
Whether, as bards have told in ancient song,
Built up by soft seducing harmonies;
Or prest together by the appetite,
      And by the power, of wrong.

Occasioned by the Battle of Waterloo
February, 1816

The Bard – whose soul is meek as dawning day,
Yet trained to judgements righteously severe,
Fervid, yet conversànt with holy fear,
As recognizing one Almighty sway:
He – whose experienced eye can pierce the array
Of past events; to whom, in vision clear,
The aspiring heads of future things appear,
Like mountain-tops whose mists have rolled away –
Assoiled from all encumbrance of our time,
10 He only, if such breathe, in strains devout
Shall comprehend this victory sublime;
Shall worthily rehearse the hideous rout,
The triumph hail, which from their peaceful clime
Angels might welcome with a choral shout!

Occasioned by the Battle of Waterloo (The last six lines intended for an Inscription) February, 1816

Intrepid sons of Albion! not by you
Is life despised; ah no, the spacious earth
Ne'er saw a race who held, by right of birth,
So many objects to which love is due:
Ye slight not life – to God and Nature true;
But death, becoming death, is dearer far,
When duty bids you bleed in open war:
Hence hath your prowess quelled that impious crew.
Heroes! – for instant sacrifice prepared;
10   Yet filled with ardour and on triumph bent
'Mid direst shocks of mortal accident –
To you who fell, and you whom slaughter spared
To guard the fallen, and consummate the event,
Your Country rears this sacred Monument!

*Invocation to the Earth
February, 1816*

I

     'Rest, rest, perturbèd Earth!
    O rest, thou doleful Mother of Mankind!'
A Spirit sang in tones more plaintive than the wind:
'From regions where no evil thing has birth
I come – thy stains to wash away,
Thy cherished fetters to unbind,
And open thy sad eyes upon a milder day.
The Heavens are thronged with martyrs that have risen
    From out thy noisome prison;
10   The penal caverns groan
With tens of thousands rent from off the tree
Of hopeful life, – by battle's whirlwind blown

Into the deserts of Eternity.
Unpitied havoc! Victims unlamented!
But not on high, where madness is resented,
And murder causes some sad tears to flow,
Though, from the widely-sweeping blow,
The choirs of Angels spread, triumphantly augmented.

II
      'False Parent of Mankind!
20   Obdurate, proud, and blind,
I sprinkle thee with soft celestial dews,
Thy lost, maternal heart to re-infuse!
Scattering this far-fetched moisture from my wings,
Upon the act a blessing I implore,
Of which the rivers in their secret springs,
The rivers stained so oft with human gore,
Are conscious; – may the like return no more!
May Discord – for a Seraph's care
Shall be attended with a bolder prayer –
30 May she, who once disturbed the seats of bliss
      These mortal spheres above,
Be chained for ever to the black abyss!
And thou, O rescued Earth, by peace and love,
And merciful desires, thy sanctity approve!'
    The Spirit ended his mysterious rite,
And the pure vision closed in darkness infinite.

The French Army in Russia 1812–13

Humanity, delighting to behold
A fond reflection of her own decay,
Hath painted Winter like a traveller old,
Propped on a staff, and, through the sullen day,
In hooded mantle, limping o'er the plain,
As though his weakness were disturbed by pain:
Or, if a juster fancy should allow

An undisputed symbol of command,
The chosen sceptre is a withered bough,
10   Infirmly grasped within a palsied hand.
These emblems suit the helpless and forlorn;
But mighty Winter the device shall scorn.
For he it was – dread Winter! who beset,
Flinging round van and rear his ghastly net,
That host, when from the regions of the Pole
They shrunk, insane ambition's barren goal –
That host, as huge and strong as e'er defied
Their God, and placed their trust in human pride!
As fathers persecute rebellious sons,
20   He smote the blossoms of their warrior youth;
He called on Frost's inexorable tooth
Life to consume in Manhood's firmest hold;
Nor spared the reverend blood that feebly runs;
For why – unless for liberty enrolled
And sacred home – ah! why should hoary Age be bold?
    Fleet the Tartar's reinless steed,
But fleeter far the pinions of the Wind,
Which from Siberian caves the Monarch freed,
And sent him forth, with squadrons of his kind,
30   And bade the Snow their ample backs bestride,
    And to the battle ride.
No pitying voice commands a halt,
No courage can repel the dire assault;
Distracted, spiritless, benumbed, and blind,
Whole legions sink – and, in one instant, find
Burial and death: look for them – and descry,
When morn returns, beneath the clear blue sky,
A soundless waste, a trackless vacancy!

On the Same Occasion

Ye Storms, resound the praises of your King!
And ye mild Seasons – in a sunny clime,
Midway on some high hill, while father Time

Looks on delighted – meet in festal ring,
And loud and long of Winter's triumph sing!
Sing he, with blossoms crowned, and fruits, and flowers,
Of Winter's breath surcharged with sleety showers,
And the dire flapping of his hoary wing!
Knit the blithe dance upon the soft green grass;
10 With feet, hands, eyes, looks, lips, report your gain;
Whisper it to the billows of the main,
And to the aërial zephyrs as they pass,
That old decrepit Winter – *He* hath slain
That Host, which rendered all your bounties vain!

Ode: 1815

I
Imagination – ne'er before content,
But aye ascending, restless in her pride
From all that martial feats could yield
To her desires, or to her hopes present –
Stooped to the Victory, on that Belgic field
Achieved, this closing deed magnificent,
    And with the embrace was satisfied.
       – Fly, ministers of Fame,
With every help that ye from earth and heaven may
    claim!
10 Bear through the world these tidings of delight!
– Hours, Days, and Months, *have* borne them in the
    sight
Of mortals, hurrying like a sudden shower
    That landward stretches from the sea,
    The morning's splendours to devour;
But this swift travel scorns the company
Of irksome change, or threats from saddening power.
    – *The shock is given – the Adversaries bleed –*
    Lo, Justice triumphs! Earth is freed!
Joyful annunciation! – it went forth –
20 It pierced the caverns of the sluggish North –

It found no barrier on the ridge
Of Andes – frozen gulfs became its bridge –
The vast Pacific gladdens with the freight –
Upon the Lakes of Asia 'tis bestowed –
The Arabian desart shapes a willing road
    Across her burning breast,
For this refreshing incense from the West! –
    – Where snakes and lions breed,
Where towns and cities thick as stars appear,
30 Wherever fruits are gathered, and where'er
The upturned soil receives the hopeful seed –
While the Sun rules, and cross the shades of night –
The unwearied arrow hath pursued its flight!
The eyes of good men thankfully give heed,
    And in its sparkling progress read
Of virtue crowned with glory's deathless meed:
Tyrants exult to hear of kingdoms won,
And slaves are pleased to learn that mighty feats are
    done;
Even the proud Realm, from whose distracted borders
40 This messenger of good was launched in air,
France, humbled France, amid her wild disorders,
Feels, and hereafter shall the truth declare,
That she too lacks not reason to rejoice,
And utter England's name with sadly-plausive voice.

II

O genuine glory, pure renown!
And well might it beseem that mighty Town
Into whose bosom earth's best treasures flow,
To whom all persecuted men retreat;
If a new Temple lift her votive brow
50 High on the shore of silver Thames – to greet
The peaceful guest advancing from afar.
Bright be the Fabric, as a star
Fresh risen, and beautiful within! – there meet
Dependence infinite, proportion just;

A Pile that Grace approves, and Time can trust
With his most sacred wealth, heroic dust.

III

     But if the valiant of this land
In reverential modesty demand,
That all observance, due to them, be paid
60 Where their serene progenitors are laid;
Kings, warriors, high-souled poets, saintlike sages,
England's illustrious sons of long, long ages;
Be it not unordained that solemn rites,
Within the circuit of those Gothic walls,
Shall be performed at pregnant intervals;
Commemoration holy that unites
The living generations with the dead;
     By the deep soul-moving sense
     Of religious eloquence, –
70   By visual pomp, and by the tie
     Of sweet and threatening harmony;
     Soft notes, awful as the omen
     Of destructive tempests coming,
     And escaping from that sadness
     Into elevated gladness;
     While the white-robed choir attendant,
     Under mouldering banners pendant,
Provoke all potent symphonies to raise
     Songs of victory and praise,
80 For them who bravely stood unhurt, or bled
With medicable wounds, or found their graves
Upon the battlefield, or under ocean's waves;
Or were conducted home in single state,
And long procession – there to lie,
Where their sons' sons, and all posterity,
Unheard by them, their deeds shall celebrate!

IV

     Nor will the God of peace and love
     Such martial service disapprove.

He guides the Pestilence – the cloud
90   Of locusts travels on his breath;
The region that in hope was ploughed
His drought consumes, his mildew taints with death;
He springs the hushed Volcano's mine,
He puts the Earthquake on her still design,
Darkens the sun, hath bade the forest sink,
And, drinking towns and cities, still can drink
Cities and towns – 'tis Thou – the work is Thine! –
The fierce Tornado sleeps within Thy courts –
He hears the word – he flies –
100   And navies perish in their ports;
For Thou art angry with Thine enemies!
For these, and mourning for our errors,
And sins, that point their terrors,
We bow our heads before Thee, and we laud
And magnify Thy name, Almighty God!
But Man is Thy most awful instrument,
In working out a pure intent;
Thou cloth'st the wicked in their dazzling mail,
And for Thy righteous purpose they prevail;
110   Thine arm from peril guards the coasts
Of them who in Thy laws delight:
Thy presence turns the scale of doubtful fight,
Tremendous God of battles, Lord of Hosts!

V
Forbear: – to Thee –
Father and Judge of all, with fervent tongue
But in a gentler strain
Of contemplation, by no sense of wrong
(Too quick and keen) incited to disdain
Of pity pleading from the heart in vain –
120   TO THEE – TO THEE,
Just God of Christianized Humanity,
Shall praises be poured forth, and thanks ascend,
That Thou hast brought our warfare to an end,
And that we need no second victory!

Blest, above measure blest,
If on Thy love our Land her hopes shall rest,
And all the Nations labour to fulfil
Thy law, and live henceforth in peace, in pure good will.

Feelings of a French Royalist, on the Disinterment of the Remains of the Duke D'Enghien

Dear Reliques! from a pit of vilest mould
Uprisen – to lodge among ancestral kings;
And to inflict shame's salutary stings
On the remorseless hearts of men grown old
In a blind worship; men perversely bold
Even to this hour, – yet, some shall now forsake
Their monstrous Idol if the dead e'er spake,
To warn the living; if truth were ever told
By aught redeemed out of the hollow grave:
10 O murdered Prince! meek, loyal, pious, brave!
The power of retribution once was given:
But 'tis a rueful thought that willow bands
So often tie the thunder-wielding hands
Of Justice sent to earth from highest Heaven!

Dion (See Plutarch)

I

Serene, and fitted to embrace,
Where'er he turned, a swan-like grace
Of haughtiness without pretence,
And to unfold a still magnificence,
Was princely Dion, in the power
And beauty of his happier hour.
And what pure homage *then* did wait
On Dion's virtues, while the lunar beam
Of Plato's genius, from its lofty sphere,
10 Fell round him in the grove of Academe,

Softening their inbred dignity austere –
  That he, not too elate
  With self-sufficing solitude,
But with majestic lowliness endued,
Might in the universal bosom reign,
And from affectionate observance gain
Help, under every change of adverse fate.

II

Five thousand warriors – O the rapturous day!
Each crowned with flowers, and armed with spear and
    shield,
Or ruder weapon which their course might yield,
To Syracuse advance in bright array.
Who leads them on? – The anxious people see
Long-exiled Dion marching at their head,
He also crowned with flowers of Sicily,
And in a white, far-beaming, corslet clad!
Pure transport undisturbed by doubt or fear
The gazers feel; and, rushing to the plain,
Salute those strangers as a holy train
Or blest procession (to the Immortals dear)
That brought their precious liberty again.
Lo! when the gates are entered, on each hand,
Down the long street, rich goblets filled with wine
  In seemly order stand,
On tables set, as if for rites divine; –
And, as the great Deliverer marches by,
He looks on festal ground with fruits bestrown;
And flowers are on his person thrown
  In boundless prodigality;
Nor doth the general voice abstain from prayer,
Invoking Dion's tutelary care,
As if a very Deity he were!

III

Mourn, hills and groves of Attica! and mourn
Ilissus, bending o'er thy classic urn!

Mourn, and lament for him whose spirit dreads
Your once sweet memory, studious walks and shades!
For him who to divinity aspired,
Not on the breath of popular applause,
But through dependence on the sacred laws
Framed in the schools where Wisdom dwelt retired,
50 Intent to trace the ideal path of right
(More fair than heaven's broad causeway paved with
        stars)
Which Dion learned to measure with sublime delight; —
But He hath overleaped the eternal bars;
And, following guides whose craft holds no consent
With aught that breathes the ethereal element,
Hath stained the robes of civil power with blood,
Unjustly shed, though for the public good.
Whence doubts that came too late, and wishes vain,
Hollow excuses, and triumphant pain;
60 And oft his cogitations sink as low
As, through the abysses of a joyless heart,
The heaviest plummet of despair can go —
But whence that sudden check? that fearful start!
        He hears an uncouth sound —
        Anon his lifted eyes
Saw, at a long-drawn gallery's dusky bound,
A Shape of more than mortal size
And hideous aspect, stalking round and round.
        A woman's garb the Phantom wore,
70   And fiercely swept the marble floor, —
        Like Auster whirling to and fro,
        His force on Caspian foam to try;
Or Boreas when he scours the snow
That skins the plains of Thessaly,
Or when aloft on Maenalus he stops
His flight, 'mid eddying pine-tree tops!

IV
So, but from toil less sign of profit reaping,
The sullen Spectre to her purpose bowed,

Sweeping – vehemently sweeping –
80 No pause admitted, no design avowed!
'Avaunt, inexplicable Guest! – avaunt,'
Exclaimed the Chieftain – 'let me rather see
The coronal that coiling vipers make;
The torch that flames with many a lurid flake,
And the long train of doleful pageantry
Which they behold, whom vengeful Furies haunt;
Who, while they struggle from the scourge to flee,
Move where the blasted soil is not unworn,
And, in their anguish, bear what other minds have
    borne!'

V

90 But Shapes that come not at an earthly call,
Will not depart when mortal voices bid;
Lords of the visionary eye whose lid,
Once raised, remains aghast, and will not fall!
Ye Gods, thought He, that servile Implement
    Obeys a mystical intent!
Your Minister would brush away
The spots that to my soul adhere;
But should she labour night and day,
They will not, cannot disappear;
100 Whence angry perturbations, – and that look
Which no philosophy can brook!

VI

Ill-fated Chief! there are whose hopes are built
Upon the ruins of thy glorious name;
Who, through the portal of one moment's guilt,
Pursue thee with their deadly aim!
O matchless perfidy! portentous lust
Of monstrous crime! – that horror-striking blade,
Drawn in defiance of the Gods, hath laid
The noble Syracusan low in dust!
110 Shuddered the walls – the marble city wept –
And sylvan places heaved a pensive sigh;

But in calm peace the appointed Victim slept,
As he had fallen in magnanimity;
Of spirit too capacious to require
That Destiny her course should change; too just
To his own native greatness to desire
That wretched boon, days lengthened by mistrust.
So were the hopeless troubles, that involved
The soul of Dion, instantly dissolved.
120 Released from life and cares of princely state,
He left this moral grafted on his Fate;
'Him only pleasure leads, and peace attends,
Him, only him, the shield of Jove defends,
Whose means are fair and spotless as his ends.'

'"*A* LITTLE *onward lend thy guiding hand*"'

'*A* LITTLE *onward lend thy guiding hand*
To these dark steps, a little further on!'
– What trick of memory to *my* voice hath brought
This mournful iteration? For though Time,
The Conqueror, crowns the Conquered, on this brow
Planting his favourite silver diadem,
Nor he, nor minister of his – intent
To run before him, hath enrolled me yet,
Though not unmenaced, among those who lean
10 Upon a living staff, with borrowed sight.
– O my own Dora, my belovèd child!
Should that day come – but hark! the birds salute
The cheerful dawn, brightening for me the east;
For me, thy natural leader, once again
Impatient to conduct thee, not as erst
A tottering infant, with compliant stoop
From flower to flower supported; but to curb
Thy nymph-like step swift-bounding o'er the lawn,
Along the loose rocks, or the slippery verge
20 Of foaming torrents. – From thy orisons
Come forth; and, while the morning air is yet

Transparent as the soul of innocent youth,
Let me, thy happy guide, now point thy way,
And now precede thee, winding to and fro,
Till we by perseverance gain the top
Of some smooth ridge, whose brink precipitous
Kindles intense desire for powers withheld
From this corporeal frame; whereon who stands
Is seized with strong incitement to push forth
30   His arms, as swimmers use, and plunge – dread thought,
For pastime plunge – into the 'abrupt abyss',
Where ravens spread their plumy vans, at ease!

And yet more gladly thee would I conduct
Through woods and spacious forests, – to behold
There, how the Original of human art,
Heaven-prompted Nature, measures and erects
Her temples, fearless for the stately work,
Though waves, to every breeze, its high-arched roof,
And storms the pillars rock. But we such schools
40   Of reverential awe will chiefly seek
In the still summer noon, while beams of light,
Reposing here, and in the aisles beyond
Traceably gliding through the dusk, recall
To mind the living presences of nuns;
A gentle, pensive, white-robed sisterhood,
Whose saintly radiance mitigates the gloom
Of those terrestrial fabrics, where they serve,
To Christ, the Sun of righteousness, espoused.

Now also shall the page of classic lore,
50   To these glad eyes from bondage freed, again
Lie open; and the book of Holy Writ,
Again unfolded, passage clear shall yield
To heights more glorious still, and into shades
More awful, where, advancing hand in hand,
We may be taught, O Darling of my care!
To calm the affections, elevate the soul,
And consecrate our lives to truth and love.

To —, on Her First Ascent to the Summit of Helvellyn

Inmate of a mountain-dwelling,
Thou hast clomb aloft, and gazed
From the watch-towers of Helvellyn;
Awed, delighted, and amazed!

Potent was the spell that bound thee
Not unwilling to obey;
For blue Ether's arms, flung round thee,
Stilled the pantings of dismay.

Lo! the dwindled woods and meadows;
10   What a vast abyss is there!
Lo! the clouds, the solemn shadows,
And the glistenings – heavenly fair!

And a record of commotion
Which a thousand ridges yield;
Ridge, and gulf, and distant ocean
Gleaming like a silver shield!

Maiden! now take flight; – inherit
Alps or Andes – they are thine!
With the morning's roseate Spirit,
20   Sweep their length of snowy line;

Or survey their bright dominions
In the gorgeous colours drest
Flung from off the purple pinions,
Evening spreads throughout the west!

Thine are all the choral fountains
Warbling in each sparry vault
Of the untrodden lunar mountains;
Listen to their songs! – or halt,

To Niphates' top invited,
30 Whither spiteful Satan steered;
Or descend where the ark alighted,
When the green earth re-appeared;

For the power of hills is on thee,
As was witnessed through thine eye
Then, when old Helvellyn won thee
To confess their majesty!

'Emperors and Kings, how oft have temples rung'

Emperors and Kings, how oft have temples rung
With impious thanksgiving, the Almighty's scorn!
How oft above their altars have been hung
Trophies that led the good and wise to mourn
Triumphant wrong, battle of battle born,
And sorrow that to fruitless sorrow clung!
Now, from Heaven-sanctioned victory, Peace is sprung;
In this firm hour Salvation lifts her horn.
Glory to arms! But, conscious that the nerve
10 Of popular reason, long mistrusted, freed
Your thrones, ye Powers, from duty fear to swerve!
Be just, be grateful; nor, the oppressor's creed
Reviving, heavier chastisement deserve
Than ever forced unpitied hearts to bleed.

Vernal Ode

'Rerum Natura tota est nusquam magis quam in minimis.'
PLIN. *Nat. Hist.*

I

Beneath the concave of an April sky,
When all the fields with freshest green were dight,
Appeared, in presence of the spiritual eye
That aids or supersedes our grosser sight,

The form and rich habiliments of One
Whose countenance bore resemblance to the sun,
When it reveals, in evening majesty,
Features half lost amid their own pure light.
Poised like a weary cloud, in middle air
10 He hung, – then floated with angelic ease
(Softening that bright effulgence by degrees)
Till he had reached a summit sharp and bare,
Where oft the venturous heifer drinks the noontide breeze.
Upon the apex of that lofty cone
Alighted, there the Stranger stood alone;
Fair as a gorgeous Fabric of the east
Suddenly raised by some enchanter's power,
Where nothing was; and firm as some old Tower
Of Britain's realm, whose leafy crest
20 Waves high, embellished by a gleaming shower!

II

Beneath the shadow of his purple wings
Rested a golden harp; – he touched the strings;
And, after prelude of unearthly sound
Poured through the echoing hills around,
He sang –
          'No wintry desolations,
Scorching blight or noxious dew,
Affect my native habitations;
Buried in glory, far beyond the scope
Of man's inquiring gaze, but to his hope
30 Imaged, though faintly, in the hue
Profound of night's ethereal blue;
And in the aspect of each radiant orb; –
Some fixed, some wandering with no timid curb;
But wandering star and fixed, to mortal eye,
Blended in absolute serenity,
And free from semblance of decline; –
Fresh as if Evening brought their natal hour,
Her darkness splendour gave, her silence power,
To testify of Love and Grace divine.

III

40 'What if those bright fires
Shine subject to decay,
Sons haply of extinguished sires,
Themselves to lose their light, or pass away
Like clouds before the wind,
Be thanks poured out to Him whose hand bestows,
Nightly, on human kind
That vision of endurance and repose.
– And though to every draught of vital breath
Renewed throughout the bounds of earth or ocean,
50 The melancholy gates of Death
Respond with sympathetic motion;
Though all that feeds on nether air,
Howe'er magnificent or fair,
Grows but to perish, and entrust
Its ruins to their kindred dust;
Yet, by the Almighty's ever-during care,
Her procreant vigils Nature keeps
Amid the unfathomable deeps;
And saves the peopled fields of earth
60 From dread of emptiness or dearth.
Thus, in their stations, lifting toward the sky
The foliaged head in cloud-like majesty,
The shadow-casting race of trees survive:
Thus, in the train of Spring, arrive
Sweet flowers; – what living eye hath viewed
Their myriads? – endlessly renewed,
Wherever strikes the sun's glad ray;
Where'er the subtle waters stray;
Wherever sportive breezes bend
70 Their course, or genial showers descend!
Mortals, rejoice! the very Angels quit
Their mansions unsusceptible of change,
Amid your pleasant bowers to sit,
And through your sweet vicissitudes to range!'

IV

O, nursed at happy distance from the cares
Of a too-anxious world, mild pastoral Muse!
That, to the sparkling crown Urania wears,
And to her sister Clio's laurel wreath,
Prefer'st a garland culled from purple heath,
80 Or blooming thicket moist with morning dews;
Was such bright Spectacle vouchsafed to me?
And was it granted to the simple ear
Of thy contented Votary
Such melody to hear!
Him rather suits it, side by side with thee,
Wrapped in a fit of pleasing indolence,
While thy tired lute hangs on the hawthorn-tree,
To lie and listen – till o'erdrowsèd sense
Sinks, hardly conscious of the influence –
90 To the soft murmur of the vagrant Bee.
– A slender sound! yet hoary Time
Doth to the *Soul* exalt it with the chime
Of all his years; – a company
Of ages coming, ages gone;
(Nations from before them sweeping,
Regions in destruction steeping,)
But every awful note in unison
With that faint utterance, which tells
Of treasure sucked from buds and bells,
100 For the pure keeping of those waxen cells;
Where She – a statist prudent to confer
Upon the common weal; a warrior bold,
Radiant all over with unburnished gold,
And armed with living spear for mortal fight;
    A cunning forager
That spreads no waste; a social builder; one
In whom all busy offices unite
With all fine functions that afford delight –
Safe through the winter storm in quiet dwells!

V

110 And is She brought within the power
Of vision? – o'er this tempting flower
Hovering until the petals stay
Her flight, and take its voice away! –
Observe each wing! – a tiny van!
The structure of her laden thigh,
How fragile! yet of ancestry
Mysteriously remote and high;
High as the imperial front of man;
The roseate bloom on woman's cheek;
120 The soaring eagle's curvèd beak;
The white plumes of the floating swan;
Old as the tiger's paw, the lion's mane
Ere shaken by that mood of stern disdain
At which the desert trembles. – Humming Bee!
Thy sting was needless then, perchance unknown,
The seeds of malice were not sown;
All creatures met in peace, from fierceness free,
And no pride blended with their dignity.
– Tears had not broken from their source;
130 Nor Anguish strayed from her Tartarean den;
The golden years maintained a course
Not undiversified though smooth and even;
We were not mocked with glimpse and shadow then,
Bright Seraphs mixed familiarly with men;
And earth and stars composed a universal heaven!

Ode to Lycoris
May, 1817

I

An age hath been when Earth was proud
Of lustre too intense
To be sustained; and Mortals bowed
The front in self-defence.
Who *then*, if Dian's crescent gleamed,

Or Cupid's sparkling arrow streamed
While on the wing the Urchin played,
Could fearlessly approach the shade?
– Enough for one soft vernal day,
10 If I, a bard of ebbing time,
And nurtured in a fickle clime,
May haunt this hornèd bay;
Whose amorous water multiplies
The flitting halcyon's vivid dyes;
And smooths her liquid breast – to show
These swan-like specks of mountain snow,
White as the pair that slid along the plains
Of heaven, when Venus held the reins!

II

In youth we love the darksome lawn
20 Brushed by the owlet's wing;
Then, Twilight is preferred to Dawn,
And Autumn to the Spring.
Sad fancies do we then affect,
In luxury of disrespect
To our own prodigal excess
Of too familiar happiness.
Lycoris (if such name befit
Thee, thee my life's celestial sign!)
When Nature marks the year's decline,
30 Be ours to welcome it;
Pleased with the harvest hope that runs
Before the path of milder suns;
Pleased while the sylvan world displays
Its ripeness to the feeding gaze;
Pleased when the sullen winds resound the knell
Of the resplendent miracle.

III

But something whispers to my heart
That, as we downward tend,
Lycoris! life requires an *art*

40 To which our souls must bend;
A skill – to balance and supply;
And, ere the flowing fount be dry,
As soon it must, a sense to sip,
Or drink, with no fastidious lip.
Then welcome, above all, the Guest
Whose smiles, diffused o'er land and sea,
Seem to recall the Deity
Of youth into the breast:
May pensive Autumn ne'er present
50 A claim to her disparagement!
While blossoms and the budding spray
Inspire us in our own decay;
Still, as we nearer draw to life's dark goal,
Be hopeful Spring the favourite of the Soul!

The Pass of Kirkstone

I
Within the mind strong fancies work,
A deep delight the bosom thrills,
Oft as I pass along the fork
Of these fraternal hills:
Where, save the rugged road, we find
No appanage of human kind,
Nor hint of man; if stone or rock
Seem not his handy-work to mock
By something cognizably shaped;
10 Mockery – or model roughly hewn,
And left as if by earthquake strewn,
Or from the Flood escaped:
Altars for Druid service fit;
(But where no fire was ever lit,
Unless the glow-worm to the skies
Thence offer nightly sacrifice)
Wrinkled Egyptian monument;
Green moss-grown tower; or hoary tent;

Tents of a camp that never shall be raised –
20 On which four thousand years have gazed!

II

Ye ploughshares sparkling on the slopes!
Ye snow-white lambs that trip
Imprisoned 'mid the formal props
Of restless ownership!
Ye trees, that may tomorrow fall
To feed the insatiate Prodigal!
Lawns, houses, chattels, groves, and fields,
All that the fertile valley shields;
Wages of folly – baits of crime,
30 Of life's uneasy game the stake,
Playthings that keep the eyes awake
Of drowsy, dotard Time; –
O care! O guilt! – O vales and plains,
Here, 'mid his own unvexed domains,
A Genius dwells, that can subdue
At once all memory of You, –
Most potent when mists veil the sky,
Mists that distort and magnify,
While the coarse rushes, to the sweeping breeze,
40 Sigh forth their ancient melodies!

III

List to those shriller notes! – *that* march
Perchance was on the blast,
When, through this Height's inverted arch,
Rome's earliest legion passed!
– They saw, adventurously impelled,
And older eyes than theirs beheld,
This block – and yon, whose church-like frame
Gives to this savage Pass its name.
Aspiring Road! that lov'st to hide
50 Thy daring in a vapoury bourn,
Not seldom may the hour return
When thou shalt be my guide:

And I (as all men may find cause,
When life is at a weary pause,
And they have panted up the hill
Of duty with reluctant will)
Be thankful, even though tired and faint,
For the rich bounties of constraint;
Whence oft invigorating transports flow
60 That choice lacked courage to bestow!

IV
My Soul was grateful for delight
That wore a threatening brow;
A veil is lifted – can she slight
The scene that opens now?
Though habitation none appear,
The greenness tells, man must be there;
The shelter – that the pérspective
Is of·the clime in which we live;
Where Toil pursues his daily round;
70 Where Pity sheds sweet tears – and Love,
In woodbine bower or birchen grove,
Inflicts his tender wound.
– Who comes not hither ne'er shall know
How beautiful the world below;
Nor can he guess how lightly leaps
The brook adown the rocky steeps.
Farewell, thou desolate Domain!
Hope, pointing to the cultured plain,
Carols like a shepherd-boy;
80 And who is she? – Can that be Joy!
Who, with a sunbeam for her guide,
Smoothly skims the meadows wide;
While Faith, from yonder opening cloud,
To hill and vale proclaims aloud,
'Whate'er the weak may dread, the wicked dare,
Thy lot, O Man, is good, thy portion fair!'

Composed upon an Evening of Extraordinary Splendour and Beauty

I

Had this effulgence disappeared
With flying haste, I might have sent,
Among the speechless clouds, a look
Of blank astonishment;
But 'tis endued with power to stay,
And sanctify one closing day,
That frail Mortality may see –
What is? – ah no, but what *can* be!
Time was when field and watery cove
10   With modulated echoes rang,
While choirs of fervent Angels sang
Their vespers in the grove;
Or, crowning, star-like, each some sovereign height,
Warbled, for heaven above and earth below,
Strains suitable to both. – Such holy rite,
Methinks, if audibly repeated now
From hill or valley, could not move
Sublimer transport, purer love,
Than doth this silent spectacle – the gleam –
20   The shadow – and the peace supreme!

II

No sound is uttered, – but a deep
And solemn harmony pervades
The hollow vale from steep to steep,
And penetrates the glades.
Far-distant images draw nigh,
Called forth by wondrous potency
Of beamy radiance, that imbues
Whate'er it strikes with gem-like hues!
In vision exquisitely clear,
30   Herds range along the mountain side;
And glistening antlers are descried;

And gilded flocks appear.
Thine is the tranquil hour, purpureal Eve!
But long as god-like wish, or hope divine,
Informs my spirit, ne'er can I believe
That this magnificence is wholly thine!
– From worlds not quickened by the sun
A portion of the gift is won;
An intermingling of Heaven's pomp is spread
40 On ground which British shepherds tread!

III

And, if there be whom broken ties
Afflict, or injuries assail,
Yon hazy ridges to their eyes
Present a glorious scale,
Climbing suffused with sunny air,
To stop – no record hath told where!
And tempting Fancy to ascend,
And with immortal Spirits blend!
– Wings at my shoulders seem to play;
50 But, rooted here, I stand and gaze
On those bright steps that heavenward raise
Their practicable way.
Come forth, ye drooping old men, look abroad,
And see to what fair countries ye are bound!
And if some traveller, weary of his road,
Hath slept since noon-tide on the grassy ground,
Ye Genii! to his covert speed;
And wake him with such gentle heed
As may attune his soul to meet the dower
60 Bestowed on this transcendent hour!

IV

Such hues from their celestial Urn
Were wont to stream before mine eye,
Where'er it wandered in the morn
Of blissful infancy.
This glimpse of glory, why renewed?

Nay, rather speak with gratitude;
For, if a vestige of those gleams
Survived, 'twas only in my dreams.
Dread Power! whom peace and calmness serve
70 No less than Nature's threatening voice,
If aught unworthy be my choice,
From THEE if I would swerve;
Oh, let Thy grace remind me of the light
Full early lost, and fruitlessly deplored;
Which, at this moment, on my waking sight
Appears to shine, by miracle restored;
My soul, though yet confined to earth,
Rejoices in a second birth!
– 'Tis past, the visionary splendour fades;
80 And night approaches with her shades.

NOTE – The multiplication of mountain-ridges, described at
the commencement of the third Stanza of this Ode as a kind of
Jacob's Ladder, leading to Heaven, is produced either by
watery vapours, or sunny haze; – in the present instance by the
latter cause. Allusions to the Ode entitled 'Intimations of
Immortality' pervade the last Stanza of the foregoing Poem.

The Longest Day
Addressed to My Daughter, Dora

Let us quit the leafy arbour,
And the torrent murmuring by;
For the sun is in his harbour,
Weary of the open sky.

Evening now unbinds the fetters
Fashioned by the glowing light;
All that breathe are thankful debtors
To the harbinger of night.

Yet by some grave thoughts attended
10 Eve renews her calm career;

For the day that now is ended,
Is the longest of the year.

Dora! sport, as now thou sportest,
On this platform, light and free;
Take thy bliss, while longest, shortest,
Are indifferent to thee!

Who would check the happy feeling
That inspires the linnet's song?
Who would stop the swallow, wheeling
20 On her pinions swift and strong?

Yet, at this impressive season,
Words which tenderness can speak
From the truths of homely reason,
Might exalt the loveliest cheek;

And, while shades to shades succeeding
Steal the landscape from the sight,
I would urge this moral pleading,
Last forerunner of 'Good night!'

SUMMER ebbs; – each day that follows
30 Is a reflux from on high,
Tending to the darksome hollows
Where the frosts of winter lie.

He who governs the creation,
In His providence, assigned
Such a gradual declination
To the life of human kind.

Yet we mark it not; – fruits redden,
Fresh flowers blow, as flowers have blown,
And the heart is loth to deaden
40 Hopes that she so long hath known.

Be thou wiser, youthful Maiden!
And when thy decline shall come,
Let not flowers, or boughs fruit-laden,
Hide the knowledge of thy doom.

Now, even now, ere wrapped in slumber,
Fix thine eyes upon the sea
That absorbs time, space, and number;
Look thou to Eternity!

Follow thou the flowing river
50 On whose breast are thither borne
All deceived, and each deceiver,
Through the gates of night and morn;

Through the year's successive portals;
Through the bounds which many a star
Marks, not mindless of frail mortals,
When his light returns from far.

Thus when thou with Time hast travelled
Toward the mighty gulf of things,
And the mazy steam unravelled
60 With thy best imaginings;

Think, if thou on beauty leanest,
Think how pitiful that stay,
Did not virtue give the meanest
Charms superior to decay.

Duty, like a strict preceptor,
Sometimes frowns, or seems to frown;
Choose her thistle for thy sceptre,
While youth's roses are thy crown.

Grasp it, – if thou shrink and tremble,
70 Fairest damsel of the green,
Thou wilt lack the only symbol
That proclaims a genuine queen;

And ensures those palms of honour
Which selected spirits wear,
Bending low before the Donor,
Lord of heaven's unchanging year!

Hint from the Mountains for Certain Political Pretenders

'Who but hails the sight with pleasure
When the wings of genius rise,
Their ability to measure
 With great enterprise;
But in man was ne'er such daring
As yon Hawk exhibits, pairing
His brave spirit with the war in
 The stormy skies!

'Mark him, how his power he uses,
10 Lays it by, at will resumes!
Mark, ere for his haunt he chooses
 Clouds and utter glooms!
There, he wheels in downward mazes;
Sunward now his flight he raises,
Catches fire, as seems, and blazes
 With uninjured plumes!' –

ANSWER

'Stranger, 'tis no act of courage
Which aloft thou dost discern;
No bold *bird* gone forth to forage
20 'Mid the tempest stern;
But such mockery as the nations
See, when public perturbations
Lift men from their native stations,
 Like yon TUFT OF FERN;

'Such it is; the aspiring creature
Soaring on undaunted wing,
(So you fancied) is by nature
    A dull helpless thing,
Dry and withered, light and yellow; –
30 *That* to be the tempest's fellow!
Wait – and you shall see how hollow
    Its endeavouring!'

Lament of Mary Queen of Scots on the Eve of a New Year

I

Smile of the Moon! – for so I name
That silent greeting from above;
A gentle flash of light that came
From her whom drooping captives love;
Or art thou of still higher birth?
Thou that didst part the clouds of earth,
My torpor to reprove!

II

Bright boon of pitying Heaven! – alas,
I may not trust thy placid cheer!
10 Pondering that Time tonight will pass
The threshold of another year;
For years to me are sad and dull;
My very moments are too full
Of hopelessness and fear.

III

And yet, the soul-awakening gleam,
That struck perchance the farthest cone
Of Scotland's rocky wilds, did seem
To visit me, and me alone;
Me, unapproached by any friend,
20 Save those who to my sorrows lend
Tears due unto their own.

IV

Tonight the church-tower bells will ring
Through these wide realms a festive peal;
To the new year a welcoming;
A tuneful offering for the weal
Of happy millions lulled in sleep;
While I am forced to watch and weep,
By wounds that may not heal.

V

Born all too high, by wedlock raised
30 Still higher – to be cast thus low!
Would that mine eyes had never gazed
On aught of more ambitious show
Than the sweet flowerets of the fields!
– It is my royal state that yields
This bitterness of woe.

VI

Yet how? – for I, if there be truth
In the world's voice, was passing fair;
And beauty, for confiding youth,
Those shocks of passion can prepare
40 That kill the bloom before its time;
And blanch, without the owner's crime,
The most resplendent hair.

VII

Unblest distinction! showered on me
To bind a lingering life in chains:
All that could quit my grasp, or flee,
Is gone; – but not the subtle stains
Fixed in the spirit; for even here
Can I be proud that jealous fear
Of what I was remains.

VIII

50 A Woman rules my prison's key;
A sister Queen, against the bent

Of law and holiest sympathy,
Detains me, doubtful of the event;
Great God, who feel'st for my distress,
My thoughts are all that I possess,
O keep them innocent!

IX
Farewell desire of human aid,
Which abject mortals vainly court!
By friends deceived, by foes betrayed,
60 Of fears the prey, of hopes the sport;
Naught but the world-redeeming Cross
Is able to supply my loss,
My burden to support.

X
Hark! the death-note of the year
Sounded by the castle-clock!
From her sunk eyes a stagnant tear
Stole forth, unsettled by the shock;
But oft the woods renewed their green,
Ere the tired head of Scotland's Queen
70 Reposed upon the block!

Sequel to 'Beggars'
Composed Many Years After

Where are they now, those wanton Boys?
For whose free range the daedal earth
Was filled with animated toys,
And implements of frolic mirth;
With tools for ready wit to guide;
And ornaments of seemlier pride,
More fresh, more bright, than princes wear;
For what one moment flung aside,
Another could repair;
10 What good or evil have they seen
Since I their pastime witnessed here,

Their daring wiles, their sportive cheer?
I ask – but all is dark between!

    They met me in a genial hour,
When universal nature breathed
As with the breath of one sweet flower, –
A time to overrule the power
Of discontent, and check the birth
Of thoughts with better thoughts at strife,
20 The most familiar bane of life
Since parting Innocence bequeathed
Mortality to Earth!
Soft clouds, the whitest of the year,
Sailed through the sky – the brooks ran clear;
The lambs from rock to rock were bounding;
With songs the budded groves resounding;
And to my heart are still endeared
The thoughts with which it then was cheered;
The faith which saw that gladsome pair
30 Walk through the fire with unsinged hair.
Or, if such faith must needs deceive –
Then, Spirits of beauty and of grace,
Associates in that eager chase;
Ye, who within the blameless mind
Your favourite seat of empire find –
Kind Spirits! may we not believe
That they, so happy and so fair
Through your sweet influence, and the care
Of pitying Heaven, at least were free
40 From touch of *deadly* injury?
Destined, whate'er their earthly doom,
For mercy and immortal bloom?

Ode to Lycoris

Enough of climbing toil! – Ambition treads
Here, as 'mid busier scenes, ground steep and rough,
Or slippery even to peril! and each step,
As we for most uncertain recompence
Mount toward the empire of the fickle clouds,
Each weary step, dwarfing the world below,
Induces, for its old familiar sights,
Unacceptable feelings of contempt,
With wonder mixed – that Man could e'er be tied,
10 In anxious bondage, to such nice array
And formal fellowship of petty things!
– Oh! 'tis the *heart* that magnifies this life,
Making a truth and beauty of her own;
And moss-grown alleys, circumscribing shades,
And gurgling rills, assist her in the work
More efficaciously than realms outspread,
As in a map, before the adventurer's gaze –
Ocean and Earth contending for regard.

The umbrageous woods are left – how far beneath!
20 But lo! where darkness seems to guard the mouth
Of yon wild cave, whose jaggèd brows are fringed
With flaccid threads of ivy, in the still
And sultry air, depending motionless.
Yet cool the space within, and not uncheered
(As whoso enters shall ere long perceive)
By stealthy influx of the timid day
Mingling with night, such twilight to compose
As Numa loved; when, in the Egerian grot,
From the sage Nymph appearing at his wish,
30 He gained whate'er a regal mind might ask,
Or need, of counsel breathed through lips divine.

Long as the heat shall rage, let that dim cave
Protect us, there deciphering as we may

Diluvian records; or the sighs of Earth
Interpreting; or counting for old Time
His minutes, by reiterated drops,
Audible tears, from some invisible source
That deepens upon fancy – more and more
Drawn toward the centre whence those sighs creep forth
40 To awe the lightness of humanity.
Or, shutting up thyself within thyself,
There let me see thee sink into a mood
Of gentler thought, protracted till thine eye
Be calm as water when the winds are gone,
And no one can tell whither. Dearest Friend!
We two have known such happy hours together
That, were power granted to replace them (fetched
From out the pensive shadows where they lie)
In the first warmth of their original sunshine,
50 Loth should I be to use it: passing sweet
Are the domains of tender memory!

The Wild Duck's Nest

The imperial Consort of the Fairy-king
Owns not a sylvan bower; or gorgeous cell
With emerald floored, and with purpureal shell
Ceilinged and roofed; that is so fair a thing
As this low structure, for the tasks of Spring,
Prepared by one who loves the buoyant swell
Of the brisk waves, yet here consents to dwell;
And spreads in stedfast peace her brooding wing.
Words cannot paint the o'ershadowing yew-tree bough,
10 And dimly-gleaming Nest, – a hollow crown
Of golden leaves inlaid with silver down,
Fine as the mother's softest plumes allow;
I gazed – and, self-accused while gazing, sighed
For human-kind, weak slaves of cumbrous pride!

A Fact, and an Imagination or, Canute and Alfred, on the Sea-Shore

The Danish Conqueror, on his royal chair,
Mustering a face of haughty sovereignty,
To aid a covert purpose, cried – 'O ye
Approaching Waters of the deep, that share
With this green isle my fortunes, come not where
Your Master's throne is set.' – Deaf was the Sea;
Her waves rolled on, respecting his decree
Less than they heed a breath of wanton air.
– Then Canute, rising from the invaded throne,
10 Said to his servile Courtiers, – 'Poor the reach,
The undisguised extent, of mortal sway!
He only is a King, and he alone
Deserves the name (this truth the billows preach)
Whose everlasting laws, sea, earth, and heaven obey.'

This just reproof the prosperous Dane
Drew from the influx of the main,
For some whose rugged northern mouths would strain
At oriental flattery;
And Canute (fact more worthy to be known)
20 From that time forth did for his brows disown
The ostentatious symbol of a crown;
Esteeming earthly royalty
Contemptible as vain.

Now hear what one of elder days,
Rich theme of England's fondest praise,
Her darling Alfred, *might* have spoken;
To cheer the remnant of his host
When he was driven from coast to coast,
Distressed and harassed, but with mind unbroken:

30 'My faithful followers, lo! the tide is spent
That rose, and steadily advanced to fill

The shores and channels, working Nature's will
Among the mazy streams that backward went,
And in the sluggish pools where ships are pent:
And now, his task performed, the flood stands still,
At the green base of many an inland hill,
In placid beauty and sublime content!
Such the repose that sage and hero find;
Such measured rest the sedulous and good
40 Of humbler name; whose souls do, like the flood
Of Ocean, press right on; or gently wind,
Neither to be diverted nor withstood,
Until they reach the bounds by Heaven assigned.'

*Placard for a Poll Bearing an Old Shirt

If money I lack,
The Shirt on my back
Shall off, and go to the hammer;
Though I sell shirt and skin
By G— I'll be in,
And raise up a radical clamour!

The Pilgrim's Dream; or,
The Star and the Glow-Worm

A Pilgrim, when the summer day
Had closed upon his weary way,
A lodging begged beneath a castle's roof;
But him the haughty Warder spurned;
And from the gate the Pilgrim turned,
To seek such covert as the field
Or heath-besprinkled copse might yield,
Or lofty wood, shower-proof.

He paced along; and, pensively,
10 Halting beneath a shady tree

Whose moss-grown root might serve for couch or seat,
Fixed on a Star his upward eye;
Then, from the tenant of the sky
He turned, and watched with kindred look,
A Glow-worm, in a dusky nook,
Apparent at his feet.

The murmur of a neighbouring stream
Induced a soft and slumbrous dream,
A pregnant dream, within whose shadowy bounds
20 He recognized the earth-born Star,
And *That* which glittered from afar;
And (strange to witness!) from the frame
Of the ethereal Orb, there came
Intelligible sounds.

Much did it taunt the humble Light
That now, when day was fled, and night
Hushed the dark earth, fast closing weary eyes,
A very reptile could presume
To show her taper in the gloom,
30 As if in rivalship with One
Who sate a ruler on his throne
Erected in the skies.

'Exalted Star!' the Worm replied,
'Abate this unbecoming pride,
Or with a less uneasy lustre shine;
Thou shrink'st as momently thy rays
Are mastered by the breathing haze;
While neither mist, nor thickest cloud
That shapes in heaven its murky shroud,
40 Hath power to injure mine.

'But not for this do I aspire
To match the spark of local fire,
That at my will burns on the dewy lawn,
With thy acknowledged glories; – No!

Yet, thus upbraided, I may show
What favours do attend me here,
Till, like thyself, I disappear
Before the purple dawn.'

When this in modest guise was said,
50   Across the welkin seemed to spread
A boding sound – for aught but sleep unfit!
Hills quaked, the rivers backward ran;
That Star, so proud of late, looked wan;
And reeled with visionary stir
In the blue depth, like Lucifer
Cast headlong to the pit!

Fire raged: and, when the spangled floor
Of ancient ether was no more,
New heavens succeeded, by the dream brought forth:
60   And all the happy Souls that rode
Transfigured through that fresh abode,
Had heretofore, in humble trust,
Shone meekly 'mid their native dust,
The Glow-worms of the earth!

This knowledge, from an Angel's voice
Proceeding, made the heart rejoice
Of Him who slept upon the open lea:
Waking at morn he murmured not;
And, till life's journey closed, the spot
70   Was to the Pilgrim's soul endeared,
Where by that dream he had been cheered
Beneath the shady tree.

Inscriptions Supposed to Be Found in and near
a Hermit's Cell
1818

I
Hopes what are they? – Beads of morning
Strung on slender blades of grass;
Or a spider's web adorning
In a strait and treacherous pass.

What are fears but voices airy?
Whispering harm where harm is not;
And deluding the unwary
Till the fatal bolt is shot!

What is glory? – in the socket
10 See how dying tapers fare!
What is pride? – a whizzing rocket
That would emulate a star.

What is friendship? – do not trust her,
Nor the vows which she has made;
Diamonds dart their brightest lustre
From a palsy-shaken head.

What is truth? – a staff rejected;
Duty? – an unwelcome clog;
Joy? – a moon by fits reflected
20 In a swamp or watery bog;

Bright, as if through ether steering,
To the Traveller's eye it shone:
He hath hailed it re-appearing –
And as quickly it is gone;

Such is Joy – as quickly hidden,
Or mis-shapen to the sight,

And by sullen weeds forbidden
To resume its native light.

What is youth? – a dancing billow,
30 (Winds behind, and rocks before!)
Age? – a drooping, tottering willow
On a flat and lazy shore.

What is peace? – when pain is over,
And love ceases to rebel,
Let the last faint sigh discover
That precedes the passing-knell!

II INSCRIBED UPON A ROCK
Pause, Traveller! whosoe'er thou be
Whom chance may lead to this retreat,
Where silence yields reluctantly
Even to the fleecy straggler's bleat;

Give voice to what my hand shall trace,
And fear not lest an idle sound
Of words unsuited to the place
Disturb its solitude profound.

I saw this Rock, while vernal air
10 Blew softly o'er the russet heath,
Uphold a Monument as fair
As church or abbey furnisheth.

Unsullied did it meet the day,
Like marble, white, like ether, pure;
As if, beneath, some hero lay,
Honoured with costliest sepulture.

My fancy kindled as I gazed;
And, ever as the sun shone forth,
The flattered structure glistened, blazed,
20 And seemed the proudest thing on earth.

But frost had reared the gorgeous Pile
Unsound as those which Fortune builds –
To undermine with secret guile,
Sapped by the very beam that gilds.

And, while I gazed, with sudden shock
Fell the whole Fabric to the ground;
And naked left this dripping Rock,
With shapeless ruin spread around!

III

Hast thou seen, with flash incessant,
Bubbles gliding under ice,
Bodied forth and evanescent,
No one knows by what device?

Such are thoughts! – A wind-swept meadow
Mimicking a troubled sea,
Such is life; and death a shadow
From the rock eternity!

IV NEAR THE SPRING OF THE HERMITAGE
Troubled long with warring notions
Long impatient of Thy rod,
I resign my soul's emotions
Unto Thee, mysterious God!

What avails the kindly shelter
Yielded by this craggy rent,
If my spirit toss and welter
On the waves of discontent?

Parching Summer hath no warrant
10 To consume this crystal Well;
Rains, that make each rill a torrent,
Neither sully it nor swell.

Thus, dishonouring not her station,
Would my Life present to Thee,

Gracious God, the pure oblation
Of divine tranquillity!

V

Not seldom, clad in radiant vest,
Deceitfully goes forth the Morn;
Not seldom Evening in the west
Sinks smilingly forsworn.

The smoothest seas will sometimes prove,
To the confiding Bark, untrue;
And, if she trust the stars above,
They can be treacherous too.

The umbrageous Oak, in pomp outspread,
10 Full oft, when storms the welkin rend,
Draws lightning down upon the head
It promised to defend.

But Thou art true, incarnate Lord,
Who didst vouchsafe for man to die;
Thy smile is sure, Thy plighted word
No change can falsify!

I bent before Thy gracious throne,
And asked for peace on suppliant knee;
And peace was given, – nor peace alone,
20 But faith sublimed to ecstasy!

*This and the Two Following Were Suggested
by Mr W. Westall's Views of the Caves, etc.,
in Yorkshire*

Pure element of waters! wheresoe'er
Thou dost forsake thy subterranean haunts,
Green herbs, bright flowers, and berry-bearing plants,
Rise into life and in thy train appear:

And, through the sunny portion of the year,
Swift insects shine, thy hovering pursuivants:
And, if thy bounty fail, the forest pants;
And hart and hind and hunter with his spear
Languish and droop together. Nor unfelt
In man's perturbèd soul thy sway benign;
And, haply, far within the marble belt
Of central earth, where tortured Spirits pine
For grace and goodness lost, thy murmurs melt
Their anguish, – and they blend sweet songs with thine.

10 *(line number)*

Malham Cove

Was the aim frustrated by force or guile,
When giants scooped from out the rocky ground,
Tier under tier, this semicirque profound?
(Giants – the same who built in Erin's isle
That Causeway with incomparable toil!) –
O, had this vast theatric structure wound
With finished sweep into a perfect round,
No mightier work had gained the plausive smile
Of all-beholding Phoebus! But, alas,
Vain earth! false world! Foundations must be laid
In Heaven; for, 'mid the wreck of IS and WAS,
Things incomplete and purposes betrayed
Make sadder transits o'er thought's optic glass
Than noblest objects utterly decayed.

10 *(line number)*

Gordale

At early dawn, or rather when the air
Glimmers with fading light, and shadowy Eve
Is busiest to confer and to bereave;
Then, pensive Votary! let thy feet repair
To Gordale-chasm, terrific as the lair

Where the young lions couch; for so, by leave
Of the propitious hour, thou mayst perceive
The local Deity, with oozy hair
And mineral crown, beside his jagged urn,
10   Recumbent: Him thou mayst behold, who hides
His lineaments by day, yet there presides,
Teaching the docile waters how to turn,
Or (if need be) impediment to spurn,
And force their passage to the salt-sea tides!

'I heard (alas! 'twas only in a dream)'

I heard (alas! 'twas only in a dream)
Strains – which, as sage Antiquity believed,
By waking ears have sometimes been received
Wafted adown the wind from lake or stream;
A most melodious requiem, a supreme
And perfect harmony of notes, achieved
By a fair Swan on drowsy billows heaved,
O'er which her pinions shed a silver gleam.
For is she not the votary of Apollo?
10   And knows she not, singing as he inspires,
That bliss awaits her which the ungenial Hollow
Of the dull earth partakes not, nor desires?
Mount, tuneful Bird, and join the immortal choirs!
She soared – and I awoke, struggling in vain to follow.

A Help for the Memory of the Grand Independent
A New Song

The Scottish Broom on Birdnest brae
Twelve tedious years ago,
When many plants strange Blossoms bore
That puzzled high and low,

A not unnatural longing felt –
What longing would you know?
Why, friend, to deck her supple twigs
With yellow in full blow.

To Lowther Castle she addressed
10 A suit both bold and sly,
(For all the Brooms of Birdnest brae
Can talk and speechify)
That flattering breezes blowing thence
Their succour might supply,
And she would instantly hang out
A flag of yellow dye.

But from the Castle's turrets blew
A chill forbidding blast,
Which the poor Broom no sooner felt
20 Than she shrank up as fast;
Her wished-for yellow she forswore,
And since that day has cast
Fond looks on colours three or four
And put forth *Blue* at last.

But now, my lads, the Election comes
In June's sunshiny hours,
When every bank in field and brae
Is clad with yellow flowers.
While faction's Blue from shop and booth
30 Tricks out her blustering powers,
Lo! smiling Nature's lavish hand
Has furnished wreaths for ours!

The River Duddon
A Series of Sonnets

The River Duddon rises upon Wrynose Fell, on the confines of
Westmoreland, Cumberland, and Lancashire; and, having
served as a boundary to the last two Counties for the space of
about twenty-five miles, enters the Irish Sea, between the Isle
of Walney and the Lordship of Millum.

TO THE REV. DR WORDSWORTH
(WITH THE SONNETS TO THE RIVER DUDDON,
AND OTHER POEMS IN THIS COLLECTION, 1820)

The Minstrels played their Christmas tune
Tonight beneath my cottage-eaves;
While, smitten by a lofty moon,
The encircling laurels, thick with leaves,
Gave back a rich and dazzling sheen,
That overpowered their natural green.

Through hill and valley every breeze
Had sunk to rest with folded wings:
Keen was the air, but could not freeze,
10   Nor check the music of the strings;
So stout and hardy were the band
That scraped the chords with strenuous hand!

And who but listened? – till was paid
Respect to every Inmate's claim:
The greeting given, the music played,
In honour of each household name,
Duly pronounced with lusty call,
And 'Merry Christmas' wished to all!

O Brother! I revere the choice
20   That took thee from thy native hills;
And it is given thee to rejoice:
Though public care full often tills

(Heaven only witness of the toil)
A barren and ungrateful soil.

Yet, would that Thou, with me and mine,
Hadst heard this never-failing rite;
And seen on other faces shine
A true revival of the light
Which Nature and these rustic Powers,
30 In simple childhood, spread through ours!

For pleasure hath not ceased to wait
On these expected annual rounds;
Whether the rich man's sumptuous gate
Call forth the unelaborate sounds,
Or they are offered at the door
That guards the lowliest of the poor.

How touching, when, at midnight, sweep
Snow-muffled winds, and all is dark,
To hear – and sink again to sleep!
40 Or, at an earlier call, to mark,
By blazing fire, the still suspense
Of self-complacent innocence;

The mutual nod, – the grave disguise
Of hearts with gladness brimming o'er;
And some unbidden tears that rise
For names once heard, and heard no more;
Tears brightened by the serenade
For infant in the cradle laid.

Ah! not for emerald fields alone,
50 With ambient streams more pure and bright
Than fabled Cytherea's zone
Glittering before the Thunderer's sight,
Is to my heart of hearts endeared
The ground where we were born and reared!

Hail, ancient Manners! sure defence,
Where they survive, of wholesome laws;
Remnants of love whose modest sense
Thus into narrow room withdraws;
Hail, Usages of pristine mould,
60 And ye that guard them, Mountains old!

Bear with me, Brother! quench the thought
That slights this passion, or condemns;
If thee fond Fancy ever brought
From the proud margin of the Thames,
And Lambeth's venerable towers,
To humbler streams, and greener bowers.

Yes, they can make, who fail to find,
Short leisure even in busiest days;
Moments, to cast a look behind,
70 And profit by those kindly rays
That through the clouds do sometimes steal,
And all the far-off past reveal.

Hence, while the imperial City's din
Beats frequent on thy satiate ear,
A pleased attention I may win
To agitations less severe,
That neither overwhelm nor cloy,
But fill the hollow vale with joy!

I
Not envying Latian shades – if yet they throw
A grateful coolness round that crystal Spring,
Blandusia, prattling as when long ago
The Sabine Bard was moved her praise to sing;
Careless of flowers that in perennial blow
Round the moist marge of Persian fountains cling;
Heedless of Alpine torrents thundering
Through ice-built arches radiant as heaven's bow;
I seek the birthplace of a native Stream. –

10 All hail, ye mountains! hail, thou morning light!
Better to breathe at large on this clear height
Than toil in needless sleep from dream to dream:
Pure flow the verse, pure, vigorous, free, and bright,
For Duddon, long-loved Duddon, is my theme!

II

Child of the clouds! remote from every taint
Of sordid industry thy lot is cast;
Thine are the honours of the lofty waste;
Not seldom, when with heat the valleys faint,
Thy handmaid Frost with spangled tissue quaint
Thy cradle decks; – to chant thy birth, thou hast
No meaner Poet than the whistling Blast,
And Desolation is thy Patron-saint!
She guards thee, ruthless Power! who would not spare
10 Those mighty forests, once the bison's screen,
Where stalked the huge deer to his shaggy lair
Through paths and alleys roofed with darkest green;
Thousands of years before the silent air
Was pierced by whizzing shaft of hunter keen!

III

How shall I paint thee? – Be this naked stone
My seat, while I give way to such intent;
Pleased could my verse, a speaking monument,
Make to the eyes of men thy features known.
But as of all those tripping lambs not one
Outruns his fellows, so hath Nature lent
To thy beginning naught that doth present
Peculiar ground for hope to build upon.
To dignify the spot that gives thee birth,
10 No sign of hoar Antiquity's esteem
Appears, and none of modern Fortune's care;
Yet thou thyself hast round thee shed a gleam
Of brilliant moss, instinct with freshness rare;
Prompt offering to thy Foster-mother, Earth!

IV

Take, cradled Nursling of the mountain, take
This parting glance, no negligent adieu!
A Protean change seems wrought while I pursue
Thy curves, a loosely-scattered chain doth make;
Or rather thou appear'st a glittering snake,
Silent, and to the gazer's eye untrue,
Thridding with sinuous lapse the rushes, through
Dwarf willows gliding, and by ferny brake.
Starts from a dizzy steep the undaunted Rill
10   Robed instantly in garb of snow-white foam;
And laughing dares the Adventurer, who hath clomb
So high, a rival purpose to fulfil;
Else let the dastard backward wend, and roam,
Seeking less bold achievement, where he will!

V

Sole listener, Duddon! to the breeze that played
With thy clear voice, I caught the fitful sound
Wafted o'er sullen moss and craggy mound –
Unfruitful solitudes, that seemed to upbraid
The sun in heaven! – but now, to form a shade
For Thee, green alders have together wound
Their foliage; ashes flung their arms around;
And birch-trees risen in silver colonnade.
And thou hast also tempted here to rise,
10   'Mid sheltering pines, this Cottage rude and grey;
Whose ruddy children, by the mother's eyes
Carelessly watched, sport through the summer day,
Thy pleased associates: – light as endless May
On infant bosoms lonely Nature lies.

VI FLOWERS

Ere yet our course was graced with social trees
It lacked not old remains of hawthorn bowers,
Where small birds warbled to their paramours;
And, earlier still, was heard the hum of bees;
I saw them ply their harmless robberies,

And caught the fragrance which the sundry flowers,
Fed by the stream with soft perpetual showers,
Plenteously yielded to the vagrant breeze.
There bloomed the strawberry of the wilderness;
10 The trembling eyebright showed her sapphire blue,
The thyme her purple, like the blush of Even;
And if the breath of some to no caress
Invited, forth they peeped so fair to view,
All kinds alike seemed favourites of Heaven.

VII

'Change me, some God, into that breathing rose!'
The love-sick Stripling fancifully sighs,
The envied flower beholding, as it lies
On Laura's breast, in exquisite repose;
Or he would pass into her bird, that throws
The darts of song from out its wiry cage;
Enraptured, – could he for himself engage
The thousandth part of what the Nymph bestows;
And what the little careless innocent
10 Ungraciously receives. Too daring choice!
There are whose calmer mind it would content
To be an unculled floweret of the glen,
Fearless of plough and scythe; or darkling wren
That tunes on Duddon's banks her slender voice.

VIII

What aspect bore the Man who roved or fled,
First of his tribe, to this dark dell – who first
In this pellucid Current slaked his thirst?
What hopes came with him? what designs were spread
Along his path? His unprotected bed
What dreams encompassed? Was the intruder nursed
In hideous usages, and rights accursed,
That thinned the living and disturbed the dead?
No voice replies; – both air and earth are mute;
10 And Thou, blue Streamlet, murmuring yield'st no more

Than a soft record, that, whatever fruit
Of ignorance thou mightst witness heretofore,
Thy function was to heal and to restore,
To soothe and cleanse, not madden and pollute!

IX THE STEPPING-STONES

The struggling Rill insensibly is grown
Into a Brook of loud and stately march,
Crossed ever and anon by plank or arch;
And, for like use, lo! what might seem a zone
Chosen for ornament – stone matched with stone
In studied symmetry, with interspace
For the clear waters to pursue their race
Without restraint. How swiftly have they flown,
Succeeding – still succeeding! Here the Child
10 Puts, when the high-swoln Flood runs fierce and wild,
His budding courage to the proof; and here
Declining Manhood learns to note the sly
And sure encroachments of infirmity,
Thinking how fast time runs, life's end how near!

X THE SAME SUBJECT

Not so that Pair whose youthful spirits dance
With prompt emotion, urging them to pass;
A sweet confusion checks the Shepherd-lass;
Blushing she eyes the dizzy flood askance;
To stop ashamed – too timid to advance;
She ventures once again – another pause!
His outstretched hand He tauntingly withdraws –
She sues for help with piteous utterance!
Chidden she chides again; the thrilling touch
10 Both feel, when he renews the wished-for aid:
Ah! if their fluttering hearts should stir too much,
Should beat too strongly, both may be betrayed.
The frolic Loves, who, from yon high rock, see
The struggle, clap their wings for victory!

XI THE FAERY CHASM

No fiction was it of the antique age:
A sky-blue stone, within this sunless cleft,
Is of the very footmarks unbereft
Which tiny Elves impressed; – on that smooth stage
Dancing with all their brilliant equipage
In secret revels – haply after theft
Of some sweet Babe – Flower stolen, and coarse Weed
    left
For the distracted Mother to assuage
Her grief with, as she might! – But, where, oh! where
10 Is traceable a vestige of the notes
That ruled those dances wild in character? –
Deep underground? Or in the upper air,
On the shrill wind of midnight? or where floats
O'er twilight fields the autumnal gossamer?

XII HINTS FOR THE FANCY

On, loitering Muse – the swift Stream chides us – on!
Albeit his deep-worn channel doth immure
Objects immense portrayed in miniature,
Wild shapes for many a strange comparison!
Niagaras, Alpine passes, and anon
Abodes of Naiads, calm abysses pure,
Bright liquid mansions, fashioned to endure
When the broad oak drops, a leafless skeleton,
And the solidities of mortal pride,
10 Palace and tower, are crumbled into dust! –
The Bard who walks with Duddon for his guide,
Shall find such toys of fancy thickly set:
Turn from the sight, enamoured Muse – we must;
And, if thou canst, leave them without regret!

XIII OPEN PROSPECT

Hail to the fields – with Dwellings sprinkled o'er,
And one small hamlet, under a green hill
Clustering, with barn and byre, and spouting mill!
A glance suffices; – should we wish for more,

Gay June would scorn us. But when bleak winds roar
Through the stiff lance-like shoots of pollard ash,
Dread swell of sound! loud as the gusts that lash
The matted forests of Ontario's shore
By wasteful steel unsmitten – then would I
10 Turn into port; and, reckless of the gale,
Reckless of angry Duddon sweeping by,
While the warm hearth exalts the mantling ale,
Laugh with the generous household heartily
At all the merry pranks of Donnerdale!

XIV

O mountain Stream! the Shepherd and his Cot
Are privileged Inmates of deep solitude;
Nor would the nicest Anchorite exclude
A field or two of brighter green, or plot
Of tillage-ground, that seemeth like a spot
Of stationary sunshine: – thou hast viewed
These only, Duddon! with their paths renewed
By fits and starts, yet this contents thee not.
Thee hath some awful Spirit impelled to leave,
10 Utterly to desert, the haunts of men,
Though simple thy companions were and few;
And through this wilderness a passage cleave
Attended but by thy own voice, save when
The clouds and fowls of the air thy way pursue!

XV

From this deep chasm, where quivering sunbeams play
Upon its loftiest crags, mine eyes behold
A gloomy NICHE, capacious, blank, and cold;
A concave free from shrubs and mosses grey;
In semblance fresh, as if, with dire affray,
Some Statue, placed amid these regions old
For tutelary service, thence had rolled,
Startling the flight of timid Yesterday!
Was it by mortals sculptured? – weary slaves
10 Of slow endeavour! or abruptly cast

Into rude shape by fire, with roaring blast
Tempestuously let loose from central caves?
Or fashioned by the turbulence of waves,
Then, when o'er highest hills the Deluge passed?

XVI AMERICAN TRADITION

Such fruitless questions may not long beguile
Or plague the fancy 'mid the sculptured shows
Conspicuous yet where Oroonoko flows;
There would the Indian answer with a smile
Aimed at the White Man's ignorance the while,
Of the GREAT WATERS telling how they rose,
Covered the plains, and, wandering where they chose,
Mounted through every intricate defile,
Triumphant. – Inundation wide and deep,
10 O'er which his Fathers urged, to ridge and steep
Else unapproachable, their buoyant way;
And carved, on mural cliff's undreaded side,
Sun, moon, and stars, and beast of chase or prey;
Whate'er they sought, shunned, loved, or deified!

XVII RETURN

A dark plume fetch me from yon blasted yew,
Perched on whose top the Danish Raven croaks;
Aloft, the imperial Bird of Rome invokes
Departed ages, shedding where he flew
Loose fragments of wild wailing, that bestrew
The clouds and thrill the chambers of the rocks;
And into silence hush the timorous flocks,
That, calmly couching while the nightly dew
Moistened each fleece, beneath the twinkling stars
10 Slept amid that lone Camp on Hardknot's height,
Whose Guardians bent the knee to Jove and Mars:
Or, near that mystic Round of Druid frame
Tardily sinking by its proper weight
Deep into patient Earth, from whose smooth breast it
    came!

XVIII SEATHWAITE CHAPEL

Sacred Religion! 'mother of form and fear,'
Dread arbitress of mutable respect,
New rites ordaining when the old are wrecked,
Or cease to please the fickle worshipper;
Mother of Love! (that name best suits thee here)
Mother of Love! for this deep vale, protect
Truth's holy lamp, pure source of bright effect,
Gifted to purge the vapoury atmosphere
That seeks to stifle it; – as in those days
10   When this low Pile a Gospel Teacher knew,
Whose good works formed an endless retinue:
A Pastor such as Chaucer's verse portrays;
Such as the heaven-taught skill of Herbert drew;
And tender Goldsmith crowned with deathless praise!

XIX TRIBUTARY STREAM

My frame hath often trembled with delight
When hope presented some far-distant good,
That seemed from heaven descending, like the flood
Of yon pure waters, from their aëry height
Hurrying, with lordly Duddon to unite;
Who, 'mid a world of images imprest
On the calm depth of his transparent breast,
Appears to cherish most that Torrent white,
The fairest, softest, liveliest of them all!
10   And seldom hath ear listened to a tune
More lulling than the busy hum of Noon,
Swoln by that voice – whose murmur musical
Announces to the thirsty fields a boon
Dewy and fresh, till showers again shall fall.

XX THE PLAIN OF DONNERDALE

The old inventive Poets, had they seen,
Or rather felt, the entrancement that detains
Thy waters, Duddon! 'mid these flowery plains;
The still repose, the liquid lapse serene,
Transferred to bowers imperishably green,

Had beautified Elysium! But these chains
Will soon be broken; – a rough course remains,
Rough as the past; where Thou, of placid mien,
Innocuous as a firstling of the flock,
10 And countenanced like a soft cerulean sky,
Shalt change thy temper; and, with many a shock
Given and received in mutual jeopardy,
Dance, like a Bacchanal, from rock to rock,
Tossing her frantic thyrsus wide and high!

XXI

Whence that low voice? – A whisper from the heart,
That told of days long past, when here I roved
With friends and kindred tenderly beloved;
Some who had early mandates to depart,
Yet are allowed to steal my path athwart
By Duddon's side; once more do we unite,
Once more beneath the kind Earth's tranquil light;
And smothered joys into new being start.
From her unworthy seat, the cloudy stall
10 Of Time, breaks forth triumphant Memory;
Her glistening tresses bound, yet light and free
As golden locks of birch, that rise and fall
On gales that breathe too gently to recall
Aught of the fading year's inclemency!

XXII TRADITION

A love-lorn Maid, at some far-distant time,
Came to this hidden pool, whose depths surpass
In crystal clearness Dian's looking-glass;
And, gazing, saw that Rose, which from the prime
Derives its name, reflected as the chime
Of echo doth reverberate some sweet sound:
The starry treasure from the blue profound
She longed to ravish; – shall she plunge, or climb
The humid precipice, and seize the guest
10 Of April, smiling high in upper air?
Desperate alternative! what fiend could dare

To prompt the thought? – Upon the steep rock's breast
The lonely Primrose yet renews its bloom,
Untouched memento of her hapless doom!

XXIII SHEEP-WASHING

Sad thoughts, avaunt! – partake we their blithe cheer
Who gathered in betimes the unshorn flock
To wash the fleece, where haply bands of rock,
Checking the stream, make a pool smooth and clear
As this we look on. Distant Mountains hear,
Hear and repeat, the turmoil that unites
Clamour of boys with innocent despites
Of barking dogs, and bleatings from strange fear.
And what if Duddon's spotless flood receive
10 Unwelcome mixtures as the uncouth noise
Thickens, the pastoral River will forgive
Such wrong; nor need *we* blame the licensed joys,
Though false to Nature's quiet equipoise:
Frank are the sports, the stains are fugitive.

XXIV THE RESTING-PLACE

Mid-noon is past; – upon the sultry mead
No zephyr breathes, no cloud its shadow throws:
If we advance unstrengthened by repose,
Farewell the solace of the vagrant reed!
This Nook – with woodbine hung and straggling weed,
Tempting recess as ever pilgrim chose,
Half grot, half arbour – proffers to enclose
Body and mind, from molestation freed,
In narrow compass – narrow as itself:
10 Or if the Fancy, too industrious Elf,
Be loth that we should breathe awhile exempt
From new incitements friendly to our task,
Here wants not stealthy prospect, that may tempt
Loose Idless to forego her wily mask.

XXV

Methinks 'twere no unprecedented feat
Should some benignant Minister of air

Lift, and encircle with a cloudy chair,
The One for whom my heart shall ever beat
With tenderest love; – or, if a safer seat
Atween his downy wings be furnished, there
Would lodge her, and the cherished burden bear
O'er hill and valley to this dim retreat!
Rough ways my steps have trod; – too rough and long
10 For her companionship; here dwells soft ease:
With sweets that she partakes not some distaste
Mingles, and lurking consciousness of wrong;
Languish the flowers; the waters seem to waste
Their vocal charm; their sparklings cease to please.

XXVI

Return, Content! for fondly I pursued,
Even when a child, the Streams – unheard, unseen;
Through tangled woods, impending rocks between;
Or, free as air, with flying inquest viewed
The sullen reservoirs whence their bold brood –
Pure as the morning, fretful, boisterous, keen,
Green as the salt-sea billows, white and green –
Poured down the hills, a choral multitude!
Nor have I tracked their course for scanty gains;
10 They taught me random cares and truant joys,
That shield from mischief and preserve from stains
Vague minds, while men are growing out of boys;
Maturer Fancy owes to their rough noise
Impetuous thoughts that brook not servile reins.

XXVII

Fallen, and diffused into a shapeless heap,
Or quietly self-buried in earth's mould,
Is that embattled House, whose massy Keep
Flung from yon cliff a shadow large and cold.
There dwelt the gay, the bountiful, the bold;
Till nightly lamentations, like the sweep
Of winds – though winds were silent – struck a deep
And lasting terror through that ancient Hold.

Its line of Warriors fled; – they shrunk when tried
10 By ghostly power: – but Time's unsparing hand
Hath plucked such foes, like weeds, from out the land;
And now, if men with men in peace abide,
All other strength the weakest may withstand,
All worse assaults may safely be defied.

XXVIII JOURNEY RENEWED

I rose while yet the cattle, heat-opprest,
Crowded together under rustling trees
Brushed by the current of the water-breeze;
And for *their* sakes, and love of all that rest,
On Duddon's margin, in the sheltering nest;
For all the startled scaly tribes that slink
Into his coverts, and each fearless link
Of dancing insects forged upon his breast;
For these, and hopes and recollections worn
10 Close to the vital seat of human clay;
Glad meetings, tender partings, that upstay
The drooping mind of absence, by vows sworn
In his pure presence near the trysting thorn –
I thanked the Leader of my onward way.

XXIX

No record tells of lance opposed to lance,
Horse charging horse, 'mid these retired domains;
Tells that their turf drank purple from the veins
Of heroes, fallen, or struggling to advance,
Till doubtful combat issued in a trance
Of victory, that struck through heart and reins
Even to the inmost seat of mortal pains,
And lightened o'er the pallid countenance.
Yet, to the loyal and the brave, who lie
10 In the blank earth, neglected and forlorn,
The passing Winds memorial tribute pay;
The Torrents chant their praise, inspiring scorn
Of power usurped; with proclamation high,
And glad acknowledgement, of lawful sway.

XXX

Who swerves from innocence, who makes divorce
Of that serene companion – a good name,
Recovers not his loss; but walks with shame,
With doubt, with fear, and haply with remorse:
And oft-times he – who, yielding to the force
Of chance-temptation, ere his journey end,
From chosen comrade turns, or faithful friend –
In vain shall rue the broken intercourse.
Not so with such as loosely wear the chain
10 That binds them, pleasant River! to thy side: –
Through the rough copse wheel thou with hasty stride;
I choose to saunter o'er the grassy plain,
Sure, when the separation has been tried,
That we, who part in love, shall meet again.

XXXI

The KIRK of ULPHA to the pilgrim's eye
Is welcome as a star, that doth present
Its shining forehead through the peaceful rent
Of a black cloud diffused o'er half the sky:
Or as a fruitful palm-tree towering high
O'er the parched waste beside an Arab's tent;
Or the Indian tree whose branches, downward bent,
Take root again, a boundless canopy.
How sweet were leisure! could it yield no more
10 Than 'mid that wave-washed Church-yard to recline,
From pastoral graves extracting thoughts divine;
Or there to pace, and mark the summits hoar
Of distant moon-lit mountains faintly shine,
Soothed by the unseen River's gentle roar.

XXXII

Not hurled precipitous from steep to steep;
Lingering no more 'mid flower-enamelled lands
And blooming thickets; nor by rocky bands
Held; but in radiant progress toward the Deep
Where mightiest rivers into powerless sleep

Sink, and forget their nature – *now* expands
Majestic Duddon, over smooth flat sands
Gliding in silence with unfettered sweep!
Beneath an ampler sky a region wide
10 Is opened round him: – hamlets, towers, and towns,
And blue-topped hills, behold him from afar;
In stately mien to sovereign Thames allied
Spreading his bosom under Kentish downs,
With commerce freighted, or triumphant war.

XXXIII CONCLUSION

But here no cannon thunders to the gale;
Upon the wave no haughty pendants cast
A crimson splendour: lowly is the mast
That rises here, and humbly spread, the sail;
While, less disturbed than in the narrow Vale
Through which with strange vicissitudes he passed,
The Wanderer seeks that receptacle vast
Where all his unambitious functions fail.
And may thy Poet, cloud-born Stream! be free –
10 The sweets of earth contentedly resigned,
And each tumultuous working left behind
At seemly distance – to advance like Thee;
Prepared, in peace of heart, in calm of mind
And soul, to mingle with Eternity!

XXXIV AFTER-THOUGHT

I THOUGHT *of Thee, my partner and my guide,*
As being past away. – Vain sympathies!
For, backward, Duddon! as I cast my eyes,
I see what was, and is, and will abide;
Still glides the Stream, and shall for ever glide;
The Form remains, the Function never dies;
While we, the brave, the mighty, and the wise,
We Men, who in our morn of youth defied
The elements, must vanish; – be it so!
10 *Enough, if something from our hands have power*
To live, and act, and serve the future hour;

And if, as toward the silent tomb we go,
Through love, through hope, and faith's transcendent dower,
We feel that we are greater than we know.

Composed During a Storm

One who was suffering tumult in his soul
Yet failed to seek the sure relief of prayer,
Went forth – his course surrendering to the care
Of the fierce wind, while mid-day lightnings prowl
Insidiously, untimely thunders growl;
While trees, dim-seen, in frenzied numbers, tear
The lingering remnant of their yellow hair,
And shivering wolves, surprised with darkness, howl
As if the sun were not. He raised his eye
10   Soul-smitten; for, that instant, did appear
Large space ('mid dreadful clouds) of purest sky,
An azure disc – shield of Tranquillity;
Invisible, unlooked-for, minister
Of providential goodness ever nigh!

'Aërial Rock – whose solitary brow'

Aërial Rock – whose solitary brow
From this low threshold daily meets my sight;
When I step forth to hail the morning light;
Or quit the stars with a lingering farewell – how
Shall Fancy pay to thee a grateful vow?
How, with the Muse's aid, her love attest?
– By planting on thy naked head the crest
Of an imperial Castle, which the plough
Of ruin shall not touch. Innocent scheme!
10   That doth presume no more than to supply
A grace the sinuous vale and roaring stream
Want, through neglect of hoar Antiquity.
Rise, then, ye votive Towers! and catch a gleam
Of golden sunset, ere it fade and die.

Written upon a Blank Leaf in 'The Compleat Angler'

While flowing rivers yield a blameless sport,
Shall live the name of Walton: Sage benign!
Whose pen, the mysteries of the rod and line
Unfolding, did not fruitlessly exhort
To reverent watching of each still report
That Nature utters from her rural shrine.
Meek, nobly versed in simple discipline –
He found the longest summer day too short,
To his loved pastime given by sedgy Lee,
Or down the tempting maze of Shawford brook –
Fairer than life itself, in this sweet Book,
The cowslip-bank and shady willow-tree;
And the fresh meads – where flowed, from every nook
Of his full bosom, gladsome Piety!

Captivity. – Mary Queen of Scots

'As the cold aspect of a sunless way
Strikes through the Traveller's frame with deadlier chill,
Oft as appears a grove, or obvious hill,
Glistening with unparticipated ray,
Or shining slope where he must never stray;
So joys, remembered without wish or will,
Sharpen the keenest edge of present ill, –
On the crushed heart a heavier burden lay.
Just Heaven, contract the compass of my mind
To fit proportion with my altered state!
Quench those felicities whose light I find
Reflected in my bosom all too late! –
O be my spirit, like my thraldom, strait;
And, like mine eyes that stream with sorrow, blind!'

To a Snow-Drop

Lone Flower, hemmed in with snows and white as they
But hardier far, once more I see thee bend
Thy forehead, as if fearful to offend,
Like an unbidden guest. Though, day by day,
Storms, sallying from the mountain-tops, waylay
The rising sun, and on the plains descend;
Yet art thou welcome, welcome as a friend
Whose zeal outruns his promise! Blue-eyed May
Shall soon behold this border thickly set
10   With bright jonquils, their odours lavishing
On the soft west-wind and his frolic peers;
Nor will I then thy modest grace forget,
Chaste Snow-drop, venturous harbinger of Spring,
And pensive monitor of fleeting years!

'I watch, and long have watched, with calm regret'

I watch, and long have watched, with calm regret
Yon slowly-sinking star – immortal Sire
(So might he seem) of all the glittering choir!
Blue ether still surrounds him – yet – and yet;
But now the horizon's rocky parapet
Is reached, where, forfeiting his bright attire,
He burns – transmuted to a dusky fire –
Then pays submissively the appointed debt
To the flying moments, and is seen no more.
10   Angels and gods! we struggle with our fate,
While health, power, glory, from their height decline,
Depressed; and then extinguished: and our state,
In this, how different, lost Star, from thine,
That no tomorrow shall our beams restore!

September, 1819

The sylvan slopes with corn-clad fields
Are hung, as if with golden shields,
Bright trophies of the sun!
Like a fair sister of the sky,
Unruffled doth the blue lake lie,
The mountains looking on.

And, sooth to say, yon vocal grove,
Albeit uninspired by love,
By love untaught to ring,
10 May well afford to mortal ear
An impulse more profoundly dear
Than music of the Spring.

For *that* from turbulence and heat
Proceeds, from some uneasy seat
In nature's struggling frame,
Some region of impatient life:
And jealousy, and quivering strife,
Therein a portion claim.

This, this is holy; – while I hear
20 These vespers of another year,
This hymn of thanks and praise,
My spirit seems to mount above
The anxieties of human love,
And earth's precarious days.

But list! – though winter storms be nigh,
Unchecked is that soft harmony:
There lives Who can provide
For all His creatures; and in Him,
Even like the radiant Seraphim,
30 These choristers confide.

September, 1819

Departing summer hath assumed
An aspect tenderly illumed,
The gentlest look of spring;
That calls from yonder leafy shade
Unfaded, yet prepared to fade,
A timely carolling.

No faint and hesitating trill,
Such tribute as to winter chill
The lonely redbreast pays!
10   Clear, loud, and lively is the din,
From social warblers gathering in
Their harvest of sweet lays.

Nor doth the example fail to cheer
Me, conscious that my leaf is sere,
And yellow on the bough: –
Fall, rosy garlands, from my head!
Ye myrtle wreaths, your fragrance shed
Around a younger brow!

Yet will I temperately rejoice;
20   Wide is the range, and free the choice
Of undiscordant themes;
Which, haply, kindred souls may prize
Not less than vernal ecstasies,
And passion's feverish dreams.

For deathless powers to verse belong,
And they like Demi-gods are strong
On whom the Muses smile;
But some their function have disclaimed,
Best pleased with what is aptliest framed
30   To enervate and defile.

Not such the initiatory strains
Committed to the silent plains
In Britain's earliest dawn:
Trembled the groves, the stars gew pale,
While all-too-daringly the veil
Of nature was withdrawn!

Nor such the spirit-stirring note
When the live chords Alcaeus smote,
Inflamed by sense of wrong;
40   Woe! woe to Tyrants! from the lyre
Broke threateningly, in sparkles dire
Of fierce vindictive song.

And not unhallowed was the page
By wingèd Love inscribed, to assuage
The pangs of vain pursuit;
Love listening while the Lesbian Maid
With finest touch of passion swayed
Her own Aeolian lute.

O ye, who patiently explore
50   The wreck of Herculanean lore,
What rapture! could ye seize
Some Theban fragment, or unroll
One precious, tender-hearted, scroll
Of pure Simonides.

That were, indeed, a genuine birth
Of poesy; a bursting forth
Of genius from the dust:
What Horace gloried to behold,
What Maro loved, shall we enfold?
60   Can haughty Time be just!

To the Lady Mary Lowther

With a selection from the Poems of Anne, Countess of Winchilsea; and extracts of similar character from other Writers;
transcribed by a female friend.

Lady! I rifled a Parnassian Cave
(But seldom trod) of mildly-gleaming ore;
And culled, from sundry beds, a lucid store
Of genuine crystals, pure as those that pave
The azure brooks, where Dian joys to lave
Her spotless limbs; and ventured to explore
Dim shades – for reliques, upon Lethe's shore,
Cast up at random by the sullen wave.
To female hands the treasures were resigned;
10   And lo this Work! – a grotto bright and clear
From stain or taint; in which thy blameless mind
May feed on thoughts though pensive not austere;
Or, if thy deeper spirit be inclined
To holy musing, it may enter here.

'When haughty expectations prostrate lie'

When haughty expectations prostrate lie,
And grandeur crouches like a guilty thing,
Oft shall the lowly weak, till nature bring
Mature release, in fair society
Survive, and Fortune's utmost anger try;
Like these frail snow-drops that together cling,
And nod their helmets, smitten by the wing
Of many a furious whirl-blast sweeping by.
Observe the faithful flowers! if small to great
10   May lead the thoughts, thus struggling used to stand
The Emathian phalanx, nobly obstinate;
And so the bright immortal Theban band,
Whom onset, fiercely urged at Jove's command,
Might overwhelm, but could not separate!

The Haunted Tree
To—

Those silver clouds collected round the sun
His mid-day warmth abate not, seeming less
To overshade than multiply his beams
By soft reflection – grateful to the sky,
To rocks, fields, woods. Nor doth our human sense
Ask, for its pleasure, screen or canopy
More ample than the time-dismantled Oak
Spreads o'er this tuft of heath, which now, attired
In the whole fulness of its bloom, affords
10   Couch beautiful as e'er for earthly use
Was fashioned; whether by the hand of Art,
That eastern Sultan, amid flowers enwrought
On silken tissue, might diffuse his limbs
In languor; or, by Nature, for repose
Of panting Wood-nymph, wearied with the chase.
O Lady! fairer in thy Poet's sight
Than fairest spiritual creature of the groves,
Approach; – and, thus invited, crown with rest
The noon-tide hour: though truly some there are
20   Whose footsteps superstitiously avoid
This venerable Tree; for, when the wind
Blows keenly, it sends forth a creaking sound
(Above the general roar of woods and crags)
Distinctly heard from far – a doleful note!
As if (so Grecian shepherds would have deemed)
The Hamadryad, pent within, bewailed
Some bitter wrong. Nor is it unbelieved,
By ruder fancy, that a troubled ghost
Haunts the old trunk; lamenting deeds of which
30   The flowery ground is conscious. But no wind
Sweeps now along this elevated ridge;
Not even a zephyr stirs; – the obnoxious Tree
Is mute; and, in his silence, would look down,
O lovely Wanderer of the trackless hills,

On thy reclining form with more delight
Than his coevals in the sheltered vale
Seem to participate, the while they view
Their own far-stretching arms and leafy heads
Vividly pictured in some glassy pool,
40   That, for a brief space, checks the hurrying stream!

On the Death of His Majesty
(*George the Third*)

Ward of the Law! – dread Shadow of a King!
Whose realm had dwindled to one stately room;
Whose universe was gloom immersed in gloom,
Darkness as thick as life o'er life could fling,
Save haply for some feeble glimmering
Of Faith and Hope – if thou, by nature's doom,
Gently hast sunk into the quiet tomb,
Why should we bend in grief, to sorrow cling,
When thankfulness were best? – Fresh-flowing tears,
10   Or, where tears flow not, sigh succeeding sigh,
Yield to such after-thought the sole reply
Which justly it can claim. The Nation hears
In this deep knell, silent for threescore years,
An unexampled voice of awful memory!

Composed on the Banks of a Rocky Stream

Dogmatic Teachers, of the snow-white fur!
Ye wrangling Schoolmen, of the scarlet hood!
Who, with a keenness not to be withstood,
Press the point home, or falter and demur,
Checked in your course by many a teasing burr;
These natural council-seats your acrid blood
Might cool; – and, as the Genius of the flood
Stoops willingly to animate and spur
Each lighter function slumbering in the brain,

10   Yon eddying balls of foam, these arrowy gleams
That o'er the pavement of the surging streams
Welter and flash, a synod might detain
With subtle speculations, haply vain,
But surely less so than your far-fetched themes!

'The stars are mansions built by Nature's hand'

The stars are mansions built by Nature's hand,
And, haply, there the spirits of the blest
Dwell, clothed in radiance, their immortal vest;
Huge Ocean shows, within his yellow strand,
A habitation marvellously planned,
For life to occupy in love and rest;
All that we see – is dome, or vault, or nest,
Or fortress, reared at Nature's sage command.
Glad thought for every season! but the Spring

10   Gave it while cares were weighing on my heart,
'Mid song of birds, and insects murmuring;
And while the youthful year's prolific art –
Of bud, leaf, blade, and flower – was fashioning
Abodes where self-disturbance hath no part.

Oxford, May 30, 1820

Ye sacred Nurseries of blooming Youth!
In whose collegiate shelter England's Flowers
Expand, enjoying through their vernal hours
The air of liberty, the light of truth;
Much have ye suffered from Time's gnawing tooth:
Yet, O ye spires of Oxford! domes and towers!
Gardens and groves! your presence overpowers
The soberness of reason; till, in sooth,
Transformed, and rushing on a bold exchange

10   I slight my own beloved Cam, to range
Where silver Isis leads my stripling feet;

Pace the long avenue, or glide adown
The stream-like windings of that glorious street –
An eager Novice robed in fluttering gown!

Oxford, May 30, 1820

Shame on this faithless heart! that could allow
Such transport, though but for a moment's space;
Not while – to aid the spirit of the place –
The crescent moon clove with its glittering prow
The clouds, or night-bird sang from shady bough;
But in plain daylight: – She, too, at my side,
Who, with her heart's experience satisfied,
Maintains inviolate its slightest vow!
Sweet Fancy! other gifts must I receive;
10 Proofs of a higher sovereignty I claim;
Take from *her* brow the withering flowers of eve,
And to that brow life's morning wreath restore;
Let *her* be comprehended in the frame
Of these illusions, or they please no more.

June, 1820

Fame tells of groves – from England far away –
Groves that inspire the Nightingale to trill
And modulate, with subtle reach of skill
Elsewhere unmatched, her ever-varying lay;
Such bold report I venture to gainsay:
For I have heard the choir of Richmond hill
Chanting, with indefatigable bill,
Strains that recalled to mind a distant day;
When, haply under shade of that same wood,
10 And scarcely conscious of the dashing oars
Plied steadily between those willowy shores,
The sweet-souled Poet of the Seasons stood –
Listening, and listening long, in rapturous mood,
Ye heavenly Birds! to your Progenitors.

A Parsonage in Oxfordshire

Where holy ground begins, unhallowed ends,
Is marked by no distinguishable line;
The turf unites, the pathways intertwine;
And, wheresoe'er the stealing footstep tends,
Garden, and that Domain where kindred, friends,
And neighbours rest together, here confound
Their several features, mingled like the sound
Of many waters, or as evening blends
With shady night. Soft airs, from shrub and flower,
10 Waft fragrant greetings to each silent grave;
And while those lofty poplars gently wave
Their tops, between them comes and goes a sky
Bright as the glimpses of eternity,
To saints accorded in their mortal hour.

Memorials of a Tour on the Continent 1820

DEDICATION (SENT WITH THESE POEMS, IN MS.,
TO —)

Dear Fellow-travellers! think not that the Muse,
To You presenting these memorial Lays,
Can hope the general eye thereon would gaze,
As on a mirror that gives back the hues
Of living Nature; no – though free to choose
The greenest bowers, the most inviting ways,
The fairest landscapes and the brightest days –
Her skill she tried with less ambitious views.
For You she wrought: Ye only can supply
10 The life, the truth, the beauty: she confides
In that enjoyment which with You abides,
Trusts to your love and vivid memory;

Thus far contented, that for You her verse
Shall lack not power the 'meeting soul to pierce!'
                                        W. WORDSWORTH.
RYDAL MOUNT, *November*, 1821.

I FISH-WOMEN. – ON LANDING AT CALAIS
'Tis said, fantastic ocean doth enfold
The likeness of whate'er on land is seen;
But, if the Nereid Sisters and their Queen,
Above whose heads the tide so long hath rolled,
The Dames resemble whom we here behold,
How fearful were it down through opening waves
To sink, and meet them in their fretted caves,
Withered, grotesque, immeasurably old,
And shrill and fierce in accent! – Fear it not:
10   For they Earth's fairest daughters do excel;
Pure undecaying beauty is their lot;
Their voices into liquid music swell,
Thrilling each pearly cleft and sparry grot,
The undisturbed abodes where Sea-nymphs dwell!

II BRUGÈS
Brugès I saw attired with golden light
(Streamed from the west) as with a robe of power:
The splendour fled; and now the sunless hour,
That, slowly making way for peaceful night,
Best suits with fallen grandeur, to my sight
Offers the beauty, the magnificence,
And sober graces, left her for defence
Against the injuries of time, the spite
Of fortune, and the desolating storms
10   Of future war. Advance not – spare to hide,
O gentle Power of darkness! these mild hues;
Obscure not yet these silent avenues
Of stateliest architecture, where the Forms
Of nun-like females, with soft motion, glide!

III BRUGÈS

The Spirit of Antiquity – enshrined
In sumptuous buildings, vocal in sweet song,
In picture, speaking with heroic tongue,
And with devout solemnities entwined –
Mounts to the seat of grace within the mind:
Hence Forms that glide with swan-like ease along,
Hence motions, even amid the vulgar throng,
To an harmonious decency confined:
As if the streets were consecrated ground,
10 The city one vast temple, dedicate
To mutual respect in thought and deed;
To leisure, to forbearances sedate;
To social cares from jarring passions freed;
A deeper peace than that in deserts found!

IV INCIDENT AT BRUGÈS

In Brugès town is many a street
  Whence busy life hath fled;
Where, without hurry, noiseless feet
  The grass-grown pavement tread.
There heard we, halting in the shade
  Flung from a Convent-tower,
A harp that tuneful prelude made
  To a voice of thrilling power.

The measure, simple truth to tell,
10   Was fit for some gay throng;
Though from the same grim turret fell
  The shadow and the song.
When silent were both voice and chords,
  The strain seemed doubly dear,
Yet sad as sweet, – for *English* words
  Had fallen upon the ear.

It was a breezy hour of eve;
  And pinnacle and spire
Quivered and seemed almost to heave,

20 Clothed with innocuous fire;
But, where we stood, the setting sun
 Showed little of his state;
And, if the glory reached the Nun,
 'Twas through an iron grate.

Not always is the heart unwise,
 Nor pity idly born,
If even a passing Stranger sighs
 For them who do not mourn.
Sad is thy doom, self-solaced dove,
30 Captive, whoe'er thou be!
Oh! what is beauty, what is love,
 And opening life to thee?

Such feeling pressed upon my soul,
 A feeling sanctified
By one soft trickling tear that stole
 From the Maiden at my side;
Less tribute could she pay than this,
 Borne gaily o'er the sea,
Fresh from the beauty and the bliss
40 Of English liberty?

V AFTER VISITING THE FIELD OF WATERLOO
A wingèd Goddess – clothed in vesture wrought
Of rainbow colours; One whose port was bold,
Whose overburdened hand could scarcely hold
The glittering crowns and garlands which it brought –
Hovered in air above the far-famed Spot.
She vanished; leaving prospect blank and cold
Of wind-swept corn that wide around us rolled
In dreary billows, wood, and meagre cot,
And monuments that soon must disappear;
10 Yet a dread local recompense we found;
While glory seemed betrayed, while patriot-zeal
Sank in our hearts, we felt as men *should* feel
With such vast hoards of hidden carnage near,
And horror breathing from the silent ground!

VI BETWEEN NAMUR AND LIEGE

What lovelier home could gentle Fancy choose?
Is this the stream, whose cities, heights, and plains,
War's favourite playground, are with crimson stains
Familiar, as the Morn with pearly dews?
The Morn, that now, along the silver MEUSE,
Spreading her peaceful ensigns, calls the swains
To tend their silent boats and ringing wains,
Or strip the bough whose mellow fruit bestrews
The ripening corn beneath it. As mine eyes
10 Turn from the fortified and threatening hill,
How sweet the prospect of yon watery glade,
With its grey rocks clustering in pensive shade –
That, shaped like old monastic turrets, rise
From the smooth meadow-ground, serene and still!

VII AIX-LA-CHAPELLE

Was it to disenchant, and to undo,
That we approached the Seat of Charlemaine?
To sweep from many an old romantic strain
That faith which no devotion may renew!
Why does this puny Church present to view
Her feeble columns? and that scanty chair!
This sword that one of our weak times might wear!
Objects of false pretence, or meanly true!
If from a traveller's fortune I might claim
10 A palpable memorial of that day,
Then would I seek the Pyrenean Breach
That ROLAND clove with huge two-handed sway,
And to the enormous labour left his name,
Where unremitting frosts the rocky crescent bleach.

VIII IN THE CATHEDRAL AT COLOGNE

O for the help of Angels to complete
This Temple – Angels governed by a plan
Thus far pursued (how gloriously!) by Man,
Studious that *He* might not disdain the seat
Who dwells in heaven! But that aspiring heat

Hath failed; and now, ye Powers! whose gorgeous wings
And splendid aspect yon emblazonings
But faintly picture, 'twere an office meet
For you, on these unfinished shafts to try
10 The midnight virtues of your harmony: –
This vast design might tempt you to repeat
Strains that call forth upon empyreal ground
Immortal Fabrics, rising to the sound
Of penetrating harps and voices sweet!

IX IN A CARRIAGE, UPON THE BANKS
OF THE RHINE

Amid this dance of objects sadness steals
O'er the defrauded heart – while sweeping by,
As in a fit of Thespian jollity,
Beneath her vine-leaf crown the green Earth reels:
Backward, in rapid evanescence, wheels
The venerable pageantry of Time,
Each beetling rampart, and each tower sublime,
And what the Dell unwillingly reveals
Of lurking cloistral arch, through trees espied
10 Near the bright River's edge. Yet why repine?
To muse, to creep, to halt at will, to gaze –
Such sweet way-faring – of life's spring the pride,
Her summer's faithful joy – *that* still is mine,
And in fit measure cheers autumnal days.

X HYMN FOR THE BOATMEN, AS THEY APPROACH
THE RAPIDS UNDER THE CASTLE OF HEIDELBERG

Jesu! bless our slender Boat,
  By the current swept along;
Loud its threatenings – let them not
  Drown the music of a song
Breathed thy mercy to implore,
Where these troubled waters roar!

Saviour, for our warning, seen
  Bleeding on that precious Rood;

If, while through the meadows green
10   Gently wound the peaceful flood,
We forgot Thee, do not Thou
Disregard Thy Suppliants now!

Hither, like yon ancient Tower
   Watching o'er the River's bed,
Fling the shadow of thy power,
   Else we sleep among the dead;
Thou who trod'st the billowy sea,
Shield us in our jeopardy!

Guide our Bark among the waves;
20   Through the rocks our passage smooth;
Where the whirlpool frets and raves
   Let Thy love its anger soothe:
All our hope is placed in Thee;
Miserere Domine!

XI THE SOURCE OF THE DANUBE

Not, like his great Compeers, indignantly
Doth DANUBE spring to life! The wandering Stream
(Who loves the Cross, yet to the Crescent's gleam
Unfolds a willing breast) with infant glee
Slips from his prison walls: and Fancy, free
To follow in his track of silver light,
Mounts on rapt wing, and with a moment's flight
Hath reached the encincture of that gloomy sea
Whose waves the Orphean lyre forbad to meet
10 In conflict; whose rough winds forgot their jars
To waft the heroic progeny of Greece;
When the first Ship sailed for the Golden Fleece –
ARGO – exalted for that daring feat
To fix in heaven her shape distinct with stars.

XII ON APPROACHING THE STAUB-BACH, LAUTERBRUNNEN

Uttered by whom, or how inspired – designed
For what strange service, does this concert reach
Our ears, and near the dwellings of mankind!
'Mid fields familiarized to human speech? –
No Mermaids warble – to allay the wind
Driving some vessel toward a dangerous beach –
More thrilling melodies; Witch answering Witch,
To chant a love-spell, never intertwined
Notes shrill and wild with art more musical:
10 Alas! that from the lips of abject Want
Or Idleness in tatters mendicant
The strain should flow – free Fancy to enthral,
And with regret and useless pity haunt
This bold, this bright, this sky-born, WATERFALL!

XIII THE FALL OF THE AAR – HANDEC

From the fierce aspect of this River, throwing
His giant body o'er the steep rock's brink,
Back in astonishment and fear we shrink:
But, gradually a calmer look bestowing,
Flowers we espy beside the torrent growing;
Flowers that peep forth from many a cleft and chink,
And, from the whirlwind of his anger, drink
Hues ever fresh, in rocky fortress blowing:
They suck – from breath that, threatening to destroy,
10 Is more benignant than the dewy eve –
Beauty, and life, and motions as of joy:
Nor doubt but HE to whom yon Pinetrees nod
Their heads in sign of worship, Nature's God,
These humbler adorations will receive.

XIV MEMORIAL NEAR THE OUTLET OF THE LAKE OF THUN

'DEM ANDENKEN MEINES FREUNDES ALOYS REDING MDCCCXVIII.'

Aloys Reding, it will be remembered, was Captain-General of the Swiss forces, which, with a courage and perseverance worthy of the cause, opposed the flagitious and too successful attempt of Buonaparte to subjugate their country.

Around a wild and woody hill
A gravelled pathway treading,
We reached a votive Stone that bears
The name of Aloys Reding.

Well judged the Friend who placed it there
For silence and protection;
And haply with a finer care
Of dutiful affection.

The Sun regards it from the West;
10 And, while in summer glory
He sets, his sinking yields a type
Of that pathetic story:

And oft he tempts the patriot Swiss
Amid the grove to linger;
Till all is dim, save this bright Stone
Touched by his golden finger.

XV COMPOSED IN ONE OF THE CATHOLIC CANTONS

Doomed as we are our native dust
To wet with many a bitter shower,
It ill befits us to disdain
The altar, to deride the fane,
Where simple Sufferers bend, in trust
To win a happier hour.

I love, where spreads the village lawn,
Upon some knee-worn cell to gaze:

Hail to the firm unmoving cross,
10 Aloft, where pines their branches toss!
And to the chapel far withdrawn,
That lurks by lonely ways!

Where'er we roam – along the brink
Of Rhine – or by the sweeping Po,
Through Alpine vale, or champain wide,
Whate'er we look on, at our side
Be Charity! – to bid us think,
And feel, if we would know.

XVI AFTER-THOUGHT
Oh Life! without thy chequered scene
Of right and wrong, of weal and woe,
Success and failure, could a ground
For magnanimity be found;
For faith, 'mid ruined hopes, serene?
Or whence could virtue flow?

Pain entered through a ghastly breach –
Nor while sin lasts must effort cease;
Heaven upon earth's an empty boast;
10 But, for the bowers of Eden lost,
Mercy has placed within our reach
A portion of God's peace.

XVII SCENE ON THE LAKE OF BRIENTZ
'What know we of the Blest above
But that they sing and that they love?'
Yet, if they ever did inspire
A mortal hymn, or shaped the choir,
Now, where those harvest Damsels float
Homeward in their rugged Boat,
(While all the ruffling winds are fled –
Each slumbering on some mountain's head)
Now, surely, hath that gracious aid
10 Been felt, that influence is displayed.

Pupils of Heaven, in order stand
The rustic Maidens, every hand
Upon a Sister's shoulder laid, –
To chant, as glides the boat along,
A simple, but a touching, song;
To chant, as Angels do above,
The melodies of Peace in love!

XVIII ENGELBERG, THE HILL OF ANGELS

For gentlest uses, oft-times Nature takes
The work of Fancy from her willing hands;
And such a beautiful creation makes
As renders needless spells and magic wands,
And for the boldest tale belief commands.
When first mine eyes beheld that famous Hill
The sacred ENGELBERG, celestial Bands,
With intermingling motions soft and still,
Hung round its top, on wings that changed their hues at
will.

10   Clouds do not name those Visitants; they were
The very Angels whose authentic lays,
Sung from that heavenly ground in middle air,
Made known the spot where piety should raise
A holy Structure to the Almighty's praise.
Resplendent Apparition! if in vain
My ears did listen, 'twas enough to gaze;
And watch the slow departure of the train,
Whose skirts the glowing Mountain thirsted to detain.

XIX OUR LADY OF THE SNOW

Meek Virgin Mother, more benign
Than fairest Star, upon the height
Of thy own mountain, set to keep
Lone vigils through the hours of sleep,
What eye can look upon thy shrine
Untroubled at the sight?

These crowded offerings as they hang
In sign of misery relieved,
Even these, without intent of theirs,
10   Report of comfortless despairs,
Of many a deep and cureless pang
And confidence deceived.

To Thee, in this aërial cleft,
As to a common centre, tend
All sufferers that no more rely
On mortal succour – all who sigh
And pine, of human hope bereft,
Nor wish for earthly friend.

And hence, O Virgin Mother mild!
20   Though plenteous flowers around thee blow,
Not only from the dreary strife
Of Winter, but the storms of life,
Thee have thy Votaries aptly styled,
OUR LADY OF THE SNOW.

Even for the Man who stops not here,
But down the irriguous valley hies,
Thy very name, O Lady! flings,
O'er blooming fields and gushing springs
A tender sense of shadowy fear,
30   And chastening sympathies!

Nor falls that intermingling shade
To summer-gladsomeness unkind:
It chastens only to requite
With gleams of fresher, purer, light;
While, o'er the flower-enamelled glade,
More sweetly breathes the wind.

But on! – a tempting downward way,
A verdant path before us lies;
Clear shines the glorious sun above;

40   Then give free course to joy and love,
     Deeming the evil of the day
     Sufficient for the wise.

XX EFFUSION IN PRESENCE OF THE PAINTED TOWER OF TELL, AT ALTORF

This Tower stands upon the spot where grew the Linden Tree against which his Son is said to have been placed, when the Father's archery was put to proof under circumstances so famous in Swiss Story.

What though the Italian pencil wrought not here,
Nor such fine skill as did the meed bestow
On Marathonian valour, yet the tear
Springs forth in presence of this gaudy show,
While narrow cares their limits overflow.
Thrice happy, burghers, peasants, warriors old,
Infants in arms, and ye, that as ye go
Homeward or schoolward, ape what ye behold;
Heroes before your time, in frolic fancy bold!

10 And when that calm Spectatress from on high
Looks down – the bright and solitary Moon,
Who never gazes but to beautify;
And snow-fed torrents, which the blaze of noon
Roused into fury, murmur a soft tune
That fosters peace, and gentleness recalls;
Then might the passing Monk receive a boon
Of saintly pleasure from these pictured walls,
While, on the warlike groups, the mellowing lustre falls.

    How blest the souls who when their trials come
20 Yield not to terror or despondency,
But face like that sweet Boy their mortal doom,
Whose head the ruddy apple tops, while he
Expectant stands beneath the linden tree:
He quakes not like the timid forest game,
But smiles – the hesitating shaft to free;

Assured that Heaven its justice will proclaim,
And to his Father give its own unerring aim.

XXI THE TOWN OF SCHWYTZ
By antique Fancy trimmed – though lowly, bred
To dignity – in thee, O SCHWYTZ! are seen
The genuine features of the golden mean;
Equality by Prudence governèd,
Or jealous Nature ruling in her stead;
And, therefore, art thou blest with peace, serene
As that of the sweet fields and meadows green
In unambitious compass round thee spread.
Majestic BERNE, high on her guardian steep,
10   Holding a central station of command,
Might well be styled this noble body's HEAD;
Thou, lodged 'mid mountainous entrenchments deep,
Its HEART; and ever may the heroic Land
Thy name, O SCHWYTZ, in happy freedom keep!

XXII ON HEARING THE 'RANZ DES VACHES' ON
THE TOP OF THE PASS OF ST GOTHARD
I listen – but no faculty of mine
Avails those modulations to detect,
Which, heard in foreign lands, the Swiss affect
With tenderest passion; leaving him to pine
(So fame reports) and die, – his sweet-breathed kine
Remembering, and green Alpine pastures decked
With vernal flowers. Yet may we not reject
The tale as fabulous. – Here while I recline,
Mindful how others by this simple Strain
10   Are moved, for me – upon this Mountain named
Of God himself from dread pre-eminence –
Aspiring thoughts, by memory reclaimed,
Yield to the Music's touching influence;
And joys of distant home my heart enchain.

XXIII FORT FUENTES

The Ruins of Fort Fuentes form the crest of a rocky eminence that rises from the plain at the head of the lake of Como, commanding views up the Valteline, and toward the town of Chiavenna. The prospect in the latter direction is characterized by melancholy sublimity. We rejoiced at being favoured with a distinct view of those Alpine heights; not, as we had expected from the breaking up of the storm, steeped in celestial glory, yet in communion with clouds floating or stationary – scatterings from heaven. The Ruin is interesting both in mass and in detail. An Inscription, upon elaborately-sculptured marble lying on the ground, records that the Fort had been erected by Count Fuentes in the year 1600, during the reign of Philip the Third; and the Chapel, about twenty years after, by one of his Descendants. Marble pillars of gateways are yet standing, and a considerable part of the Chapel walls: a smooth green turf has taken place of the pavement, and we could see no trace of altar or image; but everywhere something to remind one of former splendour, and of devastation and tumult. In our ascent we had passed abundance of wild vines intermingled with bushes: near the ruins were some ill tended, but growing willingly; and rock, turf, and fragments of the pile, are alike covered or adorned with a variety of flowers, among which the rose-coloured pink was growing in great beauty. While descending, we discovered on the ground, apart from the path, and at a considerable distance from the ruined Chapel, a statue of a Child in pure white marble, uninjured by the explosion that had driven it so far down the hill. 'How little,' we exclaimed, 'are these things valued here! Could we but transport this pretty Image to our own garden!' – Yet it seemed it would have been a pity anyone should remove it from its couch in the wilderness, which may be its own for hundreds of years. – *Extract from Journal*.

Dread hour! when, upheaved by war's sulphurous blast,
   This sweet-visaged Cherub of Parian stone
So far from the holy enclosure was cast,
   To couch in this thicket of brambles alone,

To rest where the lizard may bask in the palm
   Of his half-open hand pure from blemish or speck;

And the green, gilded snake, without troubling the calm
   Of the beautiful countenance, twine round his neck;

Where haply (kind service to Piety due!)
10   When winter the grove of its mantle bereaves,
Some bird (like our own honoured redbreast) may strew
   The desolate Slumberer with moss and with leaves.

FUENTES once harboured the good and the brave,
   Nor to her was the dance of soft pleasure unknown;
Her banners for festal enjoyment did wave
   While the thrill of her fifes through the mountains
    was blown:

Now gads the wild vine o'er the pathless ascent; –
   O silence of Nature, how deep is thy sway,
When the whirlwind of human destruction is spent,
20   Our tumults appeased, and our strifes passed away!

XXIV THE CHURCH OF SAN SALVADOR SEEN FROM THE LAKE OF LUGANO

This Church was almost destroyed by lightning a few years ago, but the altar and the image of the Patron Saint were untouched. The Mount, upon the summit of which the Church is built, stands amid the intricacies of the Lake of Lugano; and is, from a hundred points of view, its principal ornament, rising to the height of 2,000 feet, and, on one side, nearly perpendicular. The ascent is toilsome; but the traveller who performs it will be amply rewarded. Splendid fertility, rich woods and dazzling waters, seclusion and confinement of view contrasted with sea-like extent of plain fading into the sky; and this again, in an opposite quarter, with an horizon of the loftiest and boldest Alps – unite in composing a prospect more diversified by magnificence, beauty, and sublimity, than perhaps any other point in Europe, of so inconsiderable an elevation, commands.

Thou sacred Pile! whose turrets rise
From yon steep mountain's loftiest stage,
Guarded by lone San Salvador;

Sink (if thou must) as heretofore,
To sulphurous bolts a sacrifice,
But ne'er to human rage!

On Horeb's top, on Sinai, deigned
To rest the universal Lord:
Why leap the fountains from their cells
10 Where everlasting Bounty dwells? –
That, while the Creature is sustained,
His God may be adored.

Cliffs, fountains, rivers, seasons, times –
Let all remind the soul of heaven;
Our slack devotion needs them all;
And Faith – so oft of sense the thrall,
While she, by aid of Nature, climbs –
May hope to be forgiven.

Glory, and patriotic Love,
20 And all the Pomps of this frail 'spot
Which men call Earth,' have yearned to seek,
Associate with the simply meek,
Religion in the sainted grove,
And in the hallowed grot.

Thither, in time of adverse shocks,
Of fainting hopes and backward wills,
Did mighty Tell repair of old –
A Hero cast in Nature's mould,
Deliverer of the stedfast rocks
30 And of the ancient hills!

He, too, of battle-martyrs chief!
Who, to recall his daunted peers,
For victory shaped an open space,
By gathering with a wide embrace,
Into his single breast, a sheaf
Of fatal Austrian spears.

XXV THE ITALIAN ITINERANT, AND THE SWISS GOATHERD

Part I

i

Now that the farewell tear is dried,
Heaven prosper thee, be hope thy guide!
Hope be thy guide, adventurous Boy;
The wages of thy travel, joy!
Whether for London bound – to trill
Thy mountain notes with simple skill;
Or on thy head to poise a show
Of Images in seemly row;
The graceful form of milk-white Steed,
10   Or Bird that soared with Ganymede;
Or through our hamlets thou wilt bear
The sightless Milton, with his hair
Around his placid temples curled;
And Shakespeare at his side – a freight,
If clay could think and mind were weight,
For him who bore the world!
Hope be thy guide, adventurous Boy;
The wages of thy travel, joy!

ii

But thou, perhaps, (alert as free
20   Though serving sage philosophy)
Wilt ramble over hill and dale,
A Vender of the well-wrought Scale,
Whose sentient tube instructs to time
A purpose to a fickle clime:
Whether thou choose this useful part,
Or minister to finer art,
Though robbed of many a cherished dream,
And crossed by many a shattered scheme,
What stirring wonders wilt thou see
30   In the proud Isle of liberty!
Yet will the Wanderer sometimes pine

With thoughts which no delights can chase,
Recall a Sister's last embrace,
His Mother's neck entwine;
Nor shall forget the Maiden coy
That *would* have loved the bright-haired Boy!

iii

My Song, encouraged by the grace
That beams from his ingenuous face,
For this Adventurer scruples not
40 To prophesy a golden lot;
Due recompense, and safe return
To COMO's steeps – his happy bourne!
Where he, aloft in garden-glade,
Shall tend, with his own dark-eyed Maid,
The towering maize, and prop the twig
That ill supports the luscious fig;
Or feed his eye in paths sun-proof
With purple of the trellis-roof,
That through the jealous leaves escapes
50 From Cadenabbia's pendent grapes.
– Oh might he tempt that Goatherd-child
To share his wanderings! him whose look
Even yet my heart can scarcely brook,
So touchingly he smiled –
As with a rapture caught from heaven –
For unasked alms in pity given.

Part II

i

With nodding plumes, and lightly drest
Like foresters in leaf-green vest,
The Helvetian Mountaineers, on ground
60 For Tell's dread archery renowned,
Before the target stood – to claim
The guerdon of the steadiest aim.
Loud was the rifle-gun's report –

A startling thunder quick and short!
But, flying through the heights around,
Echo prolonged a tell-tale sound
Of hearts and hands alike 'prepared
The treasures they enjoy to guard!'
And, if there be a favoured hour
70 When Heroes are allowed to quit
The tomb, and on the clouds to sit
With tutelary power,
On their Descendants shedding grace –
This was the hour, and that the place.

ii
But Truth inspired the Bards of old
When of an iron age they told,
Which to unequal laws gave birth,
And drove Astraea from the earth.
– A gentle Boy (perchance with blood
80 As noble as the best endued,
But seemingly a Thing despised;
Even by the sun and air unprized;
For not a tinge or flowery streak
Appeared upon his tender cheek)
Heart-deaf to those rebounding notes,
Apart, beside his silent goats,
Sate watching in a forest shed,
Pale, ragged, with bare feet and head;
Mute as the snow upon the hill,
90 And, as the saint he prays to, still.
Ah, what avails heroic deed?
What liberty? if no defence
Be won for feeble Innocence.
Father of all! though wilful Manhood read
His punishment in soul-distress,
Grant to the morn of life its natural blessedness!

XXVI THE LAST SUPPER, BY LEONARDO DA VINCI,
IN THE REFECTORY OF THE CONVENT OF
MARIA DELLA GRAZIA – MILAN

Though searching damps and many an envious flaw
Have marred this Work; the calm ethereal grace,
The love deep-seated in the Saviour's face,
The mercy, goodness, have not failed to awe
The Elements; as they do melt and thaw
The heart of the Beholder – and erase
(At least for one rapt moment) every trace
Of disobedience to the primal law.
The annunciation of the dreadful truth
10 Made to the Twelve, survives: lip, forehead, cheek,
And hand reposing on the board in ruth
Of what it utters, while the unguilty seek
Unquestionable meanings – still bespeak
A labour worthy of eternal youth!

XXVII THE ECLIPSE OF THE SUN, 1820

High on her speculative tower
Stood Science waiting for the hour
When Sol was destined to endure
That darkening of his radiant face
Which Superstition strove to chase,
Erewhile, with rites impure.

Afloat beneath Italian skies,
Through regions fair as Paradise
We gaily passed, – till Nature wrought
10 A silent and unlooked-for change,
That checked the desultory range
Of joy and sprightly thought.

Where'er was dipped the toiling oar,
The waves danced round us as before,
As lightly, though of altered hue,
'Mid recent coolness, such as falls
At noontide from umbrageous walls
That screen the morning dew.

No vapour stretched its wings; no cloud
20 Cast far or near a murky shroud;
    The sky an azure field displayed;
    'Twas sunlight sheathed and gently charmed,
    Of all its sparkling rays disarmed,
    And as in slumber laid, –

    Or something night and day between,
    Like moonshine – but the hue was green;
    Still moonshine, without shadow, spread
    On jutting rock, and curvèd shore,
    Where gazed the peasant from his door,
30 And on the mountain's head.

    It tinged the Julian steeps – it lay,
    Lugano! on thy ample bay;
    The solemnizing veil was drawn
    O'er villas, terraces, and towers;
    To Albogasio's olive bowers,
    Porlezza's verdant lawn.

    But Fancy with the speed of fire
    Hath past to Milan's loftiest spire,
    And there alights 'mid that aërial host
40 Of Figures human and divine,
    White as the snows of Apennine
    Indúrated by frost.

    Awe-stricken she beholds the array
    That guards the Temple night and day;
    Angels she sees – that might from heaven have flown,
    And Virgin-saints, who not in vain
    Have striven by purity to gain
    The beatific crown –

    Sees long-drawn files, concentric rings
50 Each narrowing above each; – the wings,
    The uplifted palms, the silent marble lips

The starry zone of sovereign height –
All steeped in this portentous light!
All suffering dim eclipse!

Thus after Man had fallen (if aught
These perishable spheres have wrought
May with that issue be compared)
Throngs of celestial visages,
Darkening like water in the breeze,
60 A holy sadness shared.

Lo! while I speak, the labouring Sun
His glad deliverance has begun:
The cypress waves her sombre plume
More cheerily; and town and tower,
The vineyard and the olive-bower,
Their lustre re-assume!

O Ye, who guard and grace my home
While in far-distant lands we roam,
What countenance hath this Day put on for you?
70 While we look round with favoured eyes,
Did sullen mists hide lake and skies
And mountains from your view?

Or was it given you to behold
Like vision, pensive though not cold,
From the smooth breast of gay Winandermere?
Saw ye the soft yet awful veil
Spread over Grasmere's lovely dale,
Helvellyn's brow severe?

I ask in vain – and know far less
80 If sickness, sorrow, or distress
Have spared my Dwelling to this hour;
Sad blindness! but ordained to prove
Our faith in Heaven's unfailing love
And all-controlling power.

XXVIII THE THREE COTTAGE GIRLS

I

How blest the Maid whose heart – yet free
From Love's uneasy sovereignty –
Beats with a fancy running high,
Her simple cares to magnify;
Whom Labour, never urged to toil,
Hath cherished on a healthful soil;
Who knows not pomp, who heeds not pelf;
Whose heaviest sin it is to look
Askance upon her pretty Self
10   Reflected in some crystal brook;
Whom grief hath spared – who sheds no tear
But in sweet pity; and can hear
Another's praise from envy clear.

II

Such (but O lavish Nature! why
That dark unfathomable eye,
Where lurks a Spirit that replies
To stillest mood of softest skies,
Yet hints at peace to be o'erthrown,
Another's first, and then her own?)
20   Such, haply, yon ITALIAN Maid,
Our Lady's laggard Votaress,
Halting beneath the chestnut shade
To accomplish there her loveliness:
Nice aid maternal fingers lend;
A Sister serves with slacker hand;
Then, glittering like a star, she joins the festal band.

III

How blest (if truth may entertain
Coy fancy with a bolder strain)
The HELVETIAN Girl – who daily braves,
30   In her light skiff, the tossing waves,
And quits the bosom of the deep

Only to climb the rugged steep!
– Say whence that modulated shout!
From Wood-nymph of Diana's throng?
Or does the greeting to a rout
Of giddy Bacchanals belong?
Jubilant outcry! rock and glade
Resounded – but the voice obeyed
The breath of an Helvetian Maid.

IV

40 Her beauty dazzles the thick wood;
Her courage animates the flood;
Her steps the elastic green-sward meets
Returning unreluctant sweets;
The mountains (as ye heard) rejoice
Aloud, saluted by her voice!
Blithe Paragon of Alpine grace,
Be as thou art – for through thy veins
The blood of Heroes runs its race!
And nobly wilt thou brook the chains
50 That, for the virtuous, Life prepares;
The fetters which the Matron wears;
The patriot Mother's weight of anxious cares!

V

'Sweet HIGHLAND Girl! a very shower
Of beauty was thy earthly dower,'
When thou didst flit before mine eyes,
Gay Vision under sullen skies,
While Hope and Love around thee played,
Near the rough Falls of Inversneyd!
Have they, who nursed the blossom, seen
60 No breach or promise in the fruit?
Was joy, in following joy, as keen
As grief can be in grief's pursuit?
When youth had flown did hope still bless
Thy goings – or the cheerfulness
Of innocence survive to mitigate distress?

VI

But from our course why turn – to tread
A way with shadows overspread;
Where what we gladliest would believe
Is feared as what may most deceive?
70 Bright Spirit, not with amaranth crowned
But heath-bells from thy native ground.
Time cannot thin thy flowing hair,
Nor take one ray of light from Thee;
For in my Fancy thou dost share
The gift of immortality;
And there shall bloom, with Thee allied,
The Votaress by Lugano's side;
And that intrepid Nymph, on Uri's steep, descried!

XXIX THE COLUMN INTENDED BY BUONAPARTE
FOR A TRIUMPHAL EDIFICE IN MILAN, NOW
LYING BY THE WAY-SIDE IN THE SIMPLON PASS
Ambition – following down this far-famed slope
Her Pioneer, the snow-dissolving Sun,
While clarions prate of kingdoms to be won –
Perchance, in future ages, here may stop;
Taught to mistrust her flattering horoscope
By admonition from this prostrate Stone!
Memento uninscribed of Pride o'erthrown;
Vanity's hieroglyphic; a choice trope
In Fortune's rhetoric. Daughter of the Rock,
10 Rest where thy course was stayed by Power divine!
The Soul transported sees, from hint of thine,
Crimes which the great Avenger's hand provoke,
Hears combats whistling o'er the ensanguined heath:
What groans! what shrieks! what quietness in death!

XXX STANZAS COMPOSED IN THE SIMPLON PASS
Vallombrosa! I longed in thy shadiest wood
To slumber, reclined on the moss-covered floor,
To listen to ANIO'S precipitous flood,
When the stillness of evening hath deepened its roar;

To range through the Temples of PAESTUM, to muse
In POMPEII preserved by her burial in earth;
On pictures to gaze where they drank in their hues;
And murmur sweet songs on the ground of their birth!

The beauty of Florence, the grandeur of Rome,
10 Could I leave them unseen, and not yield to regret?
With a hope (and no more) for a season to come,
Which ne'er may discharge the magnificent debt?
Thou fortunate Region! whose Greatness inurned
Awoke to new life from its ashes and dust;
Twice-glorified fields! if in sadness I turned
From your infinite marvels, the sadness was just.

Now, risen ere the light-footed Chamois retires
From dew-sprinkled grass to heights guarded with snow,
Toward the mists that hang over the land of my Sires,
20 From the climate of myrtles contented I go.
My thoughts become bright like yon edging of Pines
On the steep's lofty verge: how it blackened the air!
But, touched from behind by the Sun, it now shines
With threads that seem part of his own silver hair.

Though the toil of the way with dear Friends we divide,
Though by the same zephyr our temples be fanned
As we rest in the cool orange-bower side by side,
A yearning survives which few hearts shall withstand:
Each step hath its value while homeward we move; –
30 O joy when the girdle of England appears!
What moment in life is so conscious of love,
Of love in the heart made more happy by tears?

XXXI ECHO, UPON THE GEMMI
What beast of chase hath broken from the cover?
Stern GEMMI listens to as full a cry,
As multitudinous a harmony
Of sounds as rang the heights of Latmos over,
When, from the soft couch of her sleeping Lover,

Up-starting, Cynthia skimmed the mountain-dew
In keen pursuit – and gave, where'er she flew,
Impetuous motion to the Stars above her.
A solitary Wolf-dog, ranging on
10 Through the bleak concave, wakes this wondrous chime
Of aëry voices locked in unison, –
Faint – far-off – near – deep – solemn and sublime! –
So, from the body of one guilty deed,
A thousand ghostly fears, and haunting thoughts,
    proceed!

XXXII PROCESSIONS SUGGESTED ON A SABBATH
MORNING IN THE VALE OF CHAMOUNY
To appease the Gods; or public thanks to yield;
Or to solicit knowledge of events,
Which in her breast Futurity concealed;
And that the past might have its true intents
Feelingly told by living monuments –
Mankind of yore were prompted to devise
Rites such as yet Persepolis presents
Graven on her cankered walls, solemnities
That moved in long array before admiring eyes.

10 The Hebrews thus, carrying in joyful state
Thick boughs of palm, and willows from the brook,
Marched round the altar – to commemorate
How, when their course they through the desert took,
Guided by signs which ne'er the sky forsook,
They lodged in leafy tents and cabins low;
Green boughs were borne, while, for the blast that shook
Down to the earth the walls of Jericho,
Shouts rise, and storms of sound from lifted trumpets
    blow!

And thus, in order, 'mid the sacred grove
20 Fed in the Libyan waste by gushing wells,
The priests and damsels of Ammonian Jove
Provoked responses with shrill canticles;

While, in a ship begirt with silver bells,
They round his altar bore the hornèd God,
Old Cham, the solar Deity, who dwells
Aloft, yet in a tilting vessel rode,
When universal sea the mountains overflowed.

Why speak of Roman Pomps? the haughty claims
Of Chiefs triumphant after ruthless wars;
30   The feast of Neptune – and the Cereal Games,
With images, and crowns, and empty cars;
The dancing Salii – on the shields of Mars
Smiting with fury; and a deeper dread
Scattered on all sides by the hideous jars
Of Corybantian cymbals, while the head
Of Cybelè was seen, sublimely turreted!

At length a Spirit more subdued and soft
Appeared – to govern Christian pageantries:
The Cross, in calm procession, borne aloft
40   Moved to the chant of sober litanies.
Even such, this day, came wafted on the breeze
From a long train – in hooded vestments fair
Enwrapt – and winding, between Alpine trees
Spiry and dark, around their House of prayer,
Below the icy bed of bright ARGENTIERE.

Still in the vivid freshness of a dream,
The pageant haunts me as it met our eyes!
Still, with those white-robed Shapes – a living Stream,
The glacier Pillars join in solemn guise
50   For the same service, by mysterious ties;
Numbers exceeding credible account
Of number, pure and silent Votaries
Issuing or issued from a wintry fount;
The impenetrable heart of that exalted Mount!

They, too, who send so far a holy gleam
While they the Church engird with motion slow,

A product of that awful Mountain seem,
Poured from his vaults of everlasting snow;
Not virgin lilies marshalled in bright row,
60   Not swans descending with the stealthy tide,
A livelier sisterly resemblance show
Than the fair Forms, that in long order glide,
Bear to the glacier band – those Shapes aloft descried.

Trembling, I look upon the secret springs
Of that licentious craving in the mind
To act the God among external things,
To bind, on apt suggestion, or unbind;
And marvel not that antique Faith inclined
To crowd the world with metamorphosis,
70   Vouchsafed in pity or in wrath assigned;
Such insolent temptations wouldst thou miss,
Avoid these sights; nor brood o'er Fable's dark abyss!

XXXIII ELEGIAC STANZAS

The lamented Youth, whose untimely death gave occasion to
these elegiac verses, was Frederick William Goddard, from
Boston in North America. He was in his twentieth year, and had
resided for some time with a clergyman in the neighbourhood
of Geneva for the completion of his education. Accompanied by a
fellow-pupil, a native of Scotland, he had just set out on a Swiss
tour when it was his misfortune to fall in with a friend of mine
who was hastening to join our party. The travellers, after spending a day together on the road from Berne and at Soleure, took
leave of each other at night, the young men having intended to
proceed directly to Zurich. But early in the morning my friend
found his new acquaintances, who were informed of the object
of his journey, and the friends he was in pursuit of, equipped to
accompany him. We met at Lucerne the succeeding evening, and
Mr G. and his fellow-student became in consequence our travelling companions for a couple of days. We ascended the Righi
together; and, after contemplating the sunrise from that noble
mountain, we separated at an hour and on a spot well suited to
the parting of those who were to meet no more. Our party descended through the valley of Our Lady of the Snow, and our

late companions, to Art. We had hoped to meet in a few weeks at Geneva; but on the third succeeding day (on the 21st of August) Mr Goddard perished, being overset in a boat while crossing the Lake of Zurich. His companion saved himself by swimming, and was hospitably received in the mansion of a Swiss gentleman (M. Keller) situated on the eastern coast of the lake. The corpse of poor Goddard was cast ashore on the estate of the same gentleman, who generously performed all the rites of hospitality which could be rendered to the dead as well as to the living. He caused a handsome mural monument to be erected in the church of Küsnacht, which records the premature fate of the young American, and on the shores too of the lake the traveller may read an inscription pointing out the spot where the body was deposited by the waves.

Lulled by the sound of pastoral bells,
Rude Nature's Pilgrims did we go,
From the dread summit of the Queen
Of mountains, through a deep ravine,
Where, in her holy chapel, dwells
'Our Lady of the Snow.'

The sky was blue, the air was mild;
Free were the streams and green the bowers;
As if, to rough assaults unknown,
10   The genial spot had *ever* shown
A countenance that as sweetly smiled –
The face of summer-hours.

And we were gay, our hearts at ease;
With pleasure dancing through the frame
We journeyed; all we knew of care –
Our path that straggled here and there;
Of trouble – but the fluttering breeze;
Of Winter – but a name.

If foresight could have rent the veil
20   Of three short days – but hush – no more!
Calm is the grave, and calmer none
Than that to which thy cares are gone,

Thou Victim of the stormy gale;
Asleep on ZURICH'S shore!

Oh GODDARD! – what art thou? – a name –
A sunbeam followed by a shade!
Nor more, for aught that time supplies,
The great, the experienced, and the wise:
Too much from this frail earth we claim,
30 And therefore are betrayed.

We met, while festive mirth ran wild,
Where, from a deep lake's mighty urn,
Forth slips, like an enfranchised slave,
A sea-green river, proud to lave,
With current swift and undefiled,
The towers of old LUCERNE.

We parted upon solemn ground
Far-lifted towards the unfading sky;
But all our thoughts were *then* of Earth,
40 That gives to common pleasures birth;
And nothing in our hearts we found
That prompted even a sigh.

Fetch, sympathizing Powers of air,
Fetch, ye that post o'er seas and lands,
Herbs moistened by Virginian dew,
A most untimely grave to strew,
Whose turf may never know the care
Of *kindred* human hands!

Beloved by every gentle Muse
50 He left his Transatlantic home:
Europe, a realized romance,
Had opened on his eager glance;
What present bliss! – what golden views!
What stores for years to come!

Though lodged within no vigorous frame,
His soul her daily tasks renewed,
Blithe as the lark on sun-gilt wings
High poised – or as the wren that sings
In shady places, to proclaim
60 Her modest gratitude.

Not vain is sadly-uttered praise;
The words of truth's memorial vow
Are sweet as morning fragrance shed
From flowers 'mid GOLDAU'S ruins bred;
As evening's fondly-lingering rays,
On RIGHI'S silent brow.

Lamented youth! to thy cold clay
Fit obsequies the Stranger paid;
And piety shall guard the Stone
70 Which hath not left the spot unknown
Where the wild waves resigned their prey –
And *that* which marks thy bed.

And, when thy Mother weeps for Thee
Lost Youth! a solitary Mother;
This tribute from a casual Friend
A not unwelcome aid may lend,
To feed the tender luxury,
The rising pang to smother.

XXXIV SKY-PROSPECT – FROM THE PLAIN OF FRANCE

Lo! in the burning west, the craggy nape
Of a proud Ararat! and, thereupon,
The Ark, her melancholy voyage done!
Yon rampant cloud mimics a lion's shape;
There, combats a huge crocodile – agape
A golden spear to swallow! and that brown
And massy grove, so near yon blazing town,
Stirs and recedes – destruction to escape!

Yet all is harmless – as the Elysian shades
10 Where Spirits dwell in undisturbed repose –
Silently disappears, or quickly fades:
Meek Nature's evening comment on the shows
That for oblivion take their daily birth
From all the fuming vanities of Earth!

XXXV ON BEING STRANDED NEAR THE HARBOUR OF BOULOGNE

Why cast ye back upon the Gallic shore,
Ye furious waves! a patriotic Son
Of England – who in hope her coast had won,
His project crowned, his pleasant travel o'er?
Well – let him pace this noted beach once more,
That gave the Roman his triumphal shells;
That saw the Corsican his cap and bells
Haughtily shake, a dreaming Conqueror! –
Enough: my Country's cliffs I can behold,
10 And proudly think, beside the chafing sea,
Of checked ambition, tyranny controlled,
And folly cursed with endless memory:
These local recollections ne'er can cloy;
Such ground I from my very heart enjoy!

XXXVI AFTER LANDING – THE VALLEY OF DOVER, NOVEMBER, 1820

Where be the noisy followers of the game
Which faction breeds; the turmoil where, that passed
Through Europe, echoing from the newsman's blast,
And filled our hearts with grief for England's shame?
Peace greets us; – rambling on without an aim
We mark majestic herds of cattle, free
To ruminate, couched on the grassy lea;
And hear far-off the mellow horn proclaim
The Season's harmless pastime. Ruder sound
10 Stirs not; enrapt I gaze with strange delight,
While consciousnesses, not to be disowned,
Here only serve a feeling to invite

That lifts the spirit to a calmer height,
And makes this rural stillness more profound.

XXXVII AT DOVER

From the Pier's head, musing, and with increase
Of wonder, I have watched this sea-side Town,
Under the white cliff's battlemented crown,
Hushed to a depth of more than Sabbath peace:
The streets and quays are thronged, but why disown
Their natural utterance: whence this strange release
From social noise – silence elsewhere unknown? –
A Spirit whispered, 'Let all wonder cease;
Ocean's o'erpowering murmurs have set free
10   Thy sense from pressure of life's common din;
As the dread Voice that speaks from out the sea
Of God's eternal Word, the Voice of Time
Doth deaden, shocks of tumult, shrieks of crime,
The shouts of folly, and the groans of sin.'

XXXVIII DESULTORY STANZAS, UPON RECEIVING THE PRECEDING SHEETS FROM THE PRESS

Is then the final page before me spread,
Nor further outlet left to mind or heart?
Presumptuous Book! too forward to be read,
How can I give thee licence to depart?
One tribute more; unbidden feelings start
Forth from their coverts; slighted objects rise;
My spirit is the scene of such wild art
As on Parnassus rules, when lightning flies,
Visibly leading on the thunder's harmonies.

10   All that I saw returns upon my view,
All that I heard comes back upon my ear,
All that I felt this moment doth renew;
And where the foot with no unmanly fear
Recoiled – and wings alone could travel – there
I move at ease; and meet contending themes
That press upon me, crossing the career

Of recollections vivid as the dreams
Of midnight, – cities, plains, forests, and mighty streams.

Where Mortal never breathed I dare to sit
20   Among the interior Alps, gigantic crew,
Who triumphed o'er diluvian power! – and yet
What are they but a wreck and residue,
Whose only business is to perish! – true
To which sad course, these wrinkled Sons of Time
Labour their proper greatness to subdue;
Speaking of death alone, beneath a clime
Where life and rapture flow in plenitude sublime.

Fancy hath flung for me an airy bridge
Across thy long deep Valley, furious Rhone!
30   Arch that *here* rests upon the granite ridge
Of Monte Rosa – *there* on frailer stone
Of secondary birth, the Jung-frau's cone;
And, from that arch, down-looking on the Vale
The aspect I behold of every zone;
A sea of foliage, tossing with the gale,
Blithe Autumn's purple crown, and Winter's icy mail!

Far as St Maurice, from yon eastern Forks,
Down the main avenue my sight can range:
And all its branchy vales, and all that lurks
40   Within them, church, and town, and hut, and grange,
For my enjoyment meet in vision strange;
Snows, torrents; – to the region's utmost bound,
Life, Death, in amicable interchange; –
But list! the avalanche – the hush profound
That follows – yet more awful than that awful sound!

Is not the chamois suited to his place?
The eagle worthy of her ancestry?
– Let Empires fall; but ne'er shall Ye disgrace
Your noble birthright, ye that occupy
50   Your council-seats beneath the open sky,

On Sarnen's Mount, there judge of fit and right,
In simple democratic majesty;
Soft breezes fanning your rough brows – the might
And purity of nature spread before your sight!

From this appropriate Court, renowned LUCERNE
Calls me to pace her honoured Bridge – that cheers
The Patriot's heart with pictures rude and stern,
An uncouth Chronicle of glorious years.
Like portraiture, from loftier source, endears
60 That work of kindred frame, which spans the lake
Just at the point of issue, where it fears
The form and motion of a stream to take;
Where it begins to stir, *yet* voiceless as a snake.

Volumes of sound, from the Cathedral rolled,
This long-roofed Vista penetrate – but see,
One after one, its tablets, that unfold
The whole design of Scripture history;
From the first tasting of the fatal Tree,
Till the bright Star appeared in eastern skies,
70 Announcing, ONE was born mankind to free;
His acts, His wrongs, His final sacrifice;
Lessons for every heart, a Bible for all eyes.

Our pride misleads, our timid likings kill.
– Long may these homely Works devised of old,
These simple efforts of Helvetian skill,
Aid, with congenial influence, to uphold
The State, – the Country's destiny to mould;
Turning, for them who pass, the common dust
Of servile opportunity to gold;
80 Filling the soul with sentiments august –
The beautiful, the brave, the holy, and the just!

No more; Time halts not in his noiseless march –
Nor turns, nor winds, as doth the liquid flood;

Life slips from underneath us, like that arch
Of airy workmanship whereon we stood,
Earth stretched below, heaven in our neighbourhood.
Go forth, my little Book! pursue thy way;
Go forth, and please the gentle and the good;
Nor be a whisper stifled, if it say
90   That treasures, yet untouched, may grace some future
    Lay.

The Germans on the Heights of Hochheim

Abruptly paused the strife; – the field throughout
Resting upon his arms each warrior stood,
Checked in the very act and deed of blood,
With breath suspended, like a listening scout.
O Silence! thou wert mother of a shout
That through the texture of yon azure dome
Cleaves its glad way, a cry of harvest home
Uttered to Heaven in ecstasy devout!
The barrier Rhine hath flashed, through battle-smoke,
10 On men who gaze heart-smitten by the view,
As if all Germany had felt the shock!
– Fly, wretched Gauls! ere they the charge renew
Who have seen – themselves now casting off the yoke –
The unconquerable Stream his course pursue.

On the Detraction Which Followed the Publication of a Certain Poem

See Milton's Sonnet, beginning, 'A Book was writ of late called "Tetrachordon".'

A book came forth of late, called PETER BELL;
Not negligent the style; – the matter? – good
As aught that song records of Robin Hood;
Or Roy, renowned through many a Scottish dell;
But some (who brook those hackneyed themes full well,
Nor heat, at Tam o'Shanter's name, their blood)

Waxed wroth, and with foul claws, a harpy brood,
On Bard and Hero clamorously fell.
Heed not, wild Rover once through heath and glen,
10 Who mad'st at length the better life thy choice,
Heed not such onset! nay, if praise of men
To thee appear not an unmeaning voice,
Lift up that grey-haired forehead, and rejoice
In the just tribute of thy Poet's pen!

Author's Voyage down the Rhine (*Thirty Years Ago*)

The confidence of Youth our only Art,
And Hope gay Pilot of the bold design,
We saw the living Landscapes of the Rhine,
Reach after reach, salute us and depart;
Slow sink the Spires, – and up again they start!
But who shall count the Towers as they recline
O'er the dark steeps, or on the horizon line
Striding, with shattered crests, the eye athwart?
More touching still, more perfect was the pleasure,
10 When hurrying forward till the slackening stream
Spread like a spacious Mere, we there could measure
A smooth free course along the watery gleam,
Think calmly on the past, and mark at leisure
Features which else had vanished like a dream.

*Ecclesiastical Sonnets
in Series*

PART I
FROM THE INTRODUCTION OF CHRISTIANITY INTO
BRITAIN TO THE CONSUMMATION OF THE PAPAL
DOMINION

'A verse may catch a wandering Soul, that flies
Profounder Tracts, and by a blest surprise
Convert delight into a Sacrifice.'

I Introduction

I, who accompanied with faithful pace
Cerulean Duddon from its cloud-fed spring,
And loved with spirit ruled by his to sing
Of mountain-quiet and boon nature's grace;
I, who essayed the nobler Stream to trace
Of Liberty, and smote the plausive string
Till the checked torrent, proudly triumphing,
Won for herself a lasting resting-place;
Now seek upon the heights of Time the source
10 Of a HOLY RIVER, on whose banks are found
Sweet pastoral flowers, and laurels that have crowned
Full oft the unworthy brow of lawless force;
And, for delight of him who tracks its course,
Immortal amaranth and palms abound.

II Conjectures

If there be prophets on whose spirits rest
Past things, revealed like future, they can tell
What Powers, presiding o'er the sacred well
Of Christian Faith, this savage Island blessed
With its first bounty. Wandering through the west,
Did holy Paul a while in Britain dwell,
And call the Fountain forth by miracle,
And with dread signs the nascent Stream invest?
Or He, whose bonds dropped off, whose prison doors
10 Flew open, by an Angel's voice unbarred?

Or some of humbler name, to these wild shores
Storm-driven; who, having seen the cup of woe
Pass from their Master, sojourned here to guard
The precious Current they had taught to flow?

III Trepidation of the Druids

Screams round the Arch-druid's brow the sea-mew –
    white
As Menai's foam; and toward the mystic ring
Where Augurs stand, the Future questioning,
Slowly the cormorant aims her heavy flight,
Portending ruin to each baleful rite
That, in the lapse of ages, hath crept o'er
Diluvian truths, and patriarchal lore.
Haughty the Bard: can these meek doctrines blight
His transports? wither his heroic strains?
But all shall be fulfilled; – the Julian spear
A way first opened; and, with Roman chains,
The tidings come of Jesus crucified;
They come – they spread – the weak, the suffering, hear;
Receive the faith, and in the hope abide.

IV Druidical excommunication

Mercy and Love have met thee on thy road,
Thou wretched Outcast, from the gift of fire
And food cut off by sacerdotal ire,
From every sympathy that Man bestowed!
Yet shall it claim our reverence, that to God,
Ancient of days! that to the eternal Sire,
These jealous Ministers of law aspire,
As to the one sole fount whence wisdom flowed,
Justice, and order. Tremblingly escaped,
As if with prescience of the coming storm,
That intimation when the stars were shaped;
And still, 'mid yon thick woods, the primal truth
Glimmers through many a superstitious form
That fills the Soul with unavailing ruth.

V Uncertainty

Darkness surrounds us; seeking, we are lost
On Snowdon's wilds, amid Brigantian coves,
Or where the solitary shepherd roves
Along the plain of Sarum, by the ghost
Of Time and shadows of Tradition, crost;
And where the boatman of the Western Isles
Slackens his course – to mark those holy piles
Which yet survive on bleak Iona's coast.
Nor these, nor monuments of eldest name,
10 Nor Taliesin's unforgotten lays,
Nor characters of Greek or Roman fame,
To an unquestionable Source have led;
Enough – if eyes, that sought the fountain-head
In vain, upon the growing Rill may gaze.

VI Persecution

Lament! for Diocletian's fiery sword
Works busy as the lightning; but instinct
With malice ne'er to deadliest weapon linked,
Which God's ethereal storehouses afford:
Against the Followers of the incarnate Lord
It rages; – some are smitten in the field –
Some pierced to the heart through the ineffectual shield
Of sacred home; – with pomp are others gored
And dreadful respite. Thus was Alban tried,
10 England's first Martyr, whom no threats could shake:
Self-offered victim, for his friend he died,
And for the faith; nor shall his name forsake
That Hill, whose flowery platform seems to rise
By Nature decked for holiest sacrifice.

VII Recovery

As, when a storm hath ceased, the birds regain
Their cheerfulness, and busily retrim
Their nests, or chant a gratulating hymn
To the blue ether and bespangled plain;

Even so, in many a re-constructed fane,
Have the survivors of this Storm renewed
Their holy rites with vocal gratitude:
And solemn ceremonials they ordain
To celebrate their great deliverance;
10 Most feelingly instructed 'mid their fear –
That persecution, blind with rage extreme,
May not the less, through Heaven's mild countenance,
Even in her own despite, both feed and cheer;
For all things are less dreadful than they seem.

VIII Temptations from Roman refinements

Watch, and be firm! for soul-subduing vice,
Heart-killing luxury, on your steps await.
Fair houses, baths, and banquets delicate,
And temples flashing, bright as polar ice,
Their radiance through the woods – may yet suffice
To sap your hardy virtue, and abate
Your love of Him upon whose forehead sate
The crown of thorns; whose life-blood flowed, the price
Of your redemption. Shun the insidious arts
10 That Rome provides, less dreading from her frown
Than from her wily praise, her peaceful gown,
Language, and letters; – these, though fondly viewed
As humanizing graces, are but parts
And instruments of deadliest servitude!

IX Dissensions

That heresies should strike (if truth be scanned
Presumptuously) their roots both wide and deep,
Is natural as dreams to feverish sleep.
Lo! Discord at the altar dares to stand
Uplifting toward high Heaven her fiery brand,
A cherished Priestess of the new-baptized!
But chastisement shall follow peace despised.
The Pictish cloud darkens the enervate land
By Rome abandoned; vain are suppliant cries,

10   And prayers that would undo her forced farewell;
For she returns not. – Awed by her own knell,
She casts the Britons upon strange Allies,
Soon to become more dreaded enemies
Than heartless misery called them to repel.

X Struggle of the Britons against the Barbarians

Rise! – they *have* risen: of brave Aneurin ask
How they have scourged old foes, perfidious friends:
The Spirit of Caractacus descends
Upon the Patriots, animates their task; –
Amazement runs before the towering casque
Of Arthur, bearing through the stormy field
The virgin sculptured on his Christian shield: –
Stretched in the sunny light of victory bask
The Host that followed Urien as he strode
10   O'er heaps of slain; – from Cambrian wood and moss
Druids descend, auxiliars of the Cross;
Bards, nursed on blue Plinlimmon's still abode,
Rush on the fight, to harps preferring swords,
And everlasting deeds to burning words!

XI Saxon conquest

Nor wants the cause the panic-striking aid
Of hallelujahs tost from hill to hill –
For instant victory. But Heaven's high will
Permits a second and a darker shade
Of Pagan night. Afflicted and dismayed,
The Relics of the sword flee to the mountains:
O wretched Land! whose tears have flowed like fountains;
Whose arts and honours in the dust are laid
By men yet scarcely conscious of a care
10   For other monuments than those of Earth;
Who, as the fields and woods have given them birth,
Will build their savage fortunes only there;
Content, if foss, and barrow, and the girth
Of long-drawn rampart, witness what they were.

XII Monastery of old Bangor

The oppression of the tumult – wrath and scorn –
The tribulation – and the gleaming blades –
Such is the impetuous spirit that pervades
The song of Taliesin; – Ours shall mourn
The *unarmed* Host who by their prayers would turn
The sword from Bangor's walls, and guard the store
Of Aboriginal and Roman lore,
And Christian monuments, that now must burn
To senseless ashes. Mark! how all things swerve
10 From their known course, or vanish like a dream;
Another language spreads from coast to coast;
Only perchance some melancholy Stream
And some indignant Hills old names preserve,
When laws, and creeds, and people all are lost!

XIII Casual incitement

A bright-haired company of youthful slaves,
Beautiful strangers, stand within the pale
Of a sad market, ranged for public sale,
Where Tiber's stream the immortal City laves:
ANGLI by name; and not an ANGEL waves
His wing who could seem lovelier to man's eye
Than they appear to holy Gregory;
Who, having learnt that name, salvation craves
For Them, and for their Land. The earnest Sire,
10 His questions urging, feels, in slender ties
Of chiming sound, commanding sympathies;
DE-IRIANS – he would save them from God's IRE;
Subjects of Saxon AELLA – they shall sing
Glad HALLE-lujahs to the eternal King!

XIV Glad tidings

For ever hallowed be this morning fair,
Blest be the unconscious shore on which ye tread,
And blest the silver Cross, which ye, instead
Of martial banner, in procession bear;

The Cross preceding Him who floats in air,
The pictured Saviour! – By Augustin led,
They come – and onward travel without dread,
Chanting in barbarous ears a tuneful prayer –
Sung for themselves, and those whom they would free!
10   Rich conquest waits them: – the tempestuous sea
Of Ignorance, that ran so rough and high
And heeded not the voice of clashing swords,
These good men humble by a few bare words,
And calm with fear of God's divinity.

XV Paulinus

But, to remote Northumbria's royal Hall,
Where thoughtful Edwin, tutored in the school
Of sorrow, still maintains a heathen rule,
Who comes with functions apostolical?
Mark him, of shoulders curved, and stature tall,
Black hair, and vivid eye, and meagre cheek,
His prominent feature like an eagle's beak;
A Man whose aspect doth at once appal
And strike with reverence. The Monarch leans
10   Toward the pure truths this Delegate propounds,
Repeatedly his own deep mind he sounds
With careful hesitation, – then convenes
A synod of his Councillors: – give ear,
And what a pensive Sage doth utter, hear!

XVI Persuasion

'Man's life is like a Sparrow, mighty King!
That – while at banquet with your Chiefs you sit
Housed near a blazing fire – is seen to flit
Safe from the wintry tempest. Fluttering,
Here did it enter; there, on hasty wing,
Flies out, and passes on from cold to cold;
But whence it came we know not, nor behold
Whither it goes. Even such, that transient Thing,
The human Soul; not utterly unknown

10   While in the Body lodged, her warm abode;
But from what world She came, what woe or weal
On her departure waits, no tongue hath shown;
This mystery if the Stranger can reveal,
His be a welcome cordially bestowed!'

XVII Conversion

Prompt transformation works the novel Lore;
The Council closed, the Priest in full career
Rides forth, an armèd man, and hurls a spear
To desecrate the Fane which heretofore
He served in folly. Woden falls, and Thor
Is overturned; the mace, in battle heaved
(So might they dream) till victory was achieved,
Drops, and the God himself is seen no more.
Temple and Altar sink, to hide their shame
10   Amid oblivious weeds. '*O come to me,*
Ye heavy laden!' such the inviting voice
Heard near fresh streams; and thousands, who rejoice
In the new Rite – the pledge of sanctity,
Shall, by regenerate life, the promise claim.

XVIII Apology

Nor scorn the aid which Fancy oft doth lend
The Soul's eternal interests to promote:
Death, darkness, danger, are our natural lot;
And evil Spirits *may* our walk attend
For aught the wisest know or comprehend;
Then be *good* Spirits free to breathe a note
Of elevation; let their odours float
Around these Converts; and their glories blend,
The midnight stars outshining, or the blaze
10   Of the noon-day. Nor doubt that golden cords
Of good works, mingling with the visions, raise
The Soul to purer worlds: and *who* the line
Shall draw, the limits of the power define,
That even imperfect faith to man affords?

XIX Primitive Saxon Clergy

How beautiful your presence, how benign,
Servants of God! who not a thought will share
With the vain world; who, outwardly as bare
As winter trees, yield no fallacious sign
That the firm soul is clothed with fruit divine!
Such Priest, when service worthy of his care
Has called him forth to breathe the common air,
Might seem a saintly Image from its shrine
Descended: – happy are the eyes that meet
10 The Apparition; evil thoughts are stayed
At his approach, and low-bowed necks entreat
A benediction from his voice or hand;
Whence grace, through which the heart can understand,
And vows, that bind the will, in silence made.

XX Other influences

Ah, when the Body, round which in love we clung,
Is chilled by death, does mutual service fail?
Is tender pity then of no avail?
Are intercessions of the fervent tongue
A waste of hope? – From this sad source have sprung
Rites that console the Spirit, under grief
Which ill can brook more rational relief:
Hence, prayers are shaped amiss, and dirges sung
For Souls whose doom is fixed! The way is smooth
10 For Power that travels with the human heart:
Confession ministers the pang to soothe
In him who at the ghost of guilt doth start.
Ye holy Men, so earnest in your care,
Of your own mighty instruments beware!

XXI Seclusion

Lance, shield, and sword relinquished – at his side
A bead-roll, in his hand a claspèd book,
Or staff more harmless than a shepherd's crook,
The war-worn Chieftain quits the world – to hide

His thin autumnal locks where Monks abide
In cloistered privacy. But not to dwell
In soft repose he comes. Within his cell,
Round the decaying trunk of human pride,
At morn, and eve, and midnight's silent hour,
10 Do penitential cogitations cling;
Like ivy, round some ancient elm, they twine
In grisly folds and strictures serpentine;
Yet, while they strangle, a fair growth they bring,
For recompense – their own perennial bower.

XXII *Continued*

Methinks that to some vacant hermitage
My feet would rather turn – to some dry nook
Scooped out of living rock, and near a brook
Hurled down a mountain-cove from stage to stage,
Yet tempering, for my sight, its bustling rage
In the soft heaven of a translucent pool;
Thence creeping under sylvan arches cool,
Fit haunt of shapes whose glorious equipage
Would elevate my dreams. A beechen bowl,
10 A maple dish, my furniture should be;
Crisp, yellow leaves my bed; the hooting owl
My night-watch: nor should e'er the crested fowl
From thorp or vill his matins sound for me,
Tired of the world and all its industry.

XXIII *Reproof*

But what if One, through grove or flowery mead,
Indulging thus at will the creeping feet
Of a voluptuous indolence, should meet
Thy hovering Shade, O venerable Bede!
The saint, the scholar, from a circle freed
Of toil stupendous, in a hallowed seat
Of learning, where thou heard'st the billows beat
On a wild coast, rough monitors to feed
Perpetual industry. Sublime Recluse!
10 The recreant soul, that dares to shun the debt

Imposed on human kind, must first forget
Thy diligence, thy unrelaxing use
Of a long life; and, in the hour of death,
The last dear service of thy passing breath!

*XXIV Saxon monasteries, and lights and shades of the
religion*

By such examples moved to unbought pains,
The people work like congregated bees;
Eager to build the quiet Fortresses
Where Piety, as they believe, obtains
From Heaven a *general* blessing; timely rains
Or needful sunshine; prosperous enterprise,
Justice and peace: – bold faith! yet also rise
The sacred Structures for less doubtful gains.
The Sensual think with reverence of the palms
10   Which the chaste Votaries seek, beyond the grave;
If penance be redeemable, thence alms
Flow to the poor, and freedom to the slave;
And if full oft the Sanctuary save
Lives black with guilt, ferocity it calms.

XXV Missions and travels

Not sedentary all: there are who roam
To scatter seeds of life on barbarous shores;
Or quit with zealous step their knee-worn floors
To seek the general mart of Christendom;
Whence they, like richly-laden merchants, come
To their belovèd cells: – or shall we say
That, like the Red-cross Knight, they urge their way,
To lead in memorable triumph home
Truth, their immortal Una? Babylon,
10   Learnèd and wise, hath perished utterly,
Nor leaves her Speech one word to aid the sigh
That would lament her; – Memphis, Tyre, are gone
With all their Arts, – but classic lore glides on
By these Religions saved for all posterity.

XXVI Alfred

Behold a pupil of the monkish gown,
The pious ALFRED, King to Justice dear!
Lord of the harp and liberating spear;
Mirror of Princes! Indigent Renown
Might range the starry ether for a crown
Equal to *his* deserts, who, like the year,
Pours forth his bounty, like the day doth cheer,
And awes like night with mercy-tempered frown.
Ease from this noble miser of his time
10   No moment steals; pain narrows not his cares.
Though small his kingdom as a spark or gem,
Of Alfred boasts remote Jerusalem,
And Christian India, through her wide-spread clime,
In sacred converse gifts with Alfred shares.

XXVII His descendants

When thy great soul was freed from mortal chains,
Darling of England! many a bitter shower
Fell on thy tomb; but emulative power
Flowed in thy line through undegenerate veins.
The Race of Alfred covet glorious pains
When dangers threaten, dangers ever new!
Black tempests bursting, blacker still in view!
But manly sovereignty its hold retains;
The root sincere, the branches bold to strive
10   With the fierce tempest, while, within the round
Of their protection, gentle virtues thrive;
As oft, 'mid some green plot of open ground,
Wide as the oak extends its dewy gloom,
The fostered hyacinths spread their purple bloom.

XXVIII Influence abused

Urged by Ambition, who with subtlest skill
Changes her means, the Enthusiast as a dupe
Shall soar, and as a hypocrite can stoop,
And turn the instruments of good to ill,

Moulding the credulous people to his will.
Such DUNSTAN: – from its Benedictine coop
Issues the master Mind, at whose fell swoop
The chaste affections tremble to fulfil
Their purposes. Behold, pre-signified,
10 The Might of spiritual sway! his thoughts, his dreams,
Do in the supernatural world abide:
So vaunt a throng of Followers, filled with pride
In what they see of virtues pushed to extremes,
And sorceries of talent misapplied.

XXIX Danish conquests

Woe to the Crown that doth the Cowl obey!
Dissension, checking arms that would restrain
The incessant Rovers of the northern main,
Helps to restore and spread a Pagan sway:
But Gospel-truth is potent to allay
Fierceness and rage; and soon the cruel Dane
Feels, through the influence of her gentle reign,
His native superstitions melt away.
Thus, often, when thick gloom the east o'ershrouds,
10 The full-orbed Moon, slow-climbing, doth appear
Silently to consume the heavy clouds;
How no one can resolve; but every eye
Around her sees, while air is hushed, a clear
And widening circuit of ethereal sky.

XXX Canute

A pleasant music floats along the Mere,
From Monks in Ely chanting service high,
While-as Canùte the King is rowing by:
'My Oarsmen,' quoth the mighty King, 'draw near,
That we the sweet song of the Monks may hear!'
He listens (all past conquests and all schemes
Of future vanishing like empty dreams)
Heart-touched, and haply not without a tear.
The Royal Minstrel, ere the choir is still,

10   While his free Barge skims the smooth flood along,
Gives to that rapture an accordant Rhyme.
O suffering Earth! be thankful; sternest clime
And rudest age are subject to the thrill
Of heaven-descended Piety and Song.

XXXI The Norman Conquest

The woman-hearted Confessor prepares
The evanescence of the Saxon line.
Hark! 'tis the tolling Curfew! – the stars shine;
But of the lights that cherish household cares
And festive gladness, burns not one that dares
To twinkle after that dull stroke of thine,
Emblem and instrument, from Thames to Tyne,
Of force that daunts, and cunning that ensnares!
Yet as the terrors of the lordly bell,
10   That quench, from hut to palace, lamps and fires,
Touch not the tapers of the sacred choirs;
Even so a thraldom, studious to expel
Old laws, and ancient customs to derange,
To Creed or Ritual brings no fatal change.

XXXII

Coldly we spake. The Saxons, overpowered
By wrong triumphant through its own excess,
From fields laid waste, from house and home devoured
By flames, look up to heaven and crave redress
From God's eternal justice. Pitiless
Though men be, there are angels that can feel
For wounds that death alone has power to heal,
For penitent guilt, and innocent distress.
And has a Champion risen in arms to try
10   His Country's virtue, fought, and breathes no more;
Him in their hearts the people canonize;
And far above the mine's most precious ore
The least small pittance of bare mould they prize
Scooped from the sacred earth where his dear relics lie.

XXXIII *The Council of Clermont*

'And shall,' the Pontiff asks, 'profaneness flow
From Nazareth – source of Christian piety,
From Bethlehem, from the Mounts of Agony
And glorified Ascension? Warriors, go,
With prayers and blessings we your path will sow;
Like Moses hold our hands erect, till ye
Have chased far off by righteous victory
These sons of Amalek, or laid them low!' –
'GOD WILLETH IT,' the whole assembly cry;
Shout which the enraptured multitude astounds!
The Council-roof and Clermont's towers reply; –
'God willeth it,' from hill to hill rebounds,
And, in awe-stricken Countries far and nigh,
Through 'Nature's hollow arch' that voice resounds.

XXXIV *Crusades*

The turbaned Race are poured in thickening swarms
Along the west; though driven from Aquitaine,
The Crescent glitters on the towers of Spain;
And soft Italia feels renewed alarms;
The scimitar, that yields not to the charms
Of ease, the narrow Bosphorus will disdain;
Nor long (that crossed) would Grecian hills detain
Their tents, and check the current of their arms.
Then blame not those who, by the mightiest lever
Known to the moral world, Imagination,
Upheave, so seems it, from her natural station
All Christendom: – they sweep along (was never
So huge a host!) – to tear from the Unbeliever
The precious Tomb, their haven of salvation.

XXXV *Richard I*

Redoubted King, of courage leonine,
I mark thee, Richard! urgent to equip
Thy warlike person with the staff and scrip;
I watch thee sailing o'er the midland brine;

In conquered Cyprus see thy Bride decline
Her blushing cheek, love-vows upon her lip,
And see love-emblems streaming from thy ship,
As thence she holds her way to Palestine.
My Song, a fearless homager, would attend
10   Thy thundering battle-axe as it cleaves the press
Of war, but duty summons her away
To tell – how, finding in the rash distress
Of those Enthusiasts a subservient friend,
To giddier heights hath clomb the Papal sway.

XXXVI *An interdict*

Realms quake by turns: proud Arbitress of grace,
The Church, by mandate shadowing forth the power
She arrogates o'er heaven's eternal door,
Closes the gates of every sacred place.
Straight from the sun and tainted air's embrace
All sacred things are covered: cheerful morn
Grows sad as night – no seemly garb is worn,
Nor is a face allowed to meet a face
With natural smiles of greeting. Bells are dumb;
10   Ditches are graves – funereal rites denied;
And in the churchyard he must take his bride
Who dares be wedded! Fancies thickly come
Into the pensive heart ill fortified,
And comfortless despairs the soul benumb.

XXXVII *Papal abuses*

As with the Stream our voyage we pursue,
The gross materials of this world present
A marvellous study of wild accident;
Uncouth proximities of old and new;
And bold transfigurations, more untrue
(As might be deemed) to disciplined intent
Than aught the sky's fantastic element,
When most fantastic, offers to the view.
Saw we not Henry scourged at Becket's shrine?
10   Lo! John self-stripped of his insignia: – crown,

Sceptre and mantle, sword and ring, laid down
At a proud Legate's feet! The spears that line
Baronial halls, the opprobrious insult feel;
And angry Ocean roars a vain appeal.

XXXVIII Scene in Venice

Black Demons hovering o'er his mitred head,
To Caesar's Successor the Pontiff spake;
'Ere I absolve thee, stoop! that on thy neck
Levelled with earth this foot of mine may tread.'
Then he, who to the altar had been led,
He, whose strong arm the Orient could not check,
He, who had held the Soldan at his beck,
Stooped, of all glory disinherited,
And even the common dignity of man! –
Amazement strikes the crowd: while many turn
Their eyes away in sorrow, others burn
With scorn, invoking a vindictive ban
From outraged Nature; but the sense of most
In abject sympathy with power is lost.

XXXIX Papal dominion

Unless to Peter's Chair the viewless wind
Must come and ask permission when to blow,
What further empire would it have? for now
A ghostly Domination, unconfined
As that by dreaming Bards to Love assigned,
Sits there in sober truth – to raise the low,
Perplex the wise, the strong to overthrow;
Through earth and heaven to bind and to unbind! –
Resist – the thunder quails thee! – crouch – rebuff
Shall be thy recompense! from land to land
The ancient thrones of Christendom are stuff
For occupation of a magic wand,
And 'tis the Pope that wields it: – whether rough
Or smooth his front, our world is in his hand!

PART II

TO THE CLOSE OF THE TROUBLES IN THE REIGN
OF CHARLES I

I

How soon – alas! did Man, created pure –
By Angels guarded, deviate from the line
Prescribed to duty: – woeful forfeiture
He made by wilful breach of law divine.
With like perverseness did the Church abjure
Obedience to her Lord, and haste to twine,
'Mid Heaven-born flowers that shall for aye endure,
Weeds on whose front the world had fixed her sign.
O Man, – if with thy trials thus it fares,
10   If good can smooth the way to evil choice,
From all rash censure be the mind kept free;
He only judges right who weighs, compares,
And, in the sternest sentence which his voice
Pronounces, ne'er abandons Charity.

II

From false assumption rose, and fondly hailed
By superstition, spread the Papal power;
Yet do not deem the Autocracy prevailed
Thus only, even in error's darkest hour.
She daunts, forth-thundering from her spiritual tower,
Brute rapine, or with gentle lure she tames.
Justice and Peace through Her uphold their claims;
And Chastity finds many a sheltering bower.
Realm there is none that if controuled or swayed
10   By her commands partakes not, in degree,
Of good, o'er manners, arts and arms, diffused:
Yes, to thy domination, Roman See,
Though miserably, oft monstrously, abused
By blind ambition, be this tribute paid.

III Cistertian Monastery
'Here Man more purely lives, less oft doth fall,
More promptly rises, walks with stricter heed,

More safely rests, dies happier, is freed
Earlier from cleansing fires, and gains withal
A brighter crown.' – On yon Cistertian wall
That confident assurance may be read;
And, to like shelter, from the world have fled
Increasing multitudes. The potent call
Doubtless shall cheat full oft the heart's desires;
10 Yet, while the rugged Age on pliant knee
Vows to rapt Fancy humble fealty,
A gentler life spreads round the holy spires;
Where'er they rise, the sylvan waste retires,
And aëry harvests crown the fertile lea.

IV

Deplorable his lot who tills the ground,
His whole life long tills it, with heartless toil
Of villain-service, passing with the soil
To each new Master, like a steer or hound
Or like a rooted tree, or stone earth-bound;
But mark how gladly, through their own domains,
The Monks relax or break these iron chains;
While Mercy, uttering, through their voice, a sound
Echoed in Heaven, cries out, 'Ye Chiefs, abate
10 These legalized oppressions! Man – whose name
And nature God disdained not; Man – whose soul
Christ died for – cannot forfeit his high claim
To live and move exempt from all controul
Which fellow-feeling doth not mitigate!'

V Monks and schoolmen

Record we too, with just and faithful pen,
That many hooded Cenobites there are,
Who in their private cells have yet a care
Of public quiet; unambitious Men,
Counsellors for the world, of piercing ken;
Whose fervent exhortations from afar
Move Princes to their duty, peace or war;
And oft-times in the most forbidding den

Of solitude, with love of science strong,
10   How patiently the yoke of thought they bear!
How subtly glide its finest threads along!
Spirits that crowd the intellectual sphere
With mazy boundaries, as the astronomer
With orb and cycle girds the starry throng.

VI Other benefits

And, not in vain embodied to the sight,
Religion finds even in the stern retreat
Of feudal sway her own appropriate seat;
From the collegiate pomps on Windsor's height
Down to the humbler altar, which the Knight
And his Retainers of the embattled hall
Seek in domestic oratory small,
For prayer in stillness, or the chanted rite;
Then chiefly dear, when foes are planted round,
10   Who teach the intrepid guardians of the place –
Hourly exposed to death, with famine worn,
And suffering under many a perilous wound –
How sad would be their durance, if forlorn
Of offices dispensing heavenly grace!

VII Continued

And what melodious sounds at times prevail!
And, ever and anon, how bright a gleam
Pours on the surface of the turbid Stream!
What heartfelt fragrance mingles with the gale
That swells the bosom of our passing sail!
For where, but on *this* River's margin, blow
Those flowers of chivalry, to bind the brow
Of hardihood with wreaths that shall not fail? –
Fair Court of Edward! wonder of the world!
10   I see a matchless blazonry unfurled
Of wisdom, magnanimity, and love;
And meekness tempering honourable pride;
The lamb is couching by the lion's side,
And near the flame-eyed eagle sits the dove.

VIII Crusaders

Furl we the sails, and pass with tardy oars
Through these bright regions, casting many a glance
Upon the dream-like issues – the romance
Of many-coloured life that Fortune pours
Round the Crusaders, till on distant shores
Their labours end; or they return to lie,
The vow performed, in cross-legged effigy,
Devoutly stretched upon their chancel floors.
Am I deceived? Or is their requiem chanted
By voices never mute when Heaven unties
Her inmost, softest, tenderest harmonies;
Requiem which Earth takes up with voice undaunted,
When she would tell how Brave, and Good, and Wise,
For their high guerdon not in vain have panted!

IX

As faith thus sanctified the warrior's crest
While from the Papal Unity there came,
What feebler means had failed to give, one aim
Diffused through all the regions of the West;
So does her Unity its power attest
By works of Art, that shed, on the outward frame
Of worship, glory and grace, which who shall blame
That ever looked to heaven for final rest?
Hail countless Temples! that so well befit
Your ministry; that, as ye rise and take
Form, spirit and character from holy writ,
Give to devotion, wheresoe'er awake,
Pinions of high and higher sweep, and make
The unconverted soul with awe submit.

X

Where long and deeply hath been fixed the root
In the blest soil of gospel truth, the Tree,
(Blighted or scathed though many branches be,
Put forth to wither, many a hopeful shoot)

Can never cease to bear celestial fruit.
Witness the Church that oft-times, with effect
Dear to the saints, strives earnestly to eject
Her bane, her vital energies recruit.
Lamenting, do not hopelessly repine
10   When such good work is doomed to be undone,
The conquests lost that were so hardly won: –
All promises vouchsafed by Heaven will shine
In light confirmed while years their course shall run,
Confirmed alike in progress and decline.

XI Transubstantiation

Enough! for see, with dim association
The tapers burn; the odorous incense feeds
A greedy flame; the pompous mass proceeds;
The Priest bestows the appointed consecration;
And, while the HOST is raised, its elevation
An awe and supernatural horror breeds;
And all the people bow their heads, like reeds
To a soft breeze, in lowly adoration.
This Valdo brooks not. On the banks of Rhone
10   He taught, till persecution chased him thence,
To adore the Invisible, and Him alone.
Nor are his Followers loth to seek defence,
'Mid woods and wilds, on Nature's craggy throne,
From rites that trample upon soul and sense.

XII The Vaudois

But whence came they who for the Saviour Lord
Have long borne witness as the Scriptures teach? –
Ages ere Valdo raised his voice to preach
In Gallic ears the unadulterate Word,
Their fugitive Progenitors explored
Subalpine vales, in quest of safe retreats
Where that pure Church survives, though summer heats
Open a passage to the Romish sword,
Far as it dares to follow. Herbs self-sown,

10 And fruitage gathered from the chestnut-wood,
Nourish the sufferers then; and mists, that brood
O'er chasms with new-fallen obstacles bestrown,
Protect them; and the eternal snow that daunts
Aliens, is God's good winter for their haunts.

XIII

Praised be the Rivers, from their mountain springs
Shouting to Freedom, 'Plant thy banners here!'
To harassed Piety, 'Dismiss thy fear,
And in our caverns smooth thy ruffled wings!'
Nor be unthanked their final lingerings –
Silent, but not to high-souled Passion's ear –
'Mid reedy fens wide-spread and marshes drear,
Their own creation. Such glad welcomings
As Po was heard to give where Venice rose,
10 Hailed from aloft those Heirs of truth divine
Who near his fountains sought obscure repose,
Yet came prepared as glorious lights to shine,
Should that be needed for their sacred Charge;
Blest Prisoners They, whose spirits were at large!

XIV Waldenses

Those had given earliest notice, as the lark
Springs from the ground the morn to gratulate;
Or rather rose the day to antedate,
By striking out a solitary spark,
When all the world with midnight gloom was dark. –
Then followed the Waldensian bands, whom Hate
In vain endeavours to exterminate,
Whom Obloquy pursues with hideous bark:
But they desist not; – and the sacred fire,
10 Rekindled thus, from dens and savage woods
Moves, handed on with never-ceasing care,
Through courts, through camps, o'er limitary floods;
Nor lacks this sea-girt Isle a timely share
Of the new Flame, not suffered to expire.

XV Archbishop Chicheley to Henry V

'What beast in wilderness or cultured field
The lively beauty of the leopard shows?
What flower in meadow-ground or garden grows
That to the towering lily doth not yield?
Let both meet only on thy royal shield!
Go forth, great King! claim what thy birth bestows;
Conquer the Gallic lily which thy foes
Dare to usurp; – thou hast a sword to wield,
And Heaven will crown the right.' – The mitred Sire
Thus spake – and lo! a Fleet, for Gaul addrest,
Ploughs her bold course across the wondering seas;
For, sooth to say, ambition, in the breast
Of youthful heroes, is no sullen fire,
But one that leaps to meet the fanning breeze.

XVI Wars of York and Lancaster

Thus is the storm abated by the craft
Of a shrewd Counsellor, eager to protect
The Church, whose power hath recently been checked,
Whose monstrous riches threatened. So the shaft
Of victory mounts high, and blood is quaffed
In fields that rival Cressy and Poictiers –
Pride to be washed away by bitter tears!
For deep as hell itself, the avenging draught
Of civil slaughter. Yet, while temporal power
Is by these shocks exhausted, spiritual truth
Maintains the else endangered gift of life;
Proceeds from infancy to lusty youth;
And, under cover of this woeful strife,
Gathers unblighted strength from hour to hour.

XVII Wicliffe

Once more the Church is seized with sudden fear,
And at her call is Wicliffe disinhumed:
Yea, his dry bones to ashes are consumed
And flung into the brook that travels near;

Forthwith, that ancient Voice which Streams can hear
Thus speaks (that Voice which walks upon the wind,
Though seldom heard by busy human kind) –
'As thou these ashes, little Brook! wilt bear
Into the Avon, Avon to the tide
10   Of Severn, Severn to the narrow seas,
Into main Ocean they, this deed accurst
An emblem yields to friends and enemies
How the bold Teacher's Doctrine, sanctified
By truth, shall spread, throughout the world dispersed.'

XVIII Corruptions of the higher clergy

'Woe to you, Prelates! rioting in ease
And cumbrous wealth – the shame of your estate;
You, on whose progress dazzling trains await
Of pompous horses; whom vain titles please;
Who will be served by others on their knees,
Yet will yourselves to God no service pay;
Pastors who neither take nor point the way
To Heaven; for, either lost in vanities
Ye have no skill to teach, or if ye know
10   And speak the word —' Alas! of fearful things
'Tis the most fearful when the people's eye
Abuse hath cleared from vain imaginings;
And taught the general voice to prophesy
Of Justice armed, and Pride to be laid low.

XIX Abuse of monastic power

And what is Penance with her knotted thong;
Mortification with the shirt of hair,
Wan cheek, and knees indúrated with prayer,
Vigils, and fastings rigorous as long;
If cloistered Avarice scruple not to wrong
The pious, humble, useful Secular,
And rob the people of his daily care,
Scorning that world whose blindness makes her strong?
Inversion strange! that, unto One who lives

10   For self, and struggles with himself alone,
The amplest share of heavenly favour gives;
That to a Monk allots, both in the esteem
Of God and man, place higher than to him
Who on the good of others builds his own!

XX Monastic voluptuousness

Yet more, – round many a Convent's blazing fire
Unhallowed threads of revelry are spun;
There Venus sits disguisèd like a Nun, –
While Bacchus, clothed in semblance of a Friar,
Pours out his choicest beverage high and higher
Sparkling, until it cannot choose but run
Over the bowl, whose silver lip hath won
An instant kiss of masterful desire –
To stay the precious waste. Through every brain
10   The domination of the sprightly juice
Spreads high conceits to madding Fancy dear,
Till the arched roof, with resolute abuse
Of its grave echoes, swells a choral strain,
Whose votive burden is – 'OUR KINGDOM'S HERE!'

XXI Dissolution of the monasteries

Threats come which no submission may assuage,
No sacrifice avert, no power dispute;
The tapers shall be quenched, the belfries mute,
And, 'mid their choirs unroofed by selfish rage,
The warbling wren shall find a leafy cage;
The gadding bramble hang her purple fruit;
And the green lizard and the gilded newt
Lead unmolested lives, and die of age.
The owl of evening and the woodland fox
10   For their abode the shrines of Waltham choose:
Proud Glastonbury can no more refuse
To stoop her head before these desperate shocks –
She whose high pomp displaced, as story tells,
Arimathean Joseph's wattled cells.

XXII *The same subject*

The lovely Nun (submissive, but more meek
Through saintly habit than from effort due
To unrelenting mandates that pursue
With equal wrath the steps of strong and weak)
Goes forth – unveiling timidly a cheek
Suffused with blushes of celestial hue,
While through the Convent's gate to open view
Softly she glides, another home to seek.
Not Iris, issuing from her cloudy shrine,
An Apparition more divinely bright!
Not more attractive to the dazzled sight
Those watery glories, on the stormy brine
Poured forth, while summer suns at distance shine,
And the green vales lie hushed in sober light!

XXIII *Continued*

Yet many a Novice of the cloistral shade,
And many chained by vows, with eager glee
The warrant hail, exulting to be free;
Like ships before whose keels, full long embayed
In polar ice, propitious winds have made
Unlooked-for outlet to an open sea,
Their liquid world, for bold discovery,
In all her quarters temptingly displayed!
Hope guides the young; but when the old must pass
The threshold, whither shall they turn to find
The hospitality – the alms (alas!
Alms may be needed) which that House bestowed?
Can they, in faith and worship, train the mind
To keep this new and questionable road?

XXIV *Saints*

Ye, too, must fly before a chasing hand,
Angels and Saints, in every hamlet mourned!
Ah! if the old idolatry be spurned,
Let not your radiant Shapes desert the Land:

Her adoration was not your demand,
The fond heart proffered it – the servile heart;
And therefore are ye summoned to depart,
Michael, and thou, St George, whose flaming brand
The Dragon quelled; and valiant Margaret
10 Whose rival sword a like Opponent slew:
And rapt Cecilia, seraph-haunted Queen
Of harmony; and weeping Magdalene,
Who in the penitential desert met
Gales sweet as those that over Eden blew!

XXV The virgin

Mother! whose virgin bosom was uncrost
With the least shade of thought to sin allied;
Woman! above all women glorified,
Our tainted nature's solitary boast;
Purer than foam on central ocean tost;
Brighter than eastern skies at daybreak strewn
With fancied roses, than the unblemished moon
Before her wane begins on heaven's blue coast;
Thy Image falls to earth. Yet some, I ween,
10 Not unforgiven the suppliant knee might bend,
As to a visible Power, in which did blend
All that was mixed and reconciled in Thee
Of mother's love with maiden purity,
Of high with low, celestial with terrene!

XXVI Apology

Not utterly unworthy to endure
Was the supremacy of crafty Rome;
Age after age to the arch of Christendom
Aërial keystone haughtily secure;
Supremacy from Heaven transmitted pure,
As many hold; and, therefore, to the tomb
Pass, some through fire – and by the scaffold some –
Like saintly Fisher, and unbending More.
'Lightly for both the bosom's lord did sit

10 Upon his throne;' unsoftened, undismayed
By aught that mingled with the tragic scene
Of pity or fear; and More's gay genius played
With the inoffensive sword of native wit,
Than the bare axe more luminous and keen.

XXVII Imaginative regrets

Deep is the lamentation! Not alone
From Sages justly honoured by mankind;
But from the ghostly tenants of the wind,
Demons and Spirits, many a dolorous groan
Issues for that dominion overthrown:
Proud Tiber grieves, and far-off Ganges, blind
As his own worshippers: and Nile, reclined
Upon his monstrous urn, the farewell moan
Renews. Through every forest, cave, and den,
10 Where frauds were hatched of old, hath sorrow past –
Hangs o'er the Arabian Prophet's native Waste,
Where once his airy helpers schemed and planned
'Mid spectral lakes bemocking thirsty men,
And stalking pillars built of fiery sand.

XXVIII Reflections

Grant, that by this unsparing hurricane
Green leaves with yellow mixed are torn away,
And goodly fruitage with the mother-spray;
'Twere madness – wished we, therefore, to detain,
With hands stretched forth in mollified disdain,
The 'trumpery' that ascends in bare display –
Bulls, pardons, relics, cowls black, white, and grey –
Upwhirled, and flying o'er the ethereal plain
Fast bound for Limbo Lake. And yet not choice
10 But habit rules the unreflecting herd,
And airy bonds are hardest to disown;
Hence, with the spiritual sovereignty transferred
Unto itself, the Crown assumes a voice
Of reckless mastery, hitherto unknown.

XXIX Translation of the Bible

But, to outweigh all harm, the sacred Book,
In dusty sequestration wrapt too long,
Assumes the accents of our native tongue;
And he who guides the plough, or wields the crook,
With understanding spirit now may look
Upon her records, listen to her song,
And sift her laws – much wondering that the wrong,
Which Faith has suffered, Heaven could calmly brook.
Transcendent Boon! noblest that earthly King
10   Ever bestowed to equalize and bless
Under the weight of mortal wretchedness!
But passions spread like plagues, and thousands wild
With bigotry shall tread the Offering
Beneath their feet, detested and defiled.

XXX The point at issue

For what contend the wise? – for nothing less
Than that the Soul, freed from the bonds of Sense,
And to her God restored by evidence
Of things not seen, drawn forth from their recess,
Root there, and not in forms, her holiness; –
For Faith, which to the Patriarchs did dispense
Sure guidance, ere a ceremonial fence
Was needful round men thirsting to transgress; –
For Faith, more perfect still, with which the Lord
10   Of all, Himself a Spirit, in the youth
Of Christian aspiration, deigned to fill
The temples of their hearts who, with His word
Informed, were resolute to do His will,
And worship Him in spirit and in truth.

XXXI Edward VI

'Sweet is the holiness of Youth' – so felt
Time-honoured Chaucer speaking through that Lay
By which the Prioress beguiled the way,
And many a Pilgrim's rugged heart did melt.

Hadst thou, loved Bard! whose spirit often dwelt
In the clear land of vision, but foreseen
King, child, and seraph, blended in the mien
Of pious Edward kneeling as he knelt
In meek and simple infancy, what joy
10   For universal Christendom had thrilled
Thy heart! what hopes inspired thy genius, skilled
(O great Precursor, genuine morning Star)
The lucid shafts of reason to employ,
Piercing the Papal darkness from afar!

XXXII Edward signing the warrant for the execution of Joan of Kent

The tears of man in various measure gush
From various sources; gently overflow
From blissful transport some – from clefts of woe
Some with ungovernable impulse rush;
And some, coëval with the earliest blush
Of infant passion, scarcely dare to show
Their pearly lustre – coming but to go;
And some break forth when others' sorrows crush
The sympathizing heart. Nor these, nor yet
10   The noblest drops to admiration known,
To gratitude, to injuries forgiven –
Claim Heaven's regard like waters that have wet
The innocent eyes of youthful Monarchs driven
To pen the mandates, nature doth disown.

XXXIII Revival of Popery

The saintly Youth has ceased to rule, discrowned
By unrelenting Death. O People keen
For change, to whom the new looks always green!
Rejoicing did they cast upon the ground
Their Gods of wood and stone; and, at the sound
Of counter-proclamation, now are seen,
(Proud triumph is it for a sullen Queen!)
Lifting them up, the worship to confound
Of the Most High. Again do they invoke

10 The Creature, to the Creature glory give;
Again with frankincense the altars smoke
Like those the Heathen served; and mass is sung;
And prayer, man's rational prerogative,
Runs through blind channels of an unknown tongue.

XXXIV Latimer and Ridley

How fast the Marian death-list is unrolled!
See Latimer and Ridley in the might
Of Faith stand coupled for a common flight!
One (like those prophets whom God sent of old)
Transfigured, from this kindling hath foretold
A torch of inextinguishable light;
The Other gains a confidence as bold;
And thus they foil their enemy's despite.
The penal instruments, the shows of crime,
10 Are glorified while this once-mitred pair
Of saintly Friends the 'murderer's chain partake,
Corded, and burning at the social stake:'
Earth never witnessed object more sublime
In constancy, in fellowship more fair!

XXXV Cranmer

Outstretching flame-ward his upbraided hand
(O God of mercy, may no earthly Seat
Of judgement such presumptuous doom repeat!)
Amid the shuddering throng doth Cranmer stand;
Firm as the stake to which with iron band
His frame is tied; firm from the naked feet
To the bare head. The victory is complete;
The shrouded Body to the Soul's command
Answers with more than Indian fortitude,
10 Through all her nerves with finer sense endued,
Till breath departs in blissful aspiration:
Then, 'mid the ghastly ruins of the fire,
Behold the unalterable heart entire,
Emblem of faith untouched, miraculous attestation!

XXXVI *General view of the troubles of the Reformation*

Aid, glorious Martyrs, from your fields of light,
Our mortal ken! Inspire a perfect trust
(While we look round) that Heaven's decrees are just:
Which few can hold committed to a fight
That shows, even on its better side, the might
Of proud Self-will, Rapacity, and Lust,
'Mid clouds enveloped of polemic dust,
Which showers of blood seem rather to incite
Than to allay. Anathemas are hurled
From both sides; veteran thunders (the brute test
Of truth) are met by fulminations new –
Tartarean flags are caught at, and unfurled –
Friends strike at friends – the flying shall pursue –
And Victory sickens, ignorant where to rest!

XXXVII *English reformers in exile*

Scattering, like birds escaped the fowler's net,
Some seek with timely flight a foreign strand;
Most happy, re-assembled in a land
By dauntless Luther freed, could they forget
Their Country's woes. But scarcely have they met,
Partners in faith, and brothers in distress,
Free to pour forth their common thankfulness,
Ere hope declines: – their union is beset
With speculative notions rashly sown,
Whence thickly-sprouting growth of poisonous weeds;
Their forms are broken staves; their passions, steeds
That master them. How enviably blest
Is he who can, by help of grace, enthrone
The peace of God within his single breast!

XXXVIII *Elizabeth*

Hail, Virgin Queen! o'er many an envious bar
Triumphant, snatched from many a treacherous wile!
All hail, sage Lady, whom a grateful Isle
Hath blest, respiring from that dismal war

Stilled by thy voice! But quickly from afar
Defiance breathes with more malignant aim;
And alien storms with home-bred ferments claim
Portentous fellowship. Her silver car,
By sleepless prudence ruled, glides slowly on;
10 Unhurt by violence, from menaced taint
Emerging pure, and seemingly more bright:
Ah! wherefore yields it to a foul constraint
Black as the clouds its beams dispersed, while shone,
By men and angels blest, the glorious light?

XXXIX *Eminent reformers*

Methinks that I could trip o'er heaviest soil,
Light as a buoyant bark from wave to wave,
Were mine the trusty staff that JEWEL gave
To youthful HOOKER, in familiar style
The gift exalting, and with playful smile:
For thus equipped, and bearing on his head
The Donor's farewell blessing, can he dread
Tempest, or length of way, or weight of toil? –
More sweet than odours caught by him who sails
10 Near spicy shores of Araby the blest,
A thousand times more exquisitely sweet,
The freight of holy feeling which we meet,
In thoughtful moments, wafted by the gales
From fields where good men walk, or bowers wherein
    they rest.

XL *The same*

Holy and heavenly Spirits as they are,
Spotless in life, and eloquent as wise,
With what entire affection do they prize
Their Church reformed! labouring with earnest care
To baffle all that may her strength impair;
That Church, the unperverted Gospel's seat;
In their afflictions a divine retreat;
Source of their liveliest hope, and tenderest prayer! –
The truth exploring with an equal mind,

10   In doctrine and communion they have sought
Firmly between the two extremes to steer;
But theirs the wise man's ordinary lot,
To trace right courses for the stubborn blind,
And prophesy to ears that will not hear.

XLI Distractions

Men, who have ceased to reverence, soon defy
Their forefathers; lo! sects are formed, and split
With morbid restlessness: – the ecstatic fit
Spreads wide; though special mysteries multiply,
The Saints must govern is their common cry;
And so they labour, deeming Holy Writ
Disgraced by aught that seems content to sit
Beneath the roof of settled Modesty.
The Romanist exults; fresh hope he draws
10   From the confusion, craftily incites
The overweening, personates the mad –
To heap disgust upon the worthier Cause:
Totters the Throne; the new-born Church is sad,
For every wave against her peace unites.

XLII Gunpowder Plot

Fear hath a hundred eyes that all agree
To plague her beating heart; and there is one
(Nor idlest that!) which holds communion
With things that were not, yet were *meant* to be.
Aghast within its gloomy cavity
That eye (which sees as if fulfilled and done
Crimes that might stop the motion of the sun)
Beholds the horrible catastrophe
Of an assembled Senate unredeemed
10   From subterraneous Treason's darkling power:
Merciless act of sorrow infinite!
Worse than the product of that dismal night,
When gushing, copious as a thunder-shower,
The blood of Huguenots through Paris streamed.

XLIII Illustration
The Jung-Frau and the fall of the Rhine near Schaffhausen

The Virgin-Mountain, wearing like a Queen
A brilliant crown of everlasting snow,
Sheds ruin from her sides; and men below
Wonder that aught of aspect so serene
Can link with desolation. Smooth and green,
And seeming, at a little distance, slow,
The waters of the Rhine; but on they go
Fretting and whitening, keener and more keen;
Till madness seizes on the whole wide Flood,
10   Turned to a fearful Thing whose nostrils breathe
Blasts of tempestuous smoke – wherewith he tries
To hide himself, but only magnifies;
And doth in more conspicuous torment writhe,
Deafening the region in his ireful mood.

XLIV Troubles of Charles the First

Even such the contrast that, where'er we move,
To the mind's eye Religion doth present;
Now with her own deep quietness content;
Then, like the mountain, thundering from above
Against the ancient pine-trees of the grove
And the Land's humblest comforts. Now her mood
Recalls the transformation of the flood,
Whose rage the gentle skies in vain reprove,
Earth cannot check. O terrible excess
10   Of headstrong will! Can this be Piety?
No – some fierce Maniac hath usurped her name;
And scourges England struggling to be free:
Her peace destroyed! her hopes a wilderness!
Her blessings cursed – her glory turned to shame!

XLV Laud

Prejudged by foes determined not to spare,
An old weak Man for vengeance thrown aside,
Laud, 'in the painful art of dying' tried,

(Like a poor bird entangled in a snare
Whose heart still flutters, though his wings forbear
To stir in useless struggle) hath relied
On hope that conscious innocence supplied,
And in his prison breathes celestial air.
Why tarries then thy chariot? Wherefore stay,
10   O Death! the ensanguined yet triumphant wheels,
Which thou prepar'st, full often, to convey
(What time a State with madding faction reels)
The Saint or Patriot to the world that heals
All wounds, all perturbations doth allay?

XLVI *Afflictions of England*

Harp! couldst thou venture, on thy boldest string,
The faintest note to echo which the blast
Caught from the hand of Moses as it passed
O'er Sinai's top, or from the Shepherd-king,
Early awake, by Siloa's brook, to sing
Of dread Jehovah; then, should wood and waste
Hear also of that name, and mercy cast
Off to the mountains, like a covering
Of which the Lord was weary. Weep, oh! weep,
10   Weep with the good, beholding King and Priest
Despised by that stern God to whom they raise
Their suppliant hands; but holy is the feast
He keepeth; like the firmament his ways:
His statutes like the chambers of the deep.

PART III
FROM THE RESTORATION TO THE PRESENT TIMES

I

I saw the figure of a lovely Maid
Seated alone beneath a darksome tree,
Whose fondly-overhanging canopy
Set off her brightness with a pleasing shade.
No Spirit was she; *that* my heart betrayed,
For she was one I loved exceedingly;

But while I gazed in tender reverie
(Or was it sleep that with my Fancy played?)
The bright corporeal presence – form and face –
10 Remaining still distinct grew thin and rare,
Like sunny mist; – at length the golden hair,
Shape, limbs, and heavenly features, keeping pace
Each with the other in a lingering race
Of dissolution, melted into air.

II Patriotic sympathies

Last night, without a voice, that Vision spake
Fear to my Soul, and sadness which might seem
Wholly dissevered from our present theme;
Yet, my belovèd Country! I partake
Of kindred agitations for thy sake;
Thou, too, dost visit oft my midnight dream;
Thy glory meets me with the earliest beam
Of light, which tells that Morning is awake.
If aught impair thy beauty or destroy,
10 Or but forbode destruction, I deplore
With filial love the sad vicissitude;
If thou hast fallen, and righteous Heaven restore
The prostrate, then my spring-time is renewed,
And sorrow bartered for exceeding joy.

III Charles the Second

Who comes – with rapture greeted, and caressed
With frantic love – his kingdom to regain?
Him Virtue's Nurse, Adversity, in vain
Received, and fostered in her iron breast:
For all she taught of hardiest and of best,
Or would have taught, by discipline of pain
And long privation, now dissolves amain,
Or is remembered only to give zest
To wantonness. – Away, Circean revels!
10 But for what gain? if England soon must sink
Into a gulf which all distinction levels –
That bigotry may swallow the good name,

And, with that draught, the life-blood: misery, shame,
By Poets loathed; from which Historians shrink!

IV Latitudinarianism

Yet Truth is keenly sought for, and the wind
Charged with rich words poured out in thought's
   defence;
Whether the Church inspire that eloquence,
Or a Platonic Piety confined
To the sole temple of the inward mind;
And One there is who builds immortal lays,
Though doomed to tread in solitary ways,
Darkness before and danger's voice behind;
Yet not alone, nor helpless to repel
10 Sad thoughts; for from above the starry sphere
Come secrets, whispered nightly to his ear;
And the pure spirit of celestial light
Shines through his soul – 'that he may see and tell
Of things invisible to mortal sight.'

V Walton's Book of Lives

There are no colours in the fairest sky
So fair as these. The feather, whence the pen
Was shaped that traced the lives of these good men,
Dropped from an Angel's wing. With moistened eye
We read of faith and purest charity
In Statesman, Priest, and humble Citizen:
Oh could we copy their mild virtues, then
What joy to live, what blessedness to die!
Methinks their very names shine still and bright;
10 Apart – like glow-worms on a summer night;
Or lonely tapers when from far they fling
A guiding ray; or seen – like stars on high,
Satellites burning in a lucid ring
Around meek Walton's heavenly memory.

VI Clerical integrity

Nor shall the eternal roll of praise reject
Those Unconforming; whom one rigorous day

Drives from their Cures, a voluntary prey
To poverty, and grief, and disrespect,
And some to want – as if by tempests wrecked
On a wild coast; how destitute! did They
Feel not that Conscience never can betray,
That peace of mind is Virtue's sure effect.
Their altars they forego, their homes they quit,
Fields which they love, and paths they daily trod,
And cast the future upon Providence;
As men the dictate of whose inward sense
Outweighs the world; whom self-deceiving wit
Lures not from what they deem the cause of God.

VII Persecution of the Scottish covenanters

When Alpine Vales threw forth a suppliant cry,
The majesty of England interposed
And the sword stopped; the bleeding wounds were
  closed;
And Faith preserved her ancient purity.
How little boots that precedent of good,
Scorned or forgotten, Thou canst testify,
For England's shame, O Sister Realm! from wood,
Mountain, and moor, and crowded street, where lie
The headless martyrs of the Covenant,
Slain by Compatriot-protestants that draw
From councils senseless as intolerant
Their warrant. Bodies fall by wild sword-law;
But who would force the Soul, tilts with a straw
Against a Champion cased in adamant.

VIII Acquittal of the bishops

A voice, from long-expecting thousands sent,
Shatters the air, and troubles tower and spire;
For Justice hath absolved the innocent,
And Tyranny is balked of her desire:
Up, down, the busy Thames – rapid as fire
Coursing a train of gunpowder – it went,
And transport finds in every street a vent,

Till the whole City rings like one vast choir.
The Fathers urge the People to be still,
10 With outstretched hands and earnest speech – in vain!
Yea, many, haply wont to entertain
Small reverence for the mitre's offices,
And to Religion's self no friendly will,
A Prelate's blessing ask on bended knees.

IX William the Third

Calm as an under-current, strong to draw
Millions of waves into itself, and run,
From sea to sea, impervious to the sun
And ploughing storm, the spirit of Nassau
Swerves not, (how blest if by religious awe
Swayed, and thereby enabled to contend
With the wide world's commotions) from its end
Swerves not – diverted by a casual law.
Had mortal action e'er a nobler scope?
10 The Hero comes to liberate, not defy;
And, while he marches on with stedfast hope,
Conqueror beloved! expected anxiously!
The vacillating Bondman of the Pope
Shrinks from the verdict of his stedfast eye.

X Obligations of civil to religious liberty

Ungrateful Country, if thou e'er forget
The sons who for thy civil rights have bled!
How, like a Roman, Sidney bowed his head,
And Russell's milder blood the scaffold wet;
But these had fallen for profitless regret
Had not thy holy Church her champions bred,
And claims from other worlds inspirited
The star of Liberty to rise. Nor yet
(Grave this within thy heart!) if spiritual things
10 Be lost, through apathy, or scorn, or fear,
Shalt thou thy humbler franchises support,
However hardly won or justly dear:

What came from heaven to heaven by nature clings,
And, if dissevered thence, its course is short.

XI *Sacheverel*

A sudden conflict rises from the swell
Of a proud slavery met by tenets strained
In Liberty's behalf. Fears, true or feigned,
Spread through all ranks; and lo! the Sentinel
Who loudest rang his pulpit 'larum bell,
Stands at the Bar, absolved by female eyes
Mingling their glances with grave flatteries
Lavished on *Him* – that England may rebel
Against her ancient virtue. HIGH and LOW,
10 Watchwords of Party, on all tongues are rife;
As if a Church, though sprung from heaven, must owe
To opposites and fierce extremes her life, –
Not to the golden mean, and quiet flow
Of truths that soften hatred, temper strife.

XII

Down a swift Stream, thus far, a bold design
Have we pursued, with livelier stir of heart
Than his who sees, borne forward by the Rhine,
The living landscapes greet him, and depart;
Sees spires fast sinking – up again to start!
And strives the towers to number, that recline
O'er the dark steeps, or on the horizon line
Striding with shattered crests his eye athwart.
So have we hurried on with troubled pleasure:
10 Henceforth, as on the bosom of a stream
That slackens, and spreads wide a watery gleam,
We, nothing loth a lingering course to measure,
May gather up our thoughts, and mark at leisure
How widely spread the interests of our theme.

XIII *Aspects of Christianity in America i. – The Pilgrim Fathers*

Well worthy to be magnified are they
Who, with sad hearts, of friends and country took

A last farewell, their loved abodes forsook,
And hallowed ground in which their fathers lay;
Then to the new-found World explored their way,
That so a Church, unforced, uncalled to brook
Ritual restraints, within some sheltering nook
Her Lord might worship and his word obey
In freedom. Men they were who could not bend;
10 Blest Pilgrims, surely, as they took for guide
A will by sovereign Conscience sanctified;
Blest while their Spirits from the woods ascend
Along a Galaxy that knows no end,
But in His glory who for Sinners died.

XIV ii. Continued

From Rite and Ordinance abused they fled
To Wilds where both were utterly unknown;
But not to them had Providence foreshown
What benefits are missed, what evils bred,
In worship neither raised nor limited
Save by Self-will. Lo! from that distant shore,
For Rite and Ordinance, Piety is led
Back to the Land those Pilgrims left of yore,
Led by her own free choice. So Truth and Love
10 By Conscience governed do their steps retrace. –
Fathers! your Virtues, such the power of grace,
Their spirit, in your Children, thus approve.
Transcendent over time, unbound by place,
Concord and Charity in circles move.

XV iii. concluded – American episcopacy

Patriots informed with Apostolic light
Were they who, when their Country had been freed,
Bowing with reverence to the ancient creed,
Fixed on the frame of England's Church their sight,
And strove in filial love to reunite
What force had severed. Thence they fetched the seed
Of Christian unity, and won a meed
Of praise from Heaven. To Thee, O saintly WHITE,

Patriarch of a wide-spreading family,
10 Remotest lands and unborn times shall turn,
Whether they would restore or build – to Thee,
As one who rightly taught how zeal should burn,
As one who drew from out Faith's holiest urn
The purest stream of patient Energy.

XVI

Bishops and Priests, blessèd are ye, if deep
(As yours above all offices is high)
Deep in your hearts the sense of duty lie;
Charged as ye are by Christ to feed and keep
From wolves your portion of His chosen sheep:
Labouring as ever in your Master's sight,
Making your hardest task your best delight,
What perfect glory ye in Heaven shall reap! –
But, in the solemn Office which ye sought
10 And undertook premonished, if unsound
Your practice prove, faithless though but in thought,
Bishops and Priests, think what a gulf profound
Awaits you then, if they were rightly taught
Who framed the Ordinance by your lives disowned!

XVII Places of worship

As star that shines dependent upon star
Is to the sky while we look up in love;
As to the deep fair ships which though they move
Seem fixed, to eyes that watch them from afar;
As to the sandy desert fountains are,
With palm-groves shaded at wide intervals,
Whose fruit around the sun-burnt Native falls
Of roving tired or desultory war –
Such to this British Isle her Christian Fanes,
10 Each linked to each for kindred services;
Her Spires, her Steeple-towers with glittering vanes
Far-kenned, her Chapels lurking among trees,
Where a few villagers on bended knees
Find solace which a busy world disdains.

XVIII Pastoral character

A genial hearth, a hospitable board,
And a refined rusticity, belong
To the neat mansion, where, his flock among,
The learned Pastor dwells, their watchful Lord.
Though meek and patient as a sheathèd sword;
Though pride's least lurking thought appear a wrong
To human kind; though peace be on his tongue,
Gentleness in his heart – can earth afford
Such genuine state, pre-eminence so free,
10 As when, arrayed in Christ's authority,
He from the pulpit lifts his awful hand;
Conjures, implores, and labours all he can
For re-subjecting to divine command
The stubborn spirit of rebellious man?

XIX The Liturgy

Yes, if the intensities of hope and fear
Attract us still, and passionate exercise
Of lofty thoughts, the way before us lies
Distinct with signs, through which in set career,
As through a zodiac, moves the ritual year
Of England's Church; stupendous mysteries!
Which whoso travels in her bosom, eyes
As he approaches them, with solemn cheer.
Upon that circle traced from sacred story
10 We only dare to cast a transient glance,
Trusting in hope that Others may advance
With mind intent upon the King of Glory,
From his mild advent till his countenance
Shall dissipate the seas and mountains hoary.

XX Baptism

Dear be the Church that, watching o'er the needs
Of Infancy, provides a timely shower
Whose virtue changes to a Christian Flower
A Growth from sinful Nature's bed of weeds! –

Fitliest beneath the sacred roof proceeds
The ministration; while parental Love
Looks on, and Grace descendeth from above
As the high service pledges now, now pleads.
There, should vain thoughts outspread their wings and fly
10 To meet the coming hours of festal mirth,
The tombs – which hear and answer that brief cry,
The Infant's notice of his second birth –
Recall the wandering Soul to sympathy
With what man hopes from Heaven, yet fears from Earth.

XXI Sponsors

Father! to God himself we cannot give
A holier name! then lightly do not bear
Both names conjoined, but of thy spiritual care
Be duly mindful: still more sensitive
Do Thou, in truth a second Mother, strive
Against disheartening custom, that by Thee
Watched, and with love and pious industry
Tended at need, the adopted Plant may thrive
For everlasting bloom. Benign and pure
10 This Ordinance, whether loss it would supply,
Prevent omission, help deficiency,
Or seek to make assurance doubly sure.
Shame if the consecrated Vow be found
An idle form, the Word an empty sound!

XXII Catechizing

From Little down to Least, in due degree,
Around the Pastor, each in new-wrought vest,
Each with a vernal posy at his breast,
We stood, a trembling, earnest Company!
With low soft murmur, like a distant bee,
Some spake, by thought-perplexing fears betrayed;
And some a bold unerring answer made:
How fluttered then thy anxious heart for me,
Belovèd Mother! Thou whose happy hand

10   Had bound the flowers I wore, with faithful tie:
Sweet flowers! at whose inaudible command
Her countenance, phantom-like, doth reappear:
O lost too early for the frequent tear,
And ill requited by this heartfelt sigh!

XXIII Confirmation

The Young-ones gathered in from hill and dale,
With holiday delight on every brow:
'Tis past away; far other thoughts prevail;
For they are taking the baptismal Vow
Upon their conscious selves; their own lips speak
The solemn promise. Strongest sinews fail,
And many a blooming, many a lovely, cheek
Under the holy fear of God turns pale;
While on each head His lawn-robed servant lays
10   An apostolic hand, and with prayer seals
The Covenant. The Omnipotent will raise
Their feeble Souls; and bear with *his* regrets,
Who, looking round the fair assemblage, feels
That ere the Sun goes down their childhood sets.

XXIV Confirmation continued

I saw a Mother's eye intensely bent
Upon a Maiden trembling as she knelt;
In and for whom the pious Mother felt
Things that we judge of by a light too faint:
Tell, if ye may, some star-crowned Muse, or Saint!
Tell what rushed in, from what she was relieved –
Then, when her Child the hallowing touch received,
And such vibration through the Mother went
That tears burst forth amain. Did gleams appear?
10   Opened a vision of that blissful place
Where dwells a Sister-child? And was power given
Part of her lost One's glory back to trace
Even to this Rite? For thus *She* knelt, and, ere
The summer-leaf had faded, passed to Heaven.

XXV Sacrament

By chain yet stronger must the Soul be tied:
One duty more, last stage of this ascent,
Brings to thy food, mysterious Sacrament!
The Offspring, haply at the Parent's side;
But not till They, with all that do abide
In Heaven, have lifted up their hearts to laud
And magnify the glorious name of God,
Fountain of Grace, whose Son for sinners died.
Ye, who have duly weighed the summons, pause
10 No longer; ye, whom to the saving rite
The Altar calls; come early under laws
That can secure for you a path of light
Through gloomiest shade; put on (nor dread its weight)
Armour divine, and conquer in your cause!

XXVI The Marriage ceremony

The Vested Priest before the Altar stands;
Approach, come gladly, ye prepared, in sight
Of God and chosen friends, your troth to plight
With the symbolic ring, and willing hands
Solemnly joined. Now sanctify the bands
O Father! – to the Espoused Thy blessing give,
That mutually assisted they may live
Obedient, as here taught, to Thy commands.
So prays the Church, to consecrate a Vow
10 'The which would endless matrimony make;'
Union that shadows forth and doth partake
A mystery potent human love to endow
With heavenly, each more prized for the other's sake;
Weep not, meek Bride! uplift thy timid brow.

XXVII Thanksgiving after childbirth

Woman! the Power who left His throne on high,
And deigned to wear the robe of flesh we wear,
The Power that through the straits of Infancy
Did pass dependent on maternal care,

His own humanity with Thee will share,
Pleased with the thanks that in His People's eye
Thou offerest up for safe Delivery
From Childbirth's perilous throes. And should the Heir
Of thy fond hopes hereafter walk inclined
10 To courses fit to make a mother rue
That ever he was born, a glance of mind
Cast upon this observance may renew
A better will; and, in the imagined view
Of thee thus kneeling, safety he may find.

XXVIII Visitation of the sick

The Sabbath bells renew the inviting peal;
Glad music! yet there be that, worn with pain
And sickness, listen where they long have lain,
In sadness listen. With maternal zeal
Inspired, the Church sends ministers to kneel
Beside the afflicted; to sustain with prayer,
And soothe the heart confession hath laid bare –
That pardon, from God's throne, may set its seal
On a true Penitent. When breath departs
10 From one disburdened so, so comforted,
His Spirit Angels greet; and ours be hope
That, if the Sufferer rise from his sick-bed,
Hence he will gain a firmer mind, to cope
With a bad world, and foil the Tempter's arts.

XXIX The Commination Service

Shun not this rite, neglected, yea abhorred,
By some of unreflecting mind, as calling
Man to curse man, (thought monstrous and appalling).
Go thou and hear the threatenings of the *Lord*;
Listening within His Temple see His sword
Unsheathed in wrath to strike the offender's head,
Thy own, if sorrow for thy sin be dead,
Guilt unrepented, pardon unimplored.
Two aspects bears Truth needful for salvation;

10 Who knows not *that?* – yet would this delicate age
Look only on the Gospel's brighter page:
Let light and dark duly our thoughts employ;
So shall the fearful words of Commination
Yield timely fruit of peace and love and joy.

XXX *Forms of prayer at sea*

To kneeling Worshippers no earthly floor
Gives holier invitation than the deck
Of a storm-shattered Vessel saved from Wreck
(When all that Man could do availed no more)
By Him who raised the Tempest and restrains:
Happy the crew who this have felt, and pour
Forth for His mercy, as the Church ordains,
Solemn thanksgiving. Nor will *they* implore
In vain who, for a rightful cause, give breath
10 To words the Church prescribes aiding the lip
For the heart's sake, ere ship with hostile ship
Encounters, armed for work of pain and death.
Suppliants! the God to whom your cause ye trust
Will listen, and ye know that He is just.

XXXI *Funeral service*

From the Baptismal hour, through weal and woe,
The Church extends her care to thought and deed;
Nor quits the Body when the Soul is freed,
The mortal weight cast off to be laid low.
Blest Rite for him who hears in faith, 'I know
That my Redeemer liveth,' – hears each word
That follows – striking on some kindred chord
Deep in the thankful heart; – yet tears will flow.
Man is as grass that springeth up at morn,
10 Grows green, and is cut down and withereth
Ere nightfall – truth that well may claim a sigh,
Its natural echo; but hope comes reborn
At Jesu's bidding. We rejoice, 'O Death,
Where is thy Sting? – O Grave, where is thy Victory?'

XXXII Rural ceremony

Closing the sacred Book which long has fed
Our meditations, give we to a day
Of annual joy one tributary lay;
This day, when, forth by rustic music led,
The village Children, while the sky is red
With evening lights, advance in long array
Through the still churchyard, each with garland gay,
That, carried sceptre-like, o'ertops the head
Of the proud Bearer. To the wide church-door,
Charged with these offerings which their fathers bore
For decoration in the Papal time,
The innocent Procession softly moves:—
The spirit of Laud is pleased in heaven's pure clime,
And Hooker's voice the spectacle approves!

XXXIII Regrets

Would that our scrupulous Sires had dared to leave
Less scanty measure of those graceful rites
And usages, whose due return invites
A stir of mind too natural to deceive;
Giving to Memory help when she would weave
A crown for Hope! – I dread the boasted lights
That all too often are but fiery blights,
Killing the bud o'er which in vain we grieve.
Go, seek, when Christmas snows discomfort bring,
The counter Spirit found in some gay church
Green with fresh holly, every pew a perch
In which the linnet or the thrush might sing,
Merry and loud and safe from prying search,
Strains offered only to the genial Spring.

XXXIV Mutability

From low to high doth dissolution climb,
And sink from high to low, along a scale
Of awful notes, whose concord shall not fail;
A musical but melancholy chime,

Which they can hear who meddle not with crime,
Nor avarice, nor over-anxious care.
Truth fails not; but her outward forms that bear
The longest date do melt like frosty rime,
That in the morning whitened hill and plain
10 And is no more; drop like the tower sublime
Of yesterday, which royally did wear
His crown of weeds, but could not even sustain
Some casual shout that broke the silent air,
Or the unimaginable touch of Time.

XXXV Old abbeys

Monastic Domes! following my downward way,
Untouched by due regret I marked your fall!
Now, ruin, beauty, ancient stillness, all
Dispose to judgements temperate as we lay
On our past selves in life's declining day:
For as, by discipline of Time made wise,
We learn to tolerate the infirmities
And faults of others – gently as he may,
So with our own the mild Instructor deals,
10 Teaching us to forget them or forgive.
Perversely curious, then, for hidden ill
Why should we break Time's charitable seals?
Once ye were holy, ye are holy still;
Your spirit freely let me drink, and live.

XXXVI Emigrant French clergy

Even while I speak, the sacred roofs of France
Are shattered into dust; and self-exiled
From altars threatened, levelled, or defiled,
Wander the Ministers of God, as chance
Opens a way for life, or consonance
Of faith invites. More welcome to no land
The fugitives than to the British strand,
Where priest and layman with the vigilance
Of true compassion greet them. Creed and test

10   Vanish before the unreserved embrace
Of catholic humanity: – distrest
They came, – and, while the moral tempest roars
Throughout the Country they have left, our shores
Give to their Faith a fearless resting-place.

XXXVII Congratulation

Thus all things lead to Charity, secured
By THEM who blessed the soft and happy gale
That landward urged the great Deliverer's sail,
Till in the sunny bay his fleet was moored!
Propitious hour! had we, like them, endured
Sore stress of apprehension, with a mind
–Sickened by injuries, dreading worse designed,
From month to month trembling and unassured,
How had we then rejoiced! But we have felt,
10   As a loved substance, their futurity:
Good, which they dared not hope for, we have seen;
A State whose generous will through earth is dealt;
A State – which, balancing herself between
Licence and slavish order, dares be free.

XXXVIII New churches

But liberty, and triumphs on the Main,
And laurelled armies, not to be withstood –
What serve they? if, on transitory good
Intent, and sedulous of abject gain,
The State (ah, surely not preserved in vain!)
Forbear to shape due channels which the Flood
Of sacred truth may enter – till it brood
O'er the wide realm, as o'er the Egyptian plain
The all-sustaining Nile. No more – the time
10   Is conscious of her want; through England's bounds,
In rival haste, the wished-for Temples rise!
I hear their sabbath bells' harmonious chime
Float on the breeze – the heavenliest of all sounds
That vale or hill prolongs or multiplies!

XXXIX Church to be erected

Be this the chosen site; the virgin sod,
Moistened from age to age by dewy eve,
Shall disappear, and grateful earth receive
The corner-stone from hands that build to God.
Yon reverend hawthorns, hardened to the rod
Of winter storms, yet budding cheerfully;
Those forest oaks of Druid memory,
Shall long survive, to shelter the Abode
Of genuine Faith. Where, haply, 'mid this band
10 Of daisies, shepherds sate of yore and wove
May-garlands, there let the holy altar stand
For kneeling adoration; – while – above,
Broods, visibly portrayed, the mystic Dove,
That shall protect from blasphemy the Land.

XL Continued

Mine ear has rung, my spirit sunk subdued,
Sharing the strong emotion of the crowd,
When each pale brow to dread hosannas bowed
While clouds of incense mounting veiled the rood,
That glimmered like a pine-tree dimly viewed
Through Alpine vapours. Such appalling rite
Our Church prepares not, trusting to the might
Of simple truth with grace divine imbued;
Yet will we not conceal the precious Cross,
10 Like men ashamed: the Sun with his first smile
Shall greet that symbol crowning the low Pile:
And the fresh air of incense-breathing morn
Shall wooingly embrace it; and green moss
Creep round its arms through centuries unborn.

XLI New church-yard

The encircling ground, in native turf arrayed,
Is now by solemn consecration given
To social interests, and to favouring Heaven;
And where the rugged colts their gambols played,

And wild deer bounded through the forest glade,
Unchecked as when by merry Outlaw driven,
Shall hymns of praise resound at morn and even;
And soon, full soon, the lonely Sexton's spade
Shall wound the tender sod. Encincture small,
10 But infinite its grasp of weal and woe!
Hopes, fears, in never-ending ebb and flow; –
The spousal trembling, and the 'dust to dust,'
The prayers, the contrite struggle, and the trust
That to the Almighty Father looks through all.

XLII Cathedrals, etc.

Open your gates, ye everlasting Piles!
Types of the spiritual Church which God hath reared;
Not loth we quit the newly-hallowed sward
And humble altar, 'mid your sumptuous aisles
To kneel, or thrid your intricate defiles,
Or down the nave to pace in motion slow;
Watching, with upward eye, the tall tower grow
And mount, at every step, with living wiles
Instinct – to rouse the heart and lead the will
10 By a bright ladder to the world above.
Open your gates, ye Monuments of love
Divine! thou Lincoln, on thy sovereign hill!
Thou, stately York! and Ye, whose splendours cheer
Isis and Cam, to patient Science dear!

XLIII Inside of King's College Chapel, Cambridge

Tax not the royal Saint with vain expense,
With ill-matched aims the Architect who planned –
Albeit labouring for a scanty band
Of white-robed Scholars only – this immense
And glorious Work of fine intelligence!
Give all thou canst; high Heaven rejects the lore
Of nicely-calculated less or more;
So deemed the man who fashioned for the sense
These lofty pillars, spread that branching roof

10 Self-poised, and scooped into ten thousand cells,
Where light and shade repose, where music dwells
Lingering – and wandering on as loth to die;
Like thoughts whose very sweetness yieldeth proof
That they were born for immortality.

XLIV The same

What awful pérspective! while from our sight
With gradual stealth the lateral windows hide
Their Portraitures, their stone-work glimmers, dyed
In the soft chequerings of a sleepy light.
Martyr, or King, or sainted Eremite,
Whoe'er ye be, that thus, yourselves unseen,
Imbue your prison-bars with solemn sheen,
Shine on, until ye fade with coming Night! –
But, from the arms of silence – list! O list!
10 The music bursteth into second life;
The notes luxuriate, every stone is kissed
By sound, or ghost of sound, in mazy strife;
Heart-thrilling strains, that cast, before the eye
Of the devout, a veil of ecstasy!

XLV Continued

They dreamt not of a perishable home
Who thus could build. Be mine, in hours of fear
Or grovelling thought, to seek a refuge here;
Or through the aisles of Westminster to roam;
Where bubbles burst, and folly's dancing foam
Melts, if it cross the threshold; where the wreath
Of awe-struck wisdom droops: or let my path
Lead to that younger Pile, whose sky-like dome
Hath typified by reach of daring art
10 Infinity's embrace; whose guardian crest,
The silent Cross, among the stars shall spread
As now, when She hath also seen her breast
Filled with mementos, satiate with its part
Of grateful England's overflowing Dead.

XLVI Ejaculation

Glory to God! and to the Power who came
In filial duty, clothed with love divine,
That made His human tabernacle shine
Like Ocean burning with purpureal flame;
Or like the Alpine Mount, that takes its name
From roseate hues, far kenned at morn and even,
In hours of peace, or when the storm is driven
Along the nether region's rugged frame!
Earth prompts – Heaven urges; let us seek the light,
10   Studious of that pure intercourse begun
When first our infant brows their lustre won;
So, like the Mountain, may we grow more bright
From unimpeded commerce with the Sun,
At the approach of all-involving night.

XLVII Conclusion

Why sleeps the future, as a snake enrolled,
Coil within coil, at noon-tide? For the WORD
Yields, if with unpresumptuous faith explored,
Power at whose touch the sluggard shall unfold
His drowsy rings. Look forth! – that Stream behold,
THAT STREAM upon whose bosom we have passed
Floating at ease while nations have effaced
Nations, and Death has gathered to his fold
Long lines of mighty Kings – look forth, my Soul!
10   (Nor in this vision be thou slow to trust)
The living Waters, less and less by guilt
Stained and polluted, brighten as they roll,
Till they have reached the eternal City – built
For the perfécted Spirits of the just!

To Enterprise

Keep for the Young the impassioned smile
Shed from thy countenance, as I see thee stand
High on that chalky cliff of Britain's Isle,
A slender volume grasping in thy hand –
(Perchance the pages that relate
The various turns of Crusoe's fate) –
Ah, spare the exulting smile,
And drop thy pointing finger bright
As the first flash of beacon light;
10 But neither veil thy head in shadows dim,
Nor turn thy face away
From One who, in the evening of his day,
To thee would offer no presumptuous hymn!

I
Bold Spirit! who art free to rove
Among the starry courts of Jove,
And oft in splendour dost appear
Embodied to poetic eyes,
While traversing this nether sphere,
Where Mortals call thee ENTERPRISE.
20 Daughter of Hope! her favourite Child,
Whom she to young Ambition bore,
When hunter's arrow first defiled
The grove, and stained the turf with gore;
Thee wingèd Fancy took, and nursed
On broad Euphrates' palmy shore,
And where the mightier Waters burst
From caves of Indian mountains hoar!
She wrapped thee in a panther's skin;
And Thou, thy favourite food to win,
30 The flame-eyed eagle oft wouldst scare
From her rock-fortress in mid air
With infant shout; and often sweep,
Paired with the ostrich, o'er the plain;

Or, tired with sport, wouldst sink asleep
Upon the couchant lion's mane!
With rolling years thy strength increased;
And, far beyond thy native East,
To thee, by varying titles known
As variously thy power was shown,
40   Did incense-bearing altars rise,
Which caught the blaze of sacrifice,
From suppliants panting for the skies!

II

What though this ancient Earth be trod
No more by step of Demi-god
Mounting from glorious deed to deed
As thou from clime to clime didst lead;
Yet still, the bosom beating high,
And the hushed farewell of an eye
Where no procrastinating gaze
50   A last infirmity betrays,
Prove that thy heaven-descended sway
Shall ne'er submit to cold decay.
By thy divinity impelled,
The Stripling seeks the tented field;
The aspiring Virgin kneels; and, pale
With awe, receives the hallowed veil,
A soft and tender Heroine
Vowed to severer discipline;
Inflamed by thee, the blooming Boy
60   Makes of the whistling shrouds a toy,
And of the ocean's dismal breast
A play-ground, – or a couch of rest;
'Mid the blank world of snow and ice,
Thou to his dangers dost enchain
The Chamois-chaser awed in vain
By chasm or dizzy precipice;
And hast Thou not with triumph seen
How soaring Mortals glide between
Or through the clouds, and brave the light

70 With bolder than Icarian flight?
How they, in bells of crystal, dive –
Where winds and waters cease to strive –
For no unholy visitings,
Among the monsters of the Deep;
And all the sad and precious things
Which there in ghastly silence sleep?
Or, adverse tides and currents headed,
And breathless calms no longer dreaded,
In never-slackening voyage go
80 Straight as an arrow from the bow;
And, slighting sails and scorning oars,
Keep faith with Time on distant shores?
– Within our fearless reach are placed
The secrets of the burning Waste;
Egyptian tombs unlock their dead,
Nile trembles at his fountain-head;
Thou speak'st – and lo! the polar Seas
Unbosom their last mysteries.
– But oh! what transports, what sublime reward,
90 Won from the world of mind, dost thou prepare
For philosophic Sage; or high-souled Bard
Who, for thy service trained in lonely woods,
Hath fed on pageants floating through the air,
Or calentured in depth of limpid floods;
Nor grieves – though doomed through silent night to bear
The domination of his glorious themes,
Or struggle in the net-work of thy dreams!

III
If there be movements in the Patriot's soul,
From source still deeper, and of higher worth,
100 'Tis thine the quickening impulse to control,
And in due season send the mandate forth;
Thy call a prostrate Nation can restore,
When but a single Mind resolves to crouch no more.

IV

Dread Minister of wrath!
Who to their destined punishment dost urge
The Pharaohs of the earth, the men of hardened heart!
Not unassisted by the flattering stars,
Thou strew'st temptation o'er the path
When they in pomp depart
110 With trampling horses and refulgent cars –
Soon to be swallowed by the briny surge;
Or cast, for lingering death, on unknown strands;
Or caught amid a whirl of desert sands –
An Army now, and now a living hill
That a brief while heaves with convulsive throes –
Then all is still;
Or, to forget their madness and their woes,
Wrapt in a winding-sheet of spotless snows!

V

Back flows the willing current of my Song:
120 If to provoke such doom the Impious dare,
Why should it daunt a blameless prayer?
– Bold Goddess! range our Youth among;
Nor let thy genuine impulse fail to beat
In hearts no longer young;
Still may a veteran Few have pride
In thoughts whose sternness makes them sweet;
In fixed resolves by Reason justified;
That to their object cleave like sleet
Whitening a pine tree's northern side,
130 When fields are naked far and wide,
And withered leaves, from earth's cold breast
Up-caught in whirlwinds, nowhere can find rest.

VI

But if such homage thou disdain
As doth with mellowing years agree,
One rarely absent from thy train
More humble favours may obtain

For thy contented Votary.
She, who incites the frolic lambs
In presence of their heedless dams,
140 And to the solitary fawn
Vouchsafes her lessons, bounteous Nymph
That wakes the breeze, the sparkling lymph
Doth hurry to the lawn;
She, who inspires that strain of joyance holy
Which the sweet Bird, misnamed the melancholy,
Pours forth in shady groves, shall plead for me;
And vernal mornings opening bright
With views of undefined delight,
And cheerful songs, and suns that shine
150 On busy days, with thankful nights, be mine.

VII
But thou, O Goddess! in thy favourite Isle
(Freedom's impregnable redoubt,
The wide earth's storehouse fenced about
With breakers roaring to the gales
That stretch a thousand thousand sails)
Quicken the slothful, and exalt the vile! –
Thy impulse is the life of Fame;
Glad Hope would almost cease to be
If torn from thy society;
160 And Love, when worthiest of his name,
Is proud to walk the earth with Thee!

Decay of Piety

Oft have I seen, ere Time had ploughed my cheek,
Matrons and Sires – who, punctual to the call
Of their loved Church, on fast or festival
Through the long year the House of Prayer would seek:
By Christmas snows, by visitation bleak
Of Easter winds, unscared, from hut or hall
They came to lowly bench or sculptured stall,

But with one fervour of devotion meek.
I see the places where they once were known,
10 And ask, surrounded even by kneeling crowds,
Is ancient Piety for ever flown?
Alas! even then they seemed like fleecy clouds
That, struggling through the western sky, have won
Their pensive light from a departed sun!

*(*Epitaph* [*In Grasmere Church*])

These vales were saddened with no common gloom
When good Jemima perished in her bloom;
When (such the awful will of heaven) she died
By flames breathed on her from her own fireside.
On Earth we dimly see, and but in part
We know, yet Faith sustains the sorrowing heart;
And she, the pure, the patient and the meek,
Might have fit epitaph could feelings speak;
If words could tell and monuments record
10 How treasures lost are inwardly deplored,
No name by Grief's fond eloquence adorned
More than Jemima's would be praised and mourned.
The tender virtues of her blameless life,
Bright in the Daughter, brighter in the Wife,
And in the cheerful Mother brightest shone, –
That light hath past away – the will of God be done.

To Rotha Q—

Rotha, my Spiritual Child! this head was grey
When at the sacred font for thee I stood;
Pledged till thou reach the verge of womanhood,
And shalt become thy own sufficient stay:
Too late, I feel, sweet Orphan! was the day
For stedfast hope the contract to fulfil;
Yet shall my blessing hover o'er thee still,

Embodied in the music of this Lay,
Breathed forth beside the peaceful mountain Stream
10 Whose murmur soothed thy languid Mother's ear
After her throes, this Stream of name more dear
Since thou dost bear it, – a memorial theme
For others; for thy future self, a spell
To summon fancies out of Time's dark cell.

'By Moscow self-devoted to a blaze'

By Moscow self-devoted to a blaze
Of dreadful sacrifice; by Russian blood
Lavished in fight with desperate hardihood;
The unfeeling Elements no claim shall raise
To rob our Human-nature of just praise
For what she did and suffered. Pledges sure
Of a deliverance absolute and pure
She gave, if Faith might tread the beaten ways
Of Providence. But now did the Most High
10 Exalt His still small voice; – to quell that Host
Gathered His power, a manifest ally;
He, whose heaped waves confounded the proud boast
Of Pharaoh, said to Famine, Snow, and Frost,
'Finish the strife by deadliest victory!'

To the Lady Fleming on Seeing the Foundation Preparing for the Erection of Rydal Chapel, Westmoreland

I
Blest is this Isle – our native Land;
Where battlement and moated gate
Are objects only for the hand
Of hoary Time to decorate;
Where shady hamlet, town that breathes
Its busy smoke in social wreaths,

No rampart's stern defence require,
Naught but the heaven-directed spire,
And steeple tower (with pealing bells
10 Far-heard) – our only citadels.

II
O Lady! from a noble line
Of chieftains sprung, who stoutly bore
The spear, yet gave to works divine
A bounteous help in days of yore,
(As records mouldering in the Dell
Of Nightshade haply yet may tell;)
Thee kindred aspirations moved
To build, within a vale beloved,
For Him upon whose high behests
20 All peace depends, all safety rests.

III
How fondly will the woods embrace
This daughter of thy pious care,
Lifting her front with modest grace
To make a fair recess more fair;
And to exalt the passing hour;
Or soothe it with a healing power
Drawn from the Sacrifice fulfilled,
Before this rugged soil was tilled,
Or human habitation rose
30 To interrupt the deep repose!

IV
Well may the villagers rejoice!
Nor heat, nor cold, nor weary ways,
Will be a hindrance to the voice
That would unite in prayer and praise;
More duly shall wild wandering Youth
Receive the curb of sacred truth,
Shall tottering Age, bent earthward, hear
The Promise, with uplifted ear;

And all shall welcome the new ray
40 Imparted to their sabbath-day.

V

Nor deem the Poet's hope misplaced,
His fancy cheated – that can see
A shade upon the future cast,
Of time's pathetic sanctity;
Can hear the monitory clock
Sound o'er the lake with gentle shock
At evening, when the ground beneath
Is ruffled o'er with cells of death;
Where happy generations lie,
50 Here tutored for eternity.

VI

Lives there a man whose sole delights
Are trivial pomp and city noise,
Hardening a heart that loathes or slights
What every natural heart enjoys?
Who never caught a noon-tide dream
From murmur of a running stream;
Could strip, for aught the prospect yields
To him, their verdure from the fields;
And take the radiance from the clouds
60 In which the sun his setting shrouds.

VII

A soul so pitiably forlorn,
If such do on this earth abide,
May season apathy with scorn,
May turn indifference to pride;
And still be not unblest – compared
With him who grovels, self-debarred
From all that lies within the scope
Of holy faith and Christian hope;
Or, shipwrecked, kindles on the coast
70 False fires, that others may be lost.

VIII

Alas! that such perverted zeal
Should spread on Britain's favoured ground!
That public order, private weal,
Should e'er have felt or feared a wound
From champions of the desperate law
Which from their own blind hearts they draw;
Who tempt their reason to deny
God, whom their passions dare defy,
And boast that they alone are free
80 Who reach this dire extremity!

IX

But turn we from these 'bold bad' men;
The way, mild Lady! that hath led
Down to their 'dark opprobrious den,'
Is all too rough for Thee to tread.
Softly as morning vapours glide
Down Rydal-cove from Fairfield's side,
Should move the tenor of *his* song
Who means to charity no wrong;
Whose offering gladly would accord
90 With this day's work, in thought and word.

X

Heaven prosper it! may peace, and love,
And hope, and consolation, fall,
Through its meek influence, from above,
And penetrate the hearts of all;
All who, around the hallowed Fane,
Shall sojourn in this fair domain;
Grateful to Thee, while service pure,
And ancient ordinance, shall endure,
For opportunity bestowed
100 To kneel together, and adore their God!

On the Same Occasion [*On Seeing the Foundation Preparing for the Erection of Rydal Chapel*]

Oh! gather whencesoe'er ye safely may
The help which slackening Piety requires;
Nor deem that he perforce must go astray
Who treads upon the footmarks of his sires.

Our churches, invariably perhaps, stand east and west, but *why* is by few persons *exactly* known; nor that the degree of deviation from *due* east often noticeable in the ancient ones was determined, in each particular case, by the point in the horizon at which the sun rose upon the day of the saint to whom the church was dedicated. These observances of our ancestors, and the causes of them, are the subject of the following stanzas.

When in the antique age of bow and spear
And feudal rapine clothed with iron mail,
Came ministers of peace, intent to rear
The Mother Church in yon sequestered vale;

Then, to her Patron Saint a previous rite
Resounded with deep swell and solemn close,
Through unremitting vigils of the night,
Till from his couch the wished-for Sun uprose.

He rose, and straight – as by divine command,
They, who had waited for that sign to trace
Their work's foundation, gave with careful hand
To the high altar its determined place;

Mindful of Him who in the Orient born
There lived, and on the cross His life resigned,
And who, from out the regions of the morn,
Issuing in pomp, shall come to judge mankind.

So taught *their* creed; – nor failed the eastern sky,
'Mid these more awful feelings, to infuse

The sweet and natural hopes that shall not die,
20 Long as the sun his gladsome course renews.

For us hath such prelusive vigil ceased;
Yet still we plant, like men of elder days,
Our Christian altar faithful to the east,
Whence the tall window drinks the morning rays;

That obvious emblem giving to the eye
Of meek devotion, which erewhile it gave,
That symbol of the day-spring from on high,
Triumphant o'er the darkness of the grave.

[*Translation of Virgil's Aeneid*]

ADVERTISEMENT

It is proper to premise that the first Couplet of this Translation
is adopted from Pitt; – as are likewise two Couplets in the
second Book; and three or four lines, in different parts, are
taken from Dryden. A few expressions will also be found, which,
following the Original closely, are the same as the preceding
Translators have unavoidably employed.

FIRST BOOK

Arms, and the Man I sing, the first who bore
His course to Latium from the Trojan shore,
A Fugitive of Fate: – long time was He
By Powers celestial tossed on land and sea,
Through wrathful Juno's far-famed enmity;
Much, too, from war endured; till new abodes
He planted, and in Latium fixed his Gods;
Whence flowed the Latin People; whence have come
The Alban Sires, and Walls of lofty Rome.

10   Say, Muse, what Powers were wronged, what grievance
           drove
To such extremity the Spouse of Jove,
Labouring to wrap in perils, to astound
With woes, a Man for piety renowned!
In heavenly breasts is such resentment found?

Right opposite the Italian Coast there stood
An ancient City, far from Tiber's flood,
Carthage its name; a Colony of Tyre,
Rich, strong, and bent on war with fierce desire.
No region, not even Samos, was so graced
20　By Juno's favour; here her Arms were placed,
Here lodged her Chariot; and unbounded scope,
Even then, the Goddess gave to partial hope;
Her aim (if Fate such triumph will allow)
That to this Nation all the world shall bow.
But Fame had told her that a Race, from Troy
Derived, the Tyrian ramparts would destroy;
That from this stock a People, proud in war,
And trained to spread dominion wide and far,
Should come, and through her favourite Lybian State
30　Spread utter ruin; – such the doom of Fate.
In fear of this, while busy thought recalls
The war she raised against the Trojan Walls
For her loved Argos (and, with these combined,
Worked other causes rankling in her mind,
The judgement given by Paris, and the slight
Her beauty had received on Ida's height,
The undying hatred which the Race had bred,
And honours given to ravished Ganymed),
Saturnian Juno far from Latium chased
40　The Trojans, tossed upon the watery waste;
Unhappy relics of the Grecian spear
And of the dire Achilles! Many a year
They roamed ere Fate's decision was fulfilled,
Such arduous toil it was the Roman State to build.

Sicilian headlands scarcely out of sight,
They spread the canvas with a fresh delight;
Then Juno, brooding o'er the eternal wound,
Thus inly; – 'Must I vanquished quit the ground
Of my attempt? Or impotently toil
50　To bar the Trojans from the Italian soil?
For the Fates thwart me; – yet could Pallas raise

'Mid Argive vessels a destructive blaze,
And in the Deep plunge all, for fault of one,
The desperate frenzy of Oïleus' Son;
She from the clouds the bolt of Jove might cast,
And ships and sea deliver to the blast!
Him, flames ejecting from a bosom fraught
With sulphurous fire, she in a whirlwind caught,
And on a sharp rock fixed; – but I who move
60 Heaven's Queen, the Sister and the Wife of Jove,
Wage with one Race the war I waged of yore!
Who then, henceforth, will Juno's name adore?
Her altars grace with gifts, her aid implore?'

These things revolved in fiery discontent,
Her course the Goddess to Aeolia bent,
Country of lowering clouds, where South-winds rave;
There Aeolus, within a spacious cave
With sovereign power controuls the struggling Winds,
And the sonorous Storms in durance binds.
70 Loud, loud the mountain murmurs as they wreak
Their scorn upon the barriers. On a peak
High-seated, Aeolus his sceptre sways,
Soothes their fierce temper, and their wrath allays.
This did he not, – sea, earth, and heaven's vast deep
Would follow them, entangled in the sweep;
But in black caves the Sire Omnipotent
The winds sequestered, fearing such event;
Heaped over them vast mountains, and assigned
A Monarch, that should rule the blustering kind;
80 By stedfast laws their violence restrain,
And give, on due command, a loosened rein.
As she approached, thus spake the suppliant Queen:
'Aeolus! (for the Sire of Gods and men
On thee confers the power to tranquillize
The troubled waves, or summon them to rise)
A Race, my Foes, bears o'er the troubled Sea
Troy and her conquered Gods to Italy.
Throw power into the winds; the ships submerge,

Or part, – and give their bodies to the surge.
90 Twice seven fair Nymphs await on my command,
All beautiful; – the fairest of the Band,
Deïopeia, such desert to crown,
Will I, by stedfast wedlock, make thine own;
In everlasting fellowship with thee
To dwell, and yield a beauteous progeny.'

    To this the God: 'O Queen, declare thy will
And be it mine the mandate to fulfill.
To thee I owe my sceptre, and the place
Jove's favour hath assigned me; through thy grace
100 I at the banquets of the Gods recline;
And my whole empire is a gift of thine.'

    When Aeolus had ceased, his spear he bent
Full on the quarter where the winds were pent,
And smote the mountain. – Forth, where way was made,
Rush his wild Ministers; the land pervade,
And fasten on the Deep. There Eurus, there
Notus, and Africus unused to spare
His tempests, work with congregated power,
To upturn the abyss, and roll the unwieldy waves ashore.
110 Clamour of Men ensues, and crash of shrouds,
Heaven and the day by instantaneous clouds
Are ravished from the Trojans; on the floods
Black night descends, and, palpably, there broods.
The thundering Poles incessantly unsheath
Their fires, and all things threaten instant death.

    Appalled, and with slack limbs Aeneas stands;
He groans, and heavenward lifting his clasped hands,
Exclaims: 'Thrice happy they who chanced to fall
In front of lofty Ilium's sacred Wall,
120 Their parents witnessing their end; – Oh why,
Bravest of Greeks, Tydides, could not I
Pour out my willing spirit through a wound

From thy right hand received, on Trojan ground?
Where Hector lies, subjected to the spear
Of the invincible Achilles; where
The great Sarpedon sleeps; and o'er the plain
Soft Simois whirls helmet, and shield, and men,
Throngs of the Brave in fearless combat slain!'

  While thus he spake, the Aquilonian gale
130 Smote from the front upon his driving Sail,
And heaved the thwarted billows to the sky,
Round the Ship labouring in extremity.
Help from her shattered oars in vain she craves;
Then veers the prow, exposing to the waves
Her side; and lo! a surge, to mountain height
Gathering, prepares to burst with its whole weight.
Those hang aloft, as if in air: to these
Earth is disclosed between the boiling seas
Whirled on by Notus, three encounter shocks
140 In the main sea, received from latent rocks;
Rocks stretched in dorsal ridge of rugged frame
On the Deep's surface; ALTARS is the name
By which the Italians mark them. Three the force
Of Eurus hurries from an open course
On straits and Shallows, dashes on the strand,
And girds the wreck about with heaps of sand.
Another, in which Lyeus and his Mate,
Faithful Orontes, share a common fate,
As his own eyes full plainly can discern,
150 By a huge wave is swept from prow to stern;
Headlong the Pilot falls; thrice whirled around,
The Ship is buried in the gulph profound.
Amid the boundless eddy a lost Few,
Drowning, or drowned, emerge to casual view;
On waves which planks, and arms, and Trojan wealth
  bestrew.
Over the strong-ribbed pinnace, in which sails
Ilioneus, the Hurricane prevails;
Now conquers Abas, then the Ships that hold

Valiant Achates, and Alethes old;
160 The joints all loosening in their sides, they drink
The hostile brine through many a greedy chink.

Meanwhile, what strife disturbed the roaring sea,
And for what outrages the storm was free,
Troubling the Ocean to its inmost caves,
Neptune perceived incensed; and o'er the waves
Forth-looking with a stedfast brow and eye
Raised from the Deep in placid majesty,
He saw the Trojan Galleys scattered wide,
The men they bore oppressed and terrified;
170 Waters and ruinous Heaven against their peace allied.
Nor from the Brother was concealed the heat
Of Juno's anger, and each dark deceit.
Eurus he called, and Zephyrus, – and the Pair,
Who at his bidding quit the fields of air,
He thus addressed; 'Upon your Birth and Kind
Have ye presumed with confidence so blind
As, heedless of my Godhead, to perplex
The Land with uproar, and the Sea to vex;
Which by your act, O winds! thus fiercely heaves?
180 Whom I – but better calm the troubled waves.
Henceforth, atonement shall not prove so slight
For such a trespass; to your King take flight,
And say that not to *Him*, but unto *Me*,
Fate hath assigned this watery sovereignty;
Mine is the Trident – his a rocky Hold,
Thy mansion, Eurus! – vaunting uncontrolled,
Let Aeolus there occupy his hall,
And in that prison-house the winds enthrall!'

He spake; and, quicker than the word, his will
190 Felt through the sea abates each tumid hill,
Quiets the deep, and silences the shores,
And to a cloudless heaven the sun restores.
Cymothoe shoves, with leaning Triton's aid,
The stranded Ships – or Neptune from their bed

With his own Trident lifts them; – then divides
The sluggish heaps of sand – and gently glides,
Skimming, on light smooth wheels, the level tides.
Thus oft, when a sedition hath ensued,
Arousing all the ignoble multitude,
200 Straight through the air do stones and torches fly,
With every missile frenzy can supply;
Then, if a venerable Man step forth,
Strong through acknowledged piety and worth,
Hushed at the sight into mute peace, all stand
Listening, with eyes and ears at his command;
Their minds to him are subject; and the rage
That burns within their breasts his lenient words assuage.
So fell the Sea's whole tumult, overawed
Then, when the Sire, casting his eyes abroad,
210 Turns under open Heaven his docile Steeds,
And with his flowing Chariot smoothly speeds.

The worn-out Trojans, seeking land where'er
The nearest coast invites, for Lybia steer.
There is a Bay whose deep retirement hides
The place where Nature's self a Port provides,
Framed by a friendly island's jutting sides,
Bulwark from which the billows of the Main
Recoil upon themselves, spending their force in vain.
Vast rocks are here; and, safe beneath the brows
220 Of two heaven-threatening Cliffs, the Floods repose.
Glancing aloft in bright theatric show
Woods wave, and gloomily impend below;
Right opposite this pomp of sylvan shade,
Wild crags and lowering rocks a cave have made;
Within, sweet waters gush; and all bestrown
Is the cool floor with seats of living stone;
Cell of the Nymphs, no chains, no anchors, here
Bind the tired vessels, floating without fear;
Led by Aeneas, in this shelter meet
230 Seven ships, the scanty relics of his Fleet;
The Crews, athirst with longings for the land,

Here disembark, and range the wished-for strand;
Or on the sunny shore their limbs recline,
Heavy with dropping ooze, and drenched with brine.
Achates, from a smitten flint, receives
The spark upon a bed of fostering leaves;
Dry fuel on the natural hearth he lays,
And speedily provokes a mounting blaze.
Then forth they bring, not utterly forlorn,
240   The needful implements, and injured corn,
Bruise it with stones, and by the aid of fire
Prepare the nutriment their frames require.

Meanwhile Aeneas mounts a cliff, to gain
An unobstructed prospect of the Main;
Happy if thence his wistful eyes may mark
The harassed Antheus, or some Phrygian Bark,
Or Capys, or the guardian Sign descry
Which, at the stern, Caïcus bears on high.
No Sail appears in sight, nor toiling oar;
250   Only he spies three Stags upon the shore;
Behind, whole herds are following where these lead,
And in long order through the valleys feed.
He stops – and, with the bow, he seized the store
Of swift-winged arrows which Achates bore;
And first the Leaders to his shafts have bowed
Their heads elate with branching horns; the Crowd
Are stricken next; and all the affrighted Drove
Fly in confusion to the leafy grove.
Nor from the weapons doth his hand refrain, ⎫
260   Till Seven, a Stag for every Ship, are slain, ⎬
And with their bulky bodies press the plain. ⎭
Thence to the port he hies, divides the spoil;
And deals out wine, which on Trinacria's soil,
Acestes stored for his departing Guest;
Then with these words he soothes each sorrowing breast.

'O Friends, not unacquainted with your share
Of misery, ere doomed these ills to bear!

O ye, whom worse afflictions could not bend!
Jove also hath for *these* prepared an end.
270 The voices of dread Scylla ye have heard,
Her belt of rabid mouths your prows have neared;
Ye shunned with peril the Cyclopian den,
Cast off your fears, resume the hearts of men!
Hereafter, this our present lot may be
A cherished object for pleased memory.
Through strange mishaps, through hazards manifold
And various, we our course to Latium hold;
There, Fate a settled habitation shows; –
There, Trojan empire (this, too, Fate allows)
280 Shall be revived. Endure; with patience wait;
Yourselves reserving for a happier state!'

Aeneas thus, though sick with weight of care,
Strives, by apt words their spirits to repair;
The hope he does not feel his countenance feigns,
And deep within he smothers his own pains.
They seize the Quarry; for the feast prepare;
Part use their skill the carcase to lay bare,
Stripping from off the limbs the dappled hide;
And Part the palpitating flesh divide;
290 The portions some expose to naked fire,
Some steep in cauldrons where the flames aspire.
Not wanting utensils, they spread the board;
And soon their wasted vigour is restored;
While o'er green turf diffused, in genial mood
They quaff the mellow wine, nor spare the forest food.
All hunger thus appeased, they ask in thought
For friends, with long discourses, vainly sought:
Hope, fear, and doubt contend if yet they live, ⎫
Or have endured the last; nor can receive   ⎬
300 The obsequies a duteous voice might give.   ⎭
Apart, for Lycas mourns the pious Chief;
For Amycus is touched with silent grief;
For Gyas, for Cloanthes; and the Crew
That with Orontes perished in his view.

So finished their repast, while on the crown
Of Heaven stood Jupiter; whence looking down,
He traced the sea where winged vessels glide,
Saw Lands, and shores, the Nations scattered wide;
And, lastly, from that all-commanding Height,
310 He viewed the Lybian realms with stedfast sight.
To him, revolving mortal hopes and fears,
Venus (her shining eyes suffused with tears)
Thus, sorrowing, spake: 'O Sire! who rul'st the way
Of Men and Gods with thy eternal sway,
And aw'st with thunder, what offence, unfit
For pardon, could my much-loved Son commit –
The Trojans what – thine anger to awake?
That, after such dire loss, they for the sake
Of Italy see all the world denied
320 To their tired hopes, and nowhere may abide!
For, that the Romans hence should draw their birth
As years roll round, even hence, and govern earth
With power supreme, from Teucer's Line restored
Such was (O Father, why this change?) thy word.
From this, when Troy had perished, for my grief
(Fates balancing with fates) I found relief;
Like fortune follows: – when shall thy decree
Close, mighty King, this long adversity?
– Antenor, from amid the Grecian hosts
330 Escaped, could thrid Illyria's sinuous coasts;
Pierce the Lyburnian realms; o'erclimb the Fountain
Of loud Timarus, whence the murmuring Mountain
A nine-mouthed channel to the torrent yields,
That rolls its headlong sea, a terror to the fields.
Yet to his Paduan seats he safely came;
A City built, whose People bear his name;
There hung his Trojan Arms, where now he knows
The consummation of entire repose.
But *we*, thy progeny, allowed to boast
340 Of future Heaven – betrayed, – our Navy lost –
Through wrath of One, are driven far from the Italian
     coast.

Is piety thus honoured? Doth thy grace
Thus in our hands the allotted sceptre place?'

  On whom the Sire of Gods and human Kind
Half-smiling, turned the look that stills the wind
And clears the heavens; then, touching with light kiss
His Daughter's lip, he speaks:
                           'Thy griefs dismiss:
And, Cytherea, these forebodings spare;
No wavering fates deceive the objects of thy care,
350   Lavinian Walls full surely wilt thou see,
The promised City; and, upborne by thee,
Magnanimous Aeneas yet shall range
The starry heavens; nor doth my purpose change.
He (since thy soul is troubled I will raise
Things from their depths, and open Fate's dark ways)
Shall wage dread wars in Italy, abate
Fierce Nations, build a Town and rear a State;
Till three revolving summers have beheld
His Latian kingdom, the Rutulians quelled.
360   But young Ascanius (Ilus heretofore,
Name which he held till Ilium was no more,
Now called Iülus) while the months repeat
Their course, and thirty annual orbs complete,
Shall reign, and quit Lavinium to preside
O'er Alba-longa, sternly fortified.
Here, under Chiefs of this Hectorian Race,
Three hundred years shall empire hold her place,
Ere Ilia, royal Priestess, gives to earth
From the embrace of Mars, a double birth.
370   Then Romulus, the elder, proudly drest
In tawny wolf-skin, his memorial vest,
Mavortian Walls, his Father's Seat, shall frame,
And from himself, the People Romans name.
To these I give dominion that shall climb
Unchecked by space, uncircumscribed by time;
An empire without end. Even Juno, driven
To agitate with fear earth, sea and heaven,

With better mind shall for the past atone:
Prepared with me to cherish as her own ⎫
380 The Romans, lords o'er earth, the Nation of the Gown. ⎬
So 'tis decreed. As circling times roll on ⎭
Phthia shall fall, Mycenae shall be won;
Descendants of Assaracus shall reign
O'er Argos subject to the Victor's chain.
From a fair Stem shall Trojan Caesar rise;
Ocean may terminate his power; – the skies
Can be the only limit of his fame;
A Julius he, inheriting the name
From great Iülus. Fearless shalt thou greet
390 The Ruler, when to his celestial Seat
He shall ascend, spoil-laden from the East;
He, too, a God to be with vows addressed.
Then shall a rugged Age, full long defiled
With cruel wars, grow placable and mild;
Then hoary Faith, and Vesta, shall delight ⎫
To speak their laws, Quirinus shall unite ⎬
With his twin Brother to uphold the right. ⎭
Fast shall be closed the iron-bolted Gates
Upon whose dreadful issues Janus waits
400 Within, on high-piled Arms, and from behind
With countless links of brazen chains confined
Shall Fury sit, breathing unholy threats
From his ensanguined mouth that impotently frets.'

This uttered, Maia's Son he sends from high
To embolden Tyrian hospitality;
Lest haply Dido, ignorant of fate,
Should chase the Wanderers from her rising State.
He through the azure region works the oars
Of his swift wings, and lights on Lybian Shores.
410 Prompt is he there his mission to fulfil;
The Tyrians soften, yielding to Jove's will; –
And, above all, their Queen receives a mind
Fearless of harm, and to the Trojans kind.

Aeneas, much revolving through the night,
Rose with the earliest break of friendly light;
Resolved to certify by instant quest
Who ruled the uncultured region – man or beast.
Forthwith he hides, beneath a rocky cove,
His Fleet, o'ershadowed by the pendent grove;
420   And, brandishing two javelins, quits the Bay,
Achates sole companion of his way.
While they were journeying thus, before him stood
His Mother, met within a shady wood.
The habit of a virgin did she wear;
Her aspect suitable, her gait, and air; –
Armed like a Spartan Virgin, or of mien
Such as in Thrace Harpalyce is seen,
Urging to weariness the fiery horse,
Outstripping Hebrus in his headlong course.
430   Light o'er her shoulders had she given the bow
To hang; her tresses on the wind to flow;
– A Huntress with bare knee; – a knot upbound
The folds of that loose vest, which else had swept the
    ground.
'Ho!' she exclaimed, their words preventing, 'say
Have you not seen some Huntress here astray,
One of my Sisters, with a quiver graced;
Clothed by the spotted lynx, and o'er the waste
Pressing the foaming boar, with outcry chased?'

Thus Venus; – thus her Son forthwith replied,
440   'None of thy Sisters have we here espied,
None have we heard: – O Virgin! in pure grace
Teach me to name Thee; for no mortal face
Is thine, nor bears thy voice a human sound; –
A Goddess surely, worthy to be owned
By Phoebus as a Sister – or thy Line
Is haply of the Nymphs; O Power divine
Be thou propitious! and, whoe'er thou art,
Lighten our labour; tell us in what part
Of earth we roam, who these wild precincts trace,

450   Ignorant alike of person and of place!
      Not as intruders come we: but were tost
      By winds and waters on this savage coast.
      Vouchsafe thy answer; victims oft shall fall
      By this right hand, while on thy name we call!'

      Then Venus; – 'Offerings these which I disclaim
      The Tyrian Maids who chase the sylvan game
      Bear thus a quiver slung their necks behind,
      With purple buskins thus their ankles bind;
      Learn, Wanderers, that a Punic Realm you see.
460   Tyrians the men, Agenor's progeny;
      But Lybian deem the soil; the natives are
      Haughty and fierce, intractable in war.
      Here Dido reigns; from Tyre compelled to flee
      By an unnatural Brother's perfidy;
      Deep was the wrong; nor would it aught avail
      Should we do more than skim the doleful tale.
      Sichaeus loved her as his wedded Mate,
      The richest Lord of the Phoenician State;
      A Virgin She, when from her Father's hands
470   By love induced, she passed to nuptial bands;
      Unhappy Union! for to evil prone,
      Worst of bad men, her Brother held the throne;
      Dire fury came among them, and, made bold
      By that blind appetite, the thirst of gold,
      He, feeling not, or scorning what was due
      To a Wife's tender love, Sichaeus slew;
      Rushed on him unawares, and laid him low
      Before the Altar, with an impious blow.
      His arts concealed the crime, and gave vain scope
480   In Dido's bosom to a trembling hope.
      But in a dream appeared the unburied Man,
      Lifting a visage wondrous pale and wan;
      Urged her to instant flight, and showed the Ground
      Where hoards of ancient treasure might be found,
      Needful assistance. By the Vision swayed,
      Dido looks out for fellowship and aid.

They meet, who loathe the Tyrant, or who fear;
And, as some well-trimmed Ships were lying near,
This help they seized; and o'er the water fled
490 With all Pygmalion's wealth; – a Woman at their head.
The Exiles reached the Spot, where soon your eyes
Shall see the Turrets of New Carthage rise;
There purchased BARCA; so they named the Ground
From the bull's hide whose thongs had girt it round.
Now say – who are Ye? Whence and whither bound?'

He answered, deeply sighing, 'To their springs
Should I trace back the principles of things
For you, at leisure listening to our woes,
Vesper, mid gathering shadows to repose,
500 Might lead the day, before the Tale would close.
– From ancient Troy, if haply ye have heard
The name of Troy, through various seas we steered,
Until on Lybian Shores an adverse blast
By chance not rare our shattered vessels cast.
Aeneas am I, wheresoe'er I go
Carrying the Gods I rescued from the Foe,
When Troy was overthrown. A Man you see
Famed above Earth for acts of piety;
Italy is my wished-for resting place;
510 There doth my Country lie, among a Race
Sprung from high Jove. The Phrygian Sea I tried
With thrice ten Ships which Ida's Grove supplied,
My Goddess Mother pointing out the way,
Nor did unwilling Fates oppose their sway.
Seven, scarcely, of that number now are left
By tempests torn; – myself unknown, bereft,
And destitute, explore the Lybian Waste,
Alike from Europe and from Asia chased.'
He spake; nor haply at this point had closed
520 His mournful words: but Venus interposed.

'Whoe'er thou art, I trust, the heavenly Powers
Disown thee not, so near the Punic Towers;
But hasten to the Queen's imperial Court;

Thy Friends survive; their Shjps are safe in port,
Indebted for the shelter which they find
To altered courses of the rough North-wind;
Unless fond Parents taught my simple youth
Deceitful auguries, I announce the truth.
Behold yon twelve fair Swans, a joyous troop!
530 Them did the Bird of Jove, with threatening swoop
Rout, in mid-Heaven dispersed; but now again
Have they assembled, and in ordered train
These touch, while those look down upon, the plain,
Hovering, and wheeling round with tuneful voice.
– As in recovered union all rejoice;
So, with their Crews, thy Ships in harbour lie,
Or to some haven's mouth are drawing nigh
With every Sail full-spread; but Thou proceed;
And fear no hindrance where thy path shall lead.'

540 She spake; and, as she turned away, all bright
Appeared her neck, imbued with roseate light;
And from the exalted region of her head
Ambrosial hair a sudden fragrance shed,
Odours divinely breathing; – her Vest flowed
Down to her feet; – and gait and motion showed
The unquestionable Goddess. Whom his eyes
Had seen and whom his soul could recognize,
His filial voice pursueth as she flies.

'Why dost Thou, cruel as the rest, delude
550 Thy Son with Phantoms evermore renewed?
Why not allow me hand with hand to join,
To hear thy genuine voice, and to reply with mine?'
This chiding uttered from a troubled breast,
He to the appointed walls his steps addressed.
But Venus round him threw, as on they fare,
Impenetrable veil of misty air;
That none might see, or touch them with rude hand,
Obstruct their journey, or its cause demand.
She, borne aloft, resumes the joyful road
560 That leads to Paphos – her beloved abode:

There stands her Temple; garlands fresh and fair
Breathe round a hundred Altars hung, which there
Burn with Sabean incense, scenting all the air.

They who had measured a swift course were now
Climbing, as swift, a hill of lofty brow,
That overhangs wide compass of the Town,
And on the turrets, which it fronts, looks down.
Aeneas views the City – pile on pile
Rising – a place of sordid Huts erewhile;
570 And, as he looks, the gates, the stretching ways,
The stir, the din, increasing wonder raise.
The Tyrians work – one spirit in the whole;
These stretch the walls; these labour to uproll
Stones for the Citadel, with all their might;
These, for new Structures having marked a site,
Intrench the circuit. Some on laws debate,
Or choose a Senate for the infant State;
Some dig the haven out; some toil to place
A Theatre, on deep and solid base;
580 Some from the rock hew columns, to compose
A goodly ornament for future Shows.
– Fresh summer calls the Bees such tasks to ply
Through flowery grounds, beneath a summer sky;
When first they lead their progeny abroad,
Each fit to undertake his several load;
Or in a mass the liquid produce blend,
And with pure nectar every cell distend;
Or, fast as homeward Labourers arrive,
Receive the freight they bring; or mustering, drive
590 The Drones, a sluggard people, from the hive.
Glows the vast work; while thyme-clad hills and plains
Scent the pure honey that rewards their pains.
'Oh fortunate!' the Chief, Aeneas, cries
As on the aspiring Town he casts his eyes,
'Fortunate Ye, whose walls are free to rise!'
Then, strange to tell! with mist around him thrown,
In crowds he mingles, yet is seen by none.

Within the Town, a central Grove displayed
Its ample texture of delightful shade.
600   The storm-vexed Tyrians, newly-landed, found
A hopeful sign while digging there the ground;
The head of a fierce horse from earth they drew,
By Juno's self presented to their view;
Presage of martial fame, and hardy toil
Bestowed through ages on a generous soil.
Sidonian Dido here a Structure high
Raised to the tutelary Deity,
Rich with the Offerings through the Temple poured,
And bright with Juno's Image, there adored.
610   High rose, with steps, the brazen Porch; the Beams
With brass were fastened; and metallic gleams
Flashed from the valves of brazen doors, forth-sent
While on resounding hinges to and fro they went.
Within this Grove Aeneas first beheld
A novel sight, by which his fears were quelled;
Here first gave way to hope, so long withstood,
And looked through present ill to future good.
For while, expectant of the Queen, the stores
Of that far-spreading Temple he explores;
620   Admires the strife of labour; nor forbears
To ponder o'er the lot of noble cares
Which the young City for herself prepares;
He meets the Wars of Ilium; every Fight,
In due succession, offered to his sight.
There he beholds Atrides, Priam here,
And that stern Chief who was to both severe.
He stopped; and, not without a sigh, exclaimed:
'By whom, Achates! hath not Troy been named?
What region of the earth but overflows
630   With us, and the memorials of our woes?
Lo Priamus! Here also do they raise
To virtuous deeds fit monument of praise;
Tears for the frail estate of human kind
Are shed; and mortal changes touch the mind.'
He spake (nor might the gushing tears controul);

And with an empty Picture feeds his soul.

He saw the Greeks fast flying o'er the plain,
The Trojan Youth – how in pursuit they strain!
There, o'er the Phrygians routed in the war,
640 Crested Achilles hanging from his Car.
Next, to near view the painted wall presents
The fate of Rhesus, and his snow-white tents,
In the first sleep of silent night, betrayed
To the wide-wasting sword of Diomed,
Who to the camp the fiery horses led,
Ere they from Trojan stalls had tasted food,
Or stooped their heads to drink Scamander's flood.
– The Stripling Troilus he next espied,
Flying, his arms now lost, or flung aside;
650 Ill-matched with fierce Achilles! From the fight
He, by his horses borne in desperate flight,
Cleaves to his empty Chariot, on the plain
Supinely stretched, yet grasping still the rein;
Along the earth are dragged his neck and hair;
The dust is marked by his inverted spear.
Meanwhile, with tresses long and loose, a train
Of Trojan Matrons seek Minerva's Fane
As on they bear the dedicated Veil,
They beat their own sad breasts with suppliant wail.
660 The Goddess heeds not offerings, prayers, nor cries,
And on the ground are fixed her sullen eyes.
–Thrice had incensed Achilles whirled amain
About Troy Wall, the Corse of Hector slain,
And barters now that corse for proffered gold.
What grief, the spoils and Chariot to behold!
And, suppliant, near his Friend's dead body, stands
Old Priam, stretching forth his unarmed hands!
Himself, 'mid Grecian Chiefs, he can espy;
And saw the oriental blazonry
670 Of swarthy Memnon, and the Host he heads;
Her lunar shields Penthesilea leads;
A zone her mutilated breast hath bound;

And She, exulting on the embattled ground
A Virgin Warrior, with a Virgin Train,
Dares in the peril to conflict with Men.

While on these animated pictures gazed
The Dardan Chief, enwrapt, disturbed, amazed;
With a long retinue of Youth, the Queen
Ascends the Temple; – lovely was her mien;
680 And her form beautiful as Earth has seen;
Thus, where Eurotas flows, or on the heights
Of Cynthus, where Diana oft delights
To train her Nymphs, and lead the Choirs along,
Oreads, in thousands gathering, round her throng;
Where'er she moves, where'er the Goddess bears
Her pendant sheaf of arrows, she appears
Far, far above the immortal Company;
Latona's breast is thrilled with silent ecstasy.
Even with such lofty bearing Dido passed
690 Among the busy crowd; – such looks she cast
Urging the various works, with mind intent
On future empire. Through the Porch she went,
And compassed round with armed Attendants, sate
Beneath the Temple's dome, upon a Throne of State.
There, laws she gave; divided justly there
The labour; or by lot assigned to each his share.
When, turning from the Throne a casual glance,
Aeneas saw an eager Crowd advance
With various Leaders, whom the storms of Heaven
700 Had scattered, and to other shores had driven.
With Antheus and Sergestus there appeared
The brave Cloanthes, – followers long endeared.
Joy smote his heart, joy tempered with strange awe;
Achates, in like sort, by what he saw
Was smitten; and the hands of both were bent
On instant greeting; but they feared the event.
Stifling their wish, within that cloud involved,
They wait until the mystery shall be solved –
What has befallen their Friends; upon what shore

710 The Fleet is left, and what they would implore;
For Delegates from every Ship they were,
And sought the Temple with a clamorous prayer.

All entered, – and, leave given, with tranquil breast
Ilioneus preferred their joint request:
'O Queen! empowered by Jupiter to found
A hopeful City on this desart ground;
To whom he gives the curb, and guiding rein
Of Justice, a proud People to restrain,
We, wretched Trojans, rescued from a Fleet
720 Long tossed through every Sea, thy aid entreat;
Let, at thy voice, the unhallowed fire forbear
To touch our ships; a righteous People spare;
And on our fortunes look with nearer care!
We neither seek as plunderers your abodes,
Nor would our swords molest your household Gods;
Our spirit tempts us not such course to try;
Nor do the Vanquished lift their heads so high.
There is a Country called by Men of Greece
Hesperia, strong in arms, the soil of large increase,
730 Oenotrians held it; Men of later fame
Call it Italia, from their Leader's name.
That Land we sought; when, wrapt in mist, arose
Orion, helped by every wind that blows;
Dispersed us utterly – on shallows cast;
And we, we only, gained your shores at last.
What race of man is here? Was ever yet
The unnatural treatment known which we have met?
What country bears with customs that deny,
To shipwrecked men, such hospitality
740 As the sands offer on the naked beach,
And the first quiet of the Land they reach?
– Arms were *our* greeting; yet, if ye despise
Man and *his* power, look onward, and be wise;
The Gods for right and wrong have awful memories.
A man to no one second in the care
Of justice, nor in piety and war,

Ruled over us; if yet Aeneas treads
On earth, nor has been summoned to the shades,
Fear no repentance if, in acts of grace
750   Striving with him, thou gain the foremost place.
Nor want we, in Trinacria, towns and plains,
Where, sprung from Trojan blood, Acestes reigns.
Grant leave to draw our Ships upon your Shores,
Thence to refit their shattered hulks and oars.
Were Friends and Chief restored, whom now we mourn,
We to the Italian Coast with joy would turn,
Should Italy lie open to our aim;
But if our welfare be an empty name,
And Thou, best Father of the Family
760   Of Troy, hast perished in the Lybian Sea,
And young Iülus sank, engulfed with thee,
Then be it ours, at least, to cross the foam
Of the Sicilian Deep, and seek the home
Prepared by good Acestes, whence we come.'

Thus spake Ilioneus: his Friends around
Declared their sanction by a murmuring sound.

With downcast looks, brief answer Dido made;
'Trojans, be griefs dismissed, anxieties allayed.
The pressure of occasion, and a reign
770   Yet new, exact these rigours, and constrain
The jealous vigilance my coasts maintain.
The Aenean Race, with that heroic Town –
And widely-blazing war – to whom are they unknown?
Not so obtuse the Punic breasts we bear;
Nor does the Giver of the Day so far
From this our Tyrian City yoke his Car.
But if Hesperia be your wished-for bourne,
Or to Trinacrian shores your prows would turn,
Then, with all aids that may promote your weal,
780   Ye shall depart; – but if desire ye feel,
Fixed, in this growing Realm, to share my fate,
Yours are the walls which now I elevate.

Haste, and withdraw your Galleys from the sea,
– Trojans and Tyrians shall be one to me.
Would, too, that storm-compelled as ye have been,
The Person of your Chief might here be seen!
By trusty servants shall my shores be traced
To the last confines of the Lybian Waste,
For He, the Castaway of stormy floods,
790   May roam through cities, or in savage woods.'

    Thus did the Queen administer relief
For their dejected hearts; and to the Chief,
While both were burning with desire to break
From out the darksome cloud, Achates spake.
'Son of a Goddess, what resolves ensue
From this deliverance whose effects we view?
All things are safe – thy Fleet and Friends restored
Save one, whom in our sight the Sea devoured;
All else respondent to thy Mother's word.'
800   He spake; the circumambient cloud anon
Melts and dissolves, the murky veil is gone;
And left Aeneas, as it passed away,
With godlike mien and shoulders, standing in full day.
For that same Parent of celestial race
Had shed upon his hair surpassing grace;
And, breathing o'er her Son the purple light
Of youth, had glorified his eyes, made bright,
Like those of Heaven, with joyance infinite.
So stood he forth, an unexpected Guest,
810   And, while all wondered, thus the Queen addressed.

    'He whom ye seek am I, Aeneas – flung
By storms the Lybian solitudes among.
O Sole, who for the unutterable state
Of Troy art humanly compassionate;
Who not alone a shelter dost afford
To the thin relics of the Grecian sword,
Perpetually exhausted by pursuit
Of dire mischance, of all things destitute,

But in thy purposes with them hast shared
820 City and home; – not we, who thus have fared,
Not we, not all the Dardan Race that live,
Scattered through Earth, sufficient thanks can give.
The Gods (if they the Pious watch with love,
If Justice dwell about us, or above)
And a mind conscious to itself of right,
Shall, in fit measure thy deserts requite!
What happy Age gave being to such worth?
What blessed Parents, Dido! brought thee forth?
While down their channels Rivers seaward flow,
830 While shadowy Groves sweep round the mountain's
      brow,
While ether feeds the stars, where'er be cast
My lot, whatever Land by me be traced,
Thy name, thy honour, and thy praise, shall last.'
He spake; and turning towards the Trojan Band,
Salutes Ilioneus with the better hand,
And grasps Serestus with the left – then gave
Like greeting to the rest, to Gyas brave
And brave Cloanthes.
                        Inwardly amazed,
Sidonian Dido on the Chief had gazed
840 When first he met her view; – his words like wonder
      raised.
'What Force,' said She, 'pursues thee – hath impelled
To these wild shores? In Thee have I beheld
That Trojan whom bright Venus, on the shore
Of Phrygian Simois, to Anchises bore?
And well do I recall to mind the day
When to our Sidon Teucer found his way,
An Outcast from his native Borders driven,
With hope to win new Realms by aid from Belus given,
Belus, my Father, then the conquering Lord
850 Of Cyprus newly-ravaged by his sword.
Thenceforth I knew the fate of Troy that rings
Earth round, – thy Name, and the Pelasgian kings.
Teucer himself, with liberal tongue, would raise

His Adversaries to just heights of praise,
And vaunt a Trojan lineage with fair proof;
Then welcome, noble Strangers, to our Roof!
– Me, too, like Fortune, after devious strife
Stayed in this Land, to breathe a calmer life;
From no light ills which on myself have pressed,
860   Pitying I learn to succour the distressed.'
These words pronounced, and mindful to ordain
Fit sacrifice, she issues from the Fane,
And towards the Palace leads Aeneas and his Train.
Nor less regardful of his distant Friends,
To the sea coast she hospitably sends
Twice ten selected steers, a hundred lambs
Swept from the plenteous herbage with their dams;
A hundred bristly ridges of huge swine,
And what the God bestows in sparkling wine.
870   But the interior Palace doth display
Its whole magnificence in set array;
And in the centre of a spacious Hall
Are preparations for high festival;
There, gorgeous vestments – skilfully enwrought
With Eastern purple; and huge tables – fraught
With massive argentry; there, carved in gold,
Through long, long series, the achievements bold
Of Forefathers, each imaged in his place,
From the beginning of the ancient Race.

880   Aeneas, whose parental thoughts obey
Their natural impulse, brooking no delay,
Dispatched the prompt Achates, to report
The new events, and lead Ascanius to the Court.
Ascanius, for on him the Father's mind
Now rests, as if to that sole care confined;
And bids him bring, attendant on the Boy,
The richest Presents, snatched from burning Troy;
A Robe of tissue stiff with shapes exprest
In threads of gleaming gold; an upper Vest
890   Round which acanthus twines its yellow flowers;

By Argive Helen worn in festal hours;
Her Mother Leda's wonderous gift – and brought
To Ilium from Mycenae when she sought
Those unpermitted nuptials; – thickly set
With golden gems, a twofold coronet;
And Sceptre which Ilione of yore,
Eldest of Priam's royal Daughters, wore,
And orient Pearls, which on her neck she bore.
This to perform, Achates speeds his way
900 To the Ships anchored in that peaceful Bay.

But Cytherea, studious to invent
Arts yet untried, upon new counsels bent,
Resolves that Cupid, changed in form and face
To young Ascanius, should assume his place;
Present the maddening gifts, and kindle heat
Of passion at the bosom's inmost seat.
She dreads the treacherous house, the double tongue;
She burns, she frets – by Juno's rancour stung;
The calm of night is powerless to remove
910 These cares, and thus she speaks to wingèd Love:

'O son, my strength, my power! who dost despise
(What, save thyself, none dares through earth and skies)
The giant-quelling bolts of Jove, I flee,
O son, a suppliant to thy Deity!
What perils meet Aeneas in his course,
How Juno's hate with unrelenting force
Pursues thy brother – this to thee is known;
And oft-times hast thou made my griefs thine own.
Him now the generous Dido by soft chains
920 Of bland entreaty at her court detains;
Junonian hospitalities prepare
Such apt occasion that I dread a snare.
Hence, ere some hostile god can intervene,
Would I, by previous wiles, inflame the Queen
With passion for Aeneas, such strong love
That at my beck, mine only, she shall move.

Hear, and assist; – the father's mandate calls
His young Ascanius to the Tyrian walls;
He comes, my dear delight, – and costliest things
930 Preserved from fire and flood for presents brings.
Him will I take, and in close covert keep,
'Mid groves Idalian, lulled to gentle sleep,
Or on Cythera's far-sequestered steep,
That he may neither know what hope is mine,
Nor by his presence traverse the design.
Do Thou, but for a single night's brief space,
Dissemble; be that boy in form and face!
And when enraptured Dido shall receive
Thee to her arms, and kisses interweave
940 With many a fond embrace, while joy runs high,
And goblets crown the proud festivity,
Instil thy subtle poison, and inspire,
At every touch, an unsuspected fire.'

Love, at the word, before his mother's sight
Puts off his wings, and walks, with proud delight,
Like young Iülus; but the gentlest dews
Of slumber Venus sheds, to circumfuse
The true Ascanius steeped in placid rest;
Then wafts him, cherished on her careful breast,
950 Through upper air to an Idalian glade,
Where he on soft *amaracus* is laid,
With breathing flowers embraced, and fragrant shade.
But Cupid, following cheerily his guide
Achates, with the Gifts to Carthage hied;
And, as the hall he entered, there, between
The sharers of her golden couch, was seen
Reclined in festal pomp the Tyrian queen.
The Trojans too (Aeneas at their head),
On couches lie, with purple overspread:
960 Meantime in canisters is heaped the bread,
Pellucid water for the hands is borne,
And napkins of smooth texture, finely shorn.
Within are fifty Handmaids, who prepare,

As they in order stand, the dainty fare;
And fume the household deities with store
Of odorous incense; while a hundred more
Matched with an equal number of like age,
But each of manly sex, a docile page,
Marshal the banquet, giving with due grace
970   To cup or viand its appointed place.
The Tyrians rushing in, an eager Band,
Their painted couches seek, obedient to command.
They look with wonder on the gifts – they gaze
Upon Iülus, dazzled with the rays
That from his ardent countenance are flung,
And charmed to hear his simulating tongue;
Nor pass unpraised the robe and veil divine,
Round which the yellow flowers and wandering foliage
    twine.

But chiefly Dido, to the coming ill
980   Devoted, strives in vain her vast desires to fill;
She views the gifts; upon the child then turns
Insatiable looks, and gazing burns.
To ease a father's cheated love he hung
Upon Aeneas, and around him clung;
Then seeks the queen; with her his arts he tries;
She fastens on the boy enamoured eyes,
Clasps in her arms, nor weens (O lot unblest!)
How great a god, incumbent o'er her breast,
Would fill it with his spirit. He, to please
990   His Acidalian mother, by degrees
Blots out Sichaeus, studious to remove
The dead, by influx of a living love,
By stealthy entrance of a perilous guest
Troubling a heart that had been long at rest.

Now when the viands were withdrawn, and ceased
The first division of the splendid feast,
While round a vacant board the chiefs recline,
Huge goblets are brought forth; they crown the wine;

Voices of gladness roll the walls around;
1000 Those gladsome voices from the courts rebound;
From gilded rafters many a blazing light
Depends, and torches overcome the night.
The minutes fly – till, at the queen's command,
A bowl of state is offered to her hand:
Then She, as Belus wont, and all the line
From Belus, filled it to the brim with wine;
Silence ensued. 'O Jupiter, whose care
Is hospitable Dealing, grant my prayer!
Productive day be this of lasting joy
1010 To Tyrians, and these exiles driven from Troy;
A day to future generations dear!
Let Bacchus, donor of soul-quickening cheer,
Be present; kindly Juno, be thou near!
And, Tyrians, may your choicest favours wait
Upon this hour, the bond to celebrate!'
She spake and shed an offering on the board;
Then sipped the bowl whence she the wine had poured
And gave to Bitias, urging the prompt lord;
He raised the bowl, and took a long deep draught;
1020 Then every chief in turn the beverage quaffed.

Graced with redundant hair, Iopas sings
The lore of Atlas, to resounding strings,
The labours of the Sun, the lunar wanderings;
Whence human kind, and brute; what natural powers
Engender lightning, whence are falling showers.
He chaunts Arcturus, – that fraternal twain
The glittering Bears, – the Pleiads fraught with rain;
– Why suns in winter, shunning Heaven's steep heights
Post seaward, – what impedes the tardy nights.
1030 The learnèd song from Tyrian hearers draws
Loud shouts, – the Trojans echo the applause.
– But, lengthening out the night with converse new,
Large draughts of love unhappy Dido drew;
Of Priam asked, of Hector – o'er and o'er –
What arms the son of bright Aurora wore; –

What steeds the car of Diomed could boast;
Among the Leaders of the Grecian host
How looked Achilles – their dread paramount –
'But nay – the fatal wiles, O guest, recount,
1040 Retrace the Grecian cunning from its source,
Your own grief and your Friends' – your wandering course;
For now, till this seventh summer have ye ranged
The sea, or trod the earth, to peace estranged.'

SECOND BOOK

All breathed in silence, and intensely gazed,
When from the lofty couch his voice Aeneas raised,
And thus began: 'The task which you impose
O Queen, revives unutterable woes;
How by the Grecians Troy was overturned,
And her power fell – to be for ever mourned;
Calamities which with a pitying heart
I saw, of which I formed no common part.
Oh! 'twas a miserable end! What One
10 Of all our Foes, Dolopian, Myrmidon,
Or Soldier bred in stern Ulysses' train
Such things could utter, and from tears refrain?
And hastens now from Heaven the dewy night,
And the declining stars to sleep invite.
But since such strong desire prevails to know
Our wretched fate, and Troy's last overthrow
I will attempt the theme though in my breast
Memory recoils and shudders at the test.

The Grecian Chiefs, exhausted of their strength
20 By war protracted to such irksome length,
And, from the siege repulsed, new schemes devise;
A wooden horse they build of mountain size.
Assisted by Minerva's art divine,
They frame the work, and sheathe its ribs with pine,
An offering to the Gods – that they may gain
Their home in safety; this they boldly feign,
And spread the Tale abroad; – meanwhile they hide

Selected Warriors in its gloomy side;
Throng the huge concave to its utmost den,
30 And fill that mighty Womb with armed Men.

   In sight of Troy, an Island lies, by Fame
Amply distinguished, Tenedos its name;
Potent and rich while Priam's sway endured,
Now a bare hold for keels, unsafely moored.
Here did the Greeks, when for their native land
We thought them sailed, lurk on the desart strand.
From her long grief at once the Realm of Troy
Broke loose; – the gates are opened, and with joy
We seek the Dorian Camp, and wander o'er
40 The spots forsaken, the abandoned shore.
Here, the Dolopian ground its lines presents;
And here the dread Achilles pitched his tents;
There lay the Ships drawn up along the coast,
And here we oft encountered host with host.
Meanwhile, the rest an eye of wonder lift,
Unwedded Pallas! on the fatal Gift
To thee devoted. First, Thymoetes calls
For its free ingress through disparted walls
To lodge within the Citadel – thus He
50 Treacherous, or such the course of destiny.
Capys, with some of wiser mind, would sweep
The insidious Grecian offering to the Deep,
Or to the flames subject it; or advise
To perforate and search the cavities;
Into conflicting judgements break and split
The crowd, as random thoughts the fancy hit.

   Down from the Citadel a numerous throng
Hastes with Laocoon; they sweep along,
And He, the foremost, crying from afar,
60 'What would ye? wretched Maniacs, as ye are!
Think ye the Foe departed? Or that e'er
A boon from Grecian hands can prove sincere?
Thus do ye read Ulysses? Foes unseen

Lurk in these chambers; or the huge Machine
Against the ramparts brought, by pouring down
Force from aloft, will seize upon the Town.
Let not a fair pretence your minds enthrall;
For me, I fear the Greeks and most of all
When they are offering gifts.' With mighty force
70 This said, he hurled a spear against the Horse;
It smote the curved ribs, and quivering stood
While groans made answer through the hollow wood.
We too, upon this impulse, had not Fate   ⎫
Been adverse, and our minds infatuate,   ⎬
We too, had rushed the den to penetrate,   ⎭
Streams of Argolic blood our swords had stained,
Troy, thou mightst yet have stood, and Priam's Towers
  remained.

But lo! an unknown Youth with hand to hand
Bound fast behind him, whom a boisterous Band
80 Of Dardan Swains with clamour hurrying
Force to the shore and place before the King.
Such his device when he those chains had sought
A voluntary captive, fixed in thought
Either the City to betray, or meet
Death, the sure penalty of foiled deceit.
The curious Trojans, pouring in, deride
And taunt the Prisoner, with an emulous pride.
Now see the cunning of the Greeks exprest
By guilt of One, true image of the rest!
90 For, while with helpless looks, from side to side
Anxiously cast, the Phrygian throng he eyed,
'Alas! what Land,' he cries, 'can now, what Sea,
Can offer refuge? what resource for me?
Who 'mid the Greeks no breathing-place can find,
And whom ye, Trojans, have to death consigned!'
Thus were we wrought upon; and now, with sense
Of pity touched, that checked all violence,
We cheered and urged him boldly to declare
His origin, what tidings he may bear,

100 And on what claims he ventures to confide;
   Then, somewhat eased of fear, he thus replied:

    'O King, a plain confession shall ensue
On these commands, in all things plain and true.
And first, the tongue that speaks shall not deny
My origin; a Greek by birth am I.
Fortune made Sinon wretched; – to do more,
And make him false, – *that* lies not in her power.
In converse, haply, ye have heard the name
Of Palamedes, and his glorious fame;
110 A Chief with treason falsely charged, and whom
The Achaians crushed by a nefarious doom,
And now lament when covered with the tomb.
His kinsman I; and hither by his side
Me my poor Father sent, when first these fields were
    tried.
While yet his voice the Grecian Chieftains swayed
And due respect was to his counsel paid,
Ere that high influence was with life cut short,
I did not walk ungraced by fair report.
Ulysses, envy rankling in his breast,
120 (And these are things which thousands can attest)
Thereafter turned his subtlety to give
That fatal injury, and he ceased to live.
I dragged my days in sorrow and in gloom,
And mourned my guiltless Friend, indignant at his doom;
This inwardly; and yet not always mute,
Rashly I vowed revenge – my sure pursuit,
If e'er the shores of Argos I again
Should see, victorious with my Countrymen.
Sharp hatred did these open threats excite;
130 Hence the first breathings of a deadly blight;
Hence, to appal me, accusations came,
Which still Ulysses was at work to frame;
Hence would he scatter daily 'mid the crowd
Loose hints, at will sustained or disavowed,
Beyond himself for instruments he looked,

And in this search of means no respite brooked
Till Calchas his accomplice – but the chain
Of foul devices why untwist in vain?
Why should I linger? if ye Trojans place
140 On the same level all of Argive race,
And 'tis enough to know that I am one,
Punish me; would Ulysses might look on!
And let the Atridae hear, rejoiced with what is done!'

This stirred us more, whose judgements were asleep
To all suspicion of a crime so deep
And craft so fine. Our questions we renewed;
And, trembling, thus the fiction he pursued.

'Oft did the Grecian Host the means prepare
To flee from Troy, tired with so long a war;
150 Would they had fled! but winds as often stopped
Their going, and the twisted sails were dropped;
And when this pine-ribbed Horse of monstrous size ⎫
Stood forth, a finished Work, before their eyes, ⎬
Then chiefly pealed the storm through blackened skies. ⎭
So that the Oracle its aid might lend
To quell our doubts, Eurypylus we send,
Who brought the answer of the voice divine
In these sad words given from the Delphic shrine.
– "Blood flowed, a Virgin perished to appease
160 The winds, when first for Troy ye passed the seas;
O Grecians! for return across the Flood,
Life must be paid, a sacrifice of blood."
–With this response an universal dread
Among the shuddering multitude was spread;
All quaked to think at whom the Fates had aimed
This sentence, who the Victim Phoebus claimed.
Then doth the Ithacan with tumult loud
Bring forth the Prophet Calchas to the crowd;
Asks what the Gods would have; and some, meanwhile,
170 Discern what end the Mover of the guile
Is compassing; and do not hide from me

The crime which they in mute reserve foresee.
Ten days refused he still with guarded breath
To designate the Man, to fix the death;
The Ithacan still urgent for the deed;
At last the unwilling voice announced that *I* must bleed.
All gave assent, each happy to be cleared,
By one Man's fall, of what himself had feared.
Now came the accursed day; the salted cates
180 Are spread, – the Altar for the Victim waits;
The fillets bind my temples – I took flight
Bursting my chains, I own, and through the night
Lurked among oozy swamps, and there lay hid
Till winds might cease their voyage to forbid.
And now was I compelled at once to part
With all the dear old longings of the heart,
Never to see my Country, Children, Sire,
Whom they, perchance, will for this flight require
For this offence of mine of them will make
190 An expiation, punished for my sake.
But Thee, by all the Powers who hold their seat
In Heaven, and know the truth, do I entreat
O King! and by whate'er may yet remain
Among mankind of faith without a stain,
Have pity on my woes; commiserate
A mind that ne'er deserved this wretched fate.'

His tears prevail, we spare the Suppliant's life
Pitying the man we spare, without a strife;
Even Priam's self, He first of all commands
200 To loose the fetters and unbind his hands,
Then adds these friendly words; – 'Whoe'er thou be
Henceforth forget the Grecians, lost to thee;
We claim thee now, and let me truly hear
Who moved them first this monstrous Horse to rear?
And why? Was some religious vow the aim?
Or for what use in war the Engine might they frame?'
Straight were these artful words in answer given
While he upraised his hands, now free, to Heaven.

'Eternal Fires, on you I call; O Ye!
210 And your inviolable Deity!
Altars, and ruthless swords from which I fled!
Ye fillets, worn round my devoted head!
Be it no crime if Argive sanctions cease
To awe me, – none to hate the men of Greece!
The law of Country forfeiting its hold,
Mine be the voice their secrets to unfold!
And ye, O Trojans! keep the word ye gave;
Save me, if truth I speak, and Ilium save!

The Grecian Host on Pallas still relied;
220 Nor hope had they but what her aid supplied;
But all things drooped since that ill-omened time
In which Ulysses, Author of the crime,
Was leagued with impious Diomed, to seize
That Image pregnant with your destinies;
Tore the Palladium from the Holy Fane,
The Guards who watched the Citadel first slain.
And, fearing not the Goddess, touched the Bands
Wreathed round her virgin brow, with gory hands.
Hope ebbed, strength failed the Grecians since that
day,
230 From them the Goddess turned her mind away.
This by no doubtful signs Tritonia showed,
The uplifted eyes with flames coruscant glowed,
Soon as they placed her Image in the Camp;
And trickled o'er its limbs a briny damp;
And from the ground, the Goddess (strange to hear!)
Leapt thrice, with buckler grasped, and quivering spear.
– Then Calchas bade to stretch the homeward sail,
And prophesied that Grecian Arms would fail,
Unless we for new omens should repair
240 To Argos, thither the Palladium bear;
And thence to Phrygian Shores recross the Sea,
Fraught with a more propitious Deity.
They went; but only to return in power
With favouring Gods, at some unlooked-for hour.

– So Calchas read those signs; the Horse was built
To soothe Minerva, and atone for guilt.
Compact in strength you see the Fabric rise,
A pile stupendous, towering to the skies!
This was ordained by Calchas, with intent
250 That the vast bulk its ingress might prevent,
And Ilium ne'er within her Walls enfold
Another Safeguard reverenced like the old.
For if, unawed by Pallas, ye should lift
A sacrilegious hand against the Gift,
The Phrygian Realm shall perish (May the Gods
Turn on himself the mischief he forebodes!)
But if your Town it enter – by your aid
Ascending – Asia, then, in arms arrayed
Shall storm the walls of Pelops, and a fate
260 As dire on our posterity await.'

Even so the arts of perjured Sinon gained
Belief for this, and all that he had feigned;
Thus were they won by wiles, by tears compelled
Whom not Tydides, not Achilles quelled;
Who fronted ten years' war with safe disdain,
'Gainst whom a thousand Ships had tried their strength
in vain.

To speed our fate, a thing did now appear
Yet more momentous, and of instant fear.
Laocoon, Priest by lot to Neptune, stood
270 Where to his hand a Bull poured forth its blood,
Before the Altar, in high offering slain; –
But lo! two Serpents, o'er the tranquil Main
Incumbent, roll from Tenedos, and seek
Our Coast together (shuddering do I speak);
Between the waves, their elevated breasts,
Upheaved in circling spires, and sanguine crests,
Tower o'er the flood; the parts that follow, sweep
In folds voluminous and vast, the Deep.
The agitated brine, with noisy roar

280 Attends their coming, till they touch the shore;
Sparkle their eyes suffused with blood, and quick
The tongues shot forth their hissing mouths to lick.
Dispersed with fear we fly; in close array ⎫
These move, and towards Laocoon point their way, ⎬
But first assault his Sons, their youthful prey. ⎭
– A several Snake in tortuous wreaths engrasps
Each slender frame; and fanging what it clasps
Feeds on the limbs; the Father rushes on,
Arms in his hand, for rescue; but anon
290 Himself they seize; and, coiling round his waist
Their scaly backs, they bind him, twice embraced
With monstrous spires, as with a double zone; ⎫
And, twice around his neck in tangles thrown, ⎬
High o'er the Father's head each Serpent lifts its own. ⎭
His priestly fillets then are sprinkled o'er
With sable venom and distained with gore;
And while his labouring hands the knots would rend
The cries he utters to the Heavens ascend;
Loud as a Bull – that, wounded by the axe
300 Shook off the uncertain steel, and from the altar breaks,
To fill with bellowing voice the depths of air!
– But toward the Temple slid the Hydra Pair,
Their work accomplished, and there lie concealed,
Couched at Minerva's feet, beneath her orbèd Shield.
Nor was there *One* who trembled not with fear,
Or deemed the expiation too severe,
For him whose lance had pierced the votive Steed,
Which to the Temple they resolve to lead;
There to be lodged with pomp of service high
310 And supplication, such the general cry.

Shattering the Walls, a spacious breach we make,
We cleave the bulwarks – toil which all partake,
Some to the feet the rolling wheels apply,
Some round the lofty neck the cables tie;
The Engine, pregnant with our deadly foes,
Mounts to the breach; and ever, as it goes,

Boys, mixed with Maidens, chaunt a holy song
And press to touch the cords, a happy throng.
The Town it enters thus, and threatening moves along.

320   My Country, glorious Ilium! and ye Towers,
Loved habitation of celestial Powers!
Four times it halted 'mid the gates; – a din
Of armour four times warned us from within;
Yet towards the sacred Dome with reckless mind
We still press on, and in the place assigned
Lodge the portentous Gift, through frenzy blind.

Nor failed Cassandra now to scatter wide
Words that of instant ruin prophesied.
–But Phoebus willed that none should heed her voice,
330   And we, we miserable men, rejoice,
And hang our Temples round with festal boughs,
Upon that day, the last that Fate allows.

Meanwhile had Heaven revolved with rapid flight,
And fast from Ocean climbs the punctual Night,
With boundless shade involving earth and sky
And Myrmidonian frauds; – the Trojans lie
Scattered throughout the weary Town, and keep
Unbroken quiet in the embrace of sleep.

This was the time when, furnished and arrayed,
340   Nor wanting silent moonlight's friendly aid,
From Tenedos the Grecian Navy came,
Led by the royal Galley's signal flame,
And Sinon now, our hostile fates his guard,
By stealth the dungeon of the Greeks unbarred.
Straight, by a pendant rope adown the side
Of the steep Horse, the armèd Warriors glide.
The Chiefs Thersander, Sthenelus are there,
With joy delivered to the open air;
Ulysses, Thoas, Achamas the cord
350   Lets down to earth and Helen's injured Lord,

– Pyrrhus, who from Pelides drew his birth,
And bold Machaon, first to issue forth,
Nor him forget whose skill had framed the Pile
Epeus, glorying in his prosperous wile.
They rush upon the City that lay still,
Buried in sleep and wine; the Warders kill;
And at the wide-spread Gates in triumph greet
Expectant Comrades crowding from the Fleet.

    It was the earliest hour of slumbrous rest,
360 Gift of the Gods to Man with toil opprest,
When, present to my dream, did Hector rise
And stood before me with fast-streaming eyes;
Such as he was when horse had striven with horse,
Whirling along the plain his lifeless Corse,
The thongs that bound him to the Chariot thrust
Through his swoln feet, and black with gory dust, –
A spectacle how pitiably sad!
How changed from that returning Hector, clad
In glorious spoils, Achilles' own attire!
370 From Hector hurling shipward the red Phrygian fire!
– A squalid beard, hair clotted thick with gore,
And that same throng of patriot wounds he bore,
In front of Troy received; and now, methought, ⎫
That I myself was to a passion wrought   ⎬
Of tears, which to my voice this greeting brought. ⎭
'O Light of Dardan Realms! most faithful Stay
To Trojan courage, why these lingerings of delay?
Where hast thou tarried, Hector? From what coast
Com'st thou, long wished-for? That so many lost
380 Thy kinsmen or thy friends, – such travail borne
By this afflicted City – we outworn
Behold thee. Why this undeserved disgrace?
Who thus defiled with wounds that honoured face?'
He naught to this – unwilling to detain
One, who had asked vain things, with answer vain;
But, groaning deep, 'Flee, Goddess-born,' he said,
'Snatch thyself from these flames around thee spread;

Our Enemy is master of the Walls;
Down from her elevation Ilium falls.
390   Enough for Priam; the long strife is o'er,
Nor doth our Country ask one effort more.
Could Pergamus have been defended – hence,
Even from this hand, had issued her defence;
Troy her Penates doth to thee commend,
Her sacred stores, – let these thy fates attend!
Sail under their protection for the Land
Where mighty Realms shall grow at thy command!'
– No more was uttered, but his hand he stretched,
And from the inmost Sanctuary fetched
400   The consecrated wreaths, the potency
Of Vesta, and the fires that may not die.

Meantime, wild tumult through the streets is poured,
And though apart, and 'mid thick trees embowered,
My Father's mansion stood, the loud alarms
Came pressing thither, and the clash of Arms.
Sleep fled; I climb the roof and where it rears
Its loftiest summit, stand with quickened ears.
So, when a fire by raging south winds borne
Lights on a billowy sea of ripened corn,
410   Or rapid torrent sweeps with mountain flood
The fields, the harvest prostrates, headlong bears the
    wood;
High on a rock, the unweeting Shepherd, bound,
In blank amazement, listens to the sound.
Then was apparent to *whom* faith was due,
And Grecian plots lie bare to open view.
Above the spacious palace where abode
Deiphobus, the flames in triumph rode;
Ucalegon burns next; through lurid air
Sigean Friths reflect a widening glare.
420   Clamour and clangour to the heavens arise,
The blast of trumpets mixed with vocal cries;
Arms do I snatch – weak reason scarcely knows
What aid they promise, but my spirit glows;

I burn to gather Friends, whose firm array
On to the Citadel shall force its way.
Precipitation works with desperate charms;
It seems a lovely thing to die in Arms.

    Lo Pantheus! fugitive from Grecian spears,
Apollo's Priest; – his vanquished Gods he bears;
430   The other hand his little Grandson leads,
While from the Sovereign Fort, he toward my threshold
    speeds.
'Pantheus, what hope? Which Fortress shall we try?
Where plant resistance?' He in prompt reply
Said, deeply moved, – ' 'Tis come – the final hour;
The inevitable close of Dardan power
Hath come: – we have been Trojans, Ilium was,
And the great name of Troy; now all things pass
To Argos; so wills angry Jupiter:
Within the burning Town the Grecians domineer.
440   Forth from its central stand the enormous Horse
Pours in continual stream an armèd Force;
Sinon, insulting victor, aggravates
The flames; and thousands hurry through the Gates,
Thronged, as might seem, with press of all the Hosts
That e'er Mycenae sent to Phrygian Coasts.
Others with spears in serried files blockade
The passes; – hangs, with quivering point, the blade
Unsheathed for slaughter, – scarcely to the foes
A blind and baffled fight the Warders can oppose.'

450   Urged by these words, and as the Gods inspire,
I rush into the battle and the fire,
Where sad Erinnys, where the shock of fight,
The roar, the tumult, and the groans invite;
Rypheus is with me, Epytus, the pride
Of battles, joins his aid, and to my side
Flock Dymas, Hypanis, the moon their guide;
With young Coroebus, who had lately sought
Our walls, by passion for Cassandra brought;

He led to Priam an auxiliar train,
460 His Son by wedlock, miserable Man
For whom a raving Spouse had prophesied in vain.

When these I saw collected, and intent
To face the strife with deeds of hardiment,
I thus began: 'O Champions, vainly brave
If, like myself, to dare extremes ye crave,
You see our lost condition, – not a God,
Of all the Powers by whom this Empire stood,
But hath renounced his Altar – fled from his abode.
– Ye would uphold a City wrapped in fire;
470 Die rather; – let us rush, in battle to expire.
At least one safety shall the vanquished have
If they no safety seek but in the grave.'
– Thus to their minds was fury added, – then,
Like wolves driven forth by hunger from the den,
To prowl amid blind vapours, whom the brood
Expect, their jaws all parched with thirst for blood,
Through flying darts, through pressure of the Foe,
To death, to not uncertain death, we go.
Right through the Town our midway course we bear,
480 Aided by hovering darkness, strengthened by despair.
Can words the havoc of that night express?
What power of tears may equal the distress?
An ancient City sinks to disappear;
She sinks who ruled for ages, – Far and near
The Unresisting through the streets, the abodes
Of Men and hallowed Temples of the Gods,
Are felled by massacre that takes no heed;
Nor are the Trojans only doomed to bleed;
The Vanquished sometimes to their hearts recall
490 Old virtues, and the conquering Argives fall.
Sorrow is everywhere and fiery skaith,
Fear, Anguish struggling to be rid of breath,
And Death still crowding on the shape of Death.

Androgeus, whom a numerous Force attends,

Was the first Greek we met; he rashly deems us Friends.
'What sloth,' he cries, 'retards you? Warriors haste!
Troy blazes, sacked by others, and laid waste;
And ye come lagging from your Ships the last!'
Thus he; and straight mistrusting our replies,
500 He felt himself begirt with enemies;
Voice failed – step faltered, at the dire mistake;
Like one who through a deeply tangled brake
Struggling, hath trod upon a lurking Snake,
And shrunk in terror from the unlooked-for Pest
Lifting his blue-swoln neck and wrathful crest.
Even so Androgeus, smit with sudden dread,
Recoils from what he saw, and would have fled,
Forward we rush, with arms the Troop surround,
The Men, surprised and ignorant of the ground,
510 Subdued by fear, become an easy prey;
So are we favoured in our first essay.
    With exultation here Coroebus cries,
'Behold, O Friends, how bright our destinies!
Advance; – the road which they point out is plain;
Shields let us change, and bear the insignia of the Slain,
Grecians in semblance; wiles are lawful – who
To simple valour would restrict a foe?
Themselves shall give us Arms.' When this was said
The Leader's helmet nods upon his head,
520 The emblazoned buckler on his arm is tied,
He fits an Argive falchion to his side.
The like doth Rypheus, Dymas, – all put on,
With eager haste, the spoils which they had won.
Then in the combat mingling, Heaven averse,
Amid the gloom a multitude we pierce,
And to the shades dismiss them. Others flee,
Appalled by this imagined treachery;
Some to the Ships – some to the Horse would hide.
Ah! what reap they but sorrow who confide
530 In aught to which the Gods their sanction have denied?
Behold Cassandra, Priam's royal Child,
By sacrilegious men, with hair all wild,

Dragged from Minerva's Temple! Toward the skies
The Virgin lifts in vain her glowing eyes,
Her eyes, she could no more, for Grecian bands
Had rudely manacled her tender hands.
The intolerable sight to madness stung
Coroebus; and his desperate self he flung
For speedy death the ruthless Foe among!
540 We follow, and with general shock assail
The hostile Throng: – here first our efforts fail:
While, from the summit of the lofty Fane
Darts, by the People flung, descend amain;
In miserable heaps their Friends are laid,
By show of Grecian Arms and Crests betrayed.
Wroth for the Virgin rescued, by defeat
Provoked, the Grecians from all quarters meet.
With Ajax combat there the Brother Kings;
And the Dolopian Squadron thither brings
550 Its utmost rage. Thus Winds break forth and fly
To conflict from all regions of the sky;
Notus and Zephyrus, while Eurus feeds
The strife, exulting in his orient steeds;
Woods roar, and foaming Nereus stirs the waves
Roused by his trident from their lowest caves.
They also whomsoe'er through shades of night
Our stratagem had driven to scattered flight
Now reappear – by them our Shields are known;
The simulating Javelins they disown,
560 And mark our utterance of discordant tone.
Numbers on numbers bear us down; and first
Coroebus falls; him Peneleus hath pierced
Before Minerva's Altar; next, in dust
Sinks Rhypeus, one above all Trojans just,
And righteous above all; but heavenly Powers
Ordain by lights that ill agree with ours.
Then Dymas, Hypanis are slain by Friends;
– Nor thee abundant piety defends,
O Pantheus! falling with the garland wound,
570 As fits Apollo's Priest, thy brows around.

Ashes of Ilium! and ye duteous fires,
Lit for my Friends upon their funeral pyres;
Amid your fall bear witness to my word!
I shunned no hazards of the Grecian sword,
No turns of war; with hand unsparing fought;
And earned, had Fate so willed, the death I sought.
Thence am I hurried by the rolling tide,
With Iphitus and Pelias at my side;
One bowed with years; and Pelias, from a wound
580 Given by Ulysses, halts along the ground.
New clamours rise; the Abode of Priam calls,
Besieged by thousands swarming round the walls;
Concourse how thick! as if, throughout the space
Of the whole City, war in other place
Were hushed – no death elsewhere. The Assailants wield
Above their heads shield, shell-wise locked in shield;
Climb step by step the ladders, near the side
Of the strong portal daringly applied;
The weaker hand its guardian shield presents;
590 The right is stretched to grasp the battlements.
The Dardans tug at roof and turrets high,   ⎫
Rend fragments off, and with these weapons try   ⎬
Life to preserve in such extremity,   ⎭
Roll down the massy rafters decked with gold,
Magnific splendours raised by Kings of old;
Others with naked weapons stand prepared
In thick array, the doors below to guard.

A bolder hope inspirits me to lend
My utmost aid the Palace to defend,
600 And strengthen those afflicted. From behind,   ⎫
A gateway opened, whence a passage blind   ⎬
The various Mansions of the Palace joined.   ⎭
– Unblest Andromache, while Priam reigned
Oft by this way the royal Palace gained,
A lonely Visitant; this way would tread
With young Astyanax, to his Grandsire led.
Entering the gate, I reached the roof, where stand

The Trojans, hurling darts with ineffectual hand.
A Tower there was; precipitous the site,
610 And the Pile rose to an unrivalled height;
Frequented Station, whence, in circuit wide
Troy might be seen, the Argive Fleet descried,
And all the Achaian Camp. This sovereign Tower
With irons grappling where the loftiest floor
Pressed with its beams the wall we shake, we rend,
And, in a mass of thundering ruin, send
To crush the Greeks beneath. But numbers press
To new assault with reckless eagerness:
Weapons and missiles from the ruins grow,
620 And what their hasty hands can seize they throw!

In front stands Pyrrhus, glorying in the might
Of his own weapons, while his armour bright
Casts from the portal gleams of brazen light,
So shines a Snake, when kindling, he hath crept
Forth from the winter bed in which he slept,
Swoln with a glut of poisonous herbs, – but now
Fresh from the shedding of his annual slough,
Glittering in youth, warm with instinctive fires,
He, with raised breast, involves his back in gyres,
630 Darts with his forked tongue, and toward the sun
    aspires.
Joined with redoubted Periphas, comes on
To storm the Palace fierce Automedon,
Who drove the Achillean Car; – the Bands
Of Scyros follow hurling fiery brands.
Pyrrhus himself hath seized an axe, would cleave
The ponderous doors, or from their hinges heave;
And now, reiterating stroke on stroke
Hath hewn, through plates of brass and solid oak,
A broad-mouthed entrance; – to their inmost seats
640 The long-drawn courts lie open; the retreats
Of Priam and ancestral Kings are bared
To instantaneous view; and Lo! the Guard
Stands at the threshold, for defence prepared.

But tumult spreads through all the space within;
The vaulted roofs repeat the mournful din
Of female Ululation, a strange vent
Of agony, that strikes the starry firmament!
The Matrons range with wildering step the floors;
Embrace, and print their kisses on, the doors.
650 Pyrrhus, with all his Father's might, dispels
Barriers and bolts, and living obstacles;
Force shapes her own clear way; – the doors are thrown
Off from their hinges; gates are battered down
By the onrushing Soldiery, who kill
Whom first they meet, and the broad area fill.
– Less irresistibly, o'er dams and mounds,
Burst by its rage, a foaming River bounds,
Herds sweeping with their stalls along the ravaged
    grounds.
Pyrrhus I saw with slaughter desperate;
660 The two Atridae near the Palace gate
Did I behold; and by these eyes were seen
The hundred Daughters with the Mother Queen,
And hoary-headed Priam, where he stood
Beside the Altar, staining with his blood
Fires which himself had hallowed. Hope had he
Erewhile, none equal hope, of large posterity.
There, fifty bridal chambers might be told –
Superb with trophies and barbaric gold,
All, in their pomp, lie level with the ground,
670 And where the fire is not, are Grecian Masters found.

Ask ye the fate of Priam? On that night
When captured Ilium blazed before his sight,
And the Foe, bursting through the Palace gate
Spread through the privacies of royal state,
In vain to tremulous shoulders he restored
Arms which had long forgot their ancient Lord,
And girt upon his side a useless sword;
Then, thus accoutred, forward did he hie,
As if to meet the Enemy and die.

680   – Amid the Courts, an Altar stood in view
Of the wide heavens, near which a long-lived Laurel grew
And, bending over this great Altar, made
For its Penates an embracing shade.
With all her Daughters, thronged like Doves that lie
Cowering, when storms have driven them from the sky,
Hecuba shelters in that sacred place
Where they the Statues of the Gods embrace.
But when she saw in youthful Arms arrayed
Priam himself; 'What ominous thought,' she said,
690   'Hangs, wretched Spouse, this weight on limbs decayed?
And wither wouldst thou hasten? If we were
More helpless still, this succour we might spare.
Not such Defenders doth the time demand;
Profitless here would be even Hector's hand.
Retire; this Altar can protect us all,
Or thou wilt not survive when we must fall.'
This to herself: and toward the sacred spot
She drew the aged Man, to wait their common lot.

      But see Polites, one of Priam's Sons,
700   Charged with the death which he in terror shuns!
The wounded Youth, escaped from Pyrrhus, flies
Through showers of darts, through press of enemies,
Where the long Porticos invite; the space
Of widely-vacant Courts his footsteps trace.
Him, Pyrrhus, following near and still more near,
Hath caught at with his hand, and presses with his spear;
But when at length this unremitting flight
Had brought him full before his Father's sight,
He fell – and scarcely prostrate on the ground,
710   Poured forth his life from many a streaming wound.
Here Priam, scorning death and self-regard,
His voice restrained not, nor his anger spared;
But 'Shall the Gods,' he cries, 'if Gods there be
Who note such acts, and care for piety,
Requite this heinous crime with measure true,
Nor one reward withhold that is thy due;

Who thus a Father's presence hast defiled,
And forced upon his sight the murder of a Child!
Not thus Achilles' self, from whom a tongue
720 Versed in vainglorious falsehood boasts thee sprung,
Dealt with an enemy; my prayer he heard;
A Suppliant's rights in Priam he revered,
Gave Hector back to rest within the tomb,
And me remitted to my royal home.'
This said, the aged Man a javelin cast;
With weak arm – faltering to the shield it past;
The tinkling shield the harmless point repelled,
Which, to the boss it hung from, barely held.
– Then Pyrrhus, 'To my Sire, Pelides, bear
730 These feats of mine, ill relished as they are,
Tidings of which I make thee messenger!
To him a faithful history relate
Of Neoptolemus degenerate.
Now die!' So saying, towards the Altar, through
A stream of filial blood, the tottering Sire he drew;
His left hand locked within the tangled hair
Raised, with the right, a brandished sword in air,
Then to the hilt impelled it through his side;
Thus, 'mid a blazing City, Priam died.
740 Troy falling round him, thus he closed his fate,
Once proud Lord of many an Asian State!
Upon the shore lies stretched his mangled frame,
Head from the shoulders torn, a Body without name.

Then first it was, that Horror girt me round;
Chilled my frail heart, and all my senses bound;
The image of my Father crossed my mind;
Perchance in fate with slaughtered Priam joined;
Equal in age, thus may He breathe out life,
Creusa also, my deserted Wife!
750 The Child Iülus left without defence,
And the whole House laid bare to violence!
Backward I looked, and cast my eyes before;
My Friends had failed, and courage was no more;

All, wearied out, had followed desperate aims,
Self-dashed to earth, or stifled in the flames.

Thus was I left alone; such light my guide
As the conflagrant walls and roofs supplied;
When my far-wandering eyesight chanced to meet
Helen sequestered on a lonely seat
760 Amid the Porch of Vesta; She, through dread
Of Trojan vengeance amply merited,
Of Grecian punishment, and what the ire
Of a deserted Husband might require,
Thither had flown – there sate, the common bane
Of Troy and of her Country – to obtain
Protection from the Altar, or to try
What hope might spring from trembling secrecy.
Methought my falling Country cried aloud,
And the revenge it seemed to ask, I vowed;
770 'What! shall she visit Sparta once again?
In triumph enter with a loyal Train?
Consort, and Home, and Sires and Children view
By Trojan Females served, a Phrygian retinue?
For this was Priam slain? Troy burnt? The shore
Of Dardan Seas so often drenched in gore?
Not so; for though such victory can claim
In its own nature no reward of fame,
The punishment that ends the guilty days
Even of a Woman, shall find grateful praise;
780 My soul, at least, shall of her weight be eased,
The ashes of my Countrymen appeased.'

Such words broke forth; and in my own despite
Onward I bore, when through the dreary night
Appeared my gracious Mother, vested in pure light;
Never till now before me did she shine
So much herself, so thoroughly divine;
Goddess revealed in all her beauty, love,
And majesty, as she is wont to move,
A Shape familiar to the Courts of Jove!

790 The hand she seized her touch sufficed to stay,
Then through her roseate mouth these words found
easy way.

'O Son! what pain excites a wrath so blind?
Or could all thought of me desert thy mind?
Where now is left thy Parent worn with age?
Wilt thou not rather in that search engage?
Learn with thine eyes if yet Creusa live,
And if the Boy Ascanius still survive.
Them do the Greeks environ: – that they spare,
That swords so long abstain, and flames forbear,
800 Is through the intervention of my care.
Not Spartan Helen's beauty, so abhorred
By thee, not Paris, her upbraided Lord –
The hostile Gods have laid this grandeur low,
Troy from the Gods receives her overthrow.
Look! for the impediment of misty shade
With which thy mortal sight is overlaid
I will disperse; nor thou refuse to hear
Parental mandates, nor resist through fear!
There, where thou seest block rolling upon block,
810 Mass rent from mass, and dust condensed with smoke
In billowy intermixture, Neptune smites
The walls, with labouring Trident disunites
From their foundation – tearing up, as suits
His anger, Ilium from her deepest roots.
Fiercest of all, before the Scaean Gate,
Armed Juno stands, beckoning to animate
The Bands she summons from the Argive Fleet,
Tritonian Pallas holds *her* chosen seat
High on the Citadel, – look back! see there
820 Her Aegis beaming forth a stormy glare!
The very Father, Jove himself, supplies
Strength to the Greeks, sends heaven-born enemies
Against the Dardan Arms. My Son, take flight,
And close the struggle of this dismal night!

I will not quit thy steps whate'er betide,
But to thy Father's House will safely guide.'
She ceased, and did in shades her presence hide.
Dire Faces still are seen and Deities
Adverse to Troy appear, her mighty Enemies.

830   Now was all Ilium, far as sight could trace,
Settling and sinking in the Fire's embrace,
Neptunian Troy subverted from her base.
Even so, a Mountain-Ash, long tried by shock
Of storms endured upon the native rock,
When He is doomed from rustic arms to feel
The rival blows of persevering steel,
Nods high with threatening forehead, till at length
Wounds unremitting have subdued his strength;
With groans the ancient Tree foretells his end;
840   He falls; and fragments of the mountain blend
With the precipitous ruin. – I descend
And, as the Godhead leads, 'twixt foe and fire
Advance: – the darts withdraw, the flames retire.

But when beneath her guidance I had come
Far as the Gates of the paternal Dome,
My Sire, whom first I sought and wished to bear
For safety to the Hills, disdains that care;
Nor will he now, since Troy hath fallen, consent
Life to prolong, or suffer banishment.
850   'Think Ye,' he says, 'the current of whose blood
Is unimpaired, whose vigour unsubdued,
Think Ye of flight; – that I should live, the Gods
Wish not, or they had saved me these Abodes.
Not once, but twice, this City to survive,
What need against such destiny to strive?
While thus, even thus disposed the body lies,
Depart! pronounce my funeral obsequies!
Not long shall I have here to wait for death,
A pitying Foe will rid me of my breath,
860   Will seek my spoils; and should I lie forlorn

Of sepulture, the loss may well be borne.
Full long obnoxious to the Powers divine
Life lingers out these barren years of mine;
Even since the date when me the eternal Sire
Swept with the thunderbolt, and scathed with fire.'
Thus he persists; – Creusa and her Son
Second the counter-prayer by me begun;
The total House with weeping deprecate
This weight of wilful impulse given to Fate;
870 He, all unmoved by pleadings and by tears,
Guards his resolve, and to the spot adheres.

Arms once again attract me, hurried on
In misery, and craving death alone.
'And hast thou hoped that I could move to find
A place of rest, thee, Father, left behind?
How could parental lips the guilty thought unbind?
If in so great a City Heaven ordain
Utter extinction; if thy soul retain
With stedfast longing that abrupt design
880 Which would to falling Troy add thee and thine;
That way to Death lies open; – soon will stand
Pyrrhus before thee with the reeking brand
That drank the blood of Priam; He whose hand
The Son in presence of the Father slays,
And at the Altar's base the slaughtered Father lays.
For this, benignant Mother! didst thou lead
My steps along a way from danger freed,
That I might see remorseless Men invade
The holiest places that these roofs o'ershade?
890 See Father, Consort, Son, all tinged and dyed
With mutual sprinklings, perish side by side?
Arms bring me, Friends! bring Arms! our last hour speaks,
It calls the Vanquished; cast me on the Greeks!
In rallying combat let us join; – not all,
This night, unsolaced by revenge shall fall!'

The sword resumes its place; the shield I bear;
And hurry now to reach the open air;

When on the ground before the threshold cast
Lo! where Creusa hath my feet embraced
900 And holding up Iülus, there cleaves fast!
'If thou, departing, be resolved to die,
Take us through all that in thy road may lie;
But if on Arms, already tried, attend
A single hope, then first this House defend;
On whose protection Sire and Son are thrown,
And I, the Wife that once was called thine own.'

  Such outcry filled the Mansion, when behold
A strange portent, and wonderous to be told!
All suddenly a luminous crest was seen;
910 Which, where the Boy Iülus hung between
The arms of each sad Parent, rose and shed,
Tapering aloft, a lustre from his head;
Along the hair the lambent flame proceeds
With harmless touch, and round his temples feeds.
In fear we haste, the burning tresses shake,
And from the fount the holy fire would slake;
But joyfully his hands Anchises raised,
His voice not silent as on Heaven he gazed:

  'Almighty Jupiter! if prayers have power
920 To bend thee, look on us; I seek no more;
If aught our piety deserve, Oh deign
The hope this Omen proffers to sustain;
Nor, Father, let us ask a second Sign in vain!'

  Thus spake the Sire, and scarcely ended, ere
A peal of sudden thunder, loud and clear,
Broke from the left; and shot through Heaven a Star
Trailing its torch, that sparkled from afar;
Above the roof the star, conspicuous sight,
Ran to be hid on Ida's sylvan height.
930 The long way marking with a train of light.
The furrowy track the distant sky illumes,
And far and wide are spread sulphureous fumes.

Uprisen from earth, my aged Sire implores
The Deities, the holy Star adores;
– 'Now am I conquered – now is no delay;
Gods of my Country! where Ye lead the way
'Tis not in me to hesitate or swerve;
Preserve my House, Ye Powers, this Little One preserve!
Yours is this augury; and Troy hath still
940   Life in the signs that manifest your will!
I cannot choose but yield; and now, to Thee,
O Son, a firm Associate will I be!'

He spake; and nearer through the City came
Rolling more audibly, the sea of flame.
'Now give, dear Father, to this neck the freight
Of thy old age; – the burden will be light
For which my shoulders bend; henceforth one fate,
Evil or good shall we participate.
The Boy shall journey, tripping at my side;
950   Our steps, at distance marked, will be Creusa's guide.
My Household! heed these words: upon a Mound
(To those who quit the City obvious ground)
A Temple, once by Ceres honoured, shows
Its mouldering front; hard by a Cypress grows,
Through ages guarded with religious care;
Thither, by various roads, let all repair.
Thou, Father! take these relics; let thy hand
Bear the Penates of our native land;
I may not touch them, fresh from deeds of blood,
960   Till the stream cleanse me with its living flood.'

Forthwith an ample vest my shoulders clad,
Above the vest a lion's skin was spread,
Next came the living Burden; fast in mine
His little hand Iülus doth entwine,
Following his Father with no equal pace;
Creusa treads behind; the darkest ways we trace.
And me, erewhile insensible to harms,
Whom adverse Greeks agglomerate in Arms   ⎫
Moved not, now every breath of air alarms;   ⎬
    ⎭

970 All sounds have power to trouble me with fear,
Anxious for whom I lead, and whom I bear.

Thus, till the Gates were nigh, my course I shaped,
And thought the hazards of the time escaped,
When through the gloom a noise of feet we hear,
Quick sounds that seemed to press upon the ear;
'Fly,' cries my Father, looking forth, 'Oh fly!
They come – I see their shields and dazzling panoply!'
Here, in my trepidation was I left,
Through some unfriendly Power, of mind bereft,
980 For, while I journeyed devious and forlorn,
From me, me wretched, was Creusa torn;
Whether stopped short by death, or from the road
She wandered, or sank down beneath a load
Of weariness, no vestiges made plain:
She vanished, ne'er to meet these eyes again.
Nor did I seek her lost, nor backward turn
My mind, until we reached the sacred bourne
Of ancient Ceres. All, even all, save One
Were in the spot assembled; She alone,
990 As if her melancholy fate disowned
Companion, Son, and Husband, nowhere could be found.
Who, man or God, from my reproach was free?
Had desolated Troy a heavier woe for me?
'Mid careful friends my Sire and Son I place,
With the Penates of our Phrygian race,
Deep in a winding vale; my footsteps then retrace;
Resolved the whole wide City to explore
And face the perils of the night once more.

So, with refulgent Arms begirt, I haste
1000 Toward the dark gates through which my feet had passed,
Remeasure, where I may, the beaten ground,
And turn at every step a searching eye around.
Horror prevails on all sides, while with dread
The very silence is impregnated.
Fast to my Father's Mansion I repair,
If haply, haply, She had harboured there.

Seized by the Grecians was the whole Abode:
And now, voracious fire its mastery showed,
Rolled upward by the wind in flames that meet
1010 High o'er the roof, – air rages with the heat;
Thence to the Towers I pass, where Priam held his Seat.
Already Phoenix and Ulysses kept,
As chosen Guards, the spoils of Ilium, heaped
In Juno's Temple, and the wealth that rose
Piled on the floors of vacant porticos,
Prey torn through fire from many a secret Hold,
Vests, tables of the Gods, and cups of massy gold.
And, in long order, round these treasures stand
Matrons, and Boys, and Youths, a trembling Band!

1020 Nor did I spare with fearless voice to raise
Shouts in the gloom that filled the streets and ways,
And with reduplication sad and vain,
Creusa called, again and yet again.
While thus I prosecute an endless quest
A Shape was seen, unwelcome and unblest;
Creusa's Shade appeared before my eyes,
Her Image, but of more than mortal size;
Then I, as if the power of life had passed
Into my upright hair, stood speechless and aghast.
1030 – She thus – to stop my troubles at their source:
'Dear Consort, why this fondly-desperate course?
Supernal Powers, not doubtfully, prepare
These issues; going hence thou wilt not bear
Creusa with thee; know that Fate denies
This fellowship, and this the Ruler of the skies.
Long wanderings will be thine, no home allowed;
Vast the extent of sea that must be ploughed
Ere, 'mid Hesperian fields where Tiber flows
With gentle current, thy tired keels repose.
1040 Joy meets thee there, a Realm and royal Bride,
 – For loved Creusa let thy tears be dried;
I go not where the Myrmidons abide.
No proud Dolopian Mansion shall I see

Nor shall a Grecian Dame be served by me,
Derived from Jove, and raised by thee so high,
Spouse to the Offspring of a Deity, –
Far otherwise; upon my native plains
Me the great Mother of the Gods detains.
Now, fare thee well! protect our Son, and prove
1050 By tenderness for him, our common love.'

This having said – my trouble to subdue,
Into thin air she silently withdrew;
Left me while tears were gushing from their springs,
And on my tongue a thousand hasty things;
Thrice with my arms I strove her neck to clasp,
Thrice had my hands succeeded in their grasp,
From which the Image slipped away, as light
As the swift winds, or sleep when taking flight.

Such was the close; and now the night thus spent,
1060 Back to my Friends an eager course I bent,
And here a crowd with wonder I behold
Of new Associates, concourse manifold!
Matrons, and Men, and Youths that hither hied,
For exile gathering; and from every side
The wretched people thronged and multiplied;
Prepared with mind and means their flight to speed
Across the seas, where I might choose to lead.

Now on the ridge of Ida's summit grey
Rose Lucifer, prevenient to the day.
1070 The Grecians held the Gates in close blockade,
Hope was there none of giving further aid;
I yielded, took my Father up once more,
And sought the Mountain, with the Freight I bore.

THIRD BOOK
Now when the Gods had crushed the Asian State
And Priam's race, by too severe a fate;
When they were pleased proud Ilium to destroy,
And smokes upon the ground Neptunian Troy;

The sad Survivors, from their Country driven,
Seek distant shores, impelled by signs from Heaven.
Beneath Antandros we prepare a Fleet: –
There my Companions muster at the feet
Of Phrygian Ida, dubious in our quest,
10 And where the Fates may suffer us to rest.
Scarcely had breathed the earliest summer gales
Before Anchises bid to spread the sails;
Weeping I quit the Port, my native coast,
And fields where Troy once was; and soon am tost
An Exile on the bosom of the seas,
With Friends, Son, household Gods and the great
  Deities.
Right opposite is spread a peopled Land,
Where once the fierce Lycurgus held command;
The martial Thracians plough its champain wide,
20 To Troy by hospitable rites allied,
While Fortune favoured to this coast we hied;
Where entering with unfriendly Fates, I lay
My first foundations in a hollow bay;
And call the men Aeneades, – to share
With the new Citoyens the name I bear.
To Dionaean Venus we present,
And to the Gods who aid a fresh intent,
The sacred offerings; and with honour due
Upon the shore a glossy Bull I slew
30 To the great King of Heaven. A Mount was near
Upon whose summit cornel trees uprear
Their boughs, and myrtles rough with many a spear.
Studious to deck the Altar with green shoots,
Thither I turned; and, tugging at the roots
Strove to despoil the thicket; when behold
A dire portent, and wondrous to be told!
No sooner was the shattered root laid bare
Of the first Tree I struggled to uptear,
Than from the fibres drops of blood distilled,
40 Whose blackness stained the ground:– me horror thrilled:
My frame all shuddered, and my blood was chilled.

Persisting in the attempt, I toiled to free
The flexile body of another tree,
Anxious the latent causes to explore;
And from the bark blood trickled as before.
Revolving much in mind forthwith I paid
Vows to the sylvan Nymphs, and sought the aid
Of Father Mars, spear-shaking God who yields
His stern protection to the Thracian fields;
50 That to a prosperous issue they would guide
The accident, the omen turn aside.
But, for a third endeavour, when with hands
Eagerly strained, knees pressed against the sands,
I strive the myrtle lances to uproot
With my whole strength (speak shall I, or be mute?)
From the deep tomb a mournful groan was sent
And a voice followed, uttering this lament:
'Torment me not, Aeneas. Why this pain
Given to a buried Man? O cease, refrain,
60 And spare thy pious hands this guilty stain!
Troy brought me forth, no alien to thy blood;
Nor yields a senseless trunk this sable flood.
Oh fly the cruel land; the greedy shore
Forsake with speed, for I am Polydore.
A flight of iron darts have pierced me through,
Took life, and into this sharp thicket grew.'
Then truly did I stand aghast, cold fear
Strangling my voice, and lifting up my hair.
Erewhile from Troy had Priam sent by stealth
70 This Polydore, and with him store of wealth;
Trusting the Thracian King his Son would rear:
For wretched Priam now gave way to fear,
Seeing the Town beleaguered. These alarms
Spread to the Thracian King, and when the Arms
Of Troy were quelled, to the victorious side
Of Agamemnon he his hopes allied;
Breaking through sacred laws without remorse,
Slew Polydore, and seized the gold by force.
What mischief to poor mortals has not thirst

80 Of gold created! appetite accursed!
Soon as a calmer mind I could recall
I seek the Chiefs, my Father above all;
Report the omen, and their thoughts demand.
One mind is theirs, – to quit the impious Land;
With the first breezes of the South to fly
Sick of polluted hospitality.
Forthwith on Polydore our hands bestow
A second burial, and fresh mould upthrow;
And to his Manes raise beside the mound
90 Altars, which, as they stood in mournful round,
Cerulean fillets and black cypress bound;
And with loose hair a customary Band
Of Trojan Women in the circle stand.
From cups warm milk and sacred blood we pour,
Thus to the tomb the Spirit we restore;
And with a farewell cry its future rest implore.

Then, when the sea grew calm, and gently creeps
The soft South-wind and calls us to the Deeps,
The Crew draw down our Ships; they crowd the
    Shore,
100 The Port we leave; with Cities sprinkled o'er,
Slowly the Coast recedes, and then is seen no more.

In the 'mid Deep there lies a spot of earth,
Sacred to her who gave the Nereids birth;
And to Aegean Neptune. Long was tossed
This then unfruitful ground, and driven from coast to
    coast;
But, as it floated o'er the wide-spread sea,
The Archer-God, in filial piety,
Between two Sister islands bound it fast
For Man's abode, and to defy the blast.
110 Thither we steer. At length the unruffled Place
Received our Vessels in her calm embrace.
We land – and, when the pleasant soil we trod,
Adored the City of the Delian God.

Anius, the King (whose brows were wreathed around
With laurel garlands and with fillets bound,
His sacred symbols as Apollo's Priest)
Advanced to meet us, from our ships released;
He recognized Anchises; and their hands
Gladly they join, renewing ancient Bands
120 Of Hospitality; nor longer waits
The King, but leads us to his friendly gates.

To seek the Temple was my early care;
To whose Divinity I bowed in prayer
Within the reverend Pile of ancient stone: –
'Thymbreus! painful wanderings have we known
Grant, to the weary, dwellings of their own!
A City yield, a Progeny ensure,
A habitation destined to endure! –
– To us, sad relics of the Grecian Sword,
130 (All that is left of Troy) another Troy accord!
What shall we seek? whom follow? where abide?
Vouchsafe an augury our course to guide;
Father, descend, and through our Spirits glide!'
– Then shook, or seemed to shake, the entire Abode;
A trembling seized the Laurels of the God;
The mountain rocked; and sounds with murmuring
  swell
Rolled from the Shrine; upon the ground I fell,
And heard the guiding voice our fates foretell.
'Ye patient Dardans! that same Land which bore
140 From the first Stock your Fathers heretofore;
That ancient Mother will unfold her breast
For your return, – seek *Her* with faithful quest;
So shall the Aenean Line command the earth
As long as future years to future years give birth.'

Thus Phoebus answered, and forthwith the crowd
Burst into transport vehement and loud:
All ask what Phoebus wills; and where the bourne
To which Troy's wandering Race are destined to return.

Then spake my aged Father, turning o'er
150 Traditions handed down from days of yore;
'Give ear,' he said, 'O Chieftains, while my words
Unfold the hopes this Oracle affords!
On the mid sea the Cretan Island lies,
Dear to the sovereign Lord of earth and skies;
There is the Idean Mount, and there we trace
The fountain-head, the cradle of our race.
A hundred Cities, places of command,
Rise in the circle of that fruitful land;
Thence to Rhoetean shores (if things oft heard
160 I faithfully remember) Teucer steered,
Our first progenitor; and chose a spot
His Seat of government when Troy was not;
While yet the Natives housed in valleys deep,
Ere Pergamus had risen, to crown the lofty steep.
From Crete came Cybele; from Crete we gained
All that the Mother of the Gods ordained;
The Corybantian Cymbals thence we drew,
The Idaean Grove; and faithful Silence, due
To rites mysterious; and the Lion pair
170 Ruled by the Goddess from her awful Car.
Then haste – the Mandate of the Gods obey
And to the Gnossian Realms direct our way;
But first the winds propitiate, and if Jove
From his high Throne the enterprise approve,
The third day's light shall bring our happy Fleet
To a safe harbour on the shores of Crete.'

He spake, appropriate Victims forth were led,
And by his hand upon the Altars bled;
A Bull to soothe the God who rules the Sea –
180 A Bull, O bright Apollo! fell to thee,
A sable sheep for Hyems doth he smite,
For the soft Zephyrs one of purest white.
Fame told that regions would in Crete be found
Bare of the foe, deserted tracts of ground;
Left by Idomeneus, to recent flight

Driven from those realms – his patrimonial right.
Cheered by a hope those vacant seats to gain
We quit the Ortygian Shore, and scud along the Main.
Near ridgy Naxos, traversed by a rout
190   Of madding Bacchanals with song and shout;
By green Donysa rising o'er the Deeps;
Olearos, and snow-white Parian steeps;
Flying with prosperous sail through sounds and seas
Starred with the thickly-clustering Cyclades.
Confused and various clamour rises high;
'To Crete and to our Ancestors' we cry
While Ships and Sailors each with other vie.
Still freshening from the stern the breezes blow,
And speed the Barks they chase, where'er we go;
200   Till rest is given upon the ancient Shores
Of the Curetes to their Sails and Oars.
So with keen hope I trace a circling Wall
And the new City, by a name which all
Repeat with gladness, Pergamus I call.
The thankful Citoyens I then exhort
To love their hearths, and raise a guardian Fort.
– The Fleet is drawn ashore; in eager Bands
The Settlers cultivate the allotted lands;
And some for Hymeneal rites prepare;
210   I plan our new Abodes, fit laws declare;
But pestilence now came, and tainted the wide air.
To piteous wasting were our limbs betrayed;
On trees and plants the deadly season preyed.
The men relinquished their dear lives, – or life
Remaining, dragged their frames in feeble strife.
Thereafter, Sirius clomb the sultry sky,
Parched every herb to bare sterility;
And forced the sickly corn its nurture to deny.
My anxious Sire exhorts to seek once more
220   The Delian shrine, and pardon thence implore;
Ask of the God to what these sorrows tend,
Whence we must look for aid, our voyage whither
bend.

'Twas night, and couched upon the dewy ground
The weary Animals in sleep were bound,
When those Penates which my hands had snatched
From burning Troy, while on my bed I watched,
Appeared, and stood before me, to my sight
Made manifest by copious streams of light
Poured from the body of the full-orbed Moon,
230 That through the loop-holes of my chamber shone.
Thus did they speak: 'We come, the Delegates
Of Phoebus, to foretell thy future fates:
Things which his Delian tripod to thine ear
Would have announced, through us he utters here.
When Troy was burnt we crost the billowy sea
Faithful Attendants on thy arms, and *We*
Shall raise to Heaven thy proud Posterity.
But thou thy destined wanderings stoutly bear,
And for the Mighty, mighty seats prepare;
240 These thou must leave; – Apollo ne'er designed
That thou in Crete a resting-place shouldst find.
There is a Country styled by Men of Greece
Hesperia – strong in arms – the soil of large increase,
Aenotrians held it; men of later fame
Call it Italia, from their Leader's name;
Our home is there; there lies the native place
Of Dardanus, and Iasius – whence our race.
Rise then; and to thy aged Father speak
Indubitable tidings; – bid him seek
250 The Ausonian Land, and Corithus; Jove yields
No place to us among Dictean fields.'

Upon the sacred spectacle I gazed,
And heard the utterance of the Gods, amazed.
Sleep in this visitation had no share;
Each face I saw – the fillets round their hair!
Chilled with damp fear I started from the bed,
And raised my hands and voice to heaven – then shed
On the recipient hearth untempered wine
In prompt libation to the powers divine.

260 This rite performed with joy, my Sire I sought
Charged with the message that the Gods had brought;
When I had opened all in order due
The truth found easy entrance; for he knew
The double Ancestors, the ambiguous race,
And owned his new mistake in person and in place.
Then he exclaimed 'O Son, severely tried
In all that Troy is fated to abide,
This course Cassandra's voice to me made known;
She prophesied of this, and she alone;
270 Italia oft she cried, and words outthrew
Of realms Hesperian, to our Nation due:
But how should Phrygians such a power erect?
Whom did Cassandra's sayings then affect?
Now, let us yield to Phoebus, and pursue
The happier lot he offers to our view.'
All heard with transport what my Father spake.
This habitation also we forsake;
And strait, a scanty remnant left behind,
Once more in hollow Ships we court the helpful
    wind.

280   But when along the Deep our Galleys steered,
And the last speck of land had disappeared,
And naught was visible, above, around,
Save the blank sky, and ocean without bound,
Then came a Tempest-laden Cloud that stood
Right over me, and roused the blackening flood.
The fleet is scattered, while around us rise
Billows that every moment magnifies.
Day fled, and heaven, enveloped in a night
Of stormy rains, is taken from our sight;
290 By instincts of their own the clouds are riven
And prodigal of fire – while we are driven
Far from the points we aimed at, every bark
Errant upon the waters rough and dark.
Even Palinurus owns that night and day,
Thus in each other lost, confound his way.

Three sunless days we struggle with the gales,
And for three starless nights all guidance fails;
The fourth day came, and to our wistful eyes
The far-off Land then first began to rise,
300 Lifting itself in hills that gently broke
Upon our view, and rolling clouds of smoke.
Sails drop; the Mariners, with spring and stoop
Timed to their oars, the eddying waters scoop,
The Vessels skim the waves, alive from prow to poop.

Saved from the perils of the stormy seas,
We disembark upon the Strophades;
Amid the Ionian Waters lie this pair
Of Islands, and that Grecian name they bear.
The brood of Harpies, when in fear they left
310 The doors of Phineus, – of that home bereft
And of their former tables – thither fled,
There dwelt with dire Celaeno at their head.
No plague so hideous, for impure abuse
Of upper air, did ever Styx produce,
Stirred by the anger of the Gods, to fling
From out her waves some new-born monstrous Thing.
Birds they, with virgin faces, crooked claws;
Of filthy paunch and of insatiate maws,
And pallid mien – from hunger without pause.

320 Here safe in port we saw the fields o'erspread
With beeves and goats, untended as they fed.
Prompt slaughter follows; offerings thence we pay,
And call on Jove himself to share the prey.
Then, couch by couch, along the bay we rear,
And feast well pleased upon that goodly cheer.
But, clapping loud their wings, the Harpy brood
Rush from the mountain – pounce upon our food,
Pollute the morsels which they fail to seize –
And, screaming, load with noisome scents the breeze.
330 Again – but now within a long-drawn glade
O'erhung with rocks and boughs of roughest shade

We deck our tables, and replace the fire
Upon the Altars; but, with noises dire,
From different points of Heaven, from blind retreats,
They flock – and hovering o'er defile the meats.
'War let them have,' I cried, and gave command
To stem the next foul onset, arms in hand.
Forthwith the men withdraw from sight their shields
And hide their swords where grass a covert yields,
340 But when the Harpies with loud clang once more
Gathered, and spread upon the curvèd shore,
From a tall eminence in open view
His trumpet sound of charge Misenus blew;
Then do our swords assault those Fowls obscene,
Of generation aqueous and terrene.
But what avails it? oft repeated blows
They with inviolable plumes oppose;
Baffle the steel, and, leaving stains behind
And spoil half eaten, mount upon the wind;
350 Celaeno only on a summit high
Perched – and there vented this sad prophecy.

'By war, Descendants of Laomedon!
For our slain Steers, by war would ye atone?
Why seek the blameless Harpies to expel
From regions where by right of birth they dwell?
But learn, and fast within your memories hold,
Things which to Phoebus Jupiter foretold,
Phoebus to me, and I to you unfold,
I, greatest of the Furies. Ye, who strive
360 For Italy, in Italy shall arrive;
Havens within that wished-for land, by leave
Of favouring winds, your Navy shall receive;
But do not hope to raise those promised Walls
Ere on your head the curse of hunger falls;
And, for the slaughter of our herds, your doom
Hath been your very tables to consume,
Gnawed and devoured through utter want of food!'
She spake, and, borne on wings, sought refuge in the wood.

The haughty spirits of the Men were quailed,
370　A shuddering fear through every heart prevailed;
On force of arms no longer they rely
To daunt whom prayers and vows must pacify,
Whether to Goddesses the offence were given,
Or they with dire and obscene Birds had striven.
Due Rites ordained, as on the shore he stands,
My Sire Anchises, with uplifted hands,
Invokes the greater Gods: 'Ye Powers, disarm
This threat, and from your Votaries turn the harm!'
Then bids to loose the Cables and unbind
380　The willing canvas, to the breeze resigned.

Where guides the Steersman and the south winds urge
Our rapid keels, we skim the foaming surge,
Before us opens midway in the flood
Zacynthus, shaded with luxuriant wood;
Dulichium now, and Same next appears;
And Neritos a craggy summit rears;
We shun the rocks of Ithaca, ill Nurse
Of stern Ulysses! and her soil we curse;
Then Mount Leucate shows its vapoury head;
390　Where, from his temple, Phoebus strikes with dread
The passing Mariner; but no mischance
Now feared, to that small City we advance;
Gladly we haul the sterns ashore, and throw
The biting Anchor out from every prow.

Unlooked-for land thus reached, to Jove we raise
The votive Altars which with incense blaze;
Our Youth, illustrating the Actian Strand
With Trojan games, as in their native land
Imbue their naked limbs with slippery oil,
400　And pant for mastery in athletic toil;
Well pleased so fair a voyage to have shaped
'Mid Grecian Towns on every side escaped.
Sol through his annual round meanwhile had passed,
And the Sea roughened in the wintry blast;

High on the Temple Gate a brazen shield
I fixed, which mighty Abbas used to wield;
Inscriptive verse declared, why this was done,
'*Arms from the conquering Greeks and by Aeneas won.*'
Then at my word the Ships their moorings leave,
410 And with contending oars the waters cleave;
Phaeacian Peaks beheld in air and lost
As we proceed, Epirus now we coast;
And, a Chaonian harbour won, we greet
Buthrotas, perched upon her lofty seat.

Helenus, Son of Priam, here was Chief,
(So ran the tale ill-fitted for belief),
Governed where Grecian Pyrrhus once had reigned,
Whose sceptre wielding he, therewith, had gained
Andromache his Spouse, – to nuptials led
420 Once more by one whom Troy had born and bred.
I longed to greet him, wished to hear his fate
As his own voice the Story would relate.
So from the Port in which our galleys lay,
Right toward the City I pursued my way.
A Grove there was, where by a streamlet's side
With the proud name of Simois dignified,
Andromache a solemn service paid,
(As chanced that day) invoking Hector's shade;
There did her hands the mournful gifts present
430 Before a tomb – his empty monument
Of living green-sward hallowed by her care;
And two funereal Altars, planted near,
Quickened the motion of each falling tear,
When my approach she witnessed, and could see
Our Phrygian Arms, she shrank as from a prodigy,
In blank astonishment and terror shook,
While the warm blood her tottering limbs forsook.
She swooned and long lay senseless on the ground,
Before these broken words a passage found:
440 'Was that a real Shape which met my view?
Son of a Goddess, is thy coming true?

Liv'st thou? or, if the light of life be fled,
Hector, where is he?' This she spake, – then spread
A voice of weeping through the Grove, and I
Uttered these few faint accents in disturbed reply.
'Fear not to trust thine eyes; I live indeed,
And fraught with trouble is the life I lead.
Fallen from the height, where with thy glorious Mate
Thou stood'st, Andromache, what change had Fate
450 To offer worthy of thy former state?
Say, did the Gods take pity on thy vows?
Or have they given to Pyrrhus Hector's Spouse?'

Then she with downcast look, and voice subdued:
'Thrice happy Virgin, thou of Priam's blood,
Who, in the front of Troy by timely doom,
Didst pour out life before a hostile tomb;
And, slaughtered thus, wert guarded from the wrong
Of being swept by lot amid a helpless throng!
O happiest above all who ne'er did press
460 A conquering Master's bed, in captive wretchedness!
I, since our Ilium fell, have undergone
(Wide waters crossed) whate'er Achilles' Son
Could in the arrogance of birth impose,
And faced in servitude a Mother's throes.
Hereafter, he at will the knot untied,
To seek Hermione a Spartan Bride;
And me to Trojan Helenus he gave –
Captive to Captive – if not Slave to Slave.
Whereat, Orestes with strong love inflamed
470 Of her now lost whom as a bride he claimed,
And by the Furies driven, in vengeful ire
Smote Pyrrhus at the Altar of his Sire.
He, by an unexpected blow, thus slain,
On Helenus devolved a part of his Domain,
Who called the neighbouring fields Chaonian ground,
Chaonia named the Region wide around,
From Trojan Chaon, – choosing for the site
Of a new Pergamus yon rocky height.

But thee a Stranger in a land unknown
480 What Fates have urged? What winds have hither blown?
Or say what God upon our coasts hath thrown?
Survives the Boy Ascanius? In his heart
Doth his lost Mother still retain her part?
What, Son of great Aeneas, brings he forth
In emulation of his Father's worth?
In Priam's Grandchild doth not Hector raise
High hopes to reach the virtue of past days?'

Then followed sobs and lamentations vain;
But from the City, with a numerous train,
490 Her living Consort Helenus descends;
He saw, and gave glad greeting to his Friends;
And towards his hospitable palace leads
While passion interrupts the speech it feeds.
As we advance I gratulate with joy
Their dwindling Xanthus, and their little Troy;
Their Pergamus aspiring in proud state,
As if it strove the old to emulate;
And clasp the threshold of their Scaean Gate.
Nor fails this kindred City to excite
500 In my Associates unreserved delight;
And soon in ample Porticos the King
Receives the Band with earnest welcoming;
Amid the Hall high festival we hold,
Refreshed with viands served in massy gold
And from resplendent goblets, votive wine
Flows in libations to the Powers divine.

Two joyful days thus past, the southern breeze
Once more invites my Fleet to trust the Seas;
To Helenus this suit I then prefer:
510 'Illustrious Trojan! Heaven's interpreter!
By prescient Phoebus with his spirit filled,
Skilled in the tripod, in the laurel skilled;
Skilled in the stars, and what by voice or wing
Birds to the intelligence of mortals bring;

Now mark: – to Italy my course I bend
Urged by the Gods who for this aim portend,
By every sign they give, a happy end.
The Harpy Queen, she only doth presage
A curse of famine in its utmost rage;
520 Say thou what perils I am first to shun,
What course for safe deliverance must be run?'

Then Helenus (the accustomed Victims slain)
Invoked the Gods their favour to obtain.
This done, he loosed the fillets from his head,
And took my hand; and, while a holy dread
Possessed me, onward to the Temple led,
Thy Temple, Phoebus! – from his lip then flowed
Communications of the inspiring God. –
'No common auspices (this truth is plain)
530 Conduct thee, Son of Venus! o'er the Main;
The high behests of Jove this course ordain.
But, that with safer voyage thou mayst reach
The Ausonian harbour, I will clothe in speech
Some portion of the future; Fate hath hung
Clouds o'er the rest, or Juno binds my tongue.
And first, *that* Italy, whose coasts appear,
To thy too confident belief, so near,
With havens open for thy sails, a wide
And weary distance doth from thee divide.
540 Trinacrian waves shall bend the pliant oar;
Thou, through Ausonian gulfs, a passage must explore,
Trace the Circean Isle, the infernal Pool,
Before thy City rise for stedfast rule.
Now mark these Signs, and store them in thy mind;
When, anxiously reflecting, thou shalt find
A bulky Female of the bristly Kind
On a sequestered river's margin laid,
Where Ilex branches do the ground o'ershade,
With thirty young ones couched in that Recess,
550 White as the pure white Dam whose teats they press,
There found thy City; – on *that* soil shall close

All thy solicitudes, in fixed repose.
Nor dread Celaeno's threat, the Fates shall clear
The way, and at thy call Apollo interfere.
But shun those Lands where our Ionian sea
Washes the nearest shores of Italy.
On all the coasts malignant Greeks abide;
Narycian Locrians there a Town have fortified;
Idomeneus of Crete hath compassed round
560   With soldiery the Sallentinian ground;
There, when Thessalian Philoctetes chose
His resting-place, the small Petilia rose.
And when, that sea past over, thou shalt stand
Before the Altars, kindled on the strand,
While to the Gods are offered up thy vows,
Then in a purple veil enwrap thy brows,
And sacrifice thus covered, lest the sight
Of any hostile face disturb the rite.
Be this observance kept by thee and thine,
570   And this to late posterity consign!
But when by favouring breezes wafted o'er
Thy Fleet approaches the Sicilian shore,
And dense Pelorus gradually throws
Its barriers open to invite thy prows,
That passage shunned, thy course in safety keep
By steering to the left, with ample sweep.

  ' 'Tis said when heaving Earth of yore was rent
This ground forsook the Hesperian Continent;
Nor doubt, that power to work such change might lie
580   Within the grasp of dark Antiquity.
Then flowed the sea between, and, where the force
Of roaring waves established the divorce,
Still, through the Straits, the narrow waters boil,
Dissevering Town from Town, and soil from soil.
Upon the right the dogs of Scylla fret;
The left by fell Charybdis is beset;
Thrice towards the bottom of a vast abyss
Down, headlong down the liquid precipice

She sucks the whirling billows, and, as oft,
590 Ejecting, sends them into air aloft.
But Scylla, pent within her Cavern blind,
Thrusts forth a visage of our human kind,
And draws the Ship on rocks; She, fair in show,
A woman to the waist, is foul below;
A huge Sea-Beast – with Dolphin tails, and bound
With water Wolves and Dogs her middle round!
But Thou against this jeopardy provide
Doubling Pachynus with a circuit wide;
Thus shapeless Scylla may be left unseen,
600 Unheard the yelling of her brood marine.
But, above all if Phoebus I revere
Not unenlightened, an authentic Seer,
Then, Goddess-born, (on this could I enlarge
Repeating oft and oft the solemn charge)
Adore imperial Juno, freely wait
With gifts on Juno's Altar, supplicate
Her potent favour, and subdue her hate;
So shalt thou seek, a Conqueror at last,
The Italian shore, Trinacrian dangers past!
610 Arrived at Cumae and the sacred floods
Of black Avernus resonant with woods,
Thou shalt behold the Sybil where She sits
Within her cave, rapt in ecstatic fits,
And words and characters to leaves commits.
The prophecies which on those leaves the Maid
Inscribes, are by her hands in order laid
'Mid the secluded Cavern, where they fill
Their several places, undisturbed and still.
But if a light wind entering through the door
620 Scatter the thin leaves on the rocky floor,
She to replace her prophecies will use
No diligence; all flutter where they choose,
In hopeless disconnexion loose and wild;
And they, who sought for knowledge, thus beguiled
Of her predictions, from the cave depart,
And quit the Sybil with a murmuring heart.

But thou, albeit ill-disposed to wait,
And prizing moments at their highest rate,
Though Followers chide, and ever and anon
630 The flattering winds invite thee to be gone,
Beg of the moody Prophetess to break
The silent air, and for thy guidance speak.
She will disclose the features of thy doom,
The Italian Nations, and the Wars to come;
How to escape from hardships, or endure,
And make a happy termination sure;
Enough – chains bind the rest, or clouds obscure.
Go then, nor in thy glorious progress halt,
But to the stars the Trojan name exalt!'

640　　So spake the friendly Seer, from hallowed lips,
Then orders sumptuous presents to the Ships;
Smooth ivory, massy gold, with ponderous store
Of vases fashioned from the paler ore;
And Dodonaean Cauldrons, nor withholds
The golden halberk, knit in triple folds,
That Neoptolemus erewhile had worn;
Nor his resplendent crest which waving plumes adorn.
Rich offerings also grace my Father's hands;
Horses he adds with Equerries, and Bands
650 Of Rowers, and supply of Arms commands.
– Meanwhile Anchises bids the Fleet unbind
Its sails for instant seizure of the wind.
The Interpreter of Phoebus then addressed
This gracious farewell to his ancient Guest:
'Anchises! to celestial honours led,
Beloved of Venus, whom she deigned to wed,
Care of the Gods, twice snatched from Ilium lost,
Now for Ausonia be these waters crossed!
Yet must thou only glide along the shores
660 To which I point; far lies the Land from ours
Whither Apollo's voice directs your powers:
Go, happy Parent of a pious Son,
No more – I baulk the winds that press thee on.'

Nor less Andromache, disturbed in heart
That parting now, we must for ever part,
Embroidered Vests of golden thread bestows;
A Phrygian Tunic o'er Ascanius throws;
And studious that her bounty may become
The occasion, adds rich labours of the loom:
670 'Dear Child,' she said, 'these also, to be kept
As the memorials of my hand, accept!
Last gifts of Hector's Consort, let them prove
To thee the symbols of enduring love;
Take what Andromache at parting gives,
Fair Boy! – sole Image that for me survives
Of my Astyanax, – in whom his face,
His eyes are seen, his very hands I trace;
And now, but for obstruction from the tomb,
His years had opened into kindred bloom.'
680 To these, while gushing tears bedewed my cheek,
Thus in the farewell moment did I speak:
'Live happy Ye, whose race of fortune run
Permits such life; from trials undergone
We to the like are called, by you is quiet won.
No seas have Ye to measure, nor on you
Is it imposed Ausonia to pursue,
And search for fields still flying from the view.
Lo Xanthus here in miniature! – there stands
A second Troy, the labour of your hands,
690 With happier auspices – in less degree
Exposed, I trust, to Grecian enmity.
If Tiber e'er receive me, and the sod
Of Tiber's meadows by these feet be trod,
If e'er I see our promised City rise,
These neighbouring Nations bound by ancient ties
Hesperian and Epirian, whose blood came
From Dardanus, whose lot hath been the same,
Shall make one Troy in spirit. May that care
To our Descendants pass from heir to heir!'

700   We coast the high Ceraunia, whence is found

The shortest transit to Italian ground;
Meanwhile the sun went down, and shadows spread
O'er every mountain darkened to its head.
Tired of their oars the Men no sooner reach
Earth's wished-for bosom than their limbs they stretch
On the dry margin of the murmuring Deep,
Where weariness is lost in timely sleep.
Ere Night, whose Car the Hours had yoked and reined,
Black Night, the middle of her orbit gained,
710 Up from his couch did Palinurus rise,
Looks to the wind for what it signifies,
And to each breath of air a watchful ear applies.
Next all the Stars gliding through silent Heaven
The Bears, Arcturus, and the clustered Seven,
Are noted, – and his ranging eyes behold
Magnificent Orion armed in gold.
When he perceives that all things low and high
Unite to promise fixed serenity,
He sends the summons forth; our Camp we raise, –
720 Are gone, – and every Ship her broadest wings displays.

Now, when Aurora reddened in a sky
From which the Stars had vanished, we descry
The low faint hills of distant Italy.
'Italia!' shouts Achates; round and round
'Italia' flies with gratulant rebound,
From all who see the coast, or hear the happy sound.
Not slow is Sire Anchises to entwine
With wreaths a goblet, which he filled with wine,
Then, on the Stern he took his lofty stand,
730 And cried, 'Ye Deities of sea and land
Through whom the Storms are governed, speed our way
By breezes docile to your kindliest sway!'
– With freshening impulse breathe the wished-for gales,
And, as the Ships press on with greedy sails,
Opens the Port; and, peering into sight,
Minerva's Temple tops a craggy height.
The Sails are furled by many a busy hand;

The veering prows are pointed to the Strand.
Curved into semblance of a bow, the Haven
740 Looks to the East; but not a wave thence driven
Disturbs its peacefulness; their foamy spray
Breaks upon jutting rocks that fence the Bay.
Two towering cliffs extend with gradual fall
Their arms into the Sea, and frame a wall
In whose embrace the harbour hidden lies;
And, as its shelter deepens on our eyes,
Back from the shore Minerva's Temple flies.

Four snow-white Horses, grazing the wide fields,
Are the first omen which our landing yields;
750 Then Sire Anchises – 'War thy tokens bear
O Hospitable land! The Horse is armed for war;
War do these menace, but as Steed with Steed
Oft joins in friendly yoke, the sight may breed
Fair hope that peace and concord will succeed.'
To Pallas then in clanking armour mailed,
Who hailed us first, exulting to be hailed,
Prayers we address – with Phrygian amice veiled;
And, as by Helenus enjoined, the fire
On Juno's Altar fumes – to Juno vows aspire.
760 When we had ceased this service to present
That instant, seaward are our Sail-yards bent
And we forsake the Shore – with cautious dread
Of ground by Native Grecians tenanted.

The Bay is quickly reached that draws its name
From proud Tarentum, proud to share the fame
Of Hercules though by a dubious claim:
Right opposite we ken the Structure holy
Of the Lacinian Goddess rising slowly;
Next the Caulonian Citadel appeared
770 And the Scylacian bay for Shipwrecks feared;
Lo, as along the open Main we float,
Mount Etna, yet far off! and far remote
Groans of the Sea we hear; – deep groans and strokes

Of angry billows beating upon rocks, –
And hoarse surf-clamours, – while the flood throws up
Sands from the depths of its unsettled cup.
My Sire exclaimed, 'Companions, we are caught
By fell Charybdis, – flee as ye were taught!
These, doubtless, are the rocks, the dangerous shores
780 Which Helenus denounced – away – with straining oars.'
Quick, to the left the Master Galley veers
With roaring prow, as Palinurus steers;
And for the left the bands of Rowers strive,
While every help is caught that winds can give.
The whirlpool's dizzy altitudes we scale,
For ghastly sinking when the waters fail.
The hollow rocks thrice gave a fearful cry:
Three times we saw the clashing waves fling high }
Their foam dispersed along a drizzling sky.
790 The flagging wind forsook us with the sun,
And to Cyclopian shores a darkling course we run.

The Port, which now we chance to enter, lies
By winds unruffled though of ample size;
But all too near is Etna, thundering loud;
And ofttimes casting up a pitchy cloud
Of smoke – in whirling convolutions driven,
With weight of hoary ashes, high as heaven,
And globes of flame; and sometimes he gives vent
To rocky fragments, from his entrails rent;
800 And hurls out melting substances – that fly
In thick assemblage, and confound the sky;
While groans and lamentations burdensome
Tell to the air from what a depth they come.
The enormous Mass of Etna, so 'tis said,
On lightning-scorched Enceladus was laid;
And ever pressing on the Giant's frame,
Breathes out, from fractured chimneys, fitful flame,
And, often as he turns his weary side
Murmuring Trinacria trembles far and wide, }
810 While wreaths of smoke ascend and all the welkin hide.

We, through the night, enwrapped in woods obscure,
The shock of those dire prodigies endure,
Nor could distinguish whence might come the sound;
For all the stars to ether's utmost bound
Were hidden or bedimmed, and Night withheld
The Moon, in mist and lowering fogs concealed.
    [*Desunt*: translation of lines 588–706]

Those left, we harboured on the joyless coast
Of Drepanum, here harassed long and tossed,
And here my Sire Anchises did I lose,
820 Help in my cares, and solace of my woes.
Here, O best Father! best beloved and best
Didst thou desert me when I needed rest,
Thou, from so many perils snatched in vain:
Not Helenus, though much in doleful strain
He prophesied, this sorrow did unfold,
Not dire Celaeno this distress foretold.
This trouble was my last; Celestial Powers
O Queen, have brought me to your friendly shores.'

    Sole speaker, thus Aeneas did relate
830 To a hushed audience the decrees of Fate,
His wandering course remeasured, till the close
Now reached, in silence here he found repose.

FOURTH BOOK, LINES 688—92

She who to lift her heavy eyes had tried
Faints while the deep wound gurgles at her side
Thrice on her elbow propped she strove to uphold
Her frame – thrice back upon the couch was rolled,
Then with a wandering eye in heaven's blue round
She sought the light and groaned when she had found.

EIGHTH BOOK, LINES 337—66

This scarcely uttered they advance, and straight
He shows the Altar and Carmental Gate,
Which (such the record) by its Roman name
Preserves the nymph Carmenta's ancient fame,
Who first the glories of the Trojan line
Predicted, and the noble Pallantine.
Next points he out an ample sylvan shade
Which Romulus a fit asylum made,
Turns thence, and bids Aeneas fix his eyes
10 Where under a chill rock Lupercal lies
Named from Lycaean Pan, in old Arcadian guise.
Nor left he unobserved the neighbouring wood
Of sacred Argiletum, stained with blood.
There Argos fell, his guest – the story told,
To the Tarpeian Rock their way they hold
And to the Capitol now bright with gold, –
In those far-distant times a spot forlorn
With brambles choked and rough with savage thorn.
Even then an influence of religious awe
20 The rustics felt, subdued by what they saw,
The local spirit creeping through their blood,
Even then they feared the rocks, they trembled at the
    wood.
'This grove (said he) this leaf-crowned hill – some God
How named we know not, takes for his abode,
The Arcadians think that Jove himself aloft
Hath here declared his presence oft and oft,
Shaking his lurid Aegis in their sight
And covering with fierce clouds the stormy height.
Here also see two mouldering towns that lie
30 Mournful remains of buried ancestry;
That Citadel did father Janus frame,
And Saturn this, each bears the Founder's name.

Conversing thus their onward course they bent
To poor Evander's humble tenement;

Herds range the Roman Forum; in the street
Of proud Carinae bellowing herds they meet;
When they had reached the house, he said 'This gate
Conquering Alcides entered, his plain state
This palace lodged; O guest, like him forbear
40 To frown on scanty means and homely fare;
Dare riches to despise; with aim as high
Mount thou, and train thyself for Deity.'

This said, through that low door he leads his guest,
The great Aeneas, to a couch of rest.
There propped he lay on withered leaves, o'erspread
With a bear's skin in Libyan desarts bred.

'*A volant Tribe of Bards on earth are found*'

A volant Tribe of Bards on earth are found,
Who, while the flattering Zephyrs round them play,
On 'coignes of vantage' hang their nests of clay;
How quickly from that aery hold unbound,
Dust for oblivion! To the solid ground
Of nature trusts the Mind that builds for aye;
Convinced that there, there only, she can lay
Secure foundations. As the year runs round,
Apart she toils within the chosen ring;
10 While the stars shine, or while day's purple eye
Is gently closing with the flowers of spring;
Where even the motion of an Angel's wing
Would interrupt the intense tranquillity
Of silent hills, and more than silent sky.

'Not Love, not War, nor the tumultuous swell'

Not Love, not War, nor the tumultuous swell
Of civil conflict, nor the wrecks of change,
Nor Duty struggling with afflictions strange –
Not these *alone* inspire the tuneful shell;
But where untroubled peace and concord dwell,
There also is the Muse not loth to range,
Watching the twilight smoke of cot or grange,
Skyward ascending from a woody dell.
Meek aspirations please her, lone endeavour,
And sage content, and placid melancholy;
She loves to gaze upon a crystal river –
Diaphanous because it travels slowly;
Soft is the music that would charm for ever;
The flower of sweetest smell is shy and lowly.

In the First Page of an Album by One Whose Handwriting Is Wretchedly Bad

First flowret of the year is that which shows
Its rival whiteness 'mid surrounding snows;
To guide the shining Company of Heaven,
Brightest as first, appears the star of Even;
Upon imperial brows the richest gem
Stands ever foremost in the Diadem –
How then could mortal so unfit engage
To take his Station in this leading page?
For others marshall with his pen the way
Which shall be trod in many a future day?
Why was not some fair Lady called to write
Dear words for memory, 'characters of light'?
Lines which enraptured fancy might explore
And thence create her Image? but no more;
Strangers! forgive the deed, an unsought task,
For what you look on Friendship deigned to ask.

[*Translation of Virgil's Georgic* IV. *511-15*]

Even so bewails, the poplar groves among,
Sad Philomela her evanished Young;
Whom the harsh Rustic from the nest hath torn,
An unfledged brood; but on the bough forlorn
She sits, in mournful darkness all night long;
Renews, and still renews, her doleful song,
And fills the leafy grove, complaining of her wrong.

Memory

A pen – to register; a key –
That winds through secret wards;
Are well assigned to Memory
By allegoric Bards.

As aptly, also, might be given
A Pencil to her hand;
That, softening objects, sometimes even
Outstrips the heart's demand;

That smooths foregone distress, the lines
10 Of lingering care subdues,
Long-vanished happiness refines,
And clothes in brighter hues;

Yet, like a tool of Fancy, works
Those Spectres to dilate
That startle Conscience, as she lurks
Within her lonely seat.

O! that our lives, which flee so fast,
In purity were such,
That not an image of the past
20 Should fear that pencil's touch!

Retirement then might hourly look
Upon a soothing scene,
Age steal to his allotted nook
Contented and serene;

With heart as calm as lakes that sleep,
In frosty moonlight glistening;
Or mountain rivers, where they creep
Along a channel smooth and deep,
To their own far-off murmurs listening.

'*How rich that forehead's calm expanse!*'

How rich that forehead's calm expanse!
How bright that heaven-directed glance!
– Waft her to glory, wingèd Powers,
Ere sorrow be renewed,
And intercourse with mortal hours
Bring back a humbler mood!
So looked Cecilia when she drew
An Angel from his station;
So looked; not ceasing to pursue
10   Her tuneful adoration!

But hand and voice alike are still;
No sound *here* sweeps away the will
That gave it birth: in service meek
One upright arm sustains the cheek,
And one across the bosom lies –
That rose, and now forgets to rise,
Subdued by breathless harmonies
Of meditative feeling;
Mute strains from worlds beyond the skies,
20   Through the pure light of female eyes,
Their sanctity revealing!

Recollection of the Portrait of King Henry Eighth, Trinity Lodge, Cambridge

The imperial Stature, the colossal stride,
Are yet before me; yet do I behold
The broad full visage, chest of amplest mould,
The vestments 'broidered with barbaric pride:
And lo! a poniard, at the Monarch's side,
Hangs ready to be grasped in sympathy
With the keen threatenings of that fulgent eye,
Below the white-rimmed bonnet, far-descried.
Who trembles now at thy capricious mood?
10 'Mid those surrounding Worthies, haughty King,
We rather think, with grateful mind sedate,
How Providence educeth, from the spring
Of lawless will, unlooked-for streams of good,
Which neither force shall check nor time abate!

To the Lady E. B. and the Hon. Miss P.

A STREAM, to mingle with your favourite Dee,
Along the VALE OF MEDITATION flows;
So styled by those fierce Britons, pleased to see
In Nature's face the expression of repose;
Or haply there some pious hermit chose
To live and die, the peace of heaven his aim;
To whom the wild sequestered region owes,
At this late day, its sanctifying name.
GLYN CAFAILLGAROCH, in the Cambrian tongue,
10 In ours, the VALE OF FRIENDSHIP, let *this* spot
Be named; where, faithful to a low-roofed Cot,
On Deva's banks, ye have abode so long;
Sisters in love, a love allowed to climb,
Even on this earth, above the reach of Time!

To the Torrent at the Devil's Bridge, North Wales, 1824

How art thou named? In search of what strange land,
From what huge height, descending? Can such force
Of waters issue from a British source,
Or hath not Pindus fed thee, where the band
Of Patriots scoop their freedom out, with hand
Desperate as thine? Or come the incessant shocks
From that young Stream, that smites the throbbing
    rocks
Of Viamala? There I seem to stand,
As in life's morn; permitted to behold,
From the dread chasm, woods climbing above woods,
In pomp that fades not; everlasting snows;
And skies that ne'er relinquish their repose;
Such power possess the family of floods
Over the minds of Poets, young or old!

Composed among the Ruins of a Castle in North Wales

Through shattered galleries, 'mid roofless halls,
Wandering with timid footsteps oft betrayed,
The Stranger sighs, nor scruples to upbraid
Old Time, though he, gentlest among the Thralls
Of Destiny, upon these wounds hath laid
His lenient touches, soft as light that falls,
From the wan Moon, upon the towers and walls,
Light deepening the profoundest sleep of shade.
Relic of Kings! Wreck of forgotten wars,
To winds abandoned and the prying stars,
Time *loves* thee! at his call the Seasons twine
Luxuriant wreaths around thy forehead hoar;
And, though past pomp no changes can restore,
A soothing recompence, his gift, is thine!

The Infant M— M—

Unquiet Childhood here by special grace
Forgets her nature, opening like a flower
That neither feeds nor wastes its vital power
In painful struggles. Months each other chase,
And naught untunes that Infant's voice; no trace
Of fretful temper sullies her pure cheek;
Prompt, lively, self-sufficing, yet so meek
That one enrapt with gazing on her face
(Which even the placid innocence of death
10   Could scarcely make more placid, heaven more bright)
Might learn to picture, for the eye of faith,
The Virgin, as she shone with kindred light;
A nursling couched upon her mother's knee,
Beneath some shady palm of Galilee.

Elegiac Stanzas (*Addressed to Sir G. H. B. upon the Death of His Sister-in-Law*)

O for a dirge! But why complain?
Ask rather a triumphal strain
When FERMOR'S race is run;
A garland of immortal boughs
To twine around the Christian's brows,
Whose glorious work is done.

We pay a high and holy debt;
No tears of passionate regret
Shall stain this votive lay;
10   Ill-worthy, Beaumont! were the grief
That flings itself on wild relief
When Saints have passed away.

Sad doom, at Sorrow's shrine to kneel,
For ever covetous to feel,

And impotent to bear!
Such once was hers – to think and think
On severed love, and only sink
From anguish to despair!

But nature to its inmost part
20 Faith had refined; and to her heart
A peaceful cradle given:
Calm as the dew-drop's, free to rest
Within a breeze-fanned rose's breast
Till it exhales to Heaven.

Was ever Spirit that could bend
So graciously? – that could descend,
Another's need to suit,
So promptly from her lofty throne? –
In works of love, in these alone,
30 How restless, how minute!

Pale was her hue; yet mortal cheek
Ne'er kindled with a livelier streak
When aught had suffered wrong, –
When aught that breathes had felt a wound;
Such look the Oppressor might confound,
However proud and strong.

But hushed be every thought that springs
From out the bitterness of things;
Her quiet is secure;
40 No thorns can pierce her tender feet,
Whose life was, like the violet, sweet,
As climbing jasmine, pure –

As snowdrop on an infant's grave,
Or lily heaving with the wave
That feeds it and defends;
As Vesper, ere the star hath kissed
The mountain top, or breathed the mist
That from the vale ascends.

Thou takest not away, O Death!
50   Thou strikest – absence perisheth,
Indifference is no more;
The future brightens on our sight;
For on the past hath fallen a light
That tempts us to adore.

To —, in Her Seventieth Year

Such age how beautiful! O Lady bright,
Whose mortal lineaments seem all refined
By favouring Nature and a saintly Mind
To something purer and more exquisite
Than flesh and blood; whene'er thou meet'st my sight,
When I behold thy blanched unwithered cheek,
Thy temples fringed with locks of gleaming white,
And head that droops because the soul is meek,
Thee with the welcome Snowdrop I compare;
10   That child of winter, prompting thoughts that climb
From desolation toward the genial prime;
Or with the Moon conquering earth's misty air,
And filling more and more with crystal light
As pensive Evening deepens into night.

To —

Let other bards of angels sing,
    Bright suns without a spot;
But thou art no such perfect thing:
    Rejoice that thou art not!

Heed not though none should call thee fair;
    So, Mary, let it be
If naught in loveliness compare
    With what thou art to me.

True beauty dwells in deep retreats,
10   Whose veil is unremoved
Till heart with heart in concord beats,
    And the lover is beloved.

To —

Look at the fate of summer flowers,
Which blow at daybreak, droop ere even-song;
And, grieved for their brief date, confess that ours,
Measured by what we are and ought to be,
Measured by all that, trembling, we foresee,
        Is not so long!

If human Life do pass away,
Perishing yet more swiftly than the flower,
If we are creatures of a *winter's* day;
10   What space hath Virgin's beauty to disclose
Her sweets, and triumph o'er the breathing rose?
        Not even an hour!

The deepest grove whose foliage hid
The happiest lovers Arcady might boast,
Could not the entrance of this thought forbid:
O be thou wise as they, soul-gifted Maid!
Nor rate too high what must so quickly fade,
        So soon be lost.

Then shall love teach some virtuous Youth
20   'To draw, out of the object of his eyes,'
The while on thee they gaze in simple truth,
Hues more exalted, 'a refinèd Form,'
That dreads not age, nor suffers from the worm,
        And never dies.

A Flower Garden at Coleorton Hall, Leicestershire.

Tell me, ye Zephyrs! that unfold,
While fluttering o'er this gay Recess,
Pinions that fanned the teeming mould
Of Eden's blissful wilderness,
Did only softly-stealing hours
There close the peaceful lives of flowers?

Say, when the *moving* creatures saw
All kinds commingled without fear,
Prevailed a like indulgent law
10 For the still growths that prosper here?
Did wanton fawn and kid forbear
The half-blown rose, the lily spare?

Or peeped they often from their beds
And prematurely disappeared,
Devoured like pleasure ere it spreads
A bosom to the sun endeared?
If such their harsh untimely doom,
It falls not *here* on bud or bloom.

All summer-long the happy Eve
20 Of this fair Spot her flowers may bind,
Nor e'er, with ruffled fancy, grieve,
From the next glance she casts, to find
That love for little things by Fate
Is rendered vain as love for great.

Yet, where the guardian fence is wound,
So subtly are our eyes beguiled,
We see not nor suspect a bound,
No more than in some forest wild;
The sight is free as air – or crost
30 Only by art in nature lost.

And, though the jealous turf refuse
By random footsteps to be prest,
And feed on never-sullied dews,
Ye, gentle breezes from the west,
With all the ministers of hope
Are tempted to this sunny slope!

And hither throngs of birds resort;
Some, inmates lodged in shady nests,
Some, perched on stems of stately port
40 That nod to welcome transient guests;
While hare and leveret, seen at play,
Appear not more shut out than they.

Apt emblem (for reproof of pride)
This delicate Enclosure shows
Of modest kindness, that would hide
The firm protection she bestows;
Of manners, like its viewless fence,
Ensuring peace to innocence.

Thus spake the moral Muse – her wing
50 Abruptly spreading to depart,
She left that farewell offering,
Memento for some docile heart;
That may respect the good old age
When Fancy was Truth's willing Page;
And Truth would skim the flowery glade,
Though entering but as Fancy's Shade.

Cenotaph

In affectionate remembrance of Frances Fermor, whose remains
are deposited in the church of Claines, near Worcester, this
stone is erected by her sister, Dame Margaret, wife of Sir
George Beaumont, Bart., who, feeling not less than the love of a
brother for the deceased, commends this memorial to the care
of his heirs and successors in the possession of this place.

By vain affections unenthralled,
Though resolute when duty called
To meet the world's broad eye,
Pure as the holiest cloistered nun
That ever feared the tempting sun,
Did Fermor live and die.

This Tablet, hallowed by her name,
One heart-relieving tear may claim;
But if the pensive gloom
10 Of fond regret be still thy choice,
Exalt thy spirit, hear the voice
Of Jesus from her tomb!
'I AM THE WAY, THE TRUTH, AND THE LIFE.'

To —

O dearer far than light and life are dear,
Full oft our human foresight I deplore;
Trembling, through my unworthiness, with fear
That friends, by death disjoined, may meet no more!

Misgivings, hard to vanquish or control,
Mix with the day, and cross the hour of rest;
While all the future, for thy purer soul,
With 'sober certainties' of love is blest.

That sigh of thine, not meant for human ear,
10 Tells that these words thy humbleness offend;
Yet bear me up – else faltering in the rear
Of a steep march: support me to the end.

Peace settles where the intellect is meek,
And Love is dutiful in thought and deed;
Through Thee communion with that Love I seek:
The faith Heaven strengthens where *he* moulds the
    Creed.

'While Anna's peers and early playmates tread'

While Anna's peers and early playmates tread,
In freedom, mountain-turf and river's marge;
Or float with music in the festal barge;
Rein the proud steed, or through the dance are led;
Her doom it is to press a weary bed –
Till oft her guardian Angel, to some charge
More urgent called, will stretch his wings at large,
And friends too rarely prop the languid head.
Yet, helped by Genius – untired comforter,
10   The presence even of a stuffed Owl for her
Can cheat the time; sending her fancy out
To ivied castles and to moonlight skies,
Though he can neither stir a plume, nor shout;
Nor veil, with restless film, his staring eyes.

The Contrast
The Parrot and the Wren

I
Within her gilded cage confined,
I saw a dazzling Belle,
A Parrot of that famous kind
Whose name is NON-PAREIL.

Like beads of glossy jet her eyes;
And, smoothed by Nature's skill,
With pearl or gleaming agate vies
Her finely-curvèd bill.

Her plumy mantle's living hues
10   In mass opposed to mass,
Outshine the splendour that imbues
The robes of pictured glass.

And, sooth to say, an apter Mate
Did never tempt the choice
Of feathered Thing most delicate
In figure and in voice.

But, exiled from Australian bowers,
And singleness her lot,
She trills her song with tutored powers,
20   Or mocks each casual note.

No more of pity for regrets
With which she may have striven!
Now but in wantonness she frets,
Or spite, if cause be given;

Arch, volatile, a sportive bird
By social glee inspired;
Ambitious to be seen or heard,
And pleased to be admired!

II
This moss-lined shed, green, soft, and dry,
30   Harbours a self-contented Wren,
Not shunning man's abode, though shy,
Almost as thought itself, of human ken.

Strange places, coverts unendeared,
She never tried; the very nest
In which this Child of Spring was reared
Is warmed, through winter, by her feathery breast.

To the bleak winds she sometimes gives
A slender unexpected strain;
Proof that the hermitess still lives,
40   Though she appear not, and be sought in vain.

Say, Dora! tell me, by yon placid moon,
If called to choose between the favoured pair,

Which would you be, – the bird of the saloon,
By lady-fingers tended with nice care,
Caressed, applauded, upon dainties fed,
Or Nature's DARKLING of this mossy shed?

To a Skylark

Ethereal minstrel! pilgrim of the sky!
Dost thou despise the earth where cares abound?
Or, while the wings aspire, are heart and eye
Both with thy nest upon the dewy ground?
Thy nest which thou canst drop into at will,
Those quivering wings composed, that music still!

Leave to the nightingale her shady wood;
A privacy of glorious light is thine;
Whence thou dost pour upon the world a flood
10 Of harmony, with instinct more divine;
Type of the wise who soar, but never roam;
True to the kindred points of Heaven and Home!

A Morning Exercise

Fancy, who leads the pastimes of the glad,
Full oft is pleased a wayward dart to throw;
Sending sad shadows after things not sad,
Peopling the harmless fields with signs of woe:
Beneath her sway, a simple forest cry
Becomes an echo of man's misery.

Blithe ravens croak of death; and when the owl
Tries his two voices for a favourite strain –
Tu-whit – Tu-whoo! the unsuspecting fowl
10 Forebodes mishap or seems but to complain;
Fancy, intent to harass and annoy,
Can thus pervert the evidence of joy.

Through border wilds where naked Indians stray,
Myriads of notes attest her subtle skill;
A feathered task-master cries, 'WORK AWAY!'
And, in thy iteration, 'WHIP POOR WILL!'
Is heard the spirit of a toil-worn slave,
Lashed out of life, not quiet in the grave.

What wonder? at her bidding, ancient lays
20 Steeped in dire grief the voice of Philomel;
And that fleet messenger of summer days,
The Swallow, twittered subject to like spell;
But ne'er could Fancy bend the buoyant Lark
To melancholy service – hark! O hark!

The daisy sleeps upon the dewy lawn,
Not lifting yet the head that evening bowed;
But *He* is risen, a later star of dawn,
Glittering and twinkling near yon rosy cloud;
Bright gem instinct with music, vocal spark;
30 The happiest bird that sprang out of the Ark!

Hail, blest above all kinds! – Supremely skilled
Restless with fixed to balance, high with low,
Thou leav'st the halcyon free her hopes to build
On such forbearance as the deep may show;
Perpetual flight, unchecked by earthly ties,
Leav'st to the wandering bird of paradise.

Faithful, though swift as lightning, the meek dove;
Yet more hath Nature reconciled in thee;
So constant with thy downward eye of love,
40 Yet, in aërial singleness, so free;
So humble, yet so ready to rejoice
In power of wing and never-wearied voice.

To the last point of vision, and beyond,
Mount, daring warbler! – that love-prompted strain
('Twixt thee and thine a never-failing bond)

Thrills not the less the bosom of the plain:
Yet mightst thou seem, proud privilege! to sing
All independent of the leafy spring.

How would it please old Ocean to partake,
50 With sailors longing for a breeze in vain,
The harmony thy notes most gladly make
Where earth resembles most his own domain!
Urania's self might welcome with pleased ear
These matins mounting towards her native sphere.

Chanter by heaven attracted, whom no bars
To daylight known deter from that pursuit,
'Tis well that some sage instinct, when the stars
Come forth at evening, keeps Thee still and mute;
For not an eyelid could to sleep incline
60 Wert thou among them, singing as they shine!

Ode Composed on May Morning

While from the purpling east departs
    The star that led the dawn,
Blithe Flora from her couch upstarts,
    For May is on the lawn.
A quickening hope, a freshening glee,
    Foreran the expected Power,
Whose first-drawn breath, from bush and tree,
    Shakes off that pearly shower.

All Nature welcomes Her whose sway
10   Tempers the year's extremes;
Who scattereth lustres o'er noon-day,
    Like morning's dewy gleams;
While mellow warble, sprightly trill,
    The tremulous heart excite;
And hums the balmy air to still
    The balance of delight.

Time was, blest Power! when youths and maids
　　At peep of dawn would rise,
And wander forth, in forest glades
20　　Thy birth to solemnize.
Though mute the song – to grace the rite
　　Untouched the hawthorn bough,
Thy Spirit triumphs o'er the slight;
　　Man changes, but not Thou!

Thy feathered Lieges bill and wings
　　In love's disport employ;
Warmed by thy influence, creeping things
　　Awake to silent joy:
Queen art thou still for each gay plant
30　　Where the slim wild deer roves;
And served in depths where fishes haunt
　　Their own mysterious groves.

Cloud-piercing peak, and trackless heath,
　　Instinctive homage pay;
Nor wants the dim-lit cave a wreath
　　To honour thee, sweet May!
Where cities fanned by thy brisk airs
　　Behold a smokeless sky,
Their puniest flower-pot-nursling dares
40　　To open a bright eye.

And if, on this thy natal morn,
　　The pole, from which thy name
Hath not departed, stands forlorn
　　Of song and dance and game;
Still from the village-green a vow
　　Aspires to thee addrest,
Wherever peace is on the brow,
　　Or love within the breast.

Yes! where Love nestles thou canst teach
50　　The soul to love the more;
Hearts also shall thy lessons reach
　　That never loved before.

Stript is the haughty one of pride,
　　The bashful freed from fear,
While rising, like the ocean-tide,
　　In flows the joyous year.

Hush, feeble lyre! weak words refuse
　　The service to prolong!
To yon exulting thrush the Muse
60　　Entrusts the imperfect song;
His voice shall chant, in accents clear,
　　Throughout the live-long day,
Till the first silver star appear,
　　The sovereignty of May.

To May

Though many suns have risen and set
　　Since thou, blithe May, wert born,
And Bards, who hailed thee, may forget
　　Thy gifts, thy beauty scorn;
There are who to a birthday strain
　　Confine not harp and voice,
But evermore throughout thy reign
　　Are grateful and rejoice!

Delicious odours! music sweet,
10　　Too sweet to pass away!
Oh for a deathless song to meet
　　The soul's desire – a lay
That, when a thousand years are told,
　　Should praise thee, genial Power!
Through summer heat, autumnal cold,
　　And winter's dreariest hour.

Earth, sea, thy presence feel – nor less,
　　If yon ethereal blue
With its soft smile the truth express,
20　　The heavens have felt it too.

The inmost heart of man if glad
   Partakes a livelier cheer;
And eyes that cannot but be sad
   Let fall a brightened tear.

Since thy return, through days and weeks
   Of hope that grew by stealth,
How many wan and faded cheeks
   Have kindled into health!
The Old, by thee revived, have said,
30   'Another year is ours;'
And wayworn Wanderers, poorly fed,
   Have smiled upon thy flowers.

Who tripping lisps a merry song
   Amid his playful peers?
The tender Infant who was long
   A prisoner of fond fears;
But now, when every sharp-edged blast
   Is quiet in its sheath,
His Mother leaves him free to taste
40   Earth's sweetness in thy breath.

Thy help is with the weed that creeps
   Along the humblest ground;
No cliff so bare but on its steeps
   Thy favours may be found;
But most on some peculiar nook
   That our own hands have drest,
Thou and thy train are proud to look,
   And seem to love it best.

And yet how pleased we wander forth
50   When May is whispering, 'Come!
Choose from the bowers of virgin earth
   The happiest for your home;
Heaven's bounteous love through me is spread
   From sunshine, clouds, winds, waves,
Drops on the mouldering turret's head,
   And on your turf-clad graves!'

Such greeting heard, away with sighs
 For lilies that must fade,
Or 'the rathe primrose as it dies
60 Forsaken' in the shade!
Vernal fruitions and desires
 Are linked in endless chase;
While, as one kindly growth retires,
 Another takes its place.

And what if thou, sweet May, hast known
 Mishap by worm and blight;
If expectations newly blown
 Have perished in thy sight;
If loves and joys, while up they sprung,
70 Were caught as in a snare;
Such is the lot of all the young,
 However bright and fair.

Lo! Streams that April could not check
 Are patient of thy rule;
Gurgling in foamy water-break,
 Loitering in glassy pool:
By thee, thee only, could be sent
 Such gentle mists as glide,
Curling with unconfirmed intent,
80 On that green mountain's side.

How delicate the leafy veil
 Through which yon house of God
Gleams 'mid the peace of this deep dale
 By few but shepherds trod!
And lowly huts, near beaten ways,
 No sooner stand attired
In thy fresh wreaths, than they for praise
 Peep forth, and are admired.

Season of fancy and of hope,
90 Permit not for one hour

A blossom from thy crown to drop,
   Nor add to it a flower!
Keep, lovely May, as if by touch
   Of self-restraining art,
This modest charm of not too much,
   Part seen, imagined part!

'Prithee, gentle Lady, list'

Prithee, gentle Lady, list
To a small Ventriloquist:
I whose pretty voice you hear
From this paper speaking clear
Have a Mother, once a Statue!
I, thus boldly looking at you,
Do the name of Paphus bear,
Famed Pygmalion's son and heir,
By that wondrous marble wife
10 That from Venus took her life.
Cupid's nephew then am I,
Nor unskilled his darts to ply;
But from him I craved no warrant
Coming thus to seek my parent;
Not equipped with bow and quiver
Her by menace to deliver,
But resolved with filial care
Her captivity to share.
Hence, while on your Toilet, she
20 Is doomed a Pincushion to be,
By her side I'll take my place,
As a humble Needlecase
Furnished too with dainty thread
For a Sempstress thoroughbred.
Then let both be kindly treated
Till the Term for which she's fated
Durance to sustain, be over:
So will I ensure a Lover,

Lady! to your heart's content; ⎫
30 But on harshness are you bent? ⎬
Bitterly shall you repent ⎭
When to Cyprus back I go
And take up my Uncle's bow.

'Ere with cold beads of midnight dew'

Ere with cold beads of midnight dew
   Had mingled tears of thine,
I grieved, fond Youth! that thou shouldst sue
   To haughty Geraldine.

Immoveable by generous sighs,
   She glories in a train
Who drag, beneath our native skies,
   An oriental chain.

Pine not like them with arms across,
10   Forgetting in thy care
How the fast-rooted trees can toss
   Their branches in mid air.

The humblest rivulet will take
   Its own wild liberties;
And, every day, the imprisoned lake
   Is flowing in the breeze.

Then crouch no more on suppliant knee,
   But scorn with scorn outbrave;
A Briton, even in love, should be
20   A subject, not a slave!

'Once I could hail (howe'er serene the sky)'

'Late, late yestreen I saw the new moone
Wi' the auld moone in hir arme.'
                    Ballad of Sir Patrick Spence, Percy's Reliques.

Once I could hail (howe'er serene the sky)
The Moon re-entering her monthly round,
No faculty yet given me to espy
The dusky Shape within her arms imbound,
That thin memento of effulgence lost
Which some have named her Predecessor's ghost.

Young, like the Crescent that above me shone,
Naught I perceived within it dull or dim;
All that appeared was suitable to One
10 Whose fancy had a thousand fields to skim;
To expectations spreading with wild growth,
And hope that kept with me her plighted troth.

I saw (ambition quickening at the view)
A silver boat launched on a boundless flood;
A pearly crest, like Dian's when it threw
Its brightest splendour round a leafy wood;
But not a hint from underground, no sign
Fit for the glimmering brow of Proserpine.

Or was it Dian's self that seemed to move
20 Before me? – nothing blemished the fair sight;
On her I looked whom jocund Fairies love,
Cynthia, who puts the *little* stars to flight,
And by that thinning magnifies the great,
For exaltation of her sovereign state.

And when I learned to mark the spectral Shape
As each new Moon obeyed the call of Time,
If gloom fell on me, swift was my escape;
Such happy privilege hath life's gay Prime,
To see or not to see, as best may please
30 A buoyant Spirit, and a heart at ease.

Now, dazzling Stranger! when thou meet'st my glance,
Thy dark Associate ever I discern;
Emblem of thoughts too eager to advance
While I salute my joys, thoughts sad or stern;
Shades of past bliss, or phantoms that, to gain
Their fill of promised lustre, wait in vain.

So changes mortal Life with fleeting years;
A mournful change, should Reason fail to bring
The timely insight that can temper fears,
40 And from vicissitude remove its sting;
While Faith aspires to seats in that domain
Where joys are perfect – neither wax nor wane.

'The massy Ways, carried across these heights'

The massy Ways, carried across these heights
By Roman perseverance, are destroyed,
Or hidden under ground, like sleeping worms.
How venture then to hope that Time will spare
This humble Walk? Yet on the mountain's side
A POET'S hand first shaped it; and the steps
Of that same Bard – repeated to and fro
At morn, at noon, and under moonlight skies
Through the vicissitudes of many a year –
10 Forbade the weeds to creep o'er its grey line.
No longer, scattering to the heedless winds
The vocal raptures of fresh poesy,
Shall he frequent these precincts; locked no more
In earnest converse with belovèd Friends,
Here will he gather stores of ready bliss,
As from the beds and borders of a garden
Choice flowers are gathered! But, if Power may spring
Out of a farewell yearning – favoured more
Than kindred wishes mated suitably
20 With vain regrets – the Exile would consign
This Walk, his loved possession, to the care
Of those pure Minds that reverence the Muse.

Retirement

If the whole weight of what we think and feel,
Save only far as thought and feeling blend
With action, were as nothing, patriot Friend!
From thy remonstrance would be no appeal;
But to promote and fortify the weal
Of her own Being is her paramount end;
A truth which they alone shall comprehend
Who shun the mischief which they cannot heal.
Peace in these feverish times is sovereign bliss:
10   Here, with no thirst but what the stream can slake,
And startled only by the rustling brake,
Cool air I breathe; while the unincumbered Mind,
By some weak aims at services assigned
To gentle Natures, thanks not Heaven amiss.

'The Lady whom you here behold'

The Lady whom you here behold
Was once Pygmalion's Wife,
He made her first from marble cold
And Venus gave her life.

When fate removed her from his arms
Through sundry Forms she passed;
And conquering hearts by various charms
This shape she took at last.

We caught her, true though strange the account,
10   Among a troop of Fairies,
Who nightly frisk on our green Mount
And practise strange vagaries.

Her raiment then was scant, so we
Bestowed some pains upon her;
Part for the sake of decency
And part to do her honour.

But as, no doubt, 'twas for her sins
We found her in such plight,
She shall do penance stuck with pins
20 And serve you day and night.

Composed When a Probability Existed of Our Being Obliged to Quit Rydal Mount as a Residence

The doubt to which a wavering hope had clung
Is fled; we must depart, willing or not,
Sky-piercing Hills! must bid farewell to you
And all that ye look down upon with pride,
With tenderness imbosom; to your paths,
And pleasant Dwellings, to familiar trees
And wild-flowers known as well as if our hands
Had tended them: and O pellucid Spring!
Insensibly the foretaste of this parting
10 Hath ruled my steps, and seals me to thy side,
Mindful that thou (ah! wherefore by my Muse
So long unthanked) hast cheered a simple board
With beverage pure as ever fixed the choice
Of Hermit, dubious where to scoop his cell;
Which Persian kings might envy; and thy meek
And gentle aspect oft has ministered
To finer uses. They for me must cease;
Days will pass on, the year, if years be given,
Fade, – and the moralizing mind derive
20 No lesson from the presence of a Power
By the inconstant nature we inherit
Unmatched in delicate beneficence;
For neither unremitting rains avail
To swell Thee into voice; nor longest drought
Thy bounty stints, nor can thy beauty mar,
Beauty not therefore wanting change to please
The fancy, for in spectacles unlooked for,
And transformations silently fulfilled,

What witchcraft, meek Enchantress, equals thine?
30   Not yet, perchance, translucent Spring, had tolled
The Norman curfew bell when human hands
First offered help that the deficient rock
Might overarch thee, from pernicious heat
Defended, and appropriate to man's need.
Such ties will not be severed: but, when We
Are gone, what summer Loiterer, with regard
Inquisitive, thy countenance will peruse,
Pleased to detect the dimpling stir of life,
The breathing faculty with which thou yield'st
40   (Though a mere goblet to the careless eye)
Boons inexhaustible? Who, hurrying on
With a step quickened by November's cold,
Shall pause, the skill admiring that can work
Upon thy chance-defilements – withered twigs
That, lodged within thy crystal depths, seem bright,
As if they from a silver tree had fallen;
And oaken leaves that, driven by whirling blasts,
Sank down, and lay immersed in dead repose
For Time's invisible tooth to prey upon,
50   Unsightly objects and uncoveted,
Till thou with crystal bead-drops didst encrust
Their skeletons, turned to brilliant ornaments.
But, from thy bosom, would some venturous hand
Abstract those gleaming Relics, and uplift them,
However gently, toward the vulgar air,
At once their tender brightness disappears,
Leaving the Intermeddler to upbraid
His folly. Thus (I feel it while I speak),
Thus, with the fibres of these thoughts it fares;
60   And oh! how much, of all that love creates
Or beautifies, like changes undergoes,
Suffers like loss when drawn out of the soul,
Its silent laboratory! Words should say
(Could they depict the marvels of thy cell)
How often I have marked a plumy fern
From the live rock with grace inimitable

Bending its apex toward a paler self
Reflected all in perfect lineaments –
Shadow and substance kissing point to point
70 In mutual stillness; or, if some faint breeze
Entering the cell gave restlessness to One,
The Other, glassed in thy unruffled breast,
Partook of every motion, met, retired,
And met again; such playful sympathy,
Such delicate caress as in the shape
Of this green Plant had aptly recompensed
For baffled lips and disappointed arms
And hopeless pangs, the Spirit of that Youth,
The fair Narcissus by some pitying God
80 Changed to a crimson Flower; when he, whose pride
Provoked a retribution too severe,
Had pined; upon his watery Duplicate
Wasting that love the Nymphs implored in vain.
    Thus while my Fancy wanders, Thou, clear Spring,
Moved (shall I say?) like a dear Friend who meets
A parting moment with her loveliest look,
And seemingly her happiest, look so fair
It frustrates its own purpose, and recalls
The grieved One whom it meant to send away –
90 Dost tempt me by disclosures exquisite
To linger, bending over Thee: for now,
What witchcraft, mild enchantress, may with thee
Compare! thy earthly bed a moment past
Palpable unto sight as the dry ground,
Eludes perception, not by rippling airs
Concealed, nor through effect of some impure
Upstirring; but, abstracted by a charm
Of thy own cunning, earth mysteriously
From under thee hath vanished, and slant beams
100 The silent inquest of a western Sun,
Assisting, lucid Well-Spring! Thou reveal'st
Communion without check of herbs and flowers
And the vault's hoary sides to which they clung,
Imaged in downward show; the flower, the herbs,

These not of earthly texture, and the vault
Not *there* diminutive, but through a scale
Of Vision less and less distinct, descending
To gloom impenetrable. So (if truths
The highest condescend to be set forth
110 By processes minute), even so – when thought
Wins help from something greater than herself –
Is the firm basis of habitual sense
Supplanted, not for treacherous vacancy
And blank dissociation from a world
We love, but that the residues of flesh,
Mirrored, yet not too strictly, may refine
To Spirit; for the Idealizing Soul
Time wears the features of Eternity;
And Nature deepens into Nature's God.
120   Millions of kneeling Hindoos at this day
Bow to the watery Element, adored
In their vast Stream, and if an age hath been
(As Books and haply votive Altars vouch)
When British floods were worshipped, some faint trace
Of that idolatry, through monkish rites
Transmitted far as living memory,
Might wait on Thee, a silent Monitor,
On thee, bright Spring, a bashful little-one,
Yet to the measure of thy promises
130 True, as the mightiest; upon thee, sequestered
For meditation, nor inopportune
For social interest such as I have shared.
Peace to the sober Matron who shall dip
Her Pitcher here at early dawn, by me
No longer greeted – to the tottering Sire,
For whom like service, now and then his choice,
Relieves the tedious holiday of age –
Thoughts raised above the Earth while here he sits
Feeding on sunshine – to the blushing Girl
140 Who here forgets her errand, nothing loth
To be waylaid by her Betrothed, peace
And pleasure sobered down to happiness!

But should these hills be ranged by one whose Soul
Scorning love-whispers shrinks from love itself
As Fancy's snare for female vanity,
Here may the aspirant find a trysting-place
For loftier intercourse. The Muses crowned
With wreaths that have not faded to this Hour
Sprung from high Jove, of sage Mnemosyne
150 Enamoured, so the fable runs; but they
Certes were self-taught Damsels, scattered Births
Of many a Grecian Vale, who sought not praise,
And, heedless even of listeners, warbled out
Their own emotions given to mountain air
In notes which mountain echoes would take up
Boldly, and bear away to softer life;
Hence deified as Sisters they were bound
Together in a never-dying choir;
Who with their Hippocrene and grottoed fount
160 Of Castaly, attest that Woman's heart
Was in the limpid age of this stained world
The most assured seat of fine ecstasy,
And new-born waters, deemed the happiest source
Of Inspiration for the conscious lyre.

    Lured by the crystal element in times
Stormy and fierce, the Maid of Arc withdrew
From human converse to frequent alone
The Fountain of the Fairies. What to her,
Smooth summer dreams, old favours of the place,
170 Pageant and revels of blithe Elves – to her
Whose country groaned under a foreign scourge?
She pondered murmurs that attuned her ear
For the reception of far other sounds
Than their too-happy minstrelsy, – a Voice
Reached her with supernatural mandates charged
More awful than the chambers of dark earth
Have virtue to send forth. Upon the marge
Of the benignant fountain, while she stood
Gazing intensely, the translucent lymph
180 Darkened beneath the shadow of her thoughts

As if swift clouds swept over it, or caught
War's tincture, 'mid the forest green and still,
Turned into blood before her heart-sick eye.
Erelong, forsaking all her natural haunts,
All her accustomed offices and cares
Relinquishing, but treasuring every law
And grace of feminine humanity,
The chosen Rustic urged a warlike Steed
Toward the beleaguered city, in the might
190   Of prophecy, accoutred to fulfil,
At the sword's point, visions conceived in love.
   The cloud of Rooks descending through mid air
Softens its evening uproar towards a close
Near and more near; for this protracted strain
A warning not unwelcome. Fare thee well
Emblem of equanimity and truth,
Farewell – if thy composure be not ours,
Yet as Thou still when we are gone wilt keep
Thy living Chaplet of fresh flowers and fern,
200   Cherished in shade though peeped at by the sun;
So shall our bosoms feel a covert growth
Of grateful recollections, tribute due
To thy obscure and modest attributes
To thee, dear Spring, and all-sustaining Heaven!

To —

[Dedication to 'The Miscellaneous Sonnets']

Happy the feeling from the bosom thrown
In perfect shape (whose beauty Time shall spare
Though a breath made it) like a bubble blown
For summer pastime into wanton air;
Happy the thought best likened to a stone
Of the sea-beach, when, polished with nice care,
Veins it discovers exquisite and rare,
Which for the loss of that moist gleam atone

That tempted first to gather it. That here,
10 O chief of Friends! such feelings I present
To thy regard, with thoughts so fortunate,
Were a vain notion; but the hope is dear,
That thou, if not with partial joy elate,
Wilt smile upon this gift with more than mild content!

'Fair Prime of life! were it enough to gild'

Fair Prime of life! were it enough to gild
With ready sunbeams every straggling shower;
And, if an unexpected cloud should lower,
Swiftly thereon a rainbow arch to build
For Fancy's errands, – then, from fields half-tilled
Gathering green weeds to mix with poppy flower,
Thee might thy Minions crown, and chant thy power,
Unpitied by the wise, all censure stilled.
Ah! show that worthier honours are thy due;
10 Fair Prime of life! arouse the deeper heart;
Confirm the Spirit glorying to pursue
Some path of steep ascent and lofty aim;
And, if there be a joy that slights the claim
Of grateful memory, bid that joy depart.

'Go back to antique ages, if thine eyes'

Go back to antique ages, if thine eyes
The genuine mien and character would trace
Of the rash Spirit that still holds her place,
Prompting the world's audacious vanities!
Go back, and see the Tower of Babel rise;
The pyramid extend its monstrous base,
For some Aspirant of our short-lived race,
Anxious an aëry name to immortalize.
There, too, ere wiles and politic dispute
10 Gave specious colouring to aim and act,

See the first mighty Hunter leave the brute –
To chase mankind, with men in armies packed
For his field-pastime high and absolute,
While, to dislodge his game, cities are sacked!

'Why, Minstrel, these untuneful murmurings'

'Why, Minstrel, these untuneful murmurings –
Dull, flagging notes that with each other jar?'
'Think, gentle Lady, of a Harp so far
From its own country, and forgive the strings.'
A simple answer! but even so forth springs,
From the Castalian fountain of the heart,
The Poetry of Life, and all *that* Art
Divine of words quickening insensate things.
From the submissive necks of guiltless men
10 Stretched on the block, the glittering axe recoils;
Sun, moon, and stars, all struggle in the toils
Of mortal sympathy; what wonder then
That the poor Harp distempered music yields
To its sad Lord, far from his native fields?

On Seeing a Needlecase in the Form of a Harp The Work of E. M. S.

Frowns are on every Muse's face,
   Reproaches from their lips are sent,
That mimicry should thus disgrace
   The noble Instrument.

A very Harp in all but size!
   Needles for strings in apt gradation!
Minerva's self would stigmatize
   The unclassic profanation.

Even her *own* needle that subdued
    Arachne's rival spirit,
Though wrought in Vulcan's happiest mood,
    Such honour could not merit.

And this, too, from the Laureate's Child,
    A living lord of melody!
How will her Sire be reconciled
    To the refined indignity?

I spake, when whispered a low voice,
    'Bard! moderate your ire;
Spirits of all degrees rejoice
    In presence of the lyre.

'The Minstrels of Pygmean bands,
    Dwarf Genii, moonlight-loving Fays,
Have shells to fit their tiny hands
    And suit their slender lays.

'Some, still more delicate of ear,
    Have lutes (believe my words)
Whose framework is of gossamer,
    While sunbeams are the chords.

'Gay Sylphs this miniature will court,
    Made vocal by their brushing wings,
And sullen Gnomes will learn to sport
    Around its polished strings;

'Whence strains to love-sick maiden dear,
    While in her lonely bower she tries
To cheat the thought she cannot cheer,
    By fanciful embroideries.

'Trust, angry Bard! a knowing Sprite,
    Nor think the Harp her lot deplores;
Though 'mid the stars the Lyre shine bright,
    Love *stoops* as fondly as he soars.'

To —

[Conclusion to Part II, 'Miscellaneous Sonnets']

If these brief Records, by the Muses' art
Produced as lonely Nature or the strife
That animates the scenes of public life
Inspired, may in thy leisure claim a part;
And if these Transcripts of the private heart
Have gained a sanction from thy falling tears;
Then I repent not. But my soul hath fears
Breathed from eternity; for as a dart
Cleaves the blank air, Life flies: now every day
10 Is but a glimmering spoke in the swift wheel
Of the revolving week. Away, away,
All fitful cares, all transitory zeal!
So timely Grace the immortal wing may heal,
And honour rest upon the senseless clay.

'Her only pilot the soft breeze, the boat'

Her only pilot the soft breeze, the boat
Lingers, but Fancy is well satisfied;
With keen-eyed Hope, with Memory, at her side,
And the glad Muse at liberty to note
All that to each is precious, as we float
Gently along; regardless who shall chide
If the heavens smile, and leave us free to glide,
Happy Associates breathing air remote
From trivial cares. But, Fancy and the Muse,
10 Why have I crowded this small bark with you
And others of your kind, ideal crew!
While here sits One whose brightness owes its hues
To flesh and blood; no Goddess from above,
No fleeting Spirit, but my own true Love?

To S. H.

Excuse is needless when with love sincere
Of occupation, not by fashion led,
Thou turn'st the Wheel that slept with dust o'erspread;
My nerves from no such murmur shrink, – though near,
Soft as the Dorhawk's to a distant ear,
When twilight shades darken the mountain's head.
Even She who toils to spin our vital thread
Might smile on work, O Lady, once so dear
To household virtues. Venerable Art,
10   Torn from the Poor! yet shall kind Heaven protect
Its own; though Rulers, with undue respect,
Trusting to crowded factory and mart
And proud discoveries of the intellect,
Heed not the pillage of man's ancient heart.

'*Scorn not the Sonnet; Critic, you have frowned*'

Scorn not the Sonnet; Critic, you have frowned,
Mindless of its just honours; with this key
Shakespeare unlocked his heart; the melody
Of this small lute gave ease to Petrarch's wound;
A thousand times this pipe did Tasso sound;
With it Camoëns soothed an exile's grief;
The Sonnet glittered a gay myrtle leaf
Amid the cypress with which Dante crowned
His visionary brow: a glow-worm lamp,
10   It cheered mild Spenser, called from Faery-land
To struggle through dark ways; and, when a damp
Fell round the path of Milton, in his hand
The Thing became a trumpet; whence he blew
Soul-animating strains – alas, too few!

'There is a pleasure in poetic pains'

There is a pleasure in poetic pains
Which only Poets know; – 'twas rightly said;
Whom could the Muses else allure to tread
Their smoothest paths, to wear their lightest chains?
When happiest Fancy has inspired the strains,
How oft the malice of one luckless word
Pursues the Enthusiast to the social board,
Haunts him belated on the silent plains!
Yet he repines not, if his thought stand clear,
10   At last, of hindrance and obscurity,
Fresh as the star that crowns the brow of morn;
Bright, speckless, as a softly-moulded tear
The moment it has left the virgin's eye,
Or rain-drop lingering on the pointed thorn.

'*When Philoctetes in the Lemnian isle*'

When Philoctetes in the Lemnian isle
Like a Form sculptured on a monument
Lay couched; on him or his dread bow unbent
Some wild Bird oft might settle and beguile
The rigid features of a transient smile,
Disperse the tear, or to the sigh give vent,
Slackening the pains of ruthless banishment
From his loved home, and from heroic toil.
And trust that spiritual Creatures round us move,
10   Griefs to allay which Reason cannot heal;
Yea, veriest reptiles have sufficed to prove
To fettered wretchedness, that no Bastille
Is deep enough to exclude the light of love,
Though man for brother man has ceased to feel.

To the Cuckoo

Not the whole warbling grove in concert heard
When sunshine follows shower, the breast can thrill
Like the first summons, Cuckoo! of thy bill,
With its twin notes inseparably paired.
The captive 'mid damp vaults unsunned, unaired,
Measuring the periods of his lonely doom,
That cry can reach; and to the sick man's room
Sends gladness, by no languid smile declared.
The lordly eagle-race through hostile search
10 May perish; time may come when never more
The wilderness shall hear the lion roar;
But, long as cock shall crow from household perch
To rouse the dawn, soft gales shall speed thy wing,
And thy erratic voice be faithful to the Spring!

'In my mind's eye a Temple, like a cloud'

In my mind's eye a Temple, like a cloud
Slowly surmounting some invidious hill,
Rose out of darkness: the bright Work stood still;
And might of its own beauty have been proud,
But it was fashioned and to God was vowed
By Virtues that diffused, in every part,
Spirit divine through forms of human art:
Faith had her arch – her arch, when winds blow loud,
Into the consciousness of safety thrilled;
10 And Love her towers of dread foundation laid
Under the grave of things; Hope had her spire
Star-high, and pointing still to something higher;
Trembling I gazed, but heard a voice – it said,
'Hell-gates are powerless Phantoms when *we* build.'

In the Woods of Rydal

Wild Redbreast! hadst thou at Jemima's lip
Pecked, as at mine, thus boldly, Love might say,
A half-blown rose had tempted thee to sip
Its glistening dews; but hallowed is the clay
Which the Muse warms; and I, whose head is grey,
Am not unworthy of thy fellowship;
Nor could I let one thought – one motion – slip
That might thy sylvan confidence betray.
For are we not all His without whose care
10 Vouchsafed no sparrow falleth to the ground?
Who gives His Angels wings to speed through air,
And rolls the planets through the blue profound;
Then peck or perch, fond Flutterer! nor forbear
To trust a Poet in still musings bound.

[*Two Epigrams on Byron's* Cain]

i
Critics, right honourable Bard, decree
Laurels to some, a night-shade wreath to thee,
Whose muse a sure though late revenge hath ta'en
Of harmless Abel's death, by murdering Cain.

ii
A German Haggis from receipt
Of him who cooked the death of Abel,
And sent 'warm-reeking, rich' and sweet,
From Venice to Sir Walter's table.

'Just vengeance claims thy Soul for rights invaded?'

Just vengeance claims thy Soul for rights invaded?
Lo! while before Minerva's altar quake
The conscious Tyrants, like a vengeful snake
Leaps forth the sword that lurked, with myrtles braided!
Thence to the Capitol, by Fancy aided,
The hushed design of Brutus to partake;
Or watch the hero of the Helvetian Lake
Till from that rocky couch, with pine o'ershaded,
He starts – and grasps his deadly carabine.
10   Nor let thy thirst forego the draught divine
Of Liberty, which like a liquid fountain
Refreshed Pelayo on the illustrious Mountain,
The Swede within the Dalecarlian mine,
When every hope but his was shrunk, and faded.

Filial Piety

(On the Wayside between Preston and Liverpool)

Untouched through all severity of cold;
Inviolate, whate'er the cottage hearth
Might need for comfort, or for festal mirth;
That Pile of Turf is half a century old:
Yes, Traveller! fifty winters have been told
Since suddenly the dart of death went forth
'Gainst him who raised it, – his last work on earth:
Thence has it, with the Son, so strong a hold
Upon his Father's memory, that his hands,
10   Through reverence, touch it only to repair
Its waste. – Though crumbling with each breath of air,
In annual renovation thus it stands –
Rude Mausoleum! but wrens nestle there,
And red-breasts warble when sweet sounds are rare.

The Triad

Show me the noblest Youth of present time,
Whose trembling fancy would to love give birth;
Some God or Hero, from the Olympian clime
Returned, to seek a Consort upon earth;
Or, in no doubtful prospect, let me see
The brightest star of ages yet to be,
And I will mate and match him blissfully.

I will not fetch a Naiad from a flood
Pure as herself – (song lacks not mightier power)
10 Nor leaf-crowned Dryad from a pathless wood,
Nor Sea-nymph, glistening from her coral bower;
Mere Mortals, bodied forth in vision still,
Shall with Mount Ida's triple lustre fill
The chaster coverts of a British hill.

'Appear! – obey my lyre's command!
Come, like the Graces, hand in hand!
For ye, though not by birth allied,
Are Sisters in the bond of love;
Nor shall the tongue of envious pride
20 Presume those interweavings to reprove
In you, which that fair progeny of Jove
Learned from the tuneful spheres that glide
In endless union, earth and sea above.'
– I sing in vain; – the pines have hushed their waving:
A peerless Youth expectant at my side,
Breathless as they, with unabated craving
Looks to the earth, and to the vacant air;
And, with a wandering eye that seems to chide,
Asks of the clouds what occupants they hide: –
30 But why solicit more than sight could bear,
By casting on a moment all we dare?
Invoke we those bright Beings one by one;
And what was boldly promised, truly shall be done.

'Fear not a constraining measure!
– Yielding to this gentle spell,
Lucida! from domes of pleasure,
Or from cottage-sprinkled dell,
Come to regions solitary,
Where the eagle builds her aery,
40 Above the hermit's long-forsaken cell!'
– She comes! – behold
That Figure, like a ship with snow-white sail!
Nearer she draws; a breeze uplifts her veil;
Upon her coming wait
As pure a sunshine and as soft a gale
As e'er, on herbage covering earthly mould,
Tempted the bird of Juno to unfold
His richest splendour – when his veering gait
And every motion of his starry train
50 Seem governed by a strain
Of music, audible to him alone.

'O Lady, worthy of earth's proudest throne!
Nor less, by excellence of nature, fit
Beside an unambitious hearth to sit
Domestic queen, where grandeur is unknown;
What living man could fear
The worst of Fortune's malice, wert Thou near,
Humbling that lily-stem, thy sceptre meek,
That its fair flowers may from his cheek
60 Brush the too happy tear?
– Queen, and handmaid lowly!
Whose skill can speed the day with lively cares,
And banish melancholy
By all that mind invents or hand prepares;
O Thou, against whose lip, without its smile
And in its silence even, no heart is proof;
Whose goodness, sinking deep, would reconcile
The softest Nursling of a gorgeous palace
To the bare life beneath the hawthorn-roof
70 Of Sherwood's Archer, or in caves of Wallace –

Who that hath seen thy beauty could content
His soul with but a *glimpse* of heavenly day?
Who that hath loved thee, but would lay
His strong hand on the wind, if it were bent
To take thee in thy majesty away?
– Pass onward (even the glancing deer
Till we depart intrude not here;)
That mossy slope, o'er which the woodbine throws
A canopy, is smoothed for thy repose!'

80   Glad moment is it when the throng
Of warblers in full concert strong
Strive, and not vainly strive, to rout
The lagging shower, and force coy Phoebus out,
Met by the rainbow's form divine,
Issuing from her cloudy shrine; –
So may the thrillings of the lyre
Prevail to further our desire,
While to these shades a sister Nymph I call.

   'Come, if the notes thine ear may pierce,
90   Come, youngest of the lovely Three,
Submissive to the might of verse
And the dear voice of harmony,
By none more deeply felt than Thee!'
– I sang; and lo! from pastimes virginal
She hastens to the tents
Of nature, and the lonely elements.
Air sparkles round her with a dazzling sheen;
But mark her glowing cheek, her vesture green!
And, as if wishful to disarm
100   Or to repay the potent Charm,
She bears the stringèd lute of old romance,
That cheered the trellised arbour's privacy,
And soothed war-wearied knights in raftered hall.
How vivid, yet how delicate, her glee!
So tripped the Muse, inventress of the dance;
So, truant in waste woods, the blithe Euphrosyne!

But the ringlets of that head
Why are they ungarlanded?
Why bedeck her temples less
110   Than the simplest shepherdess?
Is it not a brow inviting
Choicest flowers that ever breathed,
Which the myrtle would delight in
With Idalian rose enwreathed?
But her humility is well content
With *one* wild floweret (call it not forlorn)
FLOWER OF THE WINDS, beneath her bosom worn –
Yet more for love than ornament.

Open, ye thickets! let her fly,
120   Swift as a Thracian Nymph o'er field and height!
For She, to all but those who love her, shy,
Would gladly vanish from a Stranger's sight;
Though where she is beloved and loves,
Light as the wheeling butterfly she moves;
Her happy spirit as a bird is free,
That rifles blossoms on a tree,
Turning them inside out with arch audacity.
Alas! how little can a moment show
Of an eye where feeling plays
130   In ten thousand dewy rays;
A face o'er which a thousand shadows go!
– She stops – is fastened to that rivulet's side;
And there (while, with sedater mien,
O'er timid waters that have scarcely left
Their birthplace in the rocky cleft
She bends) at leisure may be seen
Features to old ideal grace allied,
Amid their smiles and dimples dignified –
Fit countenance for the soul of primal truth;
140   The bland composure of eternal youth!

What more changeful than the sea?
But over his great tides

Fidelity presides;
And this light-hearted Maiden constant is as he.
High is her aim as heaven above,
And wide as ether her good-will;
And, like the lowly reed, her love
Can drink its nurture from the scantiest rill:
Insight as keen as frosty star
150 Is to *her* charity no bar,
Nor interrupts her frolic graces
When she is, far from these wild places,
Encircled by familiar faces.

O the charm that manners draw,
Nature, from thy genuine law!
If from what her hand would do,
Her voice would utter, aught ensue
Untoward or unfit;
She, in benign affections pure,
160 In self-forgetfulness secure,
Sheds round the transient harm or vague mischance
A light unknown to tutored elegance:
Hers is not a cheek shame-stricken,
But her blushes are joy-flushes;
And the fault (if fault it be)
Only ministers to quicken
Laughter-loving gaiety,
And kindle sportive wit –
Leaving this Daughter of the mountains free
170 As if she knew that Oberon king of Faery
Had crossed her purpose with some quaint vagary,
And heard his viewless bands
Over their mirthful triumph clapping hands.

'Last of the Three, though eldest born,
Reveal thyself, like pensive Morn
Touched by the skylark's earliest note,
Ere humbler gladness be afloat.
But whether in the semblance drest

Of Dawn – or Eve, fair vision of the west,
180 Come with each anxious hope subdued
By woman's gentle fortitude,
Each grief, through meekness, settling into rest.
– Or I would hail thee when some high-wrought page
Of a closed volume lingering in thy hand
Has raised thy spirit to a peaceful stand
Among the glories of a happier age.'

Her brow hath opened on me – see it there,
Brightening the umbrage of her hair;
So gleams the crescent moon, that loves
190 To be descried through shady groves.
Tenderest bloom is on her cheek;
Wish not for a richer streak;
Nor dread the depth of meditative eye;
But let thy love, upon that azure field
Of thoughtfulness and beauty, yield
Its homage offered up in purity.
What wouldst thou more? In sunny glade,
Or under leaves of thickest shade,
Was such a stillness e'er diffused
200 Since earth grew calm while angels mused?
Softly she treads, as if her foot were loth
To crush the mountain dew-drops – soon to melt
On the flower's breast; as if she felt
That flowers themselves, whate'er their hue,
With all their fragrance, all their glistening,
Call to the heart for inward listening –
And though for bridal wreaths and tokens true
Welcomed wisely; though a growth
Which the careless shepherd sleeps on,
210 As fitly spring from turf the mourner weeps on –
And without wrong are cropped the marble tomb to
strew.
The Charm is over; the mute Phantoms gone,
Nor will return – but droop not, favoured Youth;
The apparition that before thee shone

Obeyed a summons covetous of truth.
From these wild rocks thy footsteps I will guide
To bowers in which thy fortune may be tried,
And one of the bright Three become thy happy Bride.

The Gleaner (*Suggested by a Picture*)

That happy gleam of vernal eyes,
Those locks from summer's golden skies,
    That o'er thy brow are shed;
That cheek – a kindling of the morn,
That lip – a rose-bud from the thorn,
    I saw; and Fancy sped
To scenes Arcadian, whispering, through soft air,
Of bliss that grows without a care,
And happiness that never flies –
10 (How can it where love never dies?)
Whispering of promise, where no blight
Can reach the innocent delight;
Where pity, to the mind conveyed
In pleasure, is the darkest shade
That Time, unwrinkled grandsire, flings
From his smoothly gliding wings.

    What mortal form, what earthly face
Inspired the pencil, lines to trace,
And mingle colours, that should breed
20 Such rapture, nor want power to feed;
For had thy charge been idle flowers,
Fair Damsel! o'er my captive mind,
To truth and sober reason blind,
'Mid that soft air, those long-lost bowers,
The sweet illusion might have hung, for hours.

    Thanks to this tell-tale sheaf of corn,
That touchingly bespeaks thee born
Life's daily tasks with them to share

Who, whether from their lowly bed
30 They rise, or rest the weary head,
Ponder the blessing they entreat
From Heaven, and *feel* what they repeat,
While they give utterance to the prayer
That asks for daily bread.

The Wishing-Gate

In the vale of Grasmere, by the side of the old highway leading
to Ambleside, is a gate, which, time out of mind, has been called
the Wishing-gate, from a belief that wishes formed or indulged
there have a favourable issue.

Hope rules a land for ever green:
All powers that serve the bright-eyed Queen
Are confident and gay;
Clouds at her bidding disappear;
Points she to aught? – the bliss draws near,
And Fancy smooths the way.

Not such the land of Wishes – there
Dwell fruitless day-dreams, lawless prayer,
And thoughts with things at strife;
10 Yet how forlorn, should *ye* depart,
Ye superstitions of the *heart*,
How poor, were human life!

When magic lore abjured its might,
Ye did not forfeit one dear right,
One tender claim abate;
Witness this symbol of your sway,
Surviving near the public way,
The rustic Wishing-gate!

Inquire not if the faery race
20 Shed kindly influence on the place,

Ere northward they retired;
If here a warrior left a spell,
Panting for glory as he fell;
    Or here a saint expired.

Enough that all around is fair,
Composed with Nature's finest care,
    And in her fondest love –
Peace to embosom and content –
To overawe the turbulent,
30   The selfish to reprove.

Yea! even the Stranger from afar,
Reclining on this moss-grown bar,
    Unknowing, and unknown,
The infection of the ground partakes,
Longing for his Beloved – who makes
    All happiness her own.

Then why should conscious Spirits fear
The mystic stirrings that are here,
    The ancient faith disclaim?
40 The local Genius ne'er befriends
Desires whose course in folly ends,
    Whose just reward is shame.

Smile if thou wilt, but not in scorn,
If some, by ceaseless pains outworn,
    Here crave an easier lot;
If some have thirsted to renew
A broken vow, or bind a true,
    With firmer, holier knot.

And not in vain, when thoughts are cast
50 Upon the irrevocable past,
    Some Penitent sincere
May for a worthier future sigh,
While trickles from his downcast eye
    No unavailing tear.

The Worldling, pining to be freed
From turmoil, who would turn or speed
    The current of his fate,
Might stop before this favoured scene,
At Nature's call, nor blush to lean
60   Upon the Wishing-gate.

The Sage, who feels how blind, how weak
Is man, though loth such help to *seek*,
    Yet, passing, here might pause,
And thirst for insight to allay
Misgiving, while the crimson day
    In quietness withdraws;

Or when the church-clock's knell profound
To Time's first step across the bound
    Of midnight makes reply;
70 Time pressing on with starry crest,
To filial sleep upon the breast
    Of dread eternity.

Farewell Lines

  'High bliss is only for a higher state',
But, surely, if severe afflictions borne
With patience merit the reward of peace,
Peace ye deserve; and may the solid good,
Sought by a wise though late exchange, and here
With bounteous hand beneath a cottage-roof
To you accorded, never be withdrawn,
Nor for the world's best promises renounced.
Most soothing was it for a welcome Friend,
10 Fresh from the crowded city, to behold
That lonely union, privacy so deep,
Such calm employments, such entire content.
So when the rain is over, the storm laid,
A pair of herons oft-times have I seen,

Upon a rocky islet, side by side,
Drying their feathers in the sun, at ease;
And so, when night with grateful gloom had fallen,
Two glow-worms in such nearness that they shared,
As seemed, their soft self-satisfying light,
20 Each with the other, on the dewy ground,
Where He that made them blesses their repose. –
When wandering among lakes and hills I note,
Once more, those creatures thus by nature paired,
And guarded in their tranquil state of life,
Even, as your happy presence to my mind
Their union brought, will they repay the debt,
And send a thankful spirit back to you,
With hope that we, dear Friends! shall meet again.

A Jewish Family (*in a Small Valley opposite St Goar, upon the Rhine*)

Genius of Raphael! if thy wings
  Might bear thee to this glen,
With faithful memory left of things
  To pencil dear and pen,
Thou wouldst forego the neighbouring Rhine,
  And all his majesty –
A studious forehead to incline
  O'er this poor family.

The Mother – her thou must have seen,
10 In spirit, ere she came
To dwell these rifted rocks between,
  Or found on earth a name;
An image, too, of that sweet Boy,
  Thy inspirations give –
Of playfulness, and love, and joy,
  Predestined here to live.

Downcast, or shooting glances far,
  How beautiful his eyes,

That blend the nature of the star
20   With that of summer skies!
I speak as if of sense beguiled;
    Uncounted months are gone,
Yet am I with the Jewish Child,
    That exquisite Saint John.

I see the dark-brown curls, the brow,
    The smooth transparent skin,
Refined, as with intent to show
    The holiness within;
The grace of parting Infancy
30   By blushes yet untamed;
Age faithful to the mother's knee,
    Nor of her arms ashamed.

Two lovely Sisters, still and sweet
    As flowers, stand side by side;
Their soul-subduing looks might cheat
    The Christian of his pride:
Such beauty hath the Eternal poured
    Upon them not forlorn,
Though of a lineage once abhorred,
40   Nor yet redeemed from scorn.

Mysterious safeguard, that, in spite
    Of poverty and wrong,
Doth here preserve a living light,
    From Hebrew fountains sprung;
That gives this ragged group to cast
    Around the dell a gleam
Of Palestine, of glory past,
    And proud Jerusalem!

The Egyptian Maid; or,
The Romance of the Water Lily

For the names and persons in the following poem see the 'History of the renowned Prince Arthur and his Knights of the Round Table;' for the rest the Author is answerable; only it may be proper to add that the Lotus, with the bust of the Goddess appearing to rise out of the full-blown flower, was suggested by the beautiful work of ancient art, once included among the Townley Marbles, and now in the British Museum.

While Merlin paced the Cornish sands,
Forth-looking toward the rocks of Scilly,
The pleased Enchanter was aware
Of a bright Ship that seemed to hang in air,
Yet was she work of mortal hands,
And took from men her name – THE WATER LILY.

Soft was the wind, that landward blew;
And, as the Moon, o'er some dark hill ascendant,
Grows from a little edge of light
To a full orb, this Pinnace bright
Became, as nearer to the coast she drew,
More glorious, with spread sail and streaming pendant.

Upon this wingèd Shape so fair
Sage Merlin gazed with admiration:
Her lineaments, thought he, surpass
Aught that was ever shown in magic glass;
Was ever built with patient care;
Or, at a touch, produced by happiest transformation.

Now, though a Mechanist, whose skill
Shames the degenerate grasp of modern science,
Grave Merlin (and belike the more
For practising occult and perilous lore)
Was subject to a freakish will
That sapped good thoughts, or scared them with defiance.

Provoked to envious spleen, he cast
An altered look upon the advancing Stranger
Whom he had hailed with joy, and cried,
'My Art shall help to tame her pride –'.
Anon the breeze became a blast,
30 And the waves rose, and sky portended danger.

With thrilling word, and potent sign
Traced on the beach, his work the Sorcerer urges;
The clouds in blacker clouds are lost,
Like spiteful Fiends that vanish, crossed
By Fiends of aspect more malign;
And the winds roused the Deep with fiercer scourges.

But worthy of the name she bore
Was this Sea-flower, this buoyant Galley;
Supreme in loveliness and grace
40 Of motion, whether in the embrace
Of trusty anchorage, or scudding o'er
The main flood roughened into hill and valley.

Behold, how wantonly she laves
Her sides, the Wizard's craft confounding;
Like something out of Ocean sprung
To be for ever fresh and young,
Breasts the sea-flashes, and huge waves
Top-gallant high, rebounding and rebounding!

But Ocean under magic heaves,
50 And cannot spare the Thing he cherished:
Ah! what avails that she was fair,
Luminous, blithe, and debonair?
The storm has stripped her of her leaves;
The Lily floats no longer! – She hath perished.

Grieve for her, she deserves no less;
So like, yet so unlike, a living Creature!
No heart had she, no busy brain;

Though loved, she could not love again;
Though pitied, *feel* her own distress;
60 Nor aught that troubles us, the fools of Nature.

Yet is there cause for gushing tears;
So richly was this Galley laden,
A fairer than herself she bore,
And, in her struggles, cast ashore;
A lovely One, who nothing hears
Of wind or wave – a meek and guileless Maiden.

Into a cave had Merlin fled
From mischief, caused by spells himself had muttered;
And while, repentant all too late,
70 In moody posture there he sate,
He heard a voice, and saw, with half-raised head,
A Visitant by whom these words were uttered:

'On Christian service this frail Bark
Sailed' (hear me, Merlin!) 'under high protection,
Though on her prow a sign of heathen power
Was carved – a Goddess with a Lily flower,
The old Egyptian's emblematic mark
Of joy immortal and of pure affection.

'Her course was for the British strand;
Her freight, it was a Damsel peerless;
80 God reigns above, and Spirits strong
May gather to avenge this wrong
Done to the Princess, and her Land
Which she in duty left, sad but not cheerless.

'And to Caerleon's loftiest tower
Soon will the Knights of Arthur's Table
A cry of lamentation send;
And all will weep who there attend,
To grace that Stranger's bridal hour,
90 For whom the sea was made unnavigable.

'Shame! should a Child of royal line
Die through the blindness of thy malice?'
Thus to the Necromancer spake
Nina, the Lady of the Lake,
A gentle Sorceress, and benign,
Who ne'er embittered any good man's chalice.

'What boots,' continued she, 'to mourn?
To expiate thy sin endeavour:
From the bleak isle where she is laid,
100   Fetched by our art, the Egyptian Maid
May yet to Arthur's court be borne
Cold as she is, ere life be fled for ever.

'My pearly Boat, a shining Light,
That brought me down that sunless river,
Will bear me on from wave to wave,
And back with her to this sea-cave; –
Then Merlin! for a rapid flight
Through air, to thee my Charge will I deliver.

'The very swiftest of thy cars
110   Must, when my part is done, be ready;
Meanwhile, for further guidance, look
Into thy own prophetic book;
And, if that fail, consult the Stars
To learn thy course; farewell! be prompt and steady.'

This scarcely spoken, she again
Was seated in her gleaming shallop,
That, o'er the yet-distempered Deep,
Pursued its way with bird-like sweep,
Or like a steed, without a rein,
120 Urged o'er the wilderness in sportive gallop.

Soon did the gentle Nina reach
That Isle without a house or haven;
Landing, she found not what she sought,

Nor saw of wreck or ruin aught
But a carved Lotus cast upon the beach
By the fierce waves, a flower in marble graven.

Sad relique, but how fair the while!
For gently each from each retreating
With backward curve, the leaves revealed
130 The bosom half, and half concealed,
Of a Divinity, that seemed to smile
On Nina, as she passed, with hopeful greeting.

No quest was hers of vague desire,
Of tortured hope and purpose shaken;
Following the margin of a bay,
She spied the lonely Cast-away,
Unmarred, unstripped of her attire,
But with closed eyes, – of breath and bloom forsaken.

Then Nina, stooping down, embraced,
140 With tenderness and mild emotion,
The Damsel, in that trance embound;
And, while she raised her from the ground,
And in the pearly shallop placed,
Sleep fell upon the air, and stilled the ocean.

The turmoil hushed, celestial springs
Of music opened, and there came a blending
Of fragrance, underived from earth,
With gleams that owed not to the sun their birth,
And that soft rustling of invisible wings
150 Which Angels make, on works of love descending.

And Nina heard a sweeter voice
Than if the Goddess of the flower had spoken:
'Thou hast achieved, fair Dame! what none
Less pure in spirit could have done;
Go, in thy enterprise rejoice!
Air, earth, sea, sky, and heaven, success betoken.'

So cheered, she left that Island bleak,
A bare rock of the Scilly cluster;
And, as they traversed the smooth brine,
160   The self-illumined Brigantine
Shed, on the Slumberer's cold wan cheek
And pallid brow, a melancholy lustre.

Fleet was their course, and when they came
To the dim cavern, whence the river
Issued into the salt-sea flood,
Merlin, as fixed in thought he stood,
Was thus accosted by the Dame:
'Behold to thee my Charge I now deliver!

'But where attends thy chariot – where?' –
170   Quoth Merlin, 'Even as I was bidden,
So have I done; as trusty as thy barge
My vehicle shall prove – O precious Charge!
If this be sleep, how soft! if death, how fair!
Much have my books disclosed, but the end is hidden.'

He spake; and gliding into view
Forth from the grotto's dimmest chamber
Came two mute Swans, whose plumes of dusky white
Changed, as the pair approached the light,
Drawing an ebon car, their hue
180 (Like clouds of sunset) into lucid amber.

Once more did gentle Nina lift
The Princess, passive to all changes:
The car received her: – then up-went
Into the ethereal element
The Birds with progress smooth and swift
As thought, when through bright regions memory ranges.

Sage Merlin, at the Slumberer's side,
Instructs the Swans their way to measure;
And soon Caerleon's towers appeared,

190   And notes of minstrelsy were heard
       From rich pavilions spreading wide,
   For some high day of long-expected pleasure.

       Awe-stricken stood both Knights and Dames
       Ere on firm ground the car alighted;
       Eftsoons astonishment was past,
       For in that face they saw the last
       Last lingering look of clay, that tames
  All pride; by which all happiness is blighted.

       Said Merlin: 'Mighty King, fair Lords,
200   Away with feast and tilt and tourney!
       Ye saw, throughout this royal House,
       Ye heard, a rocking marvellous
       Of turrets, and a clash of swords
  Self-shaken, as I closed my airy journey.

       Lo! by a destiny well known
       To mortals, joy is turned to sorrow;
       This is the wished-for Bride, the Maid
       Of Egypt, from a rock conveyed
       Where she by shipwreck had been thrown;
210   Ill sight! but grief may vanish ere the morrow.'

       'Though vast thy power, thy words are weak,'
       Exclaimed the King, 'a mockery hateful;
       Dutiful Child, her lot how hard!
       Is this her piety's reward?
       Those watery locks, that bloodless cheek!
  O winds without remorse! O shore ungrateful!

       'Rich robes are fretted by the moth;
       Towers, temples, fall by stroke of thunder;
       Will that, or deeper thoughts, abate
220   A Father's sorrow for her fate?
       He will repent him of his troth;
  His brain will burn, his stout heart split asunder.

'Alas! and I have caused this woe;
For, when my prowess from invading Neighbours
Had freed his Realm, he plighted word
That he would turn to Christ our Lord,
And his dear Daughter on a Knight bestow
Whom I should choose for love and matchless labours.

'Her birth was heathen; but a fence
230   Of holy Angels round her hovered:
A Lady added to my court
So fair, of such divine report
And worship, seemed a recompence
For fifty kingdoms by my sword recovered.

'Ask not for whom, O Champions true!
She was reserved by me her life's betrayer;
She who was meant to be a bride
Is now a corse: then put aside
Vain thoughts, and speed ye, with observance due
240   Of Christian rites, in Christian ground to lay her.'

'The tomb,' said Merlin, 'may not close
Upon her yet, earth hide her beauty;
Not froward to thy sovereign will
Esteem me, Liege! if I, whose skill
Wafted her hither, interpose
To check this pious haste of erring duty.

'My books command me to lay bare
The secret thou art bent on keeping:
Here must a high attest be given,
250   *What* Bridegroom was for her ordained by Heaven:
And in my glass significants there are
Of things that may to gladness turn this weeping.

'For this, approaching, One by One,
Thy Knights must touch the cold hand of the Virgin;
So, for the favoured One, the Flower may bloom

Once more: but, if unchangeable her doom,
If life departed be for ever gone,
Some blest assurance, from this cloud emerging,

'May teach him to bewail his loss;
260   Not with a grief that, like a vapour, rises
And melts; but grief devout that shall endure,
And a perpetual growth secure
Of purposes which no false thought shall cross,
A harvest of high hopes and noble enterprises.'

'So be it,' said the King; – 'anon,
Here, where the Princess lies, begin the trial;
Knights each in order as ye stand
Step forth.' – To touch the pallid hand
Sir Agravaine advanced; no sign he won
270   From Heaven or earth; – Sir Kaye had like denial.

Abashed, Sir Dinas turned away;
Even for Sir Percival was no disclosure;
Though he, devoutest of all Champions, ere
He reached that ebon car, the bier
Whereon diffused like snow the Damsel lay,
Full thrice had crossed himself in meek composure.

Imagine (but ye Saints! who can?)
How in still air the balance trembled –
The wishes, peradventure the despites
280   That overcame some not ungenerous Knights;
And all the thoughts that lengthened out a span
Of time to Lords and Ladies thus assembled.

What patient confidence was here!
And there how many bosoms panted!
While drawing toward the car Sir Gawaine, mailed
For tournament, his beaver vailed,
And softly touched; but, to his princely cheer
And high expectancy, no sign was granted.

Next, disencumbered of his harp,
Sir Tristram, dear to thousands as a brother,
Came to the proof, nor grieved that there ensued
No change; – the fair Izonda he had wooed
With love too true, a love with pangs too sharp,
From hope too distant, not to dread another.

Not so Sir Launcelot; – from Heaven's grace
A sign he craved, tired slave of vain contrition;
The royal Guinever looked passing glad
When his touch failed. – Next came Sir Galahad;
He paused, and stood entranced by that still face
Whose features he had seen in noontide vision.

For late, as near a murmuring stream
He rested 'mid an arbour green and shady,
Nina, the good Enchantress, shed
A light around his mossy bed;
And, at her call, a waking dream
Prefigured to his sense the Egyptian Lady.

Now, while his bright-haired front he bowed,
And stood, far-kenned by mantle furred with ermine,
As o'er the insensate Body hung
The enrapt, the beautiful, the young,
Belief sank deep into the crowd
That he the solemn issue would determine.

Nor deem it strange; the Youth had worn
That very mantle on a day of glory,
The day when he achieved that matchless feat,
The marvel of the PERILOUS SEAT,
Which whosoe'er approached of strength was shorn,
Though King or Knight the most renowned in story.

He touched with hesitating hand –
And lo! those Birds, far-famed through Love's
        dominions,

The Swans, in triumph clap their wings;
And their necks play, involved in rings,
Like sinless snakes in Eden's happy land; –
'Mine is she,' cried the Knight; – again they clapped
  their pinions.

'Mine was she – mine she is, though dead,
And to her name my soul shall cleave in sorrow;'
Whereat, a tender twilight streak
Of colour dawned upon the Damsel's cheek;
And her lips, quickening with uncertain red,
330 Seemed from each other a faint warmth to borrow.

Deep was the awe, the rapture high,
Of love emboldened, hope with dread entwining,
When, to the mouth, relenting Death
Allowed a soft and flower-like breath,
Precursor to a timid sigh,
To lifted eyelids, and a doubtful shining.

In silence did King Arthur gaze
Upon the signs that pass away or tarry;
In silence watched the gentle strife
340 Of Nature leading back to life;
Then eased his soul at length by praise
Of God, and Heaven's pure Queen – the blissful Mary.

Then said he, 'Take her to thy heart,
Sir Galahad! a treasure, that God giveth,
Bound by indissoluble ties to thee
Through mortal change and immortality;
Be happy and unenvied, thou who art
A goodly Knight that hath no peer that liveth!'

Not long the Nuptials were delayed;
350 And sage tradition still rehearses
The pomp, the glory of that hour
When toward the altar from her bower
King Arthur led the Egyptian Maid,
And Angels carolled these far-echoed verses; –

Who shrinks not from alliance
Of evil with good Powers,
To God proclaims defiance,
And mocks whom he adores.

A Ship to Christ devoted
360 From the Land of Nile did go;
Alas! the bright Ship floated,
An Idol at her prow.

By magic domination,
The Heaven-permitted vent
Of purblind mortal passion,
Was wrought her punishment.

The Flower, the Form within it,
What served they in her need?
Her port she could not win it,
370 Nor from mishap be freed.

The tempest overcame her,
And she was seen no more;
But gently, gently blame her –
She cast a Pearl ashore.

The Maid to Jesu hearkened,
And kept to Him her faith,
Till sense in death was darkened,
Or sleep akin to death.

But Angels round her pillow
380 Kept watch, a viewless band;
And, billow favouring billow,
She reached the destined strand.

Blest Pair! whate'er befall you,
Your faith in Him approve
Who from frail earth can call you
To bowers of endless love!

On the Power of Sound

Argument

The Ear addressed, as occupied by a spiritual functionary, in
communion with sounds, individual, or combined in studied
harmony. – Sources and effects of those sounds (to the close of
6th Stanza). – The power of music, whence proceeding, exemplified in the idiot. – Origin of music, and its effect in early ages
– how produced (to the middle of 10th Stanza). – The mind
recalled to sounds acting casually and severally. – Wish uttered
(11th Stanza) that these could be united into a scheme or system
for moral interests and intellectual contemplation. – (Stanza
12th). – The Pythagorean theory of numbers and music, with
their supposed power over the motions of the universe – imaginations consonant with such a theory. – Wish expressed (in 11th
Stanza) realized, in some degree, by the representation of all
sounds under the form of thanksgiving to the Creator. – (Last
Stanza) the destruction of earth and the planetary system – the
survival of audible harmony, and its support in the Divine
Nature, as revealed in Holy Writ.

I

Thy functions are ethereal,
As if within thee dwelt a glancing mind,
Organ of vision! And a Spirit aërial
Informs the cell of Hearing, dark and blind;
Intricate labyrinth, more dread for thought
To enter than oracular cave;
Strict passage, through which sighs are brought,
And whispers for the heart, their slave;
And shrieks, that revel in abuse
10 Of shivering flesh; and warbled air,
Whose piercing sweetness can unloose
The chains of frenzy, or entice a smile
Into the ambush of despair;
Hosannas pealing down the long-drawn aisle,
And requiems answered by the pulse that beats
Devoutly, in life's last retreats!

II

The headlong streams and fountains
Serve Thee, invisible Spirit, with untired powers;
Cheering the wakeful tent on Syrian mountains,
20 They lull perchance ten thousand thousand flowers.
That roar, the prowling lion's *Here I am*,
How fearful to the desert wide!
That bleat, how tender! of the dam
Calling a straggler to her side.
Shout, cuckoo! – let the vernal soul
Go with thee to the frozen zone;
Toll from thy loftiest perch, lone bell-bird, toll!
At the still hour to Mercy dear,
Mercy from her twilight throne
30 Listening to nun's faint throb of holy fear,
To sailor's prayer breathed from a darkening sea,
Or widow's cottage-lullaby.

III

Ye Voices, and ye Shadows
And Images of voice – to hound and horn
From rocky steep and rock-bestudded meadows
Flung back, and, in the sky's blue caves, reborn –
On with your pastime! till the church-tower bells
A greeting give of measured glee;
And milder echoes from their cells
40 Repeat the bridal symphony.
Then, or far earlier, let us rove
Where mists are breaking up or gone,
And from aloft look down into a cove
Besprinkled with a careless choir,
Happy milk-maids, one by one
Scattering a ditty each to her desire,
A liquid concert matchless by nice Art,
A stream as if from one full heart.

IV

Blest be the song that brightens
50 The blind man's gloom, exalts the veteran's mirth;

Unscorned the peasant's whistling breath, that lightens
His duteous toil of furrowing the green earth.
For the tired slave, Song lifts the languid oar,
And bids it aptly fall, with chime
That beautifies the fairest shore,
And mitigates the harshest clime.
Yon pilgrims see – in lagging file
They move; but soon the appointed way
A choral *Ave Marie* shall beguile,
60 And to their hope the distant shrine
Glisten with a livelier ray:
Nor friendless he, the prisoner of the mine,
Who from the well-spring of his own clear breast
Can draw, and sing his griefs to rest.

V

When civic renovation
Dawns on a kingdom, and for needful haste
Best eloquence avails not, Inspiration
Mounts with a tune, that travels like a blast
Piping through cave and battlemented tower;
70 Then starts the sluggard, pleased to meet
That voice of Freedom, in its power
Of promises, shrill, wild, and sweet!
Who, from a martial *pageant*, spreads
Incitements of a battle-day,
Thrilling the unweaponed crowd with plumeless heads? –
Even She whose Lydian airs inspire
Peaceful striving, gentle play
Of timid hope and innocent desire
Shot from the dancing Graces, as they move
80 Fanned by the plausive wings of Love.

VI

How oft along thy mazes,
Regent of sound, have dangerous Passions trod!
O Thou, through whom the temple rings with praises,
And blackening clouds in thunder speak of God,

Betray not by the cozenage of sense
Thy votaries, wooingly resigned
To a voluptuous influence
That taints the purer, better, mind;
But lead sick Fancy to a harp
90 That hath in noble tasks been tried;
And, if the virtuous feel a pang too sharp,
Soothe it into patience, – stay
The uplifted arm of Suicide;
And let some mood of thine in firm array
Knit every thought the impending issue needs,
Ere martyr burns, or patriot bleeds!

VII
As Conscience, to the centre
Of being, smites with irresistible pain,
So shall a solemn cadence, if it enter
100 The mouldy vaults of the dull idiot's brain,
Transmute him to a wretch from quiet hurled –
Convulsed as by a jarring din;
And then aghast, as at the world
Of reason partially let in
By concords winding with a sway
Terrible for sense and soul!
Or, awed he weeps, struggling to quell dismay.
Point not these mysteries to an Art
Lodged above the starry pole;
110 Pure modulations flowing from the heart
Of divine Love, where Wisdom, Beauty, Truth
With Order dwell, in endless youth?

VIII
Oblivion may not cover
All treasures hoarded by the miser, Time.
Orphean Insight! truth's undaunted lover,
To the first leagues of tutored passion climb,
When Music deigned within this grosser sphere
Her subtle essence to enfold,

And voice and shell drew forth a tear
120 Softer than Nature's self could mould.
Yet *strenuous* was the infant Age:
Art, daring because souls could feel,
Stirred nowhere but an urgent equipage
Of rapt imagination sped her march
Through the realms of woe and weal:
Hell to the lyre bowed low; the upper arch
Rejoiced that clamorous spell and magic verse
Her wan disasters could disperse.

IX
The GIFT to king Amphion
130 That walled a city with its melody
Was for belief no dream: – thy skill, Arion!
Could humanize the creatures of the sea,
Where men were monsters. A last grace he craves,
Leave for one chant; – the dulcet sound
Steals from the deck o'er willing waves,
And listening dolphins gather round.
Self-cast, as with a desperate course,
'Mid that strange audience, he bestrides
A proud One docile as a managed horse;
140 And singing, while the accordant hand
Sweeps his harp, the Master rides;
So shall he touch at length a friendly strand,
And he, with his preserver, shine star-bright
In memory, through silent night.

X
The pipe of Pan, to shepherds
Couched in the shadow of Maenalian pines,
Was passing sweet; the eyeballs of the leopards,
That in high triumph drew the Lord of vines,
How did they sparkle to the cymbal's clang!
150 While Fauns and Satyrs beat the ground
In cadence, – and Silenus swang
This way and that, with wild-flowers crowned.

To life, to *life* give back thine ear:
Ye who are longing to be rid
Of fable, though to truth subservient, hear
The little sprinkling of cold earth that fell
Echoed from the coffin-lid;
The convict's summons in the steeple's knell;
'The vain distress-gun', from a leeward shore,
160   Repeated – heard, and heard no more!

XI

For terror, joy, or pity,
Vast is the compass and the swell of notes:
From the babe's first cry to voice of regal city,
Rolling a solemn sea-like bass, that floats
Far as the woodlands – with the trill to blend
Of that shy songstress, whose love-tale
Might tempt an angel to descend,
While hovering o'er the moonlight vale.
Ye wandering Utterances, has earth no scheme,
170   No scale of moral music – to unite
Powers that survive but in the faintest dream
Of memory? – O that ye might stoop to bear
Chains, such precious chains of sight
As laboured minstrelsies through ages wear!
O for a balance fit the truth to tell
Of the Unsubstantial, pondered well!

XII

By one pervading spirit
Of tones and numbers all things are controlled,
As sages taught, where faith was found to merit
180   Initiation in that mystery old.
The heavens, whose aspect makes our minds as still
As they themselves appear to be,
Innumerable voices fill
With everlasting harmony;
The towering headlands, crowned with mist,
Their feet among the billows, know

That Ocean is a mighty harmonist;
Thy pinions, universal Air,
Ever waving to and fro,
190 Are delegates of harmony, and bear
Strains that support the Seasons in their round;
Stern Winter loves a dirge-like sound.

XIII

Break forth into thanksgiving,
Ye banded instruments of wind and chords;
Unite, to magnify the Ever-living,
Your inarticulate notes with the voice of words!
Nor hushed be service from the lowing mead,
Nor mute the forest hum of noon;
Thou too be heard, lone eagle! freed
200 From snowy peak and cloud, attune
Thy hungry barkings to the hymn
Of joy, that from her utmost walls
The six-days' Work, by flaming Seraphim
Transmits to Heaven! As Deep to Deep
Shouting through one valley calls,
All worlds, all natures, mood and measure keep
For praise and ceaseless gratulation, poured
Into the ear of God, their Lord!

XIV

A Voice to Light gave Being;
210 To Time, and Man his earth-born chronicler;
A Voice shall finish doubt and dim foreseeing,
And sweep away life's visionary stir;
The trumpet (we, intoxicate with pride,
Arm at its blast for deadly wars)
To archangelic lips applied,
The grave shall open, quench the stars.
O Silence! are Man's noisy years
No more than moments of thy life?
Is Harmony, blest queen of smiles and tears,
220 With her smooth tones and discords just,

Tempered into rapturous strife,
Thy destined bond-slave? No! though earth be dust
And vanish, though the heavens dissolve, her stay
Is in the WORD, that shall not pass away.

Written in Mrs Field's Album opposite a Pen-and-Ink Sketch in the Manner of a Rembrandt Etching Done by Edmund Field

That gloomy cave, that gothic niche,
Those trees that forward lean
As if enamoured of the brook –
How soothing is the scene!

No witchery of inky words
Can such illusions yield;
Yet all (ye Landscape Poets blush!)
Was penned by Edmund Field.

A Tradition of Oker Hill in Darley Dale, Derbyshire

'Tis said that to the brow of yon fair hill
Two Brothers clomb, and, turning face from face,
Nor one look more exchanging, grief to still
Or feed, each planted on that lofty place
A chosen Tree; then, eager to fulfil
Their courses, like two new-born rivers, they
In opposite directions urged their way
Down from the far-seen mount. No blast might kill
Or blight that fond memorial; – the trees grew,
10   And now entwine their arms; but ne'er again
Embraced those Brothers upon earth's wide plain;
Nor aught of mutual joy or sorrow knew
Until their spirits mingled in the sea
That to itself takes all, Eternity.

A Gravestone upon the Floor in the Cloisters of Worcester Cathedral

'*Miserrimus!*' and neither name nor date,
Prayer, text, or symbol, graven upon the stone;
Naught but that word assigned to the unknown,
That solitary word – to separate
From all, and cast a cloud around the fate
Of him who lies beneath. Most wretched one,
Who chose his epitaph? – Himself alone
Could thus have dared the grave to agitate,
And claim, among the dead, this awful crown;
10 Nor doubt that He marked also for his own
Close to these cloistral steps a burial-place,
That every foot might fall with heavier tread,
Trampling upon his vileness. Stranger, pass
Softly! – To save the contrite, Jesus bled.

The Russian Fugitive

PART I
Enough of rose-bud lips, and eyes
  Like harebells bathed in dew,
Of cheek that with carnation vies,
  And veins of violet hue;
Earth wants not beauty that may scorn
  A likening to frail flowers;
Yea, to the stars, if they were born
  For seasons and for hours.

Through Moscow's gates, with gold unbarred,
10 Stepped One at dead of night,
Whom such high beauty could not guard
  From meditated blight;
By stealth she passed, and fled as fast
  As doth the hunted fawn,

Nor stopped, till in the dappling east
　　Appeared unwelcome dawn.

Seven days she lurked in brake and field,
　　Seven nights her course renewed,
Sustained by what her scrip might yield,
20　　Or berries of the wood;
At length, in darkness travelling on,
　　When lowly doors were shut,
The haven of her hope she won,
　　Her Foster-mother's hut.

'To put your love to dangerous proof
　　I come,' said she, 'from far;
For I have left my Father's roof,
　　In terror of the Czar.'
No answer did the Matron give,
30　　No second look she cast,
But hung upon the Fugitive,
　　Embracing and embraced.

She led the Lady to a seat
　　Beside the glimmering fire,
Bathed duteously her wayworn feet,
　　Prevented each desire: –
The cricket chirped, the house-dog dozed,
　　And on that simple bed,
Where she in childhood had reposed,
40　　Now rests her weary head.

When she, whose couch had been the sod,
　　Whose curtain pine or thorn,
Had breathed a sigh of thanks to God,
　　Who comforts the forlorn;
While over her the Matron bent
　　Sleep sealed her eyes, and stole
Feeling from limbs with travel spent,
　　And trouble from the soul.

Refreshed, the Wanderer rose at morn,
50   And soon again was dight
In those unworthy vestments worn
    Through long and perilous flight;
And 'O beloved Nurse,' she said,
    'My thanks with silent tears
Have unto Heaven and You been paid:
    Now listen to my fears!

'Have you forgot' – and here she smiled –
    'The babbling flatteries
You lavished on me when a child
60   Disporting round your knees?
I was your lambkin, and your bird,
    Your star, your gem, your flower;
Light words, that were more lightly heard
    In many a cloudless hour!

'The blossom you so fondly praised
    Is come to bitter fruit;
A mighty One upon me gazed;
    I spurned his lawless suit,
And must be hidden from his wrath:
70   You, Foster-father dear,
Will guide me in my forward path;
    I may not tarry here!

'I cannot bring to utter woe
    Your proved fidelity.' –
'Dear Child, sweet Mistress, say not so!
    For you we both would die.'
'Nay, nay, I come with semblance feigned
    And cheek embrowned by art;
Yet, being inwardly unstained,
80   With courage will depart.'

'But whither would you, could you, flee?
    A poor Man's counsel take;

The Holy Virgin gives to me
  A thought for your dear sake;
Rest, shielded by our Lady's grace,
  And soon shall you be led
Forth to a safe abiding-place,
  Where never foot doth tread.'

PART II

The dwelling of this faithful pair
90   In a straggling village stood,
For One who breathed unquiet air
  A dangerous neighbourhood;
But wide around lay forest ground
  With thickets rough and blind;
And pine-trees made a heavy shade
  Impervious to the wind.

And there, sequestered from the sight,
  Was spread a treacherous swamp,
On which the noonday sun shed light
100   As from a lonely lamp;
And midway in the unsafe morass,
  A single Island rose
Of firm dry ground, with healthful grass
  Adorned, and shady boughs.

The Woodman knew, for such the craft
  This Russian vassal plied,
That never fowler's gun, nor shaft
  Of archer, there was tried;
A sanctuary seemed the spot
110   From all intrusion free;
And there he planned an artful Cot
  For perfect secrecy.

With earnest pains unchecked by dread
  Of Power's far-stretching hand,
The bold good Man his labour sped
  At nature's pure command;

Heart-soothed, and busy as a wren,
   While, in a hollow nook,
She moulds her sight-eluding den
120   Above a murmuring brook.

His task accomplished to his mind,
   The twain ere break of day
Creep forth, and through the forest wind
   Their solitary way;
Few words they speak, nor dare to slack
   Their pace from mile to mile,
Till they have crossed the quaking marsh,
   And reached the lonely Isle.

The sun above the pine-trees showed
130   A bright and cheerful face;
And Ina looked for her abode,
   The promised hiding-place;
She sought in vain, the Woodman smiled;
   No threshold could be seen,
Nor roof, nor window; – all seemed wild
   As it had ever been.

Advancing, you might guess an hour,
   The front with such nice care
Is masked, 'if house it be or bower,'
140   But in they entered are;
As shaggy as were wall and roof
   With branches intertwined,
So smooth was all within, air-proof,
   And delicately lined:

And hearth was there, and maple dish,
   And cups in seemly rows,
And couch – all ready to a wish
   For nurture or repose;
And Heaven doth to her virtue grant
150   That there she may abide
In solitude, with every want
   By cautious love supplied.

No queen, before a shouting crowd
   Led on in bridal state,
E'er struggled with a heart so proud,
   Entering her palace gate;
Rejoiced to bid the world farewell,
   No saintly anchoress
E'er took possession of her cell
160   With deeper thankfulness.

'Father of all, upon thy care
   And mercy am I thrown;
Be thou my safeguard!' – such her prayer
   When she was left alone,
Kneeling amid the wilderness
   When joy had passed away,
And smiles, fond efforts of distress
   To hide what they betray!

The prayer is heard, the Saints have seen,
170   Diffused through form and face,
Resolves devotedly serene;
   That monumental grace
Of Faith, which doth all passions tame
That Reason *should* control;
And shows in the untrembling frame
   A statue of the soul.

PART III

'Tis sung in ancient minstrelsy
   That Phoebus wont to wear
The leaves of any pleasant tree
180   Around his golden hair;
Till Daphne, desperate with pursuit
   Of his imperious love,
At her own prayer transformed, took root,
   A laurel in the grove.

Then did the Penitent adorn
   His brow with laurel green;

And 'mid his bright locks never shorn
No meaner leaf was seen;
And poets sage, through every age,
190   About their temples wound
The bays; and conquerors thanked the Gods,
With laurel chaplets crowned.

Into the mists of fabling Time
So far runs back the praise
Of Beauty, that disdains to climb
Along forbidden ways;
That scorns temptation; power defies
Where mutual love is not;
And to the tomb for rescue flies
200   When life would be a blot.

To this fair Votaress, a fate
More mild doth Heaven ordain
Upon her Island desolate;
And words, not breathed in vain,
Might tell what intercourse she found,
Her silence to endear;
What birds she tamed, what flowers the ground
Sent forth her peace to cheer.

To one mute Presence, above all,
210   Her soothed affections clung,
A picture on the cabin wall
By Russian usage hung –
The Mother-maid, whose countenance bright
With love abridged the day;
And, communed with by taper light,
Chased spectral fears away.

And oft, as either Guardian came,
The joy in that retreat
Might any common friendship shame,
220   So high their hearts would beat;

And to the lone Recluse, whate'er
   They brought, each visiting
Was like the crowding of the year
   With a new burst of spring.

But, when she of her Parents thought,
   The pang was hard to bear;
And, if with all things not enwrought,
   That trouble still is near.
Before her flight she had not dared
230   Their constancy to prove,
Too much the heroic Daughter feared
   The weakness of their love.

Dark is the past to them, and dark
   The future still must be,
Till pitying Saints conduct her bark
   Into a safer sea –
Or gentle Nature close her eyes,
   And set her Spirit free
From the altar of this sacrifice,
240   In vestal purity.

Yet, when above the forest-glooms
   The white swans southward passed,
High as the pitch of their swift plumes
   Her fancy rode the blast;
And bore her toward the fields of France,
   Her Father's native land,
To mingle in the rustic dance,
   The happiest of the band!

Of those belovèd fields she oft
250   Had heard her Father tell
In phrase that now with echoes soft
   Haunted her lonely cell;
She saw the hereditary bowers,
   She heard the ancestral stream;
The Kremlin and its haughty towers
   Forgotten like a dream!

PART IV

The ever-changing Moon had traced
   Twelve times her monthly round,
When through the unfrequented Waste
260   Was heard a startling sound;
A shout thrice sent from one who chased
   At speed a wounded deer,
Bounding through branches interlaced,
   And where the wood was clear.

The fainting creature took the marsh,
   And toward the Island fled,
While plovers screamed with tumult harsh
   Above his antlered head;
This, Ina saw; and, pale with fear,
270   Shrunk to her citadel;
The desperate deer rushed on, and near
   The tangled covert fell.

Across the marsh, the game in view,
   The Hunter followed fast,
Nor paused, till o'er the stag he blew
   A death-proclaiming blast;
Then, resting on her upright mind,
   Came forth the Maid – 'In me
Behold,' she said, 'a stricken Hind
280   Pursued by destiny!

'From your deportment, Sir! I deem
   That you have worn a sword,
And will not hold in light esteem
   A suffering woman's word;
There is my covert, there perchance
   I might have lain concealed,
My fortunes hid, my countenance
   Not even to you revealed.

'Tears might be shed, and I might pray,
290   Crouching and terrified,

That what has been unveiled today,
   You would in mystery hide;
But I will not defile with dust
   The knee that bends to adore
The God in heaven; – attend, be just;
   This ask I, and no more!

'I speak not of the winter's cold,
   For summer's heat exchanged,
While I have lodged in this rough hold,
300   From social life estranged;
Nor yet of trouble and alarms:
   High Heaven is my defence;
And every season has soft arms
   For injured Innocence.

'From Moscow to the Wilderness
   It was my choice to come,
Lest virtue should be harbourless,
   And honour want a home;
And happy were I, if the Czar
310   Retain his lawless will,
To end life here like this poor deer,
   Or a lamb on a green hill.'

'Are you the Maid,' the Stranger cried,
   'From Gallic parents sprung,
Whose vanishing was rumoured wide,
   Sad theme for every tongue;
Who foiled an Emperor's eager quest?
   You, Lady, forced to wear
These rude habiliments, and rest
320   Your head in this dark lair!'

But wonder, pity, soon were quelled;
   And in her face and mien
The soul's pure brightness he beheld
   Without a veil between:

He loved, he hoped, – a holy flame
    Kindled 'mid rapturous tears;
The passion of a moment came
    As on the wings of years.

'Such bounty is no gift of chance,'
330   Exclaimed he: 'righteous Heaven,
Preparing your deliverance,
    To me the charge hath given.
The Czar full oft in words and deeds
    Is stormy and self-willed;
But, when the Lady Catherine pleads,
    His violence is stilled.

'Leave open to my wish the course,
    And I to her will go;
From that humane and heavenly source,
340   Good, only good, can flow.'
Faint sanction given, the Cavalier
    Was eager to depart,
Though question followed question, dear
    To the Maiden's filial heart.

Light was his step, – his hopes, more light,
    Kept pace with his desires;
And the fifth morning gave him sight
    Of Moscow's glittering spires.
He sued: – heart-smitten by the wrong,
350   To the lorn Fugitive
The Emperor sent a pledge as strong
    As sovereign power could give.

O more than mighty change! If e'er
    Amazement rose to pain,
And joy's excess produced a fear
    Of something void and vain;
'Twas when the Parents, who had mourned
    So long the lost as dead,
Beheld their only Child returned,
360   The household floor to tread.

Soon gratitude gave way to love
  Within the Maiden's breast:
Delivered and Deliverer move
  In bridal garments drest;
Meek Catherine had her own reward;
  The Czar bestowed a dower;
And universal Moscow shared
  The triumph of that hour.

Flowers strewed the ground; the nuptial feast
370   Was held with costly state;
And there, 'mid many a noble guest,
  The Foster-parents sate;
Encouraged by the imperial eye,
  They shrank not into shade;
Great was their bliss, the honour high
  To them and nature paid!

Gold and Silver Fishes in a Vase

The soaring lark is blest as proud
  When at heaven's gate she sings;
The roving bee proclaims aloud
  Her flight by vocal wings;
While Ye, in lasting durance pent,
  Your silent lives employ
For something more than dull content,
  Though haply less than joy.

Yet might your glassy prison seem
10   A place where joy is known,
Where golden flash and silver gleam
  Have meanings of their own;
While, high and low, and all about,
  Your motions, glittering Elves!
Ye weave – no danger from without,
  And peace among yourselves.

Type of a sunny human breast
   Is your transparent cell;
Where Fear is but a transient guest,
20   No sullen Humours dwell;
Where, sensitive of every ray
   That smites this tiny sea,
Your scaly panoplies repay
   The loan with usury.

How beautiful! – Yet none knows why
   This ever-graceful change,
Renewed – renewed incessantly –
   Within your quiet range.
Is it that ye with conscious skill
30   For mutual pleasure glide;
And sometimes, not without your will,
   Are dwarfed, or magnified?

Fays, Genii of gigantic size!
   And now, in twilight dim,
Clustering like constellated eyes,
   In wings of Cherubim,
When the fierce orbs abate their glare; –
   Whate'er your forms express,
Whate'er ye seem, whate'er ye are –
40   All leads to gentleness.

Cold though your nature be, 'tis pure;
   Your birthright is a fence
From all that haughtier kinds endure
   Through tyranny of sense.
Ah! not alone by colours bright
   Are Ye to heaven allied,
When, like essential Forms of light,
   Ye mingle, or divide.

For day-dreams soft as e'er beguiled
50   Day-thoughts while limbs repose;

For moonlight fascinations mild,
   Your gift, ere shutters close –
Accept, mute Captives! thanks and praise;
   And may this tribute prove
That gentle admirations raise
   Delight resembling love.

Liberty
Sequel to the Preceding

Addressed to a friend; the gold and silver fishes having been
removed to a pool in the pleasure-ground of Rydal Mount.

'The liberty of a people consists in being governed by laws
which they have made for themselves, under whatever form it
be of government. The liberty of a private man, in being master
of his own time and actions, as far as may consist with the laws
of God and of his country. Of this latter we are here to discourse.'
– COWLEY.

Those breathing Tokens of your kind regard,
(Suspect not, Anna, that their fate is hard;
Not soon does aught to which mild fancies cling
In lonely spots, become a slighted thing;)
Those silent Inmates now no longer share,
Nor do they need, our hospitable care,
Removed in kindness from their glassy Cell
To the fresh waters of a living Well –
An elfin pool so sheltered that its rest
10 No winds disturb; the mirror of whose breast
Is smooth as clear, save where with dimples small
A fly may settle, or a blossom fall.
– *There* swims, of blazing sun and beating shower
Fearless (but how obscured!) the golden Power,
That from his bauble prison used to cast
Gleams by the richest jewel unsurpast;
And near him, darkling like a sullen Gnome,
The silver Tenant of the crystal dome;

Dissevered both from all the mysteries
20   Of hue and altering shape that charmed all eyes.
Alas! they pined, they languished while they shone;
And, if not so, what matters beauty gone
And admiration lost, by change of place
That brings to the inward creature no disgrace?
But if the change restore his birthright, then,
Whate'er the difference, boundless is the gain.
Who can divine what impulses from God
Reach the caged lark, within a town-abode,
From his poor inch or two of daisied sod?
30   O yield him back his privilege! – No sea
Swells like the bosom of a man set free;
A wilderness is rich with liberty.
Roll on, ye spouting whales, who die or keep
Your independence in the fathomless Deep!
Spread, tiny nautilus, the living sail;
Dive, at thy choice, or brave the freshening gale!
If unreproved the ambitious eagle mount
Sunward to seek the daylight in its fount,
Bays, gulfs, and ocean's Indian width, shall be,
40   Till the world perishes, a field for thee!

While musing here I sit in shadow cool,
And watch these mute Companions, in the pool,
(Among reflected boughs of leafy trees)
By glimpses caught – disporting at their ease,
Enlivened, braced, by hardy luxuries,
I ask what warrant fixed them (like a spell
Of witchcraft fixed them) in the crystal cell;
To wheel with languid motion round and round,
Beautiful, yet in mournful durance bound.
50   Their peace, perhaps, our lightest footfall marred;
On their quick sense our sweetest music jarred;
And whither could they dart, if seized with fear?
No sheltering stone, no tangled root was near.
When fire or taper ceased to cheer the room,
They wore away the night in starless gloom;

And, when the sun first dawned upon the streams,
How faint their portion of his vital beams!
Thus, and unable to complain, they fared,
While not one joy of ours by them was shared.

60   Is there a cherished bird (I venture now
To snatch a sprig from Chaucer's reverend brow) –
Is there a brilliant fondling of the cage,
Though sure of plaudits on his costly stage,
Though fed with dainties from the snow-white hand
Of a kind mistress, fairest of the land,
But gladly would escape; and, if need were,
Scatter the colours from the plumes that bear
The emancipated captive through blithe air
Into strange woods, where he at large may live
70 On best or worst which they and Nature give?
The beetle loves his unpretending track,
The snail the house he carries on his back;
The far-fetched worm with pleasure would disown
The bed we give him, though of softest down;
A noble instinct; in all kinds the same,
All ranks! What Sovereign, worthy of the name,
If doomed to breathe against his lawful will
An element that flatters him – to kill,
But would rejoice to barter outward show
80 For the least boon that freedom can bestow?

     But most the Bard is true to inborn right,
Lark of the dawn, and Philomel of night,
Exults in freedom, can with rapture vouch
For the dear blessings of a lowly couch,
A natural meal – days, months, from Nature's hand;
Time, place, and business, all at his command! –
Who bends to happier duties, who more wise
Than the industrious Poet, taught to prize,
Above all grandeur, a pure life uncrossed
90 By cares in which simplicity is lost?
That life – the flowery path that winds by stealth –

Which Horace needed for his spirit's health;
Sighed for, in heart and genius, overcome
By noise and strife, and questions wearisome,
And the vain splendours of Imperial Rome? –
Let easy mirth his social hours inspire,
And fiction animate his sportive lyre,
Attuned to verse that, crowning light Distress
With garlands, cheats her into happiness;
100 Give *me* the humblest note of those sad strains
Drawn forth by pressure of his gilded chains,
As a chance-sunbeam from his memory fell
Upon the Sabine farm he loved so well;
Or when the prattle of Blandusia's spring
Haunted his ear – he only listening –
He proud to please, above all rivals, fit
To win the palm of gaiety and wit;
He, doubt not, with involuntary dread,
Shrinking from each new favour to be shed,
110 By the world's Ruler, on his honoured head!

In a deep vision's intellectual scene,
Such earnest longings and regrets as keen
Depressed the melancholy Cowley, laid
Under a fancied yew-tree's luckless shade;
A doleful bower for penitential song,
Where Man and Muse complained of mutual wrong;
While Cam's ideal current glided by,
And antique towers nodded their foreheads high,
Citadels dear to studious privacy.
120 But Fortune, who had long been used to sport
With this tried Servant of a thankless Court,
Relenting met his wishes; and to you
The remnant of his days at least was true;
You, whom, though long deserted, he loved best;
You, Muses, books, fields, liberty, and rest!

Far happier they who, fixing hope and aim
On the humanities of peaceful fame,

Enter betimes with more than martial fire
The generous course, aspire, and still aspire;
130 Upheld by warnings heeded not too late
Stifle the contradictions of their fate,
And to one purpose cleave, their Being's godlike mate!

Thus, gifted Friend, but with the placid brow
That woman ne'er should forfeit, keep *thy* vow;
With modest scorn reject whate'er would blind
The ethereal eyesight, cramp the wingèd mind!
Then, with a blessing granted from above
To every act, word, thought, and look of love,
Life's book for Thee may lie unclosed, till age
140 Shall with a thankful tear bedrop its latest page.

Humanity

The Rocking-stones, alluded to in the beginning of the following verses, are supposed to have been used, by our British ancestors, both for judicial and religious purposes. Such stones are not uncommonly found, at this day, both in Great Britain and in Ireland.

What though the Accused, upon his own appeal
To righteous Gods when man has ceased to feel,
Or at a doubting Judge's stern command,
Before the STONE OF POWER no longer stand –
To take his sentence from the balanced Block,
As, at his touch, it rocks, or seems to rock;
Though, in the depths of sunless groves, no more
The Druid-priest the hallowed Oak adore;
Yet, for the Initiate, rocks and whispering trees
10 Do still perform mysterious offices!
And functions dwell in beast and bird that sway
The reasoning mind, or with the fancy play,
Inviting, at all seasons, ears and eyes
To watch for undelusive auguries: –
Not uninspired appear their simplest ways;
Their voices mount symbolical of praise –

To mix with hymns that Spirits make and hear;
And to fallen man their innocence is dear.
Enraptured Art draws from those sacred springs
20 Streams that reflect the poetry of things!
Where Christian Martyrs stand in hues portrayed,
That, might a wish avail, would never fade,
Borne in their hands the lily and the palm
Shed round the altar a celestial calm;
There, too, behold the lamb and guileless dove
Prest in the tenderness of virgin love
To saintly bosoms! – Glorious is the blending
Of right affections climbing or descending
Along a scale of light and life, with cares
30 Alternate; carrying holy thoughts and prayers
Up to the sovereign seat of the Most High;
Descending to the worm in charity;
Like those good Angels whom a dream of night
Gave, in the field of Luz, to Jacob's sight
All, while *he* slept, treading the pendent stairs
Earthward or heavenward, radiant messengers,
That, with a perfect will in one accord
Of strict obedience, serve the Almighty Lord;
And with untired humility forbore
40 To speed their errand by the wings they wore.

    What a fair world were ours for verse to paint,
If Power could live at ease with self-restraint!
Opinion bow before the naked sense
Of the great Vision, – faith in Providence;
Merciful over all his creatures, just
To the least particle of sentient dust;
But, fixing by immutable decrees,
Seedtime and harvest for his purposes!
Then would be closed the restless oblique eye
50 That looks for evil like a treacherous spy;
Disputes would then relax, like stormy winds
That into breezes sink; impetuous minds
By discipline endeavour to grow meek

As Truth herself, whom they profess to seek.
Then Genius, shunning fellowship with Pride,
Would braid his golden locks at Wisdom's side;
Love ebb and flow untroubled by caprice;
And not alone *harsh* tyranny would cease,
But unoffending creatures find release
60 From qualified oppression, whose defence
Rests on a hollow plea of recompence;
Thought-tempered wrongs, for each humane respect
Oft worse to bear, or deadlier in effect.
Witness those glances of indignant scorn
From some high-minded Slave, impelled to spurn
The kindness that would make him less forlorn;
Or, if the soul to bondage be subdued,
His look of pitiable gratitude!

Alas for thee, bright Galaxy of Isles,
70 Whose day departs in pomp, returns with smiles –
To greet the flowers and fruitage of a land,
As the sun mounts, by sea-born breezes fanned;
A land whose azure mountain-tops are seats
For Gods in council, whose green vales, retreats
Fit for the shades of heroes, mingling there
To breathe Elysian peace in upper air.

Though cold as winter, gloomy as the grave,
Stone-walls a prisoner make, but not a slave.
Shall man assume a property in man?
80 Lay on the moral will a withering ban?
Shame that our laws at distance still protect
Enormities, which they at home reject!
'Slaves cannot breathe in England' – yet that boast
Is but a mockery! when from coast to coast,
Though *fettered* slave be none, her floors and soil
Groan underneath a weight of slavish toil,
For the poor Many, measured out by rules
Fetched with cupidity from heartless schools,
That to an Idol, falsely called 'the Wealth

90   Of Nations', sacrifice a People's health,
Body and mind and soul; a thirst so keen
Is ever urging on the vast machine
Of sleepless Labour, 'mid whose dizzy wheels
The Power least prized is that which thinks and feels.

Then, for the pastimes of this delicate age,
And all the heavy or light vassalage
Which for their sakes we fasten, as may suit
Our varying moods, on human kind or brute,
'Twere well in little, as in great, to pause,
100   Lest Fancy trifle with eternal laws.
Not from his fellows only man may learn
Rights to compare and duties to discern!
All creatures and all objects, in degree,
Are friends and patrons of humanity.
There are to whom the garden, grove, and field,
Perpetual lessons of forbearance yield;
Who would not lightly violate the grace
The lowliest flower possesses in its place;
Nor shorten the sweet life, too fugitive,
110   Which nothing less than Infinite Power could give.

'This Lawn, a carpet all alive'

This Lawn, a carpet all alive
With shadows flung from leaves – to strive

In dance, amid a press
Of sunshine, an apt emblem yields
Of Worldlings revelling in the fields
Of strenuous idleness;

Less quick the stir when tide and breeze
Encounter, and to narrow seas
Forbid a moment's rest;
10   The medley less when boreal Lights

Glance to and fro, like aëry Sprites
   To feats of arms addrest!

Yet, spite of all this eager strife,
This ceaseless play, the genuine life
   That serves the stedfast hours,
Is in the grass beneath, that grows
Unheeded, and the mute repose
   Of sweetly-breathing flowers.

Thoughts on the Seasons

Flattered with promise of escape
   From every hurtful blast,
Spring takes, O sprightly May! thy shape,
   Her loveliest and her last.

Less fair is summer riding high
   In fierce solstitial power,
Less fair than when a lenient sky
   Brings on her parting hour.

When earth repays with golden sheaves
10   The labours of the plough,
And ripening fruits and forest leaves
   All brighten on the bough;

What pensive beauty autumn shows,
   Before she hears the sound
Of winter rushing in, to close
   The emblematic round!

Such be our Spring, our Summer such;
   So may our Autumn blend
With hoary Winter, and Life touch,
20   Through heaven-born hope, her end!

Written in the Strangers' Book at
'The Station,' opposite Bowness

My Lord and Lady Darlington,
I would not speak in snarling tone;
Nor, to you, good Lady Vane,
Would I give one moment's pain;
Nor Miss Taylor, Captain Stamp,
Would I your flights of *memory* cramp.
Yet, having spent a summer's day
On the green margin of Loch Tay,
And doubled (prospect ever bettering)
10 The mazy reaches of Loch Katerine,
And more than once been free at Luss,
Loch Lomond's beauties to discuss,
And wished, at least, to hear the blarney
Of the sly boatmen of Killarney,
And dipped my hand in dancing wave
Of Eau de Zurich, Lac Genève,
And bowed to many a major-domo
On stately terraces of Como,
And seen the Simplon's forehead hoary,
20 Reclined on Lago Maggiore,
At breathless eventide at rest
On the broad water's placid breast, –
I, not insensible, Heaven knows,
To all the charms this Station shows,
Must tell you, Captain, Lord and Ladies,
For honest worth one poet's trade is,
That your praise appears to me
Folly's own hyperbole.

'Why art thou silent! Is thy love a plant'

Why art thou silent! Is thy love a plant
Of such weak fibre that the treacherous air

Of absence withers what was once so fair?
Is there no debt to pay, no boon to grant?
Yet have my thoughts for thee been vigilant –
Bound to thy service with unceasing care,
The mind's least generous wish a mendicant
For naught but what thy happiness could spare.
Speak – though this soft warm heart, once free to hold
10   A thousand tender pleasures, thine and mine,
Be left more desolate, more dreary cold
Than a forsaken bird's-nest filled with snow
'Mid its own bush of leafless eglantine –
Speak, that my torturing doubts their end may know!

'In these fair vales hath many a Tree'

In these fair vales hath many a Tree
   At Wordsworth's suit been spared;
And from the builder's hand this Stone,
For some rude beauty of its own,
   Was rescued by the Bard:
So let it rest; and time will come
   When here the tender-hearted
May heave a gentle sigh for him,
   As one of the departed.

1830

Chatsworth! thy stately mansion, and the pride
Of thy domain, strange contrast do present
To house and home in many a craggy rent
Of the wild Peak; where new-born waters glide
Through fields whose thrifty occupants abide
As in a dear and chosen banishment,
With every semblance of entire content;
So kind is simple Nature, fairly tried!
Yet He whose heart in childhood gave her troth

10　To pastoral dales, thin-set with modest farms,
　　May learn, if judgement strengthen with his growth,
　　That, not for Fancy only, pomp hath charms;
　　And, strenuous to protect from lawless harms
　　The extremes of favoured life, may honour both.

Elegiac Musings in the Grounds of Coleorton Hall, the Seat of the Late Sir G. H. Beaumont, BART.

In these grounds stands the Parish Church, wherein is a mural monument bearing an Inscription which, in deference to the earnest request of the deceased, is confined to name, dates, and these words: – 'Enter not into judgement with thy servant, O Lord!'

With copious eulogy in prose or rhyme
Graven on the tomb we struggle against Time,
Alas, how feebly! but our feelings rise
And still we struggle when a good man dies.
Such offering BEAUMONT dreaded and forbade,
A spirit meek in self-abasement clad.
Yet *here* at least, though few have numbered days
That shunned so modestly the light of praise,
His graceful manners, and the temperate ray
10　Of that arch fancy which would round him play,
　　Brightening a converse never known to swerve
　　From courtesy and delicate reserve;
　　That sense, the bland philosophy of life,
　　Which checked discussion ere it warmed to strife;
　　Those rare accomplishments, and varied powers,
　　Might have their record among sylvan bowers.
　　Oh, fled for ever! vanished like a blast
　　That shook the leaves in myriads as it passed; –
　　Gone from this world of earth, air, sea, and sky,
20　From all its spirit-moving imagery,
　　Intensely studied with a painter's eye,

A poet's heart; and, for congenial view,
Portrayed with happiest pencil, not untrue
To common recognitions while the line
Flowed in a course of sympathy divine; –
Oh! severed, too abruptly, from delights
That all the seasons shared with equal rights; –
Rapt in the grace of undismantled age,
From soul-felt music, and the treasured page
30 Lit by that evening lamp which loved to shed
Its mellow lustre round thy honoured head;
While Friends beheld thee give with eye, voice, mien,
More than theatric force to Shakespeare's scene; –
If thou hast heard me – if thy Spirit know
Aught of these bowers and whence their pleasures flow;
If things in our remembrance held so dear,
And thoughts and projects fondly cherished here,
To thy exalted nature only seem
Time's vanities, light fragments of earth's dream –
40 Rebuke us not! – The mandate is obeyed
That said, 'Let praise be mute where I am laid;'
The holier deprecation, given in trust
To the cold marble, waits upon thy dust;
Yet have we found how slowly genuine grief
From *silent* admiration wins relief.
Too long abashed thy Name is like a rose
That doth 'within itself its sweetness close;'
A drooping daisy changed into a cup
In which her bright-eyed beauty is shut up.
50 Within these groves, where still are flitting by
Shades of the Past, oft noticed with a sigh,
Shall stand a votive Tablet, haply free,
When towers and temples fall, to speak of Thee!
If sculptured emblems of our mortal doom
Recall not there the wisdom of the Tomb,
Green ivy risen from out the cheerful earth
Will fringe the lettered stone; and herbs spring forth,
Whose fragrance, by soft dews and rain unbound,
Shall penetrate the heart without a wound;

60 While truth and love their purposes fulfil,
Commemorating genius, talent, skill,
That could not lie concealed where Thou wert known;
Thy virtues *He* must judge, and He alone,
The God upon whose mercy they are thrown.

The Poet and the Caged Turtledove

As often as I murmur here
My half-formed melodies,
Straight from her osier mansion near,
The Turtledove replies:
Though silent as a leaf before,
The captive promptly coos;
Is it to teach her own soft lore,
Or second my weak Muse?

I rather think, the gentle Dove
10 Is murmuring a reproof,
Displeased that I from lays of love
Have dared to keep aloof;
That I, a Bard of hill and dale,
Have carolled, fancy free,
As if nor dove nor nightingale
Had heart or voice for me.

If such thy meaning, O forbear,
Sweet Bird! to me wrong;
Love, blessed Love, is everywhere
20 The spirit of my song:
'Mid grove, and by the calm fireside,
Love animates my lyre –
That coo again! – 'tis not to chide,
I feel, but to inspire.

The Armenian Lady's Love

[The subject of the following poem is from the Orlandus of the
author's friend, Kenelm Henry Digby: and the liberty is taken
of inscribing it to him as an acknowledgement, however unworthy, of pleasure and instruction derived from his numerous
and valuable writings, illustrative of the piety and chivalry of the
olden time.]

I

   You have heard 'a Spanish Lady
      How she wooed an English man;'
   Hear now of a fair Armenian,
      Daughter of the proud Soldàn;
How she loved a Christian Slave, and told her pain
By word, look, deed, with hope that he might love again.

II

   'Pluck that rose, it moves my liking,'
      Said she, lifting up her veil;
   'Pluck it for me, gentle gardener,
10   Ere it wither and grow pale.'
'Princess fair, I till the ground, but may not take
From twig or bed an humbler flower, even for your sake!'

III

   'Grieved am I, submissive Christian!
      To behold thy captive state;
   Women, in your land, may pity
      (May they not?) the unfortunate.'
'Yes, kind Lady! otherwise man could not bear
Life, which to everyone that breathes is full of care.'

IV

   'Worse than idle is compassion
20   If it end in tears and sighs;
   Thee from bondage would I rescue

And from vile indignities;
Nurtured, as thy mien bespeaks, in high degree,
Look up – and help a hand that longs to set thee free.'

V

'Lady! dread the wish, nor venture
In such peril to engage;
Think how it would stir against you
Your most loving father's rage:
Sad deliverance would it be, and yoked with shame,
30   Should troubles overflow on her from whom it came.'

VI

'Generous Frank! the just in effort
Are of inward peace secure:
Hardships for the brave encountered,
Even the feeblest may endure:
If almighty grące through me thy chains unbind,
My father for slave's work may seek a slave in mind.'

VII

'Princess, at this burst of goodness,
My long-frozen heart grows warm!'
'Yet you make all courage fruitless,
40   Me to save from chance of harm:
Leading such companion I that gilded dome,
Yon minarets, would gladly leave for his worst home.'

VIII

'Feeling tunes your voice, fair Princess!
And your brow is free from scorn,
Else these words would come like mockery,
Sharper than the pointed thorn.'
'Whence the undeserved mistrust? Too wide apart
Our faith hath been, – O would that eyes could see the
heart!'

IX

'Tempt me not, I pray; my doom is
50   These base implements to wield;
Rusty lance, I ne'er shall grasp thee,
      Ne'er assoil my cobwebbed shield!
Never see my native land, nor castle towers,
Nor Her who thinking of me there counts widowed hours.'

X

'Prisoner! pardon youthful fancies;
      Wedded? If you *can*, say no!
Blessed is and be your consort;
      Hopes I cherished – let them go!
Handmaid's privilege would leave my purpose free,
60 Without another link to my felicity.'

XI

'Wedded love with loyal Christians,
      Lady, is a mystery rare;
Body, heart, and soul in union,
      Make one being of a pair.'
'Humble love in me would look for no return,
Soft as a guiding star that cheers, but cannot burn.'

XII

'Gracious Allah! by such title
      Do I dare to thank the God,
Him who thus exalts thy spirit,
70   Flower of an unchristian sod!
Or hast thou put off wings which thou in heaven dost
      wear?
What have I seen, and heard, or dreamt? where am I?
      where?'

XIII

Here broke off the dangerous converse:
      Less impassioned words might tell
How the pair escaped together,
      Tears not wanting, nor a knell

Of sorrow in her heart while through her father's door,
And from her narrow world, she passed for evermore.

XIV

But affections higher, holier,
80   Urged her steps; she shrunk from trust
In a sensual creed that trampled
Woman's birthright into dust.
Little be the wonder then, the blame be none,
If she, a timid Maid, hath put such boldness on.

XV

Judge both Fugitives with knowledge:
In those old romantic days
Mighty were the soul's commandments
To support, restrain, or raise.
Foes might hang upon their path, snakes rustle near,
90 But nothing from their inward selves had they to fear.

XVI

Thought infirm ne'er came between them,
Whether printing desert sands
With accordant steps, or gathering
Forest-fruit with social hands;
Or whispering like two reeds that in the cold moonbeam
Bend with the breeze their heads, beside a crystal stream.

XVII

On a friendly deck reposing
They at length for Venice steer;
There, when they had closed their voyage,
100   One, who daily on the pier
Watched for tidings from the East, beheld his Lord,
Fell down and clasped his knees for joy, not uttering
        word.

XVIII

Mutual was the sudden transport;
Breathless questions followed fast,

Years contracting to a moment,
    Each word greedier than the last;
'Hie thee to the Countess, friend! return with speed,
And of this Stranger speak by whom her lord was
    freed.

XIX

    'Say that I, who might have languished,
110   Drooped and pined till life was spent,
    Now before the gates of Stolberg
      My Deliverer would present
For a crowning recompense, the precious grace
Of her who in my heart still holds her ancient place.

XX

    'Make it known that my Companion
      Is of royal eastern blood,
    Thirsting after all perfection,
      Innocent, and meek, and good,
Though with misbelievers bred; but that dark night
120 Will holy Church disperse by beams of gospel-light.'

XXI

    Swiftly went that grey-haired Servant,
      Soon returned a trusty Page
    Charged with greetings, benedictions,
      Thanks and praises, each a gauge
For a sunny thought to cheer the Stranger's way,
Her virtuous scruples to remove, her fears allay.

XXII

    And how blest the Reunited,
      While beneath their castle-walls,
    Runs a deafening noise of welcome! –
130   Blest, though every tear that falls
Doth in its silence of past sorrow tell,
And makes a meeting seem most like a dear farewell.

XXIII

Through a haze of human nature,
    Glorified by heavenly light,
Looked the beautiful Deliverer
    On that overpowering sight,
While across her virgin cheek pure blushes strayed,
For every tender sacrifice her heart had made.

XXIV

    On the ground the weeping Countess
140   Knelt, and kissed the Stranger's hand;
    Act of soul-devoted homage,
        Pledge of an eternal band:
Nor did aught of future days that kiss belie,
Which, with a generous shout, the crowd did ratify.

XXV

    Constant to the fair Armenian,
        Gentle pleasures round her moved,
    Like a tutelary spirit
        Reverenced, like a sister, loved.
Christian meekness smoothed for all the path of life,
150 Who, loving most, should wiseliest love, their only strife.

XXVI

    Mute memento of that union
        In a Saxon church survives,
    Where a cross-legged Knight lies sculptured
        As between two wedded Wives –
Figures with armorial signs of race and birth,
And the vain rank the pilgrims bore while yet on earth.

Presentiments

Presentiments! they judge not right
Who deem that ye from open light
    Retire in fear of shame;

All *heaven-born* Instincts shun the touch
Of vulgar sense, – and, being such,
   Such privilege ye claim.

The tear whose source I could not guess,
The deep sigh that seemed fatherless,
   Were mine in early days;
10 And now, unforced by time to part
With fancy, I obey my heart,
   And venture on your praise.

What though some busy foes to good,
Too potent over nerve and blood,
   Lurk near you – and combine
To taint the health which ye infuse;
This hides not from the moral Muse
   Your origin divine.

How oft from you, derided Powers!
20 Comes Faith that in auspicious hours
   Builds castles, not of air:
Bodings unsanctioned by the will
Flow from your visionary skill,
   And teach us to beware.

The bosom-weight, your stubborn gift,
That no philosophy can lift,
   Shall vanish, if ye please,
Like morning mist: and, where it lay,
The spirits at your bidding play
30   In gaiety and ease.

Star-guided contemplations move
Through space, though calm, not raised above
   Prognostics that ye rule;
The naked Indian of the wild,
And haply, too, the cradled Child,
   Are pupils of your school.

But who can fathom your intents,
Number their signs or instruments?
   A rainbow, a sunbeam,
40 A subtle smell that Spring unbinds,
Dead pause abrupt of midnight winds,
   An echo, or a dream.

The laughter of the Christmas hearth
With sighs of self-exhausted mirth
   Ye feelingly reprove;
And daily, in the conscious breast,
Your visitations are a test
   And exercise of love.

When some great change gives boundless scope
50 To an exulting Nation's hope,
   Oft, startled and made wise
By your low-breathed interpretings,
The simply-meek foretaste the springs
   Of bitter contraries.

Ye daunt the proud array of war,
Pervade the lonely ocean far
   As sail hath been unfurled;
For dancers in the festive hall
What ghastly partners hath your call
60   Fetched from the shadowy world.

'Tis said that warnings ye dispense,
Emboldened by a keener sense;
   That men have lived for whom,
With dread precision, ye made clear
The hour that in a distant year
   Should knell them to the tomb.

Unwelcome insight! Yet there are
Blest times when mystery is laid bare,
   Truth shows a glorious face,

70 While on that isthmus which commands
The councils of both worlds, she stands,
   Sage Spirits! by your grace.

God, who instructs the brutes to scent
All changes of the element,
   Whose wisdom fixed the scale
Of natures, for our wants provides
By higher, sometimes humbler, guides,
   When lights of reason fail.

To B. R. Haydon, On Seeing His Picture of Napoleon Buonaparte on the Island of St Helena

Haydon! let worthier judges praise the skill
Here by thy pencil shown in truth of lines
And charm of colours; *I* applaud those signs
Of thought, that give the true poetic thrill;
That unencumbered whole of blank and still,
Sky without cloud – ocean without a wave;
And the one Man that laboured to enslave
The World, sole-standing high on the bare hill –
Back turned, arms folded, the unapparent face
10 Tinged, we may fancy, in this dreary place
With light reflected from the invisible sun
Set, like his fortunes; but not set for aye
Like them. The unguilty Power pursues his way,
And before *him* doth dawn perpetual run.

Yarrow Revisited, and Other Poems

COMPOSED (TWO EXCEPTED) DURING A TOUR IN
SCOTLAND, AND ON THE ENGLISH BORDER, IN
THE AUTUMN OF 1831

TO SAMUEL ROGERS, ESQ., AS A TESTIMONY OF
FRIENDSHIP AND ACKNOWLEDGEMENT OF
INTELLECTUAL OBLIGATIONS, THESE MEMORIALS ARE
AFFECTIONATELY INSCRIBED.
Rydal Mount, *December* 11, 1834.

The following Stanzas are a memorial of a day passed with
Sir Walter Scott and other Friends visiting the Banks of the
Yarrow under his guidance, immediately before his departure
from Abbotsford, for Naples.

The title 'Yarrow Revisited' will stand in no need of explanation
for Readers acquainted with the Author's previous poems
suggested by that celebrated Stream.

I
The gallant Youth, who may have gained,
   Or seeks, a 'winsome Marrow,'
Was but an Infant in the lap
   When first I looked on Yarrow;
Once more, by Newark's Castle-gate
   Long left without a warder,
I stood, looked, listened, and with Thee,
   Great Minstrel of the Border!

Grave thoughts ruled wide on that sweet day,
10   Their dignity installing
In gentle bosoms, while sere leaves
   Were on the bough, or falling;
But breezes played, and sunshine gleamed –
   The forest to embolden;
Reddened the fiery hues, and shot
   Transparence through the golden.

For busy thoughts the Stream flowed on
  In foamy agitation;
And slept in many a crystal pool
20 For quiet contemplation:
No public and no private care
  The freeborn mind enthralling,
We made a day of happy hours,
  Our happy days recalling.

Brisk Youth appeared, the Morn of youth,
  With freaks of graceful folly, –
Life's temperate Noon, her sober Eve,
  Her Night not melancholy;
Past, present, future, all appeared
30 In harmony united,
Like guests that meet, and some from far,
  By cordial love invited.

And if, as Yarrow, through the woods
  And down the meadow ranging,
Did meet us with unaltered face,
  Though we were changed and changing;
If, *then*, some natural shadows spread
  Our inward prospect over,
The soul's deep valley was not slow
40 Its brightness to recover.

Eternal blessings on the Muse,
  And her divine employment!
The blameless Muse, who trains her Sons
  For hope and calm enjoyment;
Albeit sickness, lingering yet,
  Has o'er their pillow brooded;
And Care waylays their steps – a Sprite
  Not easily eluded.

For thee, O SCOTT! compelled to change
50 Green Eildon-hill and Cheviot

For warm Vesuvio's vine-clad slopes;
   And leave thy Tweed and Tiviot
For mild Sorento's breezy waves;
   May classic Fancy, linking
With native Fancy her fresh aid,
   Preserve thy heart from sinking!

Oh! while they minister to thee,
   Each vying with the other,
May Health return to mellow Age,
60   With Strength, her venturous brother;
And Tiber, and each brook and rill
   Renowned in song and story,
With unimagined beauty shine,
   Nor lose one ray of glory!

For Thou, upon a hundred streams,
   By tales of love and sorrow,
Of faithful love, undaunted truth,
   Hast shed the power of Yarrow;
And streams unknown, hills yet unseen,
70   Wherever they invite Thee,
At parent Nature's grateful call,
   With gladness must requite Thee.

A gracious welcome shall be thine,
   Such looks of love and honour
As thy own Yarrow gave to me
   When first I gazed upon her;
Beheld what I had feared to see,
   Unwilling to surrender
Dreams treasured up from early days,
80   The holy and the tender.

And what, for this frail world, were all
   That mortals do or suffer,
Did no responsive harp, no pen,
   Memorial tribute offer?

Yea, what were mighty Nature's self?
  Her features, could they win us,
Unhelped by the poetic voice
  That hourly speaks within us?

Nor deem that localized Romance
90   Plays false with our affections;
Unsanctifies our tears – made sport
  For fanciful dejections:
Ah, no! the visions of the past
  Sustain the heart in feeling
Life as she is – our changeful Life,
  With friends and kindred dealing.

Bear witness, Ye, whose thoughts that day
  In Yarrow's groves were centred;
Who through the silent portal arch
100 Of mouldering Newark entered;
And clomb the winding stair that once
  Too timidly was mounted
By the 'last Minstrel,' (not the last!)
  Ere he his Tale recounted.

Flow on for ever, Yarrow Stream!
  Fulfil thy pensive duty,
Well pleased that future Bards should chant
  For simple hearts thy beauty;
To dream-light dear while yet unseen,
110 Dear to the common sunshine,
And dearer still, as now I feel,
  To memory's shadowy moonshine!

II ON THE DEPARTURE OF SIR WALTER SCOTT
FROM ABBOTSFORD, FOR NAPLES
A trouble, not of clouds, or weeping rain,
Nor of the setting sun's pathetic light
Engendered, hangs o'er Eildon's triple height:
Spirits of Power, assembled there, complain

For kindred Power departing from their sight;
While Tweed, best pleased in chanting a blithe strain,
Saddens his voice again, and yet again.
Lift up your hearts, ye Mourners! for the might
Of the whole world's good wishes with him goes;
10 Blessings and prayers in nobler retinue
Than sceptred king or laurelled conqueror knows,
Follow this wondrous Potentate. Be true,
Ye winds of ocean, and the midland sea,
Wafting your Charge to soft Parthenope!

III A PLACE OF BURIAL IN THE SOUTH OF
SCOTLAND
Part fenced by man, part by a rugged steep
That curbs a foaming brook, a Graveyard lies;
The hare's best couching-place for fearless sleep;
Which moonlit elves, far seen by credulous eyes,
Enter in dance. Of church, or sabbath ties,
No vestige now remains; yet thither creep
Bereft Ones, and in lowly anguish weep
Their prayers out to the wind and naked skies.
Proud tomb is none; but rudely-sculptured knights,
10 By humble choice of plain old times, are seen
Level with earth, among the hillocks green:
Union not sad, when sunny daybreak smites
The spangled turf, and neighbouring thickets ring
With *jubilate* from the choirs of spring!

IV ON THE SIGHT OF A MANSE IN THE SOUTH OF
SCOTLAND
Say, ye far-travelled clouds, far-seeing hills –
Among the happiest-looking homes of men
Scattered all Britain over, through deep glen,
On airy upland, and by forest rills,
And o'er wide plains cheered by the lark that trills
His sky-born warblings – does aught meet your ken
More fit to animate the Poet's pen,
Aught that more surely by its aspect fills

Pure minds with sinless envy, than the Abode
10 Of the good Priest: who, faithful through all hours
To his high charge, and truly serving God,
Has yet a heart and hand for trees and flowers,
Enjoys the walks his predecessors trod,
Nor covets lineal rights in lands and towers.

V COMPOSED IN ROSLIN CHAPEL, DURING A
STORM

The wind is now thy organist; – a clank
(We know not whence) ministers for a bell
To mark some change of service. As the swell
Of music reached its height, and even when sank
The notes, in prelude, ROSLIN! to a blank
Of silence, how it thrilled thy sumptuous roof,
Pillars, and arches, – not in vain time-proof,
Though Christian rites be wanting! From what bank
Came those live herbs? by what hand were they sown
10 Where dew falls not, where rain-drops seem unknown?
Yet in the Temple they a friendly niche
Share with their sculptured fellows, that, green-grown,
Copy their beauty more and more, and preach,
Though mute, of all things blending into one.

VI THE TROSACHS

There's not a nook within this solemn Pass,
But were an apt confessional for One
Taught by his summer spent, his autumn gone,
That Life is but a tale of morning grass
Withered at eve. From scenes of art which chase
That thought away, turn, and with watchful eyes
Feed it 'mid Nature's old felicities,
Rocks, rivers, and smooth lakes more clear than glass
Untouched, unbreathed upon. Thrice happy quest,
10 If from a golden perch of aspen spray
(October's workmanship to rival May)
The pensive warbler of the ruddy breast
That moral sweeten by a heaven-taught lay,
Lulling the year, with all its cares, to rest!

VII

The pibroch's note, discountenanced or mute;
The Roman kilt, degraded to a toy
Of quaint apparel for a half-spoilt boy;
The target mouldering like ungathered fruit;
The smoking steam-boat eager in pursuit,
As eagerly pursued; the umbrella spread
To weather-fend the Celtic herdsman's head –
All speak of manners withering to the root,
And of old honours, too, and passions high:
10 Then may we ask, though pleased that thought should range
Among the conquests of civility,
Survives imagination – to the change
Superior? Help to virtue does she give?
If not, O Mortals, better cease to live!

VIII COMPOSED IN THE GLEN OF LOCH ETIVE

'This Land of Rainbows spanning glens whose walls,
Rock-built, are hung with rainbow-coloured mists –
Of far-stretched Meres whose salt flood never rests –
Of tuneful Caves and playful Waterfalls –
Of Mountains varying momently their crests –
Proud be this Land! whose poorest huts are halls
Where Fancy entertains becoming guests;
While native song the heroic Past recalls.'
Thus, in the net of her own wishes caught,
10 The Muse exclaimed; but Story now must hide
Her trophies, Fancy crouch; the course of pride
Has been diverted, other lessons taught,
That make the Patriot-spirit bow her head
Where the all-conquering Roman feared to tread.

IX EAGLES

Composed at Dunollie Castle in the Bay of Oban.

Dishonoured Rock and Ruin! that, by law
Tyrannic, keep the Bird of Jove embarred

Like a lone criminal whose life is spared.
Vexed is he, and screams loud. The last I saw
Was on the wing; stooping, he struck with awe
Man, bird, and beast; then, with a consort paired,
From a bold headland, their loved aery's guard,
Flew high above Atlantic waves, to draw
Light from the fountain of the setting sun.
10 Such was this Prisoner once; and, when his plumes
The sea-blast ruffles as the storm comes on,
Then, for a moment, he, in spirit, resumes
His rank 'mong freeborn creatures that live free,
His power, his beauty, and his majesty.

X IN THE SOUND OF MULL
Tradition, be thou mute! Oblivion, throw
Thy veil in mercy o'er the records, hung
Round strath and mountain, stamped by the ancient
    tongue
On rock and ruin darkening as we go, –
Spots where a word, ghost-like, survives to show
What crimes from hate, or desperate love, have sprung;
From honour misconceived, or fancied wrong,
What feuds, not quenched but fed by mutual woe.
Yet, though a wild vindictive Race, untamed
10 By civil arts and labours of the pen,
Could gentleness be scorned by those fierce Men,
Who, to spread wide the reverence they claimed
For patriarchal occupations, named
Yon towering Peaks, 'Shepherds of Etive Glen?'

XI SUGGESTED AT TYNDRUM IN A STORM
Enough of garlands, of the Arcadian crook,
And all that Greece and Italy have sung
Of Swains reposing myrtle groves among!
Ours couch on naked rocks, – will cross a brook
Swoln with chill rains, nor ever cast a look
This way or that, or give it even a thought

More than by smoothest pathway may be brought
Into a vacant mind. Can written book
Teach what *they* learn? Up, hardy Mountaineer!
10 And guide the Bard, ambitious to be One
Of Nature's privy council, as thou art,
On cloud-sequestered heights, that see and hear
To what dread Powers He delegates His part
On earth, who works in the heaven of heavens, alone.

XII THE EARL OF BREADALBANE'S RUINED
MANSION, AND FAMILY BURIAL-PLACE, NEAR
KILLIN

Well sang the Bard who called the grave, in strains
Thoughtful and sad, the 'narrow house.' No style
Of fond sepulchral flattery can beguile
Grief of her sting; nor cheat, where he detains
The sleeping dust, stern Death. How reconcile
With truth, or with each other, decked remains
Of a once warm Abode, and that *new* Pile,
For the departed, built with curious pains
And mausolean pomp? Yet here they stand
10 Together, – 'mid trim walks and artful bowers,
To be looked down upon by ancient hills,
That, for the living and the dead, demand
And prompt a harmony of genuine powers;
Concord that elevates the mind, and stills.

XIII 'REST AND BE THANKFUL!'

At the Head of Glencroe.

Doubling and doubling with laborious walk,
Who, that has gained at length the wished-for Height,
This brief, this simple wayside Call can slight,
And rests not thankful? Whether cheered by talk
With some loved friend, or by the unseen hawk
Whistling to clouds and sky-born streams, that shine
At the sun's outbreak, as with light divine,
Ere they descend to nourish root and stalk

Of valley flowers. Nor, while the limbs repose,
10 Will we forget that, as the fowl can keep
Absolute stillness, poised aloft in air,
And fishes front, unmoved, the torrent's sweep, –
So may the Soul, through powers that Faith bestows,
Win rest, and ease, and peace, with bliss that Angels
        share.

XIV HIGHLAND HUT

See what gay wild flowers deck this earth-built Cot,
Whose smoke, forth-issuing whence and how it may,
Shines in the greeting of the sun's first ray
Like wreaths of vapour without stain or blot.
The limpid mountain-rill avoids it not;
And why shouldst thou? – If rightly trained and bred,
Humanity is humble, finds no spot
Which her Heaven-guided feet refuse to tread.
The walls are cracked, sunk is the flowery roof,
10 Undressed the pathway leading to the door;
But love, as Nature loves, the lonely Poor;
Search, for their worth, some gentle heart wrong-proof,
Meek, patient, kind, and, were its trials fewer,
Belike less happy. – Stand no more aloof!

XV THE HIGHLAND BROACH

The exact resemblance which the old Broach (still in use,
though rarely met with, among the Highlanders) bears to the
Roman Fibula must strike everyone, and concurs with the
plaid and kilt to recall to mind the communication which the
ancient Romans had with this remote country.

If to Tradition faith be due,
And echoes from old verse speak true,
Ere the meek Saint, Columba, bore
Glad tidings to Iona's shore,
No common light of nature blessed
The mountain region of the west,
A land where gentle manners ruled
O'er men in dauntless virtues schooled

That raised, for centuries, a bar
10   Impervious to the tide of war:
Yet peaceful Arts did entrance gain
Where haughty Force had striven in vain;
And, 'mid the works of skilful hands,
By wanderers brought from foreign lands
And various climes, was not unknown
The clasp that fixed the Roman Gown;
The Fibula, whose shape, I ween,
Still in the Highland Broach is seen,
The silver Broach of massy frame,
20   Worn at the breast of some grave Dame
On road or path, or at the door
Of fern-thatched hut on heathy moor:
But delicate of yore its mould,
And the material finest gold;
As might beseem the fairest Fair,
Whether she graced a royal chair,
Or shed, within a vaulted hall,
No fancied lustre on the wall
Where shields of mighty heroes hung,
30   While Fingal heard what Ossian sung.

The heroic Age expired – it slept
Deep in its tomb: – the bramble crept
O'er Fingal's hearth; the grassy sod
Grew on the floors his sons had trod:
Malvina! where art thou? Their state
The noblest-born must abdicate;
The fairest, while with fire and sword
Come Spoilers – horde impelling horde,
Must walk the sorrowing mountains, drest
40   By ruder hands in homelier vest.
Yet still the female bosom lent,
And loved to borrow, ornament;
Still was its inner world a place
Reached by the dews of heavenly grace;
Still pity to this last retreat

Clove fondly; to his favourite seat
Love wound his way by soft approach,
Beneath a massier Highland Broach.

When alternations came of rage
50   Yet fiercer, in a darker age;
And feuds, where, clan encountering clan,
The weaker perished to a man;
For maid and mother, when despair
Might else have triumphed, baffling prayer,
One small possession lacked not power,
Provided in a calmer hour,
To meet such need as might befall –
Roof, raiment, bread, or burial:
For woman, even of tears bereft,
60   The hidden silver Broach was left.

As generations come and go,
Their arts, their customs, ebb and flow;
Fate, fortune, sweep strong powers away,
And feeble, of themselves, decay;
What poor abodes the heir-loom hide,
In which the castle once took pride!
Tokens, once kept as boasted wealth,
If saved at all, are saved by stealth.
Lo! ships, from seas by nature barred,
70   Mount along ways by man prepared;
And in far-stretching vales, whose streams
Seek other seas, their canvas gleams.
Lo! busy towns spring up, on coasts
Thronged yesterday by airy ghosts;
Soon, like a lingering star forlorn
Among the novelties of morn,
While young delights on old encroach,
Will vanish the last Highland Broach.

But when, from out their viewless bed,
80   Like vapours, years have rolled and spread;

And this poor verse, and worthier lays,
Shall yield no light of love or praise;
Then, by the spade, or cleaving plough,
Or torrent from the mountain's brow,
Or whirlwind, reckless what his might
Entombs, or forces into light;
Blind Chance, a volunteer ally,
That oft befriends Antiquity,
And clears Oblivion from reproach,
90 May render back the Highland Broach.

XVI THE BROWNIE

[Upon a small island not far from the head of Loch Lomond,
are some remains of an ancient building, which was for several
years the abode of a solitary Individual, one of the last survivors
of the clan of Macfarlane, once powerful in that neighbourhood.
Passing along the shore opposite this island in the year 1814,
the Author learned these particulars, and that this person then
living there had acquired the appellation of 'The Brownie.' See
'The Brownie's Cell,' to which the following is a sequel.]

'How disappeared he?' Ask the newt and toad;
Ask of his fellow-men, and they will tell
How he was found, cold as an icicle,
Under an arch of that forlorn abode;
Where he, unpropped, and by the gathering flood
Of years hemmed round, had dwelt, prepared to try
Privation's worst extremities, and die
With no one near save the omnipresent God.
Verily so to live was an awful choice –
10 A choice that wears the aspect of a doom;
But in the mould of mercy all is cast
For Souls familiar with the eternal Voice;
And this forgotten Taper to the last
Drove from itself, we trust, all frightful gloom.

XVII TO THE PLANET VENUS, AN EVENING STAR

[Composed at Loch Lomond.]

Though joy attend Thee orient at the birth
Of dawn, it cheers the lofty spirit most
To watch thy course when Day-light, fled from earth,
In the grey sky hath left his lingering Ghost,
Perplexed as if between a splendour lost
And splendour slowly mustering. Since the Sun,
The absolute, the world-absorbing One,
Relinquished half his empire to the host
Emboldened by thy guidance, holy Star,
10   Holy as princely, who that looks on thee
Touching, as now, in thy humility
The mountain-borders of this seat of care,
Can question that thy countenance is bright,
Celestial Power, as much with love as light?

XVIII BOTHWELL CASTLE

(Passed unseen, on account of stormy weather.)

Immured in Bothwell's towers, at times the Brave
(So beautiful is Clyde) forgot to mourn
The liberty they lost at Bannockburn.
Once on those steeps *I* roamed at large, and have
In mind the landscape, as if still in sight;
The river glides, the woods before me wave;
Then why repine that now in vain I crave
Needless renewal of an old delight?
Better to thank a dear and long-past day
10   For joy its sunny hours were free to give
Than blame the present, that our wish hath crost.
Memory, like sleep, hath powers which dreams obey,
Dreams, vivid dreams, that are not fugitive:
How little that she cherishes is lost!

XIX PICTURE OF DANIEL IN THE LIONS' DEN, AT HAMILTON PALACE

Amid a fertile region green with wood
And fresh with rivers, well did it become
The ducal Owner, in his palace-home
To naturalize this tawny Lion brood;
Children of Art, that claim strange brotherhood
(Couched in their den) with those that roam at large
Over the burning wilderness, and charge
The wind with terror while they roar for food.
Satiate are *these*; and stilled to eye and ear;
10   Hence, while we gaze, a more enduring fear!
Yet is the Prophet calm, nor would the cave
Daunt him – if his Companions, now bedrowsed
Outstretched and listless, were by hunger roused:
Man placed him here, and God, he knows, can save.

XX THE AVON

(A feeder of the Annan.)

Avon – a precious, an immortal name!
Yet is it one that other rivulets bear
Like this unheard-of, and their channels wear
Like this contented, though unknown to Fame:
For great and sacred is the modest claim
Of Streams to Nature's love, where'er they flow;
And ne'er did Genius slight them, as they go,
Tree, flower, and green herb, feeding without blame.
But Praise can waste her voice on work of tears,
10   Anguish, and death: full oft where innocent blood
Has mixed its current with the limpid flood,
Her heaven-offending trophies Glory rears:
Never for like distinction may the good
Shrink from *thy* name, pure Rill, with unpleased ears.

XXI SUGGESTED BY A VIEW FROM AN EMINENCE IN INGLEWOOD FOREST

The forest huge of ancient Caledon
Is but a name, no more is Inglewood,

That swept from hill to hill, from flood to flood:
On her last thorn the nightly moon has shone;
Yet still, though unappropriate Wild be none,
Fair parks spread wide where Adam Bell might deign
With Clym o' the Clough, were they alive again,
To kill for merry feast their venison.
Nor wants the holy Abbot's gliding Shade
10 His church with monumental wreck bestrown;
The feudal Warrior-chief, a Ghost unlaid,
Hath still his castle, though a skeleton,
That he may watch by night, and lessons con
Of power that perishes, and rights that fade.

XXII HART'S-HORN TREE, NEAR PENRITH
Here stood an Oak, that long had borne affixed
To his huge trunk, or, with more subtle art,
Among its withering topmost branches mixed,
The palmy antlers of a hunted Hart,
Whom the Dog Hercules pursued – his part
Each desperately sustaining, till at last
Both sank and died, the life-veins of the chased
And chaser bursting here with one dire smart.
Mutual the victory, mutual the defeat!
10 High was the trophy hung with pitiless pride;
Say, rather, with that generous sympathy
That wants not, even in rudest breasts, a seat;
And, for this feeling's sake, let no one chide
Verse that would guard thy memory, HART'S-HORN
    TREE!

XXIII FANCY AND TRADITION
The Lovers took within this ancient grove
Their last embrace; beside those crystal springs
The Hermit saw the Angel spread his wings
For instant flight; the Sage in yon alcove
Sate musing; on that hill the Bard would rove,
Not mute, where now the linnet only sings:
Thus everywhere to truth Tradition clings,

Or Fancy localizes Powers we love.
Were only History licensed to take note
10 Of things gone by, her meagre monuments
Would ill suffice for persons and events:
There is an ampler page for man to quote,
A readier book of manifold contents,
Studied alike in palace and in cot.

XXIV COUNTESS' PILLAR

[On the roadside beween Penrith and Appleby, there stands a pillar with the following inscription:–

'This pillar was erected, in the year 1656, by Anne Countess Dowager of Pembroke, &c. for a memorial of her last parting with her pious mother, Margaret Countess Dowager of Cumberland, on the 2d of April, 1616; in memory whereof she hath left an annuity of £4 to be distributed to the poor of the parish of Brougham, every 2d day of April for ever, upon the stone table placed hard by. Laus Deo!']

While the Poor gather round, till the end of time
May this bright flower of Charity display
Its bloom, unfolding at the appointed day;
Flower than the loveliest of the vernal prime
Lovelier – transplanted from heaven's purest clime!
'Charity never faileth:' on that creed,
More than on written testament or deed,
The pious Lady built with hope sublime.
Alms on this stone to be dealt out, *for ever*!
10 'LAUS DEO.' Many a Stranger passing by
Has with that Parting mixed a filial sigh,
Blest its humane Memorial's fond endeavour;
And, fastening on those lines an eye tear-glazed,
Has ended, though no Clerk, with 'God be praised!'

XXV ROMAN ANTIQUITIES

(From the Roman Station at Old Penrith.)

How profitless the relics that we cull,
Troubling the last holds of ambitious Rome,

Unless they chasten fancies that presume
Too high, or idle agitations lull!
Of the world's flatteries if the brain be full,
To have no seat for thought were better doom,
Like this old helmet, or the eyeless skull
Of him who gloried in its nodding plume.
Heaven out of view, our wishes what are they?
10   Our fond regrets tenacious in their grasp?
The Sage's theory? the Poet's lay? –
Mere Fibulae without a robe to clasp;
Obsolete lamps, whose light no time recalls;
Urns without ashes, tearless lacrymals!

XXVI APOLOGY

For the Foregoing Poems

No more: the end is sudden and abrupt,
Abrupt – as without preconceived design
Was the beginning; yet the several Lays
Have moved in order, to each other bound
By a continuous and acknowledged tie
Though unapparent – like those Shapes distinct
That yet survive ensculptured on the walls
Of palaces, or temples, 'mid the wreck
Of famed Persepolis; each following each,
10   As might beseem a stately embassy,
In set array; these bearing in their hands
Ensign of civil power, weapon of war,
Or gift to be presented at the throne
Of the Great King; and others, as they go
In priestly vest, with holy offerings charged,
Or leading victims drest for sacrifice.
Nor will the Power we serve, that sacred Power,
The Spirit of humanity, disdain
A ministration humble but sincere,
20   That from a threshold loved by every Muse
Its impulse took – that sorrow-stricken door,
Whence, as a current from its fountain-head,

Our thoughts have issued, and our feelings flowed,
Receiving, willingly or not, fresh strength
From kindred sources; while around us sighed
(Life's three first seasons having passed away)
Leaf-scattering winds; and hoar-frost sprinklings fell
(Foretaste of winter) on the moorland heights;
And every day brought with it tidings new
30   Of rash change, ominous for the public weal.
Hence, if dejection has too oft encroached
Upon that sweet and tender melancholy
Which may itself be cherished and caressed
More than enough; a fault so natural
(Even with the young, the hopeful, or the gay)
For prompt forgiveness will not sue in vain.

The Primrose of the Rock

A Rock there is whose homely front
   The passing traveller slights;
Yet there the glow-worms hang their lamps,
   Like stars, at various heights;
And one coy Primrose to that Rock
   The vernal breeze invites.

What hideous warfare hath been waged,
   What kingdoms overthrown,
Since first I spied that Primrose-tuft
10   And marked it for my own;
A lasting link in Nature's chain
   From highest heaven let down!

The flowers, still faithful to the stems,
   Their fellowship renew;
The stems are faithful to the root,
   That worketh out of view;
And to the rock the root adheres
   In every fibre true.

Close clings to earth the living rock,
20   Though threatening still to fall;
The earth is constant to her sphere;
    And God upholds them all:
So blooms this lonely Plant, nor dreads
    Her annual funeral.

    .   .   .   .   .   .

Here closed the meditative strain;
    But air breathed soft that day,
The hoary mountain-heights were cheered,
    The sunny vale looked gay;
And to the Primrose of the Rock
30   I gave this after-lay.

I sang – Let myriads of bright flowers,
    Like Thee, in field and grove
Revive unenvied; – mightier far,
    Than tremblings that reprove
Our vernal tendencies to hope,
    Is God's redeeming love;

That love which changed – for wan disease,
    For sorrow that had bent
O'er hopeless dust, for withered age –
40   Their moral element,
And turned the thistles of a curse
    To types beneficent.

Sin-blighted though we are, we too,
    The reasoning Sons of Men,
From one oblivious winter called
    Shall rise, and breathe again;
And in eternal summer lose
    Our threescore years and ten.

To humbleness of heart descends
50   This prescience from on high,

The faith that elevates the just,
  Before and when they die;
And makes each soul a separate heaven,
  A court for Deity.

Composed after Reading a Newspaper of the Day

'People! your chains are severing link by link;
Soon shall the Rich be levelléd down – the Poor
Meet them half way.' Vain boast! for These, the more
They thus would rise, must low and lower sink
Till, by repentance stung, they fear to think;
While all lie prostrate, save the tyrant few
Bent in quick turns each other to undo,
And mix the poison, they themselves must drink.
Mistrust thyself, vain Country! cease to cry,
'Knowledge will save me from the threatened woe.'
For, if than other rash ones more thou know
Yet on presumptuous wing as far would fly
Above thy knowledge as they dared to go,
Thou wilt provoke a heavier penalty.

The Modern Athens

'Now that a Parthenon ascends to crown
Our Calton Hill, sage Pallas! 'tis most fit
This thy dear city by the name be known
Of Modern Athens.' But opinions split
Upon this point of taste, and Mother Wit
Cries out '"*Auld Reekie!*" *guid and honest Town
Of Edinbro*', put the sad misnomer down;
This alias of Conceit – away with it!'
Let none provoke for questionable smiles
From an outlandish Goddess the just scorn
Of thy staunch gothic Patron, grave St Giles:
– Far better than such heathen foppery
The homeliest Title thou hast ever borne
Before or since the times of, '*Wha wants me?*'

Upon the Late General Fast. March, 1832

Reluctant call it was; the rite delayed;
And in the Senate some there were who doffed
The last of their humanity, and scoffed
At providential judgements, undismayed
By their own daring. But the People prayed
As with one voice; their flinty heart grew soft
With penitential sorrow, and aloft
Their spirit mounted, crying, 'God us aid!'
Oh that with aspirations more intense,
10 Chastised by self-abasement more profound,
This People, once so happy, so renowned
For liberty, would seek from God defence
Against far heavier ill, the pestilence
Of revolution, impiously unbound!

To the Author's Portrait

Painted at Rydal Mount, by W. Pickersgill, Esq., for St John's
College, Cambridge.

Go, faithful Portrait! and where long hath knelt
Margaret, the saintly Foundress, take thy place;
And, if Time spare the colours for the grace
Which to the work surpassing skill hath dealt,
Thou, on thy rock reclined, though kingdoms melt
And states be torn up by the roots, wilt seem
To breathe in rural peace, to hear the stream,
And think and feel as once the Poet felt.
Whate'er thy fate, those features have not grown
10 Unrecognized through many a household tear
More prompt, more glad to fall than drops of dew
By morning shed around a flower half-blown;
Tears of delight, that testified how true
To life thou art, and, in thy truth, how dear!

Devotional Incitements

'Not to the earth confined,
Ascend to heaven.'

Where will they stop, those breathing Powers,
The Spirits of the new-born flowers?
They wander with the breeze, they wind
Where'er the streams a passage find;
Up from their native ground they rise
In mute aërial harmonies;
From humble violet – modest thyme –
Exhaled, the essential odours climb,
As if no space below the sky
10   Their subtle flight could satisfy:
Heaven will not tax our thoughts with pride
If like ambition be *their* guide.

Roused by this kindliest of May-showers,
The spirit-quickener of the flowers,
That with moist virtue softly cleaves
The buds, and freshens the young leaves,
The birds pour forth their souls in notes
Of rapture from a thousand throats –
Here checked by too impetuous haste,
20   While there the music runs to waste,
With bounty more and more enlarged,
Till the whole air is overcharged;
Give ear, O Man! to their appeal,
And thirst for no inferior zeal,
Thou, who canst *think*, as well as feel.

Mount from the earth; aspire! aspire!
So pleads the town's cathedral choir,
In strains that from their solemn height
Sink, to attain a loftier flight;
30   While incense from the altar breathes
Rich fragrance in embodied wreaths;

Or, flung from swinging censer, shrouds
The taper-lights, and curls in clouds
Around angelic Forms, the still
Creation of the painter's skill,
That on the service wait concealed
One moment, and the next revealed.
– Cast off your bonds, awake, arise,
And for no transient ecstasies!
40　What else can mean the visual plea
Of still or moving imagery –
The iterated summons loud,
Not wasted on the attendant crowd,
Nor wholly lost upon the throng
Hurrying the busy streets along?

　　Alas! the sanctities combined
By art to unsensualize the mind,
Decay and languish; or, as creeds
And humours change, are spurned like weeds:
50　The priests are from their altars thrust;
Temples are levelled with the dust;
And solemn rites and awful forms
Founder amid fanatic storms.
Yet evermore, through years renewed
In undisturbed vicissitude
Of seasons balancing their flight
On the swift wings of day and night,
Kind Nature keeps a heavenly door
Wide open for the scattered Poor.
60　Where flower-breathed incense to the skies
Is wafted in mute harmonies;
And ground fresh-cloven by the plough
Is fragrant with a humbler vow;
Where birds and brooks from leafy dells
Chime forth unwearied canticles,
And vapours magnify and spread
The glory of the sun's bright head –
Still constant in her worship, still

Conforming to the eternal Will,
70 Whether men sow or reap the fields,
Divine monition Nature yields,
That not by bread alone we live,
Or what a hand of flesh can give;
That every day should leave some part
Free for a sabbath of the heart:
So shall the seventh be truly blest,
From morn to eve, with hallowed rest.

'Calm is the fragrant air, and loth to lose'

Calm is the fragrant air, and loth to lose
Day's grateful warmth, though moist with falling dews.
Look for the stars, you'll say that there are none;
Look up a second time, and, one by one,
You mark them twinkling out with silvery light,
And wonder how they could elude the sight!
The birds, of late so noisy in their bowers,
Warbled a while with faint and fainter powers,
But now are silent as the dim-seen flowers:
10 Nor does the village Church-clock's iron tone
The time's and season's influence disown;
Nine beats distinctly to each other bound
In drowsy sequence – how unlike the sound
That, in rough winter, oft inflicts a fear
On fireside listeners, doubting what they hear!
The shepherd, bent on rising with the sun,
Had closed his door before the day was done,
And now with thankful heart to bed doth creep,
And joins his little children in their sleep.
20 The bat, lured forth where trees the lane o'ershade,
Flits and reflits along the close arcade;
The busy dor-hawk chases the white moth
With burring note, which Industry and Sloth
Might both be pleased with, for it suits them both.
A stream is heard – I see it not, but know

By its soft music whence the waters flow:
Wheels and the tread of hoofs are heard no more;
One boat there was, but it will touch the shore
With the next dipping of its slackened oar;
30 Faint sound, that, for the gayest of the gay,
Might give to serious thought a moment's sway,
As a last token of man's toilsome day!

Rural Illusions

Sylph was it? or a Bird more bright
    Than those of fabulous stock?
A second darted by; – and lo!
    Another of the flock,
Through sunshine flitting from the bough
    To nestle in the rock.
Transient deception! a gay freak
    Of April's mimicries!
Those brilliant strangers, hailed with joy
10   Among the budding trees,
Proved last year's leaves, pushed from the spray
    To frolic on the breeze.

Maternal Flora! show thy face,
    And let thy hand be seen,
Thy hand here sprinkling tiny flowers,
    That, as they touch the green,
Take root (so seems it) and look up
    In honour of their Queen.
Yet, sooth, those little starry specks,
20   That not in vain aspired
To be confounded with live growths,
    Most dainty, most admired,
Were only blossoms dropped from twigs
    Of their own offspring tired.

Not such the World's illusive shows;
    Her wingless flutterings,

Her blossoms which, though shed, out-brave
    The floweret as it springs,
For the undeceived, smile as they may,
30   Are melancholy things:
But gentle Nature plays her part,
    With ever-varying wiles,
And transient feignings with plain truth
    So well she reconciles,
That those fond Idlers most are pleased
    Whom oftenest she beguiles.

To — Upon the Birth of Her First-Born Child, March, 1833

'Tum porro puer, ut saevis projectus ab undis
Navita, nudus humi jacet,' &c. – LUCRETIUS.

Like a shipwrecked Sailor tost
By rough waves on a perilous coast,
Lies the Babe, in helplessness
And in tenderest nakedness,
Flung by labouring nature forth
Upon the mercies of the earth.
Can its eyes beseech? – no more
Than the hands are free to implore:
Voice but serves for one brief cry;
10   Plaint was it? or prophecy
Of sorrow that will surely come?
Omen of man's grievous doom!

    But, O Mother! by the close
Duly granted to thy throes;
By the silent thanks, now tending
Incense-like to Heaven, descending
Now to mingle and to move
With the gush of earthly love,
As a debt to that frail Creature,
20   Instrument of struggling Nature

For the blissful calm, the peace
Known but to this *one* release –
Can the pitying spirit doubt
That for human-kind springs out
From the penalty a sense
Of more than mortal recompence?

   As a floating summer cloud,
Though of gorgeous drapery proud,
To the sun-burnt traveller,
30 Or the stooping labourer,
Oft-times makes its bounty known
By its shadow round him thrown;
So, by chequerings of sad cheer,
Heavenly Guardians, brooding near,
Of their presence tell – too bright
Haply for corporeal sight!
Ministers of grace divine
Feelingly their brows incline
O'er this seeming Castaway
40 Breathing, in the light of day,
Something like the faintest breath
That has power to baffle death –
Beautiful, while very weakness
Captivates like passive meekness.

   And, sweet Mother! under warrant
Of the universal Parent,
Who repays in season due
Them who have, like thee, been true
To the filial chain let down
50 From His everlasting throne,
Angels hovering round thy couch,
With their softest whispers vouch,
That – whatever griefs may fret,
Cares entangle, sins beset,
This thy First-born, and with tears
Stain her cheek in future years –

Heavenly succour, not denied
To the babe, whate'er betide,
Will to the woman be supplied!

60   Mother! blest be thy calm ease;
Blest the starry promises, –
And the firmament benign
Hallowed be it, where they shine!
Yes, for them whose souls have scope
Ample for a wingèd hope,
And can earthward bend an ear
For needful listening, pledge is here,
That, if thy new-born Charge shall tread
In thy footsteps, and be led
70 By that other Guide, whose light
Of manly virtues, mildly bright,
Gave him first the wished-for part
In thy gentle virgin heart;
Then, amid the storms of life
Presignified by that dread strife
Whence ye have escaped together,
She may look for serene weather;
In all trials sure to find
Comfort for a faithful mind;
80 Kindlier issues, holier rest,
Than even now await her prest,
Conscious Nursling, to thy breast!

The Warning
A Sequel to the Foregoing

List, the winds of March are blowing;
Her ground-flowers shrink, afraid of showing
Their meek heads to the nipping air,
Which ye feel not, happy pair!
Sunk into a kindly sleep.
We, meanwhile, our hope will keep;

And if Time leagued with adverse Change
(Too busy fear!) shall cross its range,
Whatsoever check they bring,
10   Anxious duty hindering,
To like hope our prayers will cling.

Thus, while the ruminating spirit feeds
Upon the events of home as life proceeds,
Affections pure and holy in their source
Gain a fresh impulse, run a livelier course;
Hopes that within the Father's heart prevail,
Are in the experienced Grandsire's slow to fail;
And if the harp pleased his gay youth, it rings
To his grave touch with no unready strings,
20   While thoughts press on, and feelings overflow,
And quick words round him fall like flakes of snow.

Thanks to the Powers that yet maintain their sway,
And have renewed the tributary Lay,
Truths of the heart flock in with eager pace,
And FANCY greets them with a fond embrace;
Swift as the rising sun his beams extends
She shoots the tidings forth to distant friends;
Their gifts she hails (deemed precious, as they prove
For the unconscious Babe so prompt a love!) –
30   But from this peaceful centre of delight
Vague sympathies have urged her to take flight:
Rapt into upper regions, like the bee
That sucks from mountain heath her honey fee
Or, like the warbling lark intent to shroud
His head in sunbeams or a bowery cloud,
She soars – and here and there her pinions rest
On proud towers, like this humble cottage, blest
With a new visitant, an infant guest –
Towers where red streamers flout the breezy sky
40   In pomp foreseen by her creative eye,
When feasts shall crowd the hall, and steeple bells
Glad proclamation make, and heights and dells
Catch the blithe music as it sinks and swells,

And harboured ships, whose pride is on the sea,
Shall hoist their topmost flags in sign of glee,
Honouring the hope of noble ancestry.

But who (though neither reckoning ills assigned
By Nature, nor reviewing in the mind
The track that was, and is, and must be, worn
50   With weary feet by all of woman born) –
Shall *now* by such a gift with joy be moved,
Nor feel the fulness of that joy reproved?
Not He, whose last faint memory will command
The truth that Britain was his native land;
Whose infant soul was tutored to confide
In the cleansed faith for which her martyrs died;
Whose boyish ear the voice of her renown
With rapture thrilled; whose Youth revered the crown
Of Saxon liberty that Alfred wore,
60   Alfred, dear Babe, thy great Progenitor!
– Not He, who from her mellowed practice drew
His social sense of just, and fair, and true;
And saw, thereafter, on the soil of France
Rash Polity begin her maniac dance,
Foundations broken up, the deeps run wild,
Nor grieved to see (himself not unbeguiled) –
Woke from the dream, the dreamer to upbraid,
And learn how sanguine expectations fade
When novel trusts by folly are betrayed, –
70   To see Presumption, turning pale, refrain
From further havoc, but repent in vain, –
Good aims lie down, and perish in the road
Where guilt had urged them on with ceaseless goad,
Proofs thickening round her that on public ends
Domestic virtue vitally depends,
That civic strife can turn the happiest hearth
Into a grievous sore of self-tormenting earth.

Can such a One, dear Babe! though glad and proud
To welcome thee, repel the fears that crowd

80 Into his English breast, and spare to quake
Less for his own than for thy innocent sake?
Too late – or, should the providence of God
Lead, through dark ways by sin and sorrow trod,
Justice and peace to a secure abode,
Too soon – thou com'st into this breathing world;
Ensigns of mimic outrage are unfurled.
Who shall preserve or prop the tottering Realm?
What hand suffice to govern the state-helm?
If, in the aims of men, the surest test
90 Of good or bad (whate'er be sought for or profest)
Lie in the means required, or ways ordained,
For compassing the end, else never gained;
Yet governors and governed both are blind
To this plain truth, or fling it to the wind;
If to expedience principle must bow;
Past, future, shrinking up beneath the incumbent Now;
If cowardly concession still must feed
The thirst for power in men who ne'er concede;
Nor turn aside, unless to shape a way
100 For domination at some riper day;
If generous Loyalty must stand in awe
Of subtle Treason, in his mask of law,
Or with bravado insolent and hard,
Provoking punishment, to win reward;
If office help the factious to conspire,
And they who *should* extinguish, fan the fire –
Then, will the sceptre be a straw, the crown
Sit loosely, like the thistle's crest of down;
To be blown off at will, by Power that spares it
110 In cunning patience, from the head that wears it.

Lost people, trained to theoretic feud!
Lost above all, ye labouring multitude!
Bewildered whether ye, by slanderous tongues
Deceived, mistake calamities for wrongs;
And over fancied usurpations brood,
Oft snapping at revenge in sullen mood;

Or, from long stress of real injuries fly
To desperation for a remedy;
In bursts of outrage spread your judgements wide,
120 And to your wrath cry out, 'Be thou our guide;'
Or, bound by oaths, come forth to tread earth's floor
In marshalled thousands, darkening street and moor
With the worst shape mock-patience ever wore;
Or, to the giddy top of self-esteem
By Flatterers carried, mount into a dream
Of boundless suffrage, at whose sage behest
Justice shall rule, disorder be supprest,
And every man sit down as Plenty's Guest!
– O for a bridle bitted with remorse
130 To stop your Leaders in their headstrong course!
Oh may the Almighty scatter with His grace
These mists, and lead you to a safer place,
By paths no human wisdom can foretrace!
May He pour round you, from worlds far above
Man's feverish passions, His pure light of love,
That quietly restores the natural mien
To hope, and makes truth willing to be seen!
Else shall your blood-stained hands in frenzy reap
Fields gaily sown when promises were cheap. –
140 Why is the Past belied with wicked art,
The Future made to play so false a part,
Among a people famed for strength of mind,
Foremost in freedom, noblest of mankind?
We act as if we joyed in the sad tune
Storms make in rising, valued in the moon
Naught but her changes. Thus, ungrateful Nation!
If thou persist, and, scorning moderation,
Spread for thyself the snares of tribulation,
Whom, then, shall meekness guard? What saving skill
150 Lie in forbearance, strength in standing still?
– Soon shall the widow (for the speed of Time
Naught equals when the hours are winged with crime)
Widow, or wife, implore on tremulous knee,
From him who judged her lord, a like decree;

The skies will weep o'er old men desolate:
Ye little-ones! Earth shudders at your fate,
Outcasts and homeless orphans —

But turn, my Soul, and from the sleeping pair
Learn thou the beauty of omniscient care!
160 Be strong in faith, bid anxious thoughts lie still;
Seek for the good and cherish it – the ill
Oppose, or bear with a submissive will.

By the Sea-Side

The sun is couched, the sea-fowl gone to rest,
And the wild storm hath somewhere found a nest;
Air slumbers – wave with wave no longer strives,
Only a heaving of the deep survives,
A tell-tale motion! soon will it be laid,
And by the tide alone the water swayed.
Stealthy withdrawings, interminglings mild
Of light with shade in beauty reconciled –
Such is the prospect far as sight can range,
10 The soothing recompence, the welcome change.
Where now the ships that drove before the blast,
Threatened by angry breakers as they passed;
And by a train of flying clouds bemocked;
Or, in the hollow surge, at anchor rocked
As on a bed of death? Some lodge in peace,
Saved by His care who bade the tempest cease;
And some, too heedless of past danger, court
Fresh gales to waft them to the far-off port;
But near, or hanging sea and sky between,
20 Not one of all those wingèd powers is seen,
Seen in her course, nor 'mid this quiet heard;
Yet oh! how gladly would the air be stirred
By some acknowledgement of thanks and praise,
Soft in its temper as those vesper lays
Sung to the Virgin while accordant oars

Urge the slow bark along Calabrian shores;
A sea-born service through the mountains felt
Till into one loved vision all things melt:
Or like those hymns that soothe with graver sound
30   The gulfy coast of Norway iron-bound;
And, from the wide and open Baltic, rise
With punctual care, Lutherian harmonies.
Hush, not a voice is here! but why repine,
Now when the star of eve comes forth to shine
On British waters with that look benign?
Ye mariners, that plough your onward way,
Or in the haven rest, or sheltering bay,
May silent thanks at least to God be given
With a full heart; 'our thoughts are *heard* in heaven!'

Composed by the Sea-Shore

What mischief cleaves to unsubdued regret,
How fancy sickens by vague hopes beset;
How baffled projects on the spirit prey,
And fruitless wishes eat the heart away,
The Sailor knows; he best, whose lot is cast
On the relentless sea that holds him fast
On chance dependent, and the fickle star
Of power, through long and melancholy war.
O sad it is, in sight of foreign shores,
10   Daily to think on old familiar doors,
Hearths loved in childhood, and ancestral floors;
Or, tossed about along a waste of foam,
To ruminate on that delightful home
Which with the dear Betrothèd *was* to come;
Or came and was and is, yet meets the eye
Never but in the world of memory;
Or in a dream recalled, whose smoothest range
Is crossed by knowledge, or by dread, of change,
And if not so, whose perfect joy makes sleep
20   A thing too bright for breathing man to keep.

Hail to the virtues which that perilous life
Extracts from Nature's elemental strife;
And welcome glory won in battles fought
As bravely as the foe was keenly sought.
But to each gallant Captain and his crew
A less imperious sympathy is due,
Such as my verse now yields, while moonbeams play
On the mute sea in this unruffled bay;
Such as will promptly flow from every breast,
30 Where good men, disappointed in the quest
Of wealth and power and honours, long for rest;
Or, having known the splendours of success,
Sigh for the obscurities of happiness.

On a High Part of the Coast of Cumberland

Easter Sunday, April 7.
THE AUTHOR'S SIXTY-THIRD BIRTHDAY

The Sun, that seemed so mildly to retire,
Flung back from distant climes a streaming fire,
Whose blaze is now subdued to tender gleams,
Prelude of night's approach with soothing dreams.
Look round; – of all the clouds not one is moving;
'Tis the still hour of thinking, feeling, loving.
Silent, and stedfast as the vaulted sky,
The boundless plain of waters seems to lie: –
Comes that low sound from breezes rustling o'er
10 The grass-crowned headland that conceals the shore?
No; 'tis the earth-voice of the mighty sea,
Whispering how meek and gentle he *can* be!

Thou Power supreme! who, arming to rebuke
Offenders, dost put off the gracious look,
And clothe Thyself with terrors like the flood
Of ocean roused into his fiercest mood,
Whatever discipline Thy Will ordain
For the brief course that must for me remain;

Teach me with quick-eared spirit to rejoice
20 In admonitions of Thy softest voice!
Whate'er the path these mortal feet may trace,
Breathe through my soul the blessing of Thy grace,
Glad, through a perfect love, a faith sincere
Drawn from the wisdom that begins with fear,
Glad to expand; and, for a season, free
From finite cares, to rest absorbed in Thee!

To the Utilitarians

Avaunt this economic rage!
What would it bring? – an iron age,
When Fact with heartless search explored
Shall be Imagination's Lord,
And sway with absolute controul
The god-like Functions of the Soul.
Not *thus* can Knowledge elevate
Our Nature from her fallen state.
With sober Reason Faith unites
10 To vindicate the ideal rights
Of Human-kind – the true agreeing
Of objects with internal seeing,
Of effort with the end of Being. –

Poems Composed or Suggested During a Tour, in the Summer of 1833

[Having been prevented by the lateness of the season, in 1831, from visiting Staffa and Iona, the author made these the principal objects of a short tour in the summer of 1833, of which the following Series of Poems is a Memorial. The course pursued was down the Cumberland river Derwent, and to Whitehaven; thence (by the Isle of Man, where a few days were passed) up the Frith of Clyde to Greenock, then to Oban, Staffa, Iona; and back towards England, by Loch Awe, Inverary, Loch Goil-head, Greenock, and through parts of Renfrewshire, Ayrshire, and

Dumfrieshire, to Carlisle, and thence up the river Eden, and
homewards by Ullswater.]

I

Adieu, Rydalian Laurels! that have grown
And spread as if ye knew that days might come
When ye would shelter in a happy home,
On this fair Mount, a Poet of your own,
One who ne'er ventured for a Delphic crown
To sue the God; but, haunting your green shade
All seasons through, is humbly pleased to braid
Ground-flowers, beneath your guardianship, self-sown.
Farewell! no Minstrels now with harp new-strung
For summer wandering quit their household bowers;
Yet not for this wants Poesy a tongue
To cheer the Itinerant on whom she pours
Her spirit, while he crosses lonely moors,
Or musing sits forsaken halls among.

II

Why should the Enthusiast, journeying through this Isle,
Repine as if his hour were come too late?
Not unprotected in her mouldering state,
Antiquity salutes him with a smile,
'Mid fruitful fields that ring with jocund toil,
And pleasure-grounds where Taste, refined Co-mate
Of Truth and Beauty, strives to imitate,
Far as she may, primeval Nature's style.
Fair Land! by Time's parental love made free,
By Social Order's watchful arms embraced;
With unexampled union meet in thee,
For eye and mind, the present and the past;
With golden prospect for futurity,
If that be reverenced which ought to last.

III

They called Thee MERRY ENGLAND, in old time;
A happy people won for thee that name
With envy heard in many a distant clime;
And, spite of change, for me thou keep'st the same

Endearing title, a responsive chime
To the heart's fond belief; though some there are
Whose sterner judgements deem that word a snare
For inattentive Fancy, like the lime
Which foolish birds are caught with. Can, I ask,
10 This face of rural beauty be a mask
For discontent, and poverty, and crime;
These spreading towns a cloak for lawless will?
Forbid it, Heaven! – and MERRY ENGLAND still
Shall be thy rightful name, in prose and rhyme!

IV TO THE RIVER GRETA, NEAR KESWICK

Greta, what fearful listening! when huge stones
Rumble along thy bed, block after block:
Or, whirling with reiterated shock,
Combat, while darkness aggravates the groans:
But if thou (like Cocytus from the moans
Heard on his rueful margin) thence wert named
The Mourner, thy true nature was defamed,
And the habitual murmur that atones
For thy worst rage, forgotten. Oft as Spring
10 Decks, on thy sinuous banks, her thousand thrones,
Seats of glad instinct and love's carolling,
The concert, for the happy, then may vie
With liveliest peals of birthday harmony:
To a grieved heart, the notes are benisons.

V TO THE RIVER DERWENT

Among the mountains were we nursed, loved Stream!
Thou near the eagle's nest – within brief sail,
I, of his bold wing floating on the gale,
Where thy deep voice could lull me! Faint the beam
Of human life when first allowed to gleam
On mortal notice. – Glory of the vale,
Such thy meek outset, with a crown, though frail,
Kept in perpetual verdure by the steam
Of thy soft breath! – Less vivid wreath entwined
10 Nemean victor's brow; less bright was worn,

Meed of some Roman chief – in triumph borne
With captives chained; and shedding from his car
The sunset splendours of a finished war
Upon the proud enslavers of mankind!

VI IN SIGHT OF THE TOWN OF COCKERMOUTH

(Where the Author was born, and his Father's remains are laid.)

A point of life between my Parents' dust,
And yours, my buried Little-ones! am I;
And to those graves looking habitually
In kindred quiet I repose my trust.
Death to the innocent is more than just,
And, to the sinner, mercifully bent;
So may I hope, if truly I repent
And meekly bear the ills which bear I must:
And You, my Offspring! that do still remain,
10 Yet may outstrip me in the appointed race,
If e'er, through fault of mine, in mutual pain
We breathed together for a moment's space,
The wrong, by love provoked, let love arraign,
And only love keep in your hearts a place.

VII ADDRESS FROM THE SPIRIT OF COCKERMOUTH CASTLE

'Thou look'st upon me, and dost fondly think,
Poet! that, stricken as both are by years,
We, differing once so much, are now Compeers,
Prepared, when each has stood his time, to sink
Into the dust. Erewhile a sterner link
United us; when thou, in boyish play,
Entering my dungeon, didst become a prey
To soul-appalling darkness. Not a blink
Of light was there; – and thus did I, thy Tutor,
10 Make thy young thoughts acquainted with the grave;
While thou wert chasing the winged butterfly
Through my green courts; or climbing, a bold suitor
Up to the flowers whose golden progeny
Still round my shattered brow in beauty wave.'

VIII NUN'S WELL, BRIGHAM

The cattle crowding round this beverage clear
To slake their thirst, with reckless hoofs have trod
The encircling turf into a barren clod;
Through which the waters creep, then disappear,
Born to be lost in Derwent flowing near;
Yet, o'er the brink, and round the limestone cell
Of the pure spring (they call it the 'Nun's Well,'
Name that first struck by chance my startled ear)
A tender Spirit broods – the pensive Shade
10   Of ritual honours to this Fountain paid
By hooded Votaresses with saintly cheer;
Albeit oft the Virgin-mother mild
Looked down with pity upon eyes beguiled
Into the shedding of 'too soft a tear.'

IX TO A FRIEND

(On the banks of the Derwent.)

Pastor and Patriot! – at whose bidding rise
These modest walls, amid a flock that need,
For one who comes to watch them and to feed,
A fixed Abode – keep down presageful sighs.
Threats, which the unthinking only can despise,
Perplex the Church; but be thou firm, – be true
To thy first hope, and this good work pursue,
Poor as thou art. A welcome sacrifice
Dost Thou prepare, whose sign will be the smoke
10   Of thy new hearth; and sooner shall its wreaths,
Mounting while earth her morning incense breathes,
From wandering fiends of air receive a yoke,
And straightway cease to aspire, than God disdain
This humble tribute as ill-timed or vain.

X MARY QUEEN OF SCOTS

(Landing at the mouth of the Derwent, Workington.)

Dear to the Loves, and to the Graces vowed,
The Queen drew back the wimple that she wore;

And to the throng, that on the Cumbrian shore
Her landing hailed, how touchingly she bowed!
And like a Star (that, from a heavy cloud
Of pine-tree foliage poised in air, forth darts,
When a soft summer gale at evening parts
The gloom that did its loveliness enshroud)
She smiled; but Time, the old Saturnian seer,
10 Sighed on the wing as her foot pressed the strand,
With step prelusive to a long array
Of woes and degradations hand in hand –
Weeping captivity, and shuddering fear
Stilled by the ensanguined block of Fotheringay!

XI STANZAS SUGGESTED IN A STEAMBOAT OFF
SAINT BEES' HEADS, ON THE COAST OF
CUMBERLAND

If Life were slumber on a bed of down,
Toil unimposed, vicissitude unknown,
Sad were our lot: no hunter of the hare
Exults like him whose javelin from the lair
Has roused the lion; no one plucks the rose,
Whose proffered beauty in safe shelter blows
'Mid a trim garden's summer luxuries,
With joy like his who climbs, on hands and knees,
For some rare plant, yon Headland of St Bees.

10 This independence upon oar and sail,
This new indifference to breeze or gale,
This straight-lined progress, furrowing a flat lea,
And regular as if locked in certainty –
Depress the hours. Up, Spirit of the storm!
That Courage may find something to perform;
That Fortitude, whose blood disdains to freeze
At Danger's bidding, may confront the seas,
Firm as the towering Headlands of St Bees.

Dread cliff of Baruth! *that* wild wish may sleep,
20 Bold as if men and creatures of the Deep

Breathed the same element; too many wrecks
Have struck thy sides, too many ghastly decks
Hast thou looked down upon, that such a thought
Should here be welcome, and in verse enwrought:
With thy stern aspect better far agrees
Utterance of thanks that we have past with ease,
As millions thus shall do, the Headlands of St Bees.

Yet, while each useful Art augments her store,
What boots the gain if Nature should lose more?
30 And Wisdom, as she holds a Christian place
In man's intelligence sublimed by grace?
When Bega sought of yore the Cumbrian coast,
Tempestuous winds her holy errand crossed:
She knelt in prayer – the waves their wrath appease;
And, from her vow well weighed in Heaven's decrees,
Rose, where she touched the strand, the Chantry of
      St Bees.

'Cruel of heart were they, bloody of hand,'
Who in these Wilds then struggled for command;
The strong were merciless, without hope the weak;
40 Till this bright Stranger came, fair as day-break,
And as a cresset true that darts its length
Of beamy lustre from a tower of strength;
Guiding the mariner through troubled seas,
And cheering oft his peaceful reveries,
Like the fixed Light that crowns yon Headland of St Bees.

To aid the Votaress, miracles believed
Wrought in men's minds, like miracles achieved;
So piety took root; and Song might tell
What humanizing virtues near her cell
50 Sprang up, and spread their fragrance wide around;
How savage bosoms melted at the sound
Of gospel-truth enchained in harmonies
Wafted o'er waves, or creeping through close trees,
From her religious Mansion of St Bees.

When her sweet Voice, that instrument of love,
Was glorified, and took its place, above
The silent stars, among the angelic choir,
Her chantry blazed with sacrilegious fire,
And perished utterly; but her good deeds
60 Had sown the spot, that witnessed them, with seeds
Which lay in earth expectant, till a breeze
With quickening impulse answered their mute pleas,
And lo! a *statelier* pile, the Abbey of St Bees.

There are the naked clothed, the hungry fed;
And Charity extendeth to the dead
Her intercessions made for the soul's rest
Of tardy penitents; or for the best
Among the good (when love might else have slept,
Sickened, or died) in pious memory kept.
70 Thanks to the austere and simple Devotees,
Who, to that service bound by venial fees,
Keep watch before the altars of St Bees.

Are not, in sooth, their Requiems sacred ties
Woven out of passion's sharpest agonies,
Subdued, composed, and formalized by art,
To fix a wiser sorrow in the heart?
The prayer for them whose hour is past away
Says to the Living, profit while ye may!
A little part, and that the worst, he sees
80 Who thinks that priestly cunning holds the keys
That best unlock the secrets of St Bees.

Conscience, the timid being's inmost light,
Hope of the dawn and solace of the night,
Cheers these Recluses with a steady ray
In many an hour when judgement goes astray.
Ah! scorn not hastily their rule who try
Earth to despise, and flesh to mortify;
Consume with zeal, in wingèd ecstasies
Of prayer and praise forget their rosaries,
90 Nor hear the loudest surges of St Bees.

Yet none so prompt to succour and protect
The forlorn traveller, or sailor wrecked
On the bare coast; nor do they grudge the boon
Which staff and cockle hat and sandal shoon
Claim for the pilgrim: and, though chidings sharp
May sometimes greet the strolling minstrel's harp,
It is not then when, swept with sportive ease,
It charms a feast-day throng of all degrees,
Brightening the archway of revered St Bees.

100 How did the cliffs and echoing hills rejoice
What time the Benedictine Brethren's voice,
Imploring, or commanding with meet pride,
Summoned the Chiefs to lay their feuds aside,
And under one blest ensign serve the Lord
In Palestine. Advance, indignant Sword!
Flaming till thou from Panym hands release
That Tomb, dread centre of all sanctities
Nursed in the quiet Abbey of St Bees.

But look we now to them whose minds from far
110 Follow the fortunes which they may not share.
While in Judea Fancy loves to roam,
She helps to make a Holy-land at home:
The Star of Bethlehem from its sphere invites
To sound the crystal depth of maiden rights;
And wedded Life, through scriptural mysteries,
Heavenward ascends with all her charities,
Taught by the hooded Celibates of St Bees.

Nor be it e'er forgotten how by skill
Of cloistered Architects, free their souls to fill
120 With love of God, throughout the Land were raised
Churches, on whose symbolic beauty gazed
Peasant and mail-clad Chief with pious awe;
As at this day men seeing what they saw,
Or the bare wreck of faith's solemnities,
Aspire to more than earthly destinies;
Witness yon Pile that greets us from St Bees.

Yet more; around those Churches, gathered Towns
Safe from the feudal Castle's haughty frowns;
Peaceful abodes, where Justice might uphold
130 Her scales with even hand, and culture mould
The heart to pity, train the mind in care
For rules of life, sound as the Time could bear.
Nor dost thou fail, through abject love of ease,
Or hindrance raised by sordid purposes,
To bear thy part in this good work, St Bees.

Who with the ploughshare clove the barren moors,
And to green meadows changed the swampy shores?
Thinned the rank woods; and for the cheerful grange
Made room where wolf and boar were used to range?
140 Who taught, and showed by deeds, that gentler chains
Should bind the vassal to his lord's domains?
The thoughtful Monks, intent their God to please,
For Christ's dear sake, by human sympathies
Poured from the bosom of thy Church, St Bees!

But all availed not; by a mandate given
Through lawless will the Brotherhood was driven
Forth from their cells; their ancient House laid low
In Reformation's sweeping overthrow.
But now once more the local Heart revives,
150 The inextinguishable Spirit strives.
Oh may that Power who hushed the stormy seas,
And cleared a way for the first Votaries,
Prosper the new-born College of St Bees!

Alas! the Genius of our age, from Schools
Less humble, draws her lessons, aims, and rules.
To Prowess guided by her insight keen
Matter and Spirit are as one Machine;
Boastful Idolatress of formal skill
She in her own would merge the eternal will:
160 Better, if Reason's triumphs match with these,
Her flight before the bold credulities
That furthered the first teaching of St Bees.

XII IN THE CHANNEL, BETWEEN THE COAST OF CUMBERLAND AND THE ISLE OF MAN

Ranging the heights of Scawfell or Blackcomb,
In his lone course the Shepherd oft will pause,
And strive to fathom the mysterious laws
By which the clouds, arrayed in light or gloom,
On Mona settle, and the shapes assume
Of all her peaks and ridges. What he draws
From sense, faith, reason, fancy, of the cause,
He will take with him to the silent tomb.
Or, by his fire, a child upon his knee,
Haply the untaught Philosopher may speak
Of the strange sight, nor hide his theory
That satisfies the simple and the meek,
Blest in their pious ignorance, though weak
To cope with Sages undevoutly free.

XIII AT SEA OFF THE ISLE OF MAN

Bold words affirmed, in days when faith was strong
And doubts and scruples seldom teased the brain,
That no adventurer's bark had power to gain
These shores if he approached them bent on wrong;
For, suddenly up-conjured from the Main,
Mists rose to hide the Land – that search, though long
And eager, might be still pursued in vain.
O Fancy, what an age was *that* for song!
That age, when not by *laws* inanimate,
As men believed, the waters were impelled,
The air controlled, the stars their courses held;
But element and orb on *acts* did wait
Of *Powers* endued with visible form, instinct
With will, and to their work by passion linked.

XIV

Desire we past illusions to recall?
To reinstate wild Fancy, would we hide
Truths whose thick veil Science has drawn aside?
No, – let this Age, high as she may, instal

In her esteem the thirst that wrought man's fall,
The universe is infinitely wide;
And conquering Reason, if self-glorified,
Can nowhere move uncrossed by some new wall
Or gulf of mystery, which thou alone,
10 Imaginative Faith! canst overleap,
In progress toward the fount of Love, – the throne
Of Power whose ministers the records keep
Of periods fixed, and laws established, less
Flesh to exalt than prove its nothingness.

XV ON ENTERING DOUGLAS BAY, ISLE OF MAN

'Dignum laude virum Musa vetat mori.'

The feudal Keep, the bastions of Cohorn,
Even when they rose to check or to repel
Tides of aggressive war, oft served as well
Greedy ambition, armed to treat with scorn
Just limits; but yon Tower, whose smiles adorn
This perilous bay, stands clear of all offence;
Blest work it is of love and innocence,
A Tower of refuge built for the else forlorn.
Spare it, ye waves, and lift the mariner,
10 Struggling for life, into its saving arms!
Spare, too, the human helpers! Do they stir
'Mid your fierce shock like men afraid to die?
No; their dread service nerves the heart it warms,
And they are led by noble HILLARY.

XVI BY THE SEA-SHORE, ISLE OF MAN

Why stand we gazing on the sparkling Brine,
With wonder smit by its transparency,
And all-enraptured with its purity? –
Because the unstained, the clear, the crystalline,
Have ever in them something of benign;
Whether in gem, in water, or in sky,
A sleeping infant's brow, or wakeful eye
Of a young maiden, only not divine.

Scarcely the hand forbears to dip its palm
10 For beverage drawn as from a mountain-well.
Temptation centres in the liquid Calm;
Our daily raiment seems no obstacle
To instantaneous plunging in, deep Sea!
And revelling in long embrace with thee.

XVII ISLE OF MAN
A youth too certain of his power to wade
On the smooth bottom of this clear bright sea,
To sight so shallow, with a bather's glee,
Leapt from this rock, and but for timely aid
He, by the alluring element betrayed,
Had perished. Then might Sea-nymphs (and with sighs
Of self-reproach) have chanted elegies
Bewailing his sad fate, when he was laid
In peaceful earth: for, doubtless, he was frank,
10 Utterly in himself devoid of guile;
Knew not the double-dealing of a smile;
Nor aught that makes men's promises a blank,
Or deadly snare: and He survives to bless
The Power that saved him in his strange distress.

XVIII ISLE OF MAN
Did pangs of grief for lenient time too keen,
Grief that devouring waves had caused – or guilt
Which they had witnessed, sway the man who built
This Homestead, placed where nothing could be seen,
Naught heard, of ocean troubled or serene?
A tired Ship-soldier on paternal land,
That o'er the channel holds august command,
The dwelling raised, – a veteran Marine.
He, in disgust, turned from the neighbouring sea
10 To shun the memory of a listless life
That hung between two callings. May no strife
More hurtful here beset him, doomed though free,
Self-doomed, to worse inaction, till his eye
Shrink from the daily sight of earth and sky!

XIX *BY A RETIRED MARINER (A FRIEND OF
THE AUTHOR)

From early youth I ploughed the restless Main,
My mind as restless and as apt to change;
Through every clime and ocean did I range,
In hope at length a competence to gain;
For poor to Sea I went, and poor I still remain.
Year after year I strove, but strove in vain,
And hardships manifold did I endure,
For Fortune on me never deigned to smile;
Yet I at last a resting-place have found,
10 With just enough life's comforts to procure,
In a snug Cove on this our favoured Isle,
A peaceful spot where Nature's gifts abound;
Then sure I have no reason to complain,
Though poor to Sea I went, and poor I still remain.

XX AT BALA-SALA, ISLE OF MAN

(Supposed to be written by a Friend.)

Broken in fortune, but in mind entire
And sound in principle, I seek repose
Where ancient trees this convent-pile enclose,
In ruin beautiful. When vain desire
Intrudes on peace, I pray the eternal Sire
To cast a soul-subduing shade on me,
A grey-haired, pensive, thankful Refugee;
A shade – but with some sparks of heavenly fire
Once to these cells vouchsafed. And when I note
10 The old Tower's brow yellowed as with the beams
Of sunset ever there, albeit streams
Of stormy weather-stains that semblance wrought,
I thank the silent Monitor, and say
'Shine so, my aged brow, at all hours of the day!'

XXI TYNWALD HILL

Once on the top of Tynwald's formal mound
(Still marked with green turf circles narrowing

Stage above stage) would sit this Island's King,
The laws to promulgate, enrobed and crowned;
While, compassing the little mound around,
Degrees and Orders stood, each under each:
Now, like to things within fate's easiest reach,
The power is merged, the pomp a grave has found.
Off with yon cloud, old Snafell! that thine eye
10   Over three Realms may take its widest range;
And let, for them, thy fountains utter strange
Voices, thy winds break forth in prophecy,
If the whole State must suffer mortal change,
Like Mona's miniature of sovereignty.

XXII

Despond who will – *I* heard a voice exclaim,
'Though fierce the assault, and shattered the defence,
It cannot be that Britain's social frame,
The glorious work of time and providence,
Before a flying season's rash pretence,
Should fall; that She, whose virtue put to shame,
When Europe prostrate lay, the Conqueror's aim,
Should perish, self-subverted. Black and dense
The cloud is; but brings *that* a day of doom
10   To Liberty? Her sun is up the while,
That orb whose beams round Saxon Alfred shone:
Then laugh, ye innocent Vales! ye Streams, sweep on,
Nor let one billow of our heaven-blest Isle
Toss in the fanning wind a humbler plume.'

XXIII IN THE FIRTH OF CLYDE, AILSA CRAG

(During an Eclipse of the Sun, July 17.)

Since risen from ocean, ocean to defy,
Appeared the Crag of Ailsa, ne'er did morn
With gleaming lights more gracefully adorn
His sides, or wreathe with mist his forehead high:
Now, faintly darkening with the sun's eclipse,
Still is he seen, in lone sublimity,

Towering above the sea and little ships;
For dwarfs the tallest seem while sailing by,
Each for her haven; with her freight of Care,
10 Pleasure, or Grief, and Toil that seldom looks
Into the secret of tomorrow's fare;
Though poor, yet rich, without the wealth of books,
Or aught that watchful Love to Nature owes
For her mute Powers, fixed Forms, or transient Shows.

XXIV ON THE FIRTH OF CLYDE

(In a Steamboat.)

Arran! a single-crested Teneriffe,
A St Helena next – in shape and hue,
Varying her crowded peaks and ridges blue;
Who but must covet a cloud-seat, or skiff
Built for the air, or wingèd Hippogriff?
That he might fly, where no one could pursue,
From this dull Monster and her sooty crew;
And, as a God, light on thy topmost cliff.
Impotent wish! which reason would despise
10 If the mind knew no union of extremes,
No natural bond between the boldest schemes
Ambition frames, and heart-humilities.
Beneath stern mountains many a soft vale lies,
And lofty springs give birth to lowly streams.

XXV ON REVISITING DUNOLLY CASTLE

The captive Bird was gone; – to cliff or moor
Perchance had flown, delivered by the storm;
Or he had pined, and sunk to feed the worm:
Him found we not: but, climbing a tall tower,
There saw, impaved with rude fidelity
Of art mosaic, in a roofless floor,
An Eagle with stretched wings, but beamless eye –
An Eagle that could neither wail nor soar.
Effigy of the Vanished – (shall I dare
10 To call thee so?) or symbol of fierce deeds

And of the towering courage which past times
Rejoiced in – take, whate'er thou be, a share,
Not undeserved, of the memorial rhymes
That animate my way where'er it leads!

XXVI THE DUNOLLY EAGLE

Not to the clouds, not to the cliff, he flew;
But when a storm, on sea or mountain bred,
Came and delivered him, alone he sped
Into the castle-dungeon's darkest mew.
Now, near his master's house in open view
He dwells, and hears indignant tempests howl,
Kennelled and chained. Ye tame domestic fowl,
Beware of him! Thou, saucy cockatoo,
Look to thy plumage and thy life! – The roe,
10 Fleet as the west wind, is for *him* no quarry;
Balanced in ether he will never tarry,
Eyeing the sea's blue depths. Poor Bird! even so
Doth man of brother man a creature make
That clings to slavery for its own sad sake.

XXVII WRITTEN IN A BLANK LEAF OF MACPHERSON'S OSSIAN

Oft have I caught, upon a fitful breeze,
Fragments of far-off melodies,
With ear not coveting the whole,
A part so charmed the pensive soul:
While a dark storm before my sight
Was yielding, on a mountain height
Loose vapours have I watched, that won
Prismatic colours from the sun;
Nor felt a wish that heaven would show
10 The image of its perfect bow.
What need, then, of these finished Strains?
Away with counterfeit Remains!
An abbey in its lone recess,
A temple of the wilderness,
Wrecks though they be, announce with feeling

The majesty of honest dealing.
Spirit of Ossian! if imbound
In language thou mayst yet be found,
If aught (intrusted to the pen
20 Or floating on the tongues of men,
Albeit shattered and impaired)
Subsist thy dignity to guard,
In concert with memorial claim
Of old grey stone, and high-born name
That cleaves to rock or pillared cave
Where moans the blast, or beats the wave,
Let Truth, stern arbitress of all,
Interpret that Original,
And for presumptuous wrongs atone; –
30 Authentic words be given, or none!

Time is not blind; – yet He, who spares
Pyramid pointing to the stars,
Hath preyed with ruthless appetite
On all that marked the primal flight
Of the poetic ecstasy
Into the land of mystery.
No tongue is able to rehearse
One measure, Orpheus! of thy verse;
Musaeus, stationed with his lyre
40 Supreme among the Elysian choir,
Is, for the dwellers upon earth,
Mute as a lark ere morning's birth.
Why grieve for these, though past away
The music, and extinct the lay?
When thousands, by severer doom,
Full early to the silent tomb
Have sunk, at Nature's call; or strayed
From hope and promise, self-betrayed;
The garland withering on their brows;
50 Stung with remorse for broken vows;
Frantic – else how might they rejoice?
And friendless, by their own sad choice!

Hail, Bards of mightier grasp! on you
I chiefly call, the chosen Few,
Who cast not off the acknowledged guide,
Who faltered not, nor turned aside;
Whose lofty genius could survive
Privation, under sorrow thrive;
In whom the fiery Muse revered
60 The symbol of a snow-white beard,
Bedewed with meditative tears
Dropped from the lenient cloud of years.

Brothers in soul! though distant times
Produced you nursed in various climes,
Ye, when the orb of life had waned,
A plenitude of love retained:
Hence, while in you each sad regret
By corresponding hope was met,
Ye lingered among human kind,
70 Sweet voices for the passing wind;
Departing sunbeams, loth to stop,
Though smiling on the last hill-top!
Such to the tender-hearted maid
Even ere her joys begin to fade;
Such, haply, to the rugged chief
By fortune crushed, or tamed by grief;
Appears, on Morven's lonely shore,
Dim-gleaming through imperfect lore,
The Son of Fingal; such was blind
80 Maeonides of ampler mind;
Such Milton, to the fountain-head
Of glory by Urania led!

XXVIII CAVE OF STAFFA
We saw, but surely, in the motley crowd,
Not One of us has felt the far-famed sight;
How *could* we feel it? each the other's blight,
Hurried and hurrying, volatile and loud.
O for those motions only that invite

The Ghost of Fingal to his tuneful Cave
By the breeze entered, and wave after wave
Softly embosoming the timid light!
And by *one* Votary who at will might stand
10 Gazing and take into his mind and heart,
With undistracted reverence, the effect
Of those proportions where the almighty hand
That made the worlds, the sovereign Architect,
Has deigned to work as if with human Art!

XXIX CAVE OF STAFFA

(After the Crowd had departed.)

Thanks for the lessons of this Spot – fit school
For the presumptuous thoughts that would assign
Mechanic laws to agency divine;
And, measuring heaven by earth, would overrule
Infinite Power. The pillared vestibule,
Expanding yet precise, the roof embowed,
Might seem designed to humble man, when proud
Of his best workmanship by plan and tool.
Down-bearing with his whole Atlantic weight
10 Of tide and tempest on the Structure's base,
And flashing to that Structure's topmost height,
Ocean has proved its strength, and of its grace
In calms is conscious, finding for his freight
Of softest music some responsive place.

XXX CAVE OF STAFFA
Ye shadowy Beings, that have rights and claims
In every cell of Fingal's mystic Grot,
Where are ye? Driven or venturing to the spot,
Our fathers glimpses caught of your thin Frames,
And, by your mien and bearing, knew your names;
And they could hear *his* ghostly song who trod
Earth, till the flesh lay on him like a load,
While he struck his desolate harp without hopes or aims.
Vanished ye are, but subject to recall;

10   Why keep *we* else the instincts whose dread law
Ruled here of yore, till what men felt they saw,
Not by black arts but magic natural!
If eyes be still sworn vassals of belief,
Yon light shapes forth a Bard, that shade a Chief.

XXXI FLOWERS ON THE TOP OF THE PILLARS AT
THE ENTRANCE OF THE CAVE
Hope smiled when your nativity was cast,
Children of Summer! Ye fresh Flowers that brave
What Summer here escapes not, the fierce wave,
And whole artillery of the western blast,
Battering the Temple's front, its long-drawn nave
Smiting, as if each moment were their last.
But ye, bright Flowers, on frieze and architrave
Survive, and once again the Pile stands fast:
Calm as the Universe, from specular towers
10   Of heaven contemplated by Spirits pure
With mute astonishment, it stands sustained
Through every part in symmetry, to endure,
Unhurt, the assault of Time with all his hours,
As the supreme Artificer ordained.

XXXII IONA
On to Iona! – What can she afford
To *us* save matter for a thoughtful sigh,
Heaved over ruin with stability
In urgent contrast? To diffuse the WORD
(Thy Paramount, mighty Nature! and Time's Lord)
Her Temples rose, 'mid pagan gloom; but why,
Even for a moment, has our verse deplored
Their wrongs, since they fulfilled their destiny?
And when, subjected to a common doom
10   Of mutability, those far-famed Piles
Shall disappear from both the sister Isles,
Iona's Saints, forgetting not past days,
Garlands shall wear of amaranthine bloom,
While heaven's vast sea of voices chants their praise.

XXXIII IONA

(Upon Landing.)

How sad a welcome! To each voyager
Some ragged child holds up for sale a store
Of wave-worn pebbles, pleading on the shore
Where once came monk and nun with gentle stir,
Blessings to give, news ask, or suit prefer.
Yet is yon neat trim church a grateful speck
Of novelty amid the sacred wreck
Strewn far and wide. Think, proud Philosopher!
Fallen though she be, this Glory of the west,
10   Still on her sons, the beams of mercy shine;
And 'hopes, perhaps more heavenly bright than thine,
A grace by thee unsought and unpossest,
A faith more fixed, a rapture more divine
Shall gild their passage to eternal rest.'

XXXIV THE BLACK STONES OF IONA

[See Martin's *Voyage among the Western Isles.*]

Here on their knees men swore: the stones were black,
Black in the people's minds and words, yet they
Were at that time, as now, in colour grey.
But what is colour, if upon the rack
Of conscience souls are placed by deeds that lack
Concord with oaths? What differ night and day
Then, when before the Perjured on his way
Hell opens, and the heavens in vengeance crack
Above his head uplifted in vain prayer
10   To Saint, or Fiend, or to the Godhead whom
He had insulted – Peasant, King, or Thane?
Fly where the culprit may, guilt meets a doom;
And, from invisible worlds at need laid bare,
Come links for social order's awful chain.

XXXV

Homeward we turn. Isle of Columba's Cell,
Where Christian piety's soul-cheering spark

(Kindled from Heaven between the light and dark
Of time) shone like the morning-star, farewell! –
And fare thee well, to Fancy visible,
Remote St Kilda, lone and loved sea-mark
For many a voyage made in her swift bark,
When with more hues than in the rainbow dwell
Thou a mysterious intercourse dost hold,
10   Extracting from clear skies and air serene,
And out of sun-bright waves, a lucid veil,
That thickens, spreads, and, mingling fold with fold,
Makes known, when thou no longer canst be seen,
Thy whereabout, to warn the approaching sail.

XXXVI GREENOCK

Per me si va nella Città dolente.

We have not passed into a doleful City,
We who were led today down a grim dell,
By some too boldly named 'the Jaws of Hell:'
Where be the wretched ones, the sights for pity?
These crowded streets resound no plaintive ditty: –
As from the hive where bees in summer dwell,
Sorrow seems here excluded; and that knell,
It neither damps the gay, nor checks the witty.
Alas! too busy Rival of old Tyre,
10   Whose merchants Princes were, whose decks were
      thrones;
Soon may the punctual sea in vain respire
To serve thy need, in union with that Clyde
Whose nursling current brawls o'er mossy stones,
The poor, the lonely, herdsman's joy and pride.

XXXVII

'There!' said a Stripling, pointing with meet pride
Towards a low roof with green trees half concealed,
'Is Mosgiel Farm; and that's the very field
Where Burns ploughed up the Daisy.' Far and wide
A plain below stretched seaward, while, descried

Above sea-clouds, the Peaks of Arran rose;
And, by that simple notice, the repose
Of earth, sky, sea, and air, was vivified.
Beneath 'the random *bield* of clod or stone'
10 Myriads of daisies have shone forth in flower
Near the lark's nest, and in their natural hour
Have passed away; less happy than the One
That, by the unwilling ploughshare, died to prove
The tender charm of poetry and love.

XXXVIII THE RIVER EDEN, CUMBERLAND

Eden! till now thy beauty had I viewed
By glimpses only, and confess with shame
That verse of mine, whate'er its varying mood,
Repeats but once the sound of thy sweet name:
Yet fetched from Paradise that honour came,
Rightfully borne; for Nature gives thee flowers
That have no rivals among British bowers;
And thy bold rocks are worthy of their fame.
Measuring thy course, fair Stream! at length I pay
10 To my life's neighbour dues of neighbourhood;
But I have traced thee on thy winding way
With pleasure sometimes by this thought restrained:
For things far off we toil, while many a good
Not sought, because too near, is never gained.

XXXIX MONUMENT OF MRS HOWARD (by
    Nollekens)

In Wetheral Church, near Corby, on the banks of the Eden.

Stretched on the dying Mother's lap, lies dead
Her new-born Babe; dire ending of bright hope!
But Sculpture here, with the divinest scope
Of luminous faith, heavenward hath raised that head
So patiently; and through one hand has spread
A touch so tender for the insensate Child –
(Earth's lingering love to parting reconciled,
Brief parting, for the spirit is all but fled) –

That we, who contemplate the turns of life
10   Through this still medium, are consoled and cheered;
Feel with the Mother, think the severed Wife
Is less to be lamented than revered;
And own that Art, triumphant over strife
And pain, hath powers to Eternity endeared.

XL   SUGGESTED BY THE FOREGOING

Tranquillity! the sovereign aim wert thou
In heathen schools of philosophic lore;
Heart-stricken by stern destiny of yore
The Tragic Muse thee served with thoughtful vow;
And what of hope Elysium could allow
Was fondly seized by Sculpture, to restore
Peace to the Mourner. But when He who wore
The crown of thorns around His bleeding brow
Warmed our sad being with celestial light,
10   *Then* Arts, which still had drawn a softening grace
From shadowy fountains of the Infinite,
Communed with that Idea face to face:
And move around it now as planets run,
Each in its orbit round the central Sun.

XLI   NUNNERY

The floods are roused, and will not soon be weary;
Down from the Pennine Alps how fiercely sweeps
CROGLIN, the stately Eden's tributary!
He raves, or through some moody passage creeps
Plotting new mischief – out again he leaps
Into broad light, and sends, through regions airy,
That voice which soothed the Nuns while on the steeps
They knelt in prayer, or sang to blissful Mary.
That union ceased: then, cleaving easy walks
10   Through crags, and smoothing paths beset with danger,
Came studious Taste; and many a pensive stranger
Dreams on the banks, and to the river talks.
What change shall happen next to Nunnery Dell?
Canal, and Viaduct, and Railway, tell!

XLII STEAMBOATS, VIADUCTS, AND RAILWAYS
Motions and Means, on land and sea at war
With old poetic feeling, not for this,
Shall ye, by Poets even, be judged amiss!
Nor shall your presence, howsoe'er it mar
The loveliness of Nature, prove a bar
To the Mind's gaining that prophetic sense
Of future change, that point of vision, whence
May be discovered what in soul ye are.
In spite of all that beauty may disown
10 In your harsh features, Nature doth embrace
Her lawful offspring in Man's art; and Time,
Pleased with your triumphs o'er his brother Space,
Accepts from your bold hands the proffered crown
Of hope, and smiles on you with cheer sublime.

XLIII THE MONUMENT COMMONLY CALLED LONG
MEG AND HER DAUGHTERS, NEAR THE RIVER EDEN
A weight of awe, not easy to be borne,
Fell suddenly upon my Spirit – cast
From the dread bosom of the unknown past,
When first I saw that family forlorn.
Speak Thou, whose massy strength and stature scorn
The power of years – pre-eminent, and placed
Apart, to overlook the circle vast –
Speak, Giant-mother! tell it to the Morn
While she dispels the cumbrous shades of Night;
10 Let the Moon hear, emerging from a cloud;
At whose behest uprose on British ground
That Sisterhood, in hieroglyphic round
Forth-shadowing, some have deemed, the infinite
The inviolable God, that tames the proud!

XLIV LOWTHER
Lowther! in thy majestic Pile are seen
Cathedral pomp and grace, in apt accord
With the baronial castle's sterner mien;
Union significant of God adored,

And charters won and guarded by the sword
Of ancient honour; whence that goodly state
Of polity which wise men venerate,
And will maintain, if God his help afford.
Hourly the democratic torrent swells;
10 For airy promises and hopes suborned
The strength of backward-looking thoughts is scorned.
Fall if ye must, ye Towers and Pinnacles,
With what ye symbolize; authentic Story
Will say, Ye disappeared with England's Glory!

XLV TO THE EARL OF LONSDALE

'Magistratus indicat virum.'

Lonsdale! it were unworthy of a Guest,
Whose heart with gratitude to thee inclines,
If he should speak, by fancy touched, of signs
On thy Abode harmoniously imprest,
Yet be unmoved with wishes to attest
How in thy mind and moral frame agree
Fortitude, and that Christian Charity
Which, filling, consecrates the human breast.
And if the Motto on thy 'scutcheon teach
10 With truth, 'THE MAGISTRACY SHOWS THE MAN;'
That searching test thy public course has stood;
As will be owned alike by bad and good,
Soon as the measuring of life's little span
Shall place thy virtues out of Envy's reach.

XLVI THE SOMNAMBULIST

List, ye who pass by Lyulph's Tower
   At eve; how softly then
Doth Aira-force, that torrent hoarse,
   Speak from the woody glen!
Fit music for a solemn vale!
   And holier seems the ground
To him who catches on the gale
The spirit of a mournful tale,
   Embodied in the sound.

10 Not far from that fair site whereon
  The Pleasure-house is reared,
As story says, in antique days
  A stern-browed house appeared;
Foil to a Jewel rich in light
  There set, and guarded well;
Cage for a Bird of plumage bright,
Sweet-voiced, nor wishing for a flight
  Beyond her native dell.

To win this bright Bird from her cage,
20 To make this Gem their own,
Came Barons bold, with store of gold,
  And Knights of high renown;
But one She prized, and only one;
  Sir Eglamore was he;
Full happy season, when was known,
Ye Dales and Hills! to you alone
  Their mutual loyalty –

Known chiefly, Aira! to thy glen,
  Thy brook, and bowers of holly;
30 Where Passion caught what Nature taught,
  That all but love is folly;
Where Fact with Fancy stooped to play;
  Doubt came not, nor regret –
To trouble hours that winged their way,
As if through an immortal day
  Whose sun could never set.

  But in old times Love dwelt not long
  Sequestered with repose;
Best throve the fire of chaste desire,
40 Fanned by the breath of foes.
'A conquering lance is beauty's test,
  And proves the Lover true;'
So spake Sir Eglamore, and pressed
The drooping Emma to his breast,
  And looked a blind adieu.

They parted. – Well with him it fared
   Through wide-spread regions errant;
A knight of proof in love's behoof,
   The thirst of fame his warrant:
50 And She her happiness can build
   On woman's quiet hours;
Though faint, compared with spear and shield,
The solace beads and masses yield,
   And needlework and flowers.

Yet blest was Emma when she heard
   Her Champion's praise recounted;
Though brain would swim, and eyes grow dim,
   And high her blushes mounted;
Or when a bold heroic lay
60 She warbled from full heart;
Delightful blossoms for the *May*
Of absence! but they will not stay,
   Born only to depart.

Hope wanes with her, while lustre fills
   Whatever path he chooses;
As if his orb, that owns no curb,
   Received the light hers loses.
He comes not back; an ampler space
   Requires for nobler deeds;
70 He ranges on from place to place,
Till of his doings is no trace,
   But what her fancy breeds.

His fame may spread, but in the past
   Her spirit finds its centre;
Clear sight She has of what he was,
   And that would now content her.
'Still is he my devoted Knight?'
   The tear in answer flows;
Month falls on month with heavier weight;
80 Day sickens round her, and the night
   Is empty of repose.

In sleep She sometimes walked abroad,
  Deep sighs with quick words blending,
Like that pale Queen whose hands are seen
  With fancied spots contending;
But *she* is innocent of blood, –
  The moon is not more pure
That shines aloft, while through the wood
She thrids her way, the sounding Flood
90 Her melancholy lure!

While 'mid the fern-brake sleeps the doe,
  And owls alone are waking,
In white arrayed, glides on the Maid
  The downward pathway taking,
That leads her to the torrent's side
  And to a holly bower;
By whom on this still night descried?
By whom in that lone place espied?
  By thee, Sir Eglamore!

100 A wandering Ghost, so thinks the Knight,
  His coming step has thwarted,
Beneath the boughs that heard their vows,
  Within whose shade they parted.
Hush, hush, the busy Sleeper see!
  Perplexed her fingers seem,
As if they from the holly tree
Green twigs would pluck, as rapidly
  Flung from her to the stream.

What means the Spectre? Why intent
110 To violate the Tree,
Thought Eglamore, by which I swore
  Unfading constancy?
Here am I, and tomorrow's sun,
  To her I left, shall prove
That bliss is ne'er so surely won
As when a circuit has been run
  Of valour, truth, and love.

So from the spot whereon he stood,
　　He moved with stealthy pace;
120　And, drawing nigh, with his living eye,
　　He recognized the face;
And whispers caught, and speeches small,
　　Some to the green-leaved tree,
Some muttered to the torrent-fall; –
'Roar on, and bring him with thy call;
　　I heard, and so may He!'

Soul-shattered was the Knight, nor knew
　　If Emma's Ghost it were,
Or boding Shade, or if the Maid
130　Her very self stood there.
He touched; what followed who shall tell?
　　The soft touch snapped the thread
Of slumber – shrieking back she fell,
And the Stream whirled her down the dell
　　Along its foaming bed.

In plunged the Knight! – when on firm ground
　　The rescued Maiden lay,
Her eyes grew bright with blissful light,
　　Confusion passed away;
140　She heard, ere to the throne of grace
　　Her faithful Spirit flew,
His voice – beheld his speaking face;
And, dying, from his own embrace,
　　She felt that he was true.

So was he reconciled to life:
　　Brief words may speak the rest;
Within the dell he built a cell,
　　And there was Sorrow's guest;
In hermits' weeds repose he found,
150　From vain temptations free;
Beside the torrent dwelling – bound
By one deep heart-controlling sound,
　　And awed to piety.

Wild stream of Aira, hold thy course,
  Nor fear memorial lays,
Where clouds that spread .in solemn shade,
  Are edged with golden rays!
Dear art thou to the light of heaven,
  Though minister of sorrow;
160 Sweet is thy voice at pensive even;
And thou, in lovers' hearts forgiven,
  Shalt take thy place with Yarrow!

XLVII TO CORDELIA M————

Hallsteads, Ullswater.

Not in the mines beyond the western main,
You say, Cordelia, was the metal sought,
Which a fine skill, of Indian growth, has wrought
Into this flexible yet faithful Chain;
Nor is it silver of romantic Spain;
But from our loved Helvellyn's depths was brought,
Our own domestic mountain. Thing and thought
Mix strangely; trifles light, and partly vain,
Can prop, as you have learnt, our nobler being:
10 Yes, Lady, while about your neck is wound
(Your casual glance oft meeting) this bright cord,
What witchery, for pure gifts of inward seeing,
Lurks in it, Memory's Helper, Fancy's Lord,
For precious tremblings in your bosom found!

XLVIII

Most sweet it is with unuplifted eyes
To pace the ground, if path be there or none,
While a fair region round the traveller lies
Which he forbears again to look upon;
Pleased rather with some soft ideal scene,
The work of Fancy, or some happy tone
Of meditation, slipping in between
The beauty coming and the beauty gone.
If Thought and Love desert us, from that day
10 Let us break off all commerce with the Muse:

With Thought and Love companions of our way,
Whate'er the senses take or may refuse,
The Mind's internal heaven shall shed her dews
Of inspiration on the humblest lay.

'If this great world of joy and pain'

If this great world of joy and pain
   Revolve in one sure track;
If freedom, set, will rise again,
   And virtue, flown, come back;
Woe to the purblind crew who fill
   The heart with each day's care;
Nor gain, from past or future, skill
   To bear, and to forbear!

Love Lies Bleeding

You call it, 'Love lies bleeding,' – so you may,
Though the red Flower, not prostrate, only droops,
As we have seen it here from day to day,
From month to month, life passing not away:
A flower how rich in sadness! Even thus stoops
(Sentient by Grecian sculpture's marvellous power),
Thus leans, with hanging brow and body bent
Earthward in uncomplaining languishment,
The dying Gladiator. So, sad Flower!
10 ('Tis Fancy guides me willing to be led,
Though by a slender thread,)
So drooped Adonis, bathed in sanguine dew
Of his death-wound, when he from innocent air
The gentlest breath of resignation drew;
While Venus in a passion of despair
Rent, weeping over him, her golden hair
Spangled with drops of that celestial shower.
She suffered, as Immortals sometimes do;

But pangs more lasting far, *that* Lover knew
20　Who first, weighed down by scorn, in some lone bower
Did press this semblance of unpitied smart
Into the service of his constant heart,
His own dejection, downcast Flower! could share
With thine, and gave the mournful name which thou
　　wilt ever bear.

Companion to the Foregoing

Never enlivened with the liveliest ray
That fosters growth or checks or cheers decay,
Nor by the heaviest rain-drops more deprest,
This Flower, that first appeared as summer's guest,
Preserves her beauty 'mid autumnal leaves
And to her mournful habits fondly cleaves.
When files of stateliest plants have ceased to bloom,
One after one submitting to their doom,
When her coevals each and all are fled,
10　What keeps her thus reclined upon her lonesome bed?

　The old mythologists, more impressed than we
Of this late day by character in tree
Or herb, that claimed peculiar sympathy,
Or by the silent lapse of fountain clear,
Or with the language of the viewless air
By bird or beast made vocal, sought a cause
To solve the mystery, not in Nature's laws
But in Man's fortunes. Hence a thousand tales
Sung to the plaintive lyre in Grecian vales.
20　Nor doubt that something of their spirit swayed
The fancy-stricken Youth or heart-sick Maid,
Who, while each stood companionless and eyed
This undeparting Flower in crimson dyed,
Thought of a wound which death is slow to cure,
A fate that has endured and will endure,
And, patience coveting yet passion feeding,
Called the dejected Lingerer, *Love lies Bleeding*.

A Wren's Nest

Among the dwellings framed by birds
  In field or forest with nice care,
Is none that with the little Wren's
  In snugness may compare.

No door the tenement requires,
  And seldom needs a laboured roof;
Yet is it to the fiercest sun
  Impervious, and storm-proof.

So warm, so beautiful withal
10   In perfect fitness for its aim,
That to the Kind by special grace
  Their instinct surely came.

And when for their abodes they seek
  An opportune recess,
The hermit has no finer eye
  For shadowy quietness.

These find, 'mid ivied abbey-walls,
  A canopy in some still nook;
Others are pent-housed by a brae
20   That overhangs a brook.

There to the brooding bird her mate
  Warbles by fits his low clear song;
And by the busy streamlet both
  Are sung to all day long.

Or in sequestered lanes they build,
  Where, till the flitting bird's return,
Her eggs within the nest repose,
  Like relics in an urn.

But still, where general choice is good,
30 There is a better and a best;
And, among fairest objects, some
  Are fairer than the rest;

This, one of those small builders proved
  In a green covert, where, from out
The forehead of a pollard oak,
  The leafy antlers sprout;

For She who planned the mossy lodge,
  Mistrusting her evasive skill,
Had to a Primrose looked for aid
40 Her wishes to fulfil.

High on the trunk's projecting brow,
  And fixed an infant's span above
The budding flowers, peeped forth the nest
  The prettiest of the grove!

The treasure proudly did I show
  To some whose minds without disdain
Can turn to little things; but once
  Looked up for it in vain:

'Tis gone – a ruthless spoiler's prey,
50 Who heeds not beauty, love, or song,
'Tis gone! (so seemed it) and we grieved
  Indignant at the wrong.

Just three days after, passing by
  In clearer light the moss-built cell
I saw, espied its shaded mouth;
  And felt that all was well.

The Primrose for a veil had spread
  The largest of her upright leaves;
And thus, for purposes benign,
60 A simple flower deceives.

Concealed from friends who might disturb
   Thy quiet with no ill intent,
Secure from evil eyes and hands
   On barbarous plunder bent,

Rest, Mother-bird! and when thy young
   Take flight, and thou art free to roam,
When withered is the guardian Flower,
   And empty thy late home,

Think how ye prospered, thou and thine,
70   Amid the unviolated grove
Housed near the growing Primrose-tuft
   In foresight, or in love.

To a Child Written in Her Album

Small service is true service while it lasts:
Of humblest Friends, bright Creature! scorn not one:
The Daisy, by the shadow that it casts,
Protects the lingering dew-drop from the Sun.

Lines Written in the Album of the Countess of Lonsdale

Lady! a Pen (perhaps with thy regard,
Among the Favoured, favoured not the least)
Left, 'mid the Records of this Book inscribed,
Deliberate traces, registers of thought
And feeling, suited to the place and time
That gave them birth: – months passed, and still this
   hand,
That had not been too timid to imprint
Words which the virtues of thy Lord inspired,
Was yet not bold enough to write of Thee.
10 And why that scrupulous reserve? In sooth
The blameless cause lay in the Theme itself.

Flowers are there many that delight to strive
With the sharp wind, and seem to court the shower,
Yet are by nature careless of the sun
Whether he shine on them or not; and some,
Where'er he moves along the unclouded sky,
Turn a broad front full on his flattering beams:
Others do rather from their notice shrink,
Loving the dewy shade, – a humble band,
20 Modest and sweet, a progeny of earth,
Congenial with thy mind and character,
High-born Augusta!
                    Witness, Towers and Groves!
And Thou, wild Stream, that giv'st the honoured name
Of Lowther to this ancient Line, bear witness
From thy most secret haunts; and ye Parterres,
Which She is pleased and proud to call her own,
Witness how oft upon my noble Friend
Mute offerings, tribute from an inward sense
Of admiration and respectful love,
30 Have waited – till the affections could no more
Endure that silence, and broke out in song,
Snatches of music taken up and dropt
Like those self-solacing, those under, notes
Trilled by the redbreast, when autumnal leaves
Are thin upon the bough. Mine, only mine,
The pleasure was, and no one heard the praise,
Checked, in the moment of its issue, checked
And reprehended, by a fancied blush
From the pure qualities that called it forth.

40   Thus Virtue lives debarred from Virtue's meed;
Thus, Lady, is retiredness a veil
That, while it only spreads a softening charm
O'er features looked at by discerning eyes,
Hides half their beauty from the common gaze;
And thus, even on the exposed and breezy hill
Of lofty station, female goodness walks,
When side by side with lunar gentleness,

As in a cloister. Yet the grateful Poor
(Such the immunities of low estate,
50   Plain Nature's enviable privilege,
Her sacred recompence for many wants)
Open their hearts before Thee, pouring out
All that they think and feel, with tears of joy;
And benedictions not unheard in heaven:
And friend in the ear of friend, where speech is free
To follow truth, is eloquent as they.

Then let the Book receive in these prompt lines
A just memorial; and thine eyes consent
To read that they, who mark thy course, behold
60   A life declining with the golden light
Of summer, in the season of sere leaves;
See cheerfulness undamped by stealing Time;
See studied kindness flow with easy stream,
Illustrated with inborn courtesy;
And an habitual disregard of self
Balanced by vigilance for others' weal.

And shall the Verse not tell of lighter gifts
With these ennobling attributes conjoined
And blended, in peculiar harmony,
70   By Youth's surviving spirit? What agile grace!
A nymph-like liberty, in nymph-like form,
Beheld with wonder; whether floor or path
Thou tread; or sweep – borne on the managed steed –
Fleet as the shadows, over down or field,
Driven by strong winds at play among the clouds.

Yet one word more – one farewell word – a wish
Which came, but it has passed into a prayer –
That, as thy sun in brightness is declining,
So – at an hour yet distant for *their* sakes
80   Whose tender love, here faltering on the way
Of a diviner love, will be forgiven –
So may it set in peace, to rise again
For everlasting glory won by faith.

'Not in the lucid intervals of life'

Not in the lucid intervals of life
That come but as a curse to party-strife;
Not in some hour when Pleasure with a sigh
Of languor puts his rosy garland by;
Not in the breathing-times of that poor slave
Who daily piles up wealth in Mammon's cave –
Is Nature felt, or can be; nor do words,
Which practised talent readily affords,
Prove that her hand has touched responsive chords;
10 Nor has her gentle beauty power to move
With genuine rapture and with fervent love
The soul of Genius, if he dare to take
Life's rule from passion craved for passion's sake;
Untaught that meekness is the cherished bent
Of all the truly great and all the innocent.

    But who *is* innocent? By grace divine,
Not otherwise, O Nature! we are thine,
Through good and evil thine, in just degree
Of rational and manly sympathy.
20 To all that Earth from pensive hearts is stealing,
And Heaven is now to gladdened eyes revealing,
Add every charm the Universe can show
Through every change its aspects undergo –
Care may be respited, but not repealed;
No perfect cure grows on that bounded field.
Vain is the pleasure, a false calm the peace,
If He, through Whom alone our conflicts cease,
Our virtuous hopes without relapse advance,
Come not to speed the Soul's deliverance;
30 To the distempered Intellect refuse
His gracious help, or give what we abuse.

(*By the Side of Rydal Mere*)

The linnet's warble, sinking toward a close,
Hints to the thrush 'tis time for their repose;
The shrill-voiced thrush is heedless, and again
The monitor revives his own sweet strain;
But both will soon be mastered, and the copse
Be left as silent as the mountain-tops,
Ere some commanding star dismiss to rest
The throng of rooks, that now, from twig or nest,
(After a steady flight on home-bound wings,
10 And a last game of mazy hoverings
Around their ancient grove) with cawing noise
Disturb the liquid music's equipoise.

O Nightingale! Who ever heard thy song
Might here be moved, till Fancy grows so strong
That listening sense is pardonably cheated
Where wood or stream by thee was never greeted.
Surely, from fairest spots of favoured lands,
Were not some gifts withheld by jealous hands,
This hour of deepening darkness here would be
20 As a fresh morning for new harmony;
And lays as prompt would hail the dawn of Night:
A *dawn* she has both beautiful and bright,
When the East kindles with the full moon's light;
Not like the rising sun's impatient glow
Dazzling the mountains, but an overflow
Of solemn splendour, in mutation slow.

Wanderer by spring with gradual progress led,
For sway profoundly felt as widely spread;
To king, to peasant, to rough sailor, dear,
30 And to the soldier's trumpet-wearied ear;
How welcome wouldst thou be to this green Vale
Fairer than Tempe! Yet, sweet Nightingale!
From the warm breeze that bears thee on, alight
At will, and stay thy migratory flight;

Build, at thy choice, or sing, by pool or fount,
Who shall complain, or call thee to account?
The wisest, happiest, of our kind are they
That ever walk content with Nature's way,
God's goodness – measuring bounty as it may;
40 For whom the gravest thought of what they miss,
Chastening the fulness of a present bliss,
Is with that wholesome office satisfied,
While unrepining sadness is allied
In thankful bosoms to a modest pride.

'Soft as a cloud is yon blue Ridge'

Soft as a cloud is yon blue Ridge – the Mere
Seems firm as solid crystal, breathless, clear,
And motionless; and, to the gazer's eye,
Deeper than ocean, in the immensity
Of its vague mountains and unreal sky!
But, from the process in that still retreat,
Turn to minuter changes at our feet;
Observe how dewy Twilight has withdrawn
The crowd of daisies from the shaven lawn,
10 And has restored to view its tender green,
That, while the sun rode high, was lost beneath their
    dazzling sheen.
– An emblem this of what the sober Hour
Can do for minds disposed to feel its power!
Thus oft, when we in vain have wished away
The petty pleasures of the garish day,
Meek eve shuts up the whole usurping host
(Unbashful dwarfs each glittering at his post)
And leaves the disencumbered spirit free
To reassume a staid simplicity.

20   'Tis well – but what are helps of time and place,
When wisdom stands in need of nature's grace;
Why do good thoughts, invoked or not, descend,
Like Angels from their bowers, our virtues to befriend;

If yet Tomorrow, unbelied, may say,
'I come to open out, for fresh display,
The elastic vanities of yesterday?'

'The leaves that rustled on this oak-crowned hill'

The leaves that rustled on this oak-crowned hill,
And sky that danced among those leaves, are still;
Rest smooths the way for sleep; in field and bower
Soft shades and dews have shed their blended power
On drooping eyelid and the closing flower;
Sound is there none at which the faintest heart
Might leap, the weakest nerve of superstition start;
Save when the Owlet's unexpected scream
Pierces the ethereal vault; and ('mid the gleam
10   Of unsubstantial imagery, the dream,
From the hushed vale's realities, transferred
To the still lake) the imaginative Bird
Seems, 'mid inverted mountains, not unheard.

Grave Creature! – whether, while the moon shines
      bright
On thy wings opened wide for smoothest flight,
Thou art discovered in a roofless tower,
Rising from what may once have been a lady's bower;
Or spied where thou sitt'st moping in thy mew
At the dim centre of a churchyard yew;
20   Or, from a rifted crag or ivy tod
Deep in a forest, thy secure abode,
Thou giv'st, for pastime's sake, by shriek or shout,
A puzzling notice of thy whereabout –
May the night never come, nor day be seen,
When I shall scorn thy voice or mock thy mien!

In classic ages men perceived a soul
Of sapience in thy aspect, headless Owl!
Thee Athens reverenced in the studious grove;
And, near the golden sceptre grasped by Jove,

30 His Eagle's favourite perch, while round him sate
The Gods revolving the decrees of Fate,
Thou, too, wert present at Minerva's side:
Hark to that second larum! – far and wide
The elements have heard, and rock and cave replied.

The Labourer's Noon-Day Hymn

Up to the throne of God is borne
The voice of praise at early morn,
And He accepts the punctual hymn
Sung as the light of day grows dim.

Nor will He turn his ear aside
From holy offerings at noontide.
Then here reposing let us raise
A song of gratitude and praise.

What though our burden be not light,
10 We need not toil from morn to night;
The respite of the mid-day hour
Is in the thankful Creature's power.

Blest are the moments, doubly blest,
That, drawn from this one hour of rest,
Are with a ready heart bestowed
Upon the service of our God!

Each field is then a hallowed spot,
An altar is in each man's cot,
A church in every grove that spreads
20 Its living roof above our heads.

Look up to Heaven! the industrious Sun
Already half his race hath run;
He cannot halt nor go astray,
But our immortal Spirits may.

Lord! since his rising in the East,
If we have faltered or transgressed,
Guide, from Thy love's abundant source,
What yet remains of this day's course:

Help with Thy grace, through life's short day,
30 Our upward and our downward way;
And glorify for us the west,
Where we shall sink to final rest.

The Redbreast (*Suggested in a Westmoreland Cottage*)

Driven in by Autumn's sharpening air
From half-stripped woods and pastures bare,
Brisk Robin seeks a kindlier home:
Not like a beggar is he come,
But enters as a looked-for guest,
Confiding in his ruddy breast,
As if it were a natural shield
Charged with a blazon on the field,
Due to that good and pious deed
10 Of which we in the Ballad read.
But pensive fancies putting by,
And wild-wood sorrows, speedily
He plays the expert ventriloquist;
And, caught by glimpses now – now missed,
Puzzles the listener with a doubt
If the soft voice he throws about
Comes from within doors or without!
Was ever such a sweet confusion,
Sustained by delicate illusion?
20 He's at your elbow – to your feeling
The notes are from the floor or ceiling;
And there's a riddle to be guessed,
Till you have marked his heaving chest,

And busy throat whose sink and swell
Betray the Elf that loves to dwell
In Robin's bosom, as a chosen cell.

Heart-pleased we smile upon the Bird
If seen, and with like pleasure stirred
Commend him, when he's only heard.
30 But small and fugitive our gain
Compared with *hers* who long hath lain,
With languid limbs and patient head
Reposing on a lone sick-bed;
Where now, she daily hears a strain
That cheats her of too busy cares,
Eases her pain, and helps her prayers.
And who but this dear Bird beguiled
The fever of that pale-faced Child;
Now cooling, with his passing wing,
40 Her forehead, like a breeze of Spring:
Recalling now, with descant soft
Shed round her pillow from aloft,
Sweet thoughts of angels hovering nigh,
And the invisible sympathy
Of 'Matthew, Mark, and Luke, and John,
Blessing the bed she lies upon?'
And sometimes, just as listening ends
In slumber, with the cadence blends
A dream of that low-warbled hymn
50 Which old folk, fondly pleased to trim
Lamps of faith, now burning dim,
Say that the Cherubs carved in stone,
When clouds gave way at dead of night
And the ancient church was filled with light,
Used to sing in heavenly tone,
Above and round the sacred places
They guard, with wingèd baby-faces.

Thrice happy Creature! in all lands
Nurtured by hospitable hands:

60 Free entrance to this cot has he,
Entrance and exit both *yet* free;
And, when the keen unruffled weather
That thus brings man and bird together,
Shall with its pleasantness be past,
And casement closed and door made fast,
To keep at bay the howling blast,
He needs not fear the season's rage,
For the whole house is Robin's cage.
Whether the bird flit here or there,
70 O'er table *lilt*, or perch on chair,
Though some may frown and make a stir,
To scare him as a trespasser,
And he belike will flinch or start,
Good friends he has to take his part;
One chiefly, who with voice and look
Pleads for him from the chimney-nook,
Where sits the Dame, and wears away
Her long and vacant holiday;
With images about her heart,
80 Reflected from the years gone by,
On human nature's second infancy.

Lines Suggested by a Portrait from the Pencil of F. Stone

Beguiled into forgetfulness of care
Due to the day's unfinished task; of pen
Or book regardless, and of that fair scene
In Nature's prodigality displayed
Before my window, oftentimes and long
I gaze upon a Portrait whose mild gleam
Of beauty never ceases to enrich
The common light; whose stillness charms the air,
Or seems to charm it, into like repose;
10 Whose silence, for the pleasure of the ear,
Surpasses sweetest music. There she sits

With emblematic purity attired
In a white vest, white as her marble neck
Is, and the pillar of the throat would be
But for the shadow by the drooping chin
Cast into that recess – the tender shade,
The shade and light, both there and everywhere,
And through the very atmosphere she breathes,
Broad, clear, and toned harmoniously, with skill
20 That might from nature have been learnt in the hour
When the lone shepherd sees the morning spread
Upon the mountains. Look at her, whoe'er
Thou be that, kindling with a poet's soul,
Hast loved the painter's true Promethean craft
Intensely – from Imagination take
The treasure, – what mine eyes behold see thou,
Even though the Atlantic ocean roll between.

A silver line, that runs from brow to crown
And in the middle parts the braided hair,
30 Just serves to show how delicate a soil
The golden harvest grows in; and those eyes,
Soft and capacious as a cloudless sky
Whose azure depth their colour emulates,
Must needs be conversant with upward looks,
Prayer's voiceless service; but now, seeking naught
And shunning naught, their own peculiar life
Of motion they renounce, and with the head
Partake its inclination towards earth
In humble grace, and quiet pensiveness
40 Caught at the point where it stops short of sadness.

Offspring of soul-bewitching Art, make me
Thy confidant! say, whence derived that air
Of calm abstraction? Can the ruling thought
Be with some lover far away, or one
Crossed by misfortune, or of doubted faith?
Inapt conjecture! Childhood here, a moon
Crescent in simple loveliness serene,

Has but approached the gates of womanhood,
Not entered them; her heart is yet unpierced
50   By the blind Archer-god; her fancy free:
The fount of feeling, if unsought elsewhere,
Will not be found.
              Her right hand, as it lies
Across the slender wrist of the left arm
Upon her lap reposing, holds – but mark
How slackly, for the absent mind permits
No firmer grasp – a little wild-flower, joined
As in a posy, with a few pale ears
Of yellowing corn, the same that overtopped
And in their common birthplace sheltered it
60   Till they were plucked together; a blue flower
Called by the thrifty husbandman a weed;
But Ceres, in her garland, might have worn
That ornament, unblamed. The floweret, held
In scarcely conscious fingers, was, she knows,
(Her Father told her so) in youth's gay dawn
Her Mother's favourite; and the orphan Girl,
In her own dawn – a dawn less gay and bright,
Loves it, while there in solitary peace
She sits, for that departed Mother's sake.
70   – Not from a source less sacred is derived
(Surely I do not err) that pensive air
Of calm abstraction through the face diffused
And the whole person.
              Words have something told
More than the pencil can, and verily
More than is needed, but the precious Art
Forgives their interference – Art divine,
That both creates and fixes, in despite
Of Death and Time, the marvels it hath wrought.

Strange contrasts have we in this world of ours!
80   That posture, and the look of filial love
Thinking of past and gone, with what is left
Dearly united, might be swept away

From this fair Portrait's fleshy Archetype,
Even by an innocent fancy's slightest freak
Banished, nor ever, haply, be restored
To their lost place, or meet in harmony
So exquisite; but *here* do they abide,
Enshrined for ages. Is not then the Art
Godlike, a humble branch of the divine,
90 In visible quest of immortality,
Stretched forth with trembling hope? – In every realm,
From high Gibraltar to Siberian plains
Thousands, in each variety of tongue
That Europe knows, would echo this appeal;
One above all, a Monk who waits on God
In the magnific Convent built of yore
To sanctify the Escurial palace. He –
Guiding, from cell to cell and room to room,
A British Painter (eminent for truth
100 In character, and depth of feeling, shown
By labours that have touched the hearts of kings,
And are endeared to simple cottagers) –
Came, in that service, to a glorious work,
Our Lord's Last Supper, beautiful as when first
The appropriate Picture, fresh from Titian's hand,
Graced the Refectory: and there, while both
Stood with eyes fixed upon that masterpiece,
The hoary Father in the Stranger's ear
Breathed out these words: – 'Here daily do we sit,
110 Thanks given to God for daily bread, and here
Pondering the mischiefs of these restless times,
And thinking of my Brethren, dead, dispersed,
Or changed and changing, I not seldom gaze
Upon this solemn Company unmoved
By shock of circumstance, or lapse of years,
Until I cannot but believe that they –
They are in truth the Substance, we the Shadows.'

So spake the mild Jeronymite, his griefs
Melting away within him like a dream

120 Ere he had ceased to gaze, perhaps to speak:
And I, grown old, but in a happier land,
Domestic Portrait! have to verse consigned
In thy calm presence those heart-moving words:
Words that can soothe, more than they agitate;
Whose spirit, like the angel that went down
Into Bethesda's pool, with healing virtue
Informs the fountain in the human breast
Which by the visitation was disturbed.
– But why this stealing tear? Companion mute,
130 On thee I look, not sorrowing; fare thee well,
My Song's Inspirer, once again farewell!

The Foregoing Subject Resumed

Among a grave fraternity of Monks,
For One, but surely not for One alone,
Triumphs, in that great work, the Painter's skill,
Humbling the body, to exalt the soul;
Yet representing, amid wreck and wrong
And dissolution and decay, the warm
And breathing life of flesh, as if already
Clothed with impassive majesty, and graced
With no mean earnest of a heritage
10 Assigned to it in future worlds. Thou, too,
With thy memorial flower, meek Portraiture!
From whose serene companionship I passed
Pursued by thoughts that haunt me still; thou also –
Though but a simple object, into light
Called forth by those affections that endear
The private hearth; though keeping thy sole seat
In singleness, and little tried by time,
Creation, as it were, of yesterday –
With a congenial function art endued
20 For each and all of us, together joined
In course of nature under a low roof
By charities and duties that proceed

Out of the bosom of a wiser vow.
To a like salutary sense of awe
Or sacred wonder, growing with the power
Of meditation that attempts to weigh,
In faithful scales, things and their opposites,
Can thy enduring quiet gently raise
A household small and sensitive, – whose love,
30 Dependent as in part its blessings are
Upon frail ties dissolving or dissolved
On earth, will be revived, we trust, in heaven.

Upon Seeing a Coloured Drawing of the Bird of Paradise in an Album

Who rashly strove thy Image to portray?
Thou buoyant minion of the tropic air;
How could he think of the live creature – gay
With a divinity of colours, drest
In all her brightness, from the dancing crest
Far as the last gleam of the filmy train
Extended and extending to sustain
The motions that it graces – and forbear
To drop his pencil! Flowers of every clime
10 Depicted on these pages smile at time;
And gorgeous insects copied with nice care
Are here, and likenesses of many a shell
Tossed ashore by restless waves,
Or in the diver's grasp fetched up from caves
Where sea-nymphs might be proud to dwell:
But whose rash hand (again I ask) could dare,
'Mid casual tokens and promiscuous shows,
To circumscribe this Shape in fixed repose;
Could imitate for indolent survey,
20 Perhaps for touch profane,
Plumes that might catch, but cannot keep; a stain;
And, with cloud-streaks lightest and loftiest, share
The sun's first greeting, his last farewell ray!

Resplendent Wanderer! followed with glad eyes
Where'er her course; mysterious Bird!
To whom, by wondering Fancy stirred,
Eastern Islanders have given
A holy name – the Bird of Heaven!
And even a title higher still,
30 The Bird of God! whose blessed will
She seems performing as she flies
Over the earth and through the skies
In never-wearied search of Paradise –
Region that crowns her beauty with the name
She bears for *us* – for us how blest,
How happy at all seasons, could like aim
Uphold our Spirits urged to kindred flight
On wings that fear no glance of God's pure sight,
No tempest from His breath, their promised rest
40 Seeking with indefatigable quest
Above a world that deems itself most wise
When most enslaved by gross realities!

Airey-Force Valley

————— Not a breath of air
Ruffles the bosom of this leafy glen.
From the brook's margin, wide around, the trees
Are stedfast as the rocks; the brook itself,
Old as the hills that feed it from afar,
Doth rather deepen than disturb the calm
Where all things else are still and motionless.
And yet, even now, a little breeze, perchance
Escaped from boisterous winds that rage without,
10 Has entered, by the sturdy oaks unfelt,
But to its gentle touch how sensitive
Is the light ash! that, pendent from the brow
Of yon dim cave, in seeming silence makes
A soft eye-music of slow-waving boughs,
Powerful almost as vocal harmony
To stay the wanderer's steps and soothe his thoughts.

Written after the Death of Charles Lamb

To a good Man of most dear memory
This Stone is sacred. Here he lies apart
From the great city where he first drew breath,
Was reared and taught; and humbly earned his bread,
To the strict labours of the merchant's desk
By duty chained. Not seldom did those tasks
Tease, and the thought of time so spent depress,
His spirit, but the recompence was high;
Firm Independence, Bounty's rightful sire;
10 Affections, warm as sunshine, free as air;
And when the precious hours of leisure came,
Knowledge and wisdom, gained from converse sweet
With books, or while he ranged the crowded streets
With a keen eye, and overflowing heart:
So genius triumphed over seeming wrong,
And poured out truth in works by thoughtful love
Inspired – works potent over smiles and tears.
And as round mountain-tops the lightning plays,
Thus innocently sported, breaking forth
20 As from a cloud of some grave sympathy,
Humour and wild instinctive wit, and all
The vivid flashes of his spoken words.
From the most gentle creature nursed in fields
Had been derived the name he bore – a name,
Wherever Christian altars have been raised,
Hallowed to meekness and to innocence;
And if in him meekness at times gave way,
Provoked out of herself by troubles strange,
Many and strange, that hung about his life;
30 Still, at the centre of his being, lodged
A soul by resignation sanctified:
And if too often, self-reproached, he felt
That innocence belongs not to our kind,
A power that never ceased to abide in him,
Charity, 'mid the multitude of sins

That she can cover, left not his exposed
To an unforgiving judgement from just Heaven.
O, he was good, if e'er a good Man lived!

  • • • • • •

From a reflecting mind and sorrowing heart
40 Those simple lines flowed with an earnest wish,
Though but a doubting hope, that they might serve
Fitly to guard the precious dust of him
Whose virtues called them forth. That aim is missed;
For much that truth most urgently required
Had from a faltering pen been asked in vain:
Yet, haply, on the printed page received,
The imperfect record, there, may stand unblamed
As long as verse of mine shall breathe the air
Of memory, or see the light of love.

50 Thou wert a scorner of the fields, my Friend,
But more in show than truth; and from the fields,
And from the mountains, to thy rural grave
Transported, my soothed spirit hovers o'er
Its green untrodden turf, and blowing flowers;
And taking up a voice shall speak (though still
Awed by the theme's peculiar sanctity
Which words less free presumed not even to touch)
Of that fraternal love, whose heaven-lit lamp
From infancy, through manhood, to the last
60 Of threescore years, and to thy latest hour,
Burned on with ever-strengthening light, enshrined
Within thy bosom.
      'Wonderful' hath been
The love established between man and man,
'Passing the love of women;' and between
Man and his help-mate in fast wedlock joined
Through God, is raised a spirit and soul of love
Without whose blissful influence Paradise
Had been no Paradise; and earth were now
A waste where creatures bearing human form,

70 Direst of savage beasts, would roam in fear,
Joyless and comfortless. Our days glide on;
And let him grieve who cannot choose but grieve
That he hath been an Elm without his Vine,
And her bright dower of clustering charities,
That, round his trunk and branches, might have clung
Enriching and adorning. Unto thee,
Not so enriched, not so adorned, to thee
Was given (say rather thou of later birth
Wert given to her) a Sister – 'tis a word
80 Timidly uttered, for she *lives*, the meek,
The self-restraining, and the ever-kind;
In whom thy reason and intelligent heart
Found – for all interests, hopes, and tender cares,
All softening, humanizing, hallowing powers,
Whether withheld, or for her sake unsought –
More than sufficient recompence!
                             Her love
(What weakness prompts the voice to tell it here?)
Was as the love of mothers; and when years,
Lifting the boy to man's estate, had called
90 The long-protected to assume the part
Of a protector, the first filial tie
Was undissolved; and, in or out of sight,
Remained imperishably interwoven
With life itself. Thus, 'mid a shifting world,
Did they together testify of time
And season's difference – a double tree
With two collateral stems sprung from one root;
Such were they – such through life they *might* have been
In union, in partition only such;
100 Otherwise wrought the will of the Most High;
Yet, through all visitations and all trials,
Still they were faithful; like two vessels launched
From the same beach one ocean to explore
With mutual help, and sailing – to their league
True, as inexorable winds, or bars
Floating or fixed of polar ice, allow.

But turn we rather, let my spirit turn
With thine, O silent and invisible Friend!
To those dear intervals, nor rare nor brief,
110 When reunited, and by choice withdrawn
From miscellaneous converse, ye were taught
That the remembrance of foregone distress,
And the worse fear of future ill (which oft
Doth hang around it, as a sickly child
Upon its mother) may be both alike
Disarmed of power to unsettle present good
So prized, and things inward and outward held
In such an even balance, that the heart
Acknowledges God's grace, His mercy feels,
120 And in its depth of gratitude is still.

O gift divine of quiet sequestration!
The hermit, exercised in prayer and praise,
And feeding daily on the hope of heaven,
Is happy in his vow, and fondly cleaves
To life-long singleness; but happier far
Was to your souls, and, to the thoughts of others,
A thousand times more beautiful appeared,
Your *dual* loneliness. The sacred tie
Is broken; yet why grieve? for Time but holds
130 His moiety in trust, till Joy shall lead
To the blest world where parting is unknown.

Extempore Effusion upon the Death of
James Hogg

When first, descending from the moorlands,
I saw the Stream of Yarrow glide
Along a bare and open valley,
The Ettrick Shepherd was my guide.

When last along its banks I wandered,
Through groves that had begun to shed

Their golden leaves upon the pathways,
My steps the Border-minstrel led.

The mighty Minstrel breathes no longer,
10 'Mid mouldering ruins low he lies;
And death upon the braes of Yarrow,
Has closed the Shepherd-poet's eyes:

Nor has the rolling year twice measured,
From sign to sign, its stedfast course,
Since every mortal power of Coleridge
Was frozen at its marvellous source;

The rapt One, of the godlike forehead,
The heaven-eyed creature sleeps in earth:
And Lamb, the frolic and the gentle,
20 Has vanished from his lonely hearth.

Like clouds that rake the mountain-summits,
Or waves that own no curbing hand,
How fast has brother followed brother,
From sunshine to the sunless land!

Yet I, whose lids from infant slumber
Were earlier raised, remain to hear
A timid voice, that asks in whispers,
'Who next will drop and disappear?'

Our haughty life is crowned with darkness,
30 Like London with its own black wreath,
On which with thee, O Crabbe! forth-looking,
I gazed from Hampstead's breezy heath.

As if but yesterday departed,
Thou too art gone before; but why,
O'er ripe fruit, seasonably gathered,
Should frail survivors heave a sigh?

Mourn rather for that holy Spirit,
Sweet as the spring, as ocean deep;
For Her who, ere her summer faded,
40 Has sunk into a breathless sleep.

No more of old romantic sorrows,
For slaughtered Youth or love-lorn Maid!
With sharper grief is Yarrow smitten,
And Ettrick mourns with her their Poet dead.

*[A Cento Made by Wordsworth]

[For printing the following Piece, some reason should be given,
as not a word of it is original: it is simply a fine stanza of Akenside, connected with a still finer from Beattie, by a couplet of
Thomson. This practise, in which the author sometimes indul-
ges, of linking together, in his own mind, favourite passages
from different authors, seems in itself unobjectionable; but, as
the *publishing* such compilations might lead to confusion in
literature, he should deem himself inexcusable in giving this
specimen, were it not from a hope that it might open to others
a harmless source of *private* gratification.]

Throned in the Sun's descending car
What Power unseen diffuses far
This tenderness of mind?
What Genius smiles on yonder flood?
What God in whispers from the wood
Bids every thought be kind?

O ever-pleasing Solitude,
Companion of the wise and good,
Thy shades, thy silence, now be mine,
    Thy charms my only theme;
My haunt the hollow cliff whose Pine
    Waves o'er the gloomy stream;
Whence the sacred Owl on pinions grey
    Breaks from the rustling boughs,
And down the lone vale sails away
    To more profound repose!

'*By a blest Husband guided, Mary came*'

By a blest Husband guided, Mary came
From nearest kindred, Vernon her new name;
She came, though meek of soul, in seemly pride
Of happiness and hope, a youthful Bride.
O dread reverse! if aught *be* so, which proves
That God will chasten whom He dearly loves.
Faith bore her up through pains in mercy given,
And troubles that were each a step to Heaven:
Two Babes were laid in earth before she died;
10 A third now slumbers at the Mother's side;
Its Sister-twin survives, whose smiles afford
A trembling solace to her widowed Lord.

    Reader! if to thy bosom cling the pain
Of recent sorrow combated in vain;
Or if thy cherished grief have failed to thwart
Time still intent on his insidious part,
Lulling the mourner's best good thoughts asleep,
Pilfering regrets we would, but cannot, keep;
Bear with Him – judge *Him* gently who makes known
20 His bitter loss by this memorial Stone;
And pray that in his faithful breast the grace
Of resignation find a hallowed place.

Roman Antiquities Discovered at Bishopstone, Herefordshire

While poring Antiquarians search the ground
Upturned with curious pains, the Bard, a Seer,
Takes fire: – The men that have been reappear;
Romans for travel girt, for business gowned;
And some recline on couches, myrtle-crowned,
In festal glee: why not? For fresh and clear,
As if its hues were of the passing year,

Dawns this time-buried pavement. From that mound
Hoards may come forth of Trajans, Maximins,
10   Shrunk into coins with all their warlike toil:
Or a fierce impress issues with its foil
Of tenderness – the Wolf, whose suckling Twins
The unlettered ploughboy pities when he wins
The casual treasure from the furrowed soil.

St Catherine of Ledbury

When human touch (as monkish books attest)
Nor was applied nor could be, Ledbury bells
Broke forth in concert flung adown the dells,
And upward, high as Malvern's cloudy crest;
Sweet tones, and caught by a noble Lady blest
To rapture! Mabel listened at the side
Of her loved mistress: soon the music died,
And Catherine said, *Here I set up my rest.*
Warned in a dream, the Wanderer long had sought
10   A home that by such miracle of sound
Must be revealed: – she heard it now, or felt
The deep, deep joy of a confiding thought;
And there, a saintly Anchoress, she dwelt
Till she exchanged for heaven that happy ground.

'Desponding Father! mark this altered bough'

Desponding Father! mark this altered bough,
So beautiful of late, with sunshine warmed,
Or moist with dews; what more unsightly now,
Its blossoms shrivelled, and its fruit, if formed,
Invisible? yet Spring her genial brow
Knits not o'er that discolouring and decay
As false to expectation. Nor fret thou
At like unlovely process in the May
Of human life: a Stripling's graces blow,

10 Fade and are shed, that from their timely fall
(Misdeem it not a cankerous change) may grow
Rich mellow bearings, that for thanks shall call:
In all men, sinful is it to be slow
To hope – in Parents, sinful above all.

'Four fiery steeds impatient of the rein'

Four fiery steeds impatient of the rein
Whirled us o'er sunless ground beneath a sky
As void of sunshine, when, from that wide plain,
Clear tops of far-off mountains we descry,
Like a Sierra of cerulean Spain,
All light and lustre. Did no heart reply?
Yes, there was One; – for One, asunder fly
The thousand links of that ethereal chain;
And green vales open out, with grove and field,
10 And the fair front of many a happy Home;
Such tempting spots as into vision come
While Soldiers, weary of the arms they wield
And sick at heart of strifeful Christendom,
Gaze on the moon by parting clouds revealed.

To ————

'Miss not the occasion: by the forelock take
That subtle Power, the never-halting Time,
Lest a mere moment's putting-off should make
Mischance almost as heavy as a crime.'

'Wait, prithee, wait!' this answer Lesbia threw
Forth to her Dove, and took no further heed.
Her eye was busy, while her fingers flew
Across the harp, with soul-engrossing speed;
But from that bondage when her thoughts were freed
She rose, and toward the close-shut casement drew,
Whence the poor unregarded Favourite, true
To old affections, had been heard to plead

With flapping wing for entrance. What a shriek
10 Forced from that voice so lately tuned to a strain
Of harmony! – a shriek of terror, pain,
And self-reproach! for, from aloft, a Kite
Pounced, – and the Dove, which from its ruthless beak
She could not rescue, perished in her sight!

To the Moon (Composed by the Seaside, – on the Coast of Cumberland)

Wanderer! that stoop'st so low, and com'st so near
To human life's unsettled atmosphere;
Who lov'st with Night and Silence to partake,
So might it seem, the cares of them that wake;
And, through the cottage-lattice softly peeping,
Dost shield from harm the humblest of the sleeping;
What pleasure once encompassed those sweet names
Which yet in thy behalf the Poet claims,
An idolizing dreamer as of yore! –
10 I slight them all; and, on this sea-beat shore
Sole-sitting, only can to thoughts attend
That bid me hail thee as the SAILOR'S FRIEND;
So call thee for heaven's grace through thee made known
By confidence supplied and mercy shown,
When not a twinkling star or beacon's light
Abates the perils of a stormy night;
And for less obvious benefits, that find
Their way, with thy pure help, to heart and mind;
Both for the adventurer starting in life's prime;
20 And veteran ranging round from clime to clime,
Long-baffled hope's slow fever in his veins,
And wounds and weakness oft his labour's sole remains.

   The aspiring Mountains and the winding Streams,
Empress of Night! are gladdened by thy beams;
A look of thine the wilderness pervades,
And penetrates the forest's inmost shades;

Thou, chequering peaceably the minster's gloom,
Guid'st the pale Mourner to the lost one's tomb;
Canst reach the Prisoner – to his grated cell
30 Welcome, though silent and intangible! –
And lives there one, of all that come and go
On the great waters toiling to and fro,
One, who has watched thee at some quiet hour
Enthroned aloft in undisputed power,
Or crossed by vapoury streaks and clouds that move
Catching the lustre they in part reprove –
Nor sometimes felt a fitness in thy sway
To call up thoughts that shun the glare of day,
And make the serious happier than the gay?

40   Yes, lovely Moon! if thou so mildly bright
Dost rouse, yet surely in thy own despite,
To fiercer mood the frenzy-stricken brain,
Let me a compensating faith maintain;
That there's a sensitive, a tender, part
Which thou canst touch in every human heart,
For healing and composure. – But, as least
And mightiest billows ever have confessed
Thy domination; as the whole vast Sea
Feels through her lowest depths thy sovereignty;
50 So shines that countenance with especial grace
On them who urge the keel her *plains* to trace
Furrowing its way right onward. The most rude,
Cut off from home and country, may have stood –
Even till long gazing hath bedimmed his eye,
Or the mute rapture ended in a sigh –
Touched by accordance of thy placid cheer,
With some internal lights to memory dear,
Or fancies stealing forth to soothe the breast
Tired with its daily share of earth's unrest, –
60 Gentle awakenings, visitations meek;
A kindly influence whereof few will speak,
Though it can wet with tears the hardiest cheek.

And when thy beauty in the shadowy cave
Is hidden, buried in its monthly grave;
Then, while the Sailor, 'mid an open sea
Swept by a favouring wind that leaves thought free,
Paces the deck – no star perhaps in sight,
And nothing save the moving ship's own light
To cheer the long dark hours of vacant night –
70 Oft with his musings does thy image blend,
In his mind's eye thy crescent horns ascend,
And thou art still, O Moon, that SAILOR'S FRIEND!

To the Moon (*Rydal*)

Queen of the stars! – so gentle, so benign,
That ancient Fable did to thee assign,
When darkness creeping o'er thy silver brow
Warned thee these upper regions to forego,
Alternate empire in the shades below –
A Bard, who, lately near the wide-spread sea
Traversed by gleaming ships, looked up to thee
With grateful thoughts, doth now thy rising hail
From the close confines of a shadowy vale.
10 Glory of night, conspicuous yet serene,
Nor less attractive when by glimpses seen
Through cloudy umbrage, well might that fair face,
And all those attributes of modest grace,
In days when Fancy wrought unchecked by fear,
Down to the green earth fetch thee from thy sphere,
To sit in leafy woods by fountains clear!

O still beloved (for thine, meek Power, are charms
That fascinate the very Babe in arms,
While he, uplifted towards thee, laughs outright,
20 Spreading his little palms in his glad Mother's sight)
O still beloved, once worshipped! Time, that frowns
In his destructive flight on earthly crowns,
Spares thy mild splendour; still those far-shot beams
Tremble on dancing waves and rippling streams

With stainless touch, as chaste as then thy praise
Was sung by Virgin-choirs in festal lays;
And through dark trials still dost thou explore
Thy way for increase punctual as of yore,
When teeming Matrons – yielding to rude faith
30 In mysteries of birth and life and death
And painful struggle and deliverance – prayed
Of thee to visit then with lenient aid.
What though the rites be swept away, the fanes
Extinct that echoed to the votive strains;
Yet thy mild aspect does not, cannot, cease
Love to promote and purity and peace;
And Fancy, unreproved, even yet may trace
Faint types of suffering in thy beamless face.

Then, silent Monitress! let us – not blind
40 To worlds unthought of till the searching mind
Of Science laid them open to mankind –
Told, also, how the voiceless heavens declare
God's glory; and acknowledging thy share
In that blest charge; let us – without offence
To aught of highest, holiest, influence –
Receive whatever good 'tis given thee to dispense.
May sage and simple, catching with one eye
The moral intimations of the sky,
Learn from thy course, where'er their own be taken,
50 'To look on tempests, and be never shaken;'
To keep with faithful step the appointed way
Eclipsing or eclipsed, by night or day,
And from example of thy monthly range
Gently to brook decline and fatal change;
Meek, patient, stedfast, and with loftier scope,
Than thy revival yields, for gladsome hope!

November, 1836

Even so for me a Vision sanctified
The sway of Death; long ere mine eyes had seen
Thy countenance – the still rapture of thy mien –
When thou, dear Sister! wert become Death's Bride:
No trace of pain or languor could abide
That change: – age on thy brow was smoothed – thy cold
Wan cheek at once was privileged to unfold
A loveliness to living youth denied.
Oh! if within me hope should e'er decline,
10   The lamp of faith, lost Friend! too faintly burn;
Then may that heaven-revealing smile of thine,
The bright assurance, visibly return:
And let my spirit in that power divine
Rejoice, as, through that power, it ceased to mourn.

[*Epigram on an Event in Col. Evans's Redoubted Performances in Spain*]

The ball whizzed by, – It grazed his Ear,
   And whispered as it flew: –
'I touch – not take, so do not fear
For both, my valiant buccaneer!
   Are to the Pillory due.'

At Bologna, in Remembrance of the Late Insurrections, 1837

Ah why deceive ourselves! by no mere fit
Of sudden passion roused shall men attain
True freedom where for ages they have lain
Bound in a dark abominable pit,
With life's best sinews more and more unknit.

Here, there, a banded few who loathe the chain
May rise to break it: effort worse than vain
For thee, O great Italian nation, split
Into those jarring fractions. – Let thy scope
10   Be one fixed mind for all; thy rights approve
To thy own conscience gradually renewed;
Learn to make Time the father of wise Hope;
Then trust thy cause to the arm of Fortitude,
The light of Knowledge, and the warmth of Love.

At Bologna, in Remembrance of the Late Insurrections, 1837, continued

Hard task! exclaim the undisciplined, to lean
On Patience coupled with such slow endeavour,
That long-lived servitude must last for ever,
Perish the grovelling few, who, prest between
Wrongs and the terror of redress, would wean
Millions from glorious aims. Our chains to sever
Let us break forth in tempest now or never! –
What, is there then no space for golden mean
And gradual progress? – Twilight leads to day,
10   And, even within the burning zones of earth,
The hastiest sunrise yields a temperate ray;
The softest breeze to fairest flowers gives birth:
Think not that Prudence dwells in dark abodes,
She scans the future with the eye of gods.

At Bologna, in Remembrance of the Late Insurrections, 1837, concluded

As leaves are to the tree whereon they grow
And wither, every human generation
Is to the Being of a mighty nation,
Locked in our world's embrace through weal and woe;
Thought that should teach the zealot to forego

Rash schemes, to abjure all selfish agitation,
And seek through noiseless pains and moderation
The unblemished good they only can bestow.
Alas! with most, who weigh futurity
10   Against time present, passion holds the scales:
Hence equal ignorance of both prevails,
And nations sink; or, struggling to be free,
Are doomed to flounder on, like wounded whales
Tossed on the bosom of a stormy sea.

'Oh what a Wreck! how changed in mien and speech'

Oh what a Wreck! how changed in mien and speech!
Yet – though dread Powers, that work in mystery, spin
Entanglings of the brain; though shadows stretch
O'er the chilled heart – reflect; far, far within
Hers is a holy Being, freed from Sin.
She is not what she seems, a forlorn wretch,
But delegated Spirits comfort fetch
To Her from heights that Reason may not win.
Like Children, She is privileged to hold
10   Divine communion; both to live and move,
Whate'er to shallow Faith their ways unfold,
Inly illumined by Heaven's pitying love;
Love pitying innocence, not long to last,
In them – in Her our sins and sorrows past.

A Night Thought

Lo! where the Moon along the sky
Sails with her happy destiny;
Oft is she hid from mortal eye
          Or dimly seen,
But when the clouds asunder fly
          How bright her mien!

Far different we – a froward race,
Thousands though rich in Fortune's grace
With cherished sullenness of pace
        Their way pursue,
Ingrates who wear a smileless face
        The whole year through.

If kindred humours e'er would make
My spirit droop for drooping's sake,
From Fancy following in thy wake,
        Bright ship of heaven!
A counter impulse let me take
        And be forgiven.

The Widow on Windermere Side

I
How beautiful when up a lofty height
Honour ascends among the humblest poor,
And feeling sinks as deep! See there the door
Of One, a Widow, left beneath a weight
Of blameless debt. On evil Fortune's spite
She wasted no complaint, but strove to make
A just repayment, both for conscience-sake
And that herself and hers should stand upright
In the world's eye. Her work when daylight failed
Paused not, and through the depth of night she kept
Such earnest vigils, that belief prevailed
With some, the noble Creature never slept;
But, one by one, the hand of death assailed
Her children from her inmost heart bewept.

II
The Mother mourned, nor ceased her tears to flow,
Till a winter's noon-day placed her buried Son
Before her eyes, last child of many gone –
His raiment of angelic white, and lo!

His very feet bright as the dazzling snow
20 Which they are touching; yea far brighter, even
As that which comes, or seems to come, from heaven,
Surpasses aught these elements can show.
Much she rejoiced, trusting that from that hour
Whate'er befell she could not grieve or pine;
But the Transfigured, in and out of season,
Appeared, and spiritual presence gained a power
Over material forms that mastered reason.
Oh, gracious Heaven, in pity make her thine!

III

But why that prayer? as if to her could come
30 No good but by the way that leads to bliss
Through Death, – so judging we should judge amiss.
Since reason failed want is her threatened doom,
Yet frequent transports mitigate the gloom:
Nor of those maniacs is she one that kiss
The air or laugh upon a precipice;
No, passing through strange sufferings towards the tomb,
She smiles as if a martyr's crown were won:
Oft, when light breaks through clouds or waving trees,
With outspread arms and fallen upon her knees
40 The Mother hails in her descending Son
An Angel, and in earthly ecstasies
Her own angelic glory seems begun.

'Lo! where she stands fixed in a saint-like trance'

'Lo! where she stands fixed in a saint-like trance,
One upward hand, as if she needed rest
From rapture, lying softly on her breast!
Nor wants her eyeball an ethereal glance;
But not the less – nay more – that countenance,
While thus illumined, tells of painful strife
For a sick heart made weary of this life
By love, long crossed with adverse circumstance.

– Would She were now as when she hoped to pass
10 At God's appointed hour to them who tread
Heaven's sapphire pavement, yet breathed well content,
Well pleased, her foot should print earth's common grass,
Lived thankful for day's light, for daily bread,
For health, and time in obvious duty spent.'

To the Planet Venus

Upon its approximation (as an Evening Star) to the Earth, January, 1838.

What strong allurement draws, what spirit guides,
Thee, Vesper! brightening still, as if the nearer
Thou com'st to man's abode the spot grew dearer
Night after night? True is it Nature hides
Her treasures less and less. – Man now presides
In power, where once he trembled in his weakness;
Science advances with gigantic strides;
But are we aught enriched in love and meekness?
Aught dost thou see, bright Star! of pure and wise
10 More than in humbler times graced human story;
That makes our hearts more apt to sympathize
With heaven, our souls more fit for future glory,
When earth shall vanish from our closing eyes,
Ere we lie down in our last dormitory?

'Said Secrecy to Cowardice and Fraud'

Said Secrecy to Cowardice and Fraud,
Falsehood and Treachery, in close council met,
Deep under ground, in Pluto's cabinet,
'The frost of England's pride will soon be thawed;
Hooded the open brow that overawed
Our schemes; the faith and honour, never yet
By us with hope encountered, be upset; –
For once I burst my bands, and cry, applaud!'

Then whispered she, 'The Bill is carrying out!'
10 They heard, and, starting up, the Brood of Night
Clapped hands, and shook with glee their matted locks;
All Powers and Places that abhor the light
Joined in the transport, echoed back their shout,
Hurrah for ——, hugging his Ballot-box!

[*A Squib on Colonel Evans*]

Said red-ribboned Evans:
'My legion in Spain
Were at sixes and sevens;
Now they're famished or slain!
But no fault of mine,
For like brave Philip Sidney
In campaigning I shine,
A true Knight of his Kidney.
Sound flogging and fighting
10 No Chief, on my troth,
E'er took such delight in
As I in them both.
Fontarabbia can tell
How my eyes watched the foe,
Hernani knows well
That our feet were not slow;
Our hospitals, too,
Are matchless in story;
Where her thousands fate slew,
20 All panting for glory.'
Alas for this Hero!
His fame touched the skies,
Then fell below Zero,
Never, never to rise!
For him to Westminster
Did Prudence convey,
There safe as a Spinster
The Patriot to play.

But why be so glib on
30   His feats, or his fall?
He's got his red ribbon,
And laughs at us all.

'Hark! 'tis the Thrush, undaunted, undeprest'

Hark! 'tis the Thrush, undaunted, undeprest,
By twilight premature of cloud and rain;
Nor does that roaring wind deaden his strain
Who carols thinking of his Love and nest,
And seems, as more incited, still more blest.
Thanks; thou hast snapped a fireside Prisoner's chain,
Exulting Warbler! eased a fretted brain,
And in a moment charmed my cares to rest.
Yes, I will forth, bold Bird! and front the blast,
10 That we may sing together, if thou wilt,
So loud, so clear, my Partner through life's day,
Mute in her nest love-chosen, if not love-built
Like thine, shall gladden, as in seasons past,
Thrilled by loose snatches of the social Lay.

Composed on a May Morning, 1838

Life with yon Lambs, like day, is just begun,
Yet Nature seems to them a heavenly guide.
Does joy approach? they meet the coming tide;
And sullenness avoid, as now they shun
Pale twilight's lingering glooms, – and in the sun
Couch near their dams, with quiet satisfied;
Or gambol – each with his shadow at his side,
Varying its shape wherever he may run.
As they from turf yet hoar with sleepy dew
10 All turn, and court the shining and the green,
Where herbs look up, and opening flowers are seen;
Why to God's goodness cannot We be true,
And so, His gifts and promises between,
Feed to the last on pleasures ever new?

A Plea for Authors, May 1838

Failing impartial measure to dispense
To every suitor, Equity is lame;
And social Justice, stript of reverence
For natural rights, a mockery and a shame;
Law but a servile dupe of false pretence,
If, guarding grossest things from common claim
Now and for ever, She, to works that came
From mind and spirit, grudge a short-lived fence.
'What! lengthened privilege, a lineal tie,
10 For *Books*!' Yes, heartless Ones, or be it proved
That 'tis a fault in Us to have lived and loved
Like others, with like temporal hopes to die;
No public harm that Genius from her course
Be turned; and streams of truth dried up, even at their
    source!

A Poet to His Grandchild
Sequel to 'A Plea for Authors'

'Son of my buried Son, while thus thy hand
Is clasping mine, it saddens me to think
How Want may press thee down, and with thee sink
Thy Children left unfit, through vain demand
Of culture, even to feel or understand
My simplest Lay that to their memory
May cling; – hard fate! which haply need not be
Did Justice mould the Statutes of the Land.
A Book time-cherished and an honoured name
10 Are high rewards; but bound they nature's claim
Or Reason's? No – hopes spun in timid line
From out the bosom of a modest home
Extend through unambitious years to come,
My careless Little-one, for thee and thine!'

'*Blest Statesman He, whose Mind's unselfish will*'

Blest Statesman He, whose Mind's unselfish will
Leaves him at ease among grand thoughts: whose eye
Sees that, apart from magnanimity,
Wisdom exists not; nor the humbler skill
Of Prudence, disentangling good and ill
With patient care. What though assaults run high,
They daunt not him who holds his ministry,
Resolute, at all hazards, to fulfil
Its duties; – prompt to move, but firm to wait, –
10 Knowing, things rashly sought are rarely found;
That, for the functions of an ancient State –
Strong by her charters, free because imbound,
Servant of Providence, not slave of Fate –
Perilous is sweeping change, all chance unsound.

''*Tis He whose yester-evening's high disdain*'

'Tis He whose yester-evening's high disdain
Beat back the roaring storm – but how subdued
His day-break note, a sad vicissitude!
Does the hour's drowsy weight his glee restrain?
Or, like the nightingale, her joyous vein
Pleased to renounce, does this dear Thrush attune
His voice to suit the temper of yon Moon
Doubly depressed, setting, and in her wane?
Rise, tardy Sun! and let the Songster prove
10 (The balance trembling between night and morn
No longer) with what ecstasy upborne
He can pour forth his spirit. In heaven above,
And earth below, they best can serve true gladness
Who meet most feelingly the calls of sadness.

Valedictory Sonnet

Closing the Volume of Sonnets published in 1838.

Serving no haughty Muse, my hands have here
Disposed some cultured Flowerets (drawn from spots
Where they bloomed singly, or in scattered knots),
Each kind in several beds of one parterre;
Both to allure the casual Loiterer,
And that, so placed, my Nurslings may requite
Studious regard with opportune delight,
Nor be unthanked, unless I fondly err.
But metaphor dismissed, and thanks apart,
10 Reader, farewell! My last words let them be –
If in this book Fancy and Truth agree;
If simple Nature trained by careful Art
Through It have won a passage to thy heart;
Grant me thy love, I crave no other fee!

Protest against the Ballot

Forth rushed, from Envy sprung and Self-conceit,
A Power misnamed the SPIRIT of REFORM,
And through the astonished Island swept in storm,
Threatening to lay all Orders at her feet
That crossed her way. Now stoops she to entreat
Licence to hide at intervals her head,
Where she may work, safe, undisquieted,
In a close BOX, covert for Justice meet.
St George of England! keep a watchful eye
10 Fixed on the Suitor; frustrate her request –
Stifle her hope; for, if the the State comply,
From such Pandorian gift may come a Pest
Worse than the Dragon that bowed low his crest,
Pierced by thy spear in glorious victory.

[*Inscription on a Rock at Rydal Mount*]

Wouldst thou be gathered to Christ's chosen flock,
Shun the broad way too easily explored,
And let thy path be hewn out of the Rock,
The living Rock of God's eternal Word.

[*Sonnet to a Picture by Lucca Giordano in the Museo Borbonico at Naples*]

A sad and lovely face, with upturned eyes,
Tearless, yet full of grief. – How heavenly fair
How saintlike is the look those features wear!
Such sorrow is more lovely in its guise
Than joy itself – for underneath it lies
A calmness that betokens strength to bear
Earth's petty grievances – its toil and care: –
A spirit that can look through clouded skies,
And see the blue beyond. – Type of that grace
That lit *Her* holy features, from whose womb
Issued the blest Redeemer of our race –
How little dost thou speak of earthly gloom!
As little as the unblemished Queen of Night,
When envious clouds shut out her silver light.

'*Men of the Western World! in Fate's dark book*'

Men of the Western World! in Fate's dark book
Whence these opprobrious leaves of dire portent?
Think ye your British Ancestors forsook
Their native Land, for outrage provident;
From unsubmissive necks the bridle shook
To give, in their Descendants, freer vent
And wider range to passions turbulent,
To mutual tyranny a deadlier look?

Nay, said a voice, soft as the south wind's breath,
10 Dive through the stormy surface of the flood
To the great current flowing underneath;
Explore the countless springs of silent good;
So shall the truth be better understood,
And thy grieved Spirit brighten strong in faith.

'More may not be by human Art exprest'

More may not be by human Art exprest,
But Love, far mightier Power, can add the rest,
Add to the picture which those lines present
All that is wanting for my heart's content:
The braided hair a majesty displays
Of brow that thinks and muses while I gaze,
And O what meekness in those lips that share
A seeming intercourse with vital air,
Such faint sweet sign of life as Nature shows
10 A sleeping infant or the breathing rose;
And in that eye where others gladly see
Earth's purest light Heaven opens upon me.

Sonnets upon the Punishment of Death

In Series

I SUGGESTED BY THE VIEW OF LANCASTER CASTLE
(ON THE ROAD FROM THE SOUTH)

This Spot – at once unfolding sight so fair
Of sea and land, with yon grey towers that still
Rise up as if to lord it over air –
Might soothe in human breasts the sense of ill,
Or charm it out of memory; yea, might fill
The heart with joy and gratitude to God
For all His bounties upon man bestowed:
Why bears it then the name of 'Weeping Hill'?

Thousands, as toward yon old Lancastrian Towers,
10   A prison's crown, along this way they passed
For lingering durance or quick death with shame,
From this bare eminence thereon have cast
Their first look – blinded as tears fell in showers
Shed on their chains; and hence that doleful name.

II
Tenderly do we feel by Nature's law
For worst offenders: though the heart will heave
With indignation, deeply moved we grieve,
In afterthought, for Him who stood in awe
Neither of God nor man, and only saw,
Lost wretch, a horrible device enthroned
On proud temptations, till the victim groaned
Under the steel his hand had dared to draw.
But O, restrain compassion, if its course,
10   As oft befalls, prevent or turn aside
Judgements and aims and acts whose higher source
Is sympathy with the unforewarned, who died
Blameless – with them that shuddered o'er his grave,
And all who from the law firm safety crave.

III
The Roman Consul doomed his sons to die
Who had betrayed their country. The stern word
Afforded (may it through all time afford)
A theme for praise and admiration high.
Upon the surface of humanity
He rested not; its depths his mind explored;
He felt; but his parental bosom's lord
Was Duty, – Duty calmed his agony.
And some, we know, when they by wilful act
10   A single human life have wrongly taken,
Pass sentence on themselves, confess the fact,
And, to atone for it, with soul unshaken
Kneel at the feet of Justice, and, for faith
Broken with all mankind, solicit death.

IV

Is *Death*, when evil against good has fought
With such fell mastery that a man may dare
By deeds the blackest purpose to lay bare –
Is Death, for one to that condition brought,
For him, or anyone, the thing that ought
To be *most* dreaded? Lawgivers, beware,
Lest, capital pains remitting till ye spare
The murderer, ye, by sanction to that thought
Seemingly given, debase the general mind;
Tempt the vague will tried standards to disown,
Nor only palpable restraints unbind,
But upon Honour's head disturb the crown,
Whose absolute rule permits not to withstand
In the weak love of life his least command.

V

Not to the object specially designed,
Howe'er momentous in itself it be,
Good to promote or curb depravity,
Is the wise Legislator's view confined.
His Spirit, when most severe, is oft most kind;
As all Authority in earth depends
On Love and Fear, their several powers he blends,
Copying with awe the one Paternal mind.
Uncaught by processes in show humane,
He feels how far the act would derogate
From even the humblest functions of the State;
If she, self-shorn of Majesty, ordain
That never more shall hang upon her breath
The last alternative of Life or Death.

VI

Ye brood of conscience – Spectres! that frequent
The bad man's restless walk, and haunt his bed –
Fiends in your aspect, yet beneficent
In act, as hovering Angels when they spread

Their wings to guard the unconscious Innocent –
Slow be the Statutes of the land to share
A laxity that could not but impair
Your power to punish crime, and so prevent.
And ye, Beliefs! coiled serpent-like about
10 The adage on all tongues, 'Murder will out,'
How shall your ancient warnings work for good
In the full might they hitherto have shown,
If for deliberate shedder of man's blood
Survive not Judgement that requires his own?

VII

Before the world had past her time of youth
While polity and discipline were weak,
The precept eye for eye, and tooth for tooth,
Came forth – a light, though but as of daybreak,
Strong as could then be borne. A Master meek
Proscribed the spirit fostered by that rule,
Patience *his* law, long-suffering *his* school,
And love the end, which all through peace must seek.
But lamentably do they err who strain
10 His mandates, given rash impulse to controul
And keep vindictive thirstings from the soul,
So far that, if consistent in their scheme,
Thy must forbid the State to inflict a pain,
Making of social order a mere dream.

VIII

Fit retribution, by the moral code
Determined, lies beyond the State's embrace,
Yet, as she may, for each peculiar case
She plants well-measured terrors in the road
Of wrongful acts. Downward it is and broad,
And, the main fear once doomed to banishment,
Far oftener then, bad ushering worse event,
Blood would be spilt that in his dark abode
Crime might lie better hid. And, should the change
10 Take from the horror due to a foul deed,

Pursuit and evidence so far must fail,
And, guilt escaping, passion then might plead
In angry spirits for her old free range,
And the 'wild justice of revenge' prevail.

IX

Though to give timely warning and deter
Is one great aim of penalty, extend
Thy mental vision further and ascend
Far higher, else full surely shalt thou err.
What is a State? The wise behold in her
A creature born of time, that keeps one eye
Fixed on the statutes of Eternity,
To which her judgements reverently defer.
Speaking through Law's dispassionate voice the State
10   Endues her conscience with external life
And being, to preclude or quell the strife
Of individual will, to elevate
The grovelling mind, the erring to recall,
And fortify the moral sense of all.

X

Our bodily life, some plead, that life the shrine
Of an immortal spirit, is a gift
So sacred, so informed with light divine,
That no tribunal, though most wise to sift
Deed and intent, should turn the Being adrift
Into that world where penitential tear
May not avail, nor prayer have for God's ear
A voice – that world whose veil no hand can lift
For earthly sight. 'Eternity and Time,'
10   *They* urge, 'have interwoven claims and rights
Not to be jeopardized through foulest crime:
The sentence rule by mercy's heaven-born lights.'
Even so; but measuring not by finite sense
Infinite Power, perfect Intelligence.

XI

Ah, think how one compelled for life to abide
Locked in a dungeon needs must eat the heart
Out of his own humanity, and part
With every hope that mutual cares provide;
And, should a less unnatural doom confide
In life-long exile on a savage coast,
Soon the relapsing penitent may boast
Of yet more heinous guilt, with fiercer pride.
Hence thoughtful Mercy, Mercy sage and pure,
10   Sanctions the forfeiture that Law demands,
Leaving the final issue in *His* hands
Whose goodness knows no change, whose love is sure,
Who sees, foresees; who cannot judge amiss,
And wafts at will the contrite soul to bliss.

XII

See the Condemned alone within his cell
And prostrate at some moment when remorse
Stings to the quick, and, with resistless force,
Assaults the pride she strove in vain to quell.
Then mark him, him who could so long rebel,
The crime confessed, a kneeling Penitent
Before the Altar, where the Sacrament
Softens his heart, till from his eyes outwell
Tears of salvation. Welcome death! while Heaven
10   Does in this change exceedingly rejoice;
While yet the solemn heed the State hath given
Helps him to meet the last Tribunal's voice
In faith, which fresh offences, were he cast
On old temptations, might for ever blast.

XIII CONCLUSION

Yes, though He well may tremble at the sound
Of his own voice, who from the judgement-seat
Sends the pale Convict to his last retreat
In death; though Listeners shudder all around,
They know the dread requital's source profound;

Nor is, they feel, its wisdom obsolete –
(Would that it were!) the sacrifice unmeet
For Christian Faith. But hopeful signs abound;
The social rights of man breathe purer air;
10 Religion deepens her preventive care;
Then, moved by needless fear of past abuse,
Strike not from Law's firm hand that awful rod,
But leave it thence to drop for lack of use:
Oh, speed the blessed hour, Almighty God!

XIV APOLOGY

The formal World relaxes her cold chain
For One who speaks in numbers; ampler scope
His utterance finds; and, conscious of the gain,
Imagination works with bolder hope
The cause of grateful reason to sustain;
And, serving Truth, the heart more strongly beats
Against all barriers which his labour meets
In lofty place, or humble Life's domain.
Enough; – before us lay a painful road,
10 And guidance have I sought in duteous love
From Wisdom's heavenly Father. Hence hath flowed
Patience, with trust that, whatsoe'er the way
Each takes in this high matter, all may move
Cheered with the prospect of a brighter day.

Upon a Portrait

We gaze – nor grieve to think that we must die,
But that the precious love this friend hath sown
Within our hearts, the love whose flower hath blown
Bright as if heaven were ever in its eye,
Will pass so soon from human memory;
And not by strangers to our blood alone,
But by our best descendants be unknown,
Unthought of – this may surely claim a sigh.
Yet, blessed Art, we yield not to dejection;

10 Thou against Time so feelingly dost strive:
Where'er, preserved in this most true reflection,
An image of her soul is kept alive,
Some lingering fragrance of the pure affection,
Whose flower with us will vanish, must survive.

[*To I. F.*]

The star which comes at close of day to shine
More heavenly bright than when it leads the morn,
Is Friendship's emblem, whether the forlorn
She visiteth, or, shedding light benign
Through shades that solemnize Life's calm decline,
Doth make the happy happier. This have we
Learnt, Isabel, from thy society,
Which now we too unwillingly resign
Though for brief absence. But farewell! the page
10 Glimmers before my sight through thankful tears,
Such as start forth, not seldom, to approve
Our truth, when we, old yet unchilled by age,
Call thee, though known but for a few fleet years,
The heart-affianced sister of our love!

Poor Robin

Now when the primrose makes a splendid show,
And lilies face the March-winds in full blow,
And humbler growths as moved with one desire
Put on, to welcome spring, their best attire,
Poor Robin is yet flowerless; but how gay
With his red stalks upon this sunny day!
And, as his tufts of leaves he spreads, content
With a hard bed and scanty nourishment,
Mixed with the green, some shine not lacking power
10 To rival summer's brightest scarlet flower;
And flowers they well might seem to passers-by
If looked at only with a careless eye;

Flowers – or a richer produce (did it suit
The season) sprinklings of ripe strawberry fruit.

But while a thousand pleasures come unsought,
Why fix upon his wealth or want a thought?
Is the string touched in prelude to a lay
Of pretty fancies that would round him play
When all the world acknowledged elfin sway?
20 Or does it suit our humour to commend
Poor Robin as a sure and crafty friend,
Whose practice teaches, spite of names to show
Bright colours whether they deceive or no? –
Nay, we would simply praise the free good-will
With which, though slighted, he, on naked hill
Or in warm valley, seeks his part to fill;
Cheerful alike if bare of flowers as now,
Or when his tiny gems shall deck his brow:
Yet more, we wish that men by men despised,
30 And such as lift their foreheads overprized,
Should sometimes think, where'er they chance to spy
This child of Nature's own humility,
What recompence is kept in store or left
For all that seem neglected or bereft;
With what nice care equivalents are given,
How just, how bountiful, the hand of Heaven.

The Cuckoo-Clock

Wouldst thou be taught, when sleep has taken flight,
By a sure voice that can most sweetly tell,
How far off yet a glimpse of morning light,
And if to lure the truant back be well,
Forbear to covet a Repeater's stroke,
That, answering to thy touch, will sound the hour;
Better provide thee with a Cuckoo-clock
For service hung behind thy chamber-door;
And in due time the soft spontaneous shock,

10 The double note, as if with living power,
  Will to composure lead – or make thee blithe as bird in
    bower.

List, Cuckoo – Cuckoo! – oft though tempests howl,
  Cr nipping frost remind thee trees are bare,
How cattle pine, and droop the shivering fowl,
  Thy spirits will seem to feed on balmy air:
I speak with knowledge, – by that Voice beguiled,
  Thou wilt salute old memories as they throng
Into thy heart; and fancies, running wild
  Through fresh green fields, and budding groves among,
20 Will make thee happy, happy as a child;
  Of sunshine wilt thou think, and flowers, and song,
And breathe as in a world where nothing can go wrong.

And know – that, even for him who shuns the day
  And nightly tosses on a bed of pain;
Whose joys, from all but memory swept away,
  Must come unhoped for, if they come again;
Know – that, for him whose waking thoughts, severe
  As his distress is sharp, would scorn my theme,
The mimic notes, striking upon his ear
30 In sleep, and intermingling with his dream,
Could from sad regions send him to a dear
  Delightful land of verdure, shower and gleam,
To mock the *wandering* Voice beside some haunted stream.

O bounty without measure! while the grace
  Of Heaven doth in such wise, from humblest springs,
Pour pleasure forth, and solaces that trace
  A mazy course along familiar things,
Well may our hearts have faith that blessings come,
  Streaming from founts above the starry sky,
40 With angels when their own untroubled home
  They leave, and speed on nightly embassy
To visit earthly chambers, – and for whom?
  Yea, both for souls who God's forbearance try,
And those that seek his help, and for his mercy sigh.

The Norman Boy

High on a broad unfertile tract of forest-skirted Down,
Nor kept by Nature for herself, nor made by man his
  own,
From home and company remote and every playful joy,
Served, tending a few sheep and goats, a ragged Norman
  Boy.

Him never saw I, nor the spot; but from an English
  Dame,
Stranger to me and yet my friend, a simple notice came,
With suit that I would speak in verse of that sequestered
  child
Whom, one bleak winter's day, she met upon the dreary
  Wild.

His flock, along the woodland's edge with relics sprinkled
  o'er
10 Of last night's snow, beneath a sky threatening the fall
  of more,
Where tufts of herbage tempted each, were busy at their
  feed,
And the poor Boy was busier still, with work of anxious
  heed.

There *was* he, where of branches rent and withered and
  decayed,
For covert from the keen north wind, his hands a hut
  had made.
A tiny tenement, forsooth, and frail, as needs must be
A thing of such materials framed, by a builder such as he.

The hut stood finished by his pains, nor seemingly
  lacked aught
That skill or means of his could add, but the architect
  had wrought

Some limber twigs into a Cross, well-shaped with
   fingers nice,
20 To be engrafted on the top of his small edifice.

That Cross he now was fastening there, as the surest
   power and best
For supplying all deficiencies, all wants of the rude nest
In which, from burning heat, or tempest driving far and
   wide,
The innocent Boy, else shelterless, his lonely head must
   hide.

That Cross belike he also raised as a standard for the
   true
And faithful service of his heart in the worst that might
   ensue
Of hardship and distressful fear, amid the houseless
   waste
Where he, in his poor self so weak, by Providence was
   placed.

– Here, Lady! might I cease; but nay, let *us* before we
   part
30 With this dear holy shepherd-boy breathe a prayer of
   earnest heart,
That unto him, where'er shall lie his life's appointed
   way,
The Cross, fixed in his soul, may prove an all-sufficing
   stay.

The Poet's Dream

SEQUEL TO 'THE NORMAN BOY'

Just as those final words were penned, the sun broke out
   in power,
And gladdened all things; but, as chanced, within that
   very hour,

Air blackened, thunder growled, fire flashed from clouds
    that hid the sky,
And for the Subject of my Verse, I heaved a pensive
    sigh.

Nor could my heart by second thoughts from heaviness
    be cleared,
For bodied forth before my eyes the cross-crowned hut
    appeared;
And, while around it storm as fierce seemed troubling
    earth and air,
I saw, within, the Norman Boy kneeling alone in prayer.

The Child, as if the thunder's voice spake with articulate
    call,
10 Bowed meekly in submissive fear, before the Lord of All;
His lips were moving; and his eyes, upraised to sue for
    grace,
With soft illumination cheered the dimness of that place.

How beautiful is holiness! – what wonder if the sight,
Almost as vivid as a dream, produced a dream at night?
It came with sleep and showed the Boy, no cherub, not
    transformed,
But the poor ragged Thing whose ways my human heart
    had warmed.

Me had the dream equipped with wings, so I took him
    in my arms,
And lifted from the grassy floor, stilling his faint alarms,
And bore him high through yielding air my debt of love
    to pay,
20 By giving him for both our sakes, an hour of holiday.

I whispered, 'Yet a little while, dear Child! thou art my
    own,
To show thee some delightful thing, in country or in
    town.

What shall it be? a mirthful throng? or that holy place
and calm
St Denis, filled with royal tombs, or the Church of
Notre Dame?

'St Ouen's golden Shrine? Or choose what else would
please thee most
Of any wonder Normandy, or all proud France, can boast!'
'My Mother,' said the Boy, 'was born near to a blessèd
Tree,
The Chapel Oak of Allonville; good Angel, show it
me!'

On wings from broad and stedfast poise let loose by this
reply,
30   For Allonville, o'er down and dale, away then did we
fly;
O'er town and tower we flew, and fields in May's fresh
verdure drest;
The wings they did not flag; the Child, though grave,
was not deprest.

But who shall show, to waking sense, the gleam of light
that broke
Forth from his eyes, when first the Boy looked down on
that huge oak,
For length of days so much revered, so famous where it
stands
For twofold hallowing – Nature's care, and work of
human hands?

Strong as an Eagle with my charge I glided round and
round
The wide-spread boughs, for view of door, window, and
stair that wound
Gracefully up the gnarled trunk; nor left we unsurveyed
40   The pointed steeple peering forth from the centre of
the shade.

I lighted – opened with soft touch the chapel's iron door,
Passed softly, leading in the Boy; and while from roof to
    floor
From floor to roof all round his eyes the Child with
    wonder cast,
Pleasure on pleasure crowded in, each livelier than the
    last.

For, deftly framed within the trunk, the sanctuary
    showed,
By light of lamp and precious stones, that glimmered
    here, there glowed,
Shrine, Altar, Image, Offerings hung in sign of gratitude;
Sight that inspired accordant thoughts; and speech I
    thus renewed;

'Hither the Afflicted come, as thou hast heard thy
    Mother say,
50 And, kneeling, supplication make to our Lady de la
    Paix;
What mournful sighs have here been heard, and, when
    the voice was stopt
By sudden pangs; what bitter tears have on this
    pavement dropt!

'Poor Shepherd of the naked Down, a favoured lot is
    thine,
Far happier lot, dear Boy, than brings full many to this
    shrine;
From body pains and pains of soul thou needest no
    release,
Thy hours as they flow on are spent, if not in joy in
    peace.

'Then offer up thy heart to God in thankfulness and
    praise,
Give to Him prayers, and many thoughts, in thy most
    busy days;

And in His sight the fragile Cross, on thy small hut, will
    be
60 Holy as that which long hath crowned the Chapel of
    this Tree;

'Holy as that far seen which crowns the sumptuous
    Church in Rome
Where thousands meet to worship God under a mighty
    Dome;
He sees the bending multitude, He hears the choral
    rites,
Yet, not the less, in children's hymns and lonely prayer,
    delights.

'God for His service needeth not proud work of human
    skill;
They please Him best who labour most to do in peace
    His will:
So let us strive to live, and to our Spirits will be given
Such wings as, when our Saviour calls, shall bear us up
    to Heaven.'

The Boy no answer made by words, but, so earnest was
    his look,
70 Sleep fled, and with it fled the dream – recorded in this
    book,
Lest all that passed should melt away in silence from
    my mind,
As visions still more bright have done, and left no trace
    behind.

But oh! that Country-man of thine, whose eye, loved
    Child, can see
A pledge of endless bliss in acts of early piety,
In verse, which to thy ear might come, would treat
    this simple theme,
Nor leave untold our happy flight in that adventurous
    dream.

Alas the dream, to thee, poor Boy! to thee from whom
  it flowed,
Was nothing, scarcely can be aught, yet 'twas
  bounteously bestowed,
If I may dare to cherish hope that gentle eyes will read
80 Not loth, and listening Little-ones, heart-touched, their
  fancies feed.

At Furness Abbey

Here, where, of havoc tired and rash undoing,
Man left this Structure to become Time's prey,
A soothing spirit follows in the way
That Nature takes, her counter-work pursuing.
See how her Ivy clasps the sacred Ruin,
Fall to prevent or beautify decay;
And, on the mouldered walls, how bright, how gay,
The flowers in pearly dews their bloom renewing!
Thanks to the place, blessings upon the hour;
10 Even as I speak the rising Sun's first smile
Gleams on the grass-crowned top of yon tall Tower
Whose cawing occupants with joy proclaim
Prescriptive title to the shattered pile,
Where, Cavendish, *thine* seems nothing but a name!

Upon the Sight of the Portrait of a Female Friend

Upon those lips, those placid lips, I look
Nor grieve that they are still and mute as death;
I gaze – I read as in an Angel's Book,
And ask not speech from them, but long for breath.

On a Portrait of the Duke of Wellington upon the Field of Waterloo, by Haydon

By Art's bold privilege Warrior and War-horse stand
On ground yet strewn with their last battle's wreck;
Let the Steed glory while his Master's hand
Lies fixed for ages on his conscious neck;
But by the Chieftain's look, though at his side
Hangs that day's treasured sword, how firm a check
Is given to triumph and all human pride!
Yon trophied Mound shrinks to a shadowy speck
In his calm presence! Him the mighty deed
Elates not, brought far nearer the grave's rest,
As shows that time-worn face, for he such seed
Has sown as yields, we trust, the fruit of fame
In Heaven; hence no one blushes for thy name,
Conqueror, 'mid some sad thoughts, divinely blest!

10 (line marker)

Memorials of a Tour in Italy, 1837

TO HENRY CRABB ROBINSON

Companion! by whose buoyant Spirit cheered,
In whose experience trusting, day by day
Treasures I gained with zeal that neither feared
The toils nor felt the crosses of the way,
These records take, and happy should I be
Were but the Gift a meet Return to thee
For kindnesses that never ceased to flow,
And prompt self-sacrifice to which I owe
Far more than any heart but mine can know.

W. WORDSWORTH.
RYDAL MOUNT, *February 14th*, 1842.

The Tour of which the following Poems are very inadequate remembrances was shortened by report, too well founded, of the prevalence of Cholera at Naples. To make some amends for what was reluctantly left unseen in the South of Italy, we visited the Tuscan Sanctuaries among the Apennines, and the principal Italian Lakes among the Alps. Neither of those lakes, nor of Venice, is there any notice in these Poems, chiefly because I have touched upon them elsewhere. See, in particular, 'Descriptive Sketches,' 'Memorials of a Tour on the Continent in 1820,' and a Sonnet upon the extinction of the Venetian Republic.

I MUSINGS NEAR AQUAPENDENTE APRIL, 1837

Ye Apennines! with all your fertile vales
Deeply embosomed, and your winding shores
Of either sea, an Islander by birth,
A Mountaineer by habit, would resound
Your praise, in meet accordance with your claims
Bestowed by Nature, or from man's great deeds
Inherited: – presumptuous thought! – it fled
Like vapour, like a towering cloud, dissolved.
Not, therefore, shall my mind give way to sadness; –
10   Yon snow-white torrent-fall, plumb down it drops
Yet ever hangs or seems to hang in air,
Lulling the leisure of that high-perched town,
AQUAPENDENTE, in her lofty site
Its neighbour and its namesake – town, and flood
Forth flashing out of its own gloomy chasm
Bright sunbeams – the fresh verdure of this lawn
Strewn with grey rocks, and on the horizon's verge,
O'er intervenient waste, through glimmering haze,
Unquestionably kenned, that cone-shaped hill
20   With fractured summit, no indifferent sight
To travellers, from such comforts as are thine,
Bleak Radicofani! escaped with joy –
These are before me; and the varied scene
May well suffice, till noon-tide's sultry heat
Relax, to fix and satisfy the mind
Passive yet pleased. What! with this Broom in flower
Close at my side! She bids me fly to greet
Her sisters, soon like her to be attired
With golden blossoms opening at the feet
30   Of my own Fairfield. The glad greeting given,

Given with a voice and by a look returned
Of old companionship, Time counts not minutes
Ere, from accustomed paths, familiar fields,
The local Genius hurries me aloft,
Transported over that cloud-wooing hill,
Seat Sandal, a fond suitor of the clouds,
With dream-like smoothness, to Helvellyn's top,
There to alight upon crisp moss and range,
Obtaining ampler boon, at every step,
40 Of visual sovereignty – hills multitudinous,
(Not Apennine can boast of fairer) hills
Pride of two nations, wood and lake and plains,
And prospect right below of deep coves shaped
By skeleton arms, that, from the mountain's trunk
Extended, clasp the winds, with mutual moan
Struggling for liberty, while undismayed
The shepherd struggles with them. Onward thence
And downward by the skirt of Greenside fell,
And by Glenridding-screes, and low Glencoign,
50 Places forsaken now, though loving still
The Muses, as they loved them in the days
Of the old minstrels and the border bards. –
But here am I fast bound; and let it pass,
The simple rapture; – who that travels far
To feed his mind with watchful eyes could share
Or wish to share it? – One there surely was,
'The Wizard of the North,' with anxious hope
Brought to this genial climate, when disease
Preyed upon body and mind – yet not the less
60 Had his sunk eye kindled at those dear words
That spake of bards and minstrels; and his spirit
Had flown with mine to old Helvellyn's brow,
Where once together, in his day of strength,
We stood rejoicing, as if earth were free
From sorrow, like the sky above our heads.

    Years followed years, and when, upon the eve
Of his last going from Tweed-side, thought turned,

Or by another's sympathy was led,
To this bright land, Hope was for him no friend,
70 Knowledge no help; Imagination shaped
No promise. Still, in more than ear-deep seats,
Survives for me, and cannot but survive
The tone of voice which wedded borrowed words
To sadness not their own, when, with faint smile
Forced by intent to take from speech its edge,
He said, 'When I am there, although 'tis fair,
'Twill be another Yarrow.' Prophecy
More than fulfilled, as gay Campania's shores
Soon witnessed, and the city of seven hills,
80 Her sparkling fountains, and her mouldering tombs;
And more than all, that Eminence which showed
Her splendours, seen, not felt, the while he stood
A few short steps (painful they were) apart
From Tasso's Convent-haven, and retired grave.

Peace to their Spirits! why should Poesy
Yield to the lure of vain regret, and hover
In gloom on wings with confidence outspread
To move in sunshine? – Utter thanks, my Soul!
Tempered with awe, and sweetened by compassion
90 For them who in the shades of sorrow dwell,
That I – so near the term to human life
Appointed by man's common heritage,
Frail as the frailest, one withal (if that
Deserve a thought) but little known to fame –
Am free to rove where Nature's loveliest looks,
Art's noblest relics, history's rich bequests,
Failed to reanimate and but feebly cheered
The whole world's Darling – free to rove at will
O'er high and low, and if requiring rest,
Rest from enjoyment only.
100   Thanks poured forth
For what thus far hath blessed my wanderings, thanks
Fervent but humble as the lips can breathe
Where gladness seems a duty – let me guard

Those seeds of expectation which the fruit
Already gathered in this favoured Land
Enfolds within its core. The faith be mine,
That He who guides and governs all, approves
When gratitude, though disciplined to look
Beyond these transient spheres, doth wear a crown
110   Of earthly hope put on with trembling hand;
Nor is least pleased, we trust, when golden beams,
Reflected through the mists of age, from hours
Of innocent delight, remote or recent,
Shoot but a little way – 'tis all they can –
Into the doubtful future. Who would keep
Power must resolve to cleave to it through life,
Else it deserts him, surely as he lives.
Saints would not grieve nor guardian angels frown
If one – while tossed, as was my lot to be,
120   In a frail bark urged by two slender oars
Over waves rough and deep, that, when they broke,
Dashed their white foam against the palace walls
Of Genoa the superb – should there be led
To meditate upon his own appointed tasks,
However humble in themselves, with thoughts
Raised and sustained by memory of Him
Who oftentimes within those narrow bounds
Rocked on the surge, there tried his spirit's strength
And grasp of purpose, long ere sailed his ship
130   To lay a new world open.
                          Nor less prized
Be those impressions which incline the heart
To mild, to lowly, and to seeming weak,
Bend that way her desires. The dew, the storm –
The dew whose moisture fell in gentle drops
On the small hyssop destined to become,
By Hebrew ordinance devoutly kept,
A purifying instrument – the storm
That shook on Lebanon the cedar's top,
And as it shook, enabling the blind roots
140   Further to force their way, endowed its trunk

With magnitude and strength fit to uphold
The glorious temple – did alike proceed
From the same gracious will, were both an offspring
Of bounty infinite.
            Between Powers that aim
Higher to lift their lofty heads, impelled
By no profane ambition, Powers that thrive
By conflict, and their opposites, that trust
In lowliness – a mid-way tract there lies
Of thoughtful sentiment for every mind
150   Pregnant with good. Young, Middle-aged, and Old,
From century on to century, must have known
The emotion – nay, more fitly were it said –
The blest tranquillity that sunk so deep
Into my spirit, when I paced, enclosed
In Pisa's Campo Santo, the smooth floor
Of its Arcades paved with sepulchral slabs,
And through each window's open fret-work looked
O'er the blank Area of sacred earth
Fetched from Mount Calvary, or haply delved
160   In precincts nearer to the Saviour's tomb,
By hands of men, humble as brave, who fought
For its deliverance – a capacious field
That to descendants of the dead it holds
And to all living mute memento breathes,
More touching far than aught which on the walls
Is pictured, or their epitaphs can speak,
Of the changed City's long-departed power,
Glory, and wealth, which, perilous as they are,
Here did not kill, but nourished, Piety.
170   And, high above that length of cloistral roof,
Peering in air and backed by azure sky,
To kindred contemplations ministers
The Baptistery's dome, and that which swells
From the Cathedral pile; and with the twain
Conjoined in prospect mutable or fixed
(As hurry on in eagerness the feet,
Or pause) the summit of the Leaning-tower.

Nor less remuneration waits on him
Who having left the Cemetery stands
180 In the Tower's shadow, of decline and fall
Admonished not without some sense of fear,
Fear that soon vanishes before the sight
Of splendour unextinguished, pomp unscathed,
And beauty unimpaired. Grand in itself,
And for itself, the assemblage, grand and fair
To view, and for the mind's consenting eye
A type of age in man, upon its front
Bearing the world-acknowledged evidence
Of past exploits, nor fondly after more
190 Struggling against the stream of destiny,
But with its peaceful majesty content.
– Oh what a spectacle at every turn
The Place unfolds, from pavement skinned with moss,
Or grass-grown spaces, where the heaviest foot
Provokes no echoes, but must softly tread;
Where Solitude with Silence paired stops short
Of Desolation, and to Ruin's scythe
Decay submits not.
                But where'er my steps
Shall wander, chiefly let me cull with care
200 Those images of genial beauty, oft
Too lovely to be pensive in themselves
But by reflexion made so, which do best
And fitliest serve to crown with fragment wreaths
Life's cup when almost filled with years, like mine.
– How lovely robed in forenoon light and shade,
Each ministering to each, didst thou appear
Savona, Queen of territory fair
As aught that marvellous coast through all its length
Yields to the Stranger's eye. Remembrance holds
210 As a selected treasure thy one cliff,
That, while it wore for melancholy crest
A shattered Convent, yet rose proud to have
Clinging to its steep sides a thousand herbs
And shrubs, whose pleasant looks gave proof how kind

The breath of air can be where earth had else
Seemed churlish. And behold, both far and near,
Garden and field all decked with orange bloom,
And peach and citron, in Spring's mildest breeze
Expanding; and, along the smooth shore curved
220 Into a natural port, a tideless sea,
To that mild breeze with motion and with voice
Softly responsive; and, attuned to all
Those vernal charms of sight and sound, appeared
Smooth space of turf which from the guardian fort
Sloped seaward, turf whose tender April green,
In coolest climes too fugitive, might even here
Plead with the sovereign Sun for longer stay
Than his unmitigated beams allow,
Nor plead in vain, if beauty could preserve,
230 From mortal change, aught that is born on earth
Or doth on time depend.
                While on the brink
Of that high Convent-crested cliff I stood,
Modest Savona! over all did brood
A pure poetic Spirit – as the breeze,
Mild – as the verdure, fresh – the sunshine, bright –
Thy gentle Chiabrera! – not a stone,
Mural or level with the trodden floor,
In Church or Chapel, if my curious quest
Missed not the truth, retains a single name
240 Of young or old, warrior, or saint, or sage,
To whose dear memories his sepulchral verse
Paid simple tribute, such as might have flowed
From the clear spring of a plain English heart,
Say rather, one in native fellowship
With all who want not skill to couple grief
With praise, as genuine admiration prompts.
The grief, the praise, are severed from their dust,
Yet in his page the records of that worth
Survive, uninjured; – glory then to words,
250 Honour to word-preserving Arts, and hail
Ye kindred local influences that still,

If Hope's familiar whispers merit faith,
Await my steps when they the breezy height
Shall range of philosophic Tusculum;
Or Sabine vales explored inspire a wish
To meet the shade of Horace by the side
Of his Blandusian fount; or I invoke
His presence to point out the spot where once
He sate, and eulogized with earnest pen
260 Peace, leisure, freedom, moderate desires;
And all the immunities of rural life
Extolled, behind Vacuna's crumbling fane.
Or let me loiter, soothed with what is given,
Nor asking more, on that delicious Bay,
Parthenope's Domain – Virgilian haunt,
Illustrated with never-dying verse,
And, by the Poet's laurel-shaded tomb,
Age after age to Pilgrims from all lands
Endeared.
            And who – if not a man as cold
270 In heart as dull in brain – while pacing ground
Chosen by Rome's legendary Bards, high minds
Out of her early struggles well inspired
To localize heroic acts – could look
Upon the spots with undelighted eye,
Though even to their last syllable the Lays
And very names of those who gave them birth
Have perished? – Verily, to her utmost depth,
Imagination feels what Reason fears not
To recognize, the lasting virtue lodged
280 In those bold fictions that, by deeds assigned
To the Valerian, Fabian, Curian Race,
And others like in fame, created Powers
With attributes from History derived,
By Poesy irradiate, and yet graced,
Through marvellous felicity of skill,
With something more propitious to high aims
Than either, pent within her separate sphere,
Can oft with justice claim.

And not disdaining
Union with those primeval energies
290 To virtue consecrate, stoop ye from your height
Christian Traditions! at my Spirit's call
Descend, and, on the brow of ancient Rome
As she survives in ruin, manifest
Your glories mingled with the brightest hues
Of her memorial halo, fading, fading,
But never to be extinct while Earth endures.
O come, if undishonoured by the prayer,
From all her Sanctuaries! – Open for my feet
Ye Catacombs, give to mine eyes a glimpse
300 Of the Devout, as, 'mid your glooms convened
For safety, they of yore enclasped the Cross
On knees that ceased from trembling, or intoned
Their orisons with voices half-suppressed,
But sometimes heard, or fancied to be heard,
Even at this hour.
                    And thou Mamertine prison,
Into that vault receive me from whose depth
Issues, revealed in no presumptuous vision,
Albeit lifting human to divine,
A Saint, the Church's Rock, the mystic Keys
310 Grasped in his hand; and lo! with upright sword
Prefiguring his own impendent doom,
The Apostle of the Gentiles; both prepared
To suffer pains with heathen scorn and hate
Inflicted; – blessèd Men, for so to Heaven
They follow their dear Lord!
                              Time flows – nor winds,
Nor stagnates, nor precipitates his course,
But many a benefit borne upon his breast
For human-kind sinks out of sight, is gone,
No one knows how; nor seldom is put forth
320 An angry arm that snatches good away,
Never perhaps to reappear. The Stream
Has to our generation brought and brings
Innumerable gains; yet we, who now

Walk in the light of day, pertain full surely
To a chilled age, most pitiably shut out
From that which *is* and actuates, by forms,
Abstractions, and by lifeless fact to fact
Minutely linked with diligence uninspired,
Unrectified, unguided, unsustained,
330 By godlike insight. To this fate is doomed
Science, wide-spread and spreading still as be
Her conquests, in the world of sense made known.
So with the internal mind it fares; and so
With morals, trusting, in contempt or fear
Of vital principle's controlling law,
To her purblind guide Expediency; and so
Suffers religious faith. Elate with view
Of what is won, we overlook or scorn
The best that should keep pace with it, and must,
340 Else more and more the general mind will droop,
Even as if bent on perishing. There lives
No faculty within us which the Soul
Can spare, and humblest earthly Weal demands,
For dignity not placed beyond her reach,
Zealous co-operation of all means
Given or acquired, to raise us from the mire,
And liberate our hearts from low pursuits.
By gross Utilities enslaved we need
More of ennobling impulse from the past,
350 If to the future aught of good must come
Sounder and therefore holier than the ends
Which, in the giddiness of self-applause,
We covet as supreme. O grant the crown
That Wisdom wears, or take his treacherous staff
From Knowledge! – If the Muse, whom I have served
This day, be mistress of a single pearl
Fit to be placed in that pure diadem;
Then, not in vain, under these chestnut boughs
Reclined, shall I have yielded up my soul
360 To transports from the secondary founts
Flowing of time and place, and paid to both

Due homage; nor shall fruitlessly have striven,
By love of beauty moved, to enshrine in verse
Accordant meditations, which in times
Vexed and disordered, as our own, may shed
Influence, at least among a scattered few,
To soberness of mind and peace of heart
Friendly; as here to my repose hath been
This flowering broom's dear neighbourhood, the light
370 And murmur issuing from yon pendent flood,
And all the varied landscape. Let us now
Rise, and tomorrow greet magnificent Rome.

II THE PINE OF MONTE MARIO AT ROME
I saw far off the dark top of a Pine
Look like a cloud – a slender stem the tie
That bound it to its native earth – poised high
'Mid evening hues, along the horizon line,
Striving in peace each other to outshine.
But when I learned the Tree was living there,
Saved from the sordid axe by Beaumont's care,
Oh, what a gush of tenderness was mine!
The rescued Pine-tree, with its sky so bright
10 And cloud-like beauty, rich in thoughts of home,
Death-parted friends, and days too swift in flight,
Supplanted the whole majesty of Rome
(Then first apparent from the Pincian Height)
Crowned with St Peter's everlasting Dome.

III AT ROME
Is this, ye Gods, the Capitolian Hill?
Yon petty Steep in truth the fearful Rock,
Tarpeian named of yore, and keeping still
That name, a local Phantom proud to mock
The Traveller's expectation? – Could our Will
Destroy the ideal Power within, 'twere done
Through what men see and touch, – slaves wandering on,
Impelled by thirst of all but Heaven-taught skill.
Full oft, our wish obtained, deeply we sigh;

10 Yet not unrecompensed are they who learn,
From that depression raised, to mount on high
With stronger wing, more clearly to discern
Eternal things; and, if need be, defy
Change, with a brow not insolent, though stern.

IV AT ROME. – REGRETS. – IN ALLUSION TO NIEBUHR
AND OTHER MODERN HISTORIANS
Those old credulities, to nature dear,
Shall they no longer bloom upon the stock
Of History, stript naked as a rock
'Mid a dry desert? What is it we hear?
The glory of Infant Rome must disappear,
Her morning splendours vanish, and their place
Know them no more. If Truth, who veiled her face
With those bright beams yet hid it not, must steer
Henceforth a humbler course perplexed and slow;
10 One solace yet remains for us who came
Into this world in days when story lacked
Severe research, that in our hearts we know
How, for exciting youth's heroic flame,
Assent is power, belief the soul of fact.

V AT ROME. – REGRETS. – IN ALLUSION TO NIEBUHR
AND OTHER MODERN HISTORIANS, CONTINUED
Complacent Fictions were they, yet the same
Involved a history of no doubtful sense,
History that proves by inward evidence
From what a precious source of truth it came.
Ne'er could the boldest Eulogist have dared
Such deeds to paint, such characters to frame,
But for coeval sympathy prepared
To greet with instant faith their loftiest claim.
None but a noble people could have loved
10 Flattery in Ancient Rome's pure-minded style:
Not in like sort the Runic Scald was moved;
He, nursed 'mid savage passions that defile
Humanity, sang feats that well might call
For the blood-thirsty mead of Odin's riotous Hall.

VI PLEA FOR THE HISTORIAN

Forbear to deem the Chronicler unwise,
Ungentle, or untouched by seemly ruth,
Who, gathering up all that Time's envious tooth
Has spared of sound and grave realities,
Firmly rejects those dazzling flatteries,
Dear as they are to unsuspecting Youth,
That might have drawn down Clio from the skies
To vindicate the majesty of truth.
Such was her office while she walked with men,
10   A Muse, who, not unmindful of her Sire
All-ruling Jove, whate'er the theme might be
Revered her Mother, sage Mnemosyne,
And taught her faithful servants how the lyre
Should animate, but not mislead, the pen.

VII AT ROME

They – who have seen the noble Roman's scorn
Break forth at thought of laying down his head,
When the blank day is over, garreted
In his ancestral palace, where, from morn
To night, the desecrated floors are worn
By feet of purse-proud strangers; they – who have read
In one meek smile, beneath a peasant's shed,
How patiently the weight of wrong is borne;
They – who have heard some learned Patriot treat
10   Of freedom, with mind grasping the whole theme
From ancient Rome, downwards through that bright
        dream
Of Commonwealths, each city a starlike seat
Of rival glory; they – fallen Italy –
Nor must, nor will, nor can, despair of Thee!

VIII NEAR ROME, IN SIGHT OF ST PETER'S

Long has the dew been dried on tree and lawn;
O'er man and beast a not unwelcome boon
Is shed, the languor of approaching noon;
To shady rest withdrawing or withdrawn
Mute are all creatures, as this couchant fawn,

Save insect-swarms that hum in air afloat,
Save that the Cock is crowing, a shrill note,
Startling and shrill as that which roused the dawn.
– Heard in that hour, or when, as now, the nerve
10   Shrinks from the note as from a mis-timed thing,
Oft for a holy warning may it serve,
Charged with remembrance of *his* sudden sting,
His bitter tears, whose name the Papal Chair
And yon resplendent Church are proud to bear.

IX AT ALBANO

Days passed – and Monte Calvo would not clear
His head from mist; and, as the wind sobbed through
Albano's dripping Ilex avenue,
My dull forebodings in a Peasant's ear
Found casual vent. She said, 'Be of good cheer;
Our yesterday's procession did not sue
In vain; the sky will change to sunny blue,
Thanks to our Lady's grace.' I smiled to hear,
But not in scorn: – the Matron's Faith may lack
10   The heavenly sanction needed to ensure
Fulfilment; but, we trust, her upward track
Stops not at this low point, nor wants the lure
Of flowers the Virgin without fear may own,
For by her Son's blest hand the seed was sown.

X

Near Anio's stream, I spied a gentle Dove
Perched on an olive branch, and heard her cooing
'Mid new-born blossoms that soft airs were wooing,
While all things present told of joy and love.
But restless Fancy left that olive grove
To hail the exploratory Bird renewing
Hope for the few, who, at the world's undoing,
On the great flood were spared to live and move.
O bounteous Heaven! signs true as dove and bough
10   Brought to the ark are coming evermore,

Given though we seek them not, but, while we plough
This sea of life without a visible shore,
Do neither promise ask nor grace implore
In what alone is ours, the living Now.

XI FROM THE ALBAN HILLS, LOOKING TOWARDS ROME

Forgive, illustrious Country! these deep sighs,
Heaved less for thy bright plains and hills bestrown
With monuments decayed or overthrown,
For all that tottering stands or prostrate lies,
Than for like scenes in moral vision shown,
Ruin perceived for keener sympathies;
Faith crushed, yet proud of weeds, her gaudy crown;
Virtues laid low, and mouldering energies.
Yet why prolong this mournful strain? – Fallen Power,
10   Thy fortunes, twice exalted, might provoke
Verse to glad notes prophetic of the hour
When thou, uprisen, shalt break thy double yoke,
And enter, with prompt aid from the Most High,
On the third stage of thy great destiny.

XII NEAR THE LAKE OF THRASYMENE

When here with Carthage Rome to conflict came,
An earthquake, mingling with the battle's shock,
Checked not its rage; unfelt the ground did rock,
Sword dropped not, javelin kept its deadly aim. –
Now all is sun-bright peace. Of that day's shame,
Or glory, not a vestige seems to endure,
Save in this Rill that took from blood the name
Which yet it bears, sweet Stream! as crystal pure.
So may all trace and sign of deeds aloof
10   From the true guidance of humanity,
Through Time and Nature's influence, purify
Their spirit; or, unless they for reproof
Or warning serve, thus let them all, on ground
That gave them being, vanish to a sound.

XIII NEAR THE SAME LAKE

For action born, existing to be tried,
Powers manifold we have that intervene
To stir the heart that would too closely screen
Her peace from images to pain allied.
What wonder if at midnight, by the side
Of Sanguinetto or broad Thrasymene,
The clang of arms is heard, and phantoms glide,
Unhappy ghosts in troops by moonlight seen;
And singly thine, O vanquished Chief! whose corse,
10 Unburied, lay hid under heaps of slain:
But who is He? – the Conqueror. Would he force
His way to Rome? Ah, no, – round hill and plain
Wandering, he haunts, at fancy's strong command,
This spot – his shadowy death-cup in his hand.

XIV THE CUCKOO AT LAVERNA
MAY 25, 1837

List – 'twas the Cuckoo. – O with what delight
Heard I that voice! and catch it now, though faint,
Far off and faint, and melting into air,
Yet not to be mistaken. Hark again!
Those louder cries give notice that the Bird,
Although invisible as Echo's self,
Is wheeling hitherward. Thanks, happy Creature,
For this unthought-of greeting!
                                                While allured
From vale to hill, from hill to vale led on,
10 We have pursued, through various lands, a long
And pleasant course; flower after flower has blown,
Embellishing the ground that gave them birth
With aspects novel to my sight; but still
Most fair, most welcome, when they drank the dew
In a sweet fellowship with kinds beloved,
For old remembrance sake. And oft – where Spring
Displayed her richest blossoms among files.
Of orange-trees bedecked with glowing fruit
Ripe for the hand, or under a thick shade

20 Of Ilex, or, if better suited to the hour,
The lightsome Olive's twinkling canopy –
Oft have I heard the Nightingale and Thrush
Blending as in a common English grove
Their love-songs; but, where'er my feet might roam,
Whate'er assemblages of new and old,
Strange and familiar, might beguile the way,
A gratulation from that vagrant Voice
Was wanting; – and most happily till now.

For see, Laverna! mark the far-famed Pile,
30 High on the brink of that precipitous rock,
Implanted like a Fortress, as in truth
It is, a Christian Fortress, garrisoned
In faith and hope, and dutiful obedience,
By a few Monks, a stern society,
Dead to the world and scorning earth-born joys.
Nay – though the hopes that drew, the fears that drove,
St Francis, far from Man's resort, to abide
Among these sterile heights of Apennine,
Bound him, nor, since he raised yon House, have ceased
40 To bind his spiritual Progeny, with rules
Stringent as flesh can tolerate and live;
His milder Genius (thanks to the good God
That made us) over those severe restraints
Of mind, that dread heart-freezing discipline,
Doth sometimes here predominate, and works
By unsought means for gracious purposes;
For earth through heaven, for heaven, by changeful
    earth,
Illustrated, and mutually endeared.

Rapt though He were above the power of sense,
50 Familiarly, yet out of the cleansed heart
Of that once sinful Being overflowed
On sun, moon, stars, the nether elements,
And every shape of creature they sustain,
Divine affections; and with beast and bird

(Stilled from afar – such marvel story tells –
By casual outbreak of his passionate words,
And from their own pursuits in field or grove
Drawn to his side by look or act of love
Humane, and virtue of his innocent life)
60 He wont to hold companionship so free,
So pure, so fraught with knowledge and delight,
As to be likened in his Followers' minds
To that which our first Parents, ere the fall
From their high state darkened the Earth with fear,
Held with all Kinds in Eden's blissful bowers.

Then question not that, 'mid the austere Band,
Who breathe the air he breathed, tread where he trod,
Some true Partakers of his loving spirit
Do still survive, and, with those gentle hearts
70 Consorted, Others, in the power, the faith,
Of a baptized imagination, prompt
To catch from Nature's humblest monitors
Whate'er they bring of impulses sublime.

Thus sensitive must be the Monk, though pale
With fasts, with vigils worn, depressed by years,
Whom in a sunny glade I chanced to see,
Upon a pine-tree's storm-uprooted trunk,
Seated alone, with forehead sky-ward raised,
Hands clasped above the crucifix he wore
80 Appended to his bosom, and lips closed
By the joint pressure of his musing mood
And habit of his vow. That ancient Man –
Nor haply less the Brother whom I marked,
As we approached the Convent gate, aloft
Looking far forth from his aerial cell,
A young Ascetic – Poet, Hero, Sage,
He might have been, Lover belike he was –
If they received into a conscious ear
The notes whose first faint greeting startled me,
90 Whose sedulous iteration thrilled with joy

My heart – may have been moved like me to think,
Ah! not like me who walk in the world's ways,
On the great Prophet, styled *the Voice of One
Crying amid the wilderness*, and given,
Now that their snows must melt, their herbs and flowers
Revive, their obstinate winter pass away,
That awful name to Thee, thee, simple Cuckoo,
Wandering in solitude, and evermore
Foretelling and proclaiming, ere thou leave
100 This thy last haunt beneath Italian skies
To carry thy glad tidings over heights
Still loftier, and to climes more near the Pole.

Voice of the Desert, fare-thee-well; sweet Bird!
If that substantial title please thee more,
Farewell! – but go thy way, no need hast thou
Of a good wish sent after thee; from bower
To bower as green, from sky to sky as clear,
Thee gentle breezes waft – or airs that meet
Thy course and sport around thee softly fan –
110 Till Night, descending upon hill and vale,
Grants to thy mission a brief term of silence,
And folds thy pinions up in blest repose.

XV AT THE CONVENT OF CAMALDOLI
Grieve for the Man who hither came bereft,
And seeking consolation from above;
Nor grieve the less that skill to him was left
To paint this picture of his lady-love:
Can she, a blessèd saint, the work approve?
And O, good Brethren of the cowl, a thing
So fair, to which with peril he must cling,
Destroy in pity, or with care remove.
That bloom – those eyes – can they assist to bind
Thoughts that would stray from Heaven? The dream
10   must cease
To be; by Faith, not sight, his soul must live;
Else will the enamoured Monk too surely find

How wide a space can part from inward peace
The most profound repose his cell can give.

XVI AT THE CONVENT OF CAMALDOLI, CONTINUED

The world forsaken, all its busy cares
And stirring interests shunned with desperate flight,
All trust abandoned in the healing might
Of virtuous action; all that courage dares,
Labour accomplishes, or patience bears –
Those helps rejected, they, whose minds perceive
How subtly works man's weakness, sighs may heave
For such a One beset with cloistral snares.
Father of Mercy! rectify his view,
10 If with his vows this object ill agree;
Shed over it Thy grace, and thus subdue
Imperious passion in a heart set free: –
That earthly love may to herself be true,
Give him a soul that cleaveth unto Thee.

XVII AT THE EREMITE OR UPPER CONVENT OF CAMALDOLI

What aim had they, the Pair of Monks, in size
Enormous, dragged, while side by side they sate,
By panting steers up to this convent gate?
How, with empurpled cheeks and pampered eyes,
Dare they confront the lean austerities
Of Brethren who, here fixed, on Jesu wait
In sackcloth, and God's anger deprecate
Through all that humbles flesh and mortifies?
Strange contrast! – verily the world of dreams,
10 Where mingle, as for mockery combined,
Things in their very essences at strife,
Shows not a sight incongruous as the extremes
That everywhere, before the thoughtful mind,
Meet on the solid ground of waking life.

XVIII AT VALLOMBROSA

Thick as autumnal leaves that strew the brooks
In Vallombrosa, where Etrurian shades
High over-arched embower.

PARADISE LOST.

'Vallombrosa – I longed in thy shadiest wood
To slumber, reclined on the moss-covered floor!'
Fond wish that was granted at last, and the Flood,
That lulled me asleep, bids me listen once more.
Its murmur how soft! as it falls down the steep,
Near that Cell – yon sequestered Retreat high in air –
Where our Milton was wont lonely vigils to keep
For converse with God, sought through study and prayer.

The Monks still repeat the tradition with pride,
10   And its truth who shall doubt? for his Spirit is here;
In the cloud-piercing rocks doth her grandeur abide,
In the pines pointing heavenward her beauty austere;
In the flower-besprent meadows his genius we trace
Turned to humbler delights, in which youth might
        confide,
That would yield him fit help while prefiguring that Place
Where, if Sin had not entered, Love never had died.

When with life lengthened out came a desolate time,
And darkness and danger had compassed him round,
With a thought he would flee to these haunts of his
        prime,
20   And here once again a kind shelter be found.
And let me believe that when nightly the Muse
Did waft him to Sion, the glorified hill,
Here also, on some favoured height, he would choose
To wander, and drink inspiration at will.

Vallombrosa! of thee I first heard in the page
Of that holiest of Bards, and the name for my mind
Had a musical charm, which the winter of age
And the changes it brings had no power to unbind.

And now, ye Miltonian shades! under you
30 I repose, nor am forced from sweet fancy to part,
While your leaves I behold and the brooks they will
    strew,
And the realized vision is clasped to my heart.

Even so, and unblamed, we rejoice as we may
In Forms that must perish, frail objects of sense;
Unblamed – if the Soul be intent on the day
When the Being of Beings shall summon her hence.
For he and he only with wisdom is blest
Who, gathering true pleasures wherever they grow,
Looks up in all places, for joy or for rest,
40 To the Fountain whence Time and Eternity flow.

XIX AT FLORENCE
Under the shadow of a stately Pile,
The dome of Florence, pensive and alone,
Nor giving heed to aught that passed the while,
I stood, and gazed upon a marble stone,
The laurelled Dante's favourite seat. A throne,
In just esteem, it rivals; though no style
Be there of decoration to beguile
The mind, depressed by thought of greatness flown.
As a true man, who long had served the lyre,
10 I gazed with earnestness, and dared no more.
But in his breast the mighty Poet bore
A Patriot's heart, warm with undying fire.
Bold with the thought, in reverence I sate down,
And, for a moment, filled that empty Throne.

XX BEFORE THE PICTURE OF THE BAPTIST, BY
RAPHAEL, IN THE GALLERY AT FLORENCE
The Baptist might have been ordained to cry
Forth from the towers of that huge Pile, wherein
His Father served Jehovah; but how win
Due audience, how for aught but scorn defy
The obstinate pride and wanton revelry
Of the Jerusalem below, her sin

And folly, if they with united din
Drown not at once mandate and prophecy?
Therefore the Voice spake from the Desert, thence
10   To Her, as to her opposite in peace,
Silence, and holiness, and innocence,
To Her and to all Lands its warning sent,
Crying with earnestness that might not cease,
'Make straight a highway for the Lord – repent!'

XXI AT FLORENCE. – FROM MICHELANGELO

Rapt above earth by power of one fair face,
Hers in whose sway alone my heart delights,
I mingle with the blest on those pure heights
Where Man, yet mortal, rarely finds a place.
With Him who made the Work that Work accords
So well, that by its help and through His grace
I raise my thoughts, inform my deeds and words,
Clasping her beauty in my soul's embrace.
Thus, if from two fair eyes mine cannot turn,
10   I feel how in their presence doth abide
Light which to God is both the way and guide;
And, kindling at their lustre, if I burn,
My noble fire emits the joyful ray
That through the realms of glory shines for aye.

XXII AT FLORENCE. – FROM MICHELANGELO

Eternal Lord! eased of a cumbrous load,
And loosened from the world, I turn to Thee;
Shun, like a shattered bark, the storm, and flee
To Thy protection for a safe abode.
The crown of thorns, hands pierced upon the tree,
The meek, benign, and lacerated face,
To a sincere repentance promise grace,
To the sad soul give hope of pardon free.
With justice mark not Thou, O Light divine,
10   My fault, nor hear it with Thy sacred ear;
Neither put forth that way Thy arm severe;
Wash with Thy blood my sins; thereto incline

More readily the more my years require
Help, and forgiveness speedy and entire.

XXIII AMONG THE RUINS OF A CONVENT IN THE
APENNINES
Ye Trees! whose slender roots entwine
  Altars that piety neglects;
Whose infant arms enclasp the shrine
  Which no devotion now respects;
If not a straggler from the herd
Here ruminate, nor shrouded bird,
Chanting her low-voiced hymn, take pride
In aught that ye would grace or hide –
How sadly is your love misplaced,
10 Fair Trees, your bounty run to waste!

Ye, too, wild Flowers! that no one heeds,
And ye – full often spurned as weeds –
In beauty clothed, or breathing sweetness
From fractured arch and mouldering wall –
Do but more touchingly recall
Man's headstrong violence and Time's fleetness,
Making the precincts ye adorn
Appear to sight still more forlorn.

XXIV IN LOMBARDY
See, where his difficult way that Old Man wins
Bent by a load of Mulberry leaves! – most hard
Appears *his* lot, to the small Worm's compared,
For whom his toil with early day begins.
Acknowledging no task-master, at will
(As if her labour and her ease were twins)
She seems to work, at pleasure to lie still; –
And softly sleeps within the thread she spins.
So fare they – the Man serving as her Slave.
10 Ere long their fates do each to each conform:
Both pass into new being, – but the Worm,
Transfigured, sinks into a hopeless grave;

His volant Spirit will, he trusts, ascend
To bliss unbounded, glory without end.

XXV AFTER LEAVING ITALY

Fair Land! Thee all men greet with joy; how few,
Whose souls take pride in freedom, virtue, fame,
Part from thee without pity dyed in shame:
I could not – while from Venice we withdrew,
Led on till an Alpine strait confined our view
Within its depths, and to the shore we came
Of Lago Morto, dreary sight and name,
Which o'er sad thoughts a sadder colouring threw.
Italia! on the surface of thy spirit,
10 (Too aptly emblemed by that torpid lake)
Shall a few partial breezes only creep? –
Be its depths quickened; what thou dost inherit
Of the world's hopes, dare to fulfil; awake,
Mother of Heroes, from thy death-like sleep!

XXVI AFTER LEAVING ITALY, CONTINUED

As indignation mastered grief, my tongue
Spake bitter words; words that did ill agree
With those rich stores of Nature's imagery,
And divine Art, that fast to memory clung –
Thy gifts, magnificent Region, ever young
In the sun's eye, and in his sister's sight
How beautiful! how worthy to be sung
In strains of rapture, or subdued delight!
I feign not; witness that unwelcome shock
10 That followed the first sound of German speech,
Caught the far-winding barrier Alps among.
In that announcement, greeting seemed to mock
Parting; the casual word had power to reach
My heart, and filled that heart with conflict strong.

XXVII COMPOSED AT RYDAL ON MAY MORNING, 1838

If with old love of you, dear Hills! I share
New love of many a rival image brought
From far, forgive the wanderings of my thought:
Nor art thou wronged, sweet May! when I compare
Thy present birth-morn with thy last, so fair,
So rich to me in favours. For my lot
Then was, within the famed Egerian Grot
To sit and muse, fanned by its dewy air
Mingling with thy soft breath! That morning too,
10 Warblers I heard their joy unbosoming
Amid the sunny, shadowy, Colosseum;
Heard them, unchecked by aught of saddening hue,
For victories there won by flower-crowned Spring,
Chant in full choir their innocent Te Deum.

XXVIII THE PILLAR OF TRAJAN

Where towers are crushed, and unforbidden weeds
O'er mutilated arches shed their seeds;
And temples, doomed to milder change, unfold
A new magnificence that vies with old;
Firm in its pristine majesty hath stood
A votive Column, spared by fire and flood: –
And, though the passions of man's fretful race
Have never ceased to eddy round its base,
Not injured more by touch of meddling hands
10 Than a lone obelisk, 'mid Nubian sands,
Or aught in Syrian deserts left to save
From death the memory of the good and brave.
Historic figures round the shaft embost
Ascend, with lineaments in air not lost:
Still as he turns, the charmed spectator sees
Group winding after group with dream-like ease;
Triumphs in sun-bright gratitude displayed,
Or softly stealing into modest shade.
– So, pleased with purple clusters to entwine
20 Some lofty elm-tree, mounts the daring vine;

The woodbine so, with spiral grace, and breathes
Wide-spreading odours from her flowery wreaths.

    Borne by the Muse from rills in shepherds' ears
Murmuring but one smooth story for all years,
I gladly commune with the mind and heart
Of him who thus survives by classic art,
His actions witness, venerate his mien,
And study Trajan as by Pliny seen;
Behold how fought the Chief whose conquering sword
30 Stretched far as earth might own a single lord;
In the delight of moral prudence schooled,
How feelingly at home the Sovereign ruled;
Best of the good – in pagan faith allied
To more than Man, by virtue deified.

    Memorial Pillar! 'mid the wrecks of Time
Preserve thy charge with confidence sublime –
The exultations, pomps, and cares of Rome,
Whence half the breathing world received its doom;
Things that recoil from language; that, if shown
40 By apter pencil, from the light had flown.
A Pontiff, Trajan *here* the Gods implores,
There greets an Embassy from Indian shores;
Lo! he harangues his cohorts – *there* the storm
Of battle meets him in authentic form!
Unharnessed, naked, troops of Moorish horse
Sweep to the charge; more high, the Dacian force,
To hoof and finger mailed; – yet, high or low,
None bleed, and none lie prostrate but the foe;
In every Roman, through all turns of fate,
50 Is Roman dignity inviolate;
Spirit in him pre-eminent, who guides,
Supports, adorns, and over all presides;
Distinguished only by inherent state
From honoured Instruments that round him wait;
Rise as he may, his grandeur scorns the test
Of outward symbol, nor will deign to rest

On aught by which another is deprest.
– Alas! that One thus disciplined could toil
To enslave whole nations on their native soil;
60 So emulous of Macedonian fame,
That, when his age was measured with his aim,
He drooped, 'mid else unclouded victories,
And turned his eagles back with deep-drawn sighs.
O weakness of the Great! O folly of the Wise!

Where now the haughty Empire that was spread
With such fond hope? her very speech is dead;
Yet glorious Art the power of Time defies,
And Trajan still, through various enterprise,
Mounts, in this fine illusion, toward the skies:
70 Still are we present with the imperial Chief,
Nor cease to gaze upon the bold Relief
Till Rome, to silent marble unconfined,
Becomes with all her years a vision of the Mind.

To a Painter

All praise the Likeness by thy skill portrayed;
But 'tis a fruitless task to paint for me,
Who, yielding not to changes Time has made,
By the habitual light of memory see
Eyes unbedimmed, see bloom that cannot fade,
And smiles that from their birthplace ne'er shall flee
Into the land where ghosts and phantoms be;
And, seeing this, own nothing in its stead.
Couldst thou go back into far-distant years,
10 Or share with me, fond thought! that inward eye,
Then, and then only, Painter! could thy Art
The visual powers of Nature satisfy,
Which hold, whate'er to common sight appears,
Their sovereign empire in a faithful heart.

To a Painter

Though I beheld at first with blank surprise
This Work, I now have gazed on it so long
I see its truth with unreluctant eyes;
O, my Belovèd! I have done thee wrong,
Conscious of blessedness, but, whence it sprung,
Ever too heedless, as I now perceive:
Morn into noon did pass, noon into eve,
And the old day was welcome as the young,
As welcome, and as beautiful – in sooth
10   More beautiful, as being a thing more holy:
Thanks to thy virtues, to the eternal youth
Of all thy goodness, never melancholy;
To thy large heart and humble mind, that cast
Into one vision, future, present, past.

With a Small Present

A prized memorial this slight work may prove
As bought in charity and given in Love.

'Let more ambitious Poets take the heart'

Let more ambitious Poets take the heart
By storm, my Verse would rather win its way
With gentle violence into minds well pleased
To give it welcome with a prompt return
Of their own sweetness, as March flowers that shrink
From the sharp wind do readily yield up
Their choicest fragrance to a southern breeze,
Ruffling their bosoms with its genial breath.

'The Crescent-moon, the Star of Love'

The Crescent-moon, the Star of Love,
    Glories of evening, as ye there are seen
With but a span of sky between –
    Speak one of you, my doubts remove,
Which is the attendant Page and which the Queen?

'Though Pulpits and the Desk may fail'

Though Pulpits and the Desk may fail
To reach the hearts of worldly men;
Yet may the grace of God prevail
And touch them through the Poet's pen.

The Wishing-Gate Destroyed

'Tis gone – with old belief and dream
That round it clung, and tempting scheme
    Released from fear and doubt;
And the bright landscape too must lie,
By this blank wall, from every eye,
    Relentlessly shut out.

Bear witness ye who seldom passed
That opening – but a look ye cast
    Upon the lake below,
10 What spirit-stirring power it gained
From faith which here was entertained,
    Though reason might say no.

Blest is that ground, where, o'er the springs
Of history, Glory claps her wings,
    Fame sheds the exulting tear;

Yet earth is wide, and many a nook
Unheard of is, like this, a book
    For modest meanings dear.

It was in sooth a happy thought
20 That grafted, on so fair a spot,
        So confident a token
    Of coming good; – the charm is fled;
    Indulgent centuries spun a thread,
        Which one harsh day has broken.

Alas! for him who gave the word;
Could he no sympathy afford,
    Derived from earth or heaven,
To hearts so oft by hope betrayed;
Their very wishes wanted aid
30   Which here was freely given?

Where, for the love-lorn maiden's wound,
Will now so readily be found
    A balm of expectation?
Anxious for far-off children, where
Shall mothers breathe a like sweet air
    Of home-felt consolation?

And not unfelt will prove the loss
'Mid trivial care and petty cross
    And each day's shallow grief;
40 Though the most easily beguiled
Were oft among the first that smiled
    At their own fond belief.

If still the reckless change we mourn,
A reconciling thought may turn
    To harm that might lurk here,
Ere judgement prompted from within
Fit aims, with courage to begin,
    And strength to persevere.

Not Fortune's slave is Man: our state
50 Enjoins, while firm resolves await
   On wishes just and wise,
That strenuous action follow both,
And life be one perpetual growth
   Of heaven-ward enterprise.

So taught, so trained, we boldly face
All accidents of time and place;
   Whatever props may fail,
Trust in that sovereign law can spread
New glory o'er the mountain's head,
60   Fresh beauty through the vale.

That truth informing mind and heart,
The simplest cottager may part,
   Ungrieved, with charm and spell;
And yet, lost Wishing-gate, to thee
The voice of grateful memory
   Shall bid a kind farewell!

Upon Perusing the 'Epistle [To Sir George Howland Beaumont'] Thirty Years after its Composition

Soon did the Almighty Giver of all rest
Take those dear young Ones to a fearless nest;
And in Death's arms has long reposed the Friend
For whom this simple Register was penned.
Thanks to the moth that spared it for our eyes;
And Strangers even the slighted Scroll may prize,
Moved by the touch of kindred sympathies.
For – save the calm, repentance sheds o'er strife
Raised by remembrances of misused life,
10 The light from past endeavours purely willed
And by Heaven's favour happily fulfilled;
Save hope that we, yet bound to Earth, may share

The joys of the Departed – what so fair
As blameless pleasure, not without some tears,
Reviewed through Love's transparent veil of years?

NOTE. – Loughrigg Tarn, alluded to in the foregoing Epistle,
resembles, though much smaller in compass, the Lake Nemi, or
Speculum Dianoe as it is often called, not only in its clear waters
and circular form, and the beauty immediately surrounding it,
but also as being overlooked by the eminence of Langdale Pikes
as Lake Nemi is by that of Monte Calvo. Since this Epistle was
written Loughrigg Tarn has lost much of its beauty by the
felling of many natural clumps of wood, relics of the old forest,
particularly upon the farm called 'The Oaks', from the abundance of that tree which grew there.

It is to be regretted, upon public grounds, that Sir George
Beaumont did not carry into effect his intention of constructing
here a Summer Retreat in the style I have described; as his
taste would have set an example how buildings, with all the
accommodations modern society requires, might be introduced
even into the most secluded parts of this country without in-
juring their native character. The design was not abandoned
from failure of inclination on his part, but in consequence of
local untowardness which need not be particularized.

Epitaph in the Chapel-Yard of Langdale, Westmoreland

By playful smiles, (alas! too oft
A sad heart's sunshine) by a soft
And gentle nature, and a free
Yet modest hand of charity,
Through life was OWEN LLOYD endeared
To young and old; and how revered
Had been that pious spirit, a tide
Of humble mourners testified,
When, after pains dispensed to prove
10 The measure of God's chastening love,
Here, brought from far, his corse found rest, –
Fulfilment of his own request; –

Urged less for this Yew's shade, though he
Planted with such fond hope the tree;
Less for the love of stream and rock,
Dear as they were, than that his Flock,
When they no more their Pastor's voice
Could hear to guide them in their choice
Through good and evil, help might have,
20 Admonished, from his silent grave,
Of righteousness, of sins forgiven,
For peace on earth and bliss in heaven.

'*When Severn's sweeping Flood had overthrown*'

When Severn's sweeping Flood had overthrown
St Mary's Church, the Preacher then would cry,
'Thus, Christian people, God his might hath shown,
That ye to him your love may testify;
Haste and rebuild the Pile.' But not a stone
Resumed its place – age after age went by,
And Heaven still lacked its due, though piety
In secret did, we trust, her loss bemoan.
But now her Spirit hath put forth its claim
10 In power, and Poesy would lend her voice –
Let the New Work be worthy of its aim,
That in its beauty Cardiff may rejoice!
Oh! in the Past if cause there was for shame,
Let not our Times halt in their better choice!

'*Intent on gathering wool from hedge and brake*'

Intent on gathering wool from hedge and brake
Yon busy Little-ones rejoice that soon
A poor old Dame will bless them for the boon:
Great is their glee while flake they add to flake
With rival earnestness; far other strife
Than will hereafter move them, if they make

Pastime their idol, give their day of life
To pleasure snatched for reckless pleasure's sake.
Can pomp and show allay one heart-born grief?
10 Pains which the World inflicts can she requite?
Not for an interval however brief;
The silent thoughts that search for stedfast light,
Love from her depths, and Duty in her might,
And Faith – these only yield secure relief.

Prelude, Prefixed to the Volume Entitled 'Poems Chiefly of Early and Late Years'

In desultory walk through orchard grounds,
Or some deep chestnut grove, oft have I paused
The while a Thrush, urged rather than restrained
By gusts of vernal storm, attuned his song
To his own genial instincts; and was heard
(Though not without some plaintive tones between)
To utter, above showers of blossom swept
From tossing boughs, the promise of a calm,
Which the unsheltered traveller might receive
10 With thankful spirit. The descant, and the wind
That seemed to play with it in love or scorn,
Encouraged and endeared the strain of words
That haply flowed from me, by fits of silence
Impelled to livelier pace. But now, my Book!
Charged with those lays, and others of like mood,
Or loftier pitch if higher rose the theme,
Go, single – yet aspiring to be joined
With thy Forerunners that through many a year
Have faithfully prepared each other's way –
20 Go forth upon a mission best fulfilled
When and wherever, in this changeful world,
Power hath been given to please for higher ends
Than pleasure only; gladdening to prepare
For wholesome sadness, troubling to refine,
Calming to raise; and, by a sapient Art

Diffused through all the mysteries of our Being,
Softening the toils and pains that have not ceased
To cast their shadows on our mother Earth
Since the primeval doom. Such is the grace
30   Which, though unsued for, fails not to descend
With heavenly inspiration; such the aim
That Reason dictates; and, as even the wish
Has virtue in it, why should hope to me
Be wanting that sometimes, where fancied ills
Harass the mind and strip from off the bowers
Of private life their natural pleasantness,
A Voice – devoted to the love whose seeds
Are sown in every human breast, to beauty
Lodged within compass of the humblest sight,
40   To cheerful intercourse with wood and field,
And sympathy with man's substantial griefs –
Will not be heard in vain? And in those days
When unforeseen distress spreads far and wide
Among a People mournfully cast down,
Or into anger roused by venal words
In recklessness flung out to overturn
The judgement, and divert the general heart
From mutual good – some strain of thine, my Book!
Caught at propitious intervals, may win
50   Listeners who not unwillingly admit
Kindly emotion tending to console
And reconcile; and both with young and old
Exalt the sense of thoughtful gratitude
For benefits that still survive, by faith
In progress, under laws divine, maintained.

'Wansfell! this Household has a favoured lot'

Wansfell! this Household has a favoured lot,
Living with liberty on thee to gaze,
To watch while Morn first crowns thee with her rays,
Or when along thy breast serenely float

Evening's angelic clouds. Yet ne'er a note
Hath sounded (shame upon the Bard!) thy praise
For all that thou, as if from heaven, hast brought
Of glory lavished on our quiet days.
Bountiful Son of Earth! when we are gone
10 From every object dear to mortal sight,
As soon we shall be, may these words attest
How oft, to elevate our spirits, shone
Thy visionary majesties of light,
How in thy pensive glooms our hearts found rest.

'Glad sight wherever new with old'

Glad sight wherever new with old
Is joined through some dear homeborn tie;
The life of all that we behold
Depends upon that mystery.

Vain is the glory of the sky,
The beauty vain of field and grove
Unless, while with admiring eye
We gaze, we also learn to love.

The Eagle and the Dove

Shade of Caractacus, if spirits love
The cause they fought for in their earthly home,
To see the Eagle ruffled by the Dove
May soothe thy memory of the chains of Rome.

These children claim thee for their sire; the breath
Of thy renown, from Cambrian mountains, fans
A flame within them that despises death
And glorifies the truant youth of Vannes.

With thy own scorn of tyrants they advance,
10 But truth divine has sanctified their rage,

A silver cross enchased with Flowers of France
Their badge, attests the holy fight they wage.

The shrill defiance of the young crusade
Their veteran foes mock as an idle noise;
But unto Faith and Loyalty comes aid
From Heaven, gigantic force to beardless boys.

'*Lyre! though such power do in thy magic live*'

Lyre! though such power do in thy magic live
   As might from India's farthest plain
   Recall the not unwilling Maid,
      Assist me to detain
      The lovely Fugitive:
Check with thy notes the impulse which, betrayed
By her sweet farewell looks, I longed to aid.
Here let me gaze enrapt upon that eye,
The impregnable and awe-inspiring fort
Of contemplation, the calm port
By reason fenced from winds that sigh
Among the restless sails of vanity.
But if no wish be hers that we should part,
A humbler bliss would satisfy my heart.
      Where all things are so fair,
Enough by her dear side to breathe the air
      Of this Elysian weather;
And on or in, or near, the brook, espy
   Shade upon the sunshine lying
      Faint and somewhat pensively;
   And downward Image gaily vying
      With its upright living tree
'Mid silver clouds, and openings of blue sky
As soft almost and deep as her cerulean eye.
Nor less the joy with many a glance
Cast up the Stream or down at her beseeching,
To mark its eddying foam-balls prettily distrest

By ever-changing shape and want of rest;
    Or watch, with mutual teaching,
30   The current as it plays
        In flashing leaps and stealthy creeps
    Adown a rocky maze;
Or note (translucent summer's happiest chance!)
In the slope-channel floored with pebbles bright,
Stones of all hues, gem emulous of gem,
So vivid that they take from keenest sight
The liquid veil that seeks not to hide them.

Suggested by a Picture of the Bird of Paradise

The gentlest Poet, with free thoughts endowed,
And a true master of the glowing strain,
Might scan the narrow province with disdain
That to the Painter's skill is here allowed.
This, this the Bird of Paradise! disclaim
The daring thought, forget the name;
This the Sun's Bird, whom Glendoveers might own
As no unworthy Partner in their flight
Through seas of ether, where the ruffling sway
10 Of nether air's rude billows is unknown;
Whom Sylphs, if e'er for casual pastime they
Through India's spicy regions wing their way,
Might bow to as their Lord. What character,
O sovereign Nature! I appeal to thee,
Of all thy feathered progeny
Is so unearthly, and what shape so fair?
So richly decked in variegated down,
Green, sable, shining yellow, shadowy brown,
Tints softly with each other blended,
20 Hues doubtfully begun and ended;
Or intershooting, and to sight
Lost and recovered, as the rays of light
Glance on the conscious plumes touched here and there?

Full surely, when with such proud gifts of life
Began the pencil's strife,
O'erweening Art was caught as in a snare.

A sense of seemingly presumptuous wrong
Gave the first impulse to the Poet's song;
But, of his scorn repenting soon, he drew
30 A juster judgement from a calmer view;
And, with a spirit freed from discontent,
Thankfully took an effort that was meant
Not with God's bounty, Nature's love, to vie,
Or made with hope to please that inward eye
Which ever strives in vain itself to satisfy,
But to recall the truth by some faint trace
Of power ethereal and celestial grace,
That in the living Creature find on earth a place.

'Though the bold wings of Poesy affect'

Though the bold wings of Poesy affect
The clouds, and wheel around the mountain tops
Rejoicing, from her loftiest height she drops
Well pleased to skim the plain with wild flowers deckt,
Or muse in solemn grove whose shades protect
The lingering dew – there steals along, or stops
Watching the least small bird that round her hops,
Or creeping worm, with sensitive respect.
Her functions are they therefore less divine,
10 Her thoughts less deep, or void of grave intent
Her simplest fancies? Should that fear be thine,
Aspiring Votary, ere thy hand present
One offering, kneel before her modest shrine,
With brow in penitential sorrow bent!

'A Poet! *He hath put his heart to school*'

A Poet! – He hath put his heart to school,
Nor dares to move unpropped upon the staff
Which Art hath lodged within his hand – must laugh
By precept only, and shed tears by rule.
Thy Art be Nature; the live current quaff,
And let the groveller sip his stagnant pool,
In fear that else, when Critics grave and cool
Have killed him, Scorn should write his epitaph.
How does the Meadow-flower its bloom unfold?
10   Because the lovely little flower is free
Down to its root, and, in that freedom, bold;
And so the grandeur of the Forest-tree
Comes not by casting in a formal mould,
But from its *own* divine vitality.

'*The most alluring clouds that mount the sky*'

The most alluring clouds that mount the sky
Owe to a troubled element their forms,
Their hues to sunset. If with raptured eye
We watch their splendour, shall we covet storms,
And wish the Lord of day his slow decline
Would hasten, that such pomp may float on high?
Behold, already they forget to shine,
Dissolve – and leave to him who gazed a sigh.
Not loth to thank each moment for its boon
10   Of pure delight, come whensoe'er it may,
Peace let us seek, – to stedfast things attune
Calm expectations, leaving to the gay
And volatile their love of transient bowers,
The house that cannot pass away be ours.

In Allusion to Various Recent Histories and Notices of the French Revolution

Portentous change when History can appear
As the cool Advocate of foul device;
Reckless audacity extol, and jeer
At consciences perplexed with scruples nice!
They who bewail not, must abhor, the sneer
Born of Conceit, Power's blind Idolator;
Or haply sprung from vaunting Cowardice
Betrayed by mockery of holy fear.
Hath it not long been said the wrath of Man
10 Works not the righteousness of God? Oh bend,
Bend, ye Perverse! to judgements from on High,
Laws that lay under Heaven's perpetual ban
All principles of action that transcend
The sacred limits of humanity.

In Allusion to Various Recent Histories and Notices of the French Revolution, Continued

Who ponders National events shall find
An awful balancing of loss and gain,
Joy based on sorrow, good with ill combined,
And proud deliverance issuing out of pain
And direful throes; as if the All-ruling Mind,
With whose perfection it consists to ordain
Volcanic burst, earthquake, and hurricane,
Dealt in like sort with feeble human kind
By laws immutable. But woe for him
10 Who thus deceived shall lend an eager hand
To social havoc. Is not Conscience ours,
And Truth, whose eye guilt only can make dim;
And Will, whose office, by divine command,
Is to control and check disordered Powers?

In Allusion to Various Recent Histories and Notices of the French Revolution, Concluded

Long-favoured England! be not thou misled
By monstrous theories of alien growth,
Lest alien frenzy seize thee, waxing wroth,
Self-smitten till thy garments reek, dyed red
With thy own blood, which tears in torrents shed
Fail to wash out, tears flowing ere thy troth
Be plighted, not to ease but sullen sloth,
Or wan despair – the ghost of false hope fled
Into a shameful grave. Among thy youth,
10　My Country! if such warning be held dear,
Then shall a Veteran's heart be thrilled with joy,
One who would gather from eternal truth,
For time and season, rules that work to cheer –
Not scourge, to save the People – not destroy.

'Feel for the wrongs to universal ken'

Feel for the wrongs to universal ken
Daily exposed, woe that unshrouded lies;
And seek the Sufferer in his darkest den,
Whether conducted to the spot by sighs
And moanings, or he dwells (as if the wren
Taught him concealment) hidden from all eyes
In silence and the awful modesties
Of sorrow; – feel for all, as brother Men!
Rest not in hope want's icy chain to thaw
10　By casual boons and formal charities;
Learn to be just, just through impartial law;
Far as ye may, erect and equalize;
And, what ye cannot reach by statute, draw
Each from his fountain of self-sacrifice!

'While beams of orient light shoot wide and high'

While beams of orient light shoot wide and high,
Deep in the vale a little rural Town
Breathes forth a cloud-like creature of its own,
That mounts not toward the radiant morning sky,
But, with a less ambitious sympathy,
Hangs o'er its Parent waking to the cares,
Troubles and toils that every day prepares.
So Fancy, to the musing Poet's eye,
Endears that Lingerer. And how blest her sway
10 (Like influence never may my soul reject),
If the calm Heaven, now to its zenith decked
With glorious forms in numberless array,
To the lone shepherd on the hills disclose
Gleams from a world in which the saints repose.

To a Lady

In answer to a request that I would write her a poem upon some drawings that she had made of flowers in the island of Madeira

Fair Lady! can I sing of flowers
  That in Madeira bloom and fade,
I who ne'er sate within their bowers,
  Nor through their sunny lawns have strayed?
How they in sprightly dance are worn
  By Shepherd-groom or May-day queen,
Or holy festal pomps adorn,
  These eyes have never seen.

Yet though to me the pencil's art
10 No like remembrances can give,
Your portraits still may reach the heart
  And there for gentle pleasure live;

While Fancy ranging with free scope
    Shall on some lovely Alien set
A name with us endeared to hope,
    To peace, or fond regret.

Still as we look with nicer care,
    Some new resemblance we may trace:
A *Heart's-ease* will perhaps be there,
20   A *Speedwell* may not want its place.
And so may we, with charmèd mind
    Beholding what your skill has wrought,
Another *Star-of-Bethlehem* find,
    A new *Forget-me-not.*

From earth to heaven with motion fleet
    From heaven to earth our thoughts will pass,
A *Holy-thistle* here we meet
    And there a *Shepherd's weather-glass*;
And haply some familiar name
30   Shall grace the fairest, sweetest, plant
Whose presence cheers the drooping frame
    Of English Emigrant.

Gazing she feels its power beguile
    Sad thoughts, and breathes with easier breath;
Alas! that meek, that tender smile
    Is but a harbinger of death:
And pointing with a feeble hand
    She says, in faint words by sigh broken,
Bear for me to my native land
40   This precious Flower, true love's last token.

Grace Darling

Among the dwellers in the silent fields
The natural heart is touched, and public way
And crowded street resound with ballad strains,

Inspired by ONE whose very name bespeaks
Favour divine, exalting human love;
Whom, since her birth on bleak Northumbria's coast,
Known unto few but prized as far as known,
A single Act endears to high and low
Through the whole land – to Manhood, moved in spite
10 Of the world's freezing cares – to generous Youth –
To Infancy, that lisps her praise – to Age
Whose eye reflects it, glistening through a tear
Of tremulous admiration. Such true fame
Awaits her *now*; but, verily, good deeds
Do no imperishable record find
Save in the rolls of heaven, where hers may live
A theme for angels, when they celebrate
The high-souled virtues which forgetful earth
Has witnessed. Oh! that winds and waves could speak
20 Of things which their united power called forth
From the pure depths of her humanity!
A Maiden gentle, yet, at duty's call,
Firm and unflinching, as the Lighthouse reared
On the Island-rock, her lonely dwelling-place;
Or like the invincible Rock itself that braves,
Age after age, the hostile elements,
As when it guarded holy Cuthbert's cell.

All night the storm had raged, nor ceased, nor paused,
When, as day broke, the Maid, through misty air,
30 Espies far off a Wreck, amid the surf,
Beating on one of those disastrous isles –
Half of a Vessel, half – no more; the rest
Had vanished, swallowed up with all that there
Had for the common safety striven in vain,
Or thither thronged for refuge. With quick glance
Daughter and Sire through optic-glass discern,
Clinging about the remnant of this Ship,
Creatures – how precious in the Maiden's sight!
For whom, belike, the old Man grieves still more
40 Than for their fellow-sufferers engulfed

Where every parting agony is hushed,
And hope and fear mix not in further strife.
'But courage, Father! let us out to sea –
A few may yet be saved.' The Daughter's words,
Her earnest tone, and look beaming with faith,
Dispel the Father's doubts: nor do they lack
The noble-minded Mother's helping hand
To launch the boat; and with her blessing cheered,
And inwardly sustained by silent prayer,
50 Together they put forth, Father and Child!
Each grasps an oar, and struggling on they go –
Rivals in effort; and, alike intent
Here to elude and there surmount, they watch
The billows lengthening, mutually crossed
And shattered, and re-gathering their might;
As if the tumult, by the Almighty's will
Were, in the conscious sea, roused and prolonged
That woman's fortitude – so tried, so proved –
May brighten more and more!
                                    True to the mark,
60 They stem the current of that perilous gorge,
Their arms still strengthening with the strengthening
      heart,
Though danger, as the Wreck is neared, becomes
More imminent. Not unseen do they approach;
And rapture, with varieties of fear
Incessantly conflicting, thrills the frames
Of those who, in that dauntless energy,
Foretaste deliverance; but the least perturbed
Can scarcely trust his eyes, when he perceives
That of the pair – tossed on the waves to bring
70 Hope to the hopeless, to the dying, life –
One is a Woman, a poor earthly sister,
Or, be the Visitant other than she seems,
A guardian Spirit sent from pitying Heaven,
In woman's shape. But why prolong the tale,
Casting weak words amid a host of thoughts
Armed to repel them? Every hazard faced

And difficulty mastered, with resolve
That no one breathing should be left to perish,
This last remainder of the crew are all
80 Placed in the little boat, then o'er the deep
Are safely borne, landed upon the beach,
And, in fulfilment of God's mercy, lodged
Within the sheltering Lighthouse. – Shout, ye Waves!
Send forth a song of triumph. Waves and Winds,
Exult in this deliverance wrought through faith
In Him whose Providence your rage hath served!
Ye screaming Sea-mews, in the concert join!
And would that some immortal Voice – a Voice
Fitly attuned to all that gratitude
90 Breathes out from floor or couch, through pallid lips
Of the survivors – to the clouds might bear –
Blended with praise of that parental love,
Beneath whose watchful eye the Maiden grew
Pious and pure, modest and yet so brave,
Though young so wise, though meek so resolute –
Might carry to the clouds and to the stars,
Yea, to celestial Choirs, GRACE DARLING'S name!

Inscription for a Monument in Crosthwaite Church, in the Vale of Keswick

Ye vales and hills whose beauty hither drew
The poet's steps, and fixed him here, on you
His eyes have closed! And ye, loved books, no more
Shall Southey feed upon your precious lore,
To works that ne'er shall forfeit their renown,
Adding immortal labours of his own –
Whether he traced historic truth, with zeal
For the State's guidance, or the Church's weal,
Or Fancy, disciplined by studious art,
10 Informed his pen, or wisdom of the heart,
Or judgements sanctioned in the Patriot's mind
By reverence for the rights of all mankind.

Wide were his aims, yet in no human breast
Could private feelings meet for holier rest.
His joys, his griefs, have vanished like a cloud
From Skiddaw's top; but he to heaven was vowed
Through his industrious life, and Christian faith
Calmed in his soul the fear of change and death.

To the Rev. Christopher Wordsworth, D.D., Master of Harrow School

After the perusal of his 'Theophilus Anglicanus,' recently published.

Enlightened Teacher, gladly from thy hand
Have I received this proof of pains bestowed
By Thee to guide thy Pupils on the road
That, in our native isle, and every land,
The Church, when trusting in divine command
And in her Catholic attributes, hath trod:
O may these lessons be with profit scanned
To thy heart's wish, thy labour blest by God!
So the bright faces of the young and gay
10 Shall look more bright – the happy, happier still;
Catch, in the pauses of their keenest play,
Motions of thought which elevate the will
And, like the Spire that from your classic Hill
Points heavenward, indicate the end and way.

'So fair, so sweet, withal so sensitive'

So fair, so sweet, withal so sensitive,
Would that the little Flowers were born to live,
Conscious of half the pleasure which they give;

That to this mountain-daisy's self were known
The beauty of its star-shaped shadow, thrown
On the smooth surface of this naked stone!

And what if hence a bold desire should mount
High as the Sun, that he could take account
Of all that issues from his glorious fount!

10   So might he ken how by his sovereign aid
These delicate companionships are made;
And how he rules the pomp of light and shade;

And were the Sister-power that shines by night
So privileged, what a countenance of delight
Would through the clouds break forth on human sight!

Fond fancies! wheresoe'er shall turn thine eye
On earth, air, ocean, or the starry sky,
Converse with Nature in pure sympathy;

All vain desires, all lawless wishes quelled,
20   Be Thou to love and praise alike impelled,
Whatever boon is granted or withheld.

On the Projected Kendal and Windermere Railway

Is then no nook of English ground secure
From rash assault? Schemes of retirement sown
In youth, and 'mid the busy world kept pure
As when their earliest flowers of hope were blown,
Must perish; – how can they this blight endure?
And must he too the ruthless change bemoan
Who scorns a false utilitarian lure
'Mid his paternal fields at random thrown?
Baffle the threat, bright Scene, from Orrest-head
10   Given to the pausing traveller's rapturous glance:
Plead for thy peace, thou beautiful romance
Of nature; and, if human hearts be dead,
Speak, passing winds; ye torrents, with your strong
And constant voice, protest against the wrong.

'Proud were ye, Mountains, when, in times of old'

Proud were ye, Mountains, when, in times of old,
Your patriot sons, to stem invasive war,
Intrenched your brows; ye gloried in each scar:
Now, for your shame, a Power, the Thirst of Gold,
That rules o'er Britain like a baneful star,
Wills that your peace, your beauty, shall be sold,
And clear way made for her triumphal car
Through the beloved retreats your arms enfold!
Heard YE that Whistle? As her long-linked Train
10 Swept onwards, did the vision cross your view?
Yes, ye were startled; – and, in balance true,
Weighing the mischief with the promised gain,
Mountains, and Vales, and Floods, I call on you
To share the passion of a just disdain.

'Young England – what is then become of Old'

Young England – what is then become of Old,
Of dear Old England? Think they she is dead,
Dead to the very name? Presumption fed
On empty air! That name will keep its hold
In the true filial bosom's inmost fold
For ever. – The Spirit of Alfred, at the head
Of all who for her rights watched, toiled and bled,
Knows that this prophecy is not too bold.
What – how! shall she submit in will and deed
10 To Beardless Boys – an imitative race,
The *servum pecus* of a Gallic breed?
Dear Mother! if thou *must* thy steps retrace,
Go where at least meek Innocency dwells;
Let Babes and Sucklings be thy oracles.

To the Pennsylvanians

Days undefiled by luxury or sloth,
Firm self-denial, manners grave and staid,
Rights equal, laws with cheerfulness obeyed,
Words that require no sanction from an oath,
And simple honesty a common growth –
This high repute, with bounteous Nature's aid,
Won confidence, now ruthlessly betrayed
At will, your power the measure of your troth! –
All who revere the memory of Penn
Grieve for the land on whose wild woods his name
Was fondly grafted with a virtuous aim,
Renounced, abandoned by degenerate Men
For state-dishonour black as ever came
To upper air from Mammon's loathsome den.

The Westmoreland Girl

TO MY GRANDCHILDREN

PART I
Seek who will delight in fable,
I shall tell you truth. A Lamb
Leapt from this steep bank to follow
'Cross the brook its thoughtless dam.

Far and wide on hill and valley
Rain had fallen, unceasing rain,
And the bleating mother's Young-one
Struggled with the flood in vain:

But, as chanced, a Cottage-maiden
(Ten years scarcely had she told)
Seeing, plunged into the torrent,
Clasped the Lamb and kept her hold.

Whirled adown the rocky channel,
Sinking, rising, on they go,
Peace and rest, as seems, before them
Only in the lake below.

Oh! it was a frightful current
Whose fierce wrath the Girl had braved;
Clap your hands with joy my Hearers,
20   Shout in triumph, both are saved;

Saved by courage that with danger
Grew, by strength the gift of love,
And belike a guardian angel
Came with succour from above.

PART II

Now, to a maturer Audience,
Let me speak of this brave Child
Left among her native mountains
With wild Nature to run wild.

So, unwatched by love maternal,
30   Mother's care no more her guide,
Fared this little bright-eyed Orphan
Even while at her father's side.

Spare your blame, – remembrance makes him
Loth to rule by strict command;
Still upon his cheek are living
Touches of her infant hand,

Dear caresses given in pity,
Sympathy that soothed his grief,
As the dying mother witnessed
40   To her thankful mind's relief.

Time passed on; the Child was happy,
Like a Spirit of air she moved,

Wayward, yet by all who knew her
For her tender heart beloved.

Scarcely less than sacred passions,
Bred in house, in grove, and field,
Link her with the inferior creatures,
Urge her powers their rights to shield.

Anglers, bent on reckless pastime,
50 Learn how she can feel alike
Both for tiny harmless minnow
And the fierce and sharp-toothed pike.

Merciful protectress, kindling
Into anger or disdain;
Many a captive hath she rescued,
Others saved from lingering pain.

Listen yet awhile; – with patience
Hear the homely truths I tell,
She in Grasmere's old church-steeple
60 Tolled this day the passing bell.

Yes, the wild Girl of the mountains
To their echoes gave the sound,
Notice punctual as the minute,
Warning solemn and profound.

She, fulfilling her sire's office,
Rang alone the far-heard knell,
Tribute, by her hand, in sorrow,
Paid to One who loved her well.

When his spirit was departed,
70 On that service she went forth;
Nor will fail the like to render
When his corse is laid in earth.

What then wants the Child to temper,
In her breast, unruly fire,
To control the froward impulse
And restrain the vague desire?

Easily a pious training
And a stedfast outward power
Would supplant the weeds and cherish,
80   In their stead, each opening flower.

Thus the fearless Lamb-deliverer,
Woman-grown, meek-hearted, sage,
May become a blest example
For her sex, of every age.

Watchful as a wheeling eagle,
Constant as a soaring lark,
Should the country need a heroine,
She might prove our Maid of Arc.

Leave that thought; and here be uttered
90   Prayer that Grace divine may raise
Her humane courageous spirit
Up to heaven, through peaceful ways.

At Furness Abbey

Well have yon Railway Labourers to THIS ground
Withdrawn for noontide rest. They sit, they walk
Among the Ruins, but no idle talk
Is heard; to grave demeanour all are bound;
And from one voice a Hymn with tuneful sound
Hallows once more the long-deserted Choir
And thrills the old sepulchral earth, around.
Others look up, and with fixed eyes admire
That wide-spanned arch, wondering how it was raised,
10   To keep, so high in air, its strength and grace:

All seem to feel the spirit of the place,
And by the general reverence God is praised:
Profane Despoilers, stand ye not reproved,
While thus these simple-hearted men are moved?

Sonnet

Why should we weep or mourn, Angelic boy,
For such thou wert ere from our sight removed,
Holy, and ever dutiful – beloved
From day to day with never-ceasing joy,
And hopes as dear as could the heart employ
In aught to earth pertaining? Death has proved
His might, nor less his mercy, as behoved –
Death conscious that he only could destroy
The bodily frame. That beauty is laid low
To moulder in a far-off field of Rome;
But Heaven is now, blest Child, thy Spirit's home:
When such divine communion, which we know,
Is felt, thy Roman burial-place will be
Surely a sweet remembrancer of Thee.

10

'*Forth from a jutting ridge, around whose base*'

Forth from a jutting ridge, around whose base
Winds our deep Vale, two heath-clad Rocks ascend
In fellowship, the loftiest of the pair
Rising to no ambitious height; yet both,
O'er lake and stream, mountain and flowery mead,
Unfolding prospects fair as human eyes
Ever beheld. Up-led with mutual help,
To one or other brow of those twin Peaks
Were two adventurous Sisters wont to climb,
And took no note of the hour while thence they gazed,
The blooming heath their couch, gazed, side by side,
In speechless admiration. I, a witness

10

And frequent sharer of their calm delight
With thankful heart, to either Eminence
Gave the baptismal name each Sister bore.
Now are they parted, far as Death's cold hand
Hath power to part the Spirits of those who love
As they did love. Ye kindred Pinnacles –
That, while the generations of mankind
20 Follow each other to their hiding-place
In time's abyss, are privileged to endure
Beautiful in yourselves, and richly graced
With like command of beauty – grant your aid
For MARY'S humble, SARAH'S silent, claim,
That their pure joy in nature may survive
From age to age in blended memory.

'Yes! thou art fair, yet be not moved'

Yes! thou art fair, yet be not moved
   To scorn the declaration,
That sometimes I in thee have loved
   My fancy's own creation.

Imagination needs must stir;
   Dear Maid, this truth believe,
Minds that have nothing to confer
   Find little to perceive.

Be pleased that nature made thee fit
10   To feed my heart's devotion,
By laws to which all Forms submit
   In sky, air, earth, and ocean.

'What heavenly smiles! O Lady mine'

What heavenly smiles! O Lady mine,
Through my very heart they shine;

And, if my brow gives back their light,
Do thou look gladly on the sight;
As the clear Moon with modest pride
    Beholds her own bright beams
Reflected from the mountain's side
    And from the headlong streams.

[*Lines Inscribed in a Copy of His Poems Sent to the Queen for the Royal Library at Windsor*]

Deign, Sovereign Mistress! to accept a Lay,
    No laureate Offering of elaborate art;
But salutation taking its glad way
    From deep recesses of a loyal heart.

Queen, Wife and Mother! may All-judging Heaven
    Shower with a bounteous hand on Thee and Thine
Felicity that only can be given
    On earth to goodness blest by Grace divine.

Lady! devoutly honoured and beloved
10   Through every realm confided to thy sway;
Mayst thou pursue thy course by God approved,
    And He will teach thy People to obey;

As thou art wont, thy Sovereignty adorn
    With Woman's gentleness, yet firm and staid;
So shalt that earthly crown thy brows have worn
    Be changed for one whose glory cannot fade.

And now by duty urged, I lay this Book
    Before thy Majesty, in humble trust
That on its simplest pages Thou wilt look
20   With a benign indulgence more than just.

Nor wilt Thou blame the Poet's earnest prayer
    That issuing hence may steal into thy mind
Some solace under weight of royal care,
    Or grief – the inheritance of humankind;

For know We not that from celestial spheres,
    When Time was young, an inspiration came
(Oh! were it mine!) to hallow saddest tears,
    And help Life onward in its noblest aim.
                    your Majesty's
                        devoted Subject and Servant
                            William Wordsworth

*'Where lies the truth? has Man, in
wisdom's creed'*

Where lies the truth? has Man, in wisdom's creed,
A pitiable doom; for respite brief
A care more anxious, or a heavier grief?
Is he ungrateful, and doth little heed
God's bounty, soon forgotten; or indeed,
Must Man, with labour born, awake to sorrow
When Flowers rejoice and Larks with rival speed
Spring from their nests to bid the Sun good morrow?
They mount for rapture as their songs proclaim
10 Warbled in hearing both of earth and sky;
But o'er the contrast wherefore heave a sigh?
Like those aspirants let us soar – our aim,
Through life's worst trials, whether shocks or snares,
A happier, brighter, purer Heaven than theirs.

'I know an aged Man constrained to dwell'

I know an aged Man constrained to dwell
In a large house of public charity,
Where he abides, as in a Prisoner's cell,
With numbers near, alas! no company.

When he could creep about, at will, though poor
And forced to live on alms, this old Man fed
A Redbreast, one that to his cottage door
Came not, but in a lane partook his bread.

There, at the root of one particular tree,
10   An easy seat this worn-out Labourer found
While Robin pecked the crumbs upon his knee
Laid one by one, or scattered on the ground.

Dear intercourse was theirs, day after day;
What signs of mutual gladness when they met!
Think of their common peace, their simple play,
The parting moment and its fond regret.

Months passed in love that failed not to fulfil,
In spite of season's change, its own demand,
By fluttering pinions here and busy bill;
20   There by caresses from a tremulous hand.

Thus in the chosen spot a tie so strong
Was formed between the solitary pair,
That when his fate had housed him 'mid a throng
The Captive shunned all converse proffered there.

Wife, children, kindred, they were dead and gone;
But, if no evil hap his wishes crossed,
One living Stay was left, and in that one
Some recompence for all that he had lost.

O that the good old Man had power to prove,
30   By message sent through air or visible token,
That still he loves the Bird, and still must love;
That friendship lasts though fellowship is broken!

To Lucca Giordano

Giordano, verily thy Pencil's skill
Hath here portrayed with Nature's happiest grace
The fair Endymion couched on Latmos-hill;
And Dian gazing on the Shepherd's face
In rapture, – yet suspending her embrace,

As not unconscious with what power the thrill
Of her most timid touch his sleep would chase,
And, with his sleep, that beauty calm and still.
O may this work have found its last retreat
10   Here in a Mountain-bard's secure abode,
One to whom, yet a School-boy, Cynthia showed
A face of love which he in love would greet,
Fixed, by her smile, upon some rocky seat;
Or lured along where green-wood paths he trod.

'Who but is pleased to watch the moon on high'

Who but is pleased to watch the moon on high
Travelling where she from time to time enshrouds
Her head, and nothing loth her Majesty
Renounces, till among the scattered clouds
One with its kindling edge declares that soon
Will reappear before the uplifted eye
A Form as bright, as beautiful a moon,
To glide in open prospect through clear sky.
Pity that such a promise e'er should prove
10   False in the issue, that yon seeming space
Of sky should be in truth the stedfast face
Of a cloud flat and dense, through which must move
(By transit not unlike man's frequent doom)
The Wanderer lost in more determined gloom.

Illustrated Books and Newspapers

Discourse was deemed Man's noblest attribute,
And written words the glory of his hand;
Then followed Printing with enlarged command
For thought – dominion vast and absolute
For spreading truth, and making love expand.
Now prose and verse sunk into disrepute
Must lacquey a dumb Art that best can suit

The taste of this once-intellectual Land.
A backward movement surely have we here,
10 From manhood – back to childhood; for the age –
Back towards caverned life's first rude career.
Avaunt this vile abuse of pictured page!
Must eyes be all in all, the tongue and ear
Nothing? Heaven keep us from a lower stage!

'The unremitting voice of nightly streams'

The unremitting voice of nightly streams
That wastes so oft, we think, its tuneful powers,
If neither soothing to the worm that gleams
Through dewy grass, nor small birds hushed in bowers,
Nor unto silent leaves and drowsy flowers, –
That voice of unpretending harmony
(For who what is shall measure by what seems
To be, or not to be,
Or tax high Heaven with prodigality?)
10 Wants not a healing influence that can creep
Into the human breast, and mix with sleep
To regulate the motion of our dreams
For kindly issues – as though every clime
Was felt near murmuring brooks in earliest time;
As, at this day, the rudest swains who dwell
Where torrents roar, or hear the tinkling knell
Ot water-breaks, with grateful heart could tell.

Sonnet
(To an Octogenarian)

Affections lose their object; Time brings forth
No successors; and, lodged in memory,
If love exist no longer, it must die, –
Wanting accustomed food, must pass from earth,
Or never hope to reach a second birth.

This sad belief, the happiest that is left
To thousands, share not Thou; howe'er bereft,
Scorned, or neglected, fear not such a dearth.
Though poor and destitute of friends thou art,
10 Perhaps the sole survivor of thy race,
One to whom Heaven assigns that mournful part
The utmost solitude of age to face,
Still shall be left some corner of the heart
Where Love for living Thing can find a place.

'How beautiful the Queen of Night, on high'

How beautiful the Queen of Night, on high
Her way pursuing among scattered clouds,
Where, ever and anon, her head she shrouds
Hidden from view in dense obscurity.
But look, and to the watchful eye
A brightening edge will indicate that soon
We shall behold the struggling Moon
Break forth, – again to walk the clear blue sky.

On the Banks of a Rocky Stream

Behold an emblem of our human mind
Crowded with thoughts that need a settled home,
Yet, like to eddying balls of foam
Within this whirlpool, they each other chase
Round and round, and neither find
An outlet nor a resting-place!
Stranger, if such disquietude be thine,
Fall on thy knees and sue for help divine.

*Ode on the Installation of His Royal
Highness Prince Albert as Chancellor of the
University of Cambridge, July, 1847*

For thirst of power that Heaven disowns,
   For temples, towers, and thrones
Too long insulted by the Spoiler's shock,
   Indignant Europe cast
   Her stormy foe at last
To reap the whirlwind on a Libyan rock.
   War is passion's basest game
   Madly played to win a name:
Up starts some tyrant, Earth and Heaven to dare;
   The servile million bow;
But will the Lightning glance aside to spare
   The Despot's laurelled brow?

   War is mercy, glory, fame,
   Waged in Freedom's holy cause,
   Freedom such as man may claim
   Under God's restraining laws.
   Such is Albion's fame and glory,
   Let rescued Europe tell the story.
But, lo! what sudden cloud has darkened all
   The land as with a funeral pall?
The Rose of England suffers blight:
The Flower has drooped, the Isle's delight;
   Flower and bud together fall;
A nation's hopes lie crushed in Claremont's desolate Hall.

Time a chequered mantle wears –
   Earth awakes from wintry sleep:
Again the tree a blossom bears;
   Cease, Britannia, cease to weep!
Hark to the peals on this bright May-morn!
They tell that your future Queen is born

A Guardian Angel fluttered
Above the babe, unseen;
One word he softly uttered,
It named the future Queen;
And a joyful cry through the Island rang,
As clear and bold as the trumpet's clang,
    As bland as the reed of peace:
        'Victoria be her name!'
For righteous triumphs are the base
40 Whereon Britannia rests her peaceful fame.

Time, in his mantle's sunniest fold
Uplifted on his arms the child,
And while the fearless infant smiled,
Her happier destiny foretold: –
        'Infancy, by wisdom mild
        Trained to health and artless beauty;
        Youth, by pleasure unbeguiled
        From the lore of lofty duty;
        Womanhood, in pure renown
50   Seated on her lineal throne;
        Leaves of myrtle in her crown,
        Fresh with lustre all their own.
        Love, the treasure worth possessing
        More than all the world beside,
        This shall be her choicest blessing,
        Oft to royal hearts denied.'

That eve, the Star of Brunswick shone
        With stedfast ray benign
On Gotha's ducal roof, and on
60   The softly flowing Leine,
Nor failed to gild the spires of Bonn,
        And glittered on the Rhine.
Old Camus, too, on that prophetic night
        Was conscious of the ray;
And his willows whispered in its light,
        Not to the Zephyr's sway,

But with a Delphic life, in sight
    Of this auspicious day –
This day, when Granta hails her chosen Lord,
70   And, proud of her award,
    Confiding in that Star serene,
Welcomes the Consort of a happy Queen.

    Prince, in these collegiate bowers,
    Where science, leagued with holier truth,
    Guards the sacred heart of youth,
    Solemn monitors are ours.
    These reverend aisles, these hallowed towers,
    Raised by many a hand august,
    Are haunted by majestic Powers,
80   The Memories of the Wise and Just,
    Who, faithful to a pious trust,
    Here, in the Founder's Spirit sought
    To mould and stamp the ore of thought
    In that bold form and impress high
    That best betoken patriot loyalty.
    Not in vain those Sages taught –
    True disciples, good as great,
    Have pondered here their country's weal,
    Weighed the Future by the Past,
90   Learnt how social frames may last,
    And how a Land may rule its fate
    By constancy inviolate,
    Though worlds to their foundations reel,
The sport of factious hate or godless zeal.

    Albert, in thy race we cherish
    A nation's strength that will not perish
    While England's sceptred Line
    True to the King of Kings is found,
    Like that wise ancestor of thine
100 Who threw the Saxon shield o'er Luther's life
    When first, above the yells of bigot strife,
    The trumpet of the Living Word

Assumed a voice of deep portentous sound
From gladdened Elbe to startled Tiber heard.
  What shield more sublime
  E'er was blazoned or sung?
  And the Prince whom we greet
  From its Hero is sprung.
  Resound, resound the strain
110   That hails him for our own!
Again, again, and yet again,
For the Church, the State, the Throne!
And that Presence fair and bright,
Ever blest wherever seen,
Who deigns to grace our festal rite –
The pride of the Islands, VICTORIA THE
    QUEEN!

Preface to Poems (*1815*)

The observations prefixed to that portion of these Volumes, which was published many years ago, under the title of 'Lyrical Ballads,' have so little of a special application to the greater part, perhaps, of this collection, as subsequently enlarged and diversified, that they could not with any propriety stand as an Introduction to it. Not deeming it, however, expedient to suppress that exposition, slight and imperfect as it is, of the feelings which had determined the choice of the subjects, and the principles which had regulated the composition of those Pieces, I have transferred it to the end of the second Volume, to be attended to, or not, at the pleasure of the Reader.

In the Preface to that part of 'The Recluse,' lately published under the title of 'The Excursion,' I have alluded to a meditated arrangement of my minor Poems, which should assist the attentive Reader in perceiving their connexion with each other, and also their subordination to that Work. I shall here say a few words explanatory of this arrangement, as carried into effect in the present Volumes.

The powers requisite for the production of poetry are, first, those of observation and description, i.e. the ability to observe with accuracy things as they are in themselves, and with fidelity to describe them, unmodified by any passion or feeling existing in the mind of the Describer: whether the things depicted be actually present to the senses, or have a place only in the memory. This power, though indispensable to a Poet, is one which he employs only in submission to necessity, and never for a continuance of time; as its exercise supposes all the higher qualities of the mind to be passive, and in a state of subjection to external objects, much in the same way as the Translator or Engraver ought to be to his Original. 2dly, Sensibility, – which, the more exquisite it is, the wider will be the range of a Poet's perceptions; and the more will he be incited to observe objects, both as they exist in themselves and as re-acted upon by his own mind. (The distinction between poetic and human sensibility has been marked in the character of the Poet delineated in the original preface, before-mentioned.) 3rdly, Reflection, – which makes the Poet acquainted with the value of actions, images, thoughts, and feelings; and assists the sensibility in perceiving their connexion with each other. 4thly, Imagination and Fancy, – to modify, to create, and to associate. 5thly, Invention, – by which characters are composed out of materials supplied by observation; whether of the Poet's own heart and mind, or of external life and nature; and such incidents and situations produced as are most impressive to the imagination, and most fitted to do justice to the characters, sentiments, and passions, which the Poet undertakes to illustrate. And, lastly, Judgement, – to decide how and where, and in what degree, each of these faculties ought to be exerted; so that the less shall not be sacrificed to the greater; nor the greater, slighting the less, arrogate, to its own injury, more than its due. By judgement, also, is determined what are the laws and appropriate graces of every species of composition.

The materials of Poetry, by these powers collected and produced, are cast, by means of various moulds, into divers forms. The moulds may be enumerated, and the forms specified, in the following order. 1st, the Narrative, – including the Epopoeia, the Historic Poem, the Tale, the Romance, the Mock-heroic, and, if the spirit of Homer will tolerate such neighbourhood, that dear production of our days, the metrical Novel. Of this Class, the distinguishing mark, is, that the Narrator, however liberally his speaking agents be introduced, is himself the source from which everything primarily flows. Epic Poets, in order that their mode of composition may accord with the elevation of their subject, represent themselves as *singing* from the inspiration of the Muse, Arma virum que *cano*; but this is a fiction, in modern times, of slight value: The Iliad or the Paradise Lost would gain little in our estimation by being chaunted. The other poets who belong to this class are commonly content to *tell* their tale; – so that of the whole it may be affirmed that they neither require nor reject the accompaniment of music.

2ndly, The Dramatic, – consisting of Tragedy, Historic Drama, Comedy, and Masque; in which the poet does not appear at all in his own person, and where the whole action is carried on by speech and dialogue of the agents; music being admitted only incidentally and rarely. The Opera may be placed here, in as much as it proceeds by dialogue; though depending, to the degree that it does, upon music, it has a strong claim to be ranked with the Lyrical. The characteristic and impassioned Epistle, of which Ovid and Pope have given examples, considered as a species of monodrama, may, without impropriety, be placed in this class.

3rdly, The Lyrical, – containing the Hymn, the Ode, the Elegy, the Song, and the Ballad; in all which, for the production of their *full* effect, an accompaniment of music is indispensable.

4thly, The Idyllium, – descriptive chiefly either of the processes and appearances of external nature, as the 'Seasons' of Thomson; or of characters, manners, and sentiments, as are Shenstone's School-mistress, The Cotter's Saturday Night of Burns, The Twa Dogs of the same Author; or of these in conjunction with the appearances of Nature, as most of the pieces of Theocritus, the Allegro and Penseroso of Milton, Beattie's Minstrel, Goldsmith's 'Deserted Village.' The Epitaph, the Inscription, the Sonnet, most of the epistles of poets writing in their own persons, and all loco-descriptive poetry, belong to this class.

5thly, Didactic, – the principal object of which is direct instruction; as the Poem of Lucretius, the Georgics of Virgil, 'The Fleece' of Dyer, Mason's 'English Garden,' &c.

And, lastly, philosophical satire, like that of Horace and Juvenal; personal and occasional Satire rarely comprehending sufficient of the general in the individual to be dignified with the name of Poetry.

Out of the three last classes has been constructed a composite species, of which Young's Night Thoughts and Cowper's Task are excellent examples.

It is deducible from the above, that poems, apparently miscellaneous, may with propriety be arranged either with reference to the powers of mind *predominant* in the production of them; or to the mould in which they are cast; or, lastly, to the subjects to which they relate. From each of these considerations, the following Poems have been divided into classes; which, that the work may more obviously correspond with the course of human life, for the sake of exhibiting in it the three requisites of a legitimate whole, a beginning, a middle, and an end, have been also arranged, as far as it was possible, according to an order of time, commencing with Childhood, and terminating with Old Age, Death, and Immortality. My guiding wish was, that the small pieces of which these volumes consist, thus discriminated, might be regarded under a two-fold view; as composing an entire work within themselves, and as adjuncts to the philosophical Poem, 'The Recluse.' This arrangement has long presented itself habitually to my own mind. Nevertheless, I should have preferred to scatter the contents of these volumes at random, if I had been persuaded that, by the plan adopted, anything material would be taken from the natural effect of the pieces, individually, on the mind of the unreflecting Reader. I trust there is a sufficient variety in each class to prevent this; while, for him who reads with reflection, the arrangement will serve as a commentary unostentatiously directing his attention to my purposes, both particular and general. But, as I wish to guard against the possibility of misleading by this classification, it is proper first to remind the Reader, that certain poems are placed according to the powers of mind, in the Author's conception, predominant in the production of them; *predominant*, which implies the exertion of other faculties in less degree. Where there is more imagination than fancy in a poem it is placed under the head of imagination, and vice versa. Both the above Classes might without impropriety have been enlarged from that consisting of 'Poems founded on the Affections'; as might this latter from those, and from the class 'Proceeding from Sentiment and Reflection.' The most striking characteristics of each piece, mutual illustration, variety, and proportion, have governed me throughout.

It may be proper in this place to state, that the Extracts in the 2nd Class entitled 'Juvenile Pieces,' are in many places altered from the printed copy, chiefly by omission and compression. The slight alterations of another kind were for the most part made not long after the publication of the Poems from which the Extracts are taken. These Extracts seem to have a title to be placed here as they were the productions of youth, and represent implicitly some of the features of a youthful mind, at a time when images of nature supplied to it the place of thought, sentiment, and almost of action; or, as it will be found expressed, of a state of mind when

> the sounding cataract
> Haunted me like a passion: the tall rock,
> The mountain, and the deep and gloomy wood,
> Their colours and their forms were then to me
> An appetite, a feeling and a love,
> That had no need of a remoter charm,
> By thought supplied, or any interest
> Unborrowed from the eye –

I will own that I was much at a loss what to select of these descriptions; and perhaps it would have been better either to have reprinted the whole, or suppressed what I have given.

None of the other Classes, except those of Fancy and Imagination, require any particular notice. But a remark of general application may be made. All Poets, except the dramatic, have been in the practice of feigning that their works were composed to the music of the harp or lyre: with what degree of affectation this has been done in modern times, I leave to the judicious to determine. For my own part, I have not been disposed to violate probability so far, or to make such a large demand upon the Reader's charity. Some of these pieces are essentially lyrical; and, therefore, cannot have their due force without a supposed musical accompaniment; but, in much the greatest part, as a substitute for the classic lyre or romantic harp, I require nothing more than an animated or impassioned recitation, adapted to the subject. Poems, however humble in their kind, if they be good in that kind, cannot read themselves: the law of long syllable and short must not be so inflexible – the letter of metre must not be so impassive to the spirit of versification – as to deprive the Reader of a voluntary power to modulate, in subordination to the sense, the music of the poem; – in the same manner as his mind is left at liberty, and even summoned, to act upon its thoughts and images. But, though the accompaniment of a musical instrument be frequently dispensed with, the true Poet does not therefore abandon his privilege distinct from that of the mere Proseman;

He murmurs near the running brooks
A music sweeter than their own.

I come now to the consideration of the words Fancy and Imagination, as employed in the classification of the following Poems. 'A man,' says an intelligent Author, has 'imagination,' in proportion as he can distinctly copy in idea the impressions of sense: it is the faculty which *images* within the mind the phenomena of sensation. A man has fancy in proportion as he can call up, connect, or associate, at pleasure, those internal images (Φαυταζειν is to cause to appear) so as to complete ideal representations of absent objects. Imagination is the power of depicting, and fancy of evoking and combining. The imagination is formed by patient observation; the fancy by a voluntary activity in shifting the scenery of the mind. The more accurate the imagination, the more safely may a painter, or a poet, undertake a delineation, or a description, without the presence of the objects to be characterized. The more versatile the fancy, the more original and striking will be the decorations produced. – *British Synonyms discriminated, by W. Taylor.*

Is not this as if a man should undertake to supply an account of a building, and be so intent upon what he had discovered of the foundation as to conclude his task without once looking up at the superstructure? Here, as in other instances throughout the volume, the judicious Author's mind is enthralled by Etymology; he takes up the original word as his guide, his conductor, his escort, and too often does not perceive how soon he becomes its prisoner, without liberty to tread in any path but that to which it confines him. It is not easy to find out how imagination, thus explained, differs from distinct remembrance of images; or fancy from quick and vivid recollection of them: each is nothing more than a mode of memory. If the two words bear the above meaning, and no other, what term is left to designate that Faculty of which the Poet is 'all compact'; he whose eye glances from earth to heaven, whose spiritual attributes body-forth what his pen is prompt in turning to shape; or what is left to characterize fancy, as insinuating herself into the heart of objects with creative activity? – Imagination, in the sense of the word as giving title to a Class of the following Poems, has no reference to images that are merely a faithful copy, existing in the mind, of absent external objects; but is a word of higher import, denoting operations of the mind upon those objects, and processes of creation or of composition, governed by certain fixed laws. I proceed to illustrate my meaning by instances. A parrot *hangs* from the wires of his cage by his beak or by his claws; or a monkey from the bough of a tree by his paws or his tail. Each creature does so literally and actually. In the first Eclogue of Virgil, the Shepherd, thinking of the time when he is to take leave of his Farm, thus addresses his Goats;

Non ego vos posthac viridi projectus in antro
Dumosa *pendere* procul de rupe [videbo],

  – half way down
Hangs one who gathers samphire,

is the well-known expression of Shakespeare, delineating an ordinary image upon the Cliffs of Dover. In these two instances is a slight exertion of the faculty which I denominate imagination, in the use of one word: neither the goats nor the samphiregatherer do literally hang, as does the parrot or the monkey; but, presenting to the senses something of such an appearance, the mind in its activity, for its own gratification, contemplates them as hanging.

As when far off at Sea a Fleet descried
Hangs in the clouds, by equinoctial winds
Close sailing from Bengala or the Isles
Of Ternate or Tydore, whence Merchants bring
Their spicy drugs; they on the trading flood
Through the wide Ethiopian to the Cape
Ply, stemming nightly toward the Pole: so seemed
Far off the flying Fiend.

Here is the full strength of the imagination involved in the word, *hangs*, and exerted upon the whole image: First, the Fleet, an aggregate of many Ships, is represented as one mighty Person, whose track, we know and feel, is upon the waters; but, taking advantage of its appearance to the senses, the Poet dares to represent it as *hanging in the clouds*, both for the gratification of the mind in contemplating the image itself, and in reference to the motion and appearance of the sublime object to which it is compared.

From images of sight we will pass to those of sound:

Over his own sweet voice the Stock-dove *broods*;

of the same bird,

His voice was *buried* among trees,
Yet to be come at by the breeze;

O, Cuckoo! shall I call thee *Bird*,
Or but a wandering *Voice*?

The Stock-dove is said to *coo*, a sound well imitating the note of the bird; but, by the intervention of the metaphor *broods*, the affections are called in by the imagination to assist in marking the manner in which the Bird reiterates and prolongs her soft note, as if herself delighting to listen to it, and participating of a still and quiet satisfaction, like that which may be supposed inseparable from the continuous process of incubation. 'His voice was buried among trees,' a metaphor expressing the love of *seclusion* by which this Bird is marked; and characterizing its note as not partaking of the shrill and the piercing, and therefore more easily deadened by the intervening shade; yet a note so peculiar, and withal so pleasing, that the breeze, gifted with that love of the sound which the Poet feels, penetrates the shade in which it is entombed, and conveys it to the ear of the listener.

Shall I call thee Bird
Or but a wandering Voice?

This concise interrogation characterizes the seeming ubiquity of the voice of the Cuckoo, and dispossesses the creature almost of a corporeal existence; the imagination being tempted to this exertion of her power by a consciousness in the memory that the Cuckoo is almost perpetually heard throughout the season of Spring, but seldom becomes an object of sight.

Thus far of images independent of each other, and immediately endowed by the mind with properties that do not inhere in them, upon an incitement from properties and qualities the existence of which is inherent and obvious. These processes of imagination are carried on either by conferring additional properties upon an object, or abstracting from it some of those which it actually possesses, and thus enabling it to react upon the mind which hath performed the process, like a new existence.

I pass from the Imagination acting upon an individual image to a consideration of the same faculty employed upon images in a conjunction by which they modify each other. The Reader has already had a fine instance before him in the passage quoted from Virgil, where the apparently perilous situation of the Goat, hanging upon the shaggy precipice, is contrasted with that of the Shepherd, contemplating it from the seclusion of the Cavern in which he lies stretched at ease and in security. Take these images separately, and how unaffecting the picture compared with that produced by their being thus connected with, and opposed to, each other!

As a huge Stone is sometimes seen to lie
Couched on the bald top of an eminence,
Wonder to all who do the same espy
By what means it could thither come, and whence;
So that it seems a thing endued with sense,
Like a Sea-beast crawled forth, which on a shelf
Of rock or sand reposeth, there to sun himself.

Such seemed this Man; not all alive or dead,
Nor all asleep, in his extreme old age.

  * * * * * * *

Motionless as a cloud the old Man stood,
That heareth not the loud winds when they call,
And moveth altogether if it move at all.

In these images, the conferring, the abstracting, and the modifying powers of the Imagination, immediately and mediately acting, are all brought into conjunction. The Stone is endowed with something of the power of life to approximate it to the Sea-beast; and the Sea-beast stripped of some of its vital qualities to assimilate it to the stone; which intermediate image is thus treated for the purpose of bringing the original image, that of the stone, to a nearer resemblance to the figure and condition of the aged Man; who is divested of so much of the indications of life and motion as to bring him to the point where the two objects unite and coalesce in just comparison. After what has been said, the image of the Cloud need not be commented upon.

Thus far of an endowing or modifying power: but the Imagination also shapes and *creates*; and how? By innumerable processes; and in none does it more delight than in that of consolidating numbers into unity, and dissolving and separating unity into number, – alternations proceeding from, and governed by, a sublime consciousness of the soul in her own mighty and almost divine powers. Recur to the passage already cited from Milton. When the compact Fleet, as one Person, has been introduced 'Sailing from Bengala,' 'They,' i.e. the 'Merchants,' representing the Fleet resolved into a Multitude of Ships, 'ply' their voyage towards the extremities of the earth: 'So' (referring to the word 'As' in the commencement) 'seemed the flying Fiend;' the image of his Person acting to recombine the multitude of Ships into one body, – the point from which the comparison set out. 'So seemed,' and to whom seemed? To the heavenly Muse who dictates the poem, to the eye of the Poet's mind, and to that of the Reader, present at one moment in the wide Ethiopian, and the next in the solitudes, then first broken in upon, of the infernal regions!

Modo me Thebis, modo ponit Athenis.

Hear again this mighty Poet, – speaking of the Messiah going forth to expel from Heaven the rebellious Angels,

Attended by ten thousand, thousand Saints
He onward came: far off his coming shone, –

the retinue of Saints, and the Person of the Messiah himself, lost almost and merged in the splendour of that indefinite abstraction, 'His coming!'

As I do not mean here to treat this subject further than to throw some light upon the present Volumes, and especially upon one division of them, I shall spare myself and the Reader the trouble of considering the Imagination as it deals with thoughts and sentiments, as it regulates the composition of characters, and determines the course of actions: I will not consider it (more than I have already done by implication) as that power which, in the language of one of my most esteemed Friends, 'draws all things to one, which makes things animate or inanimate, beings with their attributes, subjects with their accessories, take one colour and serve to one effect' [Charles Lamb upon the genius of Hogarth. – W]. The grand store-house of enthusiastic and meditative Imagination, of poetical, as contradistinguished from human and dramatic Imagination, is the prophetic and lyrical parts of the holy Scriptures, and the works of Milton, to which I cannot forbear to add those of Spenser. I select these writers in preference to those of ancient Greece and Rome because the anthropomorphitism of the Pagan religion subjected the minds of the greatest poets in those countries too much to the bondage of definite form; from which the Hebrews were preserved by their abhorrence of idolatry. This abhorrence was almost as strong in our great epic Poet, both from circumstances of his life, and from the constitution of his mind. However imbued the surface might be with classical literature, he was a Hebrew in soul; and all things tended in him towards the sublime. Spenser, of a gentler nature, maintained his freedom by aid of his allegorical spirit, at one time inciting him to create persons out of abstractions; and at another, by a superior effort of genius, to give the universality and permanence of abstractions to his human beings, by means of attributes and emblems that belong to the highest moral truths and the purest sensations, – of which his character of Una is a glorious example. Of the human and dramatic Imagination the works of Shakespeare are an inexhaustible source.

I tax not you, ye Elements, with unkindness,
I never gave you Kingdoms, called you Daughters.

And if, bearing in mind the many Poets distinguished by this prime quality, whose names I omit to mention; yet justified by a recollection of the insults which the Ignorant, the Incapable, and the Presumptuous have heaped upon these and my other writings, I may be permitted to anticipate the judgement of posterity upon myself; I shall declare (censurable, I grant, if the notoriety of the fact above stated does not justify me) that I have given, in these unfavourable times, evidence of exertions of this faculty upon its worthiest objects, the external universe, the moral and religious sentiments of Man, his natural affections, and his acquired passions; which have the same ennobling tendency as the productions of men, in this kind, worthy to be holden in undying remembrance.

I dismiss this subject with observing – that, in the series of Poems placed under the head of Imagination, I have begun with one of the earliest processes of Nature in the development of this faculty. Guided by one of my own primary consciousnesses, I have represented a commutation and transfer of internal feelings, co-operating with external accidents to plant, for immortality, images of sound and sight, in the celestial soil of the Imagination. The Boy, there introduced, is listening, with something of a feverish and restless anxiety, for the recurrence of the riotous sounds which he had previously excited; and, at the moment when the intenseness of his mind is beginning to remit, he is surprised into a perception of the solemn and tranquillizing images which the Poem describes. – The Poems next in succession exhibit the faculty exerting itself upon various objects of the external universe; then follow others, where it is employed upon feelings, characters, and actions; and the Class is concluded with imaginative pictures of moral, political, and religious sentiments.

To the mode in which Fancy has already been characterized as the Power of evoking and combining, or, as my friend Mr Coleridge has styled it, 'the aggregative and associative Power,' my objection is only that the definition is too general. To aggregate and to associate, to evoke and to combine, belong as well to the Imagination as to the Fancy; but either the materials evoked and combined are different; or they are brought together under a different law, and for a different purpose. Fancy does not require that the materials which she makes use of should be susceptible of change in their constitution, from her touch; and, where they admit of modification, it is enough for her purpose if it be slight, limited, and evanescent. Directly the reverse of these, are the desires and demands of the Imagination. She recoils from everything but the plastic, the pliant, and the indefinite. She leaves it to Fancy to describe Queen Mab as coming,

In shape no bigger than an agate stone
On the fore-finger of an Alderman.

Having to speak of stature, she does not tell you that her gigantic Angel was as tall as Pompey's pillar; much less that he was twelve cubits, or twelve hundred cubits high; or that his dimensions equalled those of Teneriffe or Atlas; – because these, and if they were a million times as high, it would be the same, are bounded: The expression is, 'His stature reached the sky!' the illimitable firmament! – When the Imagination frames a comparison, if it does not strike on the first presentation, a sense of the truth of the likeness, from the moment that it is perceived, grows – and continues to grow – upon the mind; the resemblance depending less upon outline of form and feature than upon expression and effect, less upon casual and outstanding, than upon inherent and internal, properties: – moreover, the images invariably modify each other. – The law under which the processes of Fancy are carried on is as capricious as the accidents of things, and the effects are surprising, playful, ludicrous, amusing, tender, or pathetic, as the objects happen to be appositely produced or fortunately combined. Fancy depends upon the rapidity and profusion with which she scatters her thoughts and images, trusting that their number, and the felicity with which they are linked together, will make amends for the want of individual value: or she prides herself upon the curious subtlety and the successful elaboration with which she can detect their lurking affinities. If she can win you over to her purpose, and impart to you her feelings, she cares not how unstable or transitory may be her influence, knowing that it will not be out of her power to resume it upon an apt occasion. But the Imagination is conscious of an indestructible dominion; – the Soul may fall away from it, not being able to sustain its grandeur, but, if once felt and acknowledged, by no act of any other faculty of the mind can it be relaxed, impaired, or diminished. – Fancy is given to quicken and to beguile the temporal part of our Nature, Imagination to incite and to support the eternal. – Yet is it not the less true that Fancy, as she is an active, is also, under her own laws and in her own spirit, a creative faculty. In what manner Fancy ambitiously aims at a rivalship with the Imagination, and Imagination stoops to work with the materials of Fancy, might be illustrated from the compositions of all eloquent writers, whether in prose or verse; and chiefly from those of our own Country. Scarcely a page of the impassioned parts of Bishop Taylor's Works can be opened that shall not afford examples. – Referring the Reader to those inestimable Volumes, I will content myself with placing a conceit (ascribed to Lord Chesterfield) in contrast with a passage from the Paradise Lost;

The dews of the evening most carefully shun,
They are the tears of the sky for the loss of the Sun.

After the transgression of Adam, Milton, with other appearances of sympathizing Nature, thus marks the immediate consequence,

Sky lowered, and muttering thunder, some sad drops
Wept at completion of the mortal sin.

The associating link is the same in each instance; – dew or rain, not distinguishable from the liquid substance of tears, are employed as indications of sorrow. A flash of surprise is the effect in the former case, a flash of surprise and nothing more; for the nature of things does not sustain the combination. In the latter, the effects of the act, of which there is this immediate consequence and visible sign, are so momentous that the mind acknowledges the justice and reasonableness of the sympathy in Nature so manifested; and the sky weeps drops of water as if with human eyes, as 'Earth had, before, trembled from her entrails, and Nature given a second groan.'

Awe-stricken as I am by contemplating the operations of the mind of this truly divine Poet, I scarcely dare venture to add that

'An Address to an Infant,' which the Reader will find under the Class of Fancy in the present Volumes, exhibits something of this communion and interchange of instruments and functions between the two powers; and is, accordingly, placed last in the class, as a preparation for that of Imagination which follows.

Finally, I will refer to Cotton's 'Ode upon Winter,' an admirable composition though stained with some peculiarities of the age in which he lived, for a general illustration of the characteristics of Fancy. The middle part of this ode contains a most lively description of the entrance of Winter, with his retinue, as 'A palsied King,' and yet a military Monarch, – advancing for conquest with his Army; the several bodies of which, and their arms and equipments, are described with a rapidity of detail, and a profusion of *fanciful* comparisons, which indicate on the part of the Poet extreme activity of intellect, and a correspondent hurry of delightful feeling. He retires from the Foe into his fortress, where

> a magazine
> Of sovereign juice is cellared in.
> Liquor that will the siege maintain
> Should Phoebus ne'er return again.

Though myself a water-drinker, I cannot resist the pleasure of transcribing what follows, as an instance still more happy of Fancy employed in the treatment of feeling than, in its preceding passages, the Poem supplies of her management of forms.

> 'Tis that, that gives the Poet rage,
> And thaws the gelly'd blood of Age;
> Matures the Young, restores the Old,
> And makes the fainting Coward bold.

> It lays the careful head to rest,
> Calms palpitations in the breast,
> Renders our lives' misfortune sweet;
> .   .   .   .

> Then let the chill Sirocco blow,
> And gird us round with hills of snow,
> Or else go whistle to the shore,
> And make the hollow mountains roar.

Whilst we together jovial sit
Careless, and crowned with mirth and wit;
Where, though bleak winds confine us home,
Our fancies round the world shall roam.

We'll think of all the Friends we know,
And drink to all worth drinking to;
When having drunk all thine and mine,
We rather shall want healths than wine.

But where Friends fail us, we'll supply
Our friendships with our charity;
Men that remote in sorrows live,
Shall by our lusty Brimmers thrive.

We'll drink the Wanting into Wealth,
And those that languish into health,
The Afflicted into joy; the Opprest
Into security and rest.

The Worthy in disgrace shall find
Favour return again more kind,
And in restraint who stifled lie,
Shall taste the air of liberty.

The Brave shall triumph in success,
The Lovers shall have Mistresses,
Poor unregarded Virtue, praise,
And the neglected Poet, Bays.

Thus shall our healths do others good,
Whilst we ourselves do all we would;
For freed from envy and from care,
What would we be but what we are?

It remains that I should express my regret at the necessity of separating my compositions from some beautiful Poems of Mr Coleridge, with which they have been long associated in publication. The feelings, with which that joint publication was made, have been gratified; its end is answered, and the time is come when considerations of general propriety dictate the separation. Three short pieces (now first published) are the work of a Female Friend; and the Reader, to whom they may be acceptable, is indebted to me for his pleasure; if anyone regard them with dislike, or be disposed to condemn them, let the censure fall upon him, who, trusting in his own sense of their merit and their fitness for the place which they occupy, *extorted* them from the Authoress.

When I sate down to write this preface it was my intention to have made it more comprehensive; but as all that I deem necessary is expressed, I will here detain the reader no longer: – what I have further to remark shall be inserted, by way of interlude, at the close of this Volume.

ESSAY, SUPPLEMENTARY TO THE PREFACE (1815)

By this time, I trust that the judicious Reader, who has now first become acquainted with these poems, is persuaded that a very senseless outcry has been raised against them and their Author. – Casually, and very rarely only, do I see any periodical publication, except a daily newspaper; but I am not wholly unacquainted with the spirit in which my most active and persevering Adversaries have maintained their hostility; nor with the impudent falsehoods and base artifices to which they have had recourse. These, as implying a consciousness on their parts that attacks honestly and fairly conducted would be unavailing, could not but have been regarded by me with triumph; had they been accompanied with such display of talents and information as might give weight to the opinions of the Writers, whether favourable or unfavourable. But the ignorance of those who have chosen to stand forth as my enemies, as far as I am acquainted with their enmity, has unfortunately been still more gross than their disingenuousness, and their incompetence more flagrant than their malice. The effect in the eyes of the discerning is indeed ludicrous: yet, contemptible as such men are, in return for the forced compliment paid me by their long-continued notice (which, as I have appeared so rarely before the public, no one can say has been solicited) I entreat them to spare themselves. The lash, which they are aiming at my productions, does, in fact, only fall on phantoms of their own brain; which, I grant, I am innocently instrumental in raising. – By what fatality the orb of my genius (for genius none of them seem to deny me) acts upon these men like the moon upon a certain description of patients, it would be irksome to inquire; nor would it consist with the respect which I owe myself to take further notice of opponents whom I internally despise.

With the young, of both sexes, Poetry is, like love, a passion; but, for much the greater part of those who have been proud of its power over their minds, a necessity soon arises of breaking the pleasing bondage; or it relaxes of itself; – the thoughts being occupied in domestic cares, or the time engrossed by business. Poetry then becomes only an occasional recreation; while to those whose existence passes away in a course of fashionable pleasure it is a species of luxurious amusement. – In middle and declining age, a scattered number of serious persons resort to poetry, as to religion, for a protection against the pressure of trivial employments, and as a consolation for the afflictions of life. And lastly, there are many, who, having been enamoured of this art, in their youth, have found leisure, after youth was spent, to cultivate general literature; in which poetry has continued to be comprehended *as a study*.

Into the above Classes the Readers of poetry may be divided; Critics abound in them all; but from the last only can opinions be collected of absolute value, and worthy to be depended upon, as prophetic of the destiny of a new work. The young, who in nothing can escape delusion, are especially subject to it in their intercourse with poetry. The cause, not so obvious as the fact is unquestionable, is the same as that from which erroneous judgements in this art, in the minds of men of all ages, chiefly proceed; but upon Youth it operates with peculiar force. The appropriate business of poetry, (which, nevertheless, if genuine is as permanent as pure science) her appropriate employment, her privilege and her *duty*, is to treat of things not as they *are*, but as they *appear*; not as they exist in themselves, but as they *seem* to exist to the *senses* and to the *passions*. What a world of delusion does this acknowledged principle prepare for the inexperienced! what temptations to go astray are here held forth for those whose thoughts have been little disciplined by the understanding, and whose feelings revolt from the sway of reason! – When a juvenile Reader is in the height of his rapture with some vicious passage, should experience throw in doubts, or common-sense suggest suspicions, a lurking consciousness that the realities of the Muse are but shows, and that her liveliest excitements are raised by transient shocks of conflicting feeling and successive assemblages of contradictory thoughts – is ever at hand to justify extravagance, and to sanction absurdity. But, it may be asked, as these illusions are unavoidable, and no doubt eminently useful to the mind as a process, what good can be gained by making observations the tendency of which is to diminish the confidence of youth in its feelings, and thus to abridge its innocent and even profitable pleasures? The reproach implied in the question could not be warded off, if Youth were incapable of being delighted with what is truly excellent; or if these errors always terminated of themselves in due season. But, with the majority, though their force be abated, they continue through life. Moreover, the fire of youth is too vivacious an element to be extinguished or damped by a philosophical remark; and, while there is no danger that what has been said will be injurious or painful to the ardent and the confident, it may prove beneficial to those who, being enthusiastic, are, at the same time, modest and ingenuous. The intimation may unite with their own misgivings to regulate their sensibility, and to bring in, sooner than it would otherwise have arrived, a more discreet and sound judgement.

If it should excite wonder that men of ability, in later life, whose understandings have been rendered acute by practice in affairs, should be so easily and so far imposed upon when they happen to take up a new work in verse, this appears to be the cause; – that, having discontinued their attention to poetry, whatever progress may have been made in other departments of knowledge, they have not, as to this art, advanced in true discernment beyond the age of youth. If then a new poem falls in their way, whose attractions are of that kind which would have enraptured them during the heat of youth, the judgement not being improved to a degree that they shall be disgusted, they are dazzled; and prize and cherish the faults for having had power to make the present time vanish before them, and to throw the mind back, as by enchantment, into the happiest season of life. As they read, powers seem to be revived, passions are regenerated, and pleasures restored. The Book was probably taken up after an escape from the burden of business, and with a wish to forget the world, and all its vexations and anxieties. Having obtained this wish, and so much more, it is natural that they should make report as they have felt.

If Men of mature age, through want of practice, be thus easily beguiled into admiration of absurdities, extravagances, and misplaced ornaments, thinking it proper that their understandings should enjoy a holiday, while they are unbending their minds with verse, it may be expected that such Readers will resemble their former selves also in strength of prejudice, and an inaptitude to be moved by the unostentatious beauties of a pure style. In the higher poetry, an enlightened Critic chiefly looks for a reflexion of the wisdom of the heart and the grandeur of the imagination. Wherever these appear, simplicity accompanies them; Magnificence herself, when legitimate, depending upon a simplicity of her own, to regulate her ornaments. But it is a well known property of human nature that our estimates are ever governed by comparisons, of which we are conscious with various degrees of distinctness. Is it not, then, inevitable (confining these observations to the effects of style merely) that an eye, accustomed to the glaring hues of diction by which such Readers are caught and excited, will for the most part be rather repelled than attracted by an original Work the colouring of which is disposed according to a pure and refined scheme of harmony? It is in the fine arts as in the affairs of life, no man can *serve* (i.e. obey with zeal and fidelity) two Masters.

As Poetry is most just to its own divine origin when it administers the comforts and breathes the spirit of religion, they who have learned to perceive this truth, and who betake themselves to reading verse for sacred purposes, must be preserved from numerous illusions to which the two Classes of Readers, whom we have been considering, are liable. But, as the mind grows serious from the weight of life, the range of its passions is contracted accordingly; and its sympathies become so exclusive that many species of high excellence wholly escape, or but languidly excite, its notice. Besides, Men who read from religious or moral inclinations, even when the subject is of that kind which they approve, are beset with misconceptions and mistakes peculiar to themselves. Attaching so much importance to the truths which interest them, they are prone to overrate the Authors by whom these truths are expressed and enforced. They come prepared to impart so much passion to the Poet's language, that they remain unconscious how little, in fact, they receive from it. And, on the other hand, religious faith is to him who holds it so momentous a thing, and error appears to be attended with such tremendous consequences, that, if opinions touching upon religion occur which the Reader condemns, he not only cannot sympathize with them however animated the expression, but there is, for the most part, an end put to all satisfaction and enjoyment. Love, if it before existed, is converted into dislike; and the heart of the Reader is set against the Author and his book. – To these excesses, they, who from their professions ought to be the most guarded against them, are perhaps the most liable; I mean those sects whose religion, being from the calculating understanding, is cold and formal. For when Christianity, the religion of humility, is founded upon the proudest quality of our nature, what can be expected but contradictions? Accordingly, believers of this cast are at one time contemptuous; at another, being troubled as they are and must be with inward misgivings, they are jealous and suspicious; – and at all seasons, they are under temptation to supply, by the heat with which they defend their tenets, the animation which is wanting to the constitution of the religion itself.

Faith was given to man that his affections, detached from the treasures of time, might be inclined to settle upon those of eternity: – the elevation of his nature, which this habit produces on earth, being to him a presumptive evidence of a future state of existence; and giving him a title to partake of its holiness. The religious man values what he sees chiefly as an 'imperfect shadowing forth' of what he is incapable of seeing. The concerns of religion refer to indefinite objects, and are too weighty for the mind to support them without relieving itself by resting a great part of the burden upon words and symbols. The commerce between Man and his Maker cannot be carried on but by a process where much is represented in little, and the infinite Being accommodates himself to a finite capacity. In all this may be perceived the affinities between religion and poetry; – between religion – making up the deficiencies of reason by faith, and poetry – passionate for the instruction of reason; between religion – whose element is infinitude, and whose ultimate trust is the supreme of things, submitting herself to circumscription and reconciled to substitutions; and poetry – ethereal and transcendent, yet incapable to sustain her existence without sensuous incarnation. In this community of nature may be perceived also the lurking incitements of kindred error; – so that we shall find that no poetry has been more subject to distortion, than that species the argument and scope of which is religious; and no lovers of the art have gone further astray than the pious and the devout.

Whither then shall we turn for that union of qualifications which must necessarily exist before the decisions of a critic can be of absolute value? For a mind at once poetical and philosophical; for a critic whose affections are as free and kindly as the spirit of society, and whose understanding is severe as that of dispassionate government? Where are we to look for that initiatory composure of mind which no selfishness can disturb? For a natural sensibility that has been tutored into correctness without losing anything of its quickness; and for active faculties capable of answering the demands which an Author of original imagination shall make upon them, – associated with a judgement that cannot be duped into admiration by aught that is unworthy of it? – Among those and those only, who, never having suffered their youthful love of poetry to remit much of its force, have applied, to the consideration of the laws of this art, the best power of their understandings. At the same time it must be observed – that, as this Class comprehends the only judgements which are trustworthy, so does it include the most erroneous and perverse. For to be mistaught is worse than to be untaught; and no perverseness equals that which is supported by system, no errors are so difficult to root out as those which the understanding has pledged its credit to uphold. In this Class are contained

Censors, who, if they be pleased with what is good, are pleased with it only by imperfect glimpses, and upon false principles; who, should they generalize rightly to a certain point, are sure to suffer for it in the end; – who, if they stumble upon a sound rule, are fettered by misapplying it, or by straining it too far; being incapable of perceiving when it ought to yield to one of higher order. In it are found Critics too petulant to be passive to a genuine Poet, and too feeble to grapple with him; Men, who take upon them to report of the course which *he* holds whom they are utterly unable to accompany, – confounded if he turn quick upon the wing, dismayed if he soar steadily into 'the region;' – Men of palsied imaginations and indurated hearts; in whose minds all healthy action is languid, – who, therefore, feed as the many direct them, or with the many, are greedy after vicious provocatives; – Judges, whose censure is auspicious, and whose praise ominous! In this Class meet together the two extremes of best and worst.

The observations presented in the foregoing series, are of too ungracious a nature to have been made without reluctance; and were it only on this account I would invite the Reader to try them by the test of comprehensive experience. If the number of judges who can be confidently relied upon be in reality so small, it ought to follow that partial notice only, or neglect, perhaps long continued, or attention wholly inadequate to their merits – must have been the fate of most works in the higher departments of poetry; and that, on the other hand, numerous productions have blazed into popularity, and have passed away, leaving scarcely a trace behind them: – it will be, further, found that when Authors have at length raised themselves into general admiration and maintained their ground, errors and prejudices have prevailed concerning their genius and their works, which the few who are conscious of those errors and prejudices would deplore; if they were not recompensed by perceiving that there are select Spirits for whom it is ordained that their fame shall be in the world an existence like that of Virtue, which owes its being to the struggles it makes, and its vigour to the enemies whom it provokes; – a vivacious quality ever doomed to meet with opposition, and still triumphing over it; and, from the nature of its dominion, incapable of being brought to the sad conclusion of Alexander, when he wept that there were no more worlds for him to conquer.

Let us take a hasty retrospect of the poetical literature of this Country for the greater part of the last two Centuries, and see if the facts correspond with these inferences.

Who is there that can now endure to read the 'Creation' of Dubartas? Yet all Europe once resounded with his praise; he was caressed by Kings; and, when his Poem was translated into our language, the Faery Queen faded before it. The name of Spenser, whose genius is of a higher order than even that of Ariosto, is at this day scarcely known beyond the limits of the British Isles. And, if the value of his works is to be estimated from the attention now paid to them by his Countrymen, compared with that which they bestow on those of other writers, it must be pronounced small indeed.

The laurel, meed of mighty Conquerors
And Poets *sage* –

are his own words; but his wisdom has, in this particular, been his worst enemy; while, its opposite, whether in the shape of folly or madness, has been their best friend. But he was a great power; and bears a high name: the laurel has been awarded to him.

A Dramatic Author, if he write for the Stage, must adapt himself to the taste of the Audience, or they will not endure him; accordingly the mighty genius of Shakespeare was listened to. The People were delighted; but I am not sufficiently versed in Stage antiquities to determine whether they did not flock as eagerly to the representation of many pieces of contemporary Authors, wholly undeserving to appear upon the same boards. Had there been a formal contest for superiority among dramatic Writers, that Shakespeare, like his predecessors Sophocles and Euripides, would have often been subject to the mortification of seeing the prize adjudged to sorry competitors, becomes too probable when we reflect that the Admirers of Settle and Shadwell were, in a later age, as numerous, and reckoned as respectable in point of talent as those of Dryden. At all events, that

Shakespeare stooped to accommodate himself to the People, is sufficiently apparent; and one of the most striking proofs of his almost omnipotent genius, is, that he could turn to such glorious purpose those materials which the prepossessions of the age compelled him to make use of. Yet even this marvellous skill appears not to have been enough to prevent his rivals from having some advantage over him in public estimation; else how can we account for passages and scenes that exist in his works, unless upon a supposition that some of the grossest of them, a fact which in my own mind I have no doubt of, were foisted in by the Players, for the gratification of the many?

But that his Works, whatever might be their reception upon the stage, made little impression upon the ruling Intellects of the time, may be inferred from the fact that Lord Bacon, in his multifarious writings, nowhere either quotes or alludes to him. – [The learned Hakewill (a 3d edition of whose book bears date 1635) writing to refute the error 'touching Nature's perpetual and universal decay,' cites triumphantly the names of Ariosto, Tasso, Bartas, and Spenser, as instances that poetic genius had not degenerated; but he makes no mention of Shakespeare. – W.] His dramatic excellence enabled him to resume possession of the stage after the Restoration; but Dryden tells us that in his time two of Beaumont's and Fletcher's Plays was acted for one of Shakespeare's. And so faint and limited was the perception of the poetic beauties of his dramas in the time of Pope, that, in his Edition of the Plays, with a view of rendering to the general Reader a necessary service, he printed between inverted commas those passages which he thought most worthy of notice.

At this day, the French Critics have abated nothing of their aversion to this darling of our Nation: 'the English with their Bouffon de Shakespeare' is as familiar an expression among them as in the time of Voltaire. Baron Grimm is the only French writer who seems to have perceived his infinite superiority to the first names of the French Theatre; an advantage which the Parisian Critic owed to his German blood and German education. The most enlightened Italians, though well acquainted with our language, are wholly incompetent to measure the proportions of Shakespeare. The Germans only, of foreign nations, are approaching towards a knowledge and feeling of what he is. In some respects they have acquired a superiority over the fellow-countrymen of the Poet; for among us it is a current, I might say, an established opinion that Shakespeare is justly praised when he is pronounced to be 'a wild irregular genius, in whom great faults are compensated by great beauties.' How long may it be before this misconception passes away, and it becomes universally acknowledged that the judgement of Shakespeare in the selection of his materials, and in the manner in which he has made them, heterogeneous as they often are, constitute a unity of their own, and contribute all to one great end, is not less admirable than his imagination, his invention, and his intuitive knowledge of human Nature!

There is extant a small Volume of miscellaneous Poems in which Shakespeare expresses his own feelings in his own Person. It is not difficult to conceive that the Editor, George Stevens, should have been insensible to the beauties of one portion of that Volume, the Sonnets; though there is not a part of the writings of this Poet where is found in an equal compass a greater number of exquisite feelings felicitously expressed. But, from regard to the Critic's own credit, he would not have ventured to talk of an act of parliament not being strong enough to compel the perusal of these, or any production of Shakespeare [This flippant insensibility was publicly reprehended by Mr Coleridge in a course of Lectures upon Poetry given by him at the Royal Institution. For the various merits of thought and language in Shakespeare's Sonnets see Numbers 27, 29, 30, 32, 33, 54, 64, 66, 68, 73, 76, 86, 91, 92, 93, 97, 98, 105, 107, 108, 109, 111, 113, 114, 116, 117, 129, and many others. – W.], if he had not known that the people of England were ignorant of the treasures contained in those little pieces; and if he had not, moreover, shared the too common propensity of human nature to exult over a supposed fall into the mire of a genius whom he had been compelled to regard with admiration, as an inmate of the celestial regions, – 'there sitting where he durst not soar.'

Nine years before the death of Shakespeare, Milton was born; and early in life he published several small poems, which, though on their first appearance they were praised by a few of the judicious, were afterwards neglected to that degree that Pope, in his youth, could pilfer from them without danger of detection. – Whether these poems are at this day justly appreciated I will not undertake to decide: nor would it imply a severe reflection upon the mass of Readers to suppose the contrary; seeing that a Man of the acknowledged genius of Voss, the German Poet, could suffer their spirit to evaporate; and could change their character, as is done in the translation made by him of the most popular of those pieces. At all events it is certain that these Poems of Milton are now much read, and loudly praised; yet were they little heard of till more than 150 years after their publication; and of the Sonnets, Dr Johnson, as appears from Boswell's Life of him, was in the habit of thinking and speaking as contempt-uously as Stevens wrote upon those of Shakespeare.

About the time when the Pindaric Odes of Cowley and his imitators, and the productions of that class of curious thinkers whom Dr Johnson has strangely styled Metaphysical Poets, were beginning to lose something of that extravagant admiration which they had excited, the Paradise Lost made its appearance. 'Fit audience find though few,' was the petition addressed by the Poet to his inspiring Muse. I have said elsewhere that he gained more than he asked; this I believe to be true; but Dr Johnson has fallen into a gross mistake when he attempts to prove, by the sale of the work, that Milton's Countrymen were '*just* to it' upon its first appearance. Thirteen hundred Copies were sold in two years; an uncommon example, he asserts, of the prevalence of genius in opposition to so much recent enmity as Milton's public conduct had excited. But be it remembered that, if Milton's political and religious opinions, and the manner in which he announced them, had raised him many enemies, they had pro-cured him numerous friends; who, as all personal danger was passed away at the time of publication, would be eager to procure the master-work of a Man whom they revered, and whom they would be proud of praising. The demand did not immediately increase; 'for,' says Dr Johnson, 'many more Readers' (he means Persons in the habit of reading poetry) 'than were sup-plied at first the Nation did not afford.' How careless must a writer be who can make this assertion in the face of so many existing title pages to belie it! Turning to my own shelves, I find the folio of Cowley, 7th Edition, 1681. A book near it is Flatman's Poems, 4th Edition, 1686; Waller, 5th Edition, same date. The Poems of Norris of Bemerton not long after went, I believe, through nine Editions. What further demand there might be for these works I do not know, but I well remember, that 25 Years ago, the Bookseller's stalls in London swarmed with the folios of Cowley. This is not mentioned in disparagement of that able writer and amiable Man; but merely to show – that, if Milton's work was not more read, it was not because readers did not exist at the time. Only 3000 copies of the Paradise Lost sold in 11 Years; and the Nation, says Dr Johnson, had been satisfied from 1623 to 1644 [1664?], that is 41 Years, with only two Editions of the Works of Shakespeare; which probably did not together make 1000 copies; facts adduced by the critic to prove the 'paucity of Readers.' – There were Readers in multitudes; but their money went for other purposes, as their admiration was fixed elsewhere. We are authorized, then, to affirm that the reception of the Paradise Lost, and the slow progress of its fame, are proofs as striking as can be desired that the positions which I am attempting to establish are not erroneous. – [Hughes is express upon this subject; in his dedication of Spenser's Works to Lord Somers he writes thus. 'It was your Lordship's encouraging a beautiful Edition of Paradise Lost that first brought that incomparable Poem to be generally known and esteemed.' – W.] How amusing to shape to one's self such a critique as a Wit of Charles's days, or a Lord of the Miscellanies, or trading Journalist, of King William's time, would have brought forth, if he had set his faculties industriously to work upon this Poem, everywhere impregnated with *original* excellence!

So strange indeed are the obliquities of admiration, that they whose opinions are much influenced by authority will often be tempted to think that there are no fixed principles in human nature for this art to rest upon. [This opinion seems actually to have been entertained by Adam Smith, the worst critic, David Hume not excepted, that Scotland, a soil to which this sort of weed seems natural, has produced. – W.] I have been honoured by being permitted to peruse in MS. a tract composed between the period of the Revolution and the close of that Century. It is the Work of an English Peer of high accomplishments, its object to form the character and direct the studies of his Son. Perhaps nowhere does a more beautiful treatise of the kind exist. The good sense and wisdom of the thoughts, the delicacy of the feelings, and the charm of the style, are, throughout, equally conspicuous. Yet the Author, selecting among the Poets of his own Country those whom he deems most worthy of his son's perusal, particularizes only Lord Rochester, Sir John Denham, and Cowley. Writing about the same time, Shaftsbury, an Author at present unjustly depreciated, describes the English Muses as only yet lisping in their Cradles.

The arts by which Pope, soon afterwards, contrived to procure to himself a more general and a higher reputation than perhaps any English Poet ever attained during his life-time, are known to the judicious. And as well known is it to them, that the undue exertion of these arts, is the cause why Pope has for some time held a rank in literature, to which, if he had not been seduced by an over-love of immediate popularity, and had confided more in his native genius, he never could have descended. He bewitched the nation by his melody, and dazzled it by his polished style, and was himself blinded by his own success. Having wandered from humanity in his Eclogues with boyish inexperience, the praise, which these compositions obtained, tempted him into a belief that nature was not to be trusted, at least in pastoral Poetry. To prove this by example, he put his friend Gay upon writing those Eclogues which the Author intended to be burlesque. The Instigator of the work, and his Admirers, could perceive in them nothing but what was ridiculous. Nevertheless, though these Poems contain some odious and even detestable passages, the effect, as Dr Johnson well observes, 'of reality and truth became conspicuous even when the intention was to show them grovelling and degrading.' These Pastorals, ludicrous to those who prided themselves upon their refinement, in spite of those disgusting passages 'became popular, and were read with delight as just representations of rural manners and occupations.'

Something less than 60 years after the publication of the Paradise Lost appeared Thomson's Winter; which was speedily followed by his other Seasons. It is a work of inspiration; much of it is written from himself, and nobly from himself. How was it received? 'It was no sooner read,' says one of his contemporary Biographers, 'than universally admired: those only excepted who had not been used to feel, or to look for anything in poetry, beyond a *point* of satirical or epigrammatic wit, a smart *antithesis* richly trimmed with rhyme, or the softness of an *elegiac* complaint. To such his manly classical spirit could not readily commend itself; till, after a more attentive perusal, they had got the better of their prejudices, and either acquired or affected a truer taste. A few others stood aloof, merely because they had long before fixed the articles of their poetical creed, and resigned themselves to an absolute despair of ever seeing anything new and original. These were somewhat mortified to find their notions disturbed by the appearance of a poet, who seemed to owe nothing but to nature and his own genius. But, in a short time, the applause became unanimous; everyone wondering how so many pictures, and pictures so familiar, should have moved them but faintly to what they felt in his descriptions. His digressions too, the overflowings of a tender benevolent heart, charmed the reader no less; leaving him in doubt, whether he should more admire the Poet or love the Man.'

This case appears to bear strongly against us: – but we must distinguish between wonder and legitimate admiration. The subject of the work is the changes produced in the appearances of nature by the revolution of the year: and, by undertaking to write in verse, Thomson pledged himself to treat his subject as became a Poet. Now it is remarkable that, excepting a passage or two in the Windsor Forest of Pope, and some delightful pictures in the Poems of Lady Winchilsea, the Poetry of the period intervening between the publication of the Paradise Lost and the Seasons does not contain a single new image of external nature; and scarcely presents a familiar one from which it can be inferred that the eye of the Poet had been steadily fixed upon his object, much less that his feelings had urged him to work upon it in the spirit of genuine imagination. To what a low state knowledge of the most obvious and important phenomena had sunk, is evident from the style in which Dryden has executed a description of

Night in one of his Tragedies, and Pope his translation of the celebrated moon-light scene in the Iliad. A blind man, in the habit of attending accurately to descriptions casually dropped from the lips of those around him, might easily depict these appearances with more truth. Dryden's lines are vague, bombastic, and senseless;

> [CORTES *alone, in a night-gown.*
> All things are hushed as Nature's self lay dead:
> The mountains seem to nod their drowsy head:
> The little Birds in dreams their songs repeat,
> And sleeping Flowers beneath the Night-dew sweat:
> Even Lust and Envy sleep; yet Love denies
> Rest to my soul, and slumber to my eyes.
> *Dryden's Indian Emperor* – W.]

those of Pope, though he had Homer to guide him, are throughout false and contradictory. The verses of Dryden, once highly celebrated, are forgotten; those of Pope still retain their hold upon public estimation, – nay, there is not a passage of descriptive poetry, which at this day finds so many and such ardent admirers. Strange to think of an Enthusiast, as may have been the case with thousands, reciting those verses under the cope of a moon-light sky, without having his raptures in the least disturbed by a suspicion of their absurdity. – If these two distinguished Writers could habitually think that the visible universe was of so little consequence to a Poet, that it was scarcely necessary for him to cast his eyes upon it, we may be assured that those passages of the elder Poets which faithfully and poetically describe the phenomena of nature, were not at that time holden in much estimation, and that there was little accurate attention paid to these appearances.

Wonder is the natural product of Ignorance; and as the soil was *in such good condition* at the time of the publication of the Seasons, the crop was doubtless abundant. Neither individuals nor nations become corrupt all at once, nor are they enlightened in a moment. Thomson was an inspired Poet, but he could not work miracles; in cases where the art of seeing had in some degree been learned, the teacher would further the proficiency of his pupils, but he could do little *more*, though so far does vanity assist men in acts of self-deception that many would often fancy they recognized a likeness when they knew nothing of the original. Having shown that much of what his Biographer deemed genuine admiration must in fact have been blind wonderment, – how is the rest to be accounted for? – Thomson was fortunate in the very title of his Poem, which seemed to bring it home to the prepared sympathies of everyone: in the next place, notwithstanding his high powers, he writes a vicious style; and his false ornaments are exactly of that kind which would be most likely to strike the undiscerning. He likewise abounds with sentimental common-places, that from the manner in which they were brought forward bore an imposing air of novelty. In any well-used Copy of the Seasons the Book generally opens of itself with the rhapsody on love, or with one of the stories (perhaps Damon and Musidora); these also are prominent in our Collections of Extracts; and are the parts of his Works which, after all, were probably most efficient in first recommending the Author to general notice. Pope, repaying praises which he had received, and wishing to extol him to the highest, only styles him 'an elegant and philosophical Poet;' nor are we able to collect any unquestionable proofs that the true characteristics of Thomson's genius as an imaginative Poet were perceived, till the elder Warton, almost 40 Years after the publication of the Seasons, pointed them out by a note in his Essay on the life and writings of Pope. In the Castle of Indolence (of which Gray speaks so coldly) these characteristics were almost as conspicuously displayed, and in verse more harmonious and diction more pure. Yet that fine Poem was neglected on its appearance, and is at this day the delight only of a Few!

When Thomson died, Collins breathed his regrets into an Elegiac Poem, in which he pronounces a poetical curse upon *him* who should regard with insensibility the place where the Poet's remains were deposited. The Poems of the mourner himself have now passed through innumerable Editions, and are universally known; but if, when Collins died, the same kind of imprecation had been pronounced by a surviving admirer, small is the number whom it would not have comprehended. The notice which his poems attained during his life-time was so small, and of course the sale so insignificant, that not long before his death he deemed it right to repay to the Bookseller the sum which he had advanced for them, and threw the Edition into the fire.

Next in importance to the Seasons of Thomson, though at considerable distance from that work in order of time, come the Reliques of Ancient English Poetry; collected, new-modelled, and in many instances (if such a contradiction in terms may be used) composed, by the editor, Dr Percy. This Work did not steal silently into the world, as is evident from the number of legendary tales, which appeared not long after its publication; and which were modelled, as the Authors persuaded themselves, after the old Ballad. The Compilation was however ill-suited to the then existing taste of City society; and Dr Johnson, 'mid the little senate to which he gave laws, was not sparing in his exertions to make it an object of contempt. The Critic triumphed, the legendary imitators were deservedly disregarded, and, as undeservedly, their ill-imitated models sank, in this Country, into temporary neglect; while Bürger, and other able Writers of Germany, were translating, or imitating, these Reliques, and composing, with the aid of inspiration thence derived, Poems, which are the delight of the German nation. Dr Percy was so abashed by the ridicule flung upon his labours from the ignorance and insensibility of the Persons with whom he lived, that, though while he was writing under a mask he had not wanted resolution to follow his genius into the regions of true simplicity and genuine pathos (as is evinced by the exquisite ballad of Sir Cauline and by many other pieces), yet, when he appeared in his own person and character as a poetical writer, he adopted, as in the tale of the Hermit of Warkworth, a diction scarcely in any one of its features distinguishable from the vague, the glossy, and unfeeling language of his day. I mention this remarkable fact with regret, esteeming the genius of Dr Percy in this kind of writing superior to that of any other man by whom, in modern times, it has been cultivated. That even Bürger (to whom Klopstock gave, in my hearing, a commendation which he denied to Goethe and Schiller, pronouncing him to be a genuine Poet, and one of the few among the Germans whose works would last) had not the fine sensibility of Percy, might be shown from many passages, in which he has deserted his original only to go astray. For example,

Now daye was gone, and night was come,
And all were fast asleepe,
All, save the Ladye Emmeline,
Who sate in her bowre to weepe:

And soone she heard her true Love's voice
Low whispering at the walle,
Awake, awake, my deare Ladye,
'Tis I thy true-love call.

Which is thus tricked out and dilated,

Als nun die Nacht Gebirg' und Thal
Vermummt in Rabenschatten,
Und Hochburgs Lampen überall
Schon ausgeflimmert hatten,
Und alles tief entschlafen war;
Doch nur das Fräulein immerdar,
Voll Fieberangst, noch wachte,
Und seinen Ritter dachte:
Da horch! Ein süsser Liebeston
Kam leis' empor geflogen.
'Ho, Trudchen, ho! Da bin ich schon!
Frisch auf! Dich angezogen!'

But from humble ballads we must ascend to heroics.

All hail Macpherson! hail to thee, Sire of Ossian! The Phantom was begotten by the snug embrace of an impudent Highlander upon a cloud of tradition – it travelled southward, where it was greeted with acclamation, and the thin Consistence took its course through Europe, upon the breath of popular applause. The Editor of the 'Reliques' had indirectly preferred a claim to the praise of invention by not concealing that his supplementary labours were considerable: how selfish his conduct contrasted with that of the disinterested Gael, who, like Lear, gives his kingdom away, and is content to become a pensioner upon his own issue for a beggarly pittance! – Open this far-famed Book! – I have done so at random, and the beginning of the 'Epic Poem Temora,' in 8 Books, presents itself. 'The blue waves of Ullin roll in light. The green hills are covered with day. Trees shake their dusky heads in the breeze. Grey torrents pour their noisy streams. Two green hills with aged oaks surround a narrow plain. The blue course of a stream is there. On its banks stood Cairbar of Atha. His spear supports the king; the red eyes of his fear are sad. Cormac rises on his soul with all his ghastly wounds.' Precious memorandums from the pocket-book of the blind Ossian!

If it be unbecoming, as I acknowledge that for the most part it is, to speak disrespectfully of Works that have enjoyed for a length of time a widely spread reputation, without at the same time producing irrefragable proofs of their unworthiness, let me be forgiven upon this occasion. – Having had the good fortune to be born and reared in a mountainous Country, from my very childhood I have felt the falsehood that pervades the volumes imposed upon the World under the name of Ossian. From what I saw with my own eyes, I knew that the imagery was spurious. In nature everything is distinct, yet nothing defined into absolute independent singleness. In Macpherson's work it is exactly the reverse; everything (that is not stolen) is in this manner defined, insulated, dislocated, deadened, – yet nothing distinct. It will always be so when words are substituted for things. To say that the characters never could exist, that the manners are impossible, and that a dream has more substance than the whole state of society, as there depicted, is doing nothing more than pronouncing a censure which Macpherson defied; when, with the steeps of Morven before his eyes, he could talk so familiarly of his Car-borne heroes; – Of Morven, which, if one may judge from its appearance at the distance of a few miles, contains scarcely an acre of ground sufficiently accommodating for a sledge to be trailed along its surface. – Mr Malcolm Laing has ably shown that the diction of this pretended translation is a motley assembly from all quarters; but he is so fond of making out parallel passages as to call poor Macpherson to account for his very 'ands' and his 'buts!' and he has weakened his argument by conducting it as if he thought that every striking resemblance was a *conscious* plagiarism. It is enough that the coincidences are too remarkable for its being probable or possible that they could arise in different minds without communication between them. Now as the Translators of the Bible, Shakespeare, Milton, and Pope, could not be indebted to Macpherson, it follows that he must have owed his fine feathers to them; unless we are prepared gravely to assert, with Madame de Staël, that many of the characteristic beauties of our most celebrated English Poets, are derived from the ancient Fingallian; in which case the modern translator would have been but giving back to Ossian his own. – It is consistent that Lucien Buonaparte, who could censure Milton for having surrounded Satan in the infernal regions with courtly and regal splendour, should pronounce the modern Ossian to be the glory of Scotland; – a Country that has produced a Dunbar, a Buchanan, a Thomson, and a Burns! These opinions are of ill omen for the Epic ambition of him who has given them to the world.

Yet, much as these pretended treasures of antiquity have been admired, they have been wholly uninfluential upon the literature of the Country. No succeeding Writer appears to have caught from them a ray of inspiration; no Author in the least distinguished, has ventured formally to imitate them – except the Boy, Chatterton, on their first appearance. He had perceived, from the successful trials which he himself had made in literary forgery, how few critics were able to distinguish between a real ancient medal and a counterfeit of modern manufacture; and he set himself to the work of filling a Magazine with *Saxon poems*, – counterparts of those of Ossian, as like his as one of his misty stars is to another. This incapability to amalgamate with the literature of the Island, is, in my estimation, a decisive proof that the book is essentially unnatural; nor should I require any other to demonstrate it to be a forgery, audacious as worthless. – Contrast, in this respect, the effect of Macpherson's publication with the Reliques of Percy, so unassuming, so modest in their pretensions! – I have already stated how much Germany is indebted to this latter work; and for our own Country, its Poetry has been absolutely redeemed by it. I do not think that there is an able Writer in verse of the present day who would not be proud to acknowledge his obligations to the Reliques; I know that it is so with my friends; and, for myself, I am happy in this occasion to make a public avowal of my own.

Dr Johnson, more fortunate in his contempt of the labours of Macpherson than those of his modest friend, was solicited not long after to furnish Prefaces biographical and critical for some of the most eminent English Poets. The Booksellers took upon themselves to make the collection; they referred probably to the most popular miscellanies, and, unquestionably, to their Books of accounts; and decided upon the claim of Authors to be admitted into a body of the most Eminent, from the familiarity of their names with the readers of that day, and by the profits, which, from the sale of his works, each had brought and was bringing to the Trade. The Editor was allowed a limited exercise of discretion, and the Authors whom he recommended are scarcely to be mentioned without a smile. We open the volume of Prefatory Lives, and to our astonishment the *first* name we find is that of Cowley! – What is become of the Morning-star of English Poetry? Where is the bright Elizabethan Constellation? Or, if Names are more acceptable than images, where is the ever-to-be-honoured Chaucer? where is Spenser? where Sydney? and lastly where he, whose rights as a Poet, contradistinguished from those which he is universally allowed to possess as a Dramatist, we have vindicated, where Shakespeare? – These, and a multitude of others not unworthy to be placed near them, their contemporaries and successors, we have *not*. But in their stead, we have (could better be expected when precedence was to be settled by an abstract of reputation at any given period made as in the case before us?) Roscommon, and Stepney, and Phillips, and Walsh, and Smith, and Duke, and King, and Spratt – Halifax, Granville, Sheffield, Congreve, Broome, and other reputed Magnates; Writers in metre utterly worthless and useless, except for occasions like the present, when their productions are referred to as evidence what a small quantity of brain is necessary to procure a considerable stock of admiration, provided the aspirant will accommodate himself to the likings and fashions of his day.

As I do not mean to bring down this retrospect to our own times, it may with propriety be closed at the era of this distinguished event. From the literature of other ages and countries, proofs equally cogent might have been adduced that the opinions announced in the former part of this Essay are founded upon truth. It was not an agreeable office, not a prudent undertaking, to declare them, but their importance seemed to render it a duty. It may still be asked, where lies the particular relation of what has been said to these Volumes? – The question will be easily answered by the discerning Reader who is old enough to remember the taste that was prevalent when some of these Poems were first published, 17 years ago; who has also observed to what degree the Poetry of this Island has since that period been coloured by them; and who is further aware of the unremitting hostility with which, upon some principle or other, they have each and all been opposed. A sketch of my own notion of the constitution of Fame, has been given; and, as far as concerns myself, I have cause to be satisfied. The love, the admiration, the indifference, the slight, the aversion, and even the contempt, with which these Poems have been received, knowing, as I do, the source within my own mind, from which they have proceeded, and the labour and pains, which, when labour and pains appeared needful, have been bestowed upon them, – must all, if I think consistently, be received as pledges and tokens, bearing the same general impression though widely different in value; – they are all proofs that for the present time I have not laboured in vain; and afford assurances, more or less authentic, that the products of my industry will endure.

If there be one conclusion more forcibly pressed upon us than another by the review which has been given of the fortunes and fate of Poetical Works, it is this, – that every Author, as far as he is great and at the same time *original*, has had the task of *creating* the taste by which he is to be enjoyed: so has it been, so will it continue to be. This remark was long since made to me by the philosophical Friend for the separation of whose Poems from my own I have previously expressed my regret. The predecessors of an original Genius of a high order will have smoothed the way for all that he has in common with them; – and much he will have in common; but, for what is peculiarly his own, he will be called upon to clear and often to shape his own road: – he will be in the condition of Hannibal among the Alps.

And where lies the real difficulty of creating that taste by which a truly original Poet is to be relished? Is it in breaking the bonds of custom, in overcoming the prejudices of false refinement, and displacing the aversions of inexperience? Or, if he labour for an object which here and elsewhere I have proposed to myself, does it consist in divesting the Reader of the pride that induces him to dwell upon those points wherein Men differ from each other, to the exclusion of those in which all Men are alike, or the same; and in making him ashamed of the vanity that renders him insensible of the appropriate excellence which civil arrangements, less unjust than might appear, and Nature illimitable in her bounty, have conferred on Men who stand below him in the scale of society? Finally, does it lie in establishing that dominion over the spirits of Readers by which they are to be humbled and humanized, in order that they may be purified and exalted?

If these ends are to be attained by the mere communication of *knowledge*, it does *not* lie here. – TASTE, I would remind the Reader, like IMAGINATION, is a word which has been forced to extend its services far beyond the point to which philosophy would have confined them. It is a metaphor, taken from a *passive* sense of the human body, and transferred to things which are in their essence *not* passive, – to intellectual *acts* and *operations*. The word, imagination, has been overstrained, from impulses honourable to mankind, to meet the demands of the faculty which is perhaps the noblest of our nature. In the instance of taste, the process has been reversed; and from the prevalence of dispositions at once injurious and discreditable, – being no other than that selfishness which is the child of apathy, – which, as Nations decline in productive and creative power, makes them value themselves upon a presumed refinement of judging. Poverty of language is the primary cause of the use which we make of the word, imagination; but the word, Taste, has been stretched to the sense which it bears in modern Europe by habits of self-conceit, inducing that inversion in the order of things whereby a passive faculty is made paramount among the faculties conversant with the fine arts. Proportion and congruity, the requisite knowledge being supposed, are subjects upon which taste may be trusted; it is competent to this office; – for in its intercourse with these the mind is *passive*, and is affected painfully or pleasurably as by an instinct. But the profound and the exquisite in feeling, the lofty and universal in thought and imagination; or in ordinary language the pathetic and the sublime; – are neither of them, accurately speaking, objects of a faculty which could ever without a sinking in the spirit of Nations have been designated by the metaphor – *Taste*. And why? Because without the exertion of a co-operating *power* in the mind of the Reader, there can be no adequate sympathy with either of these emotions: without this auxiliar impulse elevated or profound passion cannot exist.

Passion, it must be observed, is derived from a word which signifies, *suffering*; but the connexion which suffering has with effort, with exertion, and *action*, is immediate and inseparable. How strikingly is this property of human nature exhibited by the fact, that, in popular language, to be in a passion, is to be angry! – But,

Anger in hasty *words* or *blows*
Itself discharges on its foes.

To be moved, then, by a passion, is to be excited, often to external, and always to internal, effort; whether for the continuance and strengthening of the passion, or for its suppression, accordingly as the course which it takes may be painful or pleasurable. If the latter, the soul must contribute to its support, or it never becomes vivid, – and soon languishes, and dies. And this brings us to the point. If every great Poet with whose writings men are familiar, in the highest exercise of his genius, before he can be thoroughly enjoyed, has to call forth and to communicate *power*, this service, in a still greater degree, falls upon an original Writer, at his first appearance in the world. – Of genius the only proof is, the act of doing well what is worthy to be done, and what was never done before: Of genius, in the fine arts, the only infallible sign is the widening the sphere of human sensibility, for the delight, honour, and benefit of human nature. Genius is the introduction of a new element into the intellectual universe: or, if that be not allowed, it is the application of powers to objects on which they had not before been exercised, or the employment of them in such a manner as to produce effects hitherto unknown. What is all this but an advance, or a conquest, made by the soul of the Poet? Is it to be supposed that the Reader can make progress of this kind, like an Indian Prince or General – stretched on his Palanquin, and borne by his Slaves? No, he is invigorated and inspirited by his Leader, in order that he may exert himself, for he cannot proceed in quiescence, he cannot be carried like a dead weight. Therefore to create taste is to call forth and bestow power, of which knowledge is the effect; and *there* lies the true difficulty.

As the pathetic participates of an *animal* sensation, it might seem – that, if the springs of this emotion were genuine, all men, possessed of competent knowledge of the facts and circumstances, would be instantaneously affected. And, doubtless, in the works of every true Poet will be found passages of that species of excellence, which is proved by effects immediate and universal. But there are emotions of the pathetic that are simple and direct, and others – that are complex and revolutionary; some – to which the heart yields with gentleness, others, – against which it struggles with pride: these varieties are infinite as the combinations of circumstance and the constitutions of character. Remember, also, that the medium through which, in poetry, the heart is to be affected – is language; a thing subject to endless fluctuations and arbitrary associations. The genius of the Poet melts these down for his purpose; but they retain their shape and quality to him who is not capable of exerting, within his own mind, a corresponding energy. There is also a meditative, as well as a human, pathos; an enthusiastic, as well as an ordinary, sorrow; a sadness that has its seat in the depths of reason, to which the mind cannot sink gently of itself – but to which it must descend by treading the steps of thought. And for the sublime, – if we consider what are the cares that occupy the passing day, and how remote is the practice and the course of life from the sources of sublimity, in the soul of Man, can it be wondered that there is little existing preparation for a Poet

charged with a new mission to extend its kingdom, and to aug-
ment and spread its enjoyments?

Away, then, with the senseless iteration of the word, *popular*,
applied to new works in Poetry, as if there were no test of excellence in this first of the fine arts but that all Men should run
after its productions, as if urged by an appetite, or constrained
by a spell! – The qualities of writing best fitted for eager reception are either such as startle the world into attention by their
audacity and extravagance; or they are chiefly of a superficial
kind, lying upon the surfaces of manners; or arising out of a
selection and arrangement of incidents, by which the mind is
kept upon the stretch of curiosity, and the fancy amused without
the trouble of thought. But in everything which is to send the
soul into herself, to be admonished of her weakness or to be
made conscious of her power; – wherever life and nature are
described as operated upon by the creative or abstracting virtue
of the imagination; wherever the instinctive wisdom of antiquity
and her heroic passions uniting, in the heart of the Poet, with the
meditative wisdom of later ages, have produced that accord of
sublimated humanity, which is at once a history of the remote
past and a prophetic annunciation of the remotest future, *there*,
the Poet must reconcile himself for a season to few and scattered
hearers. – Grand thoughts (and Shakespeare must often have
sighed over this truth) as they are most naturally and most fitly
conceived in solitude, so can they not be brought forth in the
midst of plaudits without some violation of their sanctity. Go to
a silent exhibition of the productions of the Sister Art, and be
convinced that the qualities which dazzle at first sight, and
kindle the admiration of the multitude, are essentially different
from those by which permanent influence is secured. Let us not
shrink from following up these principles as far as they will carry
us, and conclude with observing – that there never has been a
period, and perhaps never will be, in which vicious poetry, of
some kind or other, has not excited more zealous admiration, and
been far more generally read, than good; but this advantage
attends the good, that the *individual*, as well as the species, survives from age to age: whereas, of the depraved, though the
species be immortal the individual quickly *perishes*; the object of

present admiration vanishes, being supplanted by some other as easily produced; which, though no better, brings with it at least the irritation of novelty, – with adaptation, more or less skilful, to the changing humours of the majority of those who are most at leisure to regard poetical works when they first solicit their attention.

Is it the result of the whole that, in the opinion of the Writer, the judgement of the People is not to be respected? The thought is most injurious; and could the charge be brought against him, he would repel it with indignation. The People have already been justified, and their eulogium pronounced by implication, when it was said, above – that, of *good* Poetry, the *individual,* as well as the species, *survives.* And how does it survive but through the People? what preserves it but their intellect and their wisdom?

– Past and future, are the wings
On whose support, harmoniously conjoined,
Moves the great Spirit of human knowledge –
MS.

The voice that issues from this Spirit, is that Vox populi which the Deity inspires. Foolish must he be who can mistake for this a local acclamation, or a transitory outcry – transitory though it be for years, local though from a Nation. Still more lamentable is his error, who can believe that there is anything of divine infallibility in the clamour of that small though loud portion of the community, ever governed by factitious influence, which, under the name of the PUBLIC, passes itself, upon the unthinking, for the PEOPLE. Towards the Public, the Writer hopes that he feels as much deference as it is entitled to: but to the People, philosophically characterized, and to the embodied spirit of their knowledge, so far as it exists and moves, at the present, faithfully supported by its two wings, the past and the future, his devout respect, his reverence, is due. He offers it willingly and readily; and, this done, takes leave of his Readers, by assuring them – that, if he were not persuaded that the Contents of these Volumes, and the Work to which they are subsidiary, evinced something of the 'Vision and the Faculty divine;' and that, both in words and things, they will operate in their degree, to extend the domain of sensibility for the delight, the honour, and the benefit of human nature, notwithstanding the many happy hours which he has employed in their composition, and the manifold comforts and enjoyments they have procured to him, he would not, if a wish could do it, save them from immediate destruction; – from becoming at this moment, to the world, as a thing that had never been.

Notes

References to letters and journals are by dates rather than by page numbers of particular editions. The 1850 version of *The Prelude* (J. C. Maxwell's edition, Penguin Books, 1971) is being cited unless otherwise noted. Brackets around a title indicate that the title was not given to the poem by Wordsworth.

A number of abbreviations are used. '*I. F. note*' indicates a note dictated by Wordsworth in 1843 to Isabella Fenwick. 'W.' at the end of a note designates that it is Wordsworth's. If no date is given in parentheses, the note was contained in his last edition (1849–50); otherwise the note was contained in the editions indicated by the dates. '*PW*' refers to Ernest de Selincourt's standard edition of Wordsworth's *Poetical Works*.

In the case of other complete editions of Wordsworth's poetry the editor's name alone is cited; unless otherwise indicated, the citation can be found in the notes to the poem in question in the last edition by that editor. The dates and exact title of the complete editions can be found in the bibliography. The term 'data' refers to information about composition, publication, and categorization that is contained in the first paragraph of each head-note.

Information concerning the classical citations is taken from the Loeb Classics edition unless otherwise indicated.

THE EXCURSION

Composed between 1797 and 1814; first published in 1814.

In the *Preface to the Edition of 1814*, Wordsworth describes (in the second paragraph) the genesis of his 'philosophical poem', *The Recluse*, an account which is not quite accurate (see *PW*, V, 363). In any case, of the plan as set forth by Wordsworth, very little materialized, at least in the manner described. *The Prelude* ('That Work, addressed to a dear Friend') was finished, and published posthumously, in 1850; the first part of *The Recluse* is represented by only one Book, *Home at Grasmere*, first published in 1888; *The Excursion*, the second part, was thus the only section of *The Recluse* to be completed and the only one to be published in Wordsworth's lifetime. In de Selincourt's witty phrase (*PW*, V, 368), all that came of Wordsworth's original plan 'apart from one Book, was a Prelude to the main theme and an Excursion from it'.

The reason for this failure is usually ascribed to Coleridge's role in the projected philosophical poem, for it was Coleridge who was main promoter of what he saw as 'the first and only true philosophical poem in existence' (letter to Wordsworth, 30 May 1815). The original plan for the poem is described in Coleridge's *Table Talk* (31 July 1832):

> Then the plan laid out, and, I believe, partly suggested by me, was, that Wordsworth should assume the station of a man in mental repose, one whose principles were made up, and so prepared to deliver upon authority a system of philosophy. He was to treat man as man – a subject of eye, ear,

touch, and taste, in contact with external nature, and informing the senses from the mind, and not compounding a mind out of the senses; then he was to describe the pastoral and other states of society, assuming something of the Juvenalian spirit as he approached the high civilization of cities and towns, and opening a melancholy picture of the present state of degeneracy and vice; thence he was to infer and reveal the proof of, and necessity for, the whole state of man and society being subject to, and illustrative of, a redemptive process in operation, showing how this idea reconciled all the anomalies, and promised future glory and restoration. Something of this sort was, I think, agreed on. It is, in substance, what I have been all my life doing in my system of philosophy.

Wordsworth, however, wrote the only complete part of *The Recluse* with 'something of a dramatic form'. In *The Excursion* there were in any case speakers, 'dramatis personae', and these he gives an account of in the *I. F. note*:

... Had I been born in a class which would have deprived me of what is called a liberal education, it is not unlikely that, being strong in body, I should have taken to a way of life such as that in which my Pedlar passed the greater part of his days. At all events, I am here called upon freely to acknowledge that the character I have represented in his person is chiefly an idea of what I fancied my own character might have become in his circumstances. Nevertheless, much of what he says and does had an external existence that fell under my own youthful and subsequent observation. An individual named [James] Patrick, by birth and education a Scotchman, followed this humble occupation for many years, and afterwards settled in the Town of Kendal. He married a kinswoman of my wife's, and her sister Sarah was brought up from early childhood under this good man's eye. My own imaginations I was happy to find clothed in reality, and fresh ones suggested, by what she reported of this man's tenderness of heart, his strong and pure imagination, and his solid attainments in literature, chiefly religious whether in prose or verse. At Hawkshead also, while I was a schoolboy, there occasionally resided a Packman (the name then generally given to [persons of] this calling) with whom I had frequent conversations upon what had befallen him, and what he had observed, during his wandering life; and, as was natural, we took much to each other; and, upon the subject of *Pedlarism* in general, as *then* followed, and its favourableness to an intimate knowledge of human concerns, not merely among the humbler classes of society, I need say nothing here in addition to what is to be found in *The Excursion*, and a note attached to it.

Now for the Solitary. Of him I have much less to say. Not long after we took up our abode at Grasmere, came to reside there, from what motive I either never knew or have forgotten, a Scotchman a little past the middle of life, who had for many years been Chaplain to a Highland regiment. He was in no respect as far as I know, an interesting character, though in his appearance there was a good deal that attracted attention, as if he had been shattered in fortune and not happy in mind. Of his quondam position I availed myself, to connect with the Wanderer, also a Scotchman, a character suitable to my purpose, the elements of which I drew from several persons with whom I had been connected, and who fell under my observation during frequent residences in London at the beginning of the French Revolution. The chief of these was, one may *now* say, a Mr Fawcett, a preacher at a dissenting meeting-house at the Old Jewry. It happened to me several times to be one of his congregation through my connection with Mr Nicholson of Cateaton Street, Strand, who at a time, when I had not many acquaintances in London, used often to invite me to dine with him on Sundays; and I took that opportunity (Mr N. being a Dissenter) of going to hear Fawcett, who was an able and eloquent man. He published a Poem on War, which had a good deal of merit, and made me think more about him than I should otherwise have done. But his Christianity was probably never very deeply rooted; and, like many others in those times of like showy talents, he had not strength of character to withstand the effects of the French Revolution, and of the wild and lax opinions which had done so much towards producing it, and far more in carrying it forward in its extremes. Poor Fawcett, I have been told, became pretty much such a person as I have described; and early disappeared from the stage, having fallen into habits of intemperance, which I have heard (though I will not answer for the fact) hastened his death. Of him I need say no more: there were many like him at that time, which the world will never be without, but which were more numerous then for reasons too obvious to be dwelt upon.

The Pastor: ... I had no one individual in mind, wishing rather to embody this idea [of 'a country clergyman'] than to break in upon the simplicity of it, by traits of individual character or any peculiarity of opinion.

Wordsworth also gives an account in the *I. F. note* of the locales used in the poem, pointing out especially the divergence between the scenes of Book I ('Somersetshire or Dorsetshire') and Book II (the Lake District).

The 'Prospectus',

13 *numerous verse* Paradise Lost V, 150. 'Numerous' means *metrical*.

23 *'fit audience let me find though few'* Paradise Lost VII, 30-31: 'Still govern thou my Song, / Urania, and fit audience find, though few'.

34 *empyreal thrones* Paradise Lost II, 430.

35 *Chaos* in *Paradise Lost* an unformed region existing before the creation of the universe.

36 *Erebus* the classical underworld.

83-5 '"Not my own fears, nor the prophetic soul / Of the wide world dreaming on things to come." Shakespeare's *Sonnets*.' – W. Sonnet 107.

90 *Shedding benignant influence* Compare Paradise Lost VII, 374-5: 'the *Pleiades* before him danced / Shedding sweet influence'.

Book I

In its first form, Book I was a self-sufficient poem entitled *The Ruined Cottage*, which was never published as such but is printed in *PW*, V, 379–99.

2–3 *glared Through a pale steam* Compare *An Evening Walk* 37–8: 'noon, brooding still, / Breathed a pale steam around the glaring hill'.

7 *Determined* exactly fixed.

12 *A twilight of its own* Compare *An Evening Walk* 61: 'its own twilight'.

53 *the antique market-village* Hawkshead.

85 *nice* delicate, shy.

106 *deliberately* without haste.

108 *Athol* a mountainous district in central Scotland.

118–300 Much that is said about the youth of the Wanderer has parallels in Wordsworth's autobiographical *The Prelude*; in fact, one passage was transferred from MS to that poem.

179 *That left half-told* Compare *Il Penseroso* 109–10: 'Or call up him that left half told / The story of Cambuscan bold'.

211 *access* state, fit (of mind).

266 *sweet influence* Compare *Paradise Lost* VII, 374–5: 'the *Pleiades* before him danced / Shedding sweet influence'. See also line 90 of the 'Prospectus' of *The Excursion* (p. 39, above).

341 *much did he see of men* The former profession of the Wanderer was to bring the greatest amount of criticism and scorn upon *The Excursion*. Apparently in anticipation of this, Wordsworth here added a note defending his choice of this 'class of men, from whom my own personal knowledge emboldened me to draw this portrait'. As further evidence, Wordsworth quotes two long paragraphs from Robert Heron's *Journey in Scotland* (1793, I, 91), the most pertinent passage of which is as follows (italics added by Wordsworth):

> Their dealings form [Scottish pedlars] to great quickness of wit, and acuteness of judgement . . . As, in their peregrinations, they have opportunity of contemplating the manners of various men and various cities, they become eminently skilled in the knowledge of the world. *As they wander, each alone, through thinly inhabited districts, they form habits of reflection, and of sublime contemplation.*

343–7 *Their passions . . . chiefly those Essential . . . in the heart, That . . . Exist more simple in their elements, And speak a plainer language.* Compare the Preface to *Lyrical Ballads* (1800): 'Low and rustic life was generally chosen, because, in that situation, the essential passions of the heart . . . speak a plainer . . . language; because in that situation our elementary feelings coexist in a state of greater simplicity . . .'.

368 *within*] *without 1814–1850.* One MS reads *within*, which is undoubtedly the correct reading.

370–71 *He could afford to suffer With those whom he saw suffer* Compare *The Tempest* I, ii, 5–6: 'O, I have suffered / With those that I saw suffer'. In an unpublished memoir of Wordsworth by Barron Field, Wordsworth is quoted as remarking of Coleridge: 'He could not afford to suffer with those whom he saw suffer'.

424 *nervous* vigorous.

513-19

> [These lines] faithfully delineate, as far as they go, the character possessed in common by many women whom it has been my happiness to know in humble life; and ... several of the most touching things which she is represented as saying and doing are taken from actual observation of the distresses and trials under which different persons were suffering, some of them strangers to me, and others daily under my notice.

– I. F. note.

546 *And their place knew them not* Compare *Psalms* 103:16: 'And the place thereof shall know it no more'. See also *Paradise Lost* VII, 144.

566 *A sad reverse*

> I was born too late to have a distinct remembrance of the origin of the American war, but the state in which I represent Robert's mind to be I had frequent opportunities of observing at the commencement of our rupture with France in '93, opportunities of which I availed myself in the story of the Female Vagrant, as told in the poem on Guilt and Sorrow.

– I. F. note.

593 *deepest noon* also occurs in *The Waggoner* 6.

611 *trivial* commonplace.

703 *'trotting brooks'* Compare Burns's *To William Simpson* (1785) 87: 'Adown some trottin' burn's [brook's] meander'.

708 *bladed grass* *A Midsummer Night's Dream* I, i, 211.

830 *trick* expression, habit.

905 *reckless* with no consideration of oneself.

916 *Last human tenant* With the deletion of a MS passage about *non-human* tenants, the force of *human* tenant is lost here.

934-9 These 'Christianizing' lines were added in 1845.

Book II

9 *hospital* hostel.

99 *chariots* light four-wheeled carriages.

251 *Janus* ancient Roman god, usually represented with one head but two faces.

314-15 *'a world Not moving to his mind'* Compare George Dyer's *On the Death of Gilbert Wakefield* (1802) 118-19.

324 *dreary plain* *Paradise Lost* I, 180.

327-48 Quoted by Wordsworth in *Guide to the Lakes* 5th ed. (1835) – in the first section, 'Directions and Information for the Tourist' – with the following introduction: 'The scene in which this small piece of water [Blea Tarn] lies, suggested to the Author the following description ..., supposing the spectator to look down upon it, not from the road, but from one of its elevated sides.'

381–2 *'Shall in the grave . . . thy faithfulness'* Psalm 88:11.

443 *a Novel of Voltaire Candide, ou l'Optimisme.* The Wanderer's description of the novel as 'dull' (line 484) occasioned objections from contemporary reviewers.

555 *awfulness* impressive solemnity.

569 *ashes to ashes, dust bequeathed to dust* Compare *The Book of Common Prayer*, The Order for the Burial of the Dead: 'Earth to earth, ashes to ashes, dust to dust'.

578 *We shall not sleep, but we shall all be changed* Compare *The Book of Common Prayer*, The Order for the Burial of the Dead (1 *Corinthians* 15:51).

717–19 *there the sun . . . Rests his substantial orb* 'This is strictly accurate. On and about the 21st June, the sun, as seen from Blea Tarn, sets just between the Langdale Pikes.' – Knight.

738–826

> The account given by the Solitary toward the close of the second Book, in all that belongs to the character of the Old Man, was taken from a Grasmere Pauper, who was boarded in the last house quitting the vale on the road to Ambleside; the character of his hostess, and all that befell the poor man on the mountain, belong to Patterdale; the woman I knew well; her name was Ruth Jackson, and she was exactly such a person as I describe. The ruins of the old Chapel, among which the old man was found lying, may yet be traced, and stood upon the ridge that divides Patterdale from Boardale and Martindale, having been placed there for the convenience of both districts. The glorious appearance disclosed above and among the mountains was described partly from what my friend Mr Luff, who then lived in Patterdale, witnessed upon that melancholy occasion, and partly from what Mary and I had seen in company with Sir G. and Lady Beaumont above Hartshope Hall on our way from Patterdale to Ambleside.

– *I. F. note*. The story of the old man was also told by Dorothy Wordsworth in her account of an 'Excursion on the Banks of Ullswater, November 1805'. The ruined chapel is first described:

> Whether it was ever consecrated ground or not I do not know; but the place may be kept holy in the memory of some now living in Patterdale; for it was the means of preserving the life of a poor old man last summer, who, having gone up the mountain to gather peats together, had been overtaken by a storm, and could not find his way down again. He happened to be near the remains of the old Chapel, and, in a corner of it, he contrived, by laying turf and ling and stones in a corner of it from one wall to the other, to make a shelter from the wind, and there he sate all night. The woman who had sent him on his errand began to grow uneasy towards night, and the neighbours went out to seek him. At that time the old man had housed himself in his nest, and he heard the voices of the men, but could not make himself heard, the wind being so loud, and he

was afraid to leave the spot lest he should not be able to find it again, so he remained there all night; and they returned to their homes, giving him up for lost; but the next morning the same persons discovered him huddled up in the sheltered nook. He was at first stupefied and unable to move; yet after he had eaten and drunk, and recollected himself a little, he walked down the mountain, and did not afterwards seem to have suffered.

747 *kennel* a rude hut.

Book III

93 *lapse* flow. For previous literary use, see *Paradise Lost* VIII, 263.

112 Wordsworth here cites in a note a long passage in Latin from Thomas Burnet's *Telluris Theoria Sacra*, 2nd ed. (1689), pp. 89–91, 'expressing corresponding sentiments, excited by objects of a similar nature'.

116–17 *I should have grieved hereafter* Compare *Macbeth* V, v, 17: 'She should have died hereafter'.

143 *that huge Pile* Stonehenge, situated on Salisbury (Sarum's) Plain.

150 *Syria's marble ruins* at Palmyra.

224 *senseless* said of death or the grave (obsolete).

240–43 Such is the belief of several American Indian tribes – see Knight V, 392–3.

248 *with the gay Athenian* Ancient Athenians at one time wore brooches in the shape of the head of a cicada to show that they, supposedly like the cicada, had sprung out of the ground.

277–80 See *The Faerie Queene* I, ix, 40, for a similar argument of personified Despair.

367–405 This passage also occurs in lines 265–95 of *The Tuft of Primroses*, never published by Wordsworth.

403 *seasons' difference* *As You Like It* II, i, 6.

549 *'That all the grove and all the day was ours'* unidentified quotation.

617 *progress*] *1814–45*: process *1850*.

643–9 There is a good deal of similarity between the death of two of the poet's children in 1812 and that of those in this passage, written shortly afterwards. See *PW*, V, 419.

669 *heavy change* *Lycidas* 37.

701 Compare *The Borderers*, lines 1774–5: 'I passed in sounding on, / Through words and things, a dim and perilous way'.

720 This line also appears above, II, 832.

756 *Saturnian rule* Saturn was a legendary Roman king during an age of prosperity.

774 *fiercer zealots* the Jacobins.

776–7 Brutus quotes this saying (in Greek) from Heracles in *Dion Cassius* XLVII, 49.

785 *nice* fastidious, critical.

815 *Which, now, as infamous, I should abhor* Compare *Paradise Lost* IV, 392: 'To do what else though damned I should abhor'.

883 *this gigantic stream* the Hudson River, which has sources in the Adirondack wilderness ('desert').
884 *a city* New York.
890 *fibres* small roots.
931

A man is supposed to improve by going out into the *World*, by visiting *London*. Artificial man does; he extends with his sphere; but, alas! that sphere is microscopic; it is formed of minutiæ, and he surrenders his genuine vision to the artist, in order to embrace it in his ken. His bodily senses grow acute, even to barren and inhuman pruriency; while his mental become proportionally obtuse. The reverse is the Man of Mind: he who is placed in the sphere of Nature and of God, might be a mock at Tattersall's and Brooks's, and sneer at St James's; he would certainly be swallowed alive by the first *Pizarro* that crossed him: – But when he walks along the river of Amazons; when he rests his eye on the unrivalled Andes; when he measures the long and watered savannah; or contemplates, from a sudden promontory, the distant, vast Pacific – and feels himself a freeman in this vast theatre, and commanding each ready produced fruit of this wilderness, and each progeny of this stream – his exaltation is not less than imperial. He is as gentle, too, as he is great: his emotions of tenderness keep pace with his elevation of sentiment; for he says, 'These were made by a good Being, who unsought by me, placed me here to enjoy them.' He becomes at once a child and a king. His mind is in himself; from hence he argues, and from hence he acts, and he argues unerringly, and acts magisterially; his mind in himself is also in his God; and therefore he loves, and therefore he soars. From the notes upon 'The Hurricane' [1796], a Poem, by William Gilbert.

The Reader, I am sure, will thank me for the above quotation, which though from a strange book, is one of the finest passages of modern English prose. – W.

931 *that northern stream* the St Lawrence River.
947 *Muccawiss* whippoorwill.

Book IV

111 *visionary powers* Compare *The Prelude* II, 311: 'Thence did I drink the visionary power'.
130–31 *an easy task Earth to despise* 'See, upon this subject, Baxter's most interesting review of his own opinions and sentiments in the decline of life. It may be found (lately reprinted) in Dr Wordsworth's "Ecclesiastical Biography".' – W. Christopher Wordsworth's *Ecclesiastical Biography* (1810), V, 585–6, quotes Richard Baxter's *Narrative of the Most Memorable Passages of His Life and Times*, Book I, Part I, 213, no. 32 (1696):

I find that it is comparatively very easy to me to be loose from this world, but hard to live by faith above. To despise earth is easy to me; but not so easy to be acquainted and conversant in heaven. I have nothing in this world which I could not easily let go; but to get satisfying apprehensions of the other world is the great and grievous difficulty.

188 *deplore* mourn.

205–6 *Alas! ... time* 'This subject is treated at length in the Ode *Intimations of Immortality*.' – W.

293–4 *Wisdom ... justified* Compare *Matthew* 11:19: 'But wisdom is justified of her children'.

297 *Tartarean* infernal.

324–31 'The passage quoted from Daniel is taken from a poem addressed to the Lady Margaret, Countess of Cumberland [lines 92–9], and the two last lines, printed in italics, are by him translated from Seneca.' – W. Wordsworth then in his note quotes four stanzas from the poem.

387 *'feathery bunch'* James Hurdis's *The Favourite Village* (Bishopstone, Sussex, 1800), p. 125.

402–12 'There is in *The Excursion*, an allusion to the bleat of a lamb thus re-echoed and described, without any exaggeration as I heard it on the side of Stickle Tarn, from the precipice that stretches on to Langdale Pikes.' – *I. F. note* (to *To Joanna*).

459 *clang* *Paradise Lost* VII, 421–2: 'And soaring the air sublime / With clang despised the ground'.

489–504 This passage contains much of the wording of an entry by Thomas Wilkinson in Wordsworth's Commonplace Book of 1800:

> But take courage, return to thy Father, rise with the lark, climb the summits of thy surrounding Hills, roll the Stone in thunder from the mountain, and follow with all thy might the Wild Goats of Ben Vorlach, so shalt thou return weary to thy Cottage, and thy rest will be as quiet as mine.

517 *devious* rambling.

550 *Garry's hills* The Garry is a river in central Scotland.

602 *'the dreadful appetite of death'* unidentified quotation.

617 *death-watch* a beetle.

637 *gliding like morning mist* Compare *Paradise Lost* XII, 629: 'Gliding meteorous as Evening Mist'.

638–60 The Biblical allusions in these passages are given in Knight V, 168–9.

653–4 *blaze of light, Or cloud of darkness* Compare *Paradise Lost* III, 377–80.

671–3 The rejection was due to their worship of nature.

686–7 *Belus ... Descending* For a description of the god Belus descending to his couch, see Herodotus I, 182.

699 *The planetary Five* The five planets known to the ancients, called 'Mercuries' because they carry the orders of the gods.

719 *and sounding shores* Compare *Lycidas* 154: 'shores and sounding Seas' and Milton's *Hymn On the Morning of Christ's Nativity* 182: 'the resounding shore'.

733 *Rhapsodists* the wandering minstrels of ancient Greece.

749 *Cephisus* a river sacred to the gods to which the Greeks made offerings of hair. See Pausanias I, 37, 3.

760 *While man grows old, and dwindles, and decays* Compare Keats's *Ode to a Nightingale* (1819) 26: 'Where youth grows pale, and spectre-thin, and dies'.

828 *cultured* cultivated.

858-64 By these lines in Benjamin Robert Haydon's copy of *The Excursion* appears a note: 'Poor Keats used always to prefer this passage to all others'.

859 *A beardless youth* Apollo.

865 *a beaming Goddess* Diana, goddess of the hunt and of the moon.

910-11 Saints Fillan, Anne, and Giles are saints particularly revered by the Scottish.

956 *there is laughter at their work in heaven* Compare the description of the mixture of tongues at Babel in *Paradise Lost* XII, 59: 'great laughter was in Heaven'.

975 *fearfully devised* Compare *Psalms* 139:14: 'I am fearfully and wonderfully made'.

996 *the laughing Sage* Voltaire, crowned with laurel in Paris at 84.

1130 *the inferior Faculty* unsupported reason.

1132-40 Walter Savage Landor accused Wordsworth of plagiarizing the simile of the sea-shell. See his *A Satire upon Satirists* (1836), pp. 29n-31n.

1175-87 The cries of the ravens are described in Dorothy Wordsworth's *Journal* (for 27 July 1800).

1269 *strict necessity Paradise Lost* V, 528.

1272 This line was omitted, apparently by mistake, in the 1845 edition and afterwards. I follow de Selincourt in replacing it.

Book V

77-91 '. . . As by the waving of a magic wand, I turn the comparatively confined vale of Langdale, its Tarn, and the rude Chapel which once adorned the valley, into the stately and comparatively spacious vale of Grasmere, its Lake, and its ancient Parish Church . . .' – *I. F. note.*

80-81 *church-tower . . . tufted trees* Compare *L'Allegro* 77-8: 'Towers and Battlements it sees / Bosomed high in tufted Trees'.

138 *the sacred Pile* St Oswald's, Grasmere.

292-320 In a draft, lines 292-308 were spoken by the Solitary; lines 309-20 were added when the passage was given to the poet-narrator.

318 *If to be weak . . . miserable Paradise Lost* I, 157: 'To be weak is miserable'.

329 *graze the herb* Compare *Paradise Lost* IV, 253: 'Grazing the tender herb'.

489 *speculative height* Cowper's *The Task* I, 289.

529 *forbidding* I follow several editors in returning to this earlier reading (1814, 1827-43). Editions of 1820, 1845, and 1850 read *forbidden*.

647 *And have the dead around us*

'*Leo.* You, Sir, could help me to the history
Of half these graves?
    Priest.   For eight-score winters past,
With what I've witnessed, and with what I've heard,
Perhaps I might; ...
By turning o'er these hillocks one by one,
We two could travel, Sir, through a strange round;
Yet all in the broad highway of the world.'
                        See *The Brothers.* – W.

661 *grateful* welcome.

692 *a wedded pair*

In this nothing is introduced but what was taken from nature and real life.
The cottage is called Hackett, and stands, as described, on the southern
extremity of the ridge which separates the two Langdales; the Pair who
inhabited it were called Jonathan and Betty Yewdale. Once when our
children were ill, of whooping-cough I think, we took them for change of
air to this cottage, and were in the habit of going there to drink tea on fine
summer afternoons, so that we became intimately acquainted with the
characters, habits, and lives of these good, and, let me say, in the main,
wise people. The matron had, in her early youth, been a servant in a house
at Hawkshead, where several boys boarded, while I was a schoolboy there.
I did not remember her as having served in that capacity; but we had
many little anecdotes to tell to each other of remarkable boys, incidents
and adventures which had made a noise in their day in that small town.
These two persons afterwards settled at Rydal, where they both died.

– *I. F. note.*

824–6 These 'Christianizing' lines were added in 1845.

954 *unrequired* not summoned.

975 *And gentle "Nature ... die"* '"And suffering Nature grieved that one
should die." – Southey's *Retrospect*.' – W. (1794). Robert Southey's *The
Retrospect* 140.

978 At this line Wordsworth gave (in a note) his *Essays upon Epitaphs* as
expressing similar 'sentiments and opinions' to those in the following passage.

Book VI

11 *beauty of holiness* a biblical expression; see, for example, *Psalms* 29:2,
110:3.

18 *Besprent* sprinkled

19 *And spires whose 'silent finger points to heaven'*

An instinctive taste teaches men to build their churches in flat countries
with spire-steeples, which as they cannot be referred to any other object,
point as with silent finger to the sky and stars, and sometimes, when they
reflect the brazen light of a rich though rainy sunset, appear like a

pyramid of flame burning heavenward.' See 'The Friend', by S. T. Coleridge, No. 14, p. 223.

– W.

97 *A Visitor*

His story is here truly related: he was a school-fellow of mine for some years. He came to us when he was at least 17 years of age, very tall, robust, and full-grown. This prevented him from falling into the amusements and games of the school; consequently he gave more time to books. He was not remarkably bright or quick, but by industry he made a progress more than respectable. His parents not being wealthy enough to send him to college, when he left Hawkshead he became a schoolmaster, with a view to preparing himself for holy orders. About this time he fell in love as related in the Poem, and everything followed as there described, except that I do not know exactly when and where he died.

– *I. F. note.*

163–4 *Love will not ... By mastery* Compare *The Franklyn's Tale* 36: 'Love wol nat ben constreyned by maistrye' and *The Faerie Queene* III, i, 25: 'Ne may love be compelled by mastery'.

187 *Shedding sweet influence* *Paradise Lost* VII, 375.

213 *One*

The Miner, next described as having found his treasure after twice ten years of labour, lived in Patterdale, and the story is true to the letter. It seems to me, however, rather remarkable that the strength of mind which had supported him through this long unrewarded labour, did not enable him to bear its successful issue.

– *I. F. note.*

260 *Paradise Lost* V, 899.

273 *mixture of earth's mould* *Comus* 244.

275 *He*

The next character, to whom the Priest is led by contrast with the resoluteness displayed by the foregoing, is taken from a person born and bred in Grasmere, by name Dawson; and whose talents, disposition, and way of life were such as are here delineated. I did not know him, but all was fresh in memory when we settled in Grasmere in the beginning of the century.

– *I. F. note.*

386 *dividual being* *Paradise Lost* XII, 85. 'Dividual' means 'separate'.

405 *a pair*

From this point the conversation leads to the mention of two Individuals who, by their several fortunes, were, at different times, driven to take refuge at the small and obscure town of Hawkshead on the skirt of these mountains. Their stories I had from the dear old Dame with whom, as a schoolboy and afterwards, I lodged for nearly the space of ten years. The elder, the Jacobite, was named Drummond, and was of a high family in Scotland; the Hanoverian Whig bore the name of Vandepat, and might perhaps be a descendant of some Dutchman who had come over in the train of King William. At all events his zeal was such that he ruined himself by a contest for the representation of London or Westminster, undertaken to support his party, and retired to this corner of the world, selected, as it had been by Drummond, for that obscurity which, since visiting the Lakes became fashionable, it has no longer retained.

– I. F. note.

417 *The Stuart* Prince Charles, defeated at Culloden in 1745.

423 *lenient hand of time* Compare Bowles's *Influence of Time on Grief* (1789), 1: 'O Time, who know'st a lenient hand to lay'.

532-3 *desperate by 'too quick . . . infelicity'* Jeremy Taylor's *Holy Dying* (1651) I, v, 2.

539 *Prometheus* In Aeschylus's *Prometheus Bound*, Prometheus is punished by Zeus by being chained to a rock and having a vulture devour his liver.

543 *Tantalus* punished by his father Zeus by being placed in water which constantly recedes from his thirsty mouth. 'His race' is the house of Atreus, whose tragic story is told by Aeschylus in his 'Oresteia'.

544 *the line of Thebes* Oedipus and his children, who suffer so tragically in the plays of Sophocles.

550-51 *pomp Of circumstance* Compare *Othello* III, iii, 354: 'Pride, pomp and circumstance of glorious war'.

676 *A woman*

> This person [Aggy Fisher] lived at Town End, and was almost our next neighbour. I have little to notice concerning her beyond what is said in the Poem. She was a most striking instance how far a woman may surpass in talent, in knowledge, and culture of mind, those with and among whom she lives, and yet fall below them in Christian virtues of the heart and spirit. It seemed almost, and I say it with grief, that in proportion as she excelled in the one, she failed in the other. How frequently has one to observe in both sexes the same thing, and how mortifying is the reflection!

– I. F. note.

787

> The story that follows was told to Mrs Wordsworth and my Sister by the sister of this unhappy young woman; every particular was exactly as I have related. The party was not known to me, though she lived at Hawkshead, but it was after I left school. The Clergyman, who administered comfort to her in her distress, I knew well. Her Sister who told the story was the wife of a leading yeoman in the Vale of Grasmere, and they were an affectionate pair and greatly respected by everyone who knew them.

– I. F. note.

841 *nicest* most intricately made.

905 *pang of despised love* Compare *Hamlet* III, i, 72: 'The pangs of despised love, the law's delay'.

919–20 See *Numbers* 20:11.

1005 *Home to her mother's house* Compare *Paradise Regained* IV, 639: 'Home to his Mother's house private returned'.

1114 The story of the shepherd of Bield Crag was omitted from *The Excursion*, but is printed from MS in *PW*, V, 461–2.

1192–1267 The lines printed in brackets appeared in editions 1814–20 but were afterwards deleted. I follow several editors in including them here.

Book VII

47 *cultured* cultivated.

63 *the Priest*

> The Clergyman [Rev. Joseph Sympson] and his family . . . were, during many years, our principal associates in the Vale of Grasmere, unless I were to except our very nearest neighbours. I have entered so particularly into the main points of their history, that I will barely testify in prose that – with the single exception of the particulars of their journey to Grasmere, which, however, was exactly copied from, in another instance – the whole that I have said of them is as faithful to the truth as words can make it.

– *I. F. note.*

90 *Fair Rosamond, and the Children of the Wood* two traditional ballads (included in Percy's *Reliques*).

162 *three fair Children* In spite of what Wordsworth said in the *I. F. note* (to line 63 above) about being 'faithful to the truth', the Rev. Mr Sympson had six, not three, children.

242–91 An earlier draft of this passage occurs in *The Tuft of Primroses* (lines 146–84).

255–6 *A happy consummation . . . to be wished for* Compare *Hamlet* III, i, 63–4: ''Tis a consummation / Devoutly to be wished'.

316 *A Priest* '. . . Robert Walker, for [whom] see notes to the Duddon.' – *I. F. note.* See *PW*, III, 510–22 for Wordsworth's *Memoir of the Rev. Robert Walker*.

343 *borne* I do not follow de Selincourt in exchanging the MS reading *held* for this word.

395–481 These lines were quoted at the end of Wordsworth's unpublished *Essays Upon Epitaphs* III with the prefatory remark that the lines were 'suggested . . . by a concise epitaph which I met with some time ago in one of the most retired vales among the mountains of Westmoreland. There is nothing in the detail of the poem which is not either founded upon the epitaph or gathered from inquiries concerning the deceased, made in the neighbourhood.' See *The Prose Works*, ed. Owen and Smyser II, 93–4.

400 *a gentle Dalesman* '... The deaf man [Thomas Holme], whose epitaph may be seen in the churchyard at the head of Haweswater, and whose qualities of mind and heart, and their benign influence in conjunction with his privation, I had from his relatives on the spot.' – *I. F. note.*

486 *him* 'John Gough [1757–1825], of Kendal, a man known, far beyond this neighbourhood, for his talents and attainments in Natural History and Science.' – *I. F. note.* Gough is also celebrated by Coleridge in his *Omniana* (1812), II, 16–18.

509 *instinct with spirit* *Paradise Lost* VI, 752.

511 *Fancy, and understanding* *Paradise Lost* V, 486.

514 *in his presence, humbler knowledge* Compare *Paradise Lost* VIII, 551: 'knowledge in her presence'.

514–15 *stood Abashed* Compare *Paradise Lost* IV, 846.

536 *married to immortal verse* *L'Allegro* 137.

616–17 *That sycamore . . . tent*

> '"This Sycamore oft musical with Bees;
> *Such Tents* the Patriarchs loved."
> S. T. Coleridge.' – W. *Inscription for a Fountain on a Heath* (1802).

632–94 'Of the Infant's Grave, next noticed, I will only say, it is an exact picture of what fell under my own observation; and all persons who are intimately acquainted with Cottage Life must often have observed like instances of the workings of the domestic affections.' – *I. F. note.* The family concerned was the Greens of Grasmere.

635 *three spans long* Compare Bürger's *Pfarrer's Tochter Von Taubenhain* (1773) 135: 'Drei Spannen lang'.

695 *On a bright day – so calm and bright* Compare George Herbert's *Sunday* (1633) 1: 'O Day most calm, most bright' and *Virtue* (1633) 1: 'Sweet day, so cool, so calm, so bright'.

751 *glead* kite, a bird of prey.

758 *Tyrant* Napoleon.

810 *Tell* William Tell (died c. 1350), the Swiss patriot.

814–15 See *Book of Judges* 6:25–34.

848 *'all hoping and expecting all'* Compare *I Corinthians* 13:4–7. 'Charity . . . hopeth all things, endureth all things'.

926 *his home*

> The Pillars of the Gateway in front of the mansion remained when we first took up our abode at Grasmere. Two or three cottages still remain, which are called Knott-houses from the name of the gentleman (I have called him a knight) concerning whom these traditions survive. He was the ancestor of the Knott family, formerly considerable proprietors in the district.

– *I. F. note.*

980–82

> The 'Transit gloria mundi' is finely expressed in the Introduction to the

Foundation-charters of some of the ancient Abbeys. Some expressions here used are taken from that of the Abbey of St Mary's Furness, the translation of which is as follows:

'Considering every day the uncertainty of life, that the roses and flowers of Kings, Emperors, and Dukes, and the crowns and palms of all the great, wither and decay; and that all things, with an uninterrupted course, tend to dissolution and death: I therefore,' etc.

– W. An earlier draft of these three lines occurs in *The Tuft of Primroses* 357–9.
1027 *hour was come* John 13:1.

Book VIII

50 *irksome toil* *Paradise Lost* IX, 242–3: 'For not to irksome toil, but to delight / He made us'.

87 What follows in the discourse of the Wanderer upon the changes he had witnessed in rural life, by the introduction of machinery, is truly described from what I myself saw during my boyhood and early youth, and from what was often told me by persons of this humble calling. Happily, most happily, for these mountains, the mischief was diverted from the banks of their beautiful streams, and transferred to open and flat countries abounding in coal, where the agency of steam was found much more effectual for carrying on those demoralising works.

– *I. F. note.*
100 *thorpe and vill* homestead and small house. Also used in *Ecclesiastical Sonnets* I, xxii, 13.
111–12

In treating this subject, it was impossible not to recollect, with gratitude, the pleasing picture, which, in his Poem of the Fleece, the excellent and amiable Dyer has given of the influences of manufacturing industry upon the face of this Island. He wrote at a time when machinery was first beginning to be introduced, and his benevolent heart prompted him to augur from it nothing but good. Truth has compelled me to dwell upon the baneful effects arising out of an ill-regulated and excessive application of powers so admirable in themselves.

– W. See *The Fleece* (1757) III, 565–91, which suggested the next passage to Wordsworth.
220 See Cicero's *Tusculum Disputations* V, 23, for the neglect of Archimedes's tomb.
331 *lapse* flow; see note to III, 93 above.
377 *Buxton's* a town in the Derbyshire Dales.
413 *the Christ-cross-row* the alphabet.
483 *slender* weak.

Book IX

151 *human form divine* Compare *Paradise Lost* III, 44: 'human face divine'.

195–8 'The Chartists are well aware of this possibility, and cling to it with an ardour and perseverance which nothing but wiser and more brotherly feeling towards the many, on the part of the wealthy few, can moderate or remove.' – *I. F. note*.

226–8 This 'Christianizing' passage was added in 1845.

299 *Binding herself by statute* 'The discovery of Dr Bell affords marvellous facilities for carrying this into effect; and it is impossible to over-rate the benefit which might accrue to humanity from the universal application of this simple engine under an enlightened and conscientious government.' – W. Andrew Bell (1753–1832) was the discoverer of the 'Madras system' of education, one of many schemes being advocated at the time.

336 *Calpe's* Gibraltar. Napoleon had fairly thoroughly changed the face of Europe by that time.

363–4 *the fear Of numbers* Thomas Malthus had published his *Essay on the Principle of Population* in 1798.

392 *culture* nurture, cultivation.

409 *oppression* Napoleonic.

504 *Cultured* cultivated.

519 *sweet influence* *Paradise Lost* VII, 375.

530 *A choice repast* Compare Milton's *Sonnet* XX: 'What neat repast shall feast us, light and choice'.

537 *flood* water.

596 *blue firmament* *Paradise Lost* XI, 206.

605 *unapparent fount* Compare *Paradise Lost* VII, 103.

609 'The point here fixed upon in my imagination is half-way up the northern side of Loughrigg Fell, from which the Pastor and his companions are supposed to look upwards to the sky and mountain-tops, and round the Vale, with the lake lying immediately beneath them.' – *I. F. note*.

704 *Taranis* the central Celtic god. Andates was a Celtic goddess.

750 *if I be silent, morn or even* *Paradise Lost* V, 202.

775 *promise*

When I reported this promise of the Solitary, and long after, it was my wish, and I might say intention, that we should resume our wanderings, and pass the Borders into his native country, where, as I hoped, he might witness, in the society of the Wanderer, some religious ceremony – a sacrament, say, in the open fields, or a preaching among the mountains – which, by recalling to his mind the days of his early Childhood, when he had been present on such occasions in company with his Parents and nearest kindred, might have dissolved his heart into tenderness, and so done more towards restoring the Christian faith in which he had been educated, and, with that, contentedness and even cheerfulness of mind, than all that the Wanderer and Pastor, by their several effusions and

addresses, had been able to effect. An issue like this was in my inten
tions.

– *I. F. note.*

COMPOSED IN ONE OF THE VALLEYS OF WESTMORELAND

Composed possibly for the most part 10 April 1814; first published in 1819;
from 1820 included among 'Miscellaneous Sonnets'.

COMPOSED AT CORA LINN

Composed possibly in part 25 July 1814 (or shortly after), probably com-
pleted about (but by) 1820; first published in 1820; in 1820 included among
'Poems of the Imagination' and from 1827 among 'Memorials of a Tour in
Scotland, 1814' (a classification begun in 1827).

I. F. note: 'I had seen this celebrated waterfall twice before. But the feelings to which it had given birth were not expressed till they recurred in
presence of the object on this occasion.'

The motto verse is taken from *The Prelude* I, 214–20.

41 *Leonidas* The Spartan king who with a small force held the Pass of
Thermopylae.

42 *Devoted* doomed.

45 *Tell* William Tell (died ca. 1350), the Swiss patriot. Uri is a Swiss
Canton.

THE BROWNIE'S CELL

Composed possibly in part 5 August 1814 or shortly after (probably not
completed until about, but by, 1820); first published in 1820; in 1820 included
among 'Poems of Imagination', and from 1827 among 'Memorials of a Tour
in Scotland, 1814' (a classification begun in 1827).

I. F. note: 'The account of *The Brownie's Cell* and the Brownies was given
me by a man we met with on the banks of Loch Lomond, a little above
Tarbert, and in front of a huge mass of rock ... The place is quite a solitude,
and the surrounding scenery very striking.'

31 *a fearless Race* the Clan Macfarlane.

56 *the Patmos Saint* St John the Divine.

62 *stars ... in their courses fought* *Judges* 5:20.

71 See *The Brownie*, sequel to this poem.

89 *viewless* unseen.

92–6 Compare *Paradise Lost* IV, 275–9: 'that Nyseian Isle / Girt with the
River *Triton*, where old *Cham*, / Whom Gentiles *Ammon* call and *Libyan
Jove*, / Hid *Amalthea* and her Florid Son, / Young *Bacchus* from his Step-
dame *Rhea's* eye'. For the original story, see Diodorus Siculus, *Bibliotheca
Historica* III, 68.

EFFUSION IN THE PLEASURE-GROUND

Composed in part possibly 19 August 1814 (or shortly thereafter) and probably not completed until between 1820 and 1827; first published in 1827; from 1827 included among 'Memorials of a Tour in Scotland, 1814' (a classification begun in 1827).

I. F. note: 'I am not aware that this condemnatory effusion was ever seen by the owner of the place. He might be disposed to pay little attention to it; but were it to prove otherwise, I should be glad, for the whole exhibition is distressingly puerile.'

The 'Journal of my Fellow-Traveller' from which the prefatory passage is taken is Dorothy Wordsworth's *Recollections of a Tour Made in Scotland* (1803).

46   *The Effigies*   'On the banks of the river Nid, near Knaresborough'. – W.
55   *St Robert's cell*   a cave carved out of the cliffs along the Nid, with the effigy sculptured outside.
58   *Fountain's*   Fountain's Abbey, in Yorkshire.
97   *Memnonian strain*   the so-called statue of Memnon was supposed to give off music when struck by the first rays of the sun.

'FROM THE DARK CHAMBERS OF DEJECTION FREED'

Composed perhaps between 25 and 30 August 1814 (possibly about early October and certainly by 22 October); first published in 1815 (entitled *To* — in 1815); from 1815 included among 'Miscellaneous Sonnets'.

I. F. note: 'Composed in Edinburgh during my Scotch tour with Mary and Sara, in the year 1814. Poor Gillies never rose above that course of extravagance in which he was at that time living, and which soon reduced him to poverty and all its degrading shifts, mendicity being far from the worst.'

3   *GILLIES*   Robert Pearce Gillies (1788–1858). 'He was nephew of Lord Gillies the Scotch judge, and also of the historian of Greece.' – *I. F. note*.
5   *Bellerophon*   Upon attempting to ride Pegasus up to heaven, Bellerophon, the Corinthian hero, was thrown back to earth by Zeus.
12   *Roslin's faded grove*   Roslin is a village some six miles from Edinburgh.

YARROW VISITED

Composed probably between 2 (certainly between 1) and 16 September 1814; first published in 1815; in 1815 and 1820 included among 'Poems of the Imagination', thereafter among 'Memorials of a Tour in Scotland, 1814'.

I. F. note:

As mentioned in my verses on the death of the Ettrick Shepherd [*Extempore Effusion*], my first visit to Yarrow was in his company. We had lodged the night before at Traquhair, where Hogg had joined us ... I seldom read or think of this poem without regretting that my dear Sister was not of the party as she would have had so much delight in recalling the time when, travelling together in Scotland, we declined going in search of this celebrated stream . . .

In a letter to R. P. Gillies (23 November 1814), Wordsworth referred to an earlier poem: 'Second parts, if much inferior to the first, are always disgusting, and as I had succeeded in *Yarrow Unvisited*, I was anxious that there should be no falling off; but that was unavoidable, perhaps, from the subject, as imagination almost always transcends reality.' See also Wordsworth's *Yarrow Revisited* (p. 708).

1–4 See *Yarrow Unvisited* 49–56.

25–6 *the famous Flower Of Yarrow Vale* In the ballad *The Dowie Dens of Yarrow*, a knight is slain and compared to a cropped rose.

41–8 In a letter to Wordsworth (28 April 1815) Charles Lamb commented: 'no lovelier stanza can be found in the wide world of poetry'.

55 *Newark's Towers* setting of Scott's *The Lay of the Last Minstrel* (1805).

61 *bower of bliss* See *The Faerie Queene* II, xii, 42.

LAODAMIA

Composed for the most part (130-line version) about mid-October (certainly by 27 October) 1814; first published in 1815; in 1815 and 1820 included among 'Poems Founded on the Affections', thereafter among 'Poems of the Imagination'.

I. F. note:

Rydal Mount, 1814. Written at the same time as *Dion* and *Artegal and Elidure*. The incident of the trees growing and withering put the subject into my thoughts, and I wrote with the hope of giving it a loftier tone than, so far as I know, has been given to it by any of the Ancients who have treated of it. It cost me more trouble than almost anything of equal length I have ever written.

This poem is the fruit of Wordsworth's renewed reading of classical authors, which he undertook to prepare his son for the university. The main source for the poem is Book VI of the *Aeneid*, but use is also made of Ovid's *Heroides* XIII and Euripides's *Iphigenia in Aulis*.

4 *required* requested.

12 *expects* awaits.

48 *self-devoted* self-doomed.

59 *Redundant* copious, plentiful.

65 *consciousParcae* the Fates, aware or 'conscious' of what was transpiring.

71 *Erebus* region through which the Shades pass on the way to Hades.

79–82 Hercules successfully wrestled with Death ('the guardian monster') for the return of Alcestis alive to her husband, Admetus.

83–4 When Jason returned from the voyage of the Argo, Medea by spells rejuvenated his aging father, Aeson.

96 *pensive* serious, reflective.

112 'For this feature in the character of Protesilaus, see the *Iphigenia in Aulis* of Euripides.' – W. (1815).

120 *enchained* This word is followed by a period in all editions during Wordsworth's life, but de Selincourt argues for a comma on the strength of one manuscript.

132 See the *Iliad* II, 700.

158-63 *1845, 1849-50.*

> Ah, judge her gently who so deeply loved!
> Her, who, in reason's spite, yet without crime,
> Was in a trance of passion thus removed;
> Delivered from the galling yoke of time
> And these frail elements – to gather flowers
> Of blissful quiet 'mid unfading bowers.
>
> *1815-20.*

In 1827, Laodamia is said to be 'not without crime' and 'was doomed to wander in a grosser clime'. The reason for this revision is contained in Wordsworth's letter to his nephew, John Wordsworth (October 1831): 'As first written the heroine was dismissed to happiness in Elysium. To what purpose then the mission of Protesilaus? He exhorts her to moderate her passion; the exhortation is fruitless, and no punishment follows.' In 1832, the punishment is changed to 'to wear out her appointed time', which also consorts well enough with the *Aeneid* (see the following note).

174

> For the account of these long-lived trees, see Pliny's 'Natural History',
> ib. xvi. cap. 44; and for the features in the character of Protesilaus, see the
> 'Iphigenia in Aulis' of Euripides. Virgil places the Shade of Laodamia in
> a mournful region, among unhappy Lovers,
> ———— His Laodamia
> It Comes. ————

– W.

LINES WRITTEN ON A BLANK LEAF

Composed 13 November 1814; first published in 1815; from 1815 included among 'Epitaphs and Elegiac Pieces'.

5 *MURFITT* Reverend Matthew Murfitt, Vicar of Kendal from 1806 to 1814.

[PASSAGE FROM MARY BARKER'S *LINES*]

In late 1814 (possibly about early October but not later than probably 10 December, with some revisions about 19 February 1815) Wordsworth helped Mary Barker write *Lines Addressed to a Noble Lord* and took full credit in a letter for that part of the poem in the text (except for the bracketed matter); first published in 1815; never published separately by Wordsworth.

The entire poem consists of 188 lines and was published anonymously in 1815 as having been written 'By one of the Small Fry of the Lakes'. Mary Barker (1774–c. 1853) was a painter and friend of Robert Southey and Dorothy Wordsworth. The 'Noble Lord' of the title is Lord Byron; but the notes to the original edition of the poem are mostly an attack on Francis Jeffrey, editor of the *Edinburgh Review*.

In a letter to Sara Hutchinson (probably 10 December 1814), Wordsworth asks that his part in the poem be kept secret: '. . . I should be sorry Lord B. should think I honoured him so far. It will be suspected that I and Southey, too, had some hand in it.'

22 *epergne* table ornament.

45–52 allusions to Byron's Eastern tales.

ARTEGAL AND ELIDURE

Composed possibly about 1815 (after February); first published in 1820; from 1820 included among 'Poems Founded on the Affections'.

    I. F. note:

> Rydal Mount. This was written in the year 1815, as a token of affectionate respect for the memory of Milton. 'I have determined,' says he in [Book I of] his History of England, 'to bestow the telling over even of these reputed tales, be it for nothing else but in favour of our English Poets and Rhetoricians, who by their [art] will know how to use them judiciously.'

2 *the Trojan* In Geoffrey of Monmouth's account, Brutus, the great-grandson of Aeneas, came to England and, having destroyed a race of giants, gave his name to Britain.

5 *Julius* Julius Caesar came to England in 55 B.C.

16 Compare *The Faerie Queene* II, x, 7: 'Hideous Giants . . . / That never tasted grace, nor goodness felt'.

34–40 Guendolen, the daughter of Corineus (a Trojan who had accompanied Brutus to England), was married to Locrine, son of Brutus. Locrine divorced Guendolen, who thereupon recruited an army of her father's friends and slew Locrine, his paramour, and their daughter.

92 *'Poorly provided, poorly followèd'* unidentified quotation.

97 *Troynovant* 'New Troy' or London.

234 *Thus was a Brother by a Brother saved* Compare Milton's *History of England* I (end of the second paragraph): 'Thus was a brother saved by a brother'.

TO B. R. HAYDON

Composed probably early December 1815 (certainly not before 27 November), first published 31 March 1816 in the *Examiner*; from 1820 included among 'Miscellaneous Sonnets'.

In a letter to B. R. Haydon (21 December 1815), Wordsworth claimed this sonnet 'was occasioned, I might say inspired if there be any inspiration in it, by your Letter'. Haydon's letter (27 November 1815) speaks very highly of Wordsworth's genius and sternly of Haydon's own dedication to his art.

NOVEMBER I

Composed probably early December 1815 (the day after the previous poem); first published 28 January 1816 in the *Examiner* and the *Champion*; from 1820 included among 'Miscellaneous Sonnets'.

I. F. note: 'Suggested on the banks of the Brathay by the sight of Langdale Pikes. It is delightful to remember these moments of far-distant days, which probably would have been forgotten, if the impression had not been transferred to verse.'

SEPTEMBER, 1815

Composed probably early December 1815 (the day after the previous poem); published 11 February 1816 in the *Examiner*; from 1820 included among 'Miscellaneous Sonnets'.

In a letter to B. R. Haydon (21 December 1815), Wordsworth observed that this sonnet 'notices a . . . sensation which the revolution of the seasons impressed me with last Autumn'.

9

> This conclusion has more than once, to my great regret, excited painfully sad feelings in the hearts of young persons fond of poetry and poetic composition, by contrast of their feeble and declining health with that state of robust constitution which prompted me to rejoice in a season of frost and snow as more favourable to the Muses than summer itself.

– I. F. note.

ODE: THE MORNING OF THE DAY

Composed probably late December 1815 (after 16 December) or January (by 29 January) 1816; first published in 1816; from 1820 included among 'Poems Dedicated to National Independence and Liberty'.

I. F. note:

> The first stanza of this Ode was composed almost extempore, in front of Rydal Mount, before church-time, and on such a morning and precisely with such objects before my eyes as are here described. The view taken of Napoleon's character and proceedings is little in accordance with that taken by some historians and critical philosophers. I am glad and proud of the difference . . .

In a letter to Robert Southey (June 1816), Wordsworth commented on the ode:

> Had it been a hymn, uttering the sentiments of a *multitude*, a *stanza* would have been indispensable. But though I have called it a 'Thanks-

giving Ode', strictly speaking it is not so, but a poem composed, or supposed to be composed, on the morning of the thanksgiving, uttering the sentiments of an *individual* upon that occasion. It is a *dramatised ejaculation*; and this, if anything can, must excuse the irregular frame of the metre.

Wordsworth prefixed to the 1816 volume a long note in which he defends his treatment of the subject, especially his 'encouragement of a martial spirit'. This note is reprinted in *PW*, III, 462-4.

70 *One* Britain.

122 *discipline was passion's dire excess* '"A discipline the rule whereof is passion". Lord Brooke.' – W. (1816). Fulke Greville, Lord Brooke, *A Treatie of Wars*, stanza VII.

139 Compare Wordsworth's *To* — 1: 'O dearer far than light and life are dear'.

148 *The bold Arch-despot re-appeared* Napoleon returned from Elba in February 1815.

SIEGE OF VIENNA

Composed probably late January (certainly by 29 January) 1816; first published 4 February 1816 in the *Champion*; from 1820 included among 'Poems Dedicated to National Independence and Liberty'.

John Sobieski, the Polish King, helped drive the Turks from Vienna, 12 September 1683.

Wordsworth's *note* (1816, 1820): 'See Filicaia's Canzone, addressed to John Sobieski ... This, and his other poems on the same occasion, are superior perhaps to any lyrical pieces that contemporary events have ever given birth to, those of the Hebrew Scriptures only excepted.'

13-14 'Si, si, vincesti, O Campion forte e pio, / Per Dio vincesti, e per te vinse Iddio' – quoted by Wordsworth in his prefatory note. Line 14 is a close rendering of the italicized line.

ODE: 1814

Composed probably January or February 1816; first published in 1816; in 1820 included among 'Poems of the Imagination', from 1827 among 'Poems Dedicated to National Independence and Liberty'.

The title *Ode, 1814* replaced *Ode Composed in January 1816* in 1845. The poem itself originally was meant to refer to the fall of Napoleon at Waterloo in 1815, and Ernest de Selincourt (*PW*, III, 461) speculates that the new title was meant to refer to an earlier defeat to give balance to the series in which it was placed. The Horatian motto verse reads in English as follows:

We can give a poet's song and name the value of the lyre. Not public engravings on a marble base through which a second life is given to good men after death ... set forth more clearly one's fame than the Muses; and if poems are not silent about what you have done well, you will have had your reward.

20 *loop-hole* any opening for light or air, such as a port-hole.

96–8 A depiction of the Battle of Marathon can be found in the Stoa Poecile in Athens.

111 *Pierian Sisters* the nine Muses.

ODE ('Who rises')

All data identical with the preceding poem.

OCCASIONED BY THE BATTLE OF WATERLOO ('The Bard')

Composed probably late January (certainly by 29 January) 1816; first published 4 February 1816 in the *Champion*; from 1820 included among 'Poems Dedicated to National Independence and Liberty'.

9 '"From all this world's encumbrance did himself assoil". Spenser.' – W. *The Faerie Queene* VI, v, 37.

OCCASIONED BY THE BATTLE OF WATERLOO ('Intrepid sons')

All data identical with the preceding poem.

INVOCATION TO THE EARTH

Composed probably February 1816; first published in 1816; from 1820 included among 'Epitaphs and Elegiac Pieces'.

   I. F. note: 'Composed immediately after the *Thanksgiving Ode*, to which it may be considered as a second part.'

1 Compare *Hamlet* I, v, 183: 'Rest, rest, perturbèd spirit!'

THE FRENCH ARMY IN RUSSIA

Composed probably February 1816; first published in 1816; from 1820 included among 'Poems Dedicated to National Independence and Liberty'.

ON THE SAME OCCASION

Composed probably 1816 (possibly February, at least by July); first published in 1816; from 1820 included among 'Poems Dedicated to National Independence and Liberty'.

ODE: 1815

Composed probably 1816 (by July); first published in 1816; from 1816 to 1842 part of this ode was contained in the *Ode, the Morning of the Day*, but in 1845 it was excerpted and placed among 'Poems Dedicated to National Independence and Liberty'.

106–7] *1845*. 'But Thy most dreaded instrument, / In working out a pure intent, / Is Man – arrayed for mutual slaughter, / – Yea, Carnage is thy daughter?' *1816–32*. The claim that Carnage was the daughter of God brought forth a great deal of adverse criticism when the poem was first published.

FEELINGS OF A FRENCH ROYALIST

Composed probably 1816 (by July); first published in 1816; from 1820 included among 'Poems Dedicated to National Independence and Liberty'.

The Duke D'Enghien (1772–1804) was kidnapped, tried for conspiracy against Napoleon, and shot in March 1804. After the Restoration in 1814, his body was disinterred from its original grave in a moat and moved to the castle of Vincennes.

DION

Composed probably 1816; first published in 1820; from 1820 to 1843 included among 'Poems of Sentiment and Reflection', from 1845 among 'Poems of the Imagination'.

Wordsworth's *note* (1837):

> This poem began with the following stanza, which has been displaced on account of its detaining the reader too long from the subject, and as rather precluding, than preparing for the due effect of the allusion to the genius of Plato:
>
>> 'Fair is the Swan, whose majesty, prevailing
>> O'er breezeless water, on Locarno's lake,
>> Bears him on while proudly sailing
>> He leaves behind a moon-illumined wake:
>> Behold! the mantling spirit of reserve
>> Fashions his neck into a goodly curve;
>> An arch thrown back between luxuriant wings
>> Of whitest garniture, like fir-tree boughs
>> To which, on some unruffled morning, clings
>> A flaky weight of winter's purest snows!
>> – Behold! – as with a gushing impulse heaves
>> That downy prow, and softly cleaves
>> The mirror of the crystal flood,
>> Vanish inverted hill, and shadowy wood,
>> And pendent rocks, where'er, in gliding state,
>> Winds the mute Creature without visible Mate
>> Or Rival, save the Queen of night
>> Showering down a silver light,
>> From heaven, upon her chosen Favourite!'

In the *I. F. note* to *An Evening Walk*, Wordsworth attributed this depiction of a swan to childhood recollections of swans on Esthwaite Lake.

In Knight's edition (1896, VI, 125–9) can be found a close examination by W. A. Heard of Wordsworth's debt to Plutarch, which concludes that Wordsworth differs from his source generally in emphasizing the interior of Dion's mind over external events.

8-11 Dion was the pupil of Plato. Charles Lamb, in a letter to Dorothy Wordsworth (25 May 1820), observed: 'The story of Dion is divine – the genius of Plato falling on him like moonlight the finest thing ever expressed.'
13 *self-sufficing solitude* Compare *The Prelude* II, 77: 'The self-sufficing power of Solitude'.
43 *Ilissus* small river near Athens.
71 *Auster* the South wind.
73 *Boreas* the North wind. Maenalus was a mountain in Arcadia.

'*A* LITTLE ONWARD'

Composed probably 1816; first published in 1820; from 1820 included among 'Poems of Sentiment and Reflection'.

   I. F. note: 'The complaint in my eyes which gave occasion to this address to my daughter first showed itself as a consequence of inflammation ...'

1-2 *Samson Agonistes* 1-2.
11 *O my own Dora 1849-50*. 'O my Antigone' *1820-45*. Dora Wordsworth died in 1847.

   Antigone, the daughter of Oedipus, guided him after he blinded himself.
31 '*abrupt abyss*' a merging of *Paradise Lost* II, 409 ('the vast abrupt') and II, 405 ('The dark, unbottomed, infinite abyss').
32 *plumy vans Paradise Regained* IV, 583.

TO ─────────, ON HER FIRST ASCENT

Composed probably 1816; first published in 1820; from 1820 included among 'Poems of the Imagination'.

   I. F. note: 'Rydal Mount. 1816. The lady was Miss Blackett, then residing with Mr Montagu Burgoyne at Fox-Ghyll.'

25 *choral 1820-27*. Coral – *1832, 1849-50*. Most editions consider 'coral' a misprint and return to 'choral'.
29-30 See *Paradise Lost* III, 736-42.

'EMPERORS AND KINGS'

Composed possibly 1816; first published in 1827; from 1827 included among 'Poems Dedicated to National Independence and Liberty'.

7 *victory* probably a reference to Waterloo.
9 *nerve* strength.

VERNAL ODE

Composed 17 April 1817; first published in 1820; in 1820 included among 'Poems of the Imagination', in 1827 and 1832 among 'Poems of Sentiment and Reflection', and from 1836 among 'Poems of the Imagination'. This poem was heavily revised.

   I. F. note: 'Rydal Mount, 1817. Composed to place in view the immortality of succession where immortality is denied, as far as we know, to the individual creature.'

The motto verse is from Pliny's *Historia Naturalis* XI, i: 'Nature in her entirety is to be found nowhere more than in the smallest things.'

77 *Urania* the muse of astronomy, often depicted crowned with stars. Clio, the muse of history, was usually crowned with laurel.

91 *slender* weak.

130 *Tartarean den* the lower world where the evil are punished.

ODE TO LYCORIS ('An age hath been')

Composed probably May 1817; first published in 1820; from 1820 included among 'Poems of Sentiment and Reflection'.

I. F. note:

> The discerning reader, who is aware that in the poem of 'Ellen Irwin' I was desirous of throwing the reader at once out of the old ballad, so as, if possible, to preclude a comparison between that mode of dealing with the subject and the mode I meant to adopt – may here perhaps perceive that this poem originated in the four last lines of the first stanza. Those specks of snow, reflected in the lake and so transferred, as it were, to the sub-aqueous sky, reminded me of the swans which the fancy of the ancient classic poets yoked to the car of Venus. Hence the tenor of the whole first stanza, and the name of Lycoris, which – with some readers who think mythology and classical allusion too far-fetched and therefore more or less unnatural and affected – will tend to unrealize the sentiment that pervades these verses. But surely one who has written so much in verse as I have done may be allowed to retrace his steps in the regions of fancy which delighted him in his boyhood, when he first became acquainted with the Greek and Roman Poets.

According to Edward Dowden's note, a 'Mrs Fletcher' claimed in a letter (24 November 1847) that Wordsworth said the ode was 'suggested to him one day at Ullswater, in the year 1817, by seeing two white, sunny clouds reflected in the lake. "They looked," he said, "like two swans".'

The name Lycoris is used by Virgil (*Eclogue* X, 42) and Ovid (*Ars Amoris* III, 537), but Wordsworth makes no further use of these classical sources.

14 *The flitting halcyon's* the kingfisher.

THE PASS OF KIRKSTONE

Composed probably 27 June 1817; first published in 1820; from 1820 included among 'Poems of the Imagination' (from 1820 to 1832 entitled *Ode: The Pass of Kirkstone*).

I. F. note: 'Rydal Mount, 1817. Thoughts and feelings of many walks in all weathers by day and night over this pass, alone and with beloved friends.'

78 *cultured* cultivated.

COMPOSED UPON AN EVENING OF EXTRAORDINARY SPLENDOUR

Composed probably summer 1817; first published in 1820; from 1820 to 1832 included among 'Poems of the Imagination', from 1837 among the 'Evening Voluntaries'.

I. F. note: 'Felt and in a great measure composed upon the little mount in front of our abode at Rydal.'

49 *Wings at my shoulders seem to play* 'In these lines I am under obligation to the exquisite picture of "Jacob's Dream", by Mr Alstone, now in America.' – W.

THE LONGEST DAY

Composed probably 1817; first published in 1820; from 1820 included among 'Poems Referring to the Period of Childhood'.

I. F. note: '1817. Suggested by the sight of my Daughter (Dora) playing in front of Rydal Mount, and completed in a great measure the same afternoon. I have often wished to pair this poem upon the *longest* with one upon the *shortest* day, and regret even now that it has not been done.'

24 *exalt* heighten the colour of.

HINT FROM THE MOUNTAINS

Composed probably 1817; first published in 1820; from 1820 included among 'Poems of the Fancy'.

I. F. note: 'Bunches of fern may often be seen, wheeling about in the wind as here described. The particular bunch which suggested these verses was noticed in the Pass of Dunmail-Raise. The verses were composed in 1817, but the application is for all times and places.'

3-4 *measure With* be equal to.

LAMENT OF MARY QUEEN OF SCOTS

Composed probably 1817; first published in 1820 in the *River Duddon* volume; from 1827 included among 'Poems Founded on the Affections'.

I. F. note: 'This arose out of a flash of moonlight that struck the ground when I was approaching the steps that lead from the garden at Rydal Mount to the front of the house.'

66-7 *From her sunk eyes a stagnant tear Stole forth* '... Taken, with some loss, from a discarded poem, "The Convict" ...' – *I. F. note*. See Vol. I p. 153, lines 41-2.

SEQUEL TO 'BEGGARS'

Composed probably 1817; first published 1827; from 1827 included among 'Poems of the Imagination'.

For *Beggars*, see Vol. I, p. 516.

1 *wanton Boys* *Lear* IV, i, 38.
2 *daedal* varied. Probably taken from *The Faerie Queene* IV, x, 45.

ODE TO LYCORIS ('Enough of climbing')

Composed (as a whole) probably 1817; first published in 1820; from 1820 included among 'Poems of Sentiment and Reflection'.
I. F. note: '. . . Composed in front of Rydal Mount and during my walks in the neighbourhood.'

28 *Numa* Numa Pompilius, the legendary second king of Rome who was supposed to have received counsel from the nymph Egeria.

THE WILD DUCK'S NEST

Composed possibly 1817 (at least by 1817); first published in 1819; from 1820 included among 'Miscellaneous Sonnets'.
I. F. note: 'I observed this beautiful nest on the largest island of Rydal Water.'

A FACT, AND AN IMAGINATION

Composed possibly 1817-19; first published in 1820; from 1820 included among 'Poems of Sentiment and Reflection'.
I. F. note: 'The first and last fourteen lines of this Poem each make a sonnet, and were composed as such; but I thought that by intermediate lines they might be connected so as to make a whole. One or two expressions are taken from Milton's *History of Britain*.'

14 Compare Milton's *History of Britain*, Book VI: 'whose Eternal Laws both Heaven, Earth, and Sea obey'.

PLACARD FOR A POLL

Of doubtful authorship. If written by Wordsworth, composed probably between 21 and 28 February 1818; first published in 1896.
Written for the Westmoreland election of 1818 – see head-note to *A Help for the Memory* (below).

THE PILGRIM'S DREAM

Composed probably 1818; first published in 1820; from 1820 included among 'Poems of the Fancy'.
I. F. note:

I distinctly recollect the evening on which these verses were suggested in 1818. I was on the road between Rydal and Grasmere where glow-worms abound. A star was shining above the ridge of Loughrigg Fell just opposite. I remember a blockhead of a critic, in some Review or other, crying out against this piece. 'What so monstrous,' said he, 'as to make a

star talk to a Glow-worm?' Poor fellow, we know well from this sage observation what the primrose on the river's brim was to him.

The reference to the primrose takes us to *Peter Bell* 246-50: 'In vain, through every changeful year, / Did Nature lead him as before; / A primrose by a river's brim / A yellow primrose was to him, / And it was nothing more.'

INSCRIPTIONS SUPPOSED TO BE FOUND IN AND NEAR A HERMIT'S CELL

Composed probably 1818; first published in 1820; from 1820 included among 'Inscriptions'.

II *Inscribed upon a rock*

I. F. note: 'The monument of ice here spoken of I observed while ascending the middle road of the three ways that lead from Rydal to Grasmere. It was on my right hand, and my eyes were upon it when it fell, as told in these lines.'

III *'Hast thou seen'*

I. F. note:

Where the second quarry now is, as you pass from Rydal to Grasmere, there was formerly a length of smooth rock that sloped towards the road, on the right hand. I used to call it Tadpole Slope, from having frequently observed there the water-bubbles gliding under the ice, exactly in the shape of that creature.

SUGGESTED BY MR W. WESTALL'S VIEWS

Composed probably 1818; first published January 1819 in *Blackwood's Magazine*; from 1820 included among 'Miscellaneous Sonnets'.

William Westall (1781–1850) was a painter and friend of Wordsworth.

14 'Waters (as Mr Westall informs us in the letterpress prefixed to his admirable views) are invariably found to flow through these caverns.' – W.

MALHAM COVE

All data identical with the preceding poem. Part of a group with the preceding poem.

9 *Phoebus* the sun.

GORDALE

All data identical with the preceding poem. Part of a group with the preceding poem.

'I HEARD (ALAS! 'TWAS ONLY IN A DREAM)'

Composed probably 1818; first published in 1819; from 1820 included among 'Miscellaneous Sonnets'.

9 *votary of Apollo* Swans were considered sacred to Apollo.
11 'See the *Phaedon* of Plato, by which this sonnet was suggested.' – W. In the *Phaedo* (85), Socrates argues that the swan's last song is not a lament but is joyful in foreseeing the happiness of the next life.

A HELP FOR THE MEMORY

Composed probably 1818; first published in 1891.

This is a political satire against Henry Brougham, who ran in the Westmoreland election of 1818.

1 *The Scottish Broom on Birdnest brae* 'Brougham' is pronounced 'broom' and 'Scottish' is a joke at Brougham's claiming to be English although born in Edinburgh. Bird-nest was the nickname of Brougham Hall.
8 *yellow* the colour of the Tories. Blue was the colour of the Whigs.
9 *Lowther Castle* home of Lord Lonsdale, a Tory who was running a candidate against Brougham. The point of the second stanza is that Brougham was willing to turn-coat.

THE RIVER DUDDON

Most of the sonnets in this series were composed between 1806 and 1820 (19 were probably written in December 1818); all but number XXVII (first published in 1819 and switched to the series in 1827) were first published in 1820.

> *I. F. note:*

> ... The above series of Sonnets was the growth of many years; – the one which stands the 14th was the first produced; and others were added upon occasional visits to the Stream, or as recollections of the scenes upon its banks awakened a wish to describe them. In this manner I had proceeded insensibly, without perceiving that I was trespassing upon ground pre-occupied, as least as far as intention went, by Mr Coleridge; who, more than twenty years ago, used to speak of writing a rural Poem, to be entitled 'The Brook', of which he has given a sketch in a recent publication [*Biographia Literaria*, Chapter X].

> •   •   •   •

> I have many affecting remembrances connected with this stream. Those I forbear to mention; especially things that occurred on its banks during the later part of that visit to the seaside of which the former part is detailed in my Epistle to Sir George Beaumont.

The probable locales described in the sonnets are discussed at some length in the notes to Knight's edition (1896), volume VI.

To the Rev. Dr Wordsworth

Composed possibly Christmastide, 1819.
51 *Cytherea's zone* the magic girdle of Aphrodite, borrowed by Hera to beguile Zeus.
65 *Lambeth's* Christopher Wordsworth was rector at St Mary's, Lambeth, from 1816 to 1820.

I 'Not envying Latian shades'

4 *The Sabine Bard* Horace, who praised the Spring of Blandusia in *Odes* III, xiii.
5 *Careless* indifferent to.

II 'Child of the clouds!'

11 *the huge deer* 'The deer alluded to is the Leigh, a gigantic species long since extinct.' – W.

IV 'Take, cradled Nursling of the mountain'

7 *sinuous lapse* a combination of the 'sinuous trace' of snakes (*Paradise Lost* VII, 481) and the 'liquid Lapse' of streams (VIII, 263).

VI Flowers

9-10 'These two lines are in a great measure taken from "The Beauties of Spring, a Juvenile Poem", by the Rev Joseph Sympson [1715-1807] . . .' – W.

VII 'Change me, some God'

14 *slender* weak.

XIII Open Prospect

9 *wasteful* laying waste.

12 *mantling* sparkling.

XIV 'O mountain Stream!'

Composed possibly between 27 September and early October 1804 (fairly certainly by about March 1806); first published in 1807; in 1815 only included among 'Miscellaneous Sonnets'.
3 *nicest* strictest.

XVI American Tradition

Wordsworth's *note*: 'See Humboldt's Personal Narrative.' Alexander von Humboldt, *Personal Narrative of Travels to the Equinoctial Regions of the New Continent* (1814).

4-5 Compare Humboldt's *Travels* IV, 473: '. . . they answer with a smile as relating a fact of which a stranger, a white man only, could be ignorant . . .'.

XVII Return

2 *the Danish Raven* flag of the ancient Danes.
3 *the imperial Bird of Rome* the eagle.
10 *that lone Camp* 'The Roman fort here alluded to, called by the country people *"Hardknot Castle"* is most impressively situated half-way down the hill on the right of the road, that descends from Hardknot into Eskdale.' – W.
12 *that mystic Round* 'The Druidical Circle is about half a mile to the left of the road ascending Stone-side from the vale of Duddon: the country people call it *Sunken Church*.' – W.

XVIII Seathwaite Chapel

1 *Sacred Religion! 'mother of form and fear'* Daniel's *Musophilus* 295.
10 *a Gospel Teacher* The Rev. Robert Walker, a long biographical sketch of whom is given in Wordsworth's notes to *The River Duddon* (see *PW*, III 510–22).
12 *A Pastor such as Chaucer's verse portrays* See *The Canterbury Tales, General Prologue* 477–528.
13 See Herbert's *A Priest to the Temple* or *The Country Parson* (1652).
14 See *The Deserted Village* 137–92.

XX The Plain of Donnerdale

Composed probably between April 1807 and late October 1814 (but possibly 1817).
13 *Bacchanal* a follower of Bacchus, the god of wine. The thyrsus is a vine-covered staff, topped by a pine-cone and carried by a Bacchanal.

XXI 'Whence that low voice?'

I. F. note:

During my college vacation, and two or three years afterwards, before taking my Bachelor's degree, I was several times resident in the house of a near relative [Wordsworth's cousin, Mary] who lived in the small town of Broughton. I spent many delightful hours upon the banks of this river, which becomes an estuary about a mile from that place. The remembrances of that period are the subject of the 21st Sonnet.

XXIV The Resting-Place

4 *the vagrant reed* these sonnets of the wandering poet.
10 *the Fancy, too industrious Elf* Possibly an echo of Keats's *Ode to a*

Nightingale 8–9: 'The fancy cannot cheat so well / As she is fam'd to do, deceiving elf' (first published July 1819 in the *Annals of the Fine Arts*).

XXVI 'Return, Content! for fondly I pursued'

Composed possibly 1803–4. An earlier MS version is given in *PW*, III, 523–4.

XXVII 'Fallen, and diffused'

Composed perhaps between 1815 and 1819; first published in 1819 (not added to *The River Duddon* until 1827); in 1820 included among 'Miscellaneous Sonnets'.

I. F. note: 'The subject of the 27th is in fact taken from a tradition belonging to Rydal Hall, which once stood, as is believed, upon a rocky and woody hill on the right hand as you go from Rydal to Ambleside, and was deserted from the superstitious fear here described, and the present site fortunately chosen instead.'

XXIX 'No record tells'

10 *blank* that is, unmarked by any memorial or tombstone.

XXX 'Who swerves from innocence'

I. F. note: 'With regard to the 30th Sonnet it is odd enough that this imagination was realized in the year 1840 . . .', when Mrs Wordsworth got separated from the family party on a walk in the same area.

XXXII 'Not hurled precipitous'

2 *flower-enamelled* beautified with various-coloured flowers.

XXXIV After-Thought

7 Compare Wordsworth's *In Part from Moschus's Lament for Bion* 5: 'But we, the great, the mighty and the wise'. This line is a translation of line 102 of Moschus's *Lament*.

14 *We feel that we are greater than we know* '"And feel that I am happier than I know." – Milton [*Paradise Lost* VIII, 282]. The allusion to the Greek poet will be obvious to the Classical reader.' – W. See note to line 7 (above).

COMPOSED DURING A STORM

Composed probably February 1819 (by 6 February); first published 6 February 1819 in the *Westmorland Gazette*; from 1820 included among 'Miscellaneous Sonnets'.

I. F. note: 'Written in Rydal Woods, by the side of a torrent.'

'AËRIAL ROCK'

Composed possibly 1819 (before June); first published in 1819; from 1820 included among 'Miscellaneous Sonnets'.

I. F. note: 'A projecting point of Loughrigg, nearly in front of Rydal Mount. Thence looking at it, you are struck with the boldness of its aspect; but walking under it, you admire the beauty of its details. It is vulgarly called Holme-Scar, probably from the insulated pasture by the waterside below it.'

WRITTEN UPON A BLANK LEAF

All data identical with the preceding poem.
9 *sedgy Lee* Milton's *At a Vacation Exercise* 97.

CAPTIVITY. – MARY QUEEN OF SCOTS

All data identical with the preceding poem.

TO A SNOW-DROP

All data identical with the preceding poem.

'I WATCH, AND LONG HAVE WATCHED'

Composed possibly 1819 (before June); first published in 1819; from 1820 included among 'Miscellaneous Sonnets', except for the 1827 edition, from which the poem was apparently dropped.

I. F. note: 'Suggested in front of Rydal Mount, the rocky parapet being the summit of Loughrigg Fell opposite. Not once only, but a hundred times, have the feelings of this Sonnet been awakened by the same objects seen from the same place.'

SEPTEMBER, 1819 ('The sylvan slopes')

Composed probably September 1819; first published in 1820; from 1820 included among 'Poems of Sentiment and Reflection'.

I. F. note: 'Composed in front of Rydal Mount and during my walks in the neighbourhood.'

SEPTEMBER, 1819 ('Departing summer')

Data (including *I. F. note*) identical with the preceding poem.

14-15 *my leaf is sere, And yellow* Compare *Macbeth* V, iii, 23: 'My way of life / Is fallen into the sear, the yellow leaf'.
38 *Alcaeus* Greek lyric poet of the fifth century B.C., who wrote invectives against a tyrant.
46 *the Lesbian Maid* Sappho, whose ode to Aphrodite is alluded to in the preceding lines.
50 *The wreck of Herculanean lore* In 1752 scrolls were found in the excavations of Herculaneum; and the discovery of lost classical works was

hoped for, such as, here, a work by Simonides, Greek lyric poet of the sixth century B.C.

59 *Maro* Virgil, in whose writing no reference to Simonides can be found.

TO THE LADY MARY LOWTHER

Composed 21 December 1819; first published in 1820; from 1820 included among 'Miscellaneous Sonnets'.

The 'female friend' of the title was Sara Hutchinson.

1 *Parnassian* inspired by the Muses.

'WHEN HAUGHTY EXPECTATIONS PROSTRATE LIE'

Composed possibly 1819 (at least not later than 1819); first published in 1820 (with the title *On Seeing a Tuft of Snowdrops in a Storm*); from 1820 included among 'Miscellaneous Sonnets'.

11 *The Emathian phalanx* One group of three hundred Thebans was undefeated until overwhelmed by Philip of Macedon.

THE HAUNTED TREE

Composed probably 1819; first published in 1820; from 1820 included among 'Poems of the Imagination'.

I. F. note: '1819. This tree grew in the park of Rydal, and I have often listened to its creaking as described.'

ON THE DEATH OF HIS MAJESTY

Composed probably about (certainly not before) 29 January 1820; first published in 1820; from 1820 included among 'Miscellaneous Sonnets'.

George III, blind and insane, died 29 January 1820.

13 *threescore years* George II died in 1760.

COMPOSED ON THE BANKS OF A ROCKY STREAM

Composed possibly 1820 (before May); first published in 1820; from 1820 included among 'Miscellaneous Sonnets'.

2 *Schoolmen* medieval philosophers.

'THE STARS ARE MANSIONS BUILT'

Composed possibly 1820 (before May); first published in 1820; from 1820 included among 'Miscellaneous Sonnets'.

OXFORD, MAY 30, 1820 ('Ye sacred Nurseries')

Composed possibly 30 May 1820; first published in 1820; from 1820 included among 'Miscellaneous Sonnets'.

OXFORD, MAY 30, 1820 ('Shame on this faithless heart!')

All data identical with the preceding poem.

2 *Such transport*   See the previous sonnet.

JUNE, 1820

Composed possibly June 1820; first published in 1820; from 1820 included among 'Miscellaneous Sonnets'.

2 *Groves*   'Wallachia is the country alluded to.' – W.

10 *dashing oars*   Compare Collins's *Ode on the Death of Mr Thomson* (1749), 15: 'And oft suspend the dashing Oar'.

12 *Poet*   James Thomson (1700–1748), who is buried at Richmond.

A PARSONAGE IN OXFORDSHIRE

Composed probably 13 July 1820; first published in 1822; from 1827 included among 'Miscellaneous Sonnets'.

   I. F. note: 'This parsonage was the residence of my friend [Robert] Jones and is particularly described in another note [to *Ecclesiastical Sonnets* III, xvii – see *PW*, III, 571].'

MEMORIALS OF A TOUR ON THE CONTINENT, 1820

Composed for the most part between November 1820 and November 1821; first published in 1822 as a separate volume. Over the years four of the original poems, however, were removed and placed elsewhere, while three new poems were added (these latter will be recorded in the pertinent head-notes below).

   I. F. note:

   I set out in company with my Wife and Sister, and Mr and Mrs Monkhouse, then just married, and Miss Horrocks. These two ladies, sisters, we left at Berne, while Mr Monkhouse took the opportunity of making an excursion with us among the Alps as far as Milan. Mr H. C. Robinson joined us at Lucerne, and when this ramble was completed we rejoined at Geneva the two ladies we had left at Berne and proceeded to Paris, where Mr Monkhouse and H. C. R. left us, and where we spent five weeks, of which there is not a record in these poems.

   I. F. note (to VI):

   Details in the spirit of these sonnets are given both in Mrs Wordsworth's Journals and my Sister's, and the re-perusal of them has strengthened a wish long entertained that somebody would put together, as in one work, the notices contained in them, omitting particulars that were written down merely to aid our memory, and bringing the whole into as small a compass as is consistent with the general interests belonging to the scenes, circumstances, and objects touched on by each writer.

Dedication

Composed possibly November 1821.
1   *Fellow-travellers*   See *I. F. note* to the volume (above).
14   *'meeting soul to pierce'*   Compare Milton's *L'Allegro* 138.

I Fish-Women

Wordsworth's *note*:

> If in this Sonnet I should seem to have borne a little too hard upon the
> personal appearance of the worthy Poissardes of Calais, let me take shelter
> under the authority of my lamented friend, the late Sir George Beaumont.
> He, a most accurate observer, used to say of them, that their features and
> countenances seemed to have conformed to those of the creatures they
> dealt in; at all events the resemblance was striking.

3 , *the Nereid Sisters and their Queen*   the daughters of Nereus, among
whom was Amphitrite, wife of Poseidon.

II Brugès

12-14   Compare Mrs Wordsworth's *Journal* (13 July 1820): '. . . the quiet
stately streets, grand buildings, graceful nun-like women in their long cloaks,
treading . . . those silent avenues of majestic architecture . . .'

III Brugès

Wordsworth's note (to the preceding poem): '. . . In Brugès old images are
still paramount, and an air of monastic life among the quiet goings-on of a
thinly-peopled city is inexpressibly soothing; a pensive grace seems to be cast
over all, even the very children.'

6-7   *swan-like ease along, Hence motions*   Compare Mrs Wordsworth's
Journal (13 July 1820): 'treading with swan-like motions'.

IV Incident at Brugès

Composed 1828 (after July); first published in 1835. Until 1843 placed among
'Poems of Sentiment and Reflection' and afterwards among 'Memorials of a
Tour on the Continent'.

> *I. F. note*:

> This occurred at Brugès in the year 1828. Mr Coleridge, my daughter,
> and I made a tour together in Flanders, upon the Rhine, and returned by
> Holland. Dora and I, while taking a walk along a retired part of the town,
> heard the voice as here described, and were afterwards informed that it
> was a Convent in which were many English. We were both much touched,
> I might say affected, and Dora moved as appears in the verses.

V After Visiting the Field of Waterloo

14 *And horror breathing from the silent ground* Compare Dorothy Wordsworth's *Journal* (17 July 1820): 'and even something like horror breathed out of the ground as we stood upon it!'

VII Aix-la-Chapelle

12 *with huge two-handed sway* *Paradise Lost* VI, 251.
13 *left his name* the 'Pyrenean Breach' is called by the mountaineers the '*Brèche de Roland*'.

VIII In the Cathedral at Cologne

6 *Powers* an order of angels.
13–14 Compare *Paradise Lost* I, 710–12: 'a Fabric huge / Rose like an Exhalation, with the sound / Of Dulcet Symphonies and voices sweet'.

IX In a Carriage

3 *Thespian* Thespis was traditionally the Greek who turned the choric dance in honour of Dionysus into the first drama. Thus 'Thespian' suggests 'Bacchanalian'.

X Hymn for the Boatmen

24 *Miserere Domine!* Have mercy, O Lord! 'See the beautiful Song in Mr Coleridge's Tragedy "The Remorse" [(1797; 1812) III, i, 69–82]. Why is the harp of Quantock silent?' – W. (1822–37).

XI The Source of the Danube

1–5 'The Spring appears in a capacious Stone Basin in front of a Ducal palace . . .' – W. (1822).
8 *that gloomy sea* The Black Sea, crossed by the Argonauts. Among them was Orpheus, who calmed the sea with his lyre.

XII On Approaching the Staub-Bach

Wordsworth's *note* (1822):

'The Staub-bach' is a narrow Stream, which, after a long course on the heights, comes to the sharp edge of a somewhat overhanging precipice, overleaps it with a bound, and, after a fall of 930 feet, forms again a rivulet. The vocal powers of these musical Beggars may seem to be exaggerated; but this wild and savage air was utterly unlike any sounds I had ever heard; the notes reached me from a distance, and on what occasion they were sung I could not guess, only they seemed to belong, in some way or other, to the Waterfall – and reminded me of religious services chanted to Streams and Fountains in Pagan times.

XV Composed in one of the Catholic Cantons

Originally (before 1827) this poem formed part of XXVI, *The Church of San Salvador*.

XVI After-thought

In 1832 the first stanza of this poem was added to the previous poem, but in 1837 it was removed and a second stanza added to produce this poem.

XVII Scene on the Lake of Brientz

1–2 Edmund Waller's *While I Listen to Thy Voice* 10–12: 'For all we know/ Of what the blessed do above, / Is, that they sing, and that they love'.

XVIII Engelberg

7–10 In a letter to Lord Lonsdale (19 August 1820), Wordsworth observed: '... The Rock of Engelberg could not have been seen under more fortunate circumstances, for masses of cloud glowing with the reflection of the rays of the setting sun were hovering around it, like choirs of spirits preparing to settle upon its venerable head'.
14 *A holy Structure* the Abbey of Engelberg.

XIX Our Lady of the Snow

3 *thy own mountain* 'Mount Righi'. – W. (1822).
26 *irriguous valley* *Paradise Lost* IV, 255. 'Irriguous' means 'well-watered'.
35 *flower-enamelled* beautified with various-coloured flowers.
41–2 Compare *Matthew* 6:34: 'Sufficient unto the day is the evil thereof'.

XX Effusion

Composed perhaps spring 1822.

XXI The Town of Schwytz

9–13 'If Berne, with its spacious survey of Alps, and widely-spreading vales, and magnificent river may be called the *head*, this town, intrenched among mountains, may be called the *heart* of Switzerland ...' – Dorothy Wordsworth's *Journal* (20 August 1820).

14 'Nearly 500 years (says Ebel, speaking of the French Invasion) had elapsed, when, for the first time, foreign soldiers were seen upon the frontiers of this small Canton, to impose upon it the laws of their governors.' – W.

XXIII Fort Fuentes

The Prefatory note is largely adapted from Dorothy Wordsworth's *Journal* (5 September 1820), with one sentence from Mrs Wordsworth's *Journal*.
10-11   See the ballad *The Children in the Woods* 125-8.

XXIV The Church of San Salvador

The Prefatory note is adapted from Dorothy Wordsworth's *Journal* (27 August 1820).
20-21   '*spot Which men call Earth*'   *Comus* 5-6.
22   *Associate with*   in company with.
36   'Arnold Winkelried, at the battle of Sempach, broke an Austrian phalanx in this manner.' – W.

XXV The Italian Itinerant, and the Swiss Goatherd

8   *Images   1827. plaster-craft 1822.*
10   *Bird*   the eagle, which bore Ganymede to heaven to be the cup-bearer of Zeus.
19-50

> We [were] overtaken by a fine tall Man, who somewhat proudly addressed us in English. After twenty years' traffic in our country, he had been settled near his native place on the banks of Como, having purchased an estate near Cadenabbia, with the large sum of two thousand pounds acquired by selling barometers, looking-glasses, etc. He had been used to return to his wife every third year in the month of October. He made preparations, during the winter, for fresh travels in the spring; at the same time working with her on the small portion of land which they then possessed.

– Dorothy Wordsworth's *Journal* (6 September 1820).
67-8   '*prepared ... to guard*'   Compare Smollett's *Ode to Leven Water* (1771), 27-8: 'And hearts resolved, and hands prepared, / The blessings they enjoy to guard'. Quoted also in *Descriptive Sketches* 447-8.
78   *Astraea*   the goddess of Justice, forced to leave the world because of the degeneracy of the Iron Age.
79-90   'In one of these [sheds] we found four goats (how bright in the cool shade!) beside their keeper, then sitting on the bench, an elegant-featured boy, – dark, like an Italian, ragged, silent, pensive, and timid.' – Dorothy Wordsworth's *Journal* (20 August 1820) [as quoted in *PW*, III, 480].

XXVI The Last Supper

Wordsworth's *note*: 'This picture of the Last Supper has not only been grievously injured by time, but the greatest part of it, if not the whole, is said to have been retouched, or painted over again. These niceties may be left to connoisseurs, – I speak of it as I felt.'

11-12 *hand reposing on the board in ruth Of what it utters* 'The hand / Sang with the voice, and this the argument. Milton.' – W. (1822). *Paradise Regained* I, 171-2.

XXVII The Eclipse of the Sun

In a letter to Richard Sharp (16 April 1822) Wordsworth said he considered this poem the best of the *Memorials*: 'to be valued I think as a specimen of description in which beauty, majesty and novelty, nature and art, earth and heaven are brought together with a degree of lyrical spirit and movement which professed Odes have, in our language at least, rarely attained'.

25-26 'The mountains, (their natural hue being green) appeared as if covered with a pale green light – a mean proportional between day and *moon* light, moon-light without shadows.' – Dorothy Wordsworth's *Journal* (6 September 1820). See also Mrs Wordsworth's *Journal* (7 September 1820) for a similar description (quoted in Knight's 1896 edition).

31 *Julian steeps* the Julian or Carnic Alps bounding the plains of Venezia.

40 *Of Figures human and divine* There are three thousand white-marble statues on Milan Cathedral.

52 *The starry zone of sovereign height* 'Above the highest circle of figures is a zone of metallic stars.' – W.

67-78 'We thought of our Friends in England, probably employed, like ourselves, in tracing the course of the shadow over the sun ...' – Dorothy Wordsworth's *Journal* (6 September 1820).

XXVIII The Three Cottage Girls

22-6

> [Near Lugano] a smart looking girl was putting on her gay garments before she entered the village, where also was a festival ... Her companions were assisting to put a very beautiful silk handkerchief upon her neck. One of these, ... by the interest she seemed to take in the arrangements might be the mother of the maiden, – the other a younger sister, perhaps, who lent her aid more slackly ...

– Mrs Wordsworth's *Journal* (8 September 1820).

33 *that modulated shout* 'Before we descended into Brunnen, a pretty short-faced bright-eyed girl of 19 or 20 met us [, and after parting,] she whistled very softly – then sent forth an uncouth sound, more as from the voice of a man than a maiden – it was not a *deep* sound, but one that would be

heard in the vale and across the lake, and made the hills about us ring . . .' –
Mrs Wordsworth's *Journal* (20 August 1820).
34 *Diana's* goddess of the hunt.
53 *Sweet HIGHLAND Girl* 'See address to a Highland Girl.' –
W. (*To a Highland Girl*, Vol. I, p. 598).

XXXI *Echo, upon the Gemmi*

2 *GEMMI* a mountain pass in southern Switzerland.
6 *Cynthia* the goddess of the moon and of the hunt, who loved Endymion.
9–12

> On drawing towards the little mountain Inn, the mastiff raised such a
> tumult in the mountains as produced the effect of a large pack of well-
> toned hounds in full cry. It was a grand sound. And this reminds me of
> the fine echoes called forth by a traveller or his guide in the morning.
> They were before us, as we clomb the Gemmi. The voice was a universal
> one; and the prolonged and re-echoed notes could not have been more
> harmonious had they proceeded from the sweetest instrument.

– Mrs Wordsworth's *Journal* (13 September 1820).

XXXII *Processions*

7 *Persepolis* the ancient capital of Persia. In the ruins of the Great Hall of
Xerxes are murals of processions.
11 *Thick boughs of palm, and willows from the brook* Compare *Leviticus*
23:40: 'And ye shall take you . . . branches of palm-trees, and the boughs of
thick trees, and willows of the brook'.
21 *Ammonian Jove* The temple of Jupiter Ammon (or ram-headed 'Old
Cham') is located in the Libyan Desert. The description of the rites that
follows was probably suggested by Quintus Curtius, *De Gestis Alexandri*.
26 *yet in a tilting vessel rode* Compare *Paradise Lost* XI, 741, 743: 'the
floating Vessel . . . Rode tilting o'er the Waves'.
30 *the Cereal Games* the feast of Ceres, goddess of grain.
32 *Salii* priests of Mars.
35–6 *the head Of Cybelè . . . sublimely turreted* Cybele, the Great Mother,
was represented with a crown of towers. The Corybantes were her priests.
45 *ARGENTIERE* a glacier in the French Alps.
48 *Still, with those white-robed Shapes*

> This Procession is a part of the sacramental service performed once a
> month . . . The *Grand Festival* of the Virgin . . . was much less strik-
> ing . . . : it wanted both the simplicity of the other and the accompani-
> ment of the Glacier-columns, whose sisterly resemblance to the *moving*
> Figures gave it a most beautiful and solemn peculiarity.

– W. (1822).

XXXIII Elegiac Stanzas

3 *the Queen* 'Mount Righi – Regina Montium.' – W.
64 *GOLDAU* a village at the foot of Mount Righi destroyed by an avalanche.
67–72 Stanza added 1827.
73 'The persuasion here expressed was not groundless. The first human consolation that the afflicted Mother felt, was derived from this tribute to her son's memory . . .' – W.

XXXIV Sky-Prospect

2 *Ararat* the mountain on which Noah's ark landed after the Flood. See *Genesis* 8:4.

XXXV On Being Stranded

6 *gave the Roman his triumphal shells* '. . . Caligula . . . here terminated his western expedition, of which these sea-shells were the boasted spoils.' – W. (1822).
7 *the Corsican* Napoleon, who is depicted in this line as a fool, in 'his cap and bells'.

XXXVI After Landing

1 *the game* the trial of Queen Caroline for adultery.
6–7 *cattle, free To ruminate* 'This is a most grateful sight for an Englishman returning to his native land. Everywhere one misses in the cultivated grounds abroad, the animated and soothing accompaniment of animals ranging and selecting their own food at will.' – W. (1822). 'The scattered cattle quietly selecting their own food was a cheering and a home-feeling sight.' – Mrs Wordsworth's *Journal* (8 November 1820).

XXXVII At Dover

Composed probably early 1838; first published in 1838; added to this series in 1845.
    I. F. note: 'For the impressions on which this sonnet turns, I am indebted to the experience of my daughter, during her residence at Dover with our dear friend, Miss Fenwick.'

XXXVIII Desultory Stanzas

Composed probably March or April 1822, at the request of Henry Crabb Robinson.
19–27 'In the 3d of the desultory Stanzas I am indebted to M. Ramond

who has written with genuine feeling on these subjects.' – W. (1822). Ramon de Carbonnières, *Observations faites dans les Pyrénées* (1789).

37 *Far as ST MAURICE* 'Les Fourches, the point at which the two chains of mountains part, that inclose the Valais, which terminates at St Maurice.' – W. (1822).

51 *Sarnen's Mount*

> Sarnen, one of the two capitals of the Canton of Underwalden; the spot here alluded to is close to the town, and is called the Landenberg ... [Here] the Legislators of this division of the Canton assemble. The site, which is well described by Ebel, is one of the most beautiful in Switzerland.

– W. (1822). M. J. G. Ebel, *The Traveller's Guide through Switzerland* (1818), pp. 330–31.

56 *her honoured Bridge* 'The Bridges of Lucerne are roofed ... The Pictures are attached to the rafters; those from Scripture History, on the Cathedral Bridge, amount, according to my notes, to 240.' – W. (1822).

THE GERMANS ON THE HEIGHTS OF HOCHHEIM

Composed probably 1820; first published in 1822 in *Memorials of a Tour on the Continent* (with the title *Local Recollections on the Heights near Hochheim*); from 1827 included among 'Poems Dedicated to National Independence and Liberty'.

Wordsworth's *note*:

> The event is thus recorded in the journals of the day: 'When the Austrians took Hochheim, in one part of the engagement they got to the brow of the hill, whence they had their first view of the Rhine. They instantly halted – not a gun was fired – not a voice heard; they stood gazing on the river with those feelings which the events of the last fifteen years at once called up. Prince Schwartzenberg rode up to know the cause of this sudden stop; they then gave three cheers, rushed after the enemy, and drove them into the water.'

ON THE DETRACTION

Composed probably 1820; first published in 1820; from 1820 included among 'Miscellaneous Sonnets'.

1 *A book came forth of late, called* See the prefatory note for the Miltonic source.

AUTHOR'S VOYAGE DOWN THE RHINE

Composed probably 1820 or 1821; first published in 1822 but thereafter dropped and later adapted for the *Ecclesiastical Sonnets* (III, xii).

The Rhine voyage was made with Robert Jones in their Continental tour of 1790.

ECCLESIASTICAL SONNETS

Most of the sonnets in this series, until 1837 entitled *Ecclesiastical Sketches*, were composed in 1821 and published in 1822. Thirty sonnets, however, were added to the original 102 by 1849; the dates of composition and publication of those additional sonnets are given in the notes that follow.

Prefatory letter:

> During the month of December, 1820, I accompanied a much-beloved and honoured Friend in a walk through different parts of his estate, with a view to fix upon the site of a new Church which he intended to erect. It was one of the most beautiful mornings of a mild season, – our feelings were in harmony with the cherishing influences of the scene; and such being our purpose, we were naturally led to look back upon past events with wonder and gratitude, and on the future with hope. Not long afterwards, some of the Sonnets which will be found towards the close of this series were produced as a private memorial of that morning's occupation.
>
> The Catholic Question, which was agitated in Parliament about that time, kept my thoughts in the same course; and it struck me that certain points in the Ecclesiastical History of our Country might advantageously be presented to view in verse. Accordingly, I took up the subject, and what I now offer to the reader was the result.

> • • • • •

> Rydal Mount,   W. Wordsworth.
> *January* 24, 1822.

Wordsworth's *note*:

> For the convenience of passing from one point of the subject to another without shocks of abruptness, this work has taken the shape of a series of Sonnets: but the Reader, it is to be hoped, will find that the pictures are often so closely connected as to have jointly the effect of passages of a poem in a form of stanza to which there is no objection but one that bears upon the Poet only – its difficulty.

I. F. note:

> My purpose in writing this Series was, as much as possible, to confine my view to the introduction, progress, and operation of the Church in England, both previous and subsequent to the Reformation. The Sonnets were written long before Ecclesiastical History and points of doctrine had excited the interest with which they have been recently enquired into and discussed.

In a letter to Richard Sharp (16 April 1822), Wordsworth commented on the series:

> The *Ecclesiastical Sketches* labour under one obvious disadvantage, that they can only present themselves as a whole to the reader who is pretty

well acquainted with the history of this country; and, as separate pieces several of them suffer as poetry from the matter of fact, there being unavoidably in all history, except as it is mere suggestion, something that enslaves the Fancy.

Even though there are nevertheless, as Wordsworth added, 'several continuous strains, not in the least degree liable to this objection', Wordsworth did considerable research for this series. The sources are often mentioned by Wordsworth in his own notes recorded below, but most often sources have otherwise been indicated only when they supply exact phrasing in the poems. Those sources can be found quoted at length in the edition of the *Ecclesiastical Sonnets* (1922) edited by A. F. Potts.

The motto verse is an adaptation of George Herbert's *The Church Porch* 5-6: 'A verse may find him, who a sermon flies / And turn delight into a sacrifice.'

I, i *Introduction*

1-2 *The River Duddon* (1820).
5-6 *the nobler Stream ... Of Liberty* 'Poems Dedicated to National Independence and Liberty', a section of the 1815 edition of *Poems*.
10 *HOLY RIVER* the image is traditional: see A. F. Potts, ed., *The Ecclesiastical Sonnets* (1922), pp. 62-78, 205.
10-11 See Virgil's *Eclogues* IX, 40-41.
14 *Immortal amaranth Paradise Lost* III, 353.

I, ii *Conjectures*

6

> Stillingfleet adduces many arguments in support of this opinion, but they are unconvincing. The latter part of this Sonnet refers to a favourite notion of Roman Catholic writers, that Joseph of Arimathea and his companions brought Christianity into Britain, and built a rude church at Glastonbury; alluded to hereafter, in a passage upon the dissolution of Monasteries.

– W.
   E. Stillingfleet, *Origines Britannicae* (1685), p. 37.
9-10 *He ... unbarred* St Peter.

I, iii *Trepidation of the Druids*

1 *sea-mew* 'This water-fowl was, among the Druids, an emblem of those traditions connected with the Deluge that made an important part of their mysteries. The Cormorant was a bird of bad omen.' – W.
10 *Julian* Roman emperor A.D. 361-3.

I, iv Druidical excommunication

6   *Ancient of days*   Daniel 7:9.

I, v Uncertainty

2   *Brigantian*   the Brigantes were hill-tribes in the North of England who were unconquered by the Romans.
4   *Sarum*   Salisbury. The reference is to Stonehenge.
7   *holy piles*   the temple of Classerniss in the Western Isle of Scotland. These Isles and Iona (line 8) are treated more particularly in *The Itinerary Poems of 1833*.
10   *Taliesin's unforgotten lays*   poems of the fourteenth century attributed in Wordsworth's day to a Welsh bard of the sixth century.
11   *characters*   written letters, inscriptions.

I, vi Persecution

1   *Diocletian's fiery sword*   Roman emperor (A.D 284–305.) who persecuted the Christians.
13   *That Hill*

> This hill at St Alban's must have been an object of great interest to the imagination of the venerable Bede, who thus describes it, with a delicate feeling, delightful to meet with in that rude age, traces of which are frequent in his works: – [translation of the Latin (A. M. Sellars, 1907)] 'Adorned, or rather clothed, everywhere with flowers of many colours, nowhere steep or precipitous or of sheer descent, but with a long, smooth natural slope, like a plain, on its sides, a place altogether worthy from of old, by reason of its native beauty, to be consecrated by the blood of a blessed martyr.'

– W.

I, vii Recovery

Much of the phrasing may be influenced by M. Hanmer's translation of Eusebius, *Ecclesiastical History* (1585). See Potts, pp. 214–15.
1–4   These lines echo *Paradise Lost* IV, 432–8.
8–9   *solemn ceremonials ... great deliverance*   Compare E. Stillingfleet, *Origines Britannicae* (1685), p. 74: 'The Christians ... kept solemn festivals in memory of so great a deliverance'.

I, viii Temptations from Roman refinements

3   Compare Samuel Daniel, *Works* (ed. Alexander Grosart) IV, 90: 'faire houses, bathes, and delicate banquets'.
14   Compare Daniel, *Works* IV, 91: 'instruments of servitude'.

I, ix Dissensions

1 *heresies* such as the Pelagian.
10 *forced farewell* the Romans evacuated England to defend Rome from the barbarians.
12 *strange Allies* the Saxons, who later leagued with the Picts against the Britons.

I, x Struggle of the Britons

1 *Aneurin* a sixth-century bard and chieftain of the Godolin, a Northern British tribe.
3 *Caractacus* Caradoc, a British chieftain who held off the Romans for nine years before being betrayed and captured.
9 *Urien* a British chieftain and bard, ally to Arthur.
12 *Plinlimmon's* mountain in Central Wales.

I, xi Saxon conquest

2 *hallelujahs* 'Alluding to the victory gained under Germanus. See Bede.' – W.
   Bede's *Ecclesiastical History of England* I, xx. The Britons routed the Saxons and Picts by shouting 'Hallelujah'.
6 *Relics* survivors.
9

> The last six lines of this Sonnet are chiefly from the prose of Daniel; and here I will state (though to the Readers whom this Poem will chiefly interest it is unnecessary) that my obligations to other prose writers are frequent, – obligations which, – even if I had not a pleasure in courting, it would have been presumptuous to shun, in treating an historical subject. I must, however, particularize Fuller, to whom I am indebted in the Sonnet upon Wicliffe and in other instances. And upon the acquittal of the Seven Bishops I have done little more than versify a lively description of that event in the MS. Memoirs of the first Lord Lonsdale.

– W. The pertinent passage from Daniel, *Works* (ed. Grosart) IV, p. 101, reads: 'The Saxons . . . seemed to care for no other monuments but of earth and as born in the field would build their fortunes only there. Witness so many intrenchments, Mounds, and Burroughs raised for tombs and defences upon all the wide champions and eminent hills of this Isle.'

I, xii Monastery of old Bangor

> 'Ethelforth reached the convent of Bangor; he perceived the Monks, twelve hundred in number, offering prayers for the success of their countrymen: "If they are praying against us," he exclaimed, "they are

fighting against us"; and he ordered them to be first attacked: they were destroyed ... The noble monastery was levelled to the ground; its library ... was consumed ... ' See Turner's valuable history of the Anglo-Saxons.

.   .   .   .   .

The account Bede gives of this remarkable event, suggests a most striking warning against National and Religious prejudices.

– W.

1-2   Compare Sharon Turner's translation (*History of the Anglo Saxons* [3rd ed., 1820], I, 322n) of Taliesin: 'I saw the oppression of the tumult; the wrath and tribulation; / The blades gleaming on the bright helmets'.

4   *Taliesin*   See note to I, v, 10, above. 'Taliesin was present at the battle which preceded [the] desolation.' – W. (note to the poem).

I, xiii Casual incitement

The familiar anecdote, taken from Bede, of Gregory coming upon Angle slaves in a market at Rome.

5   *ANGLI...ANGEL*   Bede, Book II, Chapter I: '[Gregory] therefore again asked, what was the name of that nation [of the slaves]? and was answered, that they were called Angles. "Right," said he, "for they have an angelic face, and it is meet that such should be co-heirs with the Angels in heaven."'

12   *DE-IRIANS ... IRE*   Bede: '[Gregory continued] "What is the name of the province from which they are brought?" It was replied, that the natives of that province were called Deiri. "Truly are they *De Ira*," said he, "saved from wrath, and called to the mercy of Christ."'

13-14   *AELLA ... HALLE-lujahs*   Bede: '[Gregory continued] "How is the king of that province called?" They told him his name was Aelli; and he, playing upon the name, said, "Allelujah, the praise of God the Creator must be sung in those parts."'

I, xiv   Glad tidings

Also based on Bede.

6   *Augustin*   St Augustine (d. 604), first archbishop of Canterbury.

I, xv   Paulinus

5-8   'The person of Paulinus is thus described by Bede, from the memory of an eye-witness: – "Longae staturae, paululum incurvus, nigro capillo, facie macilenta, naso adunco, pertenui, venerabilis simul et terribilis aspectu."' – W. The poetic description provides a close translation.

I, xvi   Persuasion

'See the original of this speech in Bede.' – W.

6-8   Compare T. Fuller's translation in his *The Church History of Britain*

(1837), I, p. 109: '. . . It passeth from cold to cold; and whence it came, and whither it goes, we are altogether ignorant.'

I, xvii Conversion

'The Conversion of Edwin, as related by [Bede], is highly interesting – and the breaking up of this Council accompanied with an event so striking and characteristic, that I am tempted to give it at length in a translation.' – W. (note to I, xvi).

1 *Prompt transformation* Compare Bede, Book I, Chapter XVII: 'prompta transierat'.

6 *the mace* In Fuller's *Church History* I, 82, Thor is described as having 'a kingly sceptre in his right hand'.

10-11 '*O come to me, Ye heavy laden!*' *Matthew* 11:28.

12 *near fresh streams* 'The early propagators of Christianity were accustomed to preach near rivers, for the convenience of baptism.' – W.

I, xviii Apology

3 *darkness, danger* Compare *Paradise Lost* VII, 27: 'In darkness, and with dangers compast round'.

7 *odours* saints were said to give off sweet odours ('odour of sanctity') at their deaths.

9-10 *the blaze Of the noon-day* Compare *Samson Agonistes* 80: 'O dark, dark, dark, amid the blaze of noon'.

I, xix Primitive Saxon Clergy

Having spoken of the zeal, disinterestedness, and temperance of the clergy of those times, Bede thus proceeds: – [in the translation of A. M. Sellar] 'For this reason the religious habit was at that time held in great veneration; so that wheresoever any clerk or monk went, he was joyfully received by all men, as God's servant; and even if they chanced to meet him upon the way, they ran to him, and with bowed head, were glad to be signed with the cross by his hand, or blessed by his lips. Great attention was also paid to their exhortations . . .' Lib. iii. cap. 26.

– W.

5 *clothed* covered with.

I, xx Other influences

13-14 The same warning, made by Gregory to Augustine, was given in Bede.

I, xxi Seclusion

7-14 *Memoirs*, ed. Christopher Wordsworth (1851), II, 476-7: 'In the *Ecclesiastical Sonnets* the lines concerning the Monk, "Within his cell . . ."'

were suggested to me by a beautiful tree clad as thus described, which you may remember in Lady Fleming's park at Rydal, near the path to the upper waterfall.'

I, xxii Seclusion – continued

13 *thorp or vill* homestead or small house. Compare *The Excursion* VIII, 100.

I, xxiii Reproof

14 'He expired dictating the last words of a translation of St John's Gospel.' – W. (1827).

I, xxiv Saxon monasteries

2 'See, in Turner's History, vol. iii, p. 528, the account of the erection of Ramsey Monastery. Penances were removable by the performance of acts of charity and benevolence.' – W.

I, xxv Missions and travels

7–9 *like the Red-cross Knight . . . Una* See *The Faerie Queene*, Book I.

I, xxvi Alfred

4 *Mirror of Princes* Compare Daniel, *Works* (ed. Grosart), IV, p. 107: 'Alfred, the mirror of Princes'.
10 *pain narrows not his cares* 'Through the whole of his life, Alfred was subject to grievous maladies.' – W.
13–14 *Christian India . . . shares* Alfred sent an embassy to India, and gifts were exchanged.

I, xxviii Influence abused

6 *DUNSTAN* English Benedictine Abbot and Prelate of the tenth century.
7 *fell swoop* *Macbeth* IV, iii, 219.

I, xxix Danish conquests

'The violent measures carried on under the influence of *Dunstan*, for strengthening the Benedictine Order, were a leading cause of the second series of Danish invasions. – See Turner.' – W.

3 *The incessant Rovers of the northern main* The Danes.

I, xxx Canute

3 *Canute the King* Canute II (994?–1035), King of England and of Denmark.
11 *an accordant Rhyme* 'Which is still extant.' – W.

I, xxxi The Norman Conquest

1 *Confessor* Edward the Confessor (1002?–66).

I, xxxii 'Coldly we spake'

Composed possibly 1836; first published in 1837.
9 *a Champion* Hereward (flourished 1070–71), English outlaw who fought against the Normans.

I, xxxiii The Council of Clermont

Called by Pope Urban II in 1095 to proclaim the First Crusade. Much of the phrasing comes from Fuller's *Historie of the Holy Warre* I, viii.
6–8 *Like Moses . . . sons of Amalek* See *Exodus* 17:11.
14 *'Nature's hollow arch'* Fuller (*ibid*): 'What spiritual intelligencers there should be, or what echoes in the hollow arch of this world should so quickly resound news from the one side thereof to the other, belongeth not to us to dispute.'

I, xxxv Richard I

3 *staff and scrip* traditional gear of a pilgrim.
5 *thy Bride* Berenguela, daughter of Sancho VI, King of Navarre.

I, xxxvi An interdict

The interdict was called by Innocent III to punish King John for not allowing Stephen Langton in England.

I, xxxviii Scene in Venice

I. F. note on the *Ecclesiastical Sonnets*:

> [I was in] error in respect to an incident which had been selected as setting forth the height to which the power of the Popedom over temporal sovereignty had attained, and the arrogance with which it was displayed. I allude to the last sonnet but one in the first series, where Pope Alexander the Third at Venice is described as setting foot on the neck of the Emperor Barbarossa. Though this is related as a fact in history, I am told it is a mere legend of no authority.

II, i 'How soon – alas!'

Composed ?; first published in 1845.

II, ii 'From false assumption rose'

Composed probably 1842 (by 4 September); first published 1845.

In a letter to Henry Reed (4 September 1842), Wordsworth claimed he had added two sonnets 'in order to do more justice to the Papal Church for the services which she did actually render to Christianity and humanity in the middle ages'. This sonnet and II, ix are the most likely candidates.

II, iii Cistertian Monastery

1–5 '"Bonum est nos hic esse, quia homo vivit purius, cadit rarius, surgit velocius, incedit cautius, quiescit securius, moritur felicius, purgatur citius, praemiatur copiosius." – Bernard. "This sentence," says Dr Whitaker, "is usually inscribed in some conspicuous part of the Cistertian houses."' – W. Thomas D. Whitaker, *An History of the Original Parish of Whalley*, 2nd ed. (1806), p. 48.

II, iv 'Deplorable his lot who tills the ground'

Composed ?; first published in *Yarrow Revisited* (1835) with a note that it was intended for the *Ecclesiastical Sonnets*.

II, v. Monks and schoolmen

10 *yoke of thought* possibly a reference to Aquinas, 'the dumb ox'.

II, vi Other benefits

4 *the collegiate pomps on Windsor's height* St George's Chapel, Windsor, augmented by Edward III.

II, vii Other benefits – continued

7 *flowers of chivalry* In *Imitation of Juvenal* 134, Wordsworth refers to Edward the Black Prince as 'the flower of chivalry'.
13 *The lamb . . . the lion's side* See *Isaiah* 11:6. The images refer to Church and State in lines 13–14.

II, ix 'As faith thus sanctified the warrior's crest'

Composed probably 1842 (by 4 September); first published in 1845. See head-note to II, ii above. This is very likely the other of the two sonnets in question.

II, x 'Where long and deeply hath been fixed the root'
Composed possibly 1842; first published in 1845.
11 *hardly* with difficulty.

II, xi Transubstantiation
9 *Valdo* Peter Waldo, a twelfth-century merchant of Lyons, who began the Waldensian Heresy.

II, xii The Vaudois
Composed ?; first published in 1835 (see note to II, iv, above).
4 *unadulterate Word* Waldo (see notes to preceding poem) had the New Testament translated into Provençal.
5 *Their fugitive Progenitors* possibly Christians of Lyons who were persecuted in 179 by Pope Eleutherius.
7 *that pure Church* The Waldensians? See Potts, p. 255.

II, xiii 'Praised be the Rivers'
Composed ?; first published in 1835 (see note to II, iv, above).
10 *those Heirs of truth divine* There was a schism in Venice during the early seventeenth century.

II, xiv Waldenses
8 *Whom Obloquy pursues*

> The list of foul names bestowed upon those poor creatures is long and curious: – and, as is, alas! too natural, most of the opprobrious appellations are drawn from circumstances into which they were forced by their persecutors, who even consolidated their miseries into one reproachful term, calling them Patarenians, or Paturins, from *pati*, to suffer. "Dwellers with wolves, she names them, for the pine / And green Oak are their covert; as the gloom / Of night oft foils their enemy's design, / She calls them Riders on the flying broom; / Sorcerers, whose frame and aspect have become / One and the same through practices malign."

– W.

II, xv Archbishop Chicheley to Henry V
1 *cultured* cultivated.
2 *leopard* part of Norman coat of arms.
4 *lily* the French royal fleur-de-lys.

II, xvi Wars of York and Lancaster
10 *spiritual truth* the Lollard heresy.

II, xvii Wicliffe

Wordsworth acknowledged his debt in this sonnet to Fuller's *Church History* (see head-note to I, xii, above).
8-14 Compare T. Fuller, *The Church History of Britain* I, 493: 'Thus this Book hath convey'd his ashes into *Avon*; *Avon* into *Severn*; *Severn* into the *narrow Seas*; they, into the *main Ocean*. And thus the *Ashes* of *Wickliff* are the *Emblem* of his *Doctrine*, which now, is dispersed all the World over.'

II, xviii Corruptions of the higher clergy

1 *Prelates* Wordsworth probably had Cardinal Wolsey especially in mind.

II, xix Abuse of monastic power

6 *Secular* the cleric, such as the parish priest, who lives in the world (versus the 'regular', who lives in a religious order).

II, xx Monastic voluptuousness

'The close of [this] sonnet . . . is taken [from a MS., written about the year 1770] as is the verse, "where Venus sits," &c.' – W. (note to II, xxi, below).

II, xxi Dissolution of the monasteries

7-8 'These two lines are adopted from a MS., written about the year 1770, which accidentally fell into my possession.' – W.
11-14 See note to I, ii, line 6, above.

II, xxii The same subject

9 *cloudy shrine* *Paradise Lost* VII, 360.
9-10 Compare Wordsworth's *Triad* 84-5: 'The rainbow's form divine / Issuing from her cloudy shrine'.

II, xxiv Saints

6 *fond* foolish, doting.
9 *Margaret* St Margaret, a virgin and martyr of the third century, was supposed to have killed a dragon with a cross.

II, xxvi Apology

8 *Fisher . . . More* John Fisher, Bishop of Rochester and Sir Thomas More refused the Oath of Supremacy and were executed in 1535.
9-10 'Lightly . . . throne' adapted from *Romeo and Juliet* V, i, 3: 'My bosom's lord sits lightly in his throne'.

II, xxvii Imaginative regrets

6–7 *Tiber . . . Ganges . . . Nile* Europe, Asia, and Africa respectively.
11 *the Arabian Prophet's* Mahomet.

II, xxviii Reflections

6–9 *The 'trumpery' . . . Limbo Lake* Compare *Paradise Lost* III, 474–5, 489–95:

> Eremites and Friars / White, Black, and Grey, with all their trumpery. / . . . Then might ye see / Cowls, Hoods and Habits with their wearers tost / And fluttered into Rags, then Reliques, Beads, / Indulgences, Dispences, Pardons, Bulls, / The sport of Winds: all these upwhirled aloft / Fly o'er the backside of the World far off / Into a *Limbo* large and broad . . .

II, xxix Translation of the Bible

13–14 *tread . . . their feet* Compare Wordsworth's *The White Doe* 714: 'And trod the Bible beneath their feet'.

II, xxx The point at issue

Composed possibly shortly before 18 December 1826; first published in 1827.
3–4 *evidence Of things not seen* Hebrews 11:1.
7 *a ceremonial fence* the Ten Commandments.
13 *Informed* inspired.

II, xxxi Edward VI

1 *'Sweet is the holiness of youth'* *Prioress Tale*, line 61 of Wordsworth's modernized version, but not in the original.
12 *morning Star* Sir John Denham's *On Mr Abraham Cowley* 1. Wordsworth had so referred to Chaucer twice before in prose works.

II, xxxii Edward signing the warrant

Joan Butcher was burned at the stake for heresy in 1550.

II, xxxiii Revival of Popery

Composed possibly shortly before 18 December 1826; first published in 1827
7 *a sullen Queen* Queen Mary.

II, xxxiv Latimer and Ridley

Composed possibly shortly before 18 December 1826; first published in 1827.
5 *Transfigured*

'M. Latimer suffered his keeper very quietly to pull off his hose, and his other array, which to looke unto was very simple: and being stripped into his shrowd, he seemed as comely a person to them that were present, as one should lightly see: and whereas in his clothes hee appeared a withered and crooked sillie (weak) olde man, he now stood bold upright, as comely a father as one might lightly behold ... Then they brought a faggotte, kindled with fire, and laid the same downe at doctor Ridley's feete. To whome M. Latimer spake in this manner, 'Bee of good comfort, master Ridley, and play the man: wee shall this day light such a candle by God's grace in England, as I trust shall never bee put out.' – Fox's *Acts, etc.*

Similar alterations in the outward figure and deportment of persons brought to like trial were not uncommon. See note to the above passage in Dr Wordsworth's 'Ecclesiastical Biography', for an example in an humble Welsh fisherman.

– W.

11–12 *'murderer's ... stake'* unidentified quotation.

II, xxxv Cranmer

1 *upbraided*] upbraiding *1822*.
12–14 'For the belief in this fact, see the contemporary Historians.' – W. (1827–49).

II, xxxviii Elizabeth

12 *a foul constraint* the execution of Mary and additional persecution of Roman Catholics.

II, xxxix Eminent reformers

5

'On foot they went, and took Salisbury in their way, purposely to see the good Bishop, who made Mr Hooker [and his companion] sit at his own table; which Mr Hooker boasted of with much joy and gratitude when he saw his mother and friends; and at the Bishop's parting with him, the Bishop gave him good counsel and his benediction, but forgot to give him money; which when the Bishop had considered, he sent a servant in all haste to call Richard back to him, and at Richard's return, the Bishop said to him, "Richard, I sent for you back to lend you a horse which hath carried me many a mile, and I thank God with much ease", and presently delivered into his hand a walking-staff, with which he professed he had travelled through many parts of Germany; and he said, "Richard, I do not give, but lend you my horse; be sure you be honest, and bring my horse back to me, at your return this way to Oxford. And I do now give you ten groats to bear your charges to Exeter; and here is ten groats more,

which I charge you to deliver to your mother, and tell her I send her a
Bishop's benediction with it, and beg the continuance of her prayers for
me. And if you bring my horse back to me, I will give you ten groats more
to carry you on foot to the college; and so God bless you, good Richard".'
– See Walton's *Life of Richard Hooker*.
– W.
9–10 Compare *Paradise Lost* IV, 162–3: 'Odours from the spicy shore / Of
Araby the blest'.

II, xl The same

4 *Church reformed*] *1849–50*; new-born Church *1822–45*. Wordsworth
made this change to avoid offending those who thought the Reformation
restored the Church, but in a letter to Christopher Wordsworth (12 November 1846) he objected to *reformed*: 'If taken in its literal sense, as a *transformation*, it is very objectionable.' See line 13 of the following sonnet.

II, xli Distractions

11 *personates the mad* 'A common device in religious and political conflicts. – See *Strype in support of this instance*.' – W. John Strype, *Life and
Acts of Matthew Parker* (1821), Book III, chapters xiii, xvi, and *Annals of
the Reformation* (1709), Book I, chapters xxv, lii.
13 *new-born Church* See note to line 4 of the preceding sonnet.

II, xlii Gunpowder Plot

12–14 the St Bartholomew's Day massacre, a common point of comparison.

II, xliii Illustration

1 *Virgin-Mountain* 'The jung-frau.' – W. (1822). The English translation
of *Jung-frau* is 'virgin'.
8–14 '"*Voilà un enfer d'eau*," cried out a German friend of Ramond, falling
on his knees on the scaffold in front of the Waterfall. See Ramond's Translation of Coxe.' [1781] – W. (note to the poem as printed in *Memorials of a
Tour on the Continent*).

II, xlv Laud

In this age a word cannot be said in praise of Laud, or even in compassion
for his fate, without incurring a charge of bigotry; but fearless of such
imputation, I concur with Hume, 'that it is sufficient for his vindication
to observe that his errors were the most excusable of all those which
prevailed during that zealous period'. A key to the right understanding of
those parts of his conduct that brought the most odium upon him in his

own time, may be found in the following passage of his speech before the bar of the House of Peers: – 'Ever since I came in place, I have laboured nothing more than that the external public worship of God, so much slighted in divers parts of this kingdom, might be preserved, and that with as much decency and uniformity as might be. For I evidently saw that the public neglect of God's service in the outward face of it, and the nasty lying of many places dedicated to that service, *had almost cast a damp upon the true and inward worship of God, which while we live in the body, needs external helps, and all little enough to keep it in any vigour.*'
– W.

3 *'in the painful art of dying'* Peter Heylyn, *Cyprianus Anglicus* (1671), p. 496: 'So well was he studied in the art of dying . . .'
9 *Why tarries then thy chariot?* *Judges* 5:28: 'Why tarry the wheels of his chariots?'

II, xlvi *Afflictions of England*

4 *the Shepherd-king* David.
13-14 See *Psalms* 36:5-6.

III, i *'I saw the figure of a lovely Maid'*

I. F. note:

When I came to this part of the series I had the dream described in this Sonnet. The figure was that of my daughter, and the whole passed exactly as here represented. The Sonnet was composed on the middle road leading from Grasmere to Ambleside: it was begun as I left the last house of the vale, and finished, word for word as it now stands, before I came in view of Rydal.

III, iv *Latitudinarianism*

4 *Platonic Piety* Cambridge Platonists.
5 Compare *Comus* 461: 'The unpolluted temple of the mind'.
6 *One there is* Milton.
8-9 *Darkness . . . not alone* Compare *Paradise Lost* VII, 27-8: 'In darkness, and with dangers compast round . . . yet not alone'.
13-14 *'that . . . mortal sight'* Compare *Paradise Lost* III, 54-5.

III, v *Walton's Book of Lives*

In 1827, this sonnet was placed after III, xii, but was returned to this position in 1845.
2-4 *The feather . . . Angel's wing* Compare Henry Constable's *To the King of Scots* (in his *Diana*, 1594), lines 13-14: 'The pen wherewith thou dost so heavenly sing / Made of a quill pluck't from an Angel's wing'.

III, vi Clerical integrity

2 *one rigorous day*   the Act of Uniformity went into effect on 24 August 1662.

III, vii Persecution of the Scottish Covenanters

Composed possibly shortly before 18 December 1826; first published 1827.
1–3   Cromwell interposed in the persecution of the Vaudois in 1655.

III, viii Acquittal of the Bishops

'. . . I have done little more than versify a lively description . . . in the MS. Memoirs of the first Lord Lonsdale.' – W. (note to I, xi). Seven bishops who stood up to James II were tried and acquitted in June 1688.

III, ix William the Third

13   *Bondman*   James II.

III, x Obligations of Civil to Religious Liberty

3–4   *Sidney, Russell's*   Algernon Sidney and Lord William Russell were executed in 1683 for implication in the Rye House Plot.
12   *hardly*   with difficulty.

III, xi Sacheverel

Composed ?; first published in 1827.
4   *the Sentinel*   Henry Sacheverell (1674?–1724), a High-Church Tory who was tried by the House of Lords in 1709 and suspended from preaching for three years.
12   *fierce extremes*   *Paradise Lost* II, 599.

III, xii 'Down a swift Stream'

Composed possibly 1820 or 1821; first published in 1827, when it was placed at III, x until 1845, when it was placed in its present position. An earlier version was included in *Memorials of a Tour on the Continent* (1822 only).

III, xiii The Pilgrim Fathers

Composed by 1 March 1842; first published in 1842.
    Wordsworth's *note*:

> American episcopacy, in union with the church of England, strictly belongs to the general subject; and I here make my acknowledgments to

my American friends, Bishop Doane, and Mr Henry Reed of Philadelphia, for having suggested to me the propriety of adverting to it, and pointed out the virtues and intellectual qualities of Bishop White, which so eminently fitted him for the great work he undertook. Bishop White was consecrated at Lambeth, Feb. 4, 1787, by Archbishop Moore; and before his long life was closed, twenty-six bishops had been consecrated in America, by himself. For his character and opinions, see his own numerous Works, and a 'Sermon in commemoration of him, by George Washington Doane, Bishop of New Jersey.'

III, xiv Continued

Composed by 1 March 1842; first published in 1842.

III, xv Concluded - American Episcopacy

Composed by 1 March 1842; first published in 1842.
14 *patient Energy* Bishop Doane, *The Path of the Just: A Sermon in Commemoration of the Right Rev. William White* (1836), p. 17.

III, xvi 'Bishops and Priests, blessèd are ye'

Composed probably between 4 September 1842 and 27 March 1843; first published in 1845.
13 *if* In a letter to Henry Reed (10 November 1843), Wordsworth agreed to change *if* to *for* so that the phrasing should not sound, as Reed had suggested, as if the clause were conditional. But the wording was never changed in print.

III, xviii Pastoral character

'Among the benefits arising, as Mr Coleridge has well observed, from a Church establishment of endowments corresponding with the wealth of the country to which it belongs, may be reckoned as eminently important, the examples of civility and refinement which the clergy, stationed at intervals, afford to the whole people.' – W. The note continues at some length to give further reasons and examples.

III, xx Baptism

Composed possibly shortly before 18 December 1826; first published in 1827.

III, xxi Sponsors

Composed 7 December 1827; first published in 1832.
12 *make assurance doubly sure* Compare *Macbeth* IV, i, 83.

III, xxii Catechizing

9–10 'I remember my mother only in some few situations, one of which was her pinning a nosegay to my breast when I was going to say the catechism in the church, as was customary before Easter.' – *Memoirs*, ed. Christopher Wordsworth, I, 8.

III, xxiii Confirmation

Composed possibly shortly before 18 December 1826; first published in 1827.

III, xxiv Confirmation continued

Composed possibly shortly before 18 December 1826; first published in 1827.

III, xxv Sacrament

Composed possibly shortly before 18 December 1826; first published in 1827.
5–7 *with all ... name of God* Compare the *Book of Common Prayer* (Communion Service): 'Therefore with Angels and Archangels, and with all the company of heaven, we laud and magnify thy glorious Name'.

III, xxvi The Marriage ceremony

Composed by 17 August 1842; first published in 1845. Written for the series at the request of Henry Reed.
10 Spenser's *Epithalamion* 217: 'The which do endless matrimony make'.

III, xxvii Thanksgiving after childbirth

Composed shortly before 4 September 1842; first published in 1845.

III, xxviii Visitation of the Sick

Composed by 17 August 1842; first published in 1845.

III, xxix The Commination Service

Composed probably between 4 September 1842 and 27 March 1843; first published in 1845.

III, xxx Forms of prayer at sea

Composed probably between 4 September 1842 and 27 March 1843; first published in 1845.

III, xxxi Funeral service

Composed by 17 August 1842; first published in 1845. Written for the series at the request of Henry Reed.

5-6 '*I know . . . Redeemer liveth*' Book of Common Prayer (The Order for the Burial of the Dead). From *Job* 19:25.

9 *Man is as grass* Psalm 103:15: 'As for man, his days are as grass . . .'

10 *Grows green, is cut down* Book of Common Prayer (The Order for the Burial of the Dead): 'He cometh up, and is cut down, like a flower.'

13-14 '*O Death . . . thy Victory?*' I *Corinthians* 15:55.

III, xxxii Rural ceremony

In 1822 placed after III, xxii; in 1827, after III, xxv.

'This is still continued in many churches in Westmoreland. It takes place in the month of July, when the floor of the stalls is strewn with fresh rushes; and hence it is called the "Rushbearing".' – W.

III, xxxiv Mutability

10-14 Compare Wordsworth's *Fragment of a Gothic Tale* 67-71: 'The unimaginable touch of time / Or shouldering rend had split with ruin deep / Those towers that stately stood . . . / And plumed their heads with trees . . .' These lines were most likely further suggested by John Dyer's *The Ruins of Rome* (1740), lines 38-42.

14 *the unimaginable touch of time* Compare Milton's *Of Education*: 'Unimaginable touches' of music.

III, xxxv Old abbeys

10 'This is borrowed from an affecting passage in Mr George Dyer's history of Cambridge.' – W. *A History of the University and Colleges of Cambridge* (1814), I, viii: 'Time . . . teaches us to forgive and forget our own infirmities, not less than those of others . . .'

13 '. . . From a M S., written about the year 1770, which accidentally fell into my possession.' – W. See note to II, xxi, 7-8, above.

III, xxxvi Emigrant French clergy

Composed possibly shortly before 18 December 1826; first published in 1827.

III, xxxvii Congratulation

3 *the great Deliverer's* William III.

5-6 'See Burnet, who is unusually animated on the subject; the east wind, so anxiously expected and prayed for, was called "the Protestant wind".' – W. Gilbert Burnet, *History of His Own Time*, 2nd ed. (1833), III, pp. 316-17.

III, xxxviii New churches

11 *the wished-for Temples rise* In 1818 Parliament voted £1,000,000 for church-building.

III, xxxix Church to be erected

This and the two following sonnets were probably the first written of the series. The church was to be erected by Sir George Beaumont at Coleorton. See Wordsworth's Preface to the series (above).

III, xl Continued

See head-note to the preceding sonnet.
9 *conceal the precious Cross* 'The Lutherans have retained the Cross within their Churches; it is to be regretted that we have not done the same.' – W. Knight suggested that Wordsworth here means crucifix, not cross.
12 *incense-breathing morn* Gray's *Elegy* 17.

III, xli New church-yard

See head-note to III, xxxix, above.
12 *'dust to dust'* Book of Common Prayer (The Order for the Burial of the Dead).

III, xlii Cathedrals, etc.

5 *intricate defiles* See *The River Duddon* XVI, 8.
14 *Science* learning.

III, xliii Inside of King's College Chapel

Composed probably between November and December 1820.
1 *the royal Saint* Henry VI.

III, xliv The same

Composed probably between November and December 1820.

III, xlv Continued

Composed probably between November and December 1820.
8 *that younger Pile* St Paul's Cathedral

III, xlvi Ejaculation

5–6 'Some say that Monte Rosa takes its name from a belt of rock at its summit – a very unpoetical and scarcely a probable supposition.' – W.

III, xlvii Conclusion

14 Compare *Hebrews* 12:23: 'to the spirits of just men made perfect'.

TO ENTERPRISE

Composed probably 1821; first published in 1822. From 1822 to 1843 included among 'Memorials of a Tour on the Continent' (in a note to that volume, Wordsworth claimed the poem grew out of the thought behind *The Italian Itinerant*); from 1845 included among 'Poems of the Imagination'.

94 *calentured* N. C. Smith notes the unusual meaning here of 'imaged as to a man in a calenture'. A calenture is a fever, delirium.

114–16 *a living hill . . . still* '"Awhile the living hill / Heaved with convulsive throes, and all was still." Dr Darwin describing the destruction of the army of Cambyses.' – W. (1822). *The Botanic Garden* I, ii, 497–8.

145 *sweet Bird, misnamed the melancholy* the nightingale; see, for example, Milton's *Il Penseroso* 61.

DECAY OF PIETY

Composed probably 1821–22; first published in 1827; from 1827 included among 'Miscellaneous Sonnets'.

    I. F. note: 'Attendance at church on prayer-days, Wednesdays and Fridays and holidays, received a shock at the Revolution. It is now, however, happily reviving. The ancient people described in this sonnet were among the last of that pious class.'

[EPITAPH (In Grasmere Church)]

Composed probably between 25 May and 3 December 1822; first published in 1947.

    Wordsworth is supposed to have written at least the first six lines, but he most likely wrote the whole from a draft written by Edward Quillinan, husband of the deceased, Jemima Anne Deborah Quillinan.

TO ROTHA Q————

Composed probably between May 1822 and 19 November 1824 (probably about the latter date); first published in 1827; from 1827 included among 'Miscellaneous Sonnets'.

    I. F. note: 'Rotha, the daughter of my son-in-law Mr Quillinan.'

11–12 *this Stream . . . bear it* the River Rothay.

'BY MOSCOW SELF-DEVOTED TO A BLAZE'

Composed probably November or December 1822; first published in 1827; included from 1827 among 'Poems Dedicated to National Independence and Liberty'.

    In a letter to Henry Crabb Robinson (21 December 1822), Dorothy Wordsworth remarked of this sonnet that Wordsworth 'felt himself called upon to write [it] in justification of the Russians whom he felt he had injured by not giving them *their* share in the overthrow of Buonaparte, in conjunction with the elements'.

10   *Exalt*   lift up.
12–13   See *Exodus* 5–12.

TO THE LADY FLEMING

Composed probably between about mid-December (by 21 December) 1822 and 24 January 1823; first published in 1827; from 1827 to 1836 included among 'Poems of Sentiment and Reflection' and then among 'Miscellaneous Poems'.

15–16   *the Dell of Nightshade*   'Bekangs Ghyll – or dell of Nightshade – in which stands St Mary's Abbey in Low Furness.' – W.
81   *'bold bad'*   The Faerie *Queene* I, i, 37.
83   *'dark opprobrious den'*   *Paradise Lost* II, 58.

ON THE SAME OCCASION

Composed probably 1823; first published in 1827; from 1827 to 1836 included among 'Poems of Sentiment and Reflection' and then among 'Miscellaneous Poems'. The motto poem is from an unidentified source.

4   *The Mother Church*   St Oswald's, Grasmere.
27   *the day-spring from on high*   *Luke* 1:78.

[TRANSLATION OF VIRGIL'S AENEID]

Mostly translated probably between summer 1823 and about February 1824 (part possibly translated as early as 1819); part of Book I (lines 657–1043) first published 1832 in the *Philological Museum*, the remainder in 1947.

In a letter to Lord Lonsdale (9 November 1823), Wordsworth said of his translation of Book I: 'I have endeavoured to be much more literal than Dryden, or Pitt, who keeps much closer to the original than his Predecessor.'

When part of Book I was published in 1832 it was prefaced by a letter:
TO THE EDITORS OF THE
'PHILOLOGICAL MUSEUM'

Your letter reminding me of an expectation I some time since held out to you of allowing some specimens of my translation from the Æneid to be printed in the 'Philological Museum', was not very acceptable; for I had abandoned the thought of ever sending into the world any part of that experiment – for it was nothing more – an experiment begun for amusement, and I now think a less fortunate one than when I first named it to you. Having been displeased in modern translations with the additions of incongruous matter, I began to translate with a resolve to keep clear of that fault, by adding nothing; but I became convinced that a spirited translation can scarcely be accomplished in the English language without admitting a principle of compensation. On this point, however, I do not wish to insist, and merely send the following passage, taken at random from a wish to comply with your request. W. W.

'A VOLANT TRIBE OF BARDS'

Composed probably in 1823 (before May); first published in 1823, in Joanna Baillie's *Poetic Miscellanies*; from 1827 included among 'Miscellaneous Sonnets'. This poem underwent considerable revision.

3   *'coignes of vantage'*   Compare *Macbeth* I, vi, 7.

'NOT LOVE, NOT WAR'

For all data, see head-note to the preceding poem.

IN THE FIRST PAGE OF AN ALBUM

Composed 1 October 1823; first published in 1947.

12   *'characters of light'*   unidentified quotation.

[TRANSLATION OF VIRGIL'S GEORGIC IV]

Translated probably early November (by 12 November) 1823; first published in 1947.

MEMORY

Composed probably 1823; first published in 1827; from 1827 included among 'Poems of Sentiment and Reflection'.

I. F. note (to *Written in a Blank Leaf of Macpherson's Ossian*): 'suggested from apprehensions of the fate of my friend H. C. [Hartley Coleridge]'.

'HOW RICH THAT FOREHEAD'S CALM EXPANSE!'

Composed probably 1824 (possibly April–May); first published in 1827; from 1827 included among 'Poems Founded on the Affections'.

I. F. note: 'Rydal Mount, 1824. Also on M. W. [Mary Wordsworth] Mrs Wordsworth's impression is that the Poem was written at Coleorton: it was certainly suggested by a Print at Coleorton Hall.'

7-8   *she drew An Angel from his station*   Compare Dryden's *Alexander's Feast* 170: 'She drew an angel down'.

RECOLLECTION OF THE PORTRAIT OF KING HENRY VIII

Composed probably between May 1824 and April 1827; first published in 1827; from 1827 included among 'Miscellaneous Sonnets'.

TO THE LADY E. B.

Composed probably in September (by 20 September) 1824; first published in 1827; from 1827 included among 'Miscellaneous Sonnets'.

The well-known friends were Lady Eleanor Butter and the Hon. Miss Ponsonby, who lived in the vicinity of Wordsworth's friend, Robert Jones.

2 *VALE OF MEDITATION* 'Glyn Myrvr.' – W.

TO THE TORRENT AT THE DEVIL'S BRIDGE

Composed 14 September 1824; first published in 1827; from 1827 included among 'Miscellaneous Sonnets'.

In a letter to Sir George Beaumont (20 September 1824) Wordsworth commented, 'It rained heavily in the night, and we saw the waterfalls in perfection. While Dora was attempting to make a sketch from the chasm in the rain, I composed by her side the . . . address to the torrent.'

4 *Pindus* a mountain range in Northern Greece.
5 *Patriots scoop their freedom out* the Greek War of Independence.
7 *that young Stream* the Rhine.

COMPOSED AMONG THE RUINS OF A CASTLE

Composed probably 1824, possibly September; first published in 1827; from 1827 included among 'Miscellaneous Sonnets'.

Wordsworth visited Carnarvon Castle in September 1824.

THE INFANT M———— M————

Composed 12 November 1824; first published in 1827; from 1827 included among 'Miscellaneous Sonnets'.

I. F. note: '. . . Mary Monkhouse, the only daughter of our friend and cousin Thomas Monkhouse.'

ELEGIAC STANZAS (ADDRESSED TO SIR G. H. B.)

Composed probably December (on or after 5 December) 1824; first published in 1827; from 1827 included among 'Epitaphs and Elegiac Pieces'.
I. F. note:

> On Mrs Fermor. This lady had been a widow long before I knew her. Her husband was of the family of the Lady celebrated in the 'Rape of the Lock', and was, I believe, a Roman Catholic. The sorrow which his death caused her was fearful in its character as described in this poem, but was subdued in course of time by the strength of her religious faith. I have been, for many weeks at a time, an inmate with her at Coleorton Hall, as were also Mrs Wordsworth and my Sister. The truth in the sketch of her character here given was acknowledged with gratitude by her nearest relatives. She was eloquent in conversation, energetic upon public matters, open in respect to these, but slow to communicate her personal feelings; upon these she never touched in her intercourse with me, so that I could not regard myself as her confidential friend, and was accordingly surprised when I learnt she had left me a Legacy of £100, as a token of her

esteem. See, in further illustration, the second stanza inscribed upon her Cenotaph in Coleorton church.

See p. 610.
In a letter to Lady Beaumont of 25 February 1825 (quoted in Edward Dowden's edition), Mary Wordsworth remarked that the poem was 'poured forth with a deep stream of fervour that was something beyond labour, and it has required very little correction'.

TO ——————, IN HER SEVENTIETH YEAR

Composed probably December (by 9 December) 1824; first published in 1827; from 1827 included among 'Miscellaneous Sonnets'.
I. F. note: 'Lady Fitzgerald, as described to me by Lady Beaumont.'

TO —————— ('Let other bards')

Composed probably 1824; first published in 1827; from 1827 included among 'Poems Founded on the Affections'.
I. F. note: 'Rydal Mount, 1824. On Mary Wordsworth.'

TO —————— ('Look at the fate')

All data identical with the preceding poem.
I. F. note: 'Rydal Mount, 1824. Prompted by the undue importance attached to personal beauty by some dear friends of mine.' Possibly addressed to Wordsworth's daughter, Dora.

20, 22 *'To draw, out of the object of his eyes,'* ... *'a refinèd Form'* See Spenser's *Hymne in Honour of Beautie*, lines 211–15: 'But they which love indeed, look otherwise, / With pure regard and spotless true intent, / Drawing out of the object of their eyes, / A more refinèd form, which they present / Unto their mind, void of all blemishment'.

A FLOWER GARDEN

Composed probably 1824; first published in 1827; from 1827 included among 'Poems of the Fancy'.
I. F. note: 'Planned by my friend Lady Beaumont in connexion with the garden at Coleorton.'

CENOTAPH

Composed probably 1824; first published in 1842; from 1845 included among 'Epitaphs and Elegiac Pieces'.
I. F. note: 'See Elegiac Stanzas Addressed to Sir G. H. B. upon the death of his Sister-in-law.' (p. 604 above.)
In a letter to Lady Beaumont (quoted in Knight's edition [1896] VII, 136) Mary Wordsworth wrote: 'To fit the lines, intended for an urn, for a Monument, William has altered the closing stanza, which (though they are not

what he would have produced had he first cast them with a view to the Church) he hopes you will not disapprove.'

13   M S note: 'Words inscribed upon her Tomb at her own request'. The quotation is from *John* 14:6.

TO ———— ('O dearer far than light')

Composed probably late 1824 or early 1825; first published in 1827; from 1827 included among 'Poems Founded on the Affections'.
    I. F. note: 'Rydal Mount, 1824. To M. W. [Mary Wordsworth].' The poem was occasioned by the approaching death of Mrs Wordsworth's cousin, Thomas Monkhouse, who died in February 1825.

8   *'sober certainties'*   Compare *Comus* 263.

'WHILE ANNA'S PEERS AND EARLY PLAYMATES TREAD'

Composed possibly about May 1825 (not earlier); first published in 1827; from 1827 included among 'Miscellaneous Sonnets'.
    I. F. note: 'This is taken from the account given by Miss Jewsbury of the pleasure she derived, when long confined to her bed by sickness, from the inanimate object on which this Sonnet turns.' Wordsworth addressed *Liberty* to Maria Jane Jewsbury (1800–33), whom he met in May 1825.

THE CONTRAST

Composed probably 1825; first published in 1827; from 1827 included among 'Poems of the Fancy'.
    I. F. note: 'The Parrot belonged to Mrs Luff while living at Fox Ghyll. The Wren was one that haunted for many years the Summerhouse between the two terraces of Rydal Mount.'

38   *slender*   weak.

TO A SKYLARK ('Ethereal minstrel!')

Composed probably 1825; first published in 1827; from 1827 included among 'Poems of the Imagination'.
    I. F. note: 'Rydal Mount 1825. (Where there are no skylarks, but the poet is everywhere. [pencil addition])'.
    A second stanza to this poem was transferred in 1845 to *A Morning Exercise* (lines 43–8), and in the Fenwick note to the latter poem, Wordsworth asks that the last five stanzas be read with *To a Skylark*.

A MORNING EXERCISE

Composed probably 1825; first published in 1832; from 1832 included among 'Poems of the Fancy'.
    I. F. note: 'Rydal Mount, 1825. I could wish the last five stanzas of this to

be read with the poem addressed to the Skylark [*To a Skylark* ('Ethereal minstrel!')].' Lines 43–8 were transferred from *To a Skylark* in 1845.

16 'See [Charles] Waterton's "Wanderings in South America" [1825].' – W.
20 *Philomel* nightingale.
53 *Urania's* the Muse of astronomy.
60 *singing as they shine* Addison's *Ode* ('The Spacious firmament on high') 23.

ODE COMPOSED ON MAY MORNING

Composed perhaps 1826 (probably May or after); first published in 1835; from 1836–7 included among 'Poems of Sentiment and Reflection'.
 I. F. note:

> This and the following poem originated in the lines 'How delicate the leafy veil', etc. [*To May*, line 81] – My daughter and I left Rydal Mount upon a tour through our mountains with Mr and Mrs Carr in the month of May, 1826, and as we were going up the vale of Newlands I was struck with the appearance of the little Chapel gleaming through the veil of half-opened leaves; and the feeling which was then conveyed to my mind was expressed in the stanza that follows. As in the case of 'Liberty' and 'Humanity', my first intention was to write only one poem, but subsequently I broke it into two, making additions to each part so as to produce a consistent and appropriate whole.

TO MAY

Composed probably 1826 (probably May or after); first published in 1835; from 1836–7 included among 'Poems of Sentiment and Reflection'.
 In a letter to W. R. Hamilton (November 1830), Wordsworth remarked: 'As I passed through the tame and manufacture-disfigured country of Lancashire I was reminded by the faded leaves, of Spring, and threw off a few stanzas of an ode to May.' This poem was originally half of a poem; the other half was *Ode Composed on May Morning* – see head-note to the preceding poem.
59–60 *'the rathe ... Forsaken'* *Lycidas* 142.

'PRITHEE, GENTLE LADY, LIST'

Composed probably 1826 (possibly 21 December); first published in 1896.
 See the head-note to *The Lady Whom You Here Behold* (below). This poem may have also been given to Fanny Barlow, for it is contained in almost identical form in Knight's edition as inscribed to her.

'ERE WITH COLD BEADS OF MIDNIGHT DEW'

Composed probably 1826; first published in 1827; from 1827 included among 'Poems Founded on the Affections'.
 I. F. note: 'Rydal Mount 1826. Suggested by the condition of a friend.'

'ONCE I COULD HAIL (HOWE'ER SERENE THE SKY)'

Composed probably 1826; first published 1827; from 1827 to 1836–7 included among 'Epitaphs and Elegiac Pieces', from 1845 among 'Miscellaneous Pieces'.

3–4 *No faculty . . . dusky Shape* 'Afterwards, when I could not avoid seeing it, I wondered at this, and the more so because, like most children, I had been in the habit of watching the Moon through all her changes, and had often continued to gaze at it while at the full, till half blinded.' – *I. F. note.*
15 *Dian's* both the moon and the moon-goddess; also called Cynthia (line 22).
18 *Proserpine* queen of Hades.

'THE MASSY WAYS'

Composed probably 1826; first published in 1835; from 1836–7 included among 'Inscriptions'.
I. F. note: 'The walk is what we call the *Far-Terrace* beyond the summer-house at Rydal Mount. The lines were written when we were afraid of being obliged to quit the place to which we were so much attached.'

RETIREMENT

Composed probably 1826; first published in 1827; from 1827 included among 'Miscellaneous Sonnets'.

3 *patriot Friend* possibly Henry Crabb Robinson, who wrote to Wordsworth (18 February 1826) to complain of the dearth of political poems after 1814.
6 *her* the antecedent is unclear. N. C. Smith suggests the word refers to 'mind' or 'soul', as indicated by 'thought and feeling' in line 2.
14 *thanks not Heaven amiss* Compare *Comus* 177: 'And thank the gods amiss'.

'THE LADY WHOM YOU HERE BEHOLD'

Composed probably 1826; first published in 1947.
On the M S of this and '*Prithee, Gentle Lady, List*', the Rev. Herbert Hill, husband of Bertha Southey, wrote: 'The two poems above have the interest of being playful effusions of Mr Wordsworth's Muse; they were written for two dolls dressed up by Edith Southey and Dora Wordsworth . . .'

COMPOSED WHEN A PROBABILITY EXISTED

Composed probably 1826; first published 1889.

147 *The Muses* the nine Muses, goddesses who inspired song, were originally nymphs of springs and wells. Their temples were situated near the Hippocrene well (line 159) and the Castalian spring (line 160).

TO ———————— [Dedication to 'The Miscellaneous Sonnets']

Composed possibly 1826; first published in 1827; from 1827 included among 'Miscellaneous Sonnets'.

Some editors believe this sonnet was dedicated to Dorothy Wordsworth, but Ernest de Selincourt thinks it is dedicated 'almost certainly, to Mary [Wordsworth]'. This poem underwent considerable revision.

14 *with more than mild content*   '"Something less than joy, but more than dull content." – Countess of Winchelsea.' – W. *The Shepherd and the Calm* (1713), 5. See also Wordsworth's *Gold and Silver Fishes in a Vase* 7–8 (p. 683 above).

'FAIR PRIME OF LIFE!'

Composed possibly 1826; first published in 1827; from 1827 included among 'Miscellaneous Sonnets'.

I. F. note: 'Suggested by observation of the way in which a young friend, whom I do not choose to name, misspent his time and misapplied his talents. He took afterwards a better course, and became a useful member of society, respected, I believe, wherever he has been known.'

'GO BACK TO ANTIQUE AGES'

Composed possibly 1826; first published in 1827; from 1827 included among 'Poems Dedicated to National Independence and Liberty'.

5 *Tower of Babel*   See *Genesis* 11:1–9.
11 *the first mighty Hunter*   Nimrod (see *Genesis* 10:8–10).

'WHY, MINSTREL, THESE UNTUNEFUL MURMURINGS'

Composed possibly 1826; first published in 1827; from 1827 included among 'Miscellaneous Sonnets'.

6 *Castalian fountain*   fountain sacred to the Muses.

ON SEEING A NEEDLECASE

Composed probably 1827 (before May); first published in 1827; from 1827 included among 'Poems of the Fancy'.

E. M. S. was Edith May Southey, daughter of Robert Southey, Poet Laureate (line 13).

7 *Minerva's*   Roman goddess, patroness of the arts.
10 *Arachne's*   a maiden changed into a spider for challenging Athena's kill at weaving.
11 *Vulcan's*   blacksmith of the gods.
24 *slender*   weak.

TO ———— [Conclusion to Part II, 'Miscellaneous Sonnets']

Composed probably 1827 (before May); first published in 1827; from 1827 included among 'Miscellaneous Sonnets'.

3 'This line alludes to Sonnets which will be found in another Class.' – W.
9–11 *every day . . . week* this image was adapted by Thomas De Quincey for *Levana and Our Ladies of Sorrow*.

'HER ONLY PILOT THE SOFT BREEZE'

All data identical with the preceding poem.

TO S. H.

All data identical with the preceding poem.
   S. H. is Sara Hutchinson, Wordsworth's sister-in-law.

7 *She who toils to spin* Lachesis, one of the three Fates.

'SCORN NOT THE SONNET'

All data identical with the preceding poem.
   I. F. note: 'Composed, almost extempore, in a short walk on the western side of Rydal Lake.'

'*THERE IS A PLEASURE IN POETIC PAINS*'

All data identical with the preceding poem.

1–2 *There is . . . know* Cowper, *The Task* II, 285–6.

'WHEN PHILOCTETES IN THE LEMNIAN ISLE'

All data identical with the preceding poem.

1 *Philoctetes* left behind on Lemnos by the Greeks en route to Troy because of a wounded foot.

TO THE CUCKOO ('Not the whole')

All data identical with the preceding poem.

'IN MY MIND'S EYE'

All data identical with the preceding poem.

IN THE WOODS OF RYDAL

All data identical with the preceding poem. The title was added in 1837.
   Wordsworth's *note*:

> This Sonnet, as Poetry, explains itself, yet the scene of the incident having
> been a wild wood, it may be doubted, as a point of natural history

whether the bird was aware that his attentions were bestowed upon a human, or even a living, creature. But a Redbreast will perch upon the foot of a gardener at work, and alight on the handle of the spade when his hand is half upon it – this I have seen ...

1 *Jemima's* Jemima Quillinan, daughter of Edward Quillinan.

[TWO EPIGRAMS ON BYRON'S *CAIN*]

Composed possibly 1827; first published in 1896.

ii

1 *a German Haggis* allusion to Salomon Gessner's *Der Tod Abels* (1758). A *receipt* is a recipe.
3 *'warm-reeking, rich'* Burns's *To a Haggis* (1786), 18.

'JUST VENGEANCE CLAIMS THY SOUL'

Composed possibly 1827; first published 1946.

3 *The conscious Tyrants* Harmodius and Aristogiton; see note to *Translation of a Celebrated Greek Song* (Vol. I, p. 922).
7 *the hero* William Tell (died c. 1350), the Swiss patriot.
12 *Pelayo* Spanish chieftain (d. 737) who defeated the Moslems at Covadonga in 718.
13 *The Swede* Gustavus I (1496–1560), who led a rebellion against Christian II of Denmark in Dalecarlia, Sweden. He sometimes disguised himself as a miner.

FILIAL PIETY

Composed probably 5 February 1828; first published in 1829 in *The Casket*; from 1832 included among 'Miscellaneous Sonnets'.

In the *I. F. note*, Wordsworth mentions that the subject was 'communicated to [him] by the coachman in the same way' as the subject of *A Tradition of Oker Hill* – see the head-note to that poem.

In a letter to the *Athenaeum* (17 May 1890), Mr James Bromley, married to a descendant of the principals of the poem, provided additional details: 'Thomas Scarisbrick was killed by a stroke of lightning while building a turf-stack between Ormskirk and Preston in 1779. His son James finished the stack, and while he lived kept it in constant repair in memory of the father.'

THE TRIAD

Composed probably by early March 1828; first published in 1828 in *The Keepsake* (for 1829); included from 1832 among 'Poems of the Imagination'. In a letter to Mary and Dora Wordsworth in March 1828 – before publication of the poem – Wordsworth called the poem *The Promise*.

I. F. note: 'Rydal Mount, 1828. The girls Edith May Southey [born 1 May

1804], my daughter Dora [born 16 August 1804] and Sara Coleridge [born 22 December 1802].'

In a letter to Henry Reed (19–21 May 1851), Sara Coleridge observed: 'There is no truth in [the poem] as a whole, although bits of truth, glazed and magnified, are embodied in it . . .' *Sarah Coleridge and Henry Reed* (1937).

In a letter to Barron Field (20 December 1828), Wordsworth said he considered 'a great part of [the poem] as elegant and spirited as anything I have written – but I was afraid to trust my judgement, as the aery Figures are all sketched from living originals that are dear to me'.

13 *Mount Ida's triple lustre* an allusion to the judgment of Paris.

21 *that fair progeny of Jove* the three Graces, most often represented as dancing with hands interwoven (line 20).

36 *Lucida* Edith Southey.

40 *the hermit's long-forsaken cell* a possible allusion to St Herbert's Island, Derwentwater, near where the Southeys lived.

47 *bird of Juno* the peacock, sacred bird of the Capitoline temple of Juno.

90 *youngest* Dora Wordsworth. According to A. J. George, Sara Coleridge remarked in her *Memoir*: 'There is truth in the sketch of Dora, poetic truth, though such as none but a poet-father would have seen.'

106 *Euphrosyne* one of the three Graces.

114 *Idalian* of the Cyprian town, sacred to Venus.

117 *FLOWER OF THE WINDS* the anemone.

137 *Features to old ideal grace allied* according to Sara Coleridge (see head-note above), an allusion to Dora's likeness to the Memnon head in the British Museum.

174 *Last of the Three* Sara Coleridge.

THE GLEANER

Composed probably March 1828; first published in 1828 in *The Keepsake* (for 1829) with the title *The Country Girl*; included from 1832 to 1843 among 'Poems of Sentiment and Reflection' and thereafter among 'Miscellaneous Poems'.

I. F. note: 'The Painter's name I am not sure of, but I think it was Holmes.' James Holmes (1777–1860). The inspiration for the poem was apparently not exclusively pictorial; in a letter to Mary and Dora (March 1828), Wordsworth wrote: 'I have written one little piece, 34 lines, on the Picture of a beautiful Peasant Girl bearing a Sheaf of Corn. The Person I had in mind lives near the Blue Bell, Fillingham – a sweet Creature, we saw her going to Hereford.'

THE WISHING-GATE

Composed probably March 1828; first published in 1828 in *The Keepsake* (for 1829); included in 1832 among 'Poems of Sentiment and Reflection' and from 1836–7 among 'Poems of the Imagination'.

I. F. note: 'Rydal Mount, 1828. See also "Wishing Gate Destroyed".'

FAREWELL LINES

Composed perhaps 1828 (possibly May or soon after); first published in 1842; from 1845 included among 'Poems Founded on the Affections'.

I. F. note: 'These lines were designed as a farewell to Charles Lamb and his sister, who had retired from the throngs of London to comparative solitude in the village of Enfield.'

1 Thomson's *To the Rev Patrick Murdoch* (1738), 10.

A JEWISH FAMILY

Composed probably July 1828; first published in 1835; from 1836-7 included among 'Poems of the Imagination'.

I. F. note:

Coleridge, my daughter, and I, in 1828, passed a fortnight upon the banks of the Rhine, principally under the hospitable roof of Mr Aders of Gotesburg, but two days of the time we spent at St Goar in rambles among the neighbouring valleys. It was at St Goar that I saw the Jewish family here described. Though exceedingly poor, and in rags, they were not less beautiful than I have endeavoured to make them appear. We had taken a little dinner with us in a basket, and invited them to partake of it, which the mother refused to do, both for herself and children, saying it was with them a fast-day; adding diffidently, that whether such observances were right or wrong, she felt it her duty to keep them strictly. The Jews, who are numerous on this part of the Rhine, greatly surpass the German peasantry in the beauty of their features and in the intelligence of their countenances . . .

THE EGYPTIAN MAID

Composed between 20 and 28 November 1828; first published in 1835; from 1836-7 included in a separate, untitled category.

I. F. note:

'[The poem] rose out of a few words casually used in conversation by my nephew Henry Hutchinson. He was describing with great spirit the appearance and movement of a vessel which he seemed to admire more than any other he had ever seen, and said her name was the 'Water Lily'. This plant has been my delight from my boyhood, as I have seen it floating on the lake; and that conversation put me upon constructing and composing the poem. Had I not heard those words it would never have been written. The form of the stanza is new, and is nothing but a repetition of the first five lines as they were thrown off, and is perhaps not well suited to narrative, and certainly would not have been trusted to had I thought at the beginning that the poem would have gone to such a length.

47-8 *sea-flashes . . . high, rebounding* Compare Sir Thomas Herbert, *A*

Description of the Persian Monarchy (1634), p. 7: '. . . Sometimes the surges or Sea-flashes do rebound top-gallant height'.
286 *vailed* lowered.
316 *The marvel of the PERILOUS SEAT* See *Le Morte D'Arthur* III, iv; XIII, ii–iv.

ON THE POWER OF SOUND

Composed probably between December 1828 and late 1829; first published in 1835; from 1836–7 included among 'Poems of the Imagination'.

Wordsworth held this poem in very high esteem; in a letter to Alexander Dyce (23 December 1837), Wordsworth replied to a comment of Field:

> I cannot call to mind a reason why you should not think some passages in 'The Power of Sound' equal to anything I have produced; when first printed in 'Yarrow Revisited', I placed it at the end of the Volume, and in the last edition of my poems, at the close of the Poems of Imagination, indicating thereby my *own* opinion of it.

14 *pealing down the long-drawn aisle* Compare Gray's *Elegy* 39–40: 'Where through the long-drawn aisle and fretted vault / The pealing anthem swells the note of praise.'
76 *Lydian airs* Milton's *L'Allegro* 136.
126 *Hell to the lyre bowed low* an allusion to Orpheus freeing Eurydice from the underworld.
129–31 Amphion, by charming stones with his music, thus built the city of Thebes.
134–6 Compare *A Midsummer Night's Dream* II, i, 150–51: 'And heard a mermaid, on a dolphin's back, / Uttering such dulcet and harmonious breath'.
143–4 An allusion to the constellation of the Dolphin.
146 *Maenalian* Arcadian.
150–51 *beat the ground In cadence* Compare Gray's *The Progress of Poesy* 34: 'To brisk notes in cadence beating'.
159 *'The vain distress-gun'* unidentified quotation.
179 *sages* Pythagoreans.
199–202 'The lines . . . in this poem, "Thou too be heard, lone Eagle etc." were suggested near the Giant's Causeway [Ireland], or rather at the promontory of Fairhead where a pair of eagles wheeled above our heads and darted off as if to hide themselves in a blaze of sky made by the setting sun.' – *I. F. note.*
204–5 *Deep to Deep . . . calls* Psalms 42:7.
217–18 Compare *Ode : Intimations* 155–6: 'Our noisy years seem moments in the being / Of the eternal silence' and *Address to Silence* (probably by Wordsworth) 50: 'Our little years are moments of thy life'.

WRITTEN IN MRS FIELD'S ALBUM

Composed between 24 December 1828 and 26 February 1829; first published in 1947.

In a letter to Wordsworth (26 February 1829) Barron Field wrote: 'Mrs Field thanks you for writing in her Album, and my Brother is very proud of your praise.'

A TRADITION OF OKER HILL

Composed probably 1828; first published in 1828 in *The Keepsake* (for 1829); from 1832 included among 'Miscellaneous Sonnets'.

I. F. note: 'This pleasing tradition was told me by the coachman at whose side I sate while he drove down the dale, he pointing to the trees on the hill as he related the story.' In a letter to Dora Wordsworth (8 November 1830), the poet reported that when revisiting the vale he could not discover the tradition from the residents but was told the trees were named 'Wm Shore's trees from the name of the man who had planted them above 200 years ago'.

A GRAVESTONE

Composed probably 1828 (by 27 January); first published in 1828 in *The Keepsake* (for 1829); from 1832 included among 'Miscellaneous Sonnets'.

I. F. note: 'Many conjectures have been formed as to the person who lies under this stone. Nothing appears to be known for a certainty.'

1 *Miserrimus* most wretched man.

THE RUSSIAN FUGITIVE

Composed probably late 1828 (at least before 19 January 1829); first published in 1835; in 1836–7 placed by itself, and from 1845 included among 'Miscellaneous Poems'.

Wordsworth's *note*: 'Peter Henry Bruce, having given in his entertaining Memoirs the substance of this Tale, affirms that, besides the concurring reports of others, he had the story from the lady's own mouth . . .'. *Memoirs, containing an account of his travels in Germany . . . ; as also several anecdotes of the Czar, Peter I of Russia* (1782).

I. F. note: 'Early in life this story had interested me, and I often thought it would make a pleasing subject for an Opera or Musical drama.'

36 *Prevented* anticipated.
139 *'if home it be or bower'* unidentified quotation.
179–80 'From Golding's Translation of Ovid's *Metamorphoses*. See also his Dedicatory Epistle prefixed to the same work.' – W. (1835 only). Arthur Golding, trans., *Metamorphoses* (1575), I, 545: 'The leaves of every pleasant tree about his goalden heare'.
335 *the Lady Catherine* 'The famous Catherine, then bearing that name as the acknowledged Wife of Peter the Great.' – W.

GOLD AND SILVER FISHES IN A VASE

Composed probably 1829 (by 19 December); first published in 1835; from 1836–7 to 1843 included among 'Poems of Sentiment and Reflection' and thereafter among 'Miscellaneous Poems'.

I. F. note: 'They were a present from Miss Jewsbury . . .'

1–2   *lark . . . sings*   Compare *Cymbeline* II, iii, 22: '. . . The lark at heaven's gate sings'.

7–8   Compare the Countess of Winchelsea's *The Shepherd and the Calm* (1713), 5: 'Something less than joy, but more than dull content'. Quoted by Wordsworth in a note, p. 1025 above.

LIBERTY

Composed probably 1829; first published in 1835; in 1836–7 included among 'Poems of Sentiment and Reflection' and thereafter among 'Miscellaneous Poems'.

This and the following poem were originally planned as one poem – see the head-note to the following poem.

The motto is from the opening of Cowley's *Essay on Liberty*.

2   *Anna*   Mrs Fletcher (née Jewsbury).

8   *living Well*   *The Faerie Queene* I, ii, 43.

61   *a sprig from Chaucer's reverend brow*   See *The Squire's Tale* 610–17.

82   *Philomel*   nightingale.

91   *path that winds by stealth*   See Horace's *Epistles* I, xviii, 103: 'An secretum iter et fallentis semita vitae'.

103   *the Sabine farm he loved so well*   See Horace's *Odes* II, xviii.

104   *Blandusia's spring*   See Horace's *Odes* III, xiii.

111   *In a deep vision's intellectual scene*   Cowley's *The Complaint* 1. See the next six lines of Cowley's poem for background and echoes to lines 112–19 of *Liberty*.

139–40

> There is now, alas! no possibility of the anticipation, with which the above Epistle concludes, being realized: nor were the verses ever seen by the Individual for whom they were intended. She accompanied her husband, the Rev. Wm. Fletcher, to India, and died of Cholera, at the age of thirty-two or thirty-three years . . .

– W.

HUMANITY

Composed probably 1829; first published in 1835; from 1836–7 included among 'Poems of Sentiment and Reflection'.

I. F. note: 'These verses and those entitled *Liberty* were composed as one piece, which Mrs Wordsworth complained of as unwieldy and ill-proportioned; and accordingly it was divided into two on her judicious recommendation.'

32   'I am indebted here, to a passage in one of Mr Digby's valuable works.' – W. Kenelm Henry Digby (1800–80), author of *The Broadstone of Honour* (1822), his best-known work and the work probably referred to by Wordsworth in this note.

33-40 See *Genesis* 28:12–19.
78 *Stone-walls a prisoner make* Compare Lovelace's *To Althea from Prison* 25: 'Stone walls do not a prison make'.
83 *'Slaves cannot breathe in England'* Cowper's *The Task* (1785), II, 40.
89-90 *Idol, falsely called 'the Wealth Of Nations'* Compare *The Prelude* XIII, 77–8: 'idol proudly named 'The Wealth of Nations'.

'THIS LAWN, A CARPET ALL ALIVE'

All data identical with the previous poem.
I. F. note: 'This lawn is the sloping one approaching the kitchen-garden, and was made out of it. Hundreds of times have I watched the dancing of shadows amid a press of sunshine, and other beautiful appearances of light and shade, flowers and shrubs.'

6 *strenuous idleness* Compare Horace's *Epistles* I, xi, 28: 'strenua ... inertia'.

THOUGHTS ON THE SEASONS

All data identical with the previous poem.

WRITTEN IN THE STRANGERS' BOOK

Composed possibly 1829; first published in 1889.
According to Knight, the poem is a retort to the following entry in the Strangers' Book: 'Lord and Lady Darlington, Lady Vane, Miss Taylor and Captain Stamp pronounce this Lake superior to Lac de Genève, Lago de Como, Lago Maggiore, L'Eau de Zurich, Loch Lomond, Loch Katerine, or the Lakes of Killarney.'

'WHY ART THOU SILENT!'

Composed 18 January 1830; first published in 1835; from 1836–7 included among 'Miscellaneous Sonnets'.
I. F. note:

> In the month of January, when Dora and I were walking from Town-End, Grasmere, across the vale, snow being on the ground, she espied, in the thick though leafless hedge, a bird's nest half-filled with snow. Out of this comfortless appearance arose this Sonnet, which was, in fact, written without the least reference to any individual object, but merely to prove to myself that I could, if I thought fit, write in a strain that poets have been fond of.

'IN THESE FAIR VALES'

Composed 26 June 1830; first published in 1835; from 1836–7 included among 'Inscriptions'. Until 1845 entitled *Intended for a Stone in the Grounds of Rydal Mount*.

I. F. note: 'Engraven, during my absence in Italy, upon a brass plate inserted in the stone.'

1830 ('Chatsworth!')

Composed probably between 6 and 8 November 1830; first published 1835; from 1836–7 included among 'Miscellaneous Sonnets'.

ELEGIAC MUSINGS

Composed probably November (before 26 November) 1830; first published 1835; from 1836–7 included among 'Epitaphs and Elegiac Pieces'.
   I. F. note: 'These verses were in fact composed on horseback during a storm whilst I was on my way from Coleorton to Cambridge.'

41 unidentified quotation.
47 Edward Fairfax's translation (1600) of Tasso's *Godfrey of Bullogne* II, xviii: 'The Rose within herself her sweetness closed'.

THE POET AND THE CAGED TURTLEDOVE

Composed probably early December 1830; first published 1835; from 1836–7 included among 'Poems of the Fancy'.
   I. F. note: 'Rydal Mount 1830 . . . These verses were composed *ex tempore*, to the letter, in the Terrace Summer House before spoken of. It was the habit of the bird to begin cooing and murmuring whenever it heard me making my verses.'

THE ARMENIAN LADY'S LOVE

Composed probably 1830; first published 1835; from 1836–7 included among 'Poems Founded on the Affections'.

2 'See in Percy's Reliques that fine old ballad, "The Spanish Lady's Love"; from which Poem the form of stanza, as suitable to dialogue, is adopted.' – W.

PRESENTIMENTS

Composed probably 1830; first published 1835; from 1836–7 included among 'Poems of the Imagination'.

TO B. R. HAYDON, ON SEEING HIS PICTURE

Composed 11 June 1831; first published 1832; from 1832 included among 'Miscellaneous Sonnets'.
   I. F. note: 'This sonnet, though said to be written on seeing the portrait of Napoleon, was, in fact, composed some time after, extempore, in the wood at Rydal Mount.'
   In a letter to W. R. Hamilton (13 June 1831), Wordsworth claimed that

although 'written at the request of the painter ... it is no more than my sincere opinion of his excellent picture'.

9 *unapparent* unseen.

YARROW REVISITED, AND OTHER POEMS

The poems in this series were probably composed in the autumn of 1831, with the exception of numbers IV and XXIII, the dates of which are indicated in the notes below; the series was first published in 1835.

I Yarrow revisited ('The gallant Youth')

    I. F. note:

> In the autumn of 1831, my daughter and I set off from Rydal to visit Sir Walter Scott before his departure for Italy ... On Tuesday morning Sir Walter Scott accompanied us and most of the party to Newark Castle on the Yarrow. When we alighted from the carriages he walked pretty stoutly, and had great pleasure in revisiting those his favourite haunts. Of that excursion the verses "Yarrow revisited" are a memorial. Notwithstanding the romance that pervades Sir W.'s works and attaches to many of his habits, there is too much pressure of fact for these verses to harmonise as much as I could wish with the two preceding Poems [*Yarrow Unvisited* and *Yarrow Visited*].

2 *'winsome Marrow'* William Hamilton's *The Braes of Yarrow* (1724), 2; quoted in *Yarrow Unvisited* 6.
8 *Great Minstrel of the Border* Sir Walter Scott.
99 *the silent portal arch* Compare Scott's *The Lay of the Last Minstrel* (1805) 32: 'The embattled portal arch he passed'.

II On the Departure of Sir Walter Scott

Composed probably September 1831; first published 1833 in the *Literary Souvenir*.

    I. F. note:

> On our return [from Newark Castle] in the afternoon we had to cross the Tweed directly opposite Abbotsford. The wheels of our carriage grated upon the pebbles in the bed of the stream, that there flows somewhat rapidly; a rich but sad light of rather a purple than a golden hue was spread over the Eildon hills at that moment; and, thinking it probable that it might be the last time Sir Walter would cross the stream, I was not a little moved, and expressed some of my feelings in the sonnet beginning – 'A trouble, not of clouds, or weeping rain'.

H. C. Robinson considered this poem 'the most perfect sonnet in the language' (letter to James Masquerier, 19 October 1833).
14 *Parthenope* Naples, Scott's destination.

III A Place of Burial

I. F. note: 'Similar places for burial are not unfrequent in Scotland. The one that suggested this Sonnet lies on the banks of a small stream called the Wauchope that flows into the Esk near Langholme.'

14 *jubilate* an outburst of joyous triumph.

IV On the Sight of a Manse

Composed probably 1833.

I. F. note: 'The Manses in Scotland and the gardens and grounds about them have seldom that attractive appearance which is common about our English parsonages, even when the Clergyman's income falls below the average of the Scotch Minister's.'

V Composed in Roslin Chapel

I. F. note:

We were detained by incessant rain and storm at the small inn near Roslin Chapel, and I passed a great part of the day pacing to and fro in this beautiful structure, which, though not used for public service, is not allowed to go to ruin. Here this Sonnet was composed, and if it has at all done justice to the feeling which the place and the storm raging without inspired, I was as a prisoner.

VI The Trosachs

I. F. note:

As recorded in my Sister's journal, I had first seen the Trosachs in her and Coleridge's company. The sentiment that runs through this Sonnet was natural to the season in which I again saw this beautiful spot, but this and some other Sonnets that follow were coloured by the remembrance of my recent visit to Sir Walter Scott, and the melancholy errand on which he was going.

VII 'The pibroch's note'

4 *target* the Highlanders' small shield.

VIII Composed in the Glen of Loch Etive

13 *That make the Patriot-spirit bow her head* 'It was mortifying to have frequent occasions to observe the bitter hatred of the lower orders of the Highlanders to their superiors; love of country seemed to have passed into its opposite. Emigration was the only relief looked to with hope.' – *I. F. note*.

IX Eagles

Composed probably in October (by 27 October) 1831.
4 *The last I saw* 'On the wing off the Promontory of Fairhead, County of Atrim.' – *I. F. note.*

X In the Sound of Mull

14 '*Shepherds of Etive Glen*' 'In Gaelic, *Buachaill Eite.*' – W.

XII The Earl of Breadalbane's Ruined Mansion

2 '*narrow house*' Burns's *Lament of Mary, Queen of Scots* (1791), 53. Also used frequently in Macpherson's *Ossian* (1765).

XV The Highland Broach

   I. F. note:

> On ascending a hill that leads from Loch Awe towards Inverary, I fell into conversation with a woman of the humbler class who wore one of those Highland Broaches. I talked with her about it; and upon parting with her, when I said with a kindness I truly felt – 'May that Broach continue in your family through many generations to come, as you have already possessed it' – she thanked me most becomingly, and seemed not a little moved.

30 Fingal and Malvina are part of the dramatis personae of Macpherson's *Ossian*. Fingal was the hero of several Ossianic poems. Malvina was the daughter of Toscar and was betrothed to Ossian's son.
79 *viewless* incapable of being seen.

XVI The Brownie

The Brownie's Cell, mentioned in the prefatory note, can be found on page 292 above.

XVIII Bothwell Castle

1-3 'In this fortress the chief of the English nobility were confined after the battle of Bannockburn.' – W. (1835).
4 *Once on those steeps I roamed* 'In my Sister's Journal is an account of Bothwell Castle as it appeared to us at that time.' – *I. F. note.* Dorothy Wordsworth's *Recollections* (for 22 August 1803).

XIX Picture of Daniel

The picture, originally owned by Charles I, was painted by Rubens.

XX The Avon

1–2   *name ... other rivulets bear*   'There is the Shakespeare Avon, the Bristol Avon; the one that flows by Salisbury, and a small river in Wales, I believe, bear the name; Avon being in the ancient tongue the general name for river.' – *I. F. note.*
7   *Genius*   tutelary spirit of a place.

XXI Suggested by a View

I. F. note: 'The extensive forest of Inglewood has been enclosed within my memory. I was well acquainted with it in its ancient state.'
5   *unappropriate*   unpossessed.
6   *Adam Bell*   Like Clym of the Clough (line 7), a famous outlaw of the North of England. They both lived in the forest of Inglewood.
9   *wants*   lacks.

XXII Hart's-Horn Tree

Wordsworth's *note*: 'The tree has now disappeared, but I well remember its imposing appearance as it stood, in a decayed state, by the side of the high road leading from Penrith to Appleby.'

XXIII Fancy and Tradition

Composed probably 1833.

XXIV Countess' Pillar

I. F. note: 'Suggested by the recollection of Julian's Bower and other traditions connected with this ancient forest.'
10   *'LAUS DEO'*   See the inscription in the Prefatory note. Translated in line 14 as 'God be praised!'

XXV Roman Antiquities

12   *Fibulae*   broaches: see the Prefatory note to XV, *The Highland Broach* (p. 717).

XXVI Apology

9   *Persepolis*   ancient capital of Persia.
20   *threshold loved by every Muse*   Abbotsford, the home of Sir Walter Scott.
30   *rash change*   the Reform of the Parliament, in legislative process during the autumn of 1831.

THE PRIMROSE OF THE ROCK

Composed probably 1831; first published in 1835; from 1836-7 included among 'Poems of the Imagination'.

    I. F. note:

> Rydal Mount 1831. It stands on the right hand a little way leading up the middle road from Rydal to Grasmere. We have been in the habit of calling it the Glow-worm Rock from the number of glow-worms we have often seen hanging on it as described. The tuft of primrose has, I fear, been washed away by the heavy rains.

18 *fibre* small root.

COMPOSED AFTER READING A NEWSPAPER OF THE DAY

Composed probably 1831; first published in 1835; in 1836-7 included in 'Yarrow Revisited', and from 1845 among 'Sonnets Dedicated to Liberty and Order'.

THE MODERN ATHENS

Composed possibly 1831; first published in 1946.

1 *a Parthenon* an imitation of the Parthenon was built in 1822 on Calton Hill, Edinburgh. Pallas Athene was the patron goddess of Athens.
6 *"Auld Reekie"* the affectionate nickname of Edinburgh.
10 *outlandish* alien.
14 *'Wha wants me?'* the title of a satiric ballad attacking Henry Dundas, first Viscount Melville (1742-1811); possibly a reference to an earlier street-cry of Edinburgh.

UPON THE LATE GENERAL FAST

Composed possibly early 1832 (after 6 February); first published in 1832; in 1832 included among 'Epitaphs and Elegiac Pieces', in 1836-7 among 'Miscellaneous Sonnets', and from 1845 among 'Sonnets Dedicated to Liberty and Order'.

    The general fast was called to pray for relief from an outbreak of cholera.

TO THE AUTHOR'S PORTRAIT

Composed possibly September (at least by 3 October) 1832; first published in 1835; from 1836-7 included among 'Miscellaneous Sonnets'.

    I. F. note: 'The six last lines of this Sonnet are not written for poetical effect, but as a matter of fact, which, in more than one instance, could not escape my notice in the servants of the house.'

2 *Margaret* Lady Margaret Beaufort, mother of Henry VII, was the foundress of St John's College.

DEVOTIONAL INCITEMENTS

Composed probably 1832; first published in 1835; from 1836-7 included among 'Poems of the Imagination'.

The motto verse is taken from *Paradise Lost* V, 78-80: 'not to Earth confined, / But sometimes in the Air, as we, sometimes / Ascend to Heaven'.

72 *not by bread alone we live* St Luke 4:4: 'And Jesus answered [the devil] saying, It is written, That man shall not live by bread alone, but by every word of God'.

'CALM IS THE FRAGRANT AIR'

Composed probably 1832; first published in 1835; from 1835 included among 'Evening Voluntaries'.

RURAL ILLUSIONS

Composed probably 1832; first published in 1835; from 1836-7 included among 'Poems of the Fancy'.

I. F. note: 'Rydal Mount 1832. Observed a hundred times in the grounds at Rydal Mount.'

TO ———— UPON THE BIRTH OF HER FIRST-BORN CHILD

Composed probably March 1833; first published in 1835; from 1836-7 included among 'Poems of Sentiment and Reflection'.

I. F. note:

> *To I*[sabella] *W*[ordsworth] *on the birth of her first child.* Written at Moresby near Whitehaven, when I was on a visit to my son [John], then Incumbent of that small living.
>
> While I am dictating these notes to my Friend, Miss Fenwick, January 24, 1843, the Child upon whose birth these verses were written is under my roof, and is of a disposition so promising that the wishes and prayers and prophecies which I then breathed forth in verse are, through God's mercy, likely to be realized.

The motto quotation is from Lucretius, *De Rerum Natura* V, 222-3: 'Then, furthermore, a child, like a sailor thrown up by the fierce waves, lies on the ground naked', etc.

THE WARNING

Composed probably March 1833; first published in 1835; from 1836-7 included among 'Poems of Sentiment and Reflection'.

I. F. note:

> These lines were composed during the fever spread through the Nation by the Reform Bill. As the motives which led to this measure, and the good or

evil which has attended or has risen from it, will be duly appreciated by future Historians, there is no call for dwelling on the subject in this place. I will content myself with saying that the then condition of the people's mind is not, in these verses, exaggerated.

In a cancelled postscript to the *Yarrow Revisited* volume (1835), Wordsworth made the following apologia for *The Warning*:

> That Poem is indeed so little in harmony with the general tenor of his writings and with the contents of this volume in particular, that it seems to require from him some notice of plain prose. It was written for one of the best reasons which in a poetical case can be given, viz. that the author could not help writing it; and it is published because, if there ever was a time when such a warning could be of the least service to any portion of his Countrymen, that time is surely not passed away.
>
> The agitation attendant upon the introduction, and carrying of the Reform Bill has there called forth a strain of reprehension, which as far as concerns the Leaders of that agitation requires neither explanation nor apology; they are spoken of with a warmth of indignant reproof which no man free in spirit will condemn, if it will appear that the feeling has been kindled by reflective patriotism: but as to the misled multitude, if there be a word that bears hard upon them, the Author would find a difficulty in forgiving himself; for even the *semblance* of such a thought would be a deviation from his habitual feelings towards the poor and humbly employed; the greater part of his life has been passed among them, he has not been an unthinking observer of their condition, and from the strongest conviction that so many of that Class are seeking their happiness in ways which cannot lead to it those admonitions proceeded.

21 'The *Warning* was composed on horseback when I was riding from Moresby in a snow-storm.' – W. (quoted in Christopher Wordsworth's *Memoirs* II, 476).
23 This line was end-stopped in all editions during Wordsworth's life; this revision was suggested by N. C. Smith.

BY THE SEA-SIDE

Composed probably March–April 1833; first published 1835; from 1835 included among 'Evening Voluntaries'.

16 *who bade the tempest cease* See *Matthew* 8:26.
39 *'our thoughts are heard in heaven!'* Young's *Night Thoughts* (1742), II, 95.

COMPOSED BY THE SEA-SHORE

Composed probably March–April 1833; first published 1842; from 1845 included among 'Evening Voluntaries'.

I. F. note: '... Suggested during my residence under my Son's roof at Moresby, on the coast near Whitehaven ...'

ON A HIGH PART OF THE COAST OF CUMBERLAND

Composed probably 7 April 1833; first published in 1835; from 1835 included among 'Evening Voluntaries'.

I. F. note:

> The lines were composed on the road between Moresby and Whitehaven while I was on a visit to my Son, then Rector of the former place. This [and some other Voluntaries] originated in the concluding lines of the last paragraph of this Poem. With this coast I have been familiar from my earliest childhood, and remember being struck for the first time by the town and port of Whitehaven, and the white waves breaking against its quays and piers, as the whole came into view from the top of the high ground down which the road (it has since been altered) then descended abruptly. My sister, when she first heard the voice of the sea from this point, and beheld the scene spread before her, burst into tears.

TO THE UTILITARIANS

Composed probably about (at least by) 5 May 1833; first published in 1885.

In the postscript to a letter to Henry Crabb Robinson (5 May 1833), Wordsworth commented on the poem: 'Is [this poem] intelligible – I fear not – I know however my own meaning – and that's enough[?]On Manuscripts' – *Correspondence of Henry Crabb Robinson* I, p. 238.

POEMS COMPOSED OR SUGGESTED DURING A TOUR, 1833

Composed mostly summer 1833; first published in 1835; exceptions to these dates will be indicated in the notes that follow.

I. F. note: 'My companions were H. C. Robinson and my son John.'

I 'Adieu, Rydalian Laurels!'

5 *Delphic crown* a crown of laurel.

IV To the River Greta

1–4 '... The immense stones ..., by their concussion in high floods, produced the loud and awful noises described in the sonnet.' – W. (1835).
5 *Cocytus* the Greek word for 'wailing,' and one of the rivers of the Underworld.
6–7 *thence wert named The Mourner*

> Dr Whitaker has derived [the name 'Greta'] from the word of common occurrence in the North of England, *'to greet'*; signifying to lament loud, mostly with weeping, a conjecture rendered more probable from the stony and rocky channel of both the Cumberland and Yorkshire rivers.

– W.

V To the River Derwent

Composed possibly 1819 (before June); first published in 1819; from 1820 to 1832 placed among 'Miscellaneous Sonnets', in 1835 included among 'Itinerary Poems of 1833'.

Wordsworth's *note* (1835): 'This sonnet has already appeared in several editions of the author's poems; but he is tempted to reprint it in this place, as a natural introduction to the two that follow it.'

9 *wreath* a wreath of parsley was awarded the victor of the Nemean Games, one of the great contests of ancient Greece.

VI In Sight of the Town of Cockermouth

2 *my buried Little-ones* Catharine and Thomas Wordsworth.

VIII Nun's Well, Brigham

11 *By hooded Votaresses* 'Attached to the church of Brigham was formerly a chantry, which held a moiety of the manor; and in the decayed parsonage some vestiges of monastic architecture are still to be seen.' – W. (1835).

14 *'too soft a tear'* Pope's *Eloisa to Abelard* 269-70: 'Thy voice I seem in every hymn to hear; / With every bead I drop too soft a tear.'

IX To a Friend

In a letter to Lady Beaumont (1834), Wordsworth commented on the poem: 'In consequence of some discouraging thoughts – expressed by my Son [John] when he had entered upon [erecting a parsonage], I addressed to him the following Sonnet . . .'

X Mary Queen of Scots

5–8 '. . . It was among the fine Scotch firs near Ambleside, and particularly those near Green Bank, that I have over and over again paused at the sight of this image.' – *I. F. note*.

XI Stanzas Suggested in a Steamboat

Originally printed as a separate category; added to this series in 1845.
Wordsworth's *note*:

St Bees' Heads, anciently called the Cliff of Baruth, are a conspicuous sea-mark for all vessels sailing in the N.E. parts of the Irish Sea. In a bay, one side of which is formed by the southern headland, stands the village of St Bees; a place distinguished, from very early times, for its religious and scholastic foundations.

.   .   .   .   .

The form of stanza in this Poem, and something in the style of versification, are adopted from the 'St Monica', a poem of much beauty upon a monastic subject, by Charlotte Smith . . .

32 *Bega* St Bega came from Ireland about 650 and is said to have founded a small monastery.

37 *'Cruel of heart . . . bloody of hand'* Compare *King Lear* III, iv, 95: 'false of heart, light of ear, bloody of hand'.

73–81

I am aware that I am here treading upon tender ground; but to the intelligent reader I feel that no apology is due. The prayers of survivors, during passionate grief for the recent loss of relatives and friends, as the object of those prayers could no longer be the suffering body of the dying, would naturally be ejaculated for the souls of the departed; the barriers between the two worlds dissolving before the power of love and faith . . .

– W. (1835).

94 *staff and cockle hat and sandal shoon* Compare the old ballad (included in Percy's *Reliques*) *The Friar of Orders Gray* 11–12: 'O, by his cockle hat and staff, / And by his sandal shoon'. See also Ophelia's mad song, *Hamlet* IV, v, 25–6.

126 The two following stanzas were added in 1845.

142 *thoughtful* reflective; contemplative.

153 *new-born College* '. . . Recently, under the patronage of the Earl of Lonsdale, a college has been established there for the education of ministers for the English Church.' – W. (1835).

162 'See "Excursion," seventh part [lines 1008–57]; and "Ecclesiastical Sketches," second part, near the beginning [III–V].' – W.

XV On Entering Douglas Bay

The motto verse is from Horace, *Odes* IV, viii, 28: 'The Muse prevents the fame of a good man from dying'.

1 *Cohorn* Baron Menno Van Cohorn (1641–1704), a Dutch specialist in military fortifications.

14 *noble HILLARY* 'The Tower of Refuge, an ornament to Douglas Bay, was erected chiefly through the humanity and zeal of Sir William Hillary . . .' – W.

XVI By the Sea-Shore

3 'The sea-water on the coast of the Isle of Man is singularly pure and beautiful.' – W.

XVII Isle of Man ('A youth')

I. F. note: 'My son William is here the person alluded to as saving the life of the youth, and the circumstances were as mentioned in the sonnet.'

XVIII Isle of Man ('Did pangs')

3 *the man* Henry Hutchinson, Wordsworth's brother-in-law (see the following sonnet).

XIX By a Retired Mariner

Wordsworth's *note*: 'This unpretending sonnet is by a gentleman nearly connected with me, and I hope, as it falls so easily into its place, that both the writer and the reader will excuse its appearance here.'

I. F. note: 'Mary's [Wordsworth's wife's] brother Henry.' (See the previous sonnet.)

XX At Bala-Sala

3 *this convent-pile* 'Rushen Abbey'. – W.
7 *A ... thankful Refugee* 'Supposed to be written by a friend, Mr H. Cookson, who died there a few years after.' – *I. F. note.*

XXI Tynwald Hill

1 *formal mound* Each summer the Manx people met on the hill for elections.
9 *Snafell* 'The summit of this mountain is well chosen by Cowley as the scene of the "Vision", in which the spectral angel discourses with him concerning the government of Oliver Cromwell.' – W. (1835).

XXIII In the Firth of Clyde

I. F. note:

The morning of the eclipse was exquisitely beautiful while we passed the Crag as described in the sonnet. On the deck of the steamboat were several persons of the poor and labouring class, and I could not but be struck by their cheerful talk with each other, while not one of them seemed to notice the magnificent objects with which we were surrounded; and even the phenomenon of the eclipse attracted but little of their attention.

XXIV On the Firth of Clyde

I. F. note : 'The mountain outline on the north of this Island, as seen from the Firth of Clyde, is much the finest I have ever noticed in Scotland or elsewhere.'
1 *Arran* Arran, off the coast of Scotland, Teneriffe, largest of the Canary Islands, and St Helena, in the South Atlantic Ocean, are all mountainous islands.

XXV On Revisiting Dunolly Castle

See *Yarrow Revisited*, IX *Eagles* (p. 714 above).
7 *An Eagle* 'This ingenious piece of workmanship, as I afterwards learned, had been executed for their own amusement by some labourers employed about the place.' – W. (1835).

XXVII Written in a Blank Leaf

Composed probably 1824; first published in 1827; included among 'Poems of Sentiment and Reflection' until 1845, when it was placed among 'Itinerary Poems of 1833'.
39 *Musaeus* according to some legends, the son of Orpheus; according to others, a mythical singer and peer of Orpheus.
47–8 *or strayed . . . self-betrayed* '[These] verses . . . were, I am sorry to say, suggested from apprehensions of the fate of my friend, H. C. [Hartley Coleridge].' – *I. F. note.*
80 *Maeonides* Homer.

XXVIII Cave of Staffa ('*We saw*')

6 *Fingal* the hero of Macpherson's *Ossian*.

XXIX Cave of Staffa (*After the Crowd had departed.*)

  Wordsworth's *note*:

  The reader may be tempted to exclaim, How came this and the two following sonnets to be written, after the dissatisfaction expressed in the preceding one? In fact, at the risk of incurring the reasonable displeasure of the master of the steamboat, I returned to the cave, and explored it under circumstances more favourable to those imaginative impressions which it is so wonderfully fitted to make upon the mind.

6 *the roof embowed* Compare *Il Penseroso* 157: 'the high embowed Roof'

XXX Cave of Staffa ('*Ye shadowy Beings*')

6 *his ghostly song* Ossian's.

XXXI Flowers on the Top of the Pillars

  Wordsworth's *note* (1835): 'Upon the head of the columns which form the front of the cave, rests a body of decomposed basaltic matter, which was richly decorated with that large bright flower, the ox-eyed daisy.'

XXXII Iona

6 *Her Temples rose* St Columba came to Iona in 563 and founded a monastery.

XXXIII Iona (Upon Landing)

11–14 '. . . Adopted from a well-known sonnet of Russel [sic], as conveying my feeling better than any words of my own could do.' – W. (1835). Rev. Thomas Russell, *Sonnets and Miscellaneous Poems* (1789), X ('Could, then, the Babes').

XXXIV The Black Stones of Iona

'Martin's *Voyage*' in Wordsworth's prefatory note is Martin Martin's *Description of the Western Islands of Scotland* (1703), p. 259.

XXXV 'Homeward we Turn'

7 *her* Fancy's.

XXXVI Greenock

The motto verse is from Dante's *Inferno* III, 1: 'Through me is the way into the sorrowful city'.

XXXVII '"There!" said a Stripling'

I. F. note: 'Mosgiel was thus pointed out to me by a young man on the top of the coach on my way from Glasgow to Kilmarnock.'
9 Burns's *To a Mountain Daisy* (1786), 21–2.

XXXVIII The River Eden, Cumberland

4 *Repeats but once* See *Song at the Feast of Brougham Castle* 47 for the previous mention of the name.
5 *from Paradise* 'It is to be feared that there is more of the poet than the sound etymologist in this derivation of the name Eden.' – W. (1835).
6–7 *Nature gives thee flowers . . . British bowers* 'This can scarcely be true to the letter; but, without stretching the point at all, I can say that the soil and air appear more congenial with many upon the banks of this river, than I have observed in any other parts of Great Britain.' – *I. F. note*.

XLI Nunnery

I. F. note: 'I became acquainted with the walks of Nunnery when a boy . . .'

2 *Pennine Alps* 'The chain of Crossfell.' – W.

14 'At Corby, a few miles below Nunnery, the Eden is crossed by a magnificent viaduct; and another of these works is thrown over a deep glen or ravine, at a very short distance from the main stream.' – W. (1835).

XLIII *The Monument Commonly Called Long Meg*

Composed possibly January (6 January or after) 1821; first published in 1822; from 1827 to 1832 contained among 'Miscellaneous Sonnets', switched to this series in 1836-7.

Wordsworth's *note*: 'The daughters of Long Meg, placed in a perfect circle eighty yards in diameter, are seventy-two in number above ground; a little way out of the circle stands Long Meg herself, a single stone, eighteen feet high.'

XLIV *Lowther*

2 *Cathedral pomp* 'It may be questioned whether this union was in the contemplation of the Artist when he planned the Edifice. However this might be, a Poet may be excused for taking the view of the subject presented in this sonnet.' – *I. F. note.*

XLV *To the Earl of Lonsdale*

Wordsworth's *note*:

> This sonnet was written immediately after certain trials, which took place at the Cumberland Assizes, when the Earl of Lonsdale, in consequence of repeated and long-continued attacks upon his character, through the local press, had thought it right to prosecute the conductors and proprietors of three several journals. A verdict of libel was given in one case; and, in the others, the prosecutions were withdrawn, upon the individuals retracting and disavowing the charges, expressing regret that they had been made, and promising to abstain from the like in future.

The motto verse is translated in line 10.

3 *If he should speak* See the previous sonnet for the poet's speech.

XLVI *The Somnambulist*

Composed possibly 1828; first published in 1835.
I. F. note:

> This poem might be dedicated to my friends Sir G. Beaumont and Mr Rogers, jointly. While we were making an excursion together in this part of the Lake District we heard that Mr Glover, the Artist, while lodging at Lyulph's Tower, had been disturbed by a loud shriek, and upon rising he had learnt that it had come from a young woman in the house

who was in the habit of walking in her sleep: in that state she had gone downstairs, and, while attempting to open the outer door, either from some difficulty or the effect of the cold stone upon her feet, had uttered the cry which alarmed him. It seemed to us all that this might serve as a hint for a poem, and the story here told was constructed, and soon after put into verse by me as it now stands.

1 *Lyulph's Tower* 'A pleasure-house built by the late Duke of Norfolk upon the banks of Ullswater.' – W.
3 *force* 'A word used in the Lake District for Waterfall.' – W.
84 *that pale Queen* Lady Macbeth.

XLVII To Cordelia M———

Cordelia Marshall was the daughter of Dorothy Wordsworth's friend, Jane Marshall.

'IF THIS GREAT WORLD'

Composed 5 December 1833; first published in 1835; from 1836–7 included among 'Poems of Sentiment and Reflection'.
    In Wordsworth's letter to John Wordsworth (5 December 1833), the poem is entitled 'Addressed to Revolutionists of All Classes'.

LOVE LIES BLEEDING

Composed in an early (sonnet) form probably 1833; first published in 1842; from 1845 included among 'Poems of the Fancy'.

12 *Adonis* a youth beloved by Venus, who sprinkled the spot where he died with nectar, whereupon anemones and other flowers sprang up.

COMPANION TO THE FOREGOING

Composed possibly 1833, more likely 1842; first published in 1842; from 1845 included among 'Poems of the Fancy'.

A WREN'S NEST

Composed probably 1833; first published in 1835; from 1836–7 included among 'Poems of the Fancy'.
    I. F. note: 'Rydal Mount. This nest was built, as described, in a tree that grows near the pool in Dora's field next the Rydal Mount garden.'

19 *pent-housed by a brae* sheltered by a sloping bank.

TO A CHILD

Composed probably 3 July 1834; first published in 1835; in 1836–7 included among 'Inscriptions', from 1845 transferred to 'Miscellaneous Poems'.
    I. F. note: 'This quatrain was extempore on observing this image, as I had

often done, on the lawn of Rydal Mount. It was first written down in the Album of my God-daughter, Rotha Quillinan.'

LINES WRITTEN IN THE ALBUM OF THE COUNTESS OF LONSDALE

Composed 5 November 1834; first published in 1835; in 1836-7 included among 'Inscriptions' and thereafter among 'Miscellaneous Poems'.

I. F. note: 'This is a faithful picture of that amiable Lady, as she then was. The youthfulness of figure and demeanour and habits, which she retained in almost unprecedented degree, departed a very few years after, and she died without violent disease by gradual decay before she reached the period of old age.'

8 See *To the Earl of Lonsdale* above (p. 770).

'NOT IN THE LUCID INTERVALS OF LIFE'

Composed probably 1834; first published in 1835; from 1835 included among 'Evening Voluntaries'.

8-15 'The lines following "nor do words" were written with Lord Byron's character, as a Poet, before me, and that of others, his contemporaries, who wrote under like influences.' – *I. F. note*.

17, 20, 22 *O Nature . . . pensive hearts . . . every charm* Compare Burns's *To William Simpson* (1785), 79-80: 'O Nature! a' thy shows an' forms / To feeling, pensive hearts hae charms!'

(BY THE SIDE OF RYDAL MERE)

All data identical with the preceding poem.

16 *by thee was never greeted* The nightingale is not usually found north of the Trent River.

32 *Tempe* a valley in Thessaly renowned for its beauty.

'SOFT AS A CLOUD IS YON BLUE RIDGE'

All data identical with the preceding poem.

'THE LEAVES THAT RUSTLED'

All data identical with the preceding poem.

I. F. note: 'Composed by the side of Grasmere Lake. The mountains that enclose the vale, especially towards Easedale, are most favourable to the reverberation of sound.'

32 *Minerva's* Roman goddess of wisdom, later identified with Athene and often depicted with an owl, her sacred bird.

THE LABOURER'S NOON-DAY HYMN

Composed probably 1834; first published in 1835; from 1836-7 included among 'Poems of Sentiment and Reflection'.

I. F. note: '... Not being aware of any [hymns] being designed for Noon-day, I was induced to compose these verses.'

THE REDBREAST

Composed probably 1834; first published in 1835; from 1836-7 included among 'Poems Founded on the Affections'.
I. F. note:

> Rydal Mount, 1834. All our cats having been banished the house, it was soon frequented by redbreasts. Two or three of them, when the window was open, would come in, particularly when Mary was breakfasting alone. My Sister being then confined to her room by sickness as, dear creature she still is, had one that without being caged, took up its abode with her, and at night used to perch upon a nail from which a picture had hung. It used to sing and fan her face with its wings in a manner that was very touching.

10 *Of which we in the Ballad read*   See *The Children in the Wood* 125-8, in which a robin covers the bodies of children with leaves.
31 *hers*] *1836. his - 1835.* See the *I. F. note* above.
45-6 '... Part of the child's prayer, still in general use through the northern counties.' – W.
70 *lilt* move with a lively action (Northern dialect).

LINES SUGGESTED BY A PORTRAIT

Composed probably 1834; first published in 1835; from 1836-7 included among 'Poems of Sentiment and Reflection'.
I. F. note:

> This portrait has hung for many years in our principal sitting-room, and represents J[emima] Q[uillinan] as she was then a girl. The picture, though it is somewhat thinly painted, has much merit in tone and general effect; it is chiefly valuable, however, from the sentiment that pervades it. The Anecdote of the saying of the Monk in sight of Titian's picture was told in this house by Mr Wilkie, and was, I believe, first communicated to the Public in this Poem, the former portion of which I was composing at the time.

50 *the blind Archer-god* Eros, the god of love.
62 *Ceres* Roman goddess of agriculture.
97 *Escurial palace* 'The pile of buildings composing the palace and convent of San Lorenzo has, in common usage, lost its proper name in that of the *Escurial*, a village at the foot of the hill upon which the splendid edifice, built by Philip the Second, stands.' – W.
118 *Jeronymite* a hermit of any order of St Jerome.
125-6 *like the angel that went down Into Bethseda's pool* See *John* 5:2-4.

THE FOREGOING SUBJECT RESUMED

All data identical with the preceding poem.

32

> In the class entitled 'Musings', in Mr Southey's Minor Poems, is one upon his own miniature Picture, taken in childhood, and another upon a landscape painted by Gaspar Poussin. It is possible that every word of the above verses, though similar in subject, might have been written had the author been unacquainted with those beautiful effusions of poetic sentiment.

–W. Robert Southey's *On My Own Miniature Picture* (1796) and *On a Landscape of* Gaspar Poussin (1795).

UPON SEEING A COLOURED DRAWING

Composed in part 23 June 1835; first published in 1836-7; from 1836-7 included among 'Poems of Sentiment and Reflection'.

> *I. F. note:*

> I cannot forbear to record that the last seven lines of this Poem were composed in bed during the night of the day on which my sister Sara Hutchinson died about 6 p.m., and it was the thought of her innocent and beautiful life that, through faith, prompted the words – 'On wings that fear no glance of God's pure sight, / No tempest from his breath.' The reader will find two poems on pictures of this bird among my Poems. I will here observe that in a far greater number of instances than have been mentioned in these notes one Poem has, as in this case, grown out of another, either because I felt the subject had been inadequately treated, or that the thoughts and images suggested in course of composition have been such as I found interfered with the unity indispensable to every work of Art, however humble in character.

The other poem referred to is entitled *Suggested by a Picture of the Bird of Paradise*.

AIREY-FORCE VALLEY

Composed probably September 1835; first published in 1842; from 1845 placed among 'Poems of the Imagination'.

Airey Force (usually spelled Aira Force) is a waterfall near the western shore of Ullswater.

WRITTEN AFTER THE DEATH OF CHARLES LAMB

Composed partly (lines 1-38) 19 November 1835 and partly (lines 39-131) December 1835; first published in 1836 (privately printed); from 1836-7 included among 'Epitaphs and Elegiac Pieces'.

In a letter to Edward Moxon (20 November 1835), Wordsworth commented on the first thirty-eight lines:

The first objection that will strike you, and everyone, is its extreme length, especially compared with epitaphs as they are now written – but this objection might in part be obviated by engraving the lines in double column, and not in capitals.

Chiabrera has been here my model – though I am aware that Italian Churches, both on account of their size and the climate of Italy, are more favourable to long inscriptions than ours. His epitaphs are characteristic and circumstantial – so have I endeavoured to make this of mine – but I have not ventured to touch upon the most striking feature of our departed friend's character and the most affecting circumstance of his life, viz. his faithful and intense love of his Sister. Had I been pouring out an Elegy or Monody, this would and must have been done; but for seeing and feeling the sanctity of that relation as it ought to be seen and felt, lights are required which could scarcely be furnished by an Epitaph, unless it were to touch on little or nothing else.

24 *the name he bore*

This way of indicating the *name* of my lamented friend has been found fault with; perhaps rightly so; but I may say in justification of the double sense of the word, that similar allusions are not uncommon in epitaphs. One of the best in our language in verse, I ever read, was upon a person who bore the name of Palmer; and the course of the thought, throughout, turned upon the Life of the Departed, considered as a pilgrimage. Nor can I think that the objection in the present case will have much force with anyone who remembers Charles Lamb's beautiful sonnet addressed to his own name, and ending, 'No deed of mine shall shame thee, gentle name!'

– W. (1837).

25 *Christian altars* alluding to Christ as the *Agnus Dei*, or Lamb of God.

56 *peculiar sanctity* also occurs in *The Excursion* VII, 479.

62–4 *'Wonderful ... Passing the love of women'* II *Samuel* 1:26.

90–91 *the part Of a protector* Mary Lamb, ten years older than her brother, was afflicted with periods of insanity and thus required close attention by him.

EXTEMPORE EFFUSION UPON THE DEATH OF JAMES HOGG

Composed probably between 21 November and 12 December 1835; first published 12 December 1835 in the *Athenaeum*; from 1836–7 included among 'Epitaphs and Elegiac Pieces'.

I. F. note: 'These verses were written extempore, immediately after reading a notice of the Ettrick Shepherd's [Hogg's] death in the Newcastle paper ...'

Wordsworth's *note*:

Walter Scott	.	.	.	.	died 21st Sept., 1832.
S. T. Coleridge	.	.	.	.	„ 25th July, 1834.
Charles Lamb	.	.	.	.	„ 27th Dec., 1834.
Geo. Crabbe	.	.	.	.	„ 3rd Feb., 1832.
Felicia Hemans	.	.	.	.	„ 16th May, 1835.

1, 5 *When first . . . When last* See *Yarrow Visited* and *Yarrow Revisited* respectively.

10 *'Mid mouldering ruins* Sir Walter Scott, the 'Border-minstrel', was buried in Dryburgh Abbey.

11–12 James Hogg died 21 November 1835. He was the author of *The Queen's Wake* and *Private Memoirs and Confessions of a Justified Sinner.*

21 *clouds that rake the mountain-summits* 'This expression is borrowed from a sonnet by Mr G. Bell, the author of a small volume of poems lately printed at Penrith. Speaking of Skiddaw, he says, "Yon dark cloud 'rakes,' and shrouds its noble brow."' – W.? (note contained in Henry Reed's *Poetical Works of William Wordsworth* [1837]).

37 *that holy Spirit* Felicia Hemans, a minor poetess befriended by Wordsworth.

[A CENTO]

Put together possibly 1835; first published in 1835; not reprinted by Wordsworth.

The first six lines are from Mark Akenside's *Ode V, Against Suspicion* (1745), 43–8, the next two lines from James Thomson's *Hymn on Solitude* (1725), 1–2, and the last eight from James Beattie's *Retirement* (1758), 49–56.

'BY A BLEST HUSBAND GUIDED'

Composed possibly 1835; first published in 1835; from 1836–7 included among 'Epitaphs and Elegiac Pieces'.

I. F. note: 'This lady was named Carleton; she, along with a sister, was brought up in the neighbourhood of Ambleside. The epitaph, a part of it at least, is in the church at Bromsgrove, where she resided after her marriage.'

ROMAN ANTIQUITIES DISCOVERED AT BISHOPSTONE

Composed possibly 1835; first published in 1835; from 1836–7 included among 'Miscellaneous Sonnets'.

I. F. note: 'My attention to these antiquities was directed by Mr Walker, son to the itinerant Eidouranian Philosopher. The beautiful pavement was discovered within a few yards of the front door of his Parsonage . . .'

12 *suckling Twins* Romulus and Remus, the legendary founders of Rome, were suckled by a she-wolf, as often depicted on Roman coins.

ST CATHERINE OF LEDBURY

All data identical with the previous poem.

I. F. note: 'Written on a journey from Brinsop Court, Herefordshire.'

'DESPONDING FATHER!'

All data identical with the previous poem.

'FOUR FIERY STEEDS'

All data identical with the previous poem.

I. F. note: 'Suggested on the road between Preston and Lancaster where it first gives a view of the Lake country, and composed on the same day, on the roof of the coach.'

TO ———— ('"Wait, prithee, wait!"')

All data identical with the preceding poem.

I. F. note: 'The fate of this poor Dove, as described, was told to me at Brinsop Court, by the young Lady to whom I have given the name of Lesbia [Ellen Loveday Walker, daughter of the Rector of Brinsop].'

The motto verse has never been identified.

TO THE MOON (Composed by the Seaside)

Composed probably 1835; first published in 1836–7; from 1836–7 included among 'Evening Voluntaries'.

10–11 *on this sea-beat shore Sole-sitting* Compare Wordsworth's *A Narrow Girdle of Rough Stones and Crags* 38: 'Sole-sitting by the shores of old romance'.

63–4 *when thy beauty . . . in its monthly grave* Compare Wordsworth's (?) *Written in a Grotto* 4: 'When thou wert hidden in thy monthly grave'.

72 Ten lines apparently intended by Wordsworth to be added to this poem can be found in *PW*, IV, 399.

TO THE MOON (Rydal)

All data identical with the preceding poem.

50 Compare Shakespeare's *Sonnets* CXVI, 6.

NOVEMBER, 1836

Composed probably November 1836; first published in 1836–7; from 1836–7 included among 'Miscellaneous Sonnets'.

I. F. note: 'When I saw [my sister-in-law Sara Hutchinson] lying in death I could not resist the impulse to compose the sonnet that follows.' Sara Hutchinson died 23 June 1835.

In a letter to Robert Southey (24 June 1835), Wordsworth remarked: 'I saw her within an hour after her decease, in the silence and peace of death, with as heavenly an expression on her countenance as ever human creature had.'

4 *Sister* sister-in-law.

[EPIGRAM ON AN EVENT]

Composed probably between 27 October 1836 and 8 September 1837; first published in 1889.

According to Henry Crabb Robinson, Mrs Wordsworth claimed in a letter that Wordsworth thought the epigram 'not amiss as being murmured between sleep and awake over the fire while thinking of you last night'. She also claimed it 'was suggested by a paragraph in the *Courier* stating that Genl Evans has been knocked down by the Wind of a Cannon Ball' – Henry Crabb Robinson, *Reminiscences* (12 September 1837).

Colonel George de Lacy Evans (1787–1870) was a British soldier and radical M.P. See also Wordsworth's *A Squib on Colonel Evans* above (p. 816).

AT BOLOGNA

Composed perhaps 1837; first published in 1842, among the 'Memorials of a Tour in Italy, 1837', transferred in 1845 to 'Sonnets Dedicated to Liberty and Order'.

AT BOLOGNA, continued

All data identical with the previous poem.

AT BOLOGNA, concluded

All data identical with the previous poem.

'OH WHAT A WRECK'

Composed probably 1837 (at least by February 1838); first published in 1838; from 1845 included among 'Miscellaneous Sonnets'.

I. F. note: 'The sad condition of poor Mrs Southey put me upon writing this. It has afforded comfort to many persons whose friends have been similarly affected.' In a MS version, Wordsworth referred to his own sister, who was afflicted in the same way.

A NIGHT THOUGHT

Composed possibly 1837; first published in 1837 in *The Tribute*; from 1845 included among 'Poems of Sentiment and Reflection'.

I. F. note:

These verses were thrown off extempore upon leaving Mrs Luff's house at Fox-Ghyll, one evening. The good woman is not disposed to look at the bright side of things, and there happened to be present certain ladies who had reached the point of life where *youth* is ended, who seemed to contend with each other in expressing their dislike of the country and climate. One of them had been heard to say she could not endure a country where there was 'neither sunshine nor cavaliers'.

6 In 1837, an additional stanza followed the first stanza.

THE WIDOW ON WINDERMERE SIDE

Composed possibly 1837; first published in 1842; from 1845 included among 'Poems Founded on the Affections'.

I. F. note:

> The facts recorded in this Poem were given me, and the character of the person described, by my friend the Rev. R. P. Graves, who has long officiated as curate at Bowness, to the great benefit of the parish and neighbourhood. The individual was well known to him. She died before these verses were composed. It is scarcely worthwhile to notice that the stanzas are written in the sonnet form, which was adopted when I thought the matter might be included in 28 lines.

'LO! WHERE SHE STANDS'

Composed probably between 1837 and 1842; first published in 1842; from 1845 included among 'Miscellaneous Sonnets'.

Sara Coleridge's *note:* 'Dora Wordsworth', Wordsworth's daughter.

TO THE PLANET VENUS

Composed probably January 1838; first published in 1838; from 1845 included among 'Miscellaneous Sonnets'.

7 *Science*] *1845*. Knowledge: *1838*.

'SAID SECRECY TO COWARDICE AND FRAUD'

Composed probably February or March 1838; first published in 1838 as part of a note to *Protest Against the Ballot*.

3 *Pluto's* god of the Underworld.
14 *Hurrah for* ———— George Grote (1794–1871), a strong advocate of voting by ballot.

[A SQUIB ON COLONEL EVANS]

Composed probably March (by 26 March) 1838; first published 1889.

George de Lacy Evans (1787–1870) was a British soldier who fought in the Peninsular War and at Waterloo and was a radical M.P. In a letter to Henry Crabb Robinson (26 March 1838), Wordsworth observed sarcastically: 'You know of old my partiality for Evans: the squib below I let off immediately upon reading his modest self-defence speech the other day.' See also Wordsworth's *Epigram on an Event in Col. Evans's Redoubted Performances in Spain* above (p. 810).

1 *red-ribboned* Evans received the red-ribboned order of K.C.B. in August 1837 for his successful command of the British Legion supporting Queen Christina of Spain against Don Carlos.

13, 15 *Fontarabbia, Hernani* locations of two battles in which Evans was defeated.

'HARK! 'TIS THE THRUSH

Composed probably about 8 April 1838; first published in 1838; from 1845 included among 'Miscellaneous Sonnets'

In a letter to Thomas and Mary Hutchinson (18 April 1838), Mary Wordsworth claimed the sonnet was composed 'almost extempore'. 'Some of the expressions', she continued, 'he softened – otherwise it was not the labour of more than an hour, if so much – a proof, I think, that age is not making the havoc with him as he seems to apprehend.'

COMPOSED ON A MAY MORNING

Composed probably 1 May 1838; first published in 1838; from 1845 included among 'Miscellaneous Sonnets'.

A PLEA FOR AUTHORS

Composed probably May 1838; first published in 1838; from 1845 included among 'Miscellaneous Sonnets'.

Toward the end of his life Wordsworth laboured arduously for a new Copyright Bill.

A POET TO HIS GRANDCHILD

Composed probably 23 May 1838; first published in 1838 and not reprinted by Wordsworth after 1839.

4 *Thy Children left unfit*

The author of an animated article, printed in the Law Magazine, in favour of the principle of Serjeant Talfourd's Copyright Bill, precedes me in the public expression of this feeling; which had been forced too often upon my own mind, by remembering how few descendants of men eminent in literature are even known to exist.

– W. (1838).

14 *careless* carefree, unconcerned.

'BLEST STATESMAN HE'

Composed probably 1838; first published in 1838; from 1845 included among 'Sonnets Dedicated to Liberty and Order'.

14 *Perilous is sweeping change, all chance unsound* '"All change is perilous and all chance unsound." Spenser.' – W. (1838). *The Faerie Queene* V, ii, 36.

''TIS HE WHOSE YESTER-EVENING'S HIGH DISDAIN'

Composed probably 1838; first published in 1838; from 1845 included among 'Miscellaneous Sonnets'.

VALEDICTORY SONNET

All data identical with the preceding poem.

PROTEST AGAINST THE BALLOT

Composed probably 1838; first published in 1838 and not reprinted by Wordsworth after 1839.

12 *Pandorian*   In Greek legend Pandora released all evils into the world.

[INSCRIPTION ON A ROCK AT RYDAL MOUNT]
Composed probably 1838; first published in 1851.

[SONNET TO A PICTURE]

Composed probably 22 October 1839; first published 2 October 1847 in the *New York Home Journal* with the preface: 'A valuable correspondent sends us the following exquisite sonnet, to a picture by Lucca Giordano, in the Museo Borbonico, at Naples, which he says he has reason to believe was never before published'; not in the 1849-50 edition of the *Poems*.

'MEN OF THE WESTERN WORLD'

Composed probably 1839 (by 23 December); first published in 1842; from 1845 included among 'Sonnets Dedicated to Liberty and Order'.
   Wordsworth's *note* (1839):

> These lines were written several years ago, when reports prevailed of cruelties committed in many parts of America, by men making a law of their own passions. A far more formidable, as being a more deliberate mischief, has appeared among those States, which have lately broken faith with the public creditor in a manner so infamous. I cannot, however, but look at both evils under a similar relation to inherent good, and hope that the time is not distant when our brethren of the West will wipe off this stain from their name and nation.

13 *So shall the truth be better understood*   Compare Wordsworth's *'England! The Time is Come'* 3: 'The truth should now be better understood'.

'MORE MAY NOT BE BY HUMAN ART EXPREST'

Composed probably 1839-40; first published in 1942 in George Healey, ed., *Wordsworth's Pocket Notebook*.
   The portrait is thought to be of Isabella Fenwick.

SONNETS UPON THE PUNISHMENT OF DEATH

These sonnets were probably composed 1839-40; first published December 1841 in the *Quarterly Review*.
   Between 1836 and 1841 there was a good deal of discussion about revising the laws involving capital punishment. For an introduction to the issues and a commentary on the sonnets by Sir Henry Taylor, see the *Quarterly* article cited above.

I Suggested by the View of Lancaster Castle

10 *passed*   I follow de Selincourt in correcting 'past', ungrammatically used for the past tense.

III 'The Roman Consul'

1-2 Lucius Junius Brutus executed his own sons for conspiring to restore the Tarquins.

VII 'Before the world had past her time'

3 *eye for eye, and tooth for tooth* Exodus 21:24; *Leviticus* 24:20; *Deuteronomy* 19:21.
6 *Proscribed the spirit* See *Matthew* 5:38-9.

VIII 'Fit retribution'

14 *'wild justice of revenge'* Bacon's *Essays*, 'Of Revenge': 'Revenge is a kind of Wild Justice . . .'

UPON A PORTRAIT

Composed probably 1 January 1840; first published in 1851.
  'I. F.' is Isabella Fenwick.

[TO I. F.]

Composed probably February 1840; first published in 1851.
  For identification of 'I. F.' see the head-note to the previous poem.

POOR ROBIN

Composed probably March 1840; first published in 1842; from 1845 included among 'Miscellaneous Poems'.
  I. F. note: 'This little wild flower – "Poor Robin" – is here constantly courting my attention, and exciting what may be called a domestic interest with the varying aspects of its stalks and leaves and flowers.'
  Wordsworth's *note* (on the title): 'The small wild Geranium known by that name.'

THE CUCKOO-CLOCK

Composed probably between 24 March and 7 April 1840; first published in 1842; from 1845 included among 'Poems of the Imagination'.

33 *wandering Voice* Compare Wordsworth's *To the Cuckoo* ('O blithe Newcomer') 3-4: 'Shall I call thee Bird, / Or but a wandering Voice?'

THE NORMAN BOY

Composed probably between May 1840 and 1842; first published in 1842; from 1845 included among 'Poems Referring to the Period of Childhood'.
  I. F. note:

  The subject of this poem was sent to me by Mrs Ogle, to whom I was personally unknown, with a hope on her part that I might be induced to relate the incident in verse; and I do not regret that I took the trouble; for not improbably the fact is illustrative of the boy's early piety, and may concur with my other little pieces on children to produce profitable reflection among my youthful readers.

THE POET'S DREAM

All data identical with the preceding poem.

28 *The Chapel Oak of Allonville* A hollow tree in the burial ground of Allonville (near Rouen) which was transformed into a small chapel with an iron gate, staircase, and steeple, in 1696.
61 *Church* St Peter's Basilica.
73 *that Country-man* Hippolyte de la Morvonnais (1802-53), the Breton poet who has a passage of such import in his 'Solitudes'.

AT FURNESS ABBEY ('Here, where')

Composed possibly summer (not before) 1840; first published in 1845; from 1845 included among 'Miscellaneous Sonnets'.

14 *Cavendish* The Duke of Devonshire, who owned Furness Abbey, was of the Cavendish family.

UPON THE SIGHT OF THE PORTRAIT OF A FEMALE FRIEND

Composed probably 10 July 1840; first published in 1946.
  The portrait is very likely of Isabella Fenwick.

ON A PORTRAIT OF THE DUKE OF WELLINGTON

Composed 31 August 1840; first published in 1842; from 1845 included among 'Miscellaneous Sonnets'.
  I. F. note: 'This was composed while I was ascending Helvellyn in company with my daughter and her husband.'

4 *conscious* aware.

MEMORIALS OF A TOUR IN ITALY, 1837

Most of the poems in this series were written probably between December 1840 and December 1841; the series was first published in 1842; the exceptions to the above datings are given below in the head-notes to the poems.
  I. F. note:

My excellent friend H. C. Robinson readily consented to accompany me, and in March, 1837, we set off from London, to which we returned in August, earlier than my companion wished or I should myself have desired had I been, like him, a bachelor. These Memorials of that Tour touch upon but a very few of the places and objects that interested me, and, in what they do avert to, are for the most part much slighter than I could wish. More particularly do I regret that there is no notice in them of the south of France, nor of the Roman Antiquities abounding in that district ...

In Christopher Wordsworth's *Memoirs* II, 331, Henry Crabb Robinson is quoted as claiming, 'Little or nothing was written on the journey. Seeds were cast into the earth, and they took root slowly.'

I Musings near Aquapendente

Composed probably March 1841 (perhaps about 25 March).
19   *cone-shaped hill*   Monte Amiata.
22   *Radicofani*   a small village in Tuscany, east of Monte Amiata.
35–6   *over that ... the clouds*   Compare *The Prelude* (1805) VIII, 236–7: 'over that cloud-loving hill, / Seat Sandal, a fond lover of the clouds'.
47–52   originally part of Wordsworth's *Michael*.
60   *his sunk eye kindled at those dear words*   'Sir Walter Scott's ["The Wizard of the North's"] eye *did* in fact kindle at them, for [lines 50–52] were adopted from a poem of mine which nearly forty years ago was *in part* read to him, and he never forgot them.' – *I. F. note*. See previous note.
63   *once*   in August 1805.
76–7   '*When I am ... another Yarrow*'

These words were quoted to me from 'Yarrow Unvisited' [lines 55–6 adapted], by Sir Walter Scott, when I visited him at Abbotsford, a day or two before his departure for Italy: and the affecting condition in which he was when he looked upon Rome from the Janicular Mount, was reported to me by a lady who had the honour of conducting him thither.

– W. (1842).
81   *that Eminence*   Mount Gianicolo ('the Janicular Mount' of the previous note).
121   *Over waves rough and deep*   'We took boat near the lighthouse at the point of the right horn of the bay which makes a sort of natural port for Genoa; but the wind was high, and the waves long and rough, so that I did not feel quite recompensed by the view of the city, splendid as it was, for the danger apparently incurred.' – *I. F. note*.
126   *Him*   Christopher Columbus.
158–9   *sacred earth Fetched from Mount Calvary*   by Archbishop Ubaldo (fl. 1188–1200) to form the Campo Santo, or cemetery, at Pisa.
207   *Savona*   on the Gulf of Genoa.
236   *Chiabrera*   Gabriello Chiabrera (1552–1617), a number of whose epitaphs Wordsworth translated. See Vol. I, pp. 830–36.
254   *philosophic Tusculum*   an ancient city in central Italy called 'philosophic' because of Cicero's *Disputationes Tusculanae*.
257   *Blandusian fount*   See Horace's *Ode* III, xiii – translated by Wordsworth (see Vol. I, p. 141).

262   *behind Vacuna's crumbling fane*   See Horace's *Epistle* I, x, 49: 'Post fanum putre Vacunae'. Vacuna was a Sabine goddess.

265   *Parthenope's*   Naples, where Virgil lived for some time.

271–7   As in Sonnets IV–VI below, Wordsworth shows familiarity with Barthold Niebuhr's theory that early Roman history as told by Livy and others is based on works of long-forgotten poets.

305   *Mamertine prison*   the Roman dungeon in which St Peter ('the Church's Rock') and St Paul ('The Apostle of the Gentiles') are thought to have been imprisoned.

II The Pine of Monte Mario

Wordsworth's *note*:

> Within a couple of hours of my arrival at Rome, I saw from Monte Pincio, the Pine tree as described in the sonnet; and, while expressing admiration at the beauty of its appearance, I was told by an acquaintance of my fellow-traveller, who happened to join us at the moment, that a price had been paid for it by the late Sir G. Beaumont, upon condition that the proprietor should not act upon his known intention of cutting it down.

IV At Rome. – Regrets

In his *History of Rome* (1811–32), Barthold Niebuhr (1776–1831) held that legendary Roman history as told by Livy and other poets was based on previous Roman bards whose works had not survived.

V At Rome. – Regrets, continued

See head-note to the previous poem.

11   *Runic Scald*   Viking poet. Odin was the supreme god of the Norse.

VI Plea for the Historian

See head-note to the previous poem.

7   *Clio*   the muse of history, whose mother was Mnemosyne or memory.

14   '"Quem virum . . . lyra . . . / . . . sumes celebrare Clio?"' – W. Horace's *Odes* I, xii, 1–2: 'What man, Clio, will you celebrate with the lyre?'

VII At Rome

I. F. note:

> I have a private interest in this Sonnet, for I doubt whether it would ever have been written but for the lively picture given me by Anna Ricketts of

what they had witnessed of the indignation and sorrow expressed by some Italian noblemen of their acquaintance on the surrender, which circumstances had obliged them to make, of the best portion of their family mansions to strangers.

VIII Near Rome

12 *his sudden sting* St Peter's sudden pang of guilt on denying Christ for the third time. See *Matthew* 26:75.

IX At Albano

I. F. note: 'This Sonnet is founded on simple fact and was written to enlarge, if possible, the views of those who can see nothing but evil in the intercessions countenanced by the Church of Rome.'

X 'Near Anio's Stream'

6 *the exploratory Bird* Noah sent from the ark a dove which returned with an olive leaf. See *Genesis* 8:11.

XI From the Alban Hills

10 *fortunes, twice exalted* the Classical period and the Renaissance.
12 *double yoke* Both the Papal and Neapolitan governments were maintained by Austria.

XII Near the Lake of Thrasymene

1 *conflict* Hannibal defeated the Romans at this site in 217 B.C.
7 *the name* 'Sanguinetto'. – W.

XIII Near the Same Lake

9 *vanquished Chief* Gaius Flaminius (d. 217 B.C.), Roman Consul and general defeated by Hannibal.
11 *He* Hannibal, hunted by the Romans after the second Punic War, finally poisoned himself.

XIV The Cuckoo at Laverna

Composed possibly June–July 1837 (by 5 July) and revised and extended 26 March 1840.

Wordsworth's MS. note: 'In the following verses I am much indebted to a passage in a letter of one of Mrs Corbelin's relations, the thought of which was suggested to that writer by my own Poem to the Cuckoo ... transcribed at Munich, July 18, 1837.'

29 *the far-famed Pile* 'Laverna is one of the three famous Convents called the three Tuscan Sanctuaries – Camaldoli and Vallombrosa are the other two. Laverna was finished by St Francis of Assisi, and the monks are Franciscans.' – W. (MS note).

93 *the great Prophet* St John the Baptist. The quotation is from *Isaiah* 40:3 and is repeated in each gospel of the New Testament.

108–9 *gentle breezes ... softly fan* Compare *Paradise Lost* X, 93–4: 'gentle Airs ... fan the Earth'.

XV At the Convent of Camaldoli

Camaldoli is a Benedictine monastery.
   Wordsworth's *note*:

> My companion had in the year 1831 fallen in with the monk, the subject of these two sonnets, who showed him his abode among the hermits. It is from him that I received the following particulars. He was then about forty years of age, but his appearance was that of an older man. He had been a painter by profession ... The reader will perceive that these sonnets were supposed to be written when he was a young man.

XVI At the Convent of Camaldoli, continued

See the head-note to the previous poem.

XVII At the Eremite or Upper Convent

   Wordsworth's *note* (to XV): 'The society comprehends two orders, monks and hermits ... The hermitage is placed in a loftier and wilder region of the forest.'
   Wordsworth's *note*:

> In justice to the Benedictines of Camaldoli, by whom strangers are so hospitably entertained, I feel obliged to notice that I saw among them no other figures at all resembling, in size and complexion, the two Monks described in this Sonnet. What was their office, or the motive which brought them to this place of mortification, which they could not have approached without being carried in this or some other way, a feeling of delicacy prevented me from enquiring.

XVIII At Vallombrosa

   Wordsworth's *note* (1842): 'The name of Milton is pleasingly connected with Vallombrosa in many ways. The pride with which the Monk, without any previous question from me, pointed out his residence, I shall not readily forget.'
   The motto verse is from *Paradise Lost* I, 302–4.

18 *darkness ... round* *Paradise Lost* VII, 27.

XIX At Florence

In Christopher Wordsworth's *Memoirs* II, 331, Henry Crabb Robinson is recorded as describing the event: 'I recollect . . . the pleasure he expressed when I said to him "You are now sitting in Dante's chair". It faces the south transept of the cathedral at Florence.'

XX Before the Picture of the Baptist

Composed probably about (at least by) April 1840.
14 *'Make straight a highway'* See *Matthew* 3:3.

XXI At Florence. – From Michelangelo ('Rapt above earth')

Translated 22 June 1839.
  I. F. note to XXI and XXII:

> However at first these two sonnets from Michael Angelo may seem in their spirit somewhat inconsistent with each other, I have not scrupled to place them side by side as characteristic of their great author, and others with whom he lived. I feel nevertheless a wish to know at what periods of his life they were respectively composed. The latter, as it expresses, was written in his advanced years when it was natural that the Platonism that pervades the one should give way to the Christian feeling that inspired the other; between both there is more than poetic affinity.

This poem is a translation of Michelangelo's Sonnet LXXXI (*'La forza d'un bel viso a che mi sprona'*).

XXII At Florence. – From Michelangelo ('Eternal Lord!')

Translated 19 January 1840. An earlier draft, *'Rid of a vexing and a heavy Load'* was produced in 1805–7; see above (Vol. I, p. 662).
  See the *I. F. note* to the previous poem.
  A translation of Sonnet LXXIII of Michelangelo (*'Scarco d'un' importuna e grave salma'*).

XXIII Among the Ruins of a Convent

  I. F. note:

> The political revolutions of our time have multiplied, on the Continent, objects that unavoidably call forth reflections such as are expressed in these verses, but the Ruins in those countries are too recent to exhibit, in anything like an equal degree, the beauty with which time and nature have invested the remains of our Convents and Abbeys. These verses it will be observed take up the beauty long before it is matured, as one cannot but wish it may be among some of the desolations of Italy, France, and Germany.

XXVI After Leaving Italy, continued

I. F. note:

We left Italy by the way which is called the 'Nuova Strada de Allemagna' to the east of the high passes of the Alps which take you at once from Italy into Switzerland; this road leads across several smaller heights, and winds down different Vales in succession, so that it was only by the accidental sound of a few German words I was aware we had quitted Italy, and hence the unwelcome shock alluded to in the two or three last lines of the sonnet with which the imperfect series concludes.

XXVII Composed at Rydal

Composed probably 1 May 1838; first published in 1838; included in these 'Memorials' 1845.

I. F. note: '... Composed on what we call the "Far Terrace" at Rydal Mount.'

XXVIII The Pillar of Trajan

Composed probably 1825–6; first published in 1827; from 1827 to 1836–7 included among the 'Poems of Sentiment and Reflection', and from 1845 among 'Memorials of a Tour in Italy'.

I. F. note:

These verses perhaps had better be transferred to the class of 'Italian Poems'. I had observed in the Newspaper, that the Pillar of Trajan was given as a subject for a [Newdigate] prize-poem in English verse. I had a wish perhaps that my son [John], who was then an undergraduate at Oxford, should try his fortune, and I told him so; but he, not having been accustomed to write verse, wisely declined to enter on the task; whereupon I showed him these lines as a proof of what might, without difficulty, be done on such a subject.

45 Compare Forsyth (see following note), p. 251: '... here the Moorish horse, all naked and unharnessed'.

46–7 *more high ... finger mailed* 'Here and infra, see Forsyth.' – W. (1827). Joseph Forsyth, *Remarks on Antiquities, Arts, and Letters* (1816), p. 252: 'There the Taranatians, in complete mail down to the fingers and hoofs'.

48 Compare Forsyth (ibid.): '... None are wounded or slain but the foe.'

TO A PAINTER ('All praise the Likeness')

Composed probably 1840; first published in 1842; from 1845 included among 'Miscellaneous Sonnets'.

I. F. note: 'The picture [of Mrs Wordsworth] which gave rise to this ... sonnet was from the pencil of Miss M[argaret] Gillies, who resided for several weeks under our roof at Rydal Mount.'

In a letter to Dora Wordsworth (7 April 1840), Wordsworth claimed he 'never poured out anything more truly from the heart'.

TO A PAINTER ('Though I beheld')

All data identical with the preceding poem (including *I. F. note* and epistolary comment).

WITH A SMALL PRESENT

Composed probably 1840–6 (possibly early 1841); first published in 1947.

'LET MORE AMBITIOUS POETS'

Composed probably 1840–6 (possibly 1841); first published in 1947.

'THE CRESCENT-MOON'

Composed probably 25 February 1841; first published in 1842; from 1845 included among 'Evening Voluntaries'.

1 *Star of Love* Venus, the evening star.

'THOUGH PULPITS AND THE DESK MAY FAIL'

Composed 28 April 1841; first published in 1947.

THE WISHING-GATE DESTROYED

Composed probably about but by 30 August 1841; first published in 1842, included among 'Poems of the Imagination'.
Wordsworth's *note*:

> In the vale of Grasmere, by the side of the old highway leading to Ambleside, is a gate which, time out of mind, has been called the Wishing-gate.
>
> Having been told, upon what I thought good authority, that this gate had been destroyed, and the opening, where it hung, walled up, I gave vent immediately to my feelings in these stanzas. But going to the place some time after, I found, with much delight, my old favourite unmolested.

42 *fond* foolish, silly.

UPON PERUSING THE 'EPISTLE'

Composed probably 1841; first published in 1842; from 1845 included among 'Miscellaneous Poems'.
The *Epistle to Sir George Howland Beaumont* can be found above (Vol. I, p. 841).

EPITAPH IN THE CHAPEL-YARD

Composed probably 1841; first published in 1842; from 1845 included among 'Epitaphs and Elegiac Pieces'.

The Rev. Owen Lloyd (1803–41) was curate of Langdale for almost twelve years.

I. F. note:

His love for the neighbourhood in which he was born, and his sympathy with the habits and characters of the mountain yeomanry, in conjunction with irregular spirits, that unfitted him for facing duties in situations to which he was unaccustomed, induced him to accept the retired curacy of Langdale. How much he was beloved and honoured there, and with what feelings he discharged his duty under the oppression of severe malady, is set forth, though imperfectly, in this Epitaph.

'WHEN SEVERN'S SWEEPING FLOOD'

Composed 23 January 1842; first published in 1842 (privately printed), not reprinted during Wordsworth's lifetime.

Written to aid in the erection at Cardiff of a church destroyed by flood several hundred years previously.

'INTENT ON GATHERING WOOL'

Composed probably 8 March 1842; first published in 1842; from 1845 included among 'Miscellaneous Sonnets'.

I. F. note: 'Suggested by a conversation with Miss Fenwick, who along with her sister had, during their childhood, found much delight in such gatherings for the purposes here alluded to.'

PRELUDE, PREFIXED TO THE VOLUME

Composed probably 26 March 1842; first published in 1842; from 1845 included among 'Miscellaneous Poems'.

I. F. note: 'These verses were begun while I was on a visit to my son John at Brigham, and finished at Rydal.'

5 *genial* natural.

45–8

The lines towards the conclusion allude to the discontents then fomented through the country by the agitators of the Anti-Corn-Law League: the particular causes of such troubles are transitory, but disposition to excite and liability to be excited are nevertheless permanent, and therefore proper objects for the Poet's regard.

– *I. F. note.*

'WANSFELL!'

Composed probably 24 December 1842; first published in 1845; from 1845 included among 'Miscellaneous Sonnets'.

1 *Wansfell* 'The Hill that rises to the south-east, above Ambleside.' – W.

'GLAD SIGHT'

Composed probably 31 December 1842; first published in 1845; from 1845 included among 'Poems of the Fancy'.

THE EAGLE AND THE DOVE

Composed possibly 1842; first published in 1842 (in a volume entitled *La Petite Chouannerie*), and never reprinted by Wordsworth during his lifetime.
1 *Caractacus* Caradoc, the British chieftain who resisted the Romans.
5 *These children* Royalist students of the College of Vannes rebelled against Napoleon in 1815.

'LYRE! THOUGH SUCH POWER'

Composed possibly 1842; first published in 1842; from 1845 included among 'Poems of the Imagination'.
I. F. note (to *The Forsaken*): 'The natural imagery of these verses was supplied by frequent, I might say intense, observation of the Rydal torrent.'

SUGGESTED BY A PICTURE OF THE BIRD OF PARADISE

All data identical with the preceding poem.
I. F. note:

> ... Pictures of animals and other productions of nature as seen in conservatories, menageries, museums, etc., would do little for the national mind, nay they would be rather injurious to it, if the imagination were excluded by the presence of the object, more or less out of a state of nature. If it were not that we learn to talk and think of the lion and the eagle, the palm-tree and even the cedar, from the impassioned introduction of them so frequently into Holy Scripture and by great poets, and divines who write as poets, the spiritual part of our nature, and therefore the higher part of it, would derive no benefit from such intercourse with such objects.

7 *Glendoveers* beautiful sprites which are found in Robert Southey's *The Curse of Kehama* (1810). A flight 'through seas of ether' occurs in the opening of Book VII.
23 *conscious* having a share in human actions (poetical).

'THOUGH THE BOLD WINGS'

Composed possibly 1842; first published in 1842; from 1845 included among 'Miscellaneous Sonnets'.

'*A POET!* HE HATH PUT HIS HEART TO SCHOOL'

All data identical with the preceding poem.
I. F. note:

I was impelled to write this Sonnet by the disgusting frequency with which the word *artistical*, imported with other impertinences from the Germans, is employed by writers of the present day: for artistical let them substitute artificial, and the poetry written on this system, both at home and abroad, will be for the most part much better characterized.

'THE MOST ALLURING CLOUDS'

All data identical with the preceding poem.

I. F. note: 'Hundreds of times have I seen, hanging about and above the vale of Rydal, clouds that might have given birth to this Sonnet, which was thrown off on the impulse of the moment one evening when I was returning home from the favourite walk of ours along the Rotha under Loughrigg.'

IN ALLUSION TO VARIOUS RECENT HISTORIES

Composed possibly 1842; first published in 1842.

Wordsworth appears to have had Thomas Carlyle's *French Revolution* (1837) especially in mind.

9-10 *the wrath ... God Epistle of St James* 1:20.

IN ALLUSION TO VARIOUS RECENT HISTORIES, Continued

All data identical with the preceding poem.

IN ALLUSION TO VARIOUS RECENT HISTORIES, Concluded

All data identical with the preceding poem.

'FEEL FOR THE WRONGS'

Composed possibly 1842; first published in 1842; from 1845 included among 'Sonnets Dedicated to Liberty and Order'.

I. F. note: 'This sonnet is recommended to the perusal of the Anti-Corn Law Leaguers, the Political Economists, and of all those who consider that the Evils under which we groan are to be removed or palliated by measures ungoverned by moral and religious principles.'

'WHILE BEAMS OF ORIENT LIGHT'

Composed probably 1 January 1843; first published in 1845; from 1845 included among 'Miscellaneous Sonnets'.

2 *Town* 'Ambleside'. - W.

TO A LADY

Composed probably 1 January 1843; first published in 1845; from 1845 included among 'Poems of the Fancy'.

The 'Lady' of the title was Jane Wallas Penfold.

GRACE DARLING

Composed probably early March (by 24 March) 1843; first published in 1843 (privately printed); from 1845 included among 'Miscellaneous Poems'.

Grace Darling (1815–42), the daughter of a lighthouse-keeper in the Farne Islands off the coast of Northumberland, with her father rescued nine survivors of a steamboat 7 September 1838.

In a letter to Henry Reed (27 March 1843), Wordsworth claimed he wrote the poem from 'the desire I felt to do justice to the memory of a heroine, whose conduct presented some time ago a striking contrast to the inhumanity with which our countrymen shipwrecked lately upon the French coast have been mistreated'.

27 *holy Cuthbert's cell* St Cuthbert (c. 635–687) was a hermit on one of the Farne Islands.
57 *conscious* having a share in human actions (poetical).

INSCRIPTION FOR A MONUMENT IN CROSTHWAITE CHURCH

Composed possibly November (before 2 December) 1843 with revisions throughout December; first published in 1845; from 1845 included among 'Epitaphs and Elegiac Pieces'.

Robert Southey died 21 March 1843. Wordsworth discusses revisions of the poem with John Taylor Coleridge in two letters (2 and 23 December 1843).

TO THE REV. CHRISTOPHER WORDSWORTH

Composed probably 11 December 1843; first published in 1845; from 1845 included among 'Miscellaneous Sonnets'.

The Rev. Christopher Wordsworth was the poet's nephew and biographer, and later the Bishop of Lincoln.

'SO FAIR, SO SWEET'

Composed probably August 1844; first published in 1845; from 1845 included among 'Poems of Sentiment and Reflection'.

In a letter to Thomas Woodward, the biographer of William Archer Butler, R. P. Graves described the event behind the poem – a walk in July 1844:

> .. ♪When the poet's eyes were satisfied with their feast on the beauty familiar to them, they sought relief in the search, to them a happy, vital habit, for new beauty in the flower-enamelled turf at his feet. There his attention was attracted by a fair, smooth stone, of the size of an ostrich's egg, seeming to imbed at its centre, and at the same time to display a dark, star-shaped fossil of most distinct outline. Upon closer inspection this proved to be the shadow of a daisy projected upon it with extraordinary precision by the intense light of an almost vertical sun. The poet drew the

attention of the rest of the party to the minute but beautiful phenomenon, and gave expression at the time to thoughts suggested by it ...

(W. A. Butler, *Sermons, Doctrinal and Practical,* 2nd edition [1852], pp. xxv–xxvi).

ON THE PROJECTED KENDAL AND WINDERMERE RAILWAY

Composed probably 12 October 1844; first published 16 October 1844 in the *Morning Post*; from 1845 included among 'Miscellaneous Sonnets'.
1-2 *Is then ... rash assault?*

The degree and kind of attachment which many of the yeomanry feel to their small inheritances can scarcely be over-rated. Near the house of one of them stands a magnificent tree, which a neighbour of the owner advised him to fell for profit's sake. 'Fell it!' exclaimed the yeoman, 'I had rather fall on my knees and worship it.' It happens, I believe, that the intended railway would pass through this little property, and I hope that an apology for the answer will not be thought necessary by one who enters into the strength of the feeling.

– W.

'PROUD WERE YE, MOUNTAINS'

Composed probably December 1844; first published 17 December 1844 in the *Morning Post*; from 1845 included among 'Miscellaneous Sonnets'.

'YOUNG ENGLAND'

Composed probably January or February (by 9 February) 1845; first published in 1845; from 1845 included among 'Sonnets Dedicated to Liberty and Order'.
6 *Alfred* Alfred the Great (849–901), King of England.
11 *servum pecus* servile herd (see Horace's *Epistles* I, xix, 19).

TO THE PENNSYLVANIANS

Composed probably January or February (by 24 February) 1845; first published in 1845; from 1845 included among 'Sonnets Dedicated to Liberty and Order'.
In the early 1840s, the State of Pennsylvania temporarily stopped payment on state bonds, which both Wordsworth's brother, Christopher, and Miss Fenwick owned.
9 *Penn* William Penn (1644–1718), the Quaker founder of Pennsylvania.

THE WESTMORELAND GIRL

Composed 6 June 1845; first published in 1845; from 1845 included among 'Poems Referring to the Period of Childhood'.
In a letter to Henry Reed (31 July 1845), Wordsworth characterized this

poem 'as exhibiting what sort of characters our mountains breed. It is truth to the Letter.'

The heroine of the poem was identified in Knight's edition as 'Sarah Mackereth of Wyke Cottage, Grasmere'.

AT FURNESS ABBEY ('Well have you')

Composed probably 21 June 1845; first published in 1845; from 1845 included among 'Miscellaneous Sonnets'.

SONNET ('Why should we weep')

Composed between 24 December 1845 and 23 January 1846; first published in 1850; in 1850 included among 'Epitaphs and Elegiac Poems'.
1 *boy* Wordsworth's grandson Edward, almost five years old, died in Rome late in 1845.

'FORTH FROM A JUTTING RIDGE'

Composed probably 1845; first published in 1845; from 1845 included among 'Poems Upon the Naming of Places'.
16 *Now they are parted* Sara Hutchinson died 23 June 1835.

'YES! THOU ART FAIR'

Composed possibly 1845; first published in 1845; from 1845 included among 'Poems Founded on the Affections'.

'WHAT HEAVENLY SMILES!'

All data identical with the preceding poem.

[LINES INSCRIBED IN A COPY OF HIS POEMS]

Composed probably 9 January 1846; first published in 1876.

'WHERE LIES THE TRUTH?'

Composed probably 10 January 1846; first published in 1849–50, among 'Evening Voluntaries'.

In a letter to Henry Reed (23 January 1846), Wordsworth stated that this poem was occasioned by the death of his grandson, and the serious illnesses of a nephew and of his brother Christopher.

'I KNOW AN AGED MAN'

Composed probably January 1846; first published in 1849–50, among 'Miscellaneous Poems'.

TO LUCCA GIORDANO

Composed probably 11 February 1846; first published in 1849–50, among 'Evening Voluntaries'.

1 *Giordano* Lucca Giordano (1632–1705), a Neapolitan painter.
3 *Endymion* a beautiful youth who lived on Mount Latmus and with whom Diana or Cynthia, the moon-goddess fell in love.
10 The picture, which hung at Rydal Mount, was brought from Italy by the poet's son, John.

'WHO BUT IS PLEASED'

Composed probably 10 June 1846; first published in 1849–50, among 'Evening Voluntaries'.

ILLUSTRATED BOOKS AND NEWSPAPERS

Composed probably 1846; first published in 1849–50, among 'Poems of Sentiment and Reflection'.
The *Illustrated London News* began in 1842.

'THE UNREMITTING VOICE'

All data identical with the preceding poem.
8 *To be, or not to be* Hamlet III, i, 56.

SONNET (TO AN OCTOGENARIAN)

Composed probably 1846; first published in 1849–50, among 'Miscellaneous Poems'.

'HOW BEAUTIFUL THE QUEEN OF NIGHT'

Composed possibly 1846; first published in 1849–50, among 'Miscellaneous Poems'.

ON THE BANKS OF A ROCKY STREAM

Composed possibly 1846; first published in 1849–50, among 'Inscriptions'.

ODE ON THE INSTALLATION OF HIS ROYAL HIGHNESS

This ode was written by Edward Quillinan, Wordsworth's son-in-law, but was revised by Wordsworth himself; composed probably about but by 29 April 1847; first published in 1847; not reprinted by Wordsworth.
6 *a Libyan rock* Elba, where Napoleon was exiled in 1814–15, actually lies off the west coast of Italy.
22 *the Isle's delight* Princess Charlotte Augusta (1796–1817), only child of George IV, died in childbirth.
38 *Victoria* Queen Victoria, daughter of the Duke of Kent, was born in 1819.
59 *Gotha's* birthplace of Prince Albert, who later studied at Bonn.
60 *Leine* river in Northern Germany.
63 *Camus* the Cam River (also known as the Granta), which flows through Cambridge.
99 *that wise ancestor* Frederick of Saxony.

Index of Titles

Index of First Lines